Essentials of the Theory of Fiction

Essentials of the Theory of Fiction

Edited by Michael J. Hoffman and Patrick D. Murphy

Second Edition : *Duke University Press Durham 1996*

© 1996 Duke University Press

All rights reserved

Printed in the United States of America on acid-free paper ∞

Typeset in Times Roman with Scala Sans display by Keystone Typesetting, Inc.

Library of Congress Cataloging-in-Publication Data

Essentials of the theory of fiction / edited by Michael J. Hoffman and
Patrick D. Murphy. — [2nd ed.]
p.   cm.
Includes index.
ISBN 0-8223-1829-6 (alk. paper). — ISBN 0-8223-1823-7 (pbk. : alk. paper)
1. Fiction — History and criticism — Theory, etc.   I. Hoffman, Michael J. 1939-
II. Murphy, Patrick D., 1951–
PN3331.E87   1996
809.3 — dc20   96-24615
CIP

Permissions appear after the Index at the end of the volume.

Contents

Acknowledgments

L ike all books, this one was a collaborative effort, not simply because there were two editors but because others were heavily involved in advising and helping us during the editing of both the first and second editions. We should like to acknowledge the prompt, efficient, and cheerful help of Diana Dulaney and Carolyn Jentzen, who typed and prepared the first edition of the manuscript, and Joseph Register and Cathy Renwick, who helped track down information, rekey sections, and reproduce materials for the second edition. Bonnie Iwasaki-Murphy deserves thanks for her continued support and active interest in this project from inception to completion, both times.

The University of California at Davis Academic Senate Committee on Research helped with a series of grants-in-aid. We are also very grateful for the enthusiastic support and intelligent, thoughtful editing of Reynolds Smith at Duke University Press, and for his encouragement for the production of a second edition. We found especially helpful the many shrewd comments of that press's anonymous consultant readers. The second edition has benefited from the suggestions of many teachers who used the first edition, particularly Robert Chianese at California State University, Northridge. We also appreciate the careful copyediting of Barbara Norton.

Preface to the Second Edition

The success of the first edition of *Essentials of the Theory of Fiction* proved that it could serve the function for which it was primarily intended: a supplemental text for courses on fiction, especially the novel. We have been gratified to see that it also has been frequently adopted as a primary text in theory courses at both the undergraduate and graduate levels as well. But, of course, in a field such as contemporary literary theory any text quickly becomes dated. At the encouragement of our editor, Reynolds Smith, we set out to bring *Essentials* up to date and solicited comments about the efficacy of the original table of contents and about new articles or authors that ought to be included. We did not want the book to become appreciably larger, and hence more expensive, but we did want to make sure it contained the best selection possible.

We found that some of the original essays did not prove as useful as we had hoped and we thus deleted seven of them from the second edition. In their place we have added eight essays published originally between 1983 and 1990. We chose essays that covered new territories, but we also chose them because they had already proven themselves to be strong texts to which others have referred in the past five years in various books and articles. These eight new essays, like the other twenty-two to which they have been added, make lasting contributions to the dynamic and vital field of the theory of fiction. Based on our experience, we also decided to omit the topical table of contents from the second edition.

Preface to the First Edition

When we first began to pursue the idea of editing this book, we naturally did some research into our potential competition. We discovered that no collection of essays on the theory of fiction had been published for more than ten years, and that all the older editions are now out of print. The many collections of essays on literary theory are of a more general nature, usually including *some* essays on fiction; but none exist that would serve the needs of a serious student of fiction who is interested in a coverage of that field or who wants a text for his or her own students to use in a course on the novel or other prose forms.

It seemed clear, then, that there is a serious need for such a text, because of the great proliferation of courses on prose fiction at colleges and universities across the United States and because the theory of fiction is one of the burgeoning subdivisions in the thriving study of literary theory. What is needed is a single text that contains within its covers the best essays written on the major topics in the theory of fiction so that the varied study of that field can be presented at its best.

We conceive of our audience as consisting of educated general readers as well as scholars who might wish to have major texts available in a single volume. Also included in our audience are those students who can use the book as an introduction to the field and those already knowledgeable who want an opportunity to experience fiction theory more broadly. Our criteria of selection were: (1) those texts traditionally considered "classics," (2) those that represent the various concerns of the most important scholars and thinkers, (3) those that are the best in their quality of thought and exposition, and (4) those that are the most readable and well written. The reader of this book should know that we have deliberately excluded essays that we found needlessly obscure or poorly written, no matter how much they might have represented the most "advanced" thinking in the field.

Within these strictures we have proceeded with both historical and topical foci. We present the essays in chronological order of their publication. This will enable any reader who wishes to read the book through from beginning to end to gain a good overview of the developing critical discussion of fiction throughout the current century. We have also attempted to represent the topics that have defined that discussion. To aid readers, students, and teachers in following that part of the discussion, we have also developed a topical table of contents, to be found immediately after the more conventional one, with the full understanding that many of the essays cannot be neatly categorized and might well be listed in more than one category. We nonetheless hope that our classifications will prove useful and enlightening.

Some readers may wish to start the book at the beginning and continue until the end; others may wish to dip in here and there, reading those essays that they may find interesting at the moment. Instructors may wish to use the essays to introduce fictional topics in conjunction with the reading of specific stories, novellas, or novels. One of us has already used the book in typescript as exactly that kind of supplemental text, and his students found both fictional and theoretical texts to be enhanced by such a juxtaposition. The book will also work well, we believe, when used in a more advanced course that stresses primarily the historical development of the theory of fiction.

In the Introduction we attempt to introduce readers to the theory of fiction, state something briefly about the history of the field, and describe the categories and terms under which the discussion has taken place. Unlike the introductions to many anthologies, ours says comparatively little about each of the essays we have chosen and their authors, reserving that kind of discussion for the headnotes that precede each of the essays. We think that such a placement of information will prove most useful to our readers. In the headnotes we try to state something about the central concern of each essay and relate it to others in the book. In this way we attempt to show how in a discipline like literary theory such essays are always in a kind of dialogue — occasionally explicit, perhaps most often implicit — with one another.

Finally, we wish to state that each of us was involved fully with the selection of texts and the drafting of prose. Producing this book was, we strongly believe, a collaboration in the best sense of that overused word.

Introduction

W ho was the first storyteller? A lonely hunter consoling his fellows on a cold northern evening far from home? A mother calming a frightened child with tales of gods and demigods? A lover telling his intended of fantastic exploits, designed to foster his courtship? The reader can multiply the number of possibilities, but we shall never know the answer, for the impulse to tell stories is as old as the development of speech, older than the invention of writing. It has deep psychological springs we do not fully comprehend, but the need to make up characters, and to place them in worlds that are parallel to our own or are perhaps wildly at variance with it, is part of the history of all peoples, cultures, and countries; there is no known human group that has not told tales.

Oral cultures are great sources for students of the theory of fiction. Researchers have established that in those that still exist, the storyteller (or bard) is highly revered for the ability to relate from memory a number of verse narratives of enormous length, told within the regularities of meter and conventional figures of language that aid the memory, containing the stories of characters known to listeners who share in a common folklore and myth. These stories, about familiar characters in recognizable situations, do not engage their audience in the mysteries of an unresolved plot, for the listeners know the story already, have heard it told before, and are often as familiar with its events as they are with events in their own lives. Then why do they listen? Beyond the story itself, the audience concerns itself with the voice and manner of the teller of the tale; the texture and density of the story's material; the fit of the characters with the audience's expectations about how human beings, gods, demigods, and mythic heroes behave in a world something like their own. For such people — just as for ourselves — fictions have an extraordinary explanatory power; they make clear why, for instance, there are seasons, why there is an underworld for the spirits of dead ancestors, why there is one royal line of descent and not another.

We begin this collection of essays on the theory of fiction with a discussion of so-called primitive origins because we believe that the impulse to tell tales and listen to them is akin to the impulse in "literate" cultures to write stories and read them, and as Claude Lévi-Strauss has shown us in *The Savage Mind (La pensée sauvage)* the science of primitive peoples is as sophisticated in its own purposes as the science in literate cultures; so too are the fictions. Tribal members in oral cultures may or may not have detailed discussions of the nature and forms of their fictions, but clearly they do make judgments as to the adequacy of the telling of stories, and the act of judgment is, after all, an act of criticism. Questions of judgment and interpretation, in fact, inform human discourse everywhere.

While we do not claim that the theory of fiction occupies much of the attention of tribal scholars, we do claim that the interpretation of works of literature, and in particular of fictional creation, is part of the written record of all literate cultures. It has constituted an extremely large and important part of literature since the times of the ancient Hebrews and Greeks, with its beginnings in Midrashic texts and in the writings of Plato and the sophists and, ultimately, in the most important literary critical text of Western antiquity, the *Poetics* of Aristotle.

The study of literature and literary theory — by which we mean the use of rhetorical, linguistic, and structural analysis as a means of interpreting texts — has, therefore, a long tradition in Western intellectual history, one employed quite heavily during certain periods and certainly appearing during the current century as a principal form of literate intellectual activity. In its forms of analysis, literary theory has been defined to a great extent by the kinds of texts to which it has been applied. In the *Poetics* Aristotle was concerned primarily with discussing the epic poem and the two dominant forms of drama, comedy and tragedy. For the most part, these were the most important forms, along with lyric poetry, written by the ancient Greek authors that Aristotle studied. The fictions about which Aristotle could have written were, therefore, composed in verse or dialogue, not in prose, and the forms were not the prose fictional forms that dominate our time: the novel, the novella, and the short story.

Historians of literature have argued at length about which prose fictions might qualify as the first novels. There were certainly prominent examples of lengthy prose fictions in the ancient world, with *The Golden Ass* of Apuleius and Petronius's *Satyricon* coming conspicuously to mind. But while these are extended narratives in prose, they do not, for most critics, fulfill the criteria for defining a novel formally in terms of the development of plot and character. Both tales are products of the early Christian centuries and were followed by more than a millennium in which the long fictional forms consisted mainly of verse epics and romances whose subject matter was the relatively conventional material of shared folklore and myth. Indeed, with some exceptions such as the Icelandic sagas and Boccaccio's *Decameron,* extended prose fictions did not begin to flourish in England and on the European continent until the sixteenth century, in the writings of Nashe and Lyly in England, Rabelais in France, and Cervantes in Spain. Some critics have called Cervantes's *Don Quixote,* published during the early years of the seventeenth century, the first European novel, and while the adventures of the man of La Mancha have been extraordinarily influential on later forms of prose fiction — Lionel Trilling finds its theme of illusion and reality to be the essence of the novel — *Don Quixote* did not found a tradition in which those writers who came after him self-consciously thought of themselves as writing "novels." Rather, Cervantes's book summed up and parodied the tradition of medieval and Renaissance romance, with all its chivalric and courtly conventions. The self-conscious establishment of a tradition of novel writing did not come about with any lasting force until more than a century later, in an increasingly mercantile and industrial Europe where the middle classes were rapidly rising. The rising literacy that always accompanies trade and technology created an expanded reading public hungry for stories of people like themselves, in prose like that of the newspapers, journals, and scientific treatises that had come to dominate the new technology of print. For the middle classes poetry was identified with the aristocracy, except for such didactic verse as they sang in church.

England in the first half of the eighteenth century was a country dominated increasingly by trade and a mercantile middle class fortified by great prosperity, who used their profits to purchase for themselves the perquisites hitherto reserved for the landed aristocracy. The earliest British novels dramatized the rise of this new class. In addition, the development of a literate population, helped by the technology of print, made it possible for the first time for writers to earn a living through the sale of their printed works rather than through receiving patronage from a wealthy person of noble birth.

This new technology created a veritable writing industry in London, producing not only great masses of publications for science and various trades, but also the first newspapers, biographies, "confessions" of famous criminals, travel books, and ostensibly "true" accounts of how successful individuals found ways to thrive in the developing bourgeois culture. The works of Daniel Defoe are representative of this tendency; the ones we still read today were written as serious parodies of the forms developed in the popular press: *Robinson Crusoe* (1719), *A Journal of the Plague Year* (1722), and *Moll Flanders* (1722). All are written in a "non-literary" prose of great lucidity and apparent functional utility. *Moll Flanders* and *Crusoe* are often called the great precursors of the British novel and taught in courses on that genre. The other great precursor of this period, Jonathan Swift's *Gulliver's Travels* (1728), uses the form of the travel tale to parody the society of England by placing it in various guises in exotic fictional settings.

While the works of Defoe and Swift are surely wonderful exercises of the fictional imagination, they were not written by authors working self-consciously in a new literary form. Not until two decades after the appearance of Lemuel Gulliver's *Travels into Several Remote Regions of the World* did the works of two writers, Samuel Richardson and Henry Fielding, announce the development of a new form. Richardson's epistolary novels, *Pamela* (1741) and *Clarissa* (1747–48), caught the imagination of England and much of Europe because of their sympathetic and extended treatment of character and their fashionable excesses of feeling. Fielding's work as a novelist began with a parody of Richardson's *Pamela* in a travesty called *Shamela* (1741). Having found his gift for comedy, Fielding then produced two of the best early novels in British literature: *Joseph Andrews* (1742) and *Tom Jones* (1749), in each of which, but especially in the latter, he wrote justifications of his use of the new form. Calling his books comic epics in prose and rationalizing his procedures through reference to the works of classic Greek and Roman authors, Fielding more than anyone else wrote the first essays on the theory of fiction in British literature.

Although the tradition of the novel was established quite quickly and has ultimately come to dominate the common conception of "literature" for the reading public, no corresponding tradition of writings on the theory of fiction arose to follow Fielding's lead in that area. Works on literary theory continued to concentrate, as they had since Aristotle, on poetry and drama, and the main practitioners in the eighteenth century were primarily poets, such as John Dryden and Alexander Pope. The one major exception to that rule, Samuel Johnson — that extraordinary man of letters who worked in many forms including the novel — included little on the theory of fiction in his theoretical writings.

Well into the nineteenth century the novel remained for critics the step-child among literary forms, popular with the mass reading public but not considered serious in the way of the lyric or the long poem. Major British critics continued to be poets, such as Samuel Taylor Coleridge and Matthew Arnold, but again neither had much to say about the novel. In France and Russia, however, critics including Sainte-Beuve and Belinsky and the novelists Balzac and Stendhal did begin to write seriously about fiction. Nonetheless, the first writer to develop an extensive and lasting body of writing in English on the theory of fiction was the novelist Henry James, who — in a lengthy series of essays written over more than four decades and in the prefaces he wrote to the New York Edition (1907–9) of his collected works — practically invented the field, along with many of the terms and concepts still most frequently used by people who write about fiction. Indeed, for instance, the Jamesian belief in the importance of the single point of view and his belief that authors should not "intrude" by "telling" but should dramatize action became an almost tyrannical force in critical theory and novelistic practice during the first half of the twentieth century — as Wayne Booth demonstrates in *The Rhetoric of Fiction* (1961).

It may well be, however, that the most important example set by James's writings on fictional theory, as well as by his own work as an artist, is to show that the writing of fiction is not simply a form of entertainment, but a serious art form, to be ranked with the lyric, the epic, and the drama and to be taken just as seriously by its practitioners. James's monastic commitment to writing, along with his belief that the exercise of craft is a form of moral commitment — a belief he learned from Flaubert and Turgenev — was so powerful that the theory of fiction has been dominated ever since by an emphasis on craft with less thought in general given to subject matter. It seems only fitting, then, to begin our collection of essays with James's "The Art of Fiction" (1884), an essay that reads like a manifesto for the position summarized above.

The nineteenth century has come to seem the great age of narrative, particularly in the realistic novel. Even though the theory of fiction in England had to await the advent of James, by the time of his death in 1917 fiction had come to be seen as the central act of literary creation — the area of real artistic commitment. In his early essays, for instance, Ezra Pound claimed that it was again time for poets to take their craft as seriously as the novelists take theirs. While for a time poet-critics such as Pound and

T. S. Eliot continued to dominate literary theory — both of them strongly influenced by the *example* of James as an artist — from the 1920s on, major contributions were made to the theory of fiction by both scholars and practitioners.

As a result, a study of recent contributions made to the theory of fiction indicates that field to be a microcosm of both the concerns of literary theory and the general study of literature — particularly because the entire field of literature has become more and more a part of the academic enterprise. As, for instance, the study of poetry moved away from a concern with the poet's biography and the poem's subject matter, so did the study of fiction focus more on the ways the novel or story is constructed rather than on how facts of the author's life relate to details in the fiction.

While readers of this collection may wish to seek analogies between the concerns expressed in these essays and those expressed throughout the century in the study of poetry, drama, language, and rhetoric, the editors wish to focus the remainder of this introduction on the central concerns of the theory of fiction and on how they evolved throughout this century.

Genre

A number of the following essays treat an issue that has occupied many writers on fiction: that of defining the nature of each of the fictional genres. The first issue lies in deciding which works fall under the purview of the theory of fiction as distinct from theories of poetry and drama. Most writers draw the line between works written in prose and those written in verse — which is certainly the case with most of the essays in this collection. Still, some critics have claimed that Homer's *Iliad* and Chaucer's *Troilus and Criseyde* are, for instance, almost "perfect" novels, even though they are both long poems in the epic/romance traditions. Major theorists like Georg Lukács and Mikhail Bakhtin see the lines of fictional tradition as running from the epic to the novel; their major task is then to show how the two forms differ. For Bakhtin the fact that one form is written in verse, the other in prose, seems almost incidental. For other critics this distinction is crucial. Does the final distinction here become a cultural one, for example between historical cultures that use one form of discourse rather than another? Is there a difference in the way the world appears through the lenses of prose and verse?

Making distinctions among the prose fictional forms of the novel, novella, and short story has also occupied critics throughout the century. Are these distinctions simply ones of length between forms of up to 15,000 words, up to 50,000 words, or more than 50,000 words? Do these arbitrary word lengths impose formal constraints on authors, so that novels, novellas, and short stories differ in their basic characters? The short story is in fact an older form, attracting critical attention at least as early as the 1840s, in Edgar Allan Poe's classical essay on his countryman Nathaniel Hawthorne's *Twice-Told Tales,* but the novella did not emerge as a self-consciously viable form until the latter part of the nineteenth century. What does the actual word limit of the various forms mean to a writer when composing a work of fiction? What advantages does each form give writers that they cannot take advantage of in the others?

Narrative Voice and Point of View

Since the time of Henry James the related matters of narrative voice and point of view have formed a major part of the discussion of fiction. It is important to remember that both concepts are metaphoric, that the figure of point of view has to do with how the action is seen or experienced and that the figurative narrative voice is really silent and requires us to suppose from the words on the page how that voice might sound if someone were actually speaking them. Although figurative concepts, these notions have long had a powerful explanatory power for critics and readers, enabling us to understand that all narrative is written from a certain perspective and that one major fictional device is making the reader share in the experience from that perspective.

Henry James codified the concept of point of view by insisting that the narrative voice be purified of the kind of authorial commentary that he claimed interfered with the narrative flow. Moral judgments were to become implicit rather than explicit, and a single narrative perspective was to be carried through the story — either that of a character in the tale or that of a narrator whose voice was to become the flexible instrument that sustained a distance between the author and the fictional matter. Authors were not to demean their tasks by pretending that novels were merely "made up" and that they could cavalierly intervene any time they had a comment to make. The author was to become invisible, to be — in James

Joyce's famous formulation in *A Portrait of the Artist as a Young Man* — "like the God of the creation, who remains within or behind or beyond or above his handiwork, invisible, refined out of existence, indifferent, paring his fingernails."

Such extraordinary narrative purity has remained an ideal throughout much of the current century, motivating the work of such writers as Joyce, Ernest Hemingway, William Faulkner, and Virginia Woolf. So strongly did this concept take hold of critics that it was not seriously challenged until Booth's *Rhetoric of Fiction,* which pointed out that not only had some of the greatest novels never strived for such purity but that in no work of fiction did the author *ever* disappear; that judgments were always present in the narrative tone and in all the various kinds of irony available to the narrator and the "implied author." Booth's influence has not only opened up earlier novels for our greater appreciation, it has also made more accessible to us a whole host of "postmodern" novels that make no attempt to hide the fact that they were written — that, in fact, make a fetish of their artificiality. This second edition includes several new essays that focus on the narrative dimensions of fiction, a field that has received as much attention from poststructuralists as it has from structuralists. Susan Lanser advances a discussion of feminist narratology, while David Lodge distinguishes between realist and modernist narrative strategies that emphasize mimesis, or showing, and postmodernist ones that emphasize diegesis, or telling, and Henry Louis Gates, Jr., focuses on the African-American strategy of "signifying."

Plot

Discussions of plot have become much more sophisticated in recent criticism. Instead of simply seeing plot as a succession of events taking place in a narrative, critics have now begun to make important distinctions. They understand that major differences exist among the story embedded in the narrative, the actual narrative sequence (which is frequently *not* in the story's chronological order), and the various tensions between the two orders that authors have always self-consciously exploited.

In addition, there are many different types of plots, ranging from idyllic love stories to stories of war, murder, and mayhem to stories of ritual and religion to stories that are primarily intellectual discussions of ideas. And to advance the many different kinds of plots novelists employ many devices, including "flashes" forward and backward, involutions of temporal sequence, and telling the story more than once from the points of view of different characters. Such is the concern of Gérard Genette in his structuralist analysis of temporal strategies within narrative and Peter Brooks in his argument for the centrality of plot to any narrative.

Character

What exactly is a character? Is it simply that entity which, for the most part, retains the same name from the beginning to the end of the work of fiction? Are fictional characters obliged to obey the same rules of human behavior as living people of flesh and blood? If so, why, for instance, are we convinced by the characters in such novels as George Orwell's *Animal Farm,* in which animals speak and act like human beings?

What constitutes a good character? To borrow terminology from E. M. Forster's *Aspects of the Novel,* can we claim that "rounded" characters are more vivid and memorable than "flat" ones? Forster himself makes no such claim, but some of his followers have misread him as suggesting that he did. Can we really say that Leo Tolstoy's Anna Karenina (a rounded character) is more memorable than Herman Melville's Captain Ahab (a flat one) — to take two tragic characters as examples? Hardly. But the question does point out that fictional characters are defined not so much by what they are as by how they are used. The functions to which characters are put determine whether we shall see only one side of them or experience their many-sidedness. Captain Ahab's obsession is what defines him and controls the monomaniacal nature of the quest for Moby-Dick. To see him much outside of this defining obsession would soften him too much and would allow the momentum of the quest to flag. Anna Karenina's role, on the other hand, demands that we see her much more completely within a set of social situations and in many moods, for her fate is tied up with the mores of a large society and she does not assume the dominant role in it that Captain Ahab does in his. But with all their differences, both characters rank among the most memorable in the history of fiction.

The problem is made to seem even more complex when we consider comic characters, who are more often flat (Don Quixote) than round (Leopold Bloom), and characters in more recent fiction who are frequently both serious and comic, round and flat (e.g., the nameless narrator in Ralph Ellison's *Invisible Man*).

And what then do we think of the arguments made by the practitioners of the French *nouveau roman,* such as Alain Robbe-Grillet and Nathalie Sarraute, who recently claimed that the notion of character was passé, and that a new conception of the novel would have to be developed in which character no longer played a role as we know it? In such a new novel the writer could only record phenomena. What then is character: a speaking voice, a thinking mind, a feeling of spirit? The essays in *Essentials* trace the development of this continuing argument.

Fiction and Reality

The relationship of fictional worlds to those inhabited by readers has long been a subject for discussion in the theory of fiction. Are novels primarily representations of "reality," or are they all "made up"? How obliged are novelists to make what happens in their texts compare with what might have happened had the same events occurred in the "real world"? Is verisimilitude, for instance, an obligation for a writer?

Lionel Trilling claims in "Manners, Morals, and the Novel" that realism is the basic drive behind all fictional creation, that the life of individuals in society has been the stuff out of which novels have always been made. Other writers, such as George Levine, have identified realism more closely with certain periods of history (the nineteenth century) than with others (the twentieth century). Even, however, in modernist novels as different as Joyce's *Ulysses* and Faulkner's *Absalom, Absalom!,* one of the main thematic problems in each concerns the relatedness of fictional events to those of a specific moment in history, a single day, as in *Ulysses,* or a more lengthy period, as in *Absalom, Absalom!*

But can we think of fictional reality in the same terms we use in thinking about history or about our own lives? Lives in fiction are surely more carefully determined than the lives that are lived by people who read books. Few lives have recurrent patterns, or perhaps even meaning, but they tend to repeat themselves almost obsessively and do not resolve themselves into the peculiar roundedness we feel when reading a satisfying plot. Novels do not have to end in death the way all lives and most biographies do. But we do not find characters to be well portrayed and developed unless something early in the novel has prepared us for what happens later. In this way novels are highly predictable and predetermined in ways unlike the randomness we all experience when living in a contingent world.

It seems, then, that we demand that novels and stories be plausible within the terms of their own fictional world and that such plausibility be measured not against whether that universe is truly a "represented" world but whether it is analogous to our own — that if some things happen then other things will follow, just as they might were we living in a universe constructed similar to the one in that "made-up" world. This, it seems to us, is as true of works of fiction written in the great "age of realism" of Dickens, Eliot, Stendhal, or Dostoevsky as it is of the more contrived but still essentially "realistic" novels of Joyce, Woolf, Faulkner, and Gabriel García Marquez, as well as works utilizing fantastic worlds, which often provide far more "realistic" or everyday details of their world than many avant-garde fictions. Among the essays added for this second edition, those by Barbara Foley, Linda Hutcheon, and Joanne Frye are concerned with fiction and reality in very different ways. Foley treats the "documentary novel" and the problem of distinguishing the border between fact and fiction, particularly in terms of the issue of how fiction refers to the everyday world. Hutcheon discusses the postmodern variant of documentary fiction, what she terms "historiographic metafiction." And Frye explores the relationship between mimesis and gender-based readings.

Time and Space

Prose fiction is a temporal medium. It takes time for the reader of a novel to absorb its words, assimilate its concepts, and perceive its various elements. Characters are developed, and plots unfold in time. Like a symphony, a novel changes from one moment to the next, and the development of a given passage depends on other passages that have preceded it.

Novelists have often manipulated a story's temporal unfolding by telling a tale out of chronological order, and in that way exploiting the tension among story, narrative, and plot — a tension that we mentioned earlier. Even in fictions characterized primarily by straightforward, continuous chronology, the time of reading is almost always at variance with the time the plot takes to unfold; almost all novels cover a longer period of time than the number of hours even a slow reader might take to finish the book. (Even the occasional novel that tries to match reading and narrative time exactly goes therefore against the reader's expectations.) The exploitation of this tension becomes yet another device through which authors define the rhythms of their narratives. Some contemporary critics like Gérard Genette and Mieke Bal have developed elaborate typologies to describe the many ways in which the different temporal characteristics of a novel relate to one another.

Another concern of recent critics (e.g., Joseph Frank) has been to describe the ways in which certain novels attempt to use "spatial" means to gain certain effects. As applied to fiction, space is even more metaphoric than the concept of time. Painting and sculpture are spatial forms, and because they exist in space (as does an unopened book), they can be experienced "all at once" in a single and instantaneous visual perception. A painting (as distinguished from one's understanding of it) does not unfold in time; it is all there at every moment, and its parts are not sequential but physically connected.

Many modernist novels have demanded that readers experience them all at once — an obviously impossible demand, given the temporal nature of the reading experience. But like a cubist painting, whose various elements are related simply by contiguity, novels like *Ulysses* or *The Sound and the Fury* can be understood only when they are perceived "all at once," for the various elements unfold not chronologically but in a fashion that seems at first to be almost random. It is often said that you cannot read such novels for the first time unless you have already read them. In other words, you must have their facts and their stories in your head (as you would when looking at a painting) before you can understand them as their narratives unfold. All students of fiction must therefore come to terms with the different conceptions of time conveyed in a nineteenth-century novel (like *Great Expectations* or *War and Peace*), with its emphasis on history and continuity, and the more fragmented modernist novel as it breaks with such seemingly old-fashioned concepts as causality and relatedness.

We hope this discussion of certain major topics in the theory of fiction will prove helpful to students, teachers, and scholars alike. Those topics and many others like them — metaphor, myth, setting, symbolism — are raised in much greater detail in the collection of texts that follow.

As prose fiction has developed from the early experiments of Cervantes's parodies, Richardson's epistolary works, and Hawthorne's sketches to the sophisticated experiments of modernism and postmodernism, literary criticism also has evolved. It has become more sophisticated as the result of efforts by critics to explain how fictions work their magic. The essays that follow, drawn from the past hundred years, and displaying that growth and change, are essential to any study of fiction in the latter part of the twentieth century.

1 Henry James : *The Art of Fiction*

Henry James has long been recognized as the major American author to bridge the transition from nineteenth-century realism to the impressionistic and modernistic fiction of the twentieth century. He is also the most important figure in effecting the transition of the criticism of fiction from the nineteenth-century journalistic review to the twentieth-century critical essay. James wrote "The Art of Fiction" as a reply to a lecture delivered by the Victorian novelist and historian Walter Besant at the Royal Institution in London in 1884. In these excerpts from that essay, James speaks not only as an author seeking the latitude necessary to develop his own method, but also as a literary critic determined to discourage prescriptive pronouncements about "the way in which fiction should be written." James the critic wishes to encourage descriptive criticism of actual novels, "what it [the novel] thinks of itself."

James echoes Besant in arguing for the novel as "one of the *fine* arts" on the basis of its formal qualities. This position stands in contradistinction to the popular contemporary argument that for a novel to qualify as *serious* literature it must engage a topic with a high moral purpose and resolution. James states unequivocally that "the only obligation to which in advance we may hold a novel . . . is that it be interesting." He draws a clear-cut distinction here that will recur throughout modern criticism and in the essays collected in this book: the appreciation and evaluation of literary works must be based on the primacy of formal or thematic qualities.

Henry James (1843–1916) is best known for many novels that have become classics of English language literature, including *The American* (1877), *Portrait of a Lady* (1881), *The Turn of the Screw* (1898), and *The Ambassadors* (1903). He has also left us a legacy of well-known novellas and short stories, such as *Daisy Miller* (1879) and *The Beast in the Jungle* (1903). Much of his literary criticism is contained in the prefaces written for the New York edition of his works (1907–1917), which have been separately published in *The Art of the Novel* (1934), *The Future of the Novel* (1956), and other collections.

The only obligation to which in advance we may hold a novel, without incurring the accusation of being arbitrary, is that it be interesting. That general responsibility rests upon it, but it is the only one I can think of. The ways in which it is at liberty to accomplish this result (of interesting us) strike me as innumerable, and such as can only suffer from being marked out or fenced in by prescription. They are as various as the temperament of man, and they are successful in proportion as they reveal a particular mind, different from others. A novel is in its broadest definition a personal, a direct impression of life: that, to begin with, constitutes its value, which is greater or less according to the intensity of the impression. But there will be no intensity at all, and therefore no value, unless there is freedom to feel and say. The tracing of a line to be followed, of a tone to be taken, of a form to be filled out, is a limitation of that freedom and a suppression of the very thing that we are most curious about. The form, it seems to me, is to be appreciated after the fact: then the author's choice has been made, his standard has been indicated; then we can follow lines and directions and compare tones and resemblances. Then in a word we can enjoy one of the most charming of pleasures, we can estimate quality, we can apply the test of execution. The execution belongs to the author alone; it is what is most personal to him, and we measure him by that. The advantage, the luxury, as well as the torment and responsibility of the novelist, is that there is no limit to what he may attempt as an executant — no limit to his possible experiments, efforts, discoveries, successes. Here it is especially that he works, step by step, like his brother of the brush, of whom we may always say that he has painted his picture in a manner best known to himself. His manner is his secret, not necessarily a jealous one. He cannot disclose it as a general thing if he would; he would be at a loss to teach it to others. I say this with a due recollection of having insisted on the community of method of the artist who paints a picture and the artist who writes a novel. The painter *is* able to teach the rudiments of his practice, and it is possible, from the study of good work (granted the aptitude), both to learn how to paint and to learn how to write. Yet it remains true, without injury to the *rapprochement,* that the literary artist would be obliged to say to his pupil much more than the other, "Ah, well, you must do it as you can!" It is a question of degree, a matter of delicacy. If there are exact sciences, there are also exact arts, and the grammar of painting is so much more definite that it makes the difference.

I ought to add, however, that if Mr. Besant says at the beginning of his essay that the "laws of fiction may be laid down and taught with as much precision and exactness as the laws of harmony, perspective, and propor- tion," he mitigates what might appear to be an extravagance by applying his remark to "general" laws, and by expressing most of these rules in a manner with which it would certainly be unaccommodating to disagree. That the novelist must write from his experience, that his "characters must be real and such as might be met with in actual life"; that "a young lady brought up in a quiet country village should avoid descriptions of garrison life," and "a writer whose friends and personal experiences belong to the lower middle-class should carefully avoid introducing his characters into society"; that one should enter one's notes in a common-place book; that one's figures should be clear in outline; that making them clear by some trick of speech or of carriage is a bad method, and "describing them at length" is a worse one; that English Fiction should have a "conscious moral purpose"; that "it is almost impossible to estimate too highly the value of careful workmanship — that is, of style"; that "the most important point of all is the story," that "the story is everything": these are principles with most of which it is surely impossible not to sympathize. That remark about the lower middle-class writer and his knowing his place is perhaps rather chilling; but for the rest I should find it difficult to dissent from any one of these recommendations. At the same time, I should find it difficult positively to assent to them, with the exception, perhaps, of the injunction as to entering one's notes in a common-place book. They scarcely seem to me to have the quality that Mr. Besant attributes to the rules of the novelist — the "precision and exactness" of "the laws of harmony, perspective, and proportion." They are suggestive, they are even inspiring, but they are not exact, though they are doubtless as much so as the case admits of: which is a proof of that liberty of interpretation for which I just contended. For the value of these different injunctions — so beautiful and so vague — is wholly in the meaning one attaches to them. The characters, the situation, which strike one as real will be those that touch and interest one most, but the measure of reality is very difficult to fix.

. . . . Experience is never limited, and it is never complete; it is an immense sensibility, a kind of huge spider-web of the finest silken threads suspended in the chamber of consciousness, and catching every air-borne particle in its tissue. It is the very atmosphere of the mind; and when the mind is imaginative — much more when it happens to be that of a man of genius — it takes to itself the faintest hints of life, it converts the very pulses of the air into revelations. The young lady living in a village has only to be a damsel upon whom nothing is lost to make it quite unfair (as it seems to me) to declare to her that she shall have nothing to say about the military. Greater miracles have been seen than that, imagination assisting, she should speak the truth about some of these gentlemen. I remember an English novelist, a woman of genius,[1] telling me that she was much commended for the impression she had managed to give in one of her tales of the nature and way of life of the French Protestant youth. She had been asked where she learned so much about this recondite being, she had been congratulated on her peculiar opportunities. These opportunities consisted in her having once, in Paris, as she ascended a staircase, passed an open door where, in the household of a *pasteur,* some of the young Protestants were seated at table round a finished meal. The glimpse made a picture; it lasted only a moment, but that moment was experience. She had got her direct personal impression, and she turned out her type. She knew what youth was, and what Protestantism; she also had the advantage of having seen what it was to be French, so that she converted these ideas into a concrete image and produced a reality. Above all, however, she was blessed with the faculty which when you give it an inch takes an ell, and which for the artist is a much greater source of strength than any accident of residence or of place in the social scale. The power to guess the unseen from the seen, to trace the implication of things, to judge the whole piece by the pattern, the condition of feeling life in general so completely that you are well on your way to knowing any particular corner of it — this cluster of gifts may almost be said to constitute experience, and they occur in country and in town, and in the most differing stages of education. If experience consists of impressions, it may be said that impressions *are* experience, just as (have we not seen it?) they are the very air we breathe. Therefore, if I should certainly say to a novice, "Write from experience and experience only," I should feel that this was rather a tantalizing monition if I were not careful immediately to add, "Try to be one of the people on whom nothing is lost!"

I am far from intending by this to minimize the importance of exactness — of truth of detail. One can speak best from one's own taste, and I may therefore venture to say that the air of reality (solidity of specification) seems to me to be the supreme virtue of a novel — the merit on which all its other merits (including that conscious moral purpose of which Mr. Besant speaks) helplessly and submissively depend. If it be not there they are all as nothing, and if these be there, they owe their effect to the success with which the author has produced the illusion of life. The cultivation of this success, the study of this exquisite process, form, to my taste, the beginning and the end of the art of the novelist. . . . That his characters "must be clear in outline," as Mr. Besant says — he feels that down to his boots; but how he shall make them so is a secret between his good angel and himself. It would be absurdly simple if he could be taught that a great deal of "description" would make them so, or that on the contrary the absence of description and the cultivation of dialogue, or the absence of dialogue and the multiplication of "incident," would rescue him from his difficulties. Nothing, for instance, is more possible than that he be of a turn of mind for which this odd, literal opposition of description and dialogue, incident and description, has little meaning and light. People often talk of these things as if they had a kind of internecine distinctness, instead of melting into each other at every breath, and being intimately associated parts of one general effort of expression. I cannot imagine composition existing in a series of blocks, nor conceive, in any novel worth discussing at all, of a passage of description that is not in its intention narrative, a passage of dialogue that is not in its intention descriptive, a touch of truth of any sort that does not partake of the nature of incident, or an incident that derives its interest from any other source than the general and only source of the success of a work of art — that of being illustrative. A novel is a living thing, all one and continuous, like any other organism, and in proportion as it lives will it be found, I think, that in each of the parts there is something of each of the other parts. The critic who over the close texture of a finished work shall pretend to trace a geography of items will mark some frontiers as artificial, I fear, as any that have been known to history. There is an old-fashioned distinction between the novel of charac-ter and the novel of incident which must have cost many a smile to the intending fabulist who was keen about his work. It appears to me as little to the point as the equally celebrated distinction between the novel and the romance — to answer as little to any reality. There are bad novels and good novels, as there are bad pictures and good pictures; but that is the only distinction in which I see any meaning, and I can as little imagine speaking of a novel of character as I can imagine speaking of a picture of character. When one says picture one says of character, when one says novel one says of incident, and the terms may be transposed at will. What is charac-ter but the determination of incident? What is incident but the illustration of character? What is either a picture or a novel that is *not* of character? What else do we seek in it and find in it? It is an incident for a woman to stand up with her hand resting on a table and look out at you in a certain way; or if it be not an incident I think it will be hard to say what it is. At the same time it is an expression of character. If you say you don't see it (character in *that—allons donc!*), this is exactly what the artist who has reasons of his own for thinking he *does* see it undertakes to show you. When a young man makes up his mind that he has not faith enough after all to enter the church as he intended, that is an incident, though you may not hurry to the end of the chapter to see whether perhaps he doesn't change once more. I do not say that these are extraordinary or startling incidents. I do not pretend to estimate the degree of interest proceeding from them, for this will depend upon the skill of the painter. It sounds almost puerile to say that some incidents are intrinsically much more important than others, and I need not take this precaution after having professed my sympathy for the major ones in remarking that the only classification of the novel that I can understand is into that which has life and that which has it not.

The novel and the romance, the novel of incident and that of charac-ter—these clumsy separations appear to me to have been made by critics and readers for their own convenience, and to help them out of some of their occasional queer predicaments, but to have little reality or interest for the producer, from whose point of view it is of course that we are attempt-ing to consider the art of fiction. . . . If we pretend to respect the artist at all, we must allow him his freedom of choice, in the face, in particular cases, of innumerable presumptions that the choice will not fructify. Art derives a considerable part of its beneficial exercise from flying in the face of presumptions, and some of the most interesting experiments of which it is capable are hidden in the bosom of common things. Gustave Flaubert has written a story[2] about the devotion of a servant-girl to a parrot, and the production, highly finished as it is, cannot on the whole be called a suc-cess. We are perfectly free to find it flat, but I think it might have been interesting; and I, for my part, am extremely glad he should have written it; it is a contribution to our knowledge of what can be done—or what cannot. Ivan Turgenev has written a tale about a deaf and dumb serf and a lap-dog[3] and the thing is touching, loving, a little masterpiece. He struck the note of life where Gustave Flaubert missed it—he flew in the face of a presumption and achieved a victory.

So that it comes back very quickly, as I have said, to the liking: in spite of M. Zola, who reasons less powerfully than he represents, and who will not reconcile himself to this absoluteness of taste, thinking that there are certain things that people ought to like, and that they can be made to like. I am quite at a loss to imagine anything (at any rate in this manner of fiction) that people *ought* to like or dislike. Selection will be sure to take care of itself, for it has a constant motive behind it. That motive is simply experience. As people feel life, so they will feel the art that is most closely related to it. This closeness of relation is what we should never forget in talking of the effort of the novel. Many people speak of it as a factitious, artificial form, a product of ingenuity, the business of which is to alter and arrange the things that surround us, to translate them into conventional, traditional moulds. This, however, is a view of the matter which carries us but a very short way, condemns the art to an eternal repetition of a few familiar *clichés,* cuts short its development, and leads us straight up to a dead wall. Catching the very note and trick, the strange irregular rhythm of life, that is the attempt whose strenuous force keeps Fiction upon her feet. In proportion as in what she offers us we see life *without* rearrangement do we feel that we are touching the truth; in proportion as we see it *with* rearrangement do we feel that we are being put off with a substitute, a compromise and convention. It is not uncommon to hear an extraordinary assurance of remark in regard to this matter of rearranging, which is often spoken of as if it were the last word of art. Mr. Besant seems to me in danger of falling into the great error with his rather unguarded talk about "selection." Art is essentially selection, but it is a selection whose main care is to be typical, to be inclusive. . . .

Mr. Besant has some remarks on the question of "the story" which I shall not attempt to criticize, though they seem to me to contain a singular ambiguity, because I do not think I understand them. I cannot see what is meant by talking as if there were a part of a novel which is the story and part of it which for mystical reasons is not — unless indeed the distinction be made in a sense in which it is difficult to suppose that any one should attempt to convey anything. "The story," if it represents anything, represents the subject, the idea, the *donnée* of the novel; and there is surely no "school" — Mr. Besant speaks of a school — which urges that a novel should be all treatment and no subject. There must assuredly be something to treat; every school is intimately conscious of that. This sense of the story being the idea, the starting-point, of the novel, is the only one that I see in which it can be spoken of as something different from its organic whole; and since in proportion as the work is successful the idea permeates and penetrates it, informs and animates it, so that every word and every punctuation-point contribute directly to the expression, in that proportion do we lose our sense of the story being a blade which may be drawn more or less out of its sheath. The story and the novel, the idea and the form, are the needle and thread, and I never heard of a guild of tailors who recommended the use of the thread without the needle, or the needle without the thread. . . .

There is one point at which the moral sense and the artistic sense lie very near together; that is in the light of the very obvious truth that the deepest quality of a work of art will always be the quality of the mind of the producer. In proportion as that intelligence is fine will the novel, the picture, the statue partake of the substance of beauty and truth. To be constituted of such elements is, to my vision, to have purpose enough. No good novel will ever proceed from a superficial mind; that seems to me an axiom which, for the artist in fiction, will cover all needful moral ground: If the youthful aspirant take it to heart it will illuminate for him many of the mysteries of "purpose." There are many other useful things that might be said to him, but I have come to the end of my article, and can only touch them as I pass. The critic in the *Pall Mall Gazette,* whom I have already quoted, draws attention to the danger, in speaking of the art of fiction, of generalizing. The danger that he has in mind is rather, I imagine, that of particularizing, for there are some comprehensive remarks which, in addition to those embodied in Mr. Besant's suggestive lecture, might without fear of misleading him be addressed to the ingenuous student. I should remind him first of the magnificence of the form that is open to him, which offers to sight so few restrictions and such innumerable opportunities. The other arts, in comparison, appear confined and hampered; the various conditions under which they are exercised are so rigid and definite. But the only condition that I can think of attaching to the composition of the novel is, as I have already said, that it be sincere. This freedom is a splendid privilege, and the first lesson of the young novelist is to learn to be worthy of it.

Notes

1. Probably Anne Thackeray, Lady Ritchie, daughter of Thackeray, whose first novel *The Story of Elizabeth* corresponds to James's description.
2. *Un coeur simple.*
3. *Mumu.*

2 Virginia Woolf : *Mr. Bennett and Mrs. Brown*

"On or about December, 1910, human character changed." So declares Virginia Woolf in "Mr. Bennett and Mrs. Brown," originally read before The Heretics Club of Cambridge, England, on May 18, 1924. This change, she goes on to claim, has produced a corresponding change in literature which requires the discarding of old prose writing habits and the adoption through experiment of new methods for shaping original forms and styles. Henry James declared that we may require of a novel only that it be "interesting," but Woolf argues that for the modern novel to fulfill that requirement it must break with the writing strategies of turn-of-the-century English novelists and forge new ones.

Such strategies must begin and end, according to Woolf, with a concern for character: "I believe that all novels . . . deal with character, and that it is to express character — not to preach doctrines, sing songs, or celebrate the glories of the British Empire, that the form of the novel, so clumsy, verbose, and undramatic, so rich, elastic, and alive, has been evolved." Like James, Woolf emphasizes the formal qualities of fiction over its thematic qualities. She declares the Edwardians, such as Arnold Bennett, John Galsworthy, and H. G. Wells, to be in the camp of social and historical novelists who are always concerned with issues outside the life of the novel they are writing; the Georgians, such as James Joyce, E. M. Forster, and, by implication, herself, she declares to be in the camp of innovative experimentalists who seek to capture through formal invention the change in human character that she believes has occurred. Woolf thus announces that what has become known as the modernist movement is the way forward for English literature: "Tolerate the spasmodic, the obscure, the fragmentary, the failure" because these experiments signal "the verge of one of the great ages of English literature." Time has borne out Woolf's claim, but we should ask ourselves whether her claim, that only through a central focus on character can the novel advance, is truly the source of this greatness.

Virginia Woolf (1882–1941) is best known as the author of such modernist novels as *Mrs. Dalloway* (1925), *To the Lighthouse* (1927), and *The Waves* (1931). She was also a prolific essayist and literary critic, a major feminist theorist (cf. *A Room of One's Own* [1929]), a diary writer, and letter writer, as well as a member of the famous Bloomsbury Group of British intellectuals. "Mr. Bennett and Mrs. Brown" appears in her collection *The Captain's Death Bed and Other Essays* (1950).

It seems to me possible, perhaps desirable, that I may be the only person in this room who has committed the folly of writing, trying to write, or failing to write, a novel. And when I asked myself, as your invitation to speak to you about modern fiction made me ask myself, what demon whispered in my ear and urged me to my doom, a little figure rose before me — the figure of a man, or of a woman, who said, "My name is Brown. Catch me if you can."

Most novelists have the same experience. Some Brown, Smith, or Jones comes before them and says in the most seductive and charming way in the world, "Come and catch me if you can." And so, led on by this will-o'-the-wisp, they flounder through volume after volume, spending the best years of their lives in the pursuit, and receiving for the most part very little cash in exchange. Few catch the phantom; most have to be content with a scrap of her dress or a wisp of her hair.

My belief that men and women write novels because they are lured on to create some character which has thus imposed itself upon them has the sanction of Mr. Arnold Bennett. In an article from which I will quote he says, "The foundation of good fiction is character-creating and nothing else. . . . Style counts; plot counts; originality of outlook counts. But none of these counts anything like so much as the convincingness of the characters. If the characters are real the novel will have a chance; if they are not, oblivion will be its portion. . . . " And he goes on to draw the conclusion that we have no young novelists of first-rate importance at the present moment, because they are unable to create characters that are real, true, and convincing.

These are the questions that I want with greater boldness than discretion to discuss tonight. I want to make out what we mean when we talk about "character" in fiction; to say something about the question of reality which Mr. Bennett raises; and to suggest some reasons why the younger novelists fail to create characters, if, as Mr. Bennett asserts, it is true that fail they do. This will lead me, I am well aware, to make some very sweeping and some very vague assertions. For the question is an extremely difficult one. Think how little we know about character — think how little we know about art. But, to make a clearance before I begin, I will suggest that we range Edwardians and Georgians into two camps; Mr. Wells, Mr. Bennett, and Mr. Galsworthy I will call the Edwardians; Mr. Forster, Mr. Lawrence, Mr. Strachey, Mr. Joyce, and Mr. Eliot I will call the Georgians. And if I speak in the first person, with intolerable egotism, I will ask you to excuse me. I do not want to attribute to the world at large the opinions of one solitary, ill-informed, and misguided individual.

My first assertion is one that I think you will grant — that every one in this room is a judge of character. Indeed it would be impossible to live for a year without disaster unless one practised character-reading and had some skill in the art. Our marriages, our friendships depend on it; our business largely depends on it; every day questions arise which can only be solved by its help. And now I will hazard a second assertion, which is more disputable perhaps, to the effect that on or about December, 1910, human character changed.

I am not saying that one went out, as one might into a garden, and there saw that a rose had flowered, or that a hen had laid an egg. The change was not sudden and definite like that. But a change there was, nevertheless; and, since one must be arbitrary, let us date it about the year 1910. The first signs of it are recorded in the books of Samuel Butler, in *The Way of All Flesh* in particular; the plays of Bernard Shaw continue to record it. In life one can see the change, if I may use a homely illustration, in the character of one's cook. The Victorian cook lived like a leviathan in the lower depths, formidable, silent, obscure, inscrutable; the Georgian cook is a creature of sunshine and fresh air; in and out of the drawing-room, now to borrow the *Daily Herald,* now to ask advice about a hat. Do you ask for more solemn instances of the power of the human race to change? Read the *Agamemnon,* and see whether, in process of time, your sympathies are not almost entirely with Clytemnestra. Or consider the married life of the Carlyles and bewail the waste, the futility, for him and for her, of the horrible domestic tradition which made it seemly for a woman of genius to spend her time chasing beetles, scouring saucepans, instead of writing books. All human relations have shifted — those between masters and servants, husbands and wives, parents and children. And when human relations change there is at the same time a change in religion, conduct, politics, and literature. Let us agree to place one of these changes about the year 1910.

I have said that people have to acquire a good deal of skill in character-reading if they are to live a single year of life without disaster. But it is the art of the young. In middle age and in old age the art is practised mostly for its uses, and friendships and other adventures and experiments in the art of reading character are seldom made. But novelists differ from the rest of the world because they do not cease to be interested in character when they have learnt enough about it for practical purposes. They go a step further, they feel that there is something permanently interesting in character in itself. When all the practical business of life has been discharged, there is something about people which continues to seem to them of overwhelming importance, in spite of the fact that it has no bearing whatever upon their happiness, comfort, or income. The study of character becomes to them an absorbing pursuit; to impart character an obsession. And this I find it very difficult to explain: what novelists mean when they talk about character, what the impulse is that urges them so powerfully every now and then to embody their view in writing.

So, if you will allow me, instead of analysing and abstracting, I will tell you a simple story which, however pointless, has the merit of being true, of a journey from Richmond to Waterloo, in the hope that I may show you what I mean by character in itself; that you may realize the different aspects it can wear; and the hideous perils that beset you directly you try to describe it in words.

One night some weeks ago, then, I was late for the train and jumped into the first carriage I came to. As I sat down I had the strange and uncomfortable feeling that I was interrupting a conversation between two people who were already sitting there. Not that they were young or happy. Far from it. They were both elderly, the woman over sixty, the man well over forty. They were sitting opposite each other, and the man, who had been leaning over and talking emphatically to judge by his attitude and the flush on his face, sat back and became silent. I had disturbed him, and he was annoyed. The elderly lady, however, whom I will call Mrs. Brown, seemed rather relieved. She was one of those clean, threadbare old ladies whose extreme tidiness — everything buttoned, fastened, tied together, mended and brushed up — suggests more extreme poverty than rags and dirt. There was something pinched about her — a look of suffering, of apprehension, and, in addition, she was extremely small. Her feet, in their clean little boots, scarcely touched the floor. I felt that she had nobody to support her; that she had to make up her mind for herself; that, having been deserted, or left a widow, years ago, she had led an anxious, harried life, bringing up an only son, perhaps, who, as likely as not, was by this time beginning to go to the bad. All this shot through my mind as I sat down, being uncomfortable, like most people, at travelling with fellow passengers unless I have somehow or other accounted for them. Then I looked at the man. He was no relation of Mrs. Brown's I felt sure; he was of a bigger, burlier, less refined type. He was a man of business I imagined, very likely a respectable corn-chandler from the North, dressed in good blue serge with a pocket-knife and a silk handkerchief, and a stout leather bag. Obviously, however, he had an unpleasant business to settle with Mrs. Brown; a secret, perhaps sinister business, which they did not intend to discuss in my presence.

"Yes, the Crofts have had very bad luck with their servants," Mr. Smith (as I will call him) said in a considering way, going back to some earlier topic, with a view to keeping up appearances.

"Ah, poor people," said Mrs. Brown, a trifle condescendingly. "My grandmother had a maid who came when she was fifteen and stayed till she was eighty" (this was said with a kind of hurt and aggressive pride to impress us both perhaps).

"One doesn't come across that sort of thing nowadays," said Mr. Smith in conciliatory tones.

Then they were silent.

"It's odd they don't start a golf club there — I should have thought one of the young fellows would," said Mr. Smith, for the silence obviously made him uneasy.

Mrs. Brown hardly took the trouble to answer.

"What changes they're making in this part of the world," said Mr. Smith, looking out of the window, and looking furtively at me as he did so.

It was plain, from Mrs. Brown's silence, from the uneasy affability with which Mr. Smith spoke, that he had some power over her which he was exerting disagreeably. It might have been her son's downfall, or some painful episode in her past life, or her daughter's. Perhaps she was going to London to sign some document to make over some property. Obviously against her will she was in Mr. Smith's hands. I was beginning to feel a great deal of pity for her, when she said, suddenly and inconsequently:

"Can you tell me if an oak-tree dies when the leaves have been eaten for two years in succession by caterpillars?"

She spoke quite brightly, and rather precisely, in a cultivated, inquisitive voice.

Mr. Smith was startled, but relieved to have a safe topic of conversation given him. He told her a great deal very quickly about plagues of insects. He told her that he had a brother who kept a fruit farm in Kent. He told her what fruit farmers do every year in Kent, and so on, and so on. While he talked a very odd thing happened. Mrs. Brown took out her little white handkerchief and began to dab her eyes. She was crying. But she went on listening quite composedly to what he was saying, and he went on talking, a little louder, a little angrily, as if he had seen her cry often before; as if it were a painful habit. At last it got on his nerves. He stopped abruptly, looked out of the window, then leant towards her as he had been doing when I got in, and said in a bullying, menacing way, as if he would not stand any more nonsense:

"So about that matter we were discussing. It'll be all right? George will be there on Tuesday?"

"We shan't be late," said Mrs. Brown, gathering herself together with superb dignity.

Mr. Smith said nothing. He got up, buttoned his coat, reached his bag down, and jumped out of the train before it had stopped at Clapham Junction. He had got what he wanted, but he was ashamed of himself; he was glad to get out of the old lady's sight.

Mrs. Brown and I were left alone together. She sat in her corner opposite, very clean, very small, rather queer, and suffering intensely. The impression she made was overwhelming. It came pouring out like a draught, like a smell of burning. What was it composed of — that overwhelming and peculiar impression? Myriads of irrelevant and incongruous ideas crowd into one's head on such occasions; one sees the person, one sees Mrs. Brown, in the centre of all sorts of different scenes. I thought of her in a seaside house, among queer ornaments: sea-urchins, models of ships in glass cases. Her husband's medals were on the mantlepiece. She popped in and out of the room, perching on the edges of chairs, picking meals out of saucers, indulging in long, silent stares. The caterpillars and the oak-trees seemed to imply all that. And then, into this fantastic and secluded life, in broke Mr. Smith. I saw him blowing in, so to speak, on a windy day. He banged, he slammed. His dripping umbrella made a pool in the hall. They sat closeted together.

And then Mrs. Brown faced the dreadful revelation. She took her heroic decision. Early, before dawn, she packed her bag and carried it herself to the station. She would not let Smith touch it. She was wounded in her pride, unmoored from her anchorage; she came of gentlefolks who kept servants — but details could wait. The important thing was to realize her character, to steep oneself in her atmosphere. I had no time to explain why I felt it somewhat tragic, heroic, yet with a dash of the flighty and fantastic, before the train stopped, and I watched her disappear, carrying her bag, into the vast blazing station. She looked very small, very tenacious; at once very frail and very heroic. And I have never seen her again, and I shall never know what became of her.

The story ends without any point to it. But I have not told you this anecdote to illustrate either my own ingenuity or the pleasure of travelling from Richmond to Waterloo. What I want you to see in it is this. Here is a character imposing itself upon another person. Here is Mrs. Brown making someone begin almost automatically to write a novel about her. I believe that all novels begin with an old lady in the corner opposite. I believe that all novels, that is to say, deal with character, and that it is to express character — not to preach doctrines, sing songs, or celebrate the glories of the British Empire, that the form of the novel, so clumsy, verbose, and undramatic, so rich, elastic, and alive, has been evolved. To express character, I have said; but you will at once reflect that the very widest interpretation can be put upon those words. For example, old Mrs. Brown's character will strike you very differently according to the age and country in which you happen to be born. It would be easy enough to write three different versions of that incident in the train, an English, a French, and a Russian. The English writer would make the old lady into a "character"; he would bring out her oddities and mannerisms; her buttons and wrinkles; her ribbons and warts. Her personality would dominate the book. A French writer would rub out all that; he would sacrifice the individual Mrs. Brown to give a more general view of human nature; to make a more abstract, proportioned, and harmonious whole. The Russian would pierce through the flesh; would reveal the soul — the soul alone, wandering out into the Waterloo Road, asking of life some tremendous question which would sound on and on in our ears after the book was finished. And then besides age and country there is the writer's temperament to be considered. You see one thing in character, and I another. You say it means this, and I that. And when it comes to writing each makes a further selection on principles of his own. Thus Mrs. Brown can be treated in an infinite variety of ways, according to the age, country, and temperament of the writer.

But now I must recall what Mr. Arnold Bennett says. He says that it is only if the characters are real that the novel has any chance of surviving. Otherwise, die it must. But, I ask myself, what is reality? And who are the judges of reality? A character may be real to Mr. Bennett and quite unreal to me. For instance, in this article he says that Dr. Watson in *Sherlock*

Holmes is real to him: to me Dr. Watson is a sack stuffed with straw, a dummy, a figure of fun. And so it is with character after character — in book after book. There is nothing that people differ about more than the reality of characters, especially in contemporary books. But if you take a larger view I think that Mr. Bennett is perfectly right. If, that is, you think of the novels which seem to you great novels — *War and Peace, Vanity Fair, Tristram Shandy, Madame Bovary, Pride and Prejudice, The Mayor of Casterbridge, Villette* — if you think of these books, you do at once think of some character who has seemed to you so real (I do not by that mean so lifelike) that it has the power to make you think not merely of it itself, but of all sorts of things through its eyes — of religion, of love, of war, of peace, of family life, of balls in country towns, of sunsets, moonrises, the immortality of the soul. There is hardly any subject of human experience that is left out of *War and Peace* it seems to me. And in all these novels all these great novelists have brought us to see whatever they wish us to see through some character. Otherwise, they would not be novelists; but poets, historians, or pamphleteers.

But now let us examine what Mr. Bennett went on to say — he said that there was no great novelist among the Georgian writers because they cannot create characters who are real, true, and convincing. And there I cannot agree. There are reasons, excuses, possibilities which I think put a different colour upon the case. It seems so to me at least, but I am well aware that this is a matter about which I am likely to be prejudiced, sanguine, and nearsighted. I will put my view before you in the hope that you will make it impartial, judicial, and broad-minded. Why, then, is it so hard for novelists at present to create characters which seem real, not only to Mr. Bennett, but to the world at large? Why, when October comes round, do the publishers always fail to supply us with a masterpiece?

Surely one reason is that the men and women who began writing novels in 1910 or thereabouts had this great difficulty to face — that there was no English novelist living from whom they could learn their business. Mr. Conrad is a Pole; which sets him apart, and makes him, however admirable, not very helpful. Mr. Hardy has written no novel since 1895. The most prominent and successful novelists in the year 1910 were, I suppose, Mr. Wells, Mr. Bennett, and Mr. Galsworthy. Now it seems to me that to go to these men and ask them to teach you how to write a novel — how to create characters that are real — is precisely like going to a boot maker and asking him to teach you how to make a watch. Do not let me give you the impression that I do not admire and enjoy their books. They seem to me of great value, and indeed of great necessity. There are seasons when it is more important to have boots than to have watches. To drop metaphor, I think that after the creative activity of the Victorian age it was quite necessary, not only for literature but for life, that someone should write the books that Mr. Wells, Mr. Bennett, and Mr. Galsworthy have written. Yet what odd books they are! Sometimes I wonder if we are right to call them books at all. For they leave one with so strange a feeling of incompleteness and dissatisfaction. In order to complete them it seems necessary to do something — to join a society, or, more desperately, to write a cheque. That done, the restlessness is laid, the book finished; it can be put upon the shelf, and need never be read again. But with the work of other novelists it is different. *Tristram Shandy* or *Pride and Prejudice* is complete in itself; it is self-contained; it leaves one with no desire to do anything, except indeed to read the book again, and to understand it better. The difference perhaps is that both Sterne and Jane Austen were interested in things in themselves; in character, in itself; in the book in itself. Therefore everything was inside the book, nothing outside. But the Edwardians were never interested in character in itself; or in the book in itself. They were interested in something outside. Their books, then, were incomplete as books, and required that the reader should finish them, actively and practically, for himself.

. . . . With all his powers of observation, which are marvellous, with all his sympathy and humanity, which are great, Mr. Bennett has never once looked at Mrs. Brown in her corner. There she sits in the corner of the carriage — that carriage which is travelling, not from Richmond to Waterloo, but from one age of English literature to the next, for Mrs. Brown is eternal, Mrs. Brown is human nature, Mrs. Brown changes only on the surface, it is the novelists who get in and out — there she sits and not one of the Edwardian writers has so much as looked at her. They have looked very powerfully, searchingly, and sympathetically out of the window; at factories, at Utopias, even at the decoration and upholstery of the carriage; but never at her, never at life, never at human nature. And so they have developed a technique of novel-writing which suits their purpose; they have made tools and established conventions which do their business. But those tools are not our tools, and that business is not our business. For us those conventions are ruin, those tools are death.

You may well complain of the vagueness of my language. What is a convention, a tool, you may ask, and what do you mean by saying that Mr. Bennett's and Mr. Wells's and Mr. Galsworthy's conventions are the wrong conventions for the Georgians? The question is difficult: I will attempt a short cut. A convention in writing is not much different from a convention in manners. Both in life and in literature it is necessary to have some means of bridging the gulf between the hostess and her unknown guest on the one hand, the writer and his unknown reader on the other. The hostess bethinks her of the weather, for generations of hostesses have established the fact that this is a subject of universal interest in which we all believe. She begins by saying that we are having a wretched May, and, having thus got into touch with her unknown guest, proceeds to matters of greater interest. So it is in literature. The writer must get into touch with his reader by putting before him something which he recognizes, which therefore stimulates his imagination, and makes him willing to co-operate in the far more difficult business of intimacy. And it is of the highest importance that this common meeting-place should be reached easily, almost instinctively, in the dark, with one's eyes shut. Here is Mr. Bennett making use of this common ground in the passage which I have quoted. The problem before him was to make us believe in the reality of Hilda Lessways. So he began, being an Edwardian, by describing accurately and minutely the sort of house Hilda lived in, and the sort of house she saw from the window. House property was the common ground from which the Edwardians found it easy to proceed to intimacy. Indirect as it seems to us, the convention worked admirably, and thousands of Hilda Lessways were launched upon the world by this means. For that age and generation, the convention was a good one.

But now, if you will allow me to pull my own anecdote to pieces, you will see how keenly I felt the lack of a convention, and how serious a matter it is when the tools of one generation are useless for the next. The incident had made a great impression on me. But how was I to transmit it to you? All I could do was to report as accurately as I could what was said, to describe in detail what was worn, to say, despairingly, that all sorts of scenes rushed into my mind, to proceed to tumble them out pell-mell, and to describe this vivid, this overmastering impression by likening it to a draught or a smell of burning. To tell you the truth, I was also strongly tempted to manufacture a three-volume novel about the old lady's son, and his adventures crossing the Atlantic, and her daughter, and how she kept a milliner's shop in Westminister, the past life of Smith himself, and his house at Sheffield, though such stories seem to me the most dreary, irrelevant, and humbugging affairs in the world.

But if I had done that I should have escaped the appalling effort of saying what I meant. And to have got at what I meant I should have had to go back and back and back; to experiment with one thing and another; to try this sentence and that, referring each word to my vision, matching it as exactly as possible, and knowing that somehow I had to find a common ground between us, a convention which would not seem to you too odd, unreal, and far-fetched to believe in. I admit that I shirked that arduous undertaking. I let my Mrs. Brown slip through my fingers. I have told you nothing whatever about her. But that is partly the great Edwardians' fault. I asked them — they are my elders and betters — How shall I begin to describe this woman's character? And they said: "Begin by saying that her father kept a shop in Harrogate. Ascertain the rent. Ascertain the wages of shop assistants in the year 1878. Discover what her mother died of. Describe cancer. Describe calico. Describe — " But I cried: "Stop! Stop!" And I regret to say that I threw that ugly, that clumsy, that incongruous tool out of the window, for I knew that if I began describing the cancer and the calico, my Mrs. Brown, that vision to which I cling though I know no way of imparting it to you, would have been dulled and tarnished and vanished for ever.

That is what I mean by saying that the Edwardian tools are the wrong ones for us to use. They have laid an enormous stress upon the fabric of things. They have given us a house in the hope that we may be able to deduce the human beings who live there. To give them their due, they have made that house much better worth living in. But if you hold that novels are in the first place about people, and only in the second about the houses they live in, that is the wrong way to set about it. Therefore, you see, the Georgian writer had to begin by throwing away the method that was in use at the moment. He was left alone there facing Mrs. Brown without any method of conveying her to the reader. But that is inaccurate. A writer is never alone. There is always the public with him — if not on the same seat, at least in the compartment next door. Now the public is a strange travelling companion. In England it is a very suggestible and docile creature, which, once you get it to attend, will believe implicitly what it is told for a certain number of years. If you say to the public with sufficient conviction: "All women have tails, and all men humps," it will actually learn to see women with tails and men with humps, and will think it very revolutionary and probably improper if you say: "Nonsense. Monkeys have tails and camels humps. But men and women have brains, and they have hearts; they think and they feel," — that will seem to it a bad joke, and an improper one into the bargain.

In view of these facts — with these sounds in my ears and these fancies in my brain — I am not going to deny that Mr. Bennett has some reason when he complains that our Georgian writers are unable to make us believe that our characters are real. I am forced to agree that they do not pour out three immortal masterpieces with Victorian regularity every autumn. But, instead of being gloomy, I am sanguine. For this state of things is, I think, inevitable whenever from hoar old age or callow youth the convention ceases to be a means of communication between writer and reader, and becomes instead an obstacle and an impediment. At the present moment we are suffering, not from decay, but from having no code of manners which writers and readers accept as a prelude to the more exciting intercourse of friendship. The literary convention of the time is so artificial — you have to talk about the weather and nothing but the weather throughout the entire visit — that, naturally, the feeble are tempted to outrage, and the strong are led to destroy the very foundations and rules of literary society. Signs of this are everywhere apparent. Grammar is violated; syntax disintegrated; as a boy staying with an aunt for the week-end rolls in the geranium bed out of sheer desperation as the solemnities of the sabbath wear on. The more adult writers do not, of course, indulge in such wanton exhibitions of spleen. Their sincerity is desperate, and their courage tremendous; it is only that they do not know which to use, a fork or their fingers. Thus, if you read Mr. Joyce and Mr. Eliot you will be struck by the indecency of the one, and the obscurity of the other. Mr. Joyce's indecency in *Ulysses* seems to me the conscious and calculated indecency of a desperate man who feels that in order to breathe he must break the windows. At moments, when the window is broken, he is magnificent. But what a waste of energy! And, after all, how dull indecency is, when it is not the overflowing of a superabundant energy or savagery, but the determined and public-spirited act of a man who needs fresh air! Again, with the obscurity of Mr. Eliot. I think that Mr. Eliot has written some of the loveliest single lines in modern poetry. But how intolerant he is of the old usages and politenesses of society — respect for the weak, consideration for the dull! As I sun myself upon the intense and ravishing beauty of one of his lines, and reflect that I must make a dizzy and dangerous leap to the next, and so on from line to line, like an acrobat flying precariously from bar to bar, I cry out, I confess, for the old decorums, and envy the indolence of my ancestors who, instead of spinning madly through mid-air, dreamt quietly in the shade with a book. Again, in Mr. Strachey's books, *Eminent Victorians* and *Queen Victoria,* the effort and strain of writing against the grain and current of the times is visible too. It is much less visible, of course, for not only is he dealing with facts, which are stubborn things, but he has fabricated, chiefly from eighteenth-century material, a very discreet code of manners of his own, which allows him to sit at table with the highest in the land and to say a great many things under cover of that exquisite apparel which, had they gone naked, would have been chased by the men-servants from the room. Still, if you compare *Eminent Victorians* with some of Lord Macaulay's essays, though you will feel that Lord Macaulay is always wrong, and Mr. Strachey always right, you will also feel a body, a sweep, a richness in Lord Macaulay's essays which show that his age was behind him; all his strength went straight into his work; none was used for purposes of concealment or of conversion. But Mr. Strachey has had to open our eyes before he made us see; he has had to search out and sew together a very artful manner of speech; and the effort, beautifully though it is concealed, has robbed his work of some of the force that should have gone into it, and limited his scope.

For these reasons, then, we must reconcile ourselves to a season of failures and fragments. We must reflect that where so much strength is spent on finding a way of telling the truth, the truth itself is bound to reach us in rather an exhausted and chaotic condition. Ulysses, Queen Victoria, Mr. Prufrock — to give Mrs. Brown some of the names she has made famous lately — is a little pale and dishevelled by the time her rescuers reach her. And it is the sound of their axes that we hear — a vigorous and stimulating sound in my ears — unless of course you wish to sleep, when, in the bounty of his concern, Providence has provided a host of writers anxious and able to satisfy your needs.

Thus I have tried, at tedious length, I fear, to answer some of the questions which I began by asking. I have given an account of some of the difficulties which in my view beset the Georgian writer in all his forms. I have sought to excuse him. May I end by venturing to remind you of the duties and responsibilities that are yours as partners in this business of writing books, as companions in the railway carriage, as fellow travellers with Mrs. Brown? For she is just as visible to you who remain silent as to us who tell stories about her. In the course of your daily life this past week you have had far stranger and more interesting experiences than the one I have tried to describe. You have overheard scraps of talk that filled you with amazement. You have gone to bed at night bewildered by the complexity of your feelings. In one day thousands of ideas have coursed through your brains; thousands of emotions have met, collided, and disappeared in astonishing disorder. Nevertheless, you allow the writers to palm off upon you a version of all this, an image of Mrs. Brown, which has no likeness to that surprising apparition whatsoever. In your modesty you seem to consider that writers are different blood and bone from yourselves; that they know more of Mrs. Brown than you do. Never was there a more fatal mistake. It is this division between reader and writer, this humility on your part, these professional airs and graces on ours, that corrupt and emasculate the books which should be the healthy offspring of a close and equal alliance between us. Hence spring those sleek, smooth novels, those portentous and ridiculous biographies, that milk and watery criticism, those poems melodiously celebrating the innocence of roses and sheep which pass so plausibly for literature at the present time.

Your part is to insist that writers shall come down off their plinths and pedestals, and describe beautifully if possible, truthfully at any rate, our Mrs. Brown. You should insist that she is an old lady of unlimited capacity and infinite variety; capable of appearing in any place; wearing any dress; saying anything and doing heaven knows what. But the things she says and the things she does and her eyes and her nose and her speech and her silence have an overwhelming fascination, for she is, of course, the spirit we live by, life itself.

But do not expect just at present a complete and satisfactory presentment of her. Tolerate the spasmodic, the obscure, the fragmentary, the failure. Your help is invoked in a good cause. For I will make one final and surpassingly rash prediction — we are trembling on the verge of one of the great ages of English literature. But it can only be reached if we are determined never, never to desert Mrs. Brown.

3 E. M. Forster : *Flat and Round Characters*

In this brief excerpt from *Aspects of the Novel* (1927), E. M. Forster defines two basic types of characters, their qualities, functions, and importance for the development of a novel. "Flat" characters, he says, "are constructed round a single idea or quality." In addition, they undergo no change or development. If, in a sense, the flat character embodies an idea or quality, then the "round" character encompasses many ideas and qualities, undergoing change and development, as well as entertaining different ideas and characteristics. Forster uses Jane Austen to demonstrate his contention that "the test of a round character is whether it is capable of surprising in a convincing way." We may want to consider, given Forster's definitions, the relationship between the use of flat and round characters and the primacy of either formal or thematic concerns in creating particular works of fiction. If Virginia Woolf's claims have any validity, we may anticipate that modernist novels will demonstrate more attention to "round" character development, while novels that are oriented socially and thematically will rely largely on "flat" characters. Is this actually the case? Let us also consider why an author might choose either flat or round characters in a specific situation and how that choice might affect the advancement of a novel's plot or narrative structure.

E. M. Forster (1879–1970) was a major English prose stylist in the novel, the short story, and the literary essay. His most famous novels are *A Room with a View* (1908), *Howards End* (1910), and *A Passage to India* (1924). Many of his best essays are collected in *Arbinger Harvest* (1936).

We may divide characters into flat and round.

Flat characters were called "humorous" in the seventeenth century, and are sometimes called types, and sometimes caricatures. In their purest form, they are constructed round a single idea or quality: when there is more than one factor in them, we get the beginning of the curve towards the round. The really flat character can be expressed in one sentence such as "I never will desert Mr. Micawber." There is Mrs. Micawber — she says she won't desert Mr. Micawber, she doesn't, and there she is. Or: "I must conceal, even by subterfuges, the poverty of my master's house." There is Caleb Balderstone in *The Bride of Lammermoor*. He does not use the actual phrase, but it completely describes him; he has no existence outside it, no pleasures, none of the private lusts and aches that must complicate the most consistent of servitors. Whatever he does, wherever he goes, whatever lies he tells or plates he breaks, it is to conceal the poverty of his master's house. It is not his *idée fixe,* because there is nothing in him into which the idea can be fixed. He is the idea, and such life as he possesses radiates from its edges and from the scintillations it strikes when other elements in the novel impinge. Or take Proust. There are numerous flat characters in Proust, such as the Princess of Parma, or Legrandin. Each can be expressed in a single sentence, the Princess's sentence being, "I must be particularly careful to be kind." She does nothing except to be particularly careful, and those of the other characters who are more complex than herself easily see through the kindness, since it is only a by-product of the carefulness.

One great advantage of flat characters is that they are easily recognized whenever they come in — recognized by the reader's emotional eye, not by the visual eye, which merely notes the recurrence of a proper name. In Russian novels, where they so seldom occur, they would be a decided help. It is a convenience for an author when he can strike with his full force at once, and flat characters are very useful to him, since they never need reintroducing, never run away, have not to be watched for development, and provide their own atmosphere — little luminous disks of a pre-arranged size, pushed hither and thither like counters across the void or between the stars; most satisfactory.

A second advantage is that they are easily remembered by the reader afterwards. They remain in his mind as unalterable for the reason that they were not changed by circumstances; they moved through circumstances, which gives them in retrospect a comforting quality, and preserves them when the book that produced them may decay. The Countess in *Evan Harrington* furnishes a good little example here. Let us compare our memories of her with our memories of Becky Sharp. We do not remember what the Countess did or what she passed through. What is clear is her figure and the formula that surrounds it, namely, "Proud as we are of dear papa, we must conceal his memory." All her rich humour proceeds from this. She is a flat character. Becky is round. She, too, is on the make, but she cannot be summed up in a single phrase, and we remember her in connection with the great scenes through which she passed and as modified by those scenes — that is to say, we do not remember her so easily because she waxes and wanes and has facets like a human being. All of us, even the sophisticated, yearn for permanence, and to the unsophisticated permanence is the chief excuse for a work of art. We all want books to endure, to be refuges, and their inhabitants to be always the same, and flat characters tend to justify themselves on this account.

All the same, critics who have their eyes fixed severely upon daily life — as were our eyes last week — have very little patience with such renderings of human nature. Queen Victoria, they argue, cannot be summed up in a single sentence, so what excuse remains for Mrs. Micawber? One of our foremost writers, Mr. Norman Douglas, is a critic of this type, and the passage from him which I will quote puts the case against flat characters in a forcible fashion. The passage occurs in an open letter to D. H. Lawrence, with whom he is quarrelling: a doughty pair of combatants, the hardness of whose hitting makes the rest of us feel like a lot of ladies up in a pavilion. He complains that Lawrence, in a biography, has falsified the picture by employing "the novelist's touch," and he goes on to define what this is:

> It consists, I should say, in a failure to realize the complexities of the ordinary human mind; it selects for literary purposes two or three facets of a man or woman, generally the most spectacular, and therefore useful ingredients of their character and disregards all the others. Whatever fails to fit in with these specially chosen traits is eliminated — must be eliminated, for otherwise the description would not hold water. Such and such are the data: everything incompatible with those data has to go by the board. It follows that the novelist's touch argues, often logically, from a wrong premise: it takes what it likes and leaves the rest. The facets may be correct as far as they go but there are too few of them: what the author says may be true and yet by no means the truth. That is the novelist's touch. It falsifies life.

Well, the novelist's touch as thus defined is, of course, bad in biography, for no human being is simple. But in a novel it has its place: a novel that is at all complex often requires flat people as well as round, and the outcome of their collisions parallels life more accurately than Mr. Douglas implies. The case of Dickens is significant. Dickens's people are nearly all flat (Pip and David Copperfield attempt roundness, but so diffidently that they seem more like bubbles than solids). Nearly every one can be summed up in a sentence, and yet there is this wonderful feeling of human depth. Probably the immense vitality of Dickens causes his characters to vibrate a little, so that they borrow his life and appear to lead one of their own. It is a conjuring trick; at any moment we may look at Mr. Pickwick edgeways and find him no thicker than a gramophone record. But we never get the sideway view. Mr. Pickwick is far too adroit and well-trained. He always has the air of weighing something, and when he is put into the cupboard of the young ladies' school he seems as heavy as Falstaff in the buck-basket at Windsor. Part of the genius of Dickens is that he does use types and caricatures, people whom we recognize the instant they re-enter, and yet achieves effects that are not mechanical and a vision of humanity that is not shallow. Those who dislike Dickens have an excellent case. He ought to be bad. He is actually one of our big writers, and his immense success with types suggests that there may be more in flatness than the severer critics admit.

Or take H. G. Wells. With the possible exceptions of Kipps and the aunt in *Tono Bungay,* all Wells's characters are as flat as a photograph. But the photographs are agitated with such vigour that we forget their complexities lie on the surface and would disappear if it were scratched or curled up. A Wells character cannot indeed be summed up in a single phrase; he is tethered much more to observation, he does not create types. Nevertheless his people seldom pulsate by their own strength. It is the deft and powerful hands of their maker that shake them and trick the reader into a sense of depth. Good but imperfect novelists, like Wells and Dickens, are very clever at transmitting force. The part of their novel that is alive galvanizes the part that is not, and causes the characters to jump about and speak in a convincing way. They are quite different from the perfect novelist who touches all his material directly, who seems to pass the creative finger down every sentence and into every word. Richardson, Defoe, Jane Austen, are perfect in this particular way; their work may not be great but their hands are always upon it; there is not the tiny interval between the touching of the button and the sound of the bell which occurs in novels where the characters are not under direct control.

For we must admit that flat people are not in themselves as big achievements as round ones, and also that they are best when they are comic. A serious or tragic flat character is apt to be a bore. Each time he enters crying "Revenge!" or "My heart bleeds for humanity!" or whatever his formula is, our hearts sink. One of the romances of a popular contemporary writer is constructed round a Sussex farmer who says, "I'll plough up that bit of gorse." There is the farmer, there is the gorse; he says he'll plough it up, he does plough it up, but it is not like saying "I'll never desert Mr. Micawber," because we are so bored by his consistency that we do not care whether he succeeds with the gorse or fails. If his formula were analysed and connected up with the rest of the human outfit, we should not be bored any longer, the formula would cease to be the man and become an obsession in the man; that is to say he would have turned from a flat farmer into a round one. It is only round people who are fit to perform tragically for any length of time and can move us to any feelings except humour and appropriateness.

So now let us desert these two-dimensional people, and by way of transition to the round, let us go to *Mansfield Park,* and look at Lady Bertram, sitting on her sofa with pug. Pug is flat, like most animals in fiction. He is once represented as straying into a rosebed in a cardboard kind of way, but that is all, and during most of the book his mistress seems to be cut out of the same simple material as her dog. Lady Bertram's formula is, "I am kindly, but must not be fatigued," and she functions out of it. But at the end there is a catastrophe. Her two daughters come to grief—to the worst grief known to Miss Austen's universe, far worse than the Napoleonic wars. Julia elopes; Maria, who is unhappily married, runs off with a lover. What is Lady Bertram's reaction? The sentence describing it is significant: "Lady Bertram did not think deeply, but, guided by Sir Thomas, she thought justly on all important points, and she saw therefore in all its enormity, what had happened, and neither endeavoured herself, nor required Fanny to advise her, to think little of guilt and infamy." These are strong words, and they used to worry me because I thought Jane Austen's moral sense was getting out of hand. She may, and of course does, deprecate guilt and infamy herself, and she duly causes all possible distress in the minds of Edmund and Fanny, but has she any right to agitate calm, consistent Lady Bertram? Is not it like giving pug three faces and setting him to guard the gates of Hell? Ought not her ladyship to remain on the sofa saying, "This is a dreadful and sadly exhausting business about Julia and Maria, but where is Fanny gone? I have dropped another stitch"?

I used to think this, through misunderstanding Jane Austen's method—exactly as Scott misunderstood it when he congratulated her for painting on a square of ivory. She is a miniaturist, but never two-dimensional. All her characters are round, or capable of rotundity. Even Miss Bates has a mind, even Elizabeth Eliot a heart, and Lady Bertram's moral fervour ceases to vex us when we realize this: the disk has suddenly extended and become a little globe. When the novel is closed, Lady Bertram goes back to the flat, it is true; the dominant impression she leaves can be summed up in a formula. But that is not how Jane Austen conceived her, and the freshness of her reappearances are due to this. Why do the characters in Jane Austen give us a slightly new pleasure each time they come in, as opposed to the merely repetitive pleasure that is caused by a character in Dickens? Why do they combine so well in a conversation, and draw one another out without seeming to do so, and never perform? The answer to this question can be put in several ways: that, unlike Dickens, she was a real artist, that she never stooped to caricature, etc. But the best reply is that her characters though smaller than his are more highly organized. They function all round, and even if her plot made greater demands on them than it does, they would still be adequate. Suppose that Louisa Musgrove had broken her neck on the Cobb. The description of her death would have been feeble and ladylike — physical violence is quite beyond Miss Austen's powers — but the survivors would have reacted properly as soon as the corpse was carried away, they would have brought into view new sides of their character, and though *Persuasion* would have been spoiled as a book, we should know more than we do about Captain Wentworth and Anne. All the Jane Austen characters are ready for an extended life, for a life which the scheme of her books seldom requires them to lead, and that is why they lead their actual lives so satisfactorily. Let us return to Lady Bertram and the crucial sentence. See how subtly it modulates from her formula into an area where the formula does not work. "Lady Bertram did not think deeply." Exactly: as per formula. "But guided by Sir Thomas she thought justly on all important points." Sir Thomas' guidance, which is part of the formula, remains, but it pushes her ladyship towards an independent and undesired morality. "She saw therefore in all its enormity what had happened." This is the moral fortissimo — very strong but carefully introduced. And then follows a most artful decrescendo, by means of negatives. "She neither endeavoured herself, nor required Fanny to advise her, to think little of guilt or infamy." The formula is reappearing, because as a rule she does try to minimize trouble, and does require Fanny to advise her how to do this; indeed Fanny has done nothing else for the last ten years. The words, though they are negatived, remind us of this, her normal state is again in view, and she has in a single sentence been inflated into a round character and collapsed back into a flat one. How Jane Austen can write! In a few words she has extended Lady Bertram, and by so doing she has increased the probability of the elopements of Maria and Julia. I say probability because the elopements belong to the domain of violent physical action, and here, as already indicated, Jane Austen is feeble and ladylike. Except in her schoolgirl novels, she cannot stage a crash. Everything violent has to take place "off" — Louisa's accident and Marianne Dashwood's putrid throat are the nearest exceptions — and consequently all the comments on the elopement must be sincere and convincing, otherwise we should doubt whether it occurred. Lady Bertram helps us to believe that her daughters have run away, and they have to run away, or there would be no apotheosis for Fanny. It is a little point, and a little sentence, yet it shows us how delicately a great novelist can modulate into the round.

All through her works we find these characters, apparently so simple and flat, never needing reintroduction and yet never out of depth — Henry Tilney, Mr. Woodhouse, Charlotte Lucas. She may label her characters "Sense," "Pride," "Sensibility," "Prejudice," but they are not tethered to those qualities.

As for the round characters proper, they have already been defined by implication and no more need be said. All I need do is to give some examples of people in books who seem to me round so that the definition can be tested afterwards:

All the principal characters in *War and Peace,* all the Dostoevsky characters, and some of the Proust — for example, the old family servant, the Duchess of Guermantes, M. de Charlus, and Saint Loup; Madame Bovary — who, like Moll Flanders, has her book to herself, and can expand and secrete unchecked; some people in Thackeray — for instance, Becky and Beatrix; some in Fielding — Parson Adams, Tom Jones; and some in Charlotte Brontë, most particularly Lucy Snowe. (And many more — this is not a catalogue.) The test of a round character is whether it is capable of surprising in a convincing way. If it never surprises, it is flat. If it does not convince, it is a flat pretending to be round. It has the incalculability of life about it — life within the pages of a book. And by using it sometimes alone, more often in combination with the other kind, the novelist achieves his task of acclimatization and harmonizes the human race with the other aspects of his work.

4 M. M. Bakhtin : *Epic and Novel*

Toward a Methodology for the Study of the Novel

Mikhail Bakhtin began writing about literature in the 1920s, but only recently has his work been translated into English. These translations have produced wide-spread interest in what has become termed the "dialogic method." In this excerpt from "Epic and Novel," written in 1941, Bakhtin presents his conception of genre, in particular that of the novel, and he introduces some concepts which guide his method. For him a key difficulty and major point of interest in analyzing the novel lies in its being still a young genre that is developing and changing: "Of all the major genres only the novel is younger than writing and the book: it alone is organically receptive to new forms of mute perception, that is, to reading." Of major significance here is Bakhtin's argument that the novel is a *new* genre, qualitatively different from the epic in direct contrast to the claims of numerous other critics. Also important is Bakhtin's concept of the novel's ability to incorporate and satirize other genres as well as its own various styles: "This ability of the novel to criticize itself is a remarkable feature of this ever-developing genre."

In many ways, Bakhtin's excitement over the novel as a developing genre that "has become the leading hero in the dream of literary development" echoes Virginia Woolf's claims for modernist literature in the 1920s. For both writers the ability to experiment and innovate is an essential feature of literary leadership. One should also note that Bakhtin claims that the old poetics — that is, old literary theory — is inadequate to describe the modern novel. A new genre calls for new critical methods and viewpoints, ones that must begin as a descriptive poetics of the novels actually being written. Bakhtin sketches the characteristics of this genre by contrasting the novel with the epic, focusing on source material, the role of the narrator, the treatment of the hero, and the genre's relationship to the present.

Mikhail Bakhtin (1895–1975) has become famous as the founder of the di-alogic method in literary criticism, as developed in books and essays written over a sixty-year period. The authorship of a few works remains contested, primarily *Marxism and the Philosophy of Language* (1929; trans. 1973), attributed to V. N. Voloshinov. He is definitely the author of *Art and Answerability* (trans. 1990), *The Dialogic Imagination* (1975; trans. 1981), *Problems of Dostoevsky's Poetics* (1929; trans. 1984), *Rabelais and His World* (1965; trans. 1968), *Speech Genres and Other Late Essays* (1979; trans. 1986), and *Toward a Philosophy of the Act* (trans. 1993).

The study of the novel as a genre is distinguished by peculiar difficulties. This is due to the unique nature of the object itself: the novel is the sole genre that continues to develop, that is as yet uncompleted. The forces that define it as a genre are at work before our very eyes: the birth and development of the novel as a genre takes place in the full light of the historical day. The generic skeleton of the novel is still far from having hardened, and we cannot foresee all its plastic possibilities.

We know other genres, as genres, in their completed aspect, that is, as more or less fixed pre-existing forms into which one may then pour artistic experience. The primordial process of their formation lies outside historically documented observation. We encounter the epic as a genre that has not only long since completed its development, but one that is already antiquated. With certain reservations we can say the same for the other major genres, even for tragedy. The life they have in history, the life with which we are familiar, is the life they have lived as already completed genres, with a hardened and no longer flexible skeleton. Each of them has developed its own canon that operates in literature as an authentic historical force.

All these genres, or in any case their defining features, are considerably older than written language and the book, and to the present day they retain their ancient oral and auditory characteristics. Of all the major genres only the novel is younger than writing and the book: it alone is organically receptive to new forms of mute perception, that is, to reading. But of critical importance here is the fact that the novel has no canon of its own, as do other genres; only individual examples of the novel are historically active, not a generic canon as such. Studying other genres is analogous to studying dead languages; studying the novel, on the other hand, is like studying languages that are not only alive, but still young.

This explains the extraordinary difficulty inherent in formulating a theory of the novel. For such a theory has at its heart an object of study completely different from that which theory treats in other genres. The novel is not merely one genre among other genres. Among genres long since completed and in part already dead, the novel is the only developing genre. It is the only genre that was born and nourished in a new era of world history and therefore it is deeply akin to that era, whereas the other major genres entered that era as already fixed forms, as an inheritance, and only now are they adapting themselves — some better, some worse — to the new conditions of their existence. Compared with them, the novel appears to be a creature from an alien species. It gets on poorly with other genres. It fights for its own hegemony in literature; wherever it triumphs, the other older genres go into decline. Significantly, the best book on the history of the ancient novel — that by Erwin Rohde[1] — does not so much recount the history of the novel as it does illustrate the process of disintegration that affected all major genres in antiquity.

The mutual interaction of genres within a single unified literary period is a problem of great interest and importance. In certain eras — the Greek classical period, the Golden Age of Roman literature, the neoclassical period — all genres in "high" literature (that is, the literature of ruling social groups) harmoniously reinforce each other to a significant extent; the whole of literature, conceived as a totality of genres, becomes an organic unity of the highest order. But it is characteristic of the novel that it never enters into this whole, it does not participate in any harmony of the genres. In these eras the novel has an unofficial existence, outside "high" literature. Only already completed genres, with fully formed and well-defined generic contours, can enter into such a literature as a hierarchically organized, organic whole. They can mutually delimit and mutually complement each other, while yet preserving their own generic natures. Each is a unit, and all units are interrelated by virtue of certain features of deep structure that they all have in common.

The great organic poetics of the past — those of Aristotle, Horace, Boileau — are permeated with a deep sense of the wholeness of literature and of the harmonious interaction of all genres contained within this whole. It is as if they literally hear this harmony of the genres. In this is their strength — the inimitable, all-embracing fullness and exhaustiveness of such poetics. And they all, as a consequence, ignore the novel. Scholarly poetics of the nineteenth century lack this integrity: they are eclectic, descriptive; their aim is not a living and organic fullness but rather an abstract and encyclopedic comprehensiveness. They do not concern themselves with the actual possibility of specific genres coexisting within the living whole of literature in a given era; they are concerned rather with their coexistence in a maximally complete anthology. Of course these poetics can no longer ignore the novel — they simply add it (albeit in a place of honor) to already existing genres (and thus it enters the roster as merely one genre among many; in literature conceived as a living whole, on the other hand, it would have to be included in a completely different way).

We have already said that the novel gets on poorly with other genres. There can be no talk of a harmony deriving from mutual limitation and complementariness. The novel parodies other genres (precisely in their role as genres); it exposes the conventionality of their forms and their language; it squeezes out some genres and incorporates others into its own peculiar structure, reformulating and reaccentuating them. Historians of literature sometimes tend to see in this merely the struggle of literary tendencies and schools. Such struggles of course exist, but they are peripheral phenomena and historically insignificant. Behind them one must be sensitive to the deeper and deeper and more truly historical struggle of genres, the establishment and growth of a generic skeleton of literature.

Of particular interest are those eras when the novel becomes the dominant genre. All literature is then caught up in the process of "becoming," and in a special kind of "generic criticism." This occurred several times in the Hellenic period, again during the late middle ages and the Renaissance, but with special force and clarity beginning in the second half of the eighteenth century. In an era when the novel reigns supreme, almost all the remaining genres are to a greater or lesser extent "novelized": drama (for example Ibsen, Hauptmann, the whole of Naturalist drama), epic poetry (for example, *Childe Harold* and especially Byron's *Don Juan*), even lyric poetry (as an extreme example, Heine's lyrical verse). Those genres that stubbornly preserve their old canonic nature begin to appear stylized. In general any strict adherence to a genre begins to feel like a stylization, a stylization taken to the point of parody, despite the artistic intent of the author. In an environment where the novel is the dominant genre, the conventional languages of strictly canonical genres begin to sound in new ways, which are quite different from the ways they sounded in those eras when the novel was *not* included in "high" literature.

Parodic stylizations of canonized genres and styles occupy an essential place in the novel. In the era of the novel's creative ascendency — and even more so in the periods of preparation preceding this era — literature was flooded with parodies and travesties of all the high genres (parodies precisely of genres, and not of individual authors or schools) — parodies that are the precursors, "companions" to the novel, in their own way studies for it. But it is characteristic that the novel does not permit any of these various individual manifestations of itself to stabilize. Throughout its entire history there is a consistent parodying or travestying of dominant or fashionable novels that attempt to become models for the genre: parodies on the chivalric romance of adventure (*Dit d'aventures,* the first such parody, belongs to the thirteenth century), on the Baroque novel, the pastoral novel (Sorel's *Le berger extravagant*),[2] the Sentimental novel (Fielding, and *The Second Grandison*[3] of Musäus) and so forth. This ability of the novel to criticize itself is a remarkable feature of this ever-developing genre.

What are the salient features of this novelization of other genres suggested by us above? They become more free and flexible, their language renews itself by incorporating extraliterary heteroglossia and the "novelistic" layers of literary language, they become dialogized, permeated with laughter, irony, humor, elements of self-parody and finally—this is the most important thing—the novel inserts into these other genres an indeterminacy, a certain semantic open-endedness, a living contact with unfinished, still-evolving contemporary reality (the open-ended present). As we will see below, all these phenomena are explained by the transposition of other genres into this new and peculiar zone for structuring artistic models (a zone of contact with the present in all its open-endedness), a zone that was first appropriated by the novel.

It is of course impossible to explain the phenomenon of novelization purely by reference to the direct and unmediated influence of the novel itself. Even where such influence can be precisely established and demonstrated, it is intimately interwoven with those direct changes in reality itself that also determine the novel and that condition its dominance in a given era. The novel is the only developing genre and therefore it reflects more deeply, more essentially, more sensitively and rapidly, reality itself in the process of its unfolding. Only that which is itself developing can comprehend development as a process. The novel has become the leading hero in the drama of literary development in our time precisely because it best of all reflects the tendencies of a new world still in the making; it is, after all, the only genre born of this new world and in total affinity with it. In many respects the novel has anticipated, and continues to anticipate, the future development of literature as a whole. In the process of becoming the dominant genre, the novel sparks the renovation of all other genres, it infects them with its spirit of process and inconclusiveness. It draws them ineluctably into its orbit precisely because this orbit coincides with the basic direction of the development of literature as a whole. In this lies the exceptional importance of the novel, as an object of study for the theory as well as the history of literature.

Unfortunately, historians of literature usually reduce this struggle between the novel and other already completed genres, all these aspects of novelization, to the actual real-life struggle among "schools" and "trends." A novelized poem, for example, they call a "romantic poem" (which of course it is) and believe that in so doing they have exhausted the subject. They do not see beneath the superficial hustle and bustle of literary process the major and crucial fates of literature and language, whose great heroes turn out to be first and foremost genres, and whose "trends" and "schools" are but second- or third-rank protagonists.

The utter inadequacy of literary theory is exposed when it is forced to deal with the novel. In the case of other genres literary theory works confidently and precisely, since there is a finished and already formed object, definite and clear. These genres preserve their rigidity and canonic quality in all classical eras of their development; variations from era to era, from trend to trend or school to school are peripheral and do not affect their ossified generic skeleton. Right up to the present day, in fact, theory dealing with these already completed genres can add almost nothing to Aristotle's formulations. Aristotle's poetics, although occasionally so deeply embedded as to be almost invisible, remains the stable foundation for the theory of genres. Everything works as long as there is no mention of the novel. But the existence of novelized genres already leads theory into a blind alley. Faced with the problem of the novel, genre theory must submit to a radical restructuring.

Thanks to the meticulous work of scholars, a huge amount of historical material has accumulated and many questions concerning the evolution of various types of novels have been clarified — but the problem of the novel genre as a whole has not yet found anything like a satisfactory principled resolution. The novel continues to be seen as one genre among many; attempts are made to distinguish it as an already completed genre from other already completed genres, to discover its internal canon — one that would function as a well-defined system of rigid generic factors. In the vast majority of cases, work on the novel is reduced to mere cataloging, a description of all variants on the novel — albeit as comprehensive as possible. But the results of these descriptions never succeed in giving us as much as a hint of comprehensive formula for the novel as a genre. In addition, the experts have not managed to isolate a single definite, stable characteristic of the novel — without adding a reservation, which immediately disqualifies it altogether as a generic characteristic.

Some examples of such "characteristics with reservations" would be: the novel is a multilayered genre (although there also exist magnificent single-layered novels); the novel is a precisely plotted and dynamic genre (although there also exist novels that push to its literary limits the art of pure description); the novel is a complicated genre (although novels are mass produced as pure and frivolous entertainment like no other genre); the novel is a love story (although the greatest examples of the European novel are utterly devoid of the love element); the novel is a prose genre (although there exist excellent novels in verse). One could of course mention a large number of additional "generic characteristics" for the novel similar to those given above, which are immediately annulled by some reservation innocently appended to them.

Of considerably more interest and consequence are those normative definitions of the novel offered by novelists themselves, who produce a specific novel and then declare it the only correct, necessary and authentic form of the novel. Such, for instance, is Rousseau's foreword to his *La nouvelle Héloïse,* Wieland's to his *Agathon,*[4] Wezel's to his *Tobias Knouts;*[5] in such a category belong the numerous declarations and statements of principle by the romantics on *Wilhelm Meister, Lucinde,* and other texts. Such statements are not attempts to incorporate all the possible variants of the novel into a single eclectic definition, but are themselves part and parcel of the living evolution of the novel as a genre. Often they deeply and faithfully reflect the novel's struggle with other genres and with itself (with other dominant and fashionable variants of the novel) at a particular point in its development. They come closer to an understanding of the peculiar position of the novel in literature, a position that is not commensurate with that of other genres.

Especially significant in this connection is a series of statements that accompanied the emergence of a new novel-type in the eighteenth century. The series opens with Fielding's reflections on the novel and its hero in *Tom Jones.* It continues in Wieland's foreword to *Agathon,* and the most essential link in the series is Blankenburg's *Versuch über den Roman.*[6] By the end of this series we have, in fact, that theory of the novel later formulated by Hegel. In all these statements, each reflecting the novel in one of its critical stages (*Tom Jones, Agathon, Wilhelm Meister*), the following prerequisites for the novel are characteristic: (1) the novel should not be "poetic," as the word "poetic" is used in other genres of imaginative literature; (2) the hero of a novel should not be "heroic" in either the epic or the tragic sense of the word: he should combine in himself negative as well as positive features, low as well as lofty, ridiculous as well as serious; (3) the hero should not be portrayed as an already completed and unchanging person but as one who is evolving and developing, a person who learns from life; (4) the novel should become for the contemporary world what the epic was for the ancient world (an idea that Blankenburg expressed very precisely, and that was later repeated by Hegel).

All these positive prerequisites have their substantial and productive side — taken together, they constitute a criticism (from the novel's point of view) of other genres and of the relationship these genres bear to reality: their stilted heroizing, their narrow and unlifelike poeticalness, their monotony and abstractness, the prepackaged and unchanging nature of their heroes. We have here, in fact, a rigorous critique of the literariness and poeticalness inherent in other genres and also in the predecessors of the contemporary novel (the heroic Baroque novel and the Sentimental novels of Richardson). These statements are reinforced significantly by the practice of these novelists themselves. Here the novel — its texts as well as the theory connected with it — emerges consciously and unambiguously as a genre that is both critical and self-critical, one fated to revise the fundamental concepts of literariness and poeticalness dominant at the time. On the one hand, the contrast of novel with epic (and the novel's opposition to the epic) is but one moment in the criticism of other literary genres (in particular, a criticism of epic heroization); but on the other hand, this contrast aims to elevate the significance of the novel, making of it the dominant genre in contemporary literature.

The positive prerequisites mentioned above constitute one of the highpoints in the novel's coming to self-consciousness. They do not yet of course provide a theory of the novel. These statements are also not distinguished by any great philosophical depth. They do however illustrate the nature of the novel as a genre no less — if perhaps no more — than do other existing theories of the novel.

I will attempt below to approach the novel precisely as a genre-in-the-making, one in the vanguard of all modern literary development. I am not constructing here a functional definition of the novelistic canon in literary history, that is, a definition that would make of it a system of fixed generic characteristics. Rather, I am trying to grope my way toward the basic structural characteristics of this most fluid of genres, characteristics that might determine the direction of its peculiar capacity for change and of its influence and effect on the rest of literature.

I find three basic characteristics that fundamentally distinguish the novel in principle from other genres: (1) its stylistic three-dimensionality, which is linked with the multi-languaged consciousness realized in the novel; (2) the radical change it effects in the temporal coordinates of the literary image; (3) the new zone opened by the novel for structuring literary images, namely, the zone of maximal contact with the present (with contemporary reality) in all its open-endedness.

These three characteristics of the novel are all organically interrelated and have all been powerfully affected by a very specific rupture in the history of European civilization: its emergence from a socially isolated and culturally deaf semipatriarchal society, and its entrance into international and interlingual contacts and relationships. A multitude of different languages, cultures and times became available to Europe, and this became a decisive factor in its life and thought.

In another work[7] I have already investigated the first stylistic peculiarity of the novel, the one resulting from the active polyglossia of the new world, the new culture and its new creative literary consciousness. I will summarize here only the basic points.

Polyglossia had always existed (it is more ancient than pure, canonic monoglossia), but it had not been a factor in literary creation; an artistically conscious choice between languages did not serve as the creative center of the literary and language process. Classical Greeks had a feeling both for "languages" and for the epochs of language, for the various Greek literary dialects (tragedy is a polyglot genre), but creative consciousness was realized in closed, pure languages (although in actual fact they were mixed). Polyglossia was appropriated and canonized among all the genres.

The new cultural and creative consciousness lives in an actively polyglot world. The world becomes polyglot, once and for all and irreversibly. The period of national languages, coexisting but closed and deaf to each other, comes to an end. Languages throw light on each other: one language can, after all, see itself only in the light of another language. The naive and stubborn coexistence of "languages" within a given national language also comes to an end — that is, there is no more peaceful coexistence between territorial dialects, social and professional dialects and jargons, literary language, generic languages within literary language, epochs in language and so forth.

All this set into motion a process of active, mutual cause-and-effect and interillumination. Words and language began to have a different feel to them; objectively they ceased to be what they had once been. Under these conditions of external and internal interillumination, each given language — even if its linguistic composition (phonetics, vocabulary, morphology, etc.) were to remain absolutely unchanged — is, as it were, reborn, becoming qualitatively a different thing for the consciousness that creates in it.

In this actively polyglot world, completely new relationships are established between language and its object (that is, the real world) — and this is fraught with enormous consequences for all the already completed genres that had been formed during eras of closed and deaf monoglossia. In contrast to other major genres, the novel emerged and matured precisely when intense activization of external and internal polyglossia was at the peak of its activity; this is its native element. The novel could therefore assume leadership in the process of developing and renewing literature in its linguistic and stylistic dimension.

In the above-mentioned work I tried to elucidate the profound stylistic originality of the novel, which is determined by its connection with polyglossia.

Let us move on to the two other characteristics, both concerned with the thematic aspect of structure in the novel as a genre. These characteristics can be best brought out and clarified through a comparison of the novel with the epic.

The epic as a genre in its own right may, for our purposes, be characterized by three constitutive features: (1) a national epic past — in Goethe's and Schiller's terminology the "absolute past" — serves as the subject for the epic;[8] (2) national tradition (not personal experience and the free thought that grows out of it) serves as the source for the epic; (3) an absolute epic distance separates the epic world from contemporary reality, that is, from the time in which the singer (the author and his audience) lives.

Let us now touch upon several artistic features related to the above. The absence of internal conclusiveness and exhaustiveness creates a sharp increase in demands for an *external* and *formal* completedness and exhaustiveness, especially in regard to plot line. The problems of a beginning, an end, and "fullness" of plot are posed anew. The epic is indifferent to formal beginnings and can remain incomplete (that is, where it concludes is almost arbitrary). The absolute past is closed and completed in the whole as well as in any of its parts. It is, therefore, possible to take any part and offer it as the whole. One cannot embrace, in a single epic, the entire world of the absolute past (although it is unified from a plot standpoint) — to do so would mean a retelling of the whole of national tradition, and it is sufficiently difficult to embrace even a significant portion of it. But this is no great loss, because the structure of the whole is repeated in each part, and each part is complete and circular like the whole. One may begin the story at almost any moment, and finish at almost any moment. The *Iliad* is a random excerpt from the Trojan cycle. Its ending (the burial of Hector) could not possibly be the ending from a novelistic point of view. But epic completedness suffers not the slightest as a result. The specific "impulse to end" — How does the war end? Who wins? What will happen to Achilles? and so forth — is absolutely excluded from the epic by both internal and external motifs (the plot-line of the tradition was already known to everyone). This specific "impulse to continue" (what will happen next?) and the "impulse to end" (how will it end?) are characteristic only for the novel and are possible only in a zone where there is proximity and contact; in a zone of distanced images they are impossible.

In distanced images we have the whole event, and plot interest (that is, the condition of not knowing) is impossible. The novel, however, speculates in what is unknown. The novel devises various forms and methods for employing the surplus knowledge that the author has, that which the hero does not know or does not see. It is possible to utilize this authorial surplus in an external way, manipulating the narrative, or it can be used to complete the image of an individual (an externalization that is peculiarly novelistic). But there is another possibility in this surplus that creates further problems.

The distinctive features of the novelistic zone emerge in various ways in various novels. A novel need not raise any problematic questions at all. Take, for example, the adventuristic "boulevard" romance. There is no philosophy in it, no social or political problems, no psychology. Consequently none of these spheres provides any contact with the inconclusive events of our own contemporary reality. The absence of distance and of a zone of contact are utilized here in a different way: in place of our tedious lives we are offered a surrogate, true, but it is the surrogate of a fascinating and brilliant life. We can experience these adventures, identify with these heroes; such novels almost become a substitute for our own lives. Nothing of the sort is possible in the epic and other distanced genres. And here we encounter the specific danger inherent in the novelistic zone of contact: we ourselves may actually enter the novel (whereas we could never enter an epic or other distanced genre). It follows that we might substitute for our own life an obsessive reading of novels, or dreams based on novelistic models (the hero of [Dostoevsky's] *White Nights*); Bovaryism becomes possible, the real-life appearance of fashionable heroes taken from novels — disillusioned, demonic and so forth. Other genres are capable of generating such phenomena only after having been novelized, that is, after having been transposed to the novelistic zone of contact (for example, the verse narratives of Byron).

Yet another phenomenon in the history of the novel — and one of extreme importance — is connected with this new temporal orientation and with this zone of contact: it is the novel's special relationship with extraliterary genres, with the genres of everyday life and with ideological genres. In its earliest stages, the novel and its preparatory genres had relied upon various extraliterary forms of personal and social reality, and especially those of rhetoric (there is a theory that actually traces the novel back to rhetoric). And in later stages of its development the novel makes wide and substantial use of letters, diaries, confessions, the forms and methods of rhetoric associated with recently established courts and so forth. Since it is constructed in a zone of contact with the incomplete events of a particular present, the novel often crosses the boundary of what we strictly call fictional literature — making use first of a moral confession, then of a philosophical tract, then of manifestos that are openly political, then degenerating into the raw spirituality of a confession, a "cry of the soul" that has not yet found its formal contours. These phenomena are precisely what characterize the novel as a developing genre. After all, the boundaries between fiction and nonfiction, between literature and nonliterature and so forth are not laid up in heaven. Every specific situation is historical. And the growth of literature is not merely development and change within the fixed boundaries of any given definition; the boundaries themselves are constantly changing. The shift of boundaries between various strata (including literature) in a culture is an extremely slow and complex process. Isolated border violations of any given specific definition (such as those mentioned above) are only symptomatic of this larger process, which occurs at a great depth. These symptoms of change appear considerably more often in the novel than they do elsewhere, as the novel is a developing genre; they are sharper and more significant because the novel is in the vanguard of change. The novel may thus serve as a document for gauging the lofty and still distant destinies of literature's future unfolding.

But the changes that take place in temporal orientation, and in the zone where images are constructed, appear nowhere more profoundly and inevitably than in the process of restructuring the image of the individual in literature. Within the bounds of the present article, however, I can touch on this great and complex question only briefly and superficially.

The individual in the high distanced genres is an individual of the absolute past and of the distanced image. As such he is a fully finished and completed being. This has been accomplished on a lofty heroic level, but what is complete is also something hopelessly ready-made; he is all there, from beginning to end he coincides with himself, he is absolutely equal to himself. He is, furthermore, completely externalized. There is not the slightest gap between his authentic essence and its external manifestation. All his potential, all his possibilities are realized utterly in his external social position, in the whole of his fate and even in his external appearance; outside of this predetermined fate and predetermined position there is nothing. He has already become everything that he could become, and he could become only that which he has already become. He is entirely externalized in the most elementary, almost literal sense: everything in him is exposed and loudly expressed: his internal world and all his external characteristics, his appearance and his actions all lie on a single plane. His view of himself coincides completely with others' views of him — the view of his society (his community), the epic singer and the audience also coincide.

In this context, mention should be made of the problem of self-praise that comes up in Plutarch and others. "I myself," in an environment that is distanced, exists not *in* itself or for *itself* but for the self's descendents, for the memory such a self anticipates in its descendents. I acknowledge myself, an image that is my own, but on this distanced plane of memory such a consciousness of self is alienated from "me." I see myself through the eyes of another. This coincidence of forms — the view I have of myself as self, and the view I have of myself as other — bears an integral, and therefore naive, character — there is no gap between the two. We have as yet no confession, no exposing of self. The one doing the depicting coincides with the one being depicted.[9]

He sees and knows in himself only the things that others see and know in him. Everything that another person — the author — is able to say about him he can say about himself, and vice versa. There is nothing to seek for in him, nothing to guess at, he can neither be exposed nor provoked; he is all of a piece, he has no shell, there is no nucleus within. Furthermore, the epic hero lacks any ideological initiative (heroes and author alike lack it). The epic world knows only a single and unified world view, obligatory and indubitably true for heroes as well as for authors and audiences. Neither world view nor language can, therefore, function as factors for limiting and determining human images, or their individualization. In the epic, characters are bounded, preformed, individualized by their various situations and destinies, but not by varying "truths." Not even the gods are separated from men by a special truth: they have the same language, they all share the same world view, the same fate, the same extravagant externalization.

These traits of the epic character, shared by and large with other highly distanced genres, are responsible for the exclusive beauty, wholeness, crystal clarity and artistic completedness of this image of man. But at the same time such traits account for his limitations and his obvious woodenness under conditions obtaining in a later period of human existence.

The destruction of epic distance and the transferral of the image of an individual from the distanced plane to the zone of contact with the inconclusive events of the present (and consequently of the future) result in a radical restructuring of the image of the individual in the novel — and consequently in all literature. Folklore and popular-comic sources for the novel played a huge role in this process. Its first and essential step was the comic familiarization of the image of man. Laughter destroyed epic distance; it began to investigate man freely and familiarly, to turn him inside out, expose the disparity between his surface and his center, between his potential and his reality. A dynamic authenticity was introduced into the image of man, dynamics of inconsistency and tension between various factors of this image; man ceased to coincide with himself, and consequently men ceased to be exhausted entirely by the plots that contain them. Of these inconsistencies and tensions laughter plays up, first of all, the comic sides (but not only the comic sides); in the serio-comical genres of antiquity, images of a new order emerge — for example, the imposing, newly and more complexly integrated heroic image of Socrates.

Characteristic here is the artistic structuring of an image out of durable popular masks — masks that had great influence on the novelistic image of man during the most important stages of the novel's development (the serio-comical genres of antiquity, Rabelais, Cervantes). Outside his destiny, the epic and tragic hero is nothing; he is, therefore, a function of the plot fate assigns him; he cannot become the hero of another destiny or another plot. On the contrary, popular masks — Maccus, Pulcinello, Harlequin — are able to assume any destiny and can figure into any situation (they often do so within the limits of a single play), but they cannot exhaust their possibilities by those situations alone; they always retain, in any situation and in any destiny, a happy surplus of their own, their own rudimentary but inexhaustible human face. Therefore these masks can function and speak independent of the plot; but, moreover, it is precisely in these excursions outside the plot proper — in the Atellan *trices*,[10] in the *lazzi*[11] of Italian comedy — that they best of all reveal a face of their own. Neither an epic nor a tragic hero could ever step out in his own character during a pause in the plot or during an intermission: he has no face for it, no gesture, no language. In this is his strength and his limitation. The epic and tragic hero is the hero who, by his very nature, must perish. Popular masks, on the contrary, never perish: not a single plot in Atellan, Italian, or Italianized French comedies provides for, or could ever provide for, the actual death of a Maccus, a Pulcinello, or a Harlequin. However, one frequently witnesses their fictive comic deaths (with subsequent resurrections). These are heroes of free improvisation and not heroes of tradition, heroes of a life process that is imperishable and forever renewing itself, forever contemporary — these are not heroes of an absolute past.

These masks and their structure (the noncoincidence with themselves, and with any given situation — the surplus, the inexhaustibility of their self and the like), have had, we repeat, an enormous influence on the development of the novelistic image of man. This structure is preserved even in the novel, although in a more complex, deeply meaningful and serious (or serio-comical) form.

One of the basic internal themes of the novel is precisely the theme of the hero's inadequacy to his fate or his situation. The individual is either greater than his fate, or less than his condition as a man. He cannot become once and for all a clerk, a landowner, a merchant, a fiancé, a jealous lover, a father and so forth. If the hero of a novel actually becomes something of the sort — that is, if he completely coincides with his situation and his fate (as do generic, everyday heroes, the majority of secondary characters in a novel) — then the surplus inhering in the human condition is realized in the main protagonist. The way in which this surplus will actually be realized grows out of the author's orientation toward form and content, that is, the ways he sees and depicts individuals. It is precisely the zone of contact with an inconclusive present (and consequently with the future) that creates the necessity of this incongruity of a man with himself. There always remains in him unrealized potential and unrealized demands. The future exists, and this future ineluctably touches upon the individual, has its roots in him.

An individual cannot be completely incarnated into the flesh of existing sociohistorical categories. There is no mere form that would be able to incarnate once and forever all of his human possibilities and needs, no form in which he could exhaust himself down to the last word, like the tragic epic hero; no form that he could fill to the very brim, and yet at the same time not splash over the brim. There always remains an unrealized surplus of humanness; there always remains a need for the future, and a place for his future must be found. All existing clothes are always too tight, and thus comical, on a man. But this surplus of un-fleshed-out humanness may be realized not only in the hero, but also in the author's point of view (as, for example, in Gogol). Reality as we have it in the novel is only one of many possible realities; it is not inevitable, not arbitrary, it bears within itself other possibilities.

The epic wholeness of an individual disintegrates in a novel in other ways as well. A crucial tension develops between the external and the internal man, and as a result of the subjectivity of the individual becomes an object of experimentation and representation — and first of all on the humorous familiarizing plane. Coordination breaks down between the various aspects: man for himself alone and man in the eyes of others. This disintegration of the integrity that an individual had possessed in epic (and in tragedy) combines in the novel with the necessary preparatory steps toward a new, complex wholeness on a higher level of human development.

Finally, in a novel the individual acquires the ideological and linguistic initiative necessary to change the nature of his own image (there is a new and higher type of individualization of the image). In the antique stage of novelistic development there appeared remarkable examples of such hero-ideologues — the image of Socrates, the image of a laughing Epicurus in the so-called "Hypocratic" novel, the deeply novelized image of Diogenes in the thoroughly dialogized literature of the cynics and in Menippean satire (where it closely approximates the image of the popular mask), and, finally, the image of Menippius in Lucian. As a rule, the hero of a novel is always more or less an ideologue.

What all this suggests is a somewhat abstract and crude schematization for restructuring the image of an individual in the novel.

We will summarize with some conclusions.

The present, in its all open-endedness, taken as a starting point and center for artistic and ideological orientation, is an enormous revolution in the creative consciousness of man. In the European world this reorientation and destruction of the old hierarchy of temporalities received its crucial generic expression on the boundary between classic antiquity and Hellenism, and in the new world during the late middle ages and Renaissance. The fundamental constituents of the novel as a genre were formed in these eras, although some of the separate elements making up the novel were present much earlier, and the novel's roots must ultimately be sought in folklore. In these eras all other major genres had already long since come to completion, they were already old and almost ossified genres. They were all permeated from top to bottom with a more ancient hierarchization of temporalities. The novel, from the very beginning, developed as a genre that had at its core a new way of conceptualizing time. The absolute past, tradition, hierarchical distance played no role in the formation of the novel as a genre (such spatiotemporal categories did play a role, though insignificant, in certain periods of the novel's development, when it was slightly influenced by the epic — for example in the Baroque novel). The novel took shape precisely at the point when epic distance was disintegrating, when both the world and man were assuming a degree of comic familiarity, when the object of artistic representation was being degraded to the level of a contemporary reality that was inconclusive and fluid. From the very beginning the novel was structured not in the distanced image of the absolute past but in the zone of direct contact with inconclusive present-day reality. At its core lay personal experience and free creative imagination. Thus a new, sober artistic-prose novelistic image and a new critical scientific perception came into being simultaneously. From the very beginning, then, the novel was made of different clay than the other already completed genres; it is a different breed, and with it and in it is born the future of all literature. Once it came into being, it could never be merely one genre among others, and it could not erect rules for interrelating with others in peaceful and harmonious co-existence. In the presence of the novel, all other genres somehow have a different resonance. A lengthy battle for the novelization of the other genres began, a battle to drag them into a zone of contact with reality. The course of this battle has been complex and tortuous.

The novelization of literature does not imply attaching to already completed genres a generic canon that is alien to them, not theirs. The novel, after all, has no canon of its own. It is, by its very nature, not canonic. It is plasticity itself. It is a genre that is ever questing, ever examining itself and subjecting its established forms to review. Such, indeed, is the only possibility open to a genre that structures itself in a zone of direct contact with developing reality. Therefore, the novelization of other genres does not imply their subjection of an alien generic canon; on the contrary, novelization implies their liberation from all that serves as a brake on their unique development, from all that would change them along with the novel into some sort of stylization of forms that have outlived themselves.

I have developed my various positions in this essay in a somewhat abstract way. There have been few illustrations, and even these were taken only from an ancient period in the novel's development. My choice was determined by the fact that the significance of that period has been greatly underestimated. When people talk about the ancient period of the novel they have traditionally had in mind the "Greek novel" alone. The ancient period of the novel is enormously significant for a proper understanding of the genre. But in ancient times the novel could not really develop all its potential; this potential came to light only in the modern world. We indicated that in several works of antiquity, the inconclusive present begins to sense a greater proximity to the future than to the past. The absence of a temporal perspective in ancient society assured that this process of reorientation toward a real future could not complete itself; after all, there was no real concept of a future. Such a reorientation occurred for the first time during the Renaissance. In that era, the present (that is, a reality that was contemporaneous) for the first time began to sense itself not only as an incomplete continuation of the past, but as something like a new and heroic beginning. To re-interpret reality on the level of the contemporary present now meant not only to degrade, but to raise reality into a new and heroic sphere. It was in the Renaissance that the present first began to feel with great clarity and awareness an incomparably closer proximity and kinship to the future than to the past.

The process of the novel's development has not yet come to an end. It is currently entering a new phase. For our era is characterized by an extraordinary complexity and a deepening in our perception of the world; there is an unusual growth in demands on human discernment, on mature objectivity and the critical faculty. These are features that will shape the further development of the novel as well.

Notes

1. Erwin Rohde (1845–1898), *Der griechische Roman und seine Vorläufer* (1876, but many later editions, most recently published by F. Olds [Hildesheim, 1960]), one of the greatest monuments of nineteenth-century classical scholarship in Germany. It has never really been superseded. But see: Ben F. Perry, *The Ancient Romances* (Berkeley, 1967) and Arthur Heiserman, *The Novel before the Novel* (Chicago, 1977). (Translator's note)

2. Charles Sorel (1599–1674), an important figure in the reaction to the *preciosité* of such figures as Honoré d'Urfé (1567–1625), whose *L'Astrée* (1607–1627), a monstrous 5,500-page volume overflowing with highflown language, is parodied in *Le berger extravagant* (1627). The latter book's major protagonist is a dyed-in-the-wool Parisian who reads too many pastoral novels; intoxicated by these, he attempts to live the rustic life as they describe it — with predictably comic results. (Translator's note)

3. Johann Karl August Musäus (1735–1787), along with Tieck and Brentano, one of the great collectors of German folktales and author of several *Kunstmärchen* of his own (translated into English by Carlyle). Reference here is to his *Grandison der Zweite* (1760–1762, rewritten as *Der deutsche Grandison,* 1781–1782), a satire on Richardson. (Translator's note)

4. Christoph Martin Wieland (1733–1813) is the author of *Geschichte des Agathon* (1767, first of many versions), an autobiographical novel in the guise of a Greek romance, considered by many to be the first in the long line of German *Bildungsromane.* (Translator's note)

5. Reference here is to Johann Carl Wezel (1747–1819), *Lebensgeschichte Tobias Knouts, des Weisen, sonst der Stammler genannt* (1773), a novel that has not received the readership it deserves. A four-volume reprint was published by Metzler (Stuttgart, Afterword by Viktor Lange) in 1971. Also see Elizabeth Holzberg-Pfenniger, *Der desorientierte Erzähler: Studien zu J. C. Wezels Lebensgeschichte des Tobias Knauts* (Bern, 1976). (Translator's note)

6. Friedrich von Blankenburg (1744–1796), *Versuch über den Roman* (1774), an enormous work (over 500 pages) that attempts to define the novel in terms of a rudimentary psychology, a concern for *Tugend* in the heroes. A facsimile edition was published by Metzler (Stuttgart) in 1965. Little is known about Blankenburg, who is

also the author of an unfinished novel with the imposing title *Beytrage zur Geschichte deutschen Reichs und deutschen Sitten,* the first part of which appeared a year after the *Versuch* in 1775. (Translator's note)

7. Cf. the article "From the Prehistory of Novelistic Discourse" in *The Dialogic Imagination.*

8. Reference here is to "Über epische und dramatische Dichtung," cosigned by Schiller and Goethe, but probably written by the latter in 1797, although not published until 1827. The actual term used by Goethe for what Bakhtin is calling "absolute past" is *vollkommen vergangen,* which is opposed not to the novel, but to drama, which is defined as *vollkommen gegenwärtig.* The essay can be found in Goethe's *Sämtliche Werke* (Stuttgart and Berlin: Jubilaums-Ausgabe, 1902–1907), vol. 36, pp. 149–52. (Translator's note)

9. Epic disintegrates when the search begins for a new point of view on one's own self (without any admixture of others' points of view). The expressive novelistic gesture arises as a departure from a norm, but the "error" of this norm immediately reveals how important it is for subjectivity. First there is a departure from a norm, and then the problematicalness of the norm itself.

10. *Trices* are thought to have been interludes in the action of the Atellanae during which the masks often stepped out of character.

11. *Lazzi* were what we might now call "routines" or "numbers" that were not part of the ongoing action of the plot.

5 Joseph Frank : *Spatial Form in Modern Literature*

Joseph Frank broke new critical ground in his 1945 study of Djuna Barnes's *Nightwood,* analyzing a crucial technique of modernist literature, the substitution of spatial relationships for temporal progression as a formal metaphor of thematic development. Here we reprint the first half of Frank's essay, in which he presents his general conception of modern "spatial form." Starting with Gustave Flaubert and recognizing his efforts to duplicate the simultaneity of action possible in drama and later in film, Frank comments that "since language proceeds in time, it is impossible to approach this simultaneity of perception except by breaking up temporal sequence." According to Frank, "spatialization of form in the novel" provides an alternative to the chronological development normal to verbal structures, which can be read only in a linear fashion through time, unlike painting and the plastic arts, which can be visually apprehended instantaneously. Frank claims that while in poetry spatialization led to the "disappearance of coherent sequence . . . the novel, with its larger unit of meaning, can preserve coherent sequence within the unit of meaning and break up only the timeflow of narrative."

While Flaubert introduces this method, it does not become a dominant form, according to Frank, until James Joyce's *Ulysses* and Marcel Proust's *A la recherche du temps perdu* (one might want to compare Frank's treatment of this novel with Gérard Genette's later in this collection). Frank sees these two authors as embodying the more common approach to spatialization, one in which the authors "accept the naturalistic principle, presenting their characters in terms of those commonplace details, those descriptions of circumstance and environment, that we have come to regard as verisimilar." Barnes, on the other hand, breaks with this tendency to present a literary equivalent of abstractionism. Although Frank does not allude to it, one might well compare Barnes's abstractionist spatialization with the experimental work of another expatriate American modernist, Gertrude Stein.

Frank's conception of spatial form has become a classical critical statement, one emended and developed by numerous other critics. But we should ask ourselves if spatialization is limited to being a formal principle of modernist fiction or if it can be integrated into a discussion of more traditional methods of plot development.

In 1963, Joseph Frank (b. 1918), who spent most of his career at Princeton

University, published *The Widening Gyre,* a full-length presentation of the critical conceptions contained in "Spatial Form in Modern Literature." He has also authored and edited other works, including four volumes of a projected five-volume biography of Dostoevsky and *The Idea of Spatial Form: Essays on Literature and Culture* (1991).

For a study of esthetic form in the modern novel, Flaubert's famous county fair scene in *Madame Bovary* is a convenient point of departure. This scene has been justly praised for its mordant caricature of bourgeois pomposity, its portrayal — unusually sympathetic for Flaubert — of the bewildered old servant, and its burlesque of the pseudo-romantic rhetoric by which Rodolphe woos the sentimental Emma. At present, it is enough to notice the method by which Flaubert handles the scene — a method we might as well call cinematographic, since this analogy comes immediately to mind. As Flaubert sets the scene, there is action going on simultaneously at three levels, and the physical position of each level is a fair index to its spiritual significance. On the lowest plane, there is the surging, jostling mob in the street, mingling with the livestock brought to the exhibition; raised slightly above the street by a platform are the speechmaking officials, bombastically reeling off platitudes to the attentive multitudes; and on the highest level of all, from a window overlooking the spectacle, Rodolphe and Emma are watching the proceedings and carrying on their amorous conversation, in phrases as stilted as those regaling the crowds. Albert Thibaudet has compared this scene to the medieval mystery play, in which various related actions occur simultaneously on different stage levels; but this acute comparison refers to Flaubert's intention rather than to his method. "Everything should sound simultaneously," Flaubert later wrote, in commenting on this scene, "one should hear the bellowing of the cattle, the whisperings of the lovers and the rhetoric of the officials all at the same time."[1]

But since language proceeds in time, it is impossible to approach this simultaneity of perception except by breaking up temporal sequence. And this is exactly what Flaubert does: he dissolves sequence by cutting back and forth between the various levels of action in a slowly-rising crescendo until — at the climax of the scene — Rodolphe's Chateaubriand-esque phrases are read at almost the same moment as the names of prize winners for raising the best pigs. Flaubert takes care to underline this satiric similarity by description, as well as by juxtaposition, as if he were afraid the reflexive relations of the two actions would not be grasped: "From magnetism, by slow degrees, Rodolphe had arrived at affinities, and while M. le Président was citing Cincinnatus at his plow, Diocletian planting his cabbages, and the emperors of China ushering in the new year with sowing-festivals, the young man was explaining to the young woman that these irresistible attractions sprang from some anterior existence."

This scene illustrates, on a small scale, what we mean by the spatialization of form in a novel. For the duration of the scene, at least, the time-flow of the narrative is halted: attention is fixed on the interplay of relationships within the limited time-area. These relationships are juxtaposed independently of the progress of the narrative; and the full significance of the scene is given only by the reflexive relations among the units of meaning. In Flaubert's scene, however, the unit of meaning is not, as in modern poetry, a word-group or a fragment of an anecdote, but the totality of each level of action taken as an integer: the unit is so large that the scene can be read with an illusion of complete understanding, yet with a total unawareness of the "dialectic of platitude" (Thibaudet) interweaving all levels, and finally linking them together with devastating irony. In other words, the struggle towards spatial form in Pound and Eliot resulted in the disappearance of coherent sequence after a few lines; but the novel, with its larger unit of meaning, can preserve coherent sequence within the unit of meaning and break up only the time-flow of narrative. (Because of this difference, readers of modern poetry are practically forced to read reflexively to get any literal sense, while readers of a novel like *Nightwood,* for example, are led to expect narrative sequence by the deceptive normality of language sequence within the unit of meaning). But this does not affect the parallel between esthetic form in modern poetry and the form of Flaubert's scene: both can be properly understood only when their units of meaning are apprehended reflexively, in an instant of time.

Flaubert's scene, although interesting in itself, is of minor importance to his novel as a whole, and is skillfully blended back into the main narrative structure after fulfilling its satiric function. But Flaubert's method was taken over by James Joyce, and applied on a gigantic scale in the composition of *Ulysses.* Joyce composed his novel of an infinite number of references and cross-references which relate to one another independently of the time-sequence of the narrative; and, before the book fits together into any meaningful pattern, these references must be connected by the reader and viewed as a whole. Ultimately, if we are to believe Stuart Gilbert, these systems of references form a complete picture of practically everything under the sun, from the stages of man's life and the organs of the human body to the colors of the spectrum; but these structures are far more important for Joyce, as Harry Levin has remarked, than they could ever possibly be for the reader. Students of Joyce, fascinated by his erudition, have usually applied themselves to exegesis. Unfortunately, such considerations have little to do with the perceptual form of Joyce's novel.

Joyce's most obvious intention in *Ulysses* is to give the reader a picture of Dublin seen as a whole—to re-recreate the sights and sounds, the people and places, of a typical Dublin day, much as Flaubert had re-created his provincial county fair. And, like Flaubert, Joyce wanted his depiction to have the same unified impact, the same sense of simultaneous activity occurring in different places. Joyce, as a matter of fact, frequently makes use of the same method as Flaubert—cutting back and forth between different actions occurring at the same time—and usually does so to obtain the same ironic effect. But Joyce had the problem of creating this impression of simultaneity for the life of a whole teeming city, and of maintaining it—or rather of strengthening it—through hundreds of pages that must be read as a sequence. To meet this problem, Joyce was forced to go far beyond what Flaubert had done; while Flaubert had maintained a clear-cut narrative line, except in the county-fair scene, Joyce breaks up his narrative and transforms the very structure of his novel into an instrument of his esthetic intention.

Joyce conceived *Ulysses* as a modern epic; and in the epic, as Stephen Dedalus tells us in *A Portrait of the Artist as a Young Man,* "the personality of the artist, at first sight a cry or a cadence and then a fluid and lambent narrative, finally refines itself out of existence, impersonalizes itself, so to speak . . . the artist, like the God of creation, remains within or beyond or above his handiwork, invisible, refined out of existence, indifferent, paring his fingernails." The epic is thus synonymous for Joyce with the complete self-effacement of the author; and, with his usual uncompromising rigor, Joyce carries this implication further than anyone had dared before. He assumes—what is obviously not true—that his readers are Dubliners, intimately acquainted with Dublin life and the personal history of his characters. This allows him to refrain from giving any direct information about his characters: such information would immediately have betrayed the presence of an omniscient author. What Joyce does, instead, is to present the elements of his narrative—the relations between

Stephen and his family, between Bloom and his wife, between Stephen and Bloom and the Dedalus family — in fragments, as they are thrown out unexplained in the course of casual conversation, or as they lie embedded in the various strata of symbolic reference; and the same is true of all the allusions to Dublin life, history, and the external events of the twenty-four hours during which the novel takes place. In other words, all the factual background — so conveniently summarized for the reader in an ordinary novel — must be reconstructed from fragments, sometimes hundreds of pages apart, scattered through the book. As a result, the reader is forced to read *Ulysses* in exactly the same manner as he reads modern poetry — continually fitting fragments together and keeping allusions in mind until, by reflexive reference, he can link them to their complements.

Joyce intended, in this way, to build up in the reader's mind a sense of Dublin as a totality, including all the relations of the characters to one another and all the events which enter their consciousness. As the reader progresses through the novel, connecting allusions and references spatially, gradually becoming aware of the pattern of relationships, this sense was to be imperceptibly acquired; and, at the conclusion of the novel, it might almost be said that Joyce literally wanted the reader to become a Dubliner. For this is what Joyce demands: that the reader have at hand the same instinctive knowledge of Dublin life, the same sense of Dublin as a huge, surrounding organism, which the Dubliner possesses as a birthright. It is such knowledge which, at any one moment of time, gives him a knowledge of Dublin's past and present as a whole; and it is only such knowledge which might enable the reader, like the characters, to place all the references in their proper context. This, it should be realized, is practically the equivalent of saying that Joyce cannot be read — he can only be re-read. A knowledge of the whole is essential to an understanding of any part; but, unless one is a Dubliner, such knowledge can be obtained only after the book has been read, when all the references are fitted into their proper place and grasped as a unity. Although the burdens placed on the reader by this method of composition may seem insuperable, the fact remains that Joyce, in his unbelievably laborious fragmentation of narrative structure, proceeded on the assumption that a unified spatial apprehension of his work would ultimately be possible.

In a far more subtle manner than with Joyce and Flaubert, the same principle of composition is at work in Marcel Proust. Since Proust himself tells us that, before all else, his novel will have imprinted on it "a form which usually remains invisible, the form of Time," it may seem strange to speak of Proust in connection with spatial form. He has, almost invariably, been considered the novelist of time *par excellence:* the literary interpreter of that Bergsonian "real time" intuited by the sensibility, as distinguished from the abstract, chronological time of the conceptual intelligence. To stop at this point, however, is to miss what Proust himself considered the deepest significance of his work. Obsessed with the ineluctability of time, Proust was suddenly visited by certain quasi-mystical experiences — described in detail in the last volume of his work, "Le temps retrouvé" — which, by providing him with a spiritual technique for transcending time, enabled him to escape what he considered to be time's domination. By writing a novel, by translating the transcendent, extratemporal quality of these experiences to the level of esthetic form, Proust hoped to reveal their nature to the world — for they seemed to him a clue to the ultimate secrets of reality. And not only should the world learn about these experiences indirectly, by reading a descriptive account of them, but, through his novel, it would feel their impact on the sensibility as Proust himself had felt it.

To define the method by which this is accomplished, one must first understand clearly the precise nature of the Proustian revelation. Each such experience, Proust tells us, is marked by a feeling that "the permanent essence of things, usually concealed, is set free and our true self, which had long seemed dead but was not dead in other ways, awakes, takes on fresh life as it receives the celestial nourishment brought to it." This celestial nourishment consists of some sound, or odor, or other sensory stimulus, "sensed anew, simultaneously in the present and the past." But why should these moments seem so overwhelmingly valuable that Proust calls them celestial? Because, Proust observes, his imagination could only operate on the past; and the material presented to his imagination, therefore, lacked any sensuous immediacy. But, at certain moments, the physical sensations of the past came flooding back to fuse with the present; and, in these moments, Proust believed that he grasped a reality "real without being of the present moment, ideal but not abstract." Only in these moments did he attain his most cherished ambition — "to seize, isolate, immobilize for the duration of a lightning flash" what otherwise he could not apprehend, "namely: a fragment of time in its pure state." For a person experiencing this moment, Proust adds, the word "death" no longer has meaning. "Situated outside the scope of time, what could he fear from the future?"

The significance of this experience, though obscurely hinted at throughout the book, is made explicit only in the concluding pages which describe the final appearance of the narrator at the reception of the Princesse de Guermantes. The narrator decides to dedicate the remainder of his life to re-creating these experiences in a work of art; and this work will differ essentially from all others because, at its foundation, will be a vision of reality that has been refracted through an extra-temporal perspective. Viewing Proust as the last and most debilitated of a long line of neurasthenic esthetes, many critics have found in this decision to create a work of art merely the final step in his flight from the burdens of reality. Edmund Wilson, ordinarily so discerning, links up this view with Proust's ambition to conquer time, assuming that Proust hoped to oppose time by establishing something — a work of art — impervious to its flux; but this somewhat ingenuous interpretation scarcely does justice to Proust's own conviction, expressed with special intensity in the last volume of his work, that he was fulfilling a prophetic mission. It was not the work of art *qua* work of art that Proust cared about — his contempt for the horde of faddish scribblers was unbounded — but a work of art which should stand as a monument to his personal conquest of time. This his own work could do not simply because it was a work of art, but because it was at once the vehicle through which he conveyed his vision and the concrete substance of that vision shaped by a method which compels the reader to re-experience its exact effect.

The prototype of this method, like the analysis of the revelatory moment, occurs during the reception at the Princesse de Guermantes. After spending years in a sanatorium, losing touch almost completely with the fashionable world of the earlier volumes, the narrator comes out of seclusion to attend the reception. He finds himself bewildered by the changes in social position, and the even more striking changes in character and personality among his former friends. According to some socially minded critics, Proust intended to paint here the invasion of French aristocratic society by the upper bourgeoisie, and the gradual breakdown of all social and moral standards caused by the First World War. No doubt this process is incidentally described at some length; but, as the narrator takes great pains to tell us, it is far from being the most important meaning of the scene. What strikes the narrator, almost with the force of a blow, is this: in trying to recognize old friends under the masks which, as he feels, the years have welded to them, he is jolted for the first time into a consciousness of the passage of time. When a young man addresses the narrator respectfully, instead of familiarly, as if he were an elderly gentleman, the narrator realizes suddenly that he has become an elderly gentleman; but for him the passage of time had gone unperceived up until that moment. To become conscious of time, the narrator begins to understand, it had first been necessary to remove himself from his accustomed environment — or, what amounts to the same thing, from the stream of time acting on that environment — and then to plunge back into the stream after a lapse of years. In so doing, the narrator found himself presented with two images — the world as he had formerly known it, and the world, transformed by time, that he now saw before him; and when these two images are juxtaposed, the narrator discovers, the passage of time is suddenly experienced through its visible effects. Habit, that universal soporific, ordinarily conceals the passage of time from those who have gone their accustomed ways: at any one moment of time the changes are so minute as to be imperceptible: "Other people," Proust writes, "never cease to change places in relation to ourselves. In the imperceptible, but eternal march of the world, we regard them as motionless in a moment of vision, too short for us to perceive the motion that is sweeping them on. But we have only to select in our memory two pictures taken of them at different moments, close enough together however for them not to have altered in themselves — perceptibly, that is to say — and the difference between the two pictures is a measure of the displacement that they have undergone in relation to us." By comparing these two images in a moment of time, the passage of time can be experienced concretely, in the impact of its visible effects on the sensibility, rather than as a mere gap counted off in numbers. And this discovery provides the narrator with a method which, in T. S. Eliot's phrase, is an "objective correlative" to the visionary apprehension of the fragment of "pure time" intuited in the revelatory moment.

When the narrator discovers this method of communicating his experience of the revelatory moment, he decides, as we have already said, to incorporate it in a novel. But the novel the narrator decides to write has just been finished by the reader; and its form is controlled by the method that the narrator has outlined in its concluding pages. The reader, in other words, is substituted for the narrator, and is placed by the author throughout the book in the same position as the narrator occupies before his own experience at the reception of the Princesse de Guermantes. This is done by the discontinuous presentation of character — a simple device which, nevertheless, is the clue to the form of Proust's vast structure. Every reader soon notices that Proust does not follow any of his characters through the whole course of his novel: they appear and reappear, in various stages of their lives, but hundreds of pages sometimes go by between the time they are last seen and the time they reappear; and when they do turn up again, the passage of time has invariably changed them in some decisive way. Instead of being submerged in the stream of time — which, for Proust, would be the equivalent of presenting a character progressively, in a continuous line of development — the reader is confronted with various snapshots of the characters "motionless in a moment of vision," taken at different stages in their lives; and the reader, in juxtaposing these images, experiences the effects of the passage of time exactly as the narrator had done. As he had promised, therefore, Proust does stamp his novel indelibly with the form of time; but we are now in a position to understand exactly what he meant by the promise.

To experience the passage of time, Proust learned, it was necessary to rise above it, and to grasp both past and present simultaneously in a moment of what he called "pure time." But "pure time," obviously, is not time at all — it is perception in a moment of time, that is to say, space. And, by the discontinuous presentation of character, Proust forces the reader to juxtapose disparate images of his characters spatially, in a moment of time, so that the experience of time's passage will be fully communicated to their sensibility. There is a striking analogy here between Proust's method and that of his beloved impressionist painters; but this analogy goes far deeper than the usual comments about the "impressionism" of Proust's style. The Impressionist painters juxtaposed pure tones on the canvas, instead of mixing them on the palette, in order to leave the blending of colors to the eye of the spectator. Similarly, Proust gives us what might be called pure views of his characters — views of them "motionless in a moment of vision" in various phases of their lives — and allows the sensibility of the reader to fuse these views into a unity. Each view must be apprehended by the reader as a unit; and Proust's purpose is only achieved when these units of meaning are referred to each other reflexively in a moment of time. As with Joyce and the modern poets, we see that spatial form is also the structural scaffolding of Proust's labyrinthine masterpiece.

The name of Djuna Barnes is not unknown to those readers who followed, with any care, the stream of pamphlets, books, magazines, and anthologies that poured forth to enlighten America in the feverish days of literary expatriation. Miss Barnes, it is true, must always have remained a somewhat enigmatic figure even to the most attentive reader. Born in New York State, she spent most of her time abroad in England and France; and the glimpses one catches of her in the memoirs of the period are brief and unrevealing. She appears in the *Dial* from time to time with a drawing or a poem; she crops up now and again in some anthology of advance-guard writers — the usual agglomeration of people who are later to become famous, or to sink into the melancholy oblivion of frustrated promise. Before the publication of *Nightwood,* indeed, one might have been inclined to place her name in the latter group. For, while she has a book of short stories and an earlier novel to her credit, neither of them prepares one for the maturity of achievement so conspicuous in every line of her latest work.

Of the fantastical quality of her imagination, of the gift for imagery which, as T. S. Eliot has said, gives one a sense of horror and doom akin to Elizabethan tragedy; of the epigrammatic incisiveness of her phrasing and her penchant, also akin to the Elizabethans, for dealing with the more scabrous manifestations of human fallibility — of all these there is evidence in *Ryder,* Miss Barnes's first novel. But all this might well have resulted only in a momentary flare-up of capricious brilliance, whose radiance would have been as dazzling as it was insubstantial. *Ryder,* it must be confessed, is an anomalous creation from any point of view. Although Miss Barnes's unusual qualities gradually emerge from its kaleidoscope of moods and styles, these qualities are still, so to speak, held in solution, or at best placed in the service of a literary *jeu d'esprit.* Only in *Nightwood* do they finally crystallize into a definitive and comprehensible pattern.

Many critics — not least among them T. S. Eliot himself — have paid tribute to *Nightwood*'s compelling intensity, its head-and-shoulders superiority, simply as a stylistic phenomenon, to most of the works that currently pass for literature. But *Nightwood*'s reputation at present is similar, in many respects, to that of *The Waste Land* in 1922 — it is known as a collection of striking passages, some of breathtaking poetic quality, appealing chiefly to connoisseurs of somewhat gamey literary items. Such a reputation, it need hardly be remarked, is not conducive to intelligent appreciation or understanding. Thanks to critics like F. R. Leavis, Cleanth Brooks, and F. O. Matthiessen, we are now able to approach *The Waste Land* as a work of art, rather than as a battleground for opposing poetic theories or as a curious piece of literary esoterica; and it is time that such a process should be at least begun for *Nightwood*.

Before dealing with *Nightwood* in detail, however, we must make certain broad distinctions between it and the novels already considered. While the structural principle of *Nightwood* is the same as in *Ulysses* and *A la recherche du temps perdu* — spatial form, obtained by means of reflexive reference — there are marked differences in technique that will be obvious to every reader. Taking an analogy from another art, we can say that these differences are similar to the differences between the work of Cézanne and the compositions of a later abstract painter like Braque. What characterizes the work of Cézanne, above all, is the tension between two conflicting but deeply-rooted tendencies: on the one hand, a struggle to attain esthetic form — conceived of by Cézanne as a self-enclosed unity of form-and-color harmonies — and, on the other hand, the desire to create this form through the recognizable depiction of natural objects. Later artists, abandoning Cézanne's efforts to achieve form in terms of natural objects, took over only his preoccupation with formal harmonies, omitting natural objects altogether or presenting them in some distorted manner.

Like Cézanne, Proust and Joyce accept the naturalistic principle, presenting their characters in terms of those commonplace details, those descriptions of circumstance and environment, that we have come to regard as verisimilar. At the same time, we have seen, they intended to control the ebullience of their naturalistic detail by the unity of spatial apprehension. But in *Nightwood,* as in the work of Braque and the later abstract painters, the naturalistic principle is totally abandoned: no attempt is made to convince us that the characters are actual flesh-and-blood human beings. We are asked only to accept their world as we accept an abstract painting or, to return to literature, as we accept a Shakespearian play — as an autonomous pattern giving us an individual vision of reality, rather than what we might consider its exact reflection.

To illustrate the transition that takes place in *Nightwood* let us examine an interesting passage from Proust, where the process can be caught at a rudimentary level. In describing Robert de Saint-Loup, an important character in the early sections of the novel, the narrator tells us that he could see concealed "beneath a courtier's smile his warrior's thirst for action — when I examined him I could see how closely the vigorous structure of his triangular face must have been modelled on that of his ancestors' faces, a face devised rather for an ardent bowman than for a delicate student.

Beneath his fine skin the bold construction, the feudal architecture were apparent. His head made one think of those old dungeon keeps on which the disused battlements are still to be seen, although inside they have been converted into libraries." When the reader comes across this passage, he has already learned a considerable number of facts about Saint-Loup. He is, for one thing, a member of the Guermantes family, one of the oldest and most aristocratic in the French nobility and still the acknowledged leaders of Parisian society. Unlike their feudal ancestors, however, the Guermantes have no real influence over the internal affairs of France under the Third Republic. Saint-Loup, for another thing, is by way of being a family black sheep: seemingly uninterested in social success, a devoted student of Nietzsche and Proudhon, we are told that his head was full of "socialistic spoutings," and that he was "imbued with the most profound contempt for his caste." Knowing these facts from earlier sections of the novel, the reader accepts the passage quoted above simply as a trenchant summation of Saint-Loup's character. But so precisely do the images in this passage apply to everything the reader has learned about Saint-Loup, so exactly do they communicate the central impression of his personality, that it would be possible to derive a total knowledge of his character solely from the images without attaching them to a set of external social and historical details.

Images of this kind are commoner in poetry than in prose — more particularly, since we are speaking of character description, in dramatic poetry. In Shakespeare and the Elizabethans, descriptions of character are not "realistic" as we understand the word today: they are not a collection of circumstantial details whose bare conglomeration is assumed to form a definition. The dramatic poet, rather, defined both the physical and psychological aspects of character at one stroke, in an image or series of images. Here is Antony, for example, as Shakespeare presents him in the opening scene of *Antony and Cleopatra:*

> Nay, but this dotage of our general's
> O'erflows the measure: those his goodly eyes
> That o'er the files and musters of the war
> Have glow'd like plated Mars, now bend, now turn,
> The office and devotion of their view
> Upon a tawny front: his captain's heart,
> Which in the scuffles of great fights hath burst

The buckles on his breast, reneges all temper,
And is become the bellows and the fan
To cool a gipsy's lust.

And then, to complete the picture, Antony is contemptuously called "the triple pillar of the world transformed into a strumpet's fool." Or, to take a more modern example, from a poet strongly influenced by the Elizabethans, here is the twentieth-century everyman:

He, the young man carbuncular, arrives,
A small house agent's clerk, with one bold stare,
One of the low on whom assurance sits
As a silk hat on a Bradford millionaire.

As Ramon Fernandez has remarked of similar character descriptions in the work of George Meredith, images of this kind analyze without dissociating; they describe character but, at the same time, hold fast to the unity of personality, without splintering it to fragments in trying to seize the secret of its integration.

Writing of this order, charged with symbolic overtones, piercing through the cumbrous mass of naturalistic detail to express the essence of character in an image, is the antithesis to what we are accustomed in the novel. Ordinary novels, as T. S. Eliot justly observes in his preface to *Nightwood*, "obtain what reality they have largely from an accurate rendering of the noises that human beings currently make in their daily simple needs of communication; and what part of a novel is not composed of these noises consists of a prose which is no more alive than that of a competent newspaper writer or government official." Miss Barnes abandons any pretensions to this kind of verisimilitude, just as modern artists have abandoned any attempt at naturalistic representation; and the result is a world as strange to the reader, at first sight, as the world of abstract art was to its first spectators. Since the selection of detail in *Nightwood* is governed, not by the logic of verisimilitude, but by the demands of the *décor* necessary to enhance the symbolic significance of the characters, the novel has baffled even its most fascinated admirers. Perhaps we can clear up some of the mystery by applying our method of reflexive reference, instead of approaching the book, as most of its readers have done, expecting to find a coherent temporal pattern of narrative.

Since *Nightwood* lacks a narrative structure in the ordinary sense, it cannot be reduced to any sequence of action for purposes of explanation. One can, if one chooses, follow the narrator in Proust through the various stages of his social career; one can, with some difficulty, follow Leopold Bloom's epic journey through Dublin; but no such reduction is possible in *Nightwood.* As Dr. O'Connor remarks to Nora Flood, with his desperate gaiety, "I have a narrative, but you will be put to it to find it." Strictly speaking, the doctor is wrong — he has a static situation, not a narrative, and no matter how hard the reader looks he will find only the various facets of this situation explored from different angles. The eight chapters of *Nightwood* are like searchlights, probing the darkness each from a different direction, yet ultimately focusing on and illuminating the same entanglement of the human spirit. In the first four chapters we are introduced to each of the important persons — Felix Volkbein, Nora Flood, Robin Vote, Jenny Petherbridge, and Dr. O'Connor. The next three chapters are, for the most part, long monologues by the doctor, through which the developments of the earlier chapters begin to take on meaning. The last chapter, only a few pages long, has the effect of a coda, giving us what we have already come to feel is the only possible termination. And these chapters are knit together, not by the progress of any action — either physical action, or, as in a stream-of-consciousness novel, the act of thinking — but by the continual reference and cross-reference of images and symbols which must be referred to each other spatially throughout the time-act of reading.

Note

1. This discussion of the county-fair scene owes a good deal to Albert Thibaudet's *Gustave Flaubert,* probably the best critical study yet written on the subject. The quotation from Flaubert's letter is used by Thibaudet and has been translated from his book.

6 Lionel Trilling : *Manners, Morals, and the Novel*

Lionel Trilling concerns himself with the moral dimension of good literature. Trilling understands this dimension as constituting the entire historical and cultural context for each work of fiction. What he calls manners refers to "a culture's hum and buzz of implication," which can be heard in the background of any contemporaneous reading of a novel but is often lost when we read a novel from another time period or culture. Trilling focuses on American manners, beginning with the hypothesis "that our attitude toward manners is the expression of a particular conception of reality" and that "all literature tends to be concerned with the question of reality." According to Trilling the answer to that question lies in manners: "The novel, then, is a perpetual quest for reality, the field of its research being always the social world, the material of its analysis being always manners as the indication of the direction of man's soul."

From these observations Trilling concludes that such a novel of manners has not yet established itself in America with the key exceptions of Henry James's and William Faulkner's novels. Instead, American writers have concerned themselves with depicting reality through the portrayal of appearance, and the resulting literature has tended to substitute programmatic generalities for a rounded look at specific characters. In the novels of the 1930s and 1940s sociology has replaced psychology as a method of cultural analysis. The remedy, according to Trilling, lies in a renewed commitment to "moral realism." While recognizing that the novel is often an ungainly, flawed literary form, he states that "its greatness and its practical usefulness lay in its unremitting work of involving the reader himself in the moral life, inviting him to put his own motives under examination, suggesting that reality is not as his conventional education had led him to see it." It is particularly instructive to note the degree to which Trilling's remarks parallel those of Virginia Woolf, even as her emphasis is on form and his on subject matter. Yet both are concerned with human character and with how a focus on the individual is the best way to record the characteristics of an age.

Lionel Trilling (1905–1975), who taught at Columbia University, was one of the important liberal voices in twentieth-century literary criticism. Many of his essays are collected in *The Liberal Imagination* (1950) (from which "Manners, Morals, and the Novel" is taken), *Beyond Culture* (1965), and *Sincerity and Authenticity* (1971).

The invitation that was made to me to address you this evening[1] was couched in somewhat uncertain terms. Time, place, and cordiality were perfectly clear, but when it came to the subject our hosts were not able to specify just what they wanted me to talk about. They wanted me to consider literature in its relation to manners — by which, as they relied on me to understand, they did not really mean *manners*. They did not mean, that is, the rules of personal intercourse in our culture; and yet such rules were by no means irrelevant to what they did mean. Nor did they quite mean manners in the sense of *mores,* customs, although, again, these did bear upon the subject they had in mind.

I understood them perfectly, as I would not have understood them had they been more definite. For they were talking about a nearly indefinable subject.

Somewhere below all the explicit statements that a people makes through its art, religion, architecture, legislation, there is a dim mental region of intention of which it is very difficult to become aware. We now and then get a strong sense of its existence when we deal with the past, not by reason of its presence in the past but by reason of its absence. As we read the great formulated monuments of the past, we notice that we are reading them without the accompaniment of something that always goes along with the formulated monuments of the present. The voice of multifarious intention and activity is stilled, all the buzz of implication which always surrounds us in the present, coming to us from what never gets fully stated, coming in the tone of greetings and the tone of quarrels, in slang and humor and popular songs, in the way children play, in the gesture the waiter makes when he puts down the plate, in the nature of the very food we prefer.

Some of the charm of the past consists of the quiet — the great distracting buzz of implication has stopped and we are left only with what has been fully phrased and precisely stated. And part of the melancholy of the past comes from our knowledge that the huge, unrecorded hum of implication was once there and left no trace — we feel that because it is evanescent it is especially human. We feel, too, that the truth of the great preserved monuments of the past does not fully appear without it. From letters and diaries, from the remote, unconscious corners of the great works themselves, we try to guess what the sound of the multifarious implication was and what it meant.

Or when we read the conclusions that are drawn about our own culture by some gifted foreign critic — or by some stupid native one — who is equipped only with a knowledge of our books, when we try in vain to say what is wrong, when in despair we say that he has read the books "out of context," then we are aware of the matter I have been asked to speak about tonight.

What I understand by manners, then, is a culture's hum and buzz of implication. I mean the whole evanescent context in which its explicit statements are made. It is that part of a culture which is made up of half-uttered or unuttered or unutterable expressions of value. They are hinted at by small actions, sometimes by the arts of dress or decoration, sometimes by tone, gesture, emphasis, or rhythm, sometimes by the words that are used with a special frequency or a special meaning. They are the things that for good or bad draw the people of a culture together and that separate them from the people of another culture. They make the part of a culture which is not art, or religion, or morals, or politics, and yet it relates to all these highly formulated departments of culture. It is modified by them; it modifies them; it is generated by them; it generates them. In this part of culture assumption rules, which is often so much stronger than reason.

The right way to begin to deal with such a subject is to gather together as much of its detail as we possibly can. Only by doing so will we become fully aware of what the gifted foreign critic or the stupid native one is not aware of, that in any complex culture there is not a single system of manners but a conflicting variety of manners, and that one of the jobs of a culture is the adjustment of this conflict.

But the nature of our present occasion does not permit this accumulation of detail and so I shall instead try to drive toward a generalization and a hypothesis which, however wrong they turn out to be, may at least permit us to circumscribe the subject. I shall try to generalize the subject of American manners by talking about the attitude of Americans toward the subject of manners itself. And since in a complex culture there are, as I say, many different systems of manners and since I cannot talk about them all, I shall select the manners and the attitude toward manners of the literate, reading, responsible middle class of people who are ourselves. I specify that they be reading people because I shall draw my conclusions from the novels they read. The hypothesis I propose is that our attitude toward manners is the expression of a particular conception of reality.

All literature tends to be concerned with the question of reality — I mean quite simply the old opposition between reality and appearance, between what really is and what merely seems. "Don't you *see?*" is the question we want to shout at Oedipus as he stands before us and before fate in the pride of his rationalism. And at the end of *Oedipus Rex* he demonstrates in a particularly direct way that he now sees what he did not see before. "Don't you *see?*" we want to shout again at Lear and Gloucester, the two deceived, self-deceiving fathers: blindness again, resistance to the clear claims of reality, the seduction by mere appearance. The same with Othello — reality is right under your stupid nose, how *dare* you be such a gull? So with Molière's Orgon — my good man, my honest citizen, merely *look* at Tartuffe and you will know what's what. So with Milton's Eve — "Woman, watch out! Don't you see — anyone can see — that's a *snake!*"

The problem of reality is central, and in a special way, to the great forefather of the novel, the great book of Cervantes, whose four hundredth birthday was celebrated in 1947. There are two movements of thought in *Don Quixote,* two different and opposed notions of reality. One is the movement which leads toward saying that the world of ordinary practicality *is* reality in its fullness. It is the reality of the present moment in all its powerful immediacy of hunger, cold, and pain, making the past and the future, and all ideas, of no account. When the conceptual, the ideal, and the fanciful come into conflict with this, bringing their notions of the past and the future, then disaster results. For one thing, the ordinary proper ways of life are upset — the chained prisoners are understood to be good men and are released, the whore is taken for a lady. There is general confusion. As for the ideal, the conceptual, the fanciful, or romantic — whatever you want to call it — it fares even worse: it is shown to be ridiculous.

Thus one movement of the novel. But Cervantes changed horses in midstream and found that he was riding Rosinante. Perhaps at first not quite consciously — although the new view is latent in the old from the very beginning — Cervantes begins to show that the world of tangible reality is not the real reality after all. The real reality is rather the wildly conceiving, the madly fantasying mind of the Don: people change, practical reality changes, when they come into its presence.

In any genre it may happen that the first great example contains the whole potentiality of the genre. It has been said that all philosophy is a footnote to Plato. It can be said that all prose fiction is a variation on the theme of *Don Quixote.* Cervantes sets for the novel the problem of appearance and reality: the shifting and conflict of social classes becomes the field of the problem of knowledge, of how we know and of how reliable our knowledge is, which at that very moment of history is vexing the philosophers and scientists. And the poverty of the Don suggests that the novel is born with the appearance of money as a social element — money, the great solvent of the solid fabric of the old society, the great generator of illusion. Or, which is to say much the same thing, the novel is born in response to snobbery.

Snobbery is not the same thing as pride of class. Pride of class may not please us but we must at least grant that it reflects a social function. A man who exhibited class pride — in the day when it was possible to do so — may have been puffed up about what he *was,* but this ultimately depended on what he *did.* Thus, aristocratic pride was based ultimately on the ability to fight and administer. No pride is without fault, but pride of class may be thought of as today we think of pride of profession, toward which we are likely to be lenient.

Snobbery is pride in status without pride in function. And it is an uneasy pride of status. It always asks, "Do I belong — do I really belong? And does he belong? And if I am observed talking to him, will it make me seem to belong or not to belong?" It is the peculiar vice not of aristocratic societies, which have their own appropriate vices, but of bourgeois democratic societies. For us the legendary strongholds of snobbery are the Hollywood studios, where two thousand dollars a week dare not talk to three hundred dollars a week for fear he be taken for nothing more than fifteen hundred dollars a week. The dominant emotions of snobbery are uneasiness, self-consciousness, self-defensiveness, the sense that one is not quite real but can in some way acquire reality.

Money is the medium that, for good or bad, makes for a fluent society. It does not make for an equal society but for one in which there is a constant shifting of classes, a frequent change in the personnel of the dominant class. In a shifting society great emphasis is put on appearance — I am using the word now in the common meaning, as when people say that "a good appearance is very important in getting a job." To appear to be established is one of the ways of becoming established. The old notion of the solid merchant who owns far more than he shows increasingly gives way to the ideal of signalizing status by appearance, by showing more than you have: status in a democratic society is presumed to come not with power but with the tokens of power. Hence the development of what Tocqueville saw as a mark of democratic culture, what he called the "hypocrisy of luxury" — instead of the well-made peasant article and the well-made middle-class article, we have the effort of all articles to appear as the articles of the very wealthy.

And a shifting society is bound to generate an interest in appearance in the philosophical sense. When Shakespeare lightly touched on the matter that so largely preoccupies the novelist — that is, the movement from one class to another — and created Malvolio, he immediately involved the question of social standing with the problem of appearance and reality. Malvolio's daydreams of bettering his position present themselves to him as reality, and in revenge his enemies conspire to convince him that he is literally mad and that the world is not as he sees it. The predicament of the characters in *A Midsummer Night's Dream* and of Christopher Sly seems to imply that the meeting of social extremes and the establishment of a person of low class in the privileges of a high class always suggested to Shakespeare's mind some radical instability of the senses and the reason.

The characteristic work of the novel is to record the illusion that snobbery generates and to try to penetrate to the truth which, as the novel assumes, lies hidden beneath all the false appearances. Money, snobbery, the ideal of status, these become in themselves the objects of fantasy, the support of the fantasies of love, freedom, charm, power, as in *Madame Bovary*, whose heroine is the sister, at a three-centuries' remove, of Don Quixote. The greatness of *Great Expectations* begins in its title: modern society bases itself on great expectations which, if ever they are realized, are found to exist by reason of a sordid, hidden reality. The real thing is not the gentility of Pip's life but the hulks and the murder and the rats and decay in the cellarage of the novel.

An English writer, recognizing the novel's central concern with snobbery, recently cried out half-ironically against it. "Who cares whether Pamela finally exasperates Mr. B. into marriage, whether Mr. Elton is more or less than moderately genteel, whether it is sinful for Pendennis nearly to kiss the porter's daughter, whether young men from Boston can ever be as truly refined as middle-aged women in Paris, whether the District Officer's fiancée ought to see so much of Dr. Aziz, whether Lady Chatterley ought to be made love to by the gamekeeper, even if he was an officer during the war? Who cares?"

The novel, of course, tells us much more about life than this. It tells us about the look and feel of things, how things are done and what things are worth and what they cost and what the odds are. If the English novel in its special concern with class does not, as the same writer says, explore the deeper layers of personality, then the French novel in exploring these layers must start and end in class, and the Russian novel, exploring the ultimate possibilities of spirit, does the same — every situation in Dostoevski, no matter how spiritual, starts with a point of social pride and a certain number of rubles. The great novelists knew that manners indicate the largest intentions of men's souls as well as the smallest and they are perpetually concerned to catch the meaning of every dim implicit hint.

The novel, then, is a perpetual quest for reality, the field of its research being always the social world, the material of its analysis being always manners as the indication of the direction of man's soul. When we understand this we can understand the pride of profession that moved D. H. Lawrence to say, "Being a novelist, I consider myself superior to the saint, the scientist, the philosopher and the poet. The novel is the one bright book of life."

Now the novel as I have described it has never really established itself in America. Not that we have not had very great novels but that the novel in America diverges from its classic intention, which, as I have said, is the investigation of the problem of reality beginning in the social field. The fact is that American writers of genius have not turned their minds to society. Poe and Melville were quite apart from it; the reality they sought was only tangential to society. Hawthorne was acute when he insisted that he did not write novels but romances — he thus expressed his awareness of the lack of social texture in his work. Howells never fulfilled himself because, although he saw the social subject clearly, he would never take it with full seriousness. In America in the nineteenth century, Henry James was alone in knowing that to scale the moral and aesthetic heights in the novel one had to use the ladder of social observation.

There is a famous passage in James's life of Hawthorne in which James enumerates the things which are lacking to give the American novel the thick social texture of the English novel — no state; barely a specific national name; no sovereign; no court; no aristocracy; no church; no clergy; no army; no diplomatic service; no country gentlemen; no palaces; no castles; no manors; no old country houses; no parsonages; no thatched cottages; no ivied ruins; no cathedrals; no great universities; no public schools; no political society; no sporting class — no Epsom, no Ascot! That is, no sufficiency of means for the display of a variety of manners, no opportunity for the novelist to do his job of searching out reality, not enough complication of appearance to make the job interesting. Another great American novelist of very different temperament had said much the same thing some decades before: James Fenimore Cooper found that American manners were too simple and dull to nourish the novelist.

This is cogent but it does not explain the condition of the American novel at the present moment. For life in America has increasingly thickened since the nineteenth century. It has not, to be sure, thickened so much as to permit our undergraduates to understand the characters of Balzac, to understand, that is, life in a crowded country where the competitive pressures are great, forcing intense passions to express themselves fiercely and yet within the limitations set by a strong and complicated tradition of manners. Still, life here has become more complex and more pressing. And even so we do not have the novel that touches significantly on society, on manners. Whatever the virtues of Dreiser may be, he could not report the social fact with the kind of accuracy it needs. Sinclair Lewis is shrewd, but no one, however charmed with him as a social satirist, can believe that he does more than a limited job of social understanding. John Dos Passos sees much, sees it often in the great way of Flaubert, but can never use social fact as more than either backdrop or "condition." Of our novelists today perhaps only William Faulkner deals with society as the field of tragic reality and he has the disadvantage of being limited to a provincial scene.

It would seem that Americans have a kind of resistance to looking closely at society. They appear to believe that to touch accurately on the matter of class, to take full note of snobbery, is somehow to demean themselves. It is as if we felt that one cannot touch pitch without being defiled — which, of course, may possibly be the case. Americans will not deny that we have classes and snobbery, but they seem to hold it to be indelicate to take precise cognizance of these phenomena. Consider that Henry James is, among a large part of our reading public, still held to be at fault for noticing society as much as he did. Consider the conversation that has, for some interesting reason, become a part of our literary folklore. Scott Fitzgerald said to Ernest Hemingway, "The very rich are different from us." Hemingway replied, "Yes, they have more money." I have seen the exchange quoted many times and always with the intention of suggesting that Fitzgerald was infatuated by wealth and had received a salutary rebuke from his democratic friend. But the truth is that after a certain point quantity of money does indeed change into quality of personality: in an important sense the very rich *are* different from us. So are the very power-ful, the very gifted, the very poor. Fitzgerald was right, and almost for that remark alone he must surely have been received in Balzac's bosom in the heaven of novelists.

It is of course by no means true that the American reading class has no interest in society. Its interest fails only before society as it used to be represented by the novel. And if we look at the commercially successful serious novels of the last decade, we see that almost all of them have been written from an intense social awareness — it might be said that our pres-ent definition of a serious book is one which holds before us some image of society to consider and condemn. What is the situation of the dis-possessed Oklahoma farmer and whose fault it is, what situation the Jew finds himself in, what it means to be a Negro, how one gets a bell for Adano, what is the advertising business really like, what it means to be insane and how society takes care of you or fails to do so — these are the matters which are believed to be most fertile for the novelist, and certainly they are the subjects most favored by our reading class.

The public is probably not deceived about the quality of most of these books. If the question of quality is brought up, the answer is likely to be: no, they are not great, they are not imaginative, they are not "literature." But there is an unexpressed addendum: and perhaps they are all the better for not being imaginative, for not being literature — they are not literature, they are reality, and *in a time like this* what we need is reality in large doses.

When, generations from now, the historian of our times undertakes to describe the assumptions of our culture, he will surely discover that the word *reality* is of central importance in his understanding of us. He will observe that for some of our philosophers the meaning of the word was a good deal in doubt, but that for our political writers, for many of our literary critics, and for most of our reading public, the word did not open discussion but, rather, closed it. Reality, as conceived by us, is whatever is external and hard, gross, unpleasant. Involved in its meaning is the idea of power conceived in a particular way. Some time ago I had occasion to remark how, in the critical estimates of Theodore Dreiser, it is always being said that Dreiser has many faults but that it cannot be denied that he has great power. No one ever says "a kind of power." Power is assumed to be always "brute" power, crude, ugly, and undiscriminating, the way an elephant appears to be. It is seldom understood to be the way an elephant actually is, precise and discriminating; or the way electricity is, swift and absolute and scarcely embodied.

The word *reality* is a honorific word and the future historian will naturally try to discover our notion of its pejorative opposite, appearance, mere appearance. He will find it in our feeling about the internal; whenever we detect evidences of style and thought we suspect that reality is being a little betrayed, that "mere subjectivity" is creeping in. There follows from this our feeling about complication, modulation, personal idiosyncrasy, and about social forms, both the great and the small.

Having gone so far, our historian is then likely to discover a puzzling contradiction. For we claim that the great advantage of reality is its hard, bedrock, concrete quality, yet everything we say about it tends toward the abstract and it almost seems that what we want to find in reality is abstraction itself. Thus we believe that one of the unpleasant bedrock facts is social class, but we become extremely impatient if ever we are told that social class is indeed so real that it produces actual difference of personality. The very people who talk most about class and its evils think that Fitzgerald was bedazzled and Hemingway right. Or again, it might be observed that in the degree that we speak in praise of the "individual" we have contrived that our literature should have no individuals in it — no people, that is, who are shaped by our liking for the interesting and memorable and special and precious.

Here, then, is our generalization: that in proportion as we have committed ourselves to our particular idea of reality we have lost our interest in manners. For the novel this is a definitive condition because it is inescapably true that in the novel manners make men. It does not matter in what sense the word manners is taken — it is equally true of the sense which so much interested Proust or of the sense which interested Dickens or, indeed, of the sense which interested Homer. The Duchesse de Guermantes, unable to delay departure for the dinner party to receive properly from her friend Swann the news that he is dying but able to delay to change the black slippers her husband objects to; Mr. Pickwick and Sam Weller; Priam and Achilles — they exist by reason of their observed manners.

So true is this, indeed, so creative is the novelist's awareness of manners, that we may say that it is a function of his love. It is some sort of love that Fielding has for Squire Western that allows him to note the great, gross details which bring the insensitive sentient man into existence for us. If that is true, we are forced to certain conclusions about our literature and about the particular definition of reality which has shaped it. The reality we admire tells us that the observation of manners is trivial and even malicious, that there are things much more important for the novel to consider. As a consequence our social sympathies have indeed broadened, but in proportion as they have done so we have lost something of our power of love, for our novels can never create characters who truly exist. We make public demands for love, for we know that broad social feeling should be infused with warmth, and we receive a kind of public product which we try to believe is not cold potatoes. The reviewers of Helen Howe's novel of a few years ago, *We Happy Few,* thought that its satiric first part, an excellent comment on the manners of a small but significant segment of society, was ill-natured and unsatisfactory, but they approved the second part, which is the record of the heroine's self-accusing effort to come into communication with the great soul of America. Yet it should have been clear that the satire had its source in a kind of affection, in a real community of feeling, and told the truth, while the second part, said to be so "warm," was mere abstraction, one more example of our public idea of ourselves and our national life. John Steinbeck is generally praised both for his reality and his warmheartedness, but in *The Wayward Bus* the lower-class characters receive a doctrinaire affection in proportion to the suffering and sexuality which define their existence, while the ill-observed middle-class characters are made to submit not only to moral judgment but to the withdrawal of all fellow-feeling, being mocked for their very misfortunes and almost for their susceptibility to death. Only a little thought or even less feeling is required to perceive that the basis of his creation is the coldest response to abstract ideas.

Two novelists of the older sort had a prevision of our present situation. In Henry James's *The Princess Casamassima* there is a scene in which the heroine is told about the existence of a conspiratorial group of revolutionaries pledged to the destruction of all existing society. She has for some time been drawn by a desire for social responsibility; she has wanted to help "the people," she has longed to discover just such a group as she now hears about, and she exclaims in joy, "Then it's real, it's solid!" We are intended to hear the Princess's glad cry with the knowledge that she is a woman who despises herself, "that in the darkest hour of her life she sold herself for a title and a fortune. She regards her doing so as such a terrible piece of frivolity that she can never for the rest of her days be serious enough to make up for it." She seeks out poverty, suffering, sacrifice, and death because she believes that these things alone are real; she comes to believe that art is contemptible; she withdraws her awareness and love from the one person of her acquaintance who most deserves them, and she increasingly scorns whatever suggests variety and modulation, and is more and more dissatisfied with the humanity of the present in her longing for the more perfect humanity of the future. It is one of the great points that the novel makes that with each passionate step that she takes toward what she calls the real, the solid, she in fact moves further away from the life-giving reality.

In E. M. Forster's *The Longest Journey* there is a young man named Stephen Wonham who, although a gentleman born, has been carelessly brought up and has no real notion of the responsibilities of his class. He has a friend, a country laborer, a shepherd, and on two occasions he outrages the feelings of certain intelligent, liberal, democratic people in the book by his treatment of this friend. Once, when the shepherd reneges on a bargain, Stephen quarrels with him and knocks him down; and in the matter of the loan of a few shillings he insists that the money be paid back to the last farthing. The intelligent, liberal, democratic people know that this is not the way to act to the poor. But Stephen cannot think of the shepherd as the poor nor, although he is a country laborer, as an object of research by J. L. and Barbara Hammond; he is rather a reciprocating subject in a relationship of affection — as we say, a friend — and therefore liable to anger and required to pay his debts. But this view is held to be deficient in intelligence, liberalism, and democracy.

In these two incidents we have the premonition of our present cultural and social situation, the passionate self-reproachful addiction to a "strong" reality which must limit its purview to maintain its strength, the replacement by abstraction of natural, direct human feeling. It is worth noting, by the way, how clear is the line by which the two novels descend from *Don Quixote* — how their young heroes come into life with large preconceived ideas and are knocked about in consequence; how both are concerned with the problem of appearance and reality, *The Longest Journey* quite explicitly, *The Princess Casamassima* by indirection; how both evoke the question of the nature of reality by contriving a meeting and conflict of diverse social classes and take scrupulous note of the differences of manners. Both have as their leading characters people who are specifically and passionately concerned with social injustice and both agree in saying that to act against social injustice is right and noble but that to choose to act so does not settle all moral problems but on the contrary generates new ones of an especially difficult sort.

I have elsewhere given the name of moral realism to the perception of the dangers of the moral life itself. Perhaps at no other time has the enterprise of moral realism ever been so much needed, for at no other time have so many people committed themselves to moral righteousness. We have the books that point out the bad conditions, that praise us for taking progressive attitudes. We have no books that raise questions in our minds not only about conditions but about ourselves, that lead us to refine our motives and ask what might lie behind our good impulses.

There is nothing so very terrible in discovering that something does lie behind. Nor does it need a Freud to make the discovery. Here is a publicity release sent out by one of our oldest and most respectable publishing houses. Under the heading "What Makes Books Sell?" it reads, "Blank & Company reports that the current interest in horror stories has attracted a great number of readers to John Dash's novel . . . because of its depiction of Nazi brutality. Critics and readers alike have commented on the stark realism of Dash's handling of the torture scenes in the book. The publishers originally envisaged a woman's market because of the love story, now find men reading the book because of the other angle." This does not suggest a more than usual depravity in the male reader, for "the other angle" has always had a fascination, no doubt a bad one, even for those who would not themselves commit or actually witness an act of torture. I cite the extreme example only to suggest that something may indeed lie behind our sober, intelligent interest in moral politics. In this instance the pleasure in the cruelty is protected and licensed by moral indignation. In other instances moral indignation, which has been said to be the favorite emotion of the middle class, may be in itself an exquisite pleasure. To understand this does not invalidate moral indignation but only sets up the conditions on which it ought to be entertained, only says when it is legitimate and when not.

But, the answer comes, however important it may be for moral realism to raise questions in our minds about our motives, is it not at best a matter of secondary importance? Is it not of the first importance that we be given a direct and immediate report on the reality that is daily being brought to dreadful birth? The novels that have done this have effected much practical good, bringing to consciousness the latent feelings of many people, making it harder for them to be unaware or indifferent, creating an atmosphere in which injustice finds it harder to thrive. To speak of moral realism is all very well. But it is an elaborate, even fancy, phrase and it is to be suspected of having the intention of sophisticating the simple reality that is easily to be conceived. Life presses us so hard, time is so short, the suffering of the world is so huge, simple, unendurable — anything that complicates our moral fervor in dealing with reality as we immediately see it and wish to drive headlong upon it must be regarded with some impatience.

True enough: and therefore any defense of what I have called moral realism must be made not in the name of some highflown fineness of feeling but in the name of simple social practicality. And there is indeed a simple social fact to which moral realism has a simple practical relevance, but it is a fact very difficult for us nowadays to perceive. It is that the moral passions are even more willful and imperious and impatient than the self-seeking passions. All history is at one in telling us that their tendency is to be not only liberating but also restrictive.

It is probable that at this time we are about to make great changes in our social system. The world is ripe for such changes and if they are not made in the direction of greater social liberality, the direction forward, they will almost of necessity be made in the direction backward, of a terrible social niggardliness. We all know which of those directions we want. But it is not enough to want it, not even enough to work for it — we must want it and work for it with intelligence. Which means that we must be aware of the dangers which lie in our most generous wishes. Some paradox of our natures leads us, when once we have made our fellow men the objects of our enlightened interest, to go on to make them the objects of our pity, then of our wisdom, ultimately of our coercion. It is to prevent this corruption, the most ironic and tragic that man knows, that we stand in need of the moral realism which is the product of the free play of the moral imagination.

For our time the most effective agent of the moral imagination has been the novel of the last two hundred years. It was never, either aesthetically or morally, a perfect form and its faults and failures can be quickly enumerated. But its greatness and its practical usefulness lay in its unremitting work of involving the reader himself in the moral life, inviting him to put his own motives under examination, suggesting that reality is not as his conventional education has led him to see it. It taught us, as no other genre ever did, the extent of human variety and the value of this variety. It was the literary form to which the emotions of understanding and forgiveness were indigenous, as if by the definition of the form itself. At the moment its impulse does not seem strong, for there never was a time when the virtues of its greatness were so likely to be thought of as weaknesses. Yet there never was a time when its particular activity was so much needed, was of so much practical, political, and social use — so much so that if its impulse does not respond to the need, we shall have reason to be sad not only over a waning form of art but also over our waning freedom.

Note

1. This essay was read at the Conference on the Heritage of the English-speaking Peoples and Their Responsibilities, at Kenyon College, September 1947.

Roland Barthes begins his critique of French literature with an assertion that "Narration, as a form common to both the Novel and to History, does remain, in general, the choice or the expression of an historical moment." Barthes attacks the concept that the nineteenth-century form of the chronologically narrated novel is synonymous with "writing." He notes that in French, the preterite form of the verb, "obsolete in spoken French," is used in writing literature and that its linguistic nature "calls for a sequence of events, that is, for an intelligible Narrative." According to Barthes, a grammatical structure, representing a particular mode of bourgeois perception, dominates the writing of novels. This structure presents an orderly, coherent view of history and life, but one that Barthes argues is false and misleading. The preterite, then, prevents the engagement of literature with the open-ended present, because it portrays the values of a particular class and period of history as universal values, just as the use of third-person narration presents an apparently authoritative and truthful narrator. (As Seymour Chatman demonstrates in his essay in this volume, the creation of nonnarrated stories and unreliable narrators subverts this convention.)

For Barthes, the novel is a temporary literary phenomenon, a bourgeois product challenged by the modernist efforts to write a new kind of novel: "Modernism begins with the search for a Literature which is no longer possible." As with a number of other French critics after World War II who were heavily influenced by Marxism and existentialism, for Barthes the novel was an integral part of bourgeois society. In order to fight that society one could not use the novel but had to proclaim its "death" and replace it with "writing"; i.e., other forms of literature that were not enslaved by the conventions of bourgeois narration. Can a historically determined form of literature, such as the "bourgeois novel," be used to express new experiences that have never before been expressed, including criticism of the very society that spawned the literary genre? Or must literature in its search for expressing the new reflect that discovery in new techniques of narration and characterization?

Roland Barthes, born in France in 1915, gained an extraordinary reputation as a brilliant, eclectic, and prolific cultural critic before his death in 1980. Identified with a number of critical movements, his method always remained uniquely individual, as in such works as *Writing Degree Zero* (1953; trans. 1967) (the source for this essay), *The Pleasure of the Text* (1973; trans. 1975), *S/Z* (1970; trans. 1974), *Mythologies* (1957; trans. 1972), and *Camera Lucida* (1980; trans. 1981).

The Novel and History have been closely related in the very century which witnessed their greatest development. Their link in depth, that which should allow us to understand at once Balzac and Michelet, is that in both we find the construction of an autarkic world which elaborates its own dimensions and limits, and organizes within these its own Time, its own Space, its population, its own set of objects and its myths.

This sphericity of the great works of the nineteenth century found its expression in those long recitatives, the Novel and History, which are, as it were, plane projections of a curved and organic world of which the serial story which came into being at that precise moment, presents, through its involved complications, a degraded image. And yet narration is not necessarily a law of the form. A whole period could conceive novels in letters, for instance; and another can evolve a practice of History by means of analyses. Therefore Narration, as a form common to both the Novel and to History, does remain, in general, the choice or the expression of an historical moment.

Obsolete in spoken French, the preterite, which is the cornerstone of Narration, always signifies the presence of Art; it is a part of a ritual of Letters. Its function is no longer that of a tense. The part it plays is to reduce reality to a point of time, and to abstract, from the depth of a multiplicity of experiences, a pure verbal act, freed from the existential roots of knowledge, and directed towards a logical link with other acts, other processes, a general movement of the world: it aims at maintaining a hierarchy in the realm of facts. Through the preterite, the verb implicitly belongs with a causal chain, it partakes of a set of related and oriented actions, it functions as the algebraic sign of an intention. Allowing as it does an ambiguity between temporality and causality, it calls for a sequence of events, that is, for an intelligible Narrative. This is why it is the ideal instrument for every construction of a world; it is the unreal time of cosmogonies, myths, History and Novels. It presupposes a world which is constructed, elaborated, self-sufficient, reduced to significant lines, and not one which has been sent sprawling before us, for us to take or leave. Behind the preterite there always lurks a demiurge, a God or a reciter. The world is not unexplained since it is told like a story; each one of its accidents is but a circumstance, and the preterite is precisely this operative sign whereby the narrator reduces the exploded reality to a slim and pure logos, without density, without volume, without spread, and whose sole function is to unite as rapidly as possible a cause and an end. When the historian states that the duc de Guise died on December 23rd, 1588, or when the novelist relates that the Marchioness went out at five o'clock,[1] such actions emerge from a past without substance; purged of the uncertainty of existence, they have the stability and outline of an algebra, they are a recollection, but a useful recollection, the interest of which far surpasses its duration.

So that finally the preterite is the expression of an order, and consequently of a euphoria. Thanks to it, reality is neither mysterious nor absurd; it is clear, almost familiar, repeatedly gathered up and contained in the hand of a creator; it is subjected to the ingenious pressure of his freedom. For all the great storytellers of the nineteenth century, the world may be full of pathos but it is not derelict, since it is a grouping of coherent relations, since there is no overlapping between the written facts, since he who tells the story has the power to do away with the opacity and the solitude of the existences which made it up, since he can in all sentences bear witness to a communication and a hierarchy of actions and since, to tell the truth, these very actions can be reduced to mere signs.

The narrative past is therefore a part of a security system for Belles-Lettres. Being the image of an order, it is one of those numerous formal pacts made between the writer and society for the justification of the former and the serenity of the latter. The preterite *signifies* a creation: that is, it proclaims and imposes it. Even from the depth of the most sombre realism, it has a reassuring effect because, thanks to it, the verb expresses a closed, well-defined, substantival act, the Novel has a name, it escapes the terror of an expression without laws: reality becomes slighter and more familiar, it fits within a style, it does not outrun language. Literature remains the currency in use in a society apprised, by the very form of words, of the meaning of what it consumes. On the contrary, when the Narrative is rejected in favour of other literary genres, or when, within the narration, the preterite is replaced by less ornamental forms, fresher, more full-blooded and nearer to speech (the present tense or the present perfect), Literature becomes the receptacle of existence in all its density and no longer of its meaning alone. The acts it recounts are still separated from History, but no longer from people.

We now understand what is profitable and what is intolerable in the preterite as used in the Novel: it is a lie made manifest, it delineates an area of plausibility which reveals the possible in the very act of unmasking it as false. The teleology common to the Novel and to narrated History is the alienation of the facts: the preterite is the very act by which society affirms its possession of its past and its possibility. It creates a content credible, yet flaunted as an illusion; it is the ultimate term of a formal dialectics which clothes an unreal fact in the garb first of truth then of a lie denounced as such. This has to be related to a certain mythology of the universal typifying the bourgeois society of which the Novel is a characteristic product; it involves giving to the imaginary the formal guarantee of the real, but while preserving in the sign the ambiguity of a double object, at once believable and false. This operation occurs constantly in the whole of Western art, in which the false is equal to the true, not through any agnosticism or poetic duplicity, but because the true is supposed to contain a germ of the universal, or to put it differently, an essence capable of fecundating by mere reproduction, several orders of things among which some differ by their remoteness and some by their fictitious character.

It is thanks to an expedient of the same kind that the triumphant bourgeoisie of the last century was able to look upon its values as universal and to carry over to sections of society which were absolutely heterogeneous to it all the Names which were parts of its ethos. This is strictly how myths function, and the Novel — and within the Novel, the preterite — are mythological objects in which there is, superimposed upon an immediate intention, a second-order appeal to a corpus of dogmas, or better, to a pedagogy, since what is sought is to impart an essence in the guise of an artefact. In order to grasp the significance of the preterite, we have but to compare the Western art of the novel with a certain Chinese tradition, for instance, in which art lies solely in the perfection with which reality is imitated. But in this tradition no sign, absolutely nothing, must allow any distinction to be drawn between the natural and the artificial objects: this wooden walnut must not impart to me, along with the image of a walnut, the intention of conveying to me the art which gave birth to it. Whereas on the contrary this is what writing does in the novel. Its task is to put the mask in place and at the same time to point it out.

This ambiguous function disclosed in the preterite is found in another fact relating to this type of writing: the third person in the Novel. The reader will perhaps recall a novel by Agatha Christie in which all the invention consisted in concealing the murderer beneath the use of the first person of the narrative. The reader looked for him behind every "he" in the plot: he was all the time hidden under the "I." Agatha Christie knew perfectly well that, in the novel, the "I" is usually a spectator, and that it is the "he" who is an actor. Why? The "he" is a typical novelistic convention; like the narrative tense, it signifies and carries through the action of the novel; if the third person is absent, the novel is powerless to come into being, and even wills its own destruction. The "he" is a formal manifestation of the myth, and we have just seen that, in the West at least, there is no art which does not point to its own mask. The third person, like the preterite, therefore performs this service for the art of the novel, and supplies its consumers with the security born of a credible fabrication which is yet constantly held up as false.

Less ambiguous, the "I" is thereby less typical of the novel: it is therefore at the same time the most obvious solution, when the narration remains on this side of convention (Proust's work, for instance, purports to be a mere introduction to Literature), and the most sophisticated, when the "I" takes its place beyond convention and attempts to destroy it, by conferring on the narrative the spurious naturalness of taking the reader into its confidence (such is the guileful air of some stories by Gide). In the same way the use of the "he" in a novel involves two opposed systems of ethics: since it represents an unquestioned convention, it attracts the most conformist and the least dissatisfied, as well as those others who have decided that, finally, this convention is necessary to the novelty of their work. In any case, it is the sign of an intelligible pact between society and the author; but it is also, for the latter, the most important means he has of building the world in the way that he chooses. It is therefore more than a literary experiment: it is a human act which connects creation to History or to existence.

In Balzac for instance, the multiplicity of "he"s, this vast network of characters, slight in terms of solid flesh, but consistent by the duration of their acts, reveals the existence of a world of which History is the first datum. The Balzacian "he" is not the end-product of a development starting from some transformed and generalized "I"; it is the original and crude element of the novel, the material, not the outcome, the creative activity: there is no Balzacian history prior to the history of each third person in the novels of Balzac. His "he" is analogous to Caesar's "he":

the third person here brings about a kind of algebraic state of the action, in which existence plays the smallest possible part, in favour of elements which connect, clarify, or show the tragedy inherent in human relationships. Conversely — or at any rate previously — the function of "he" in the novel can be that of expressing an existential experience. In many modern novelists the history of the man is identified with the course of the conjugation: starting from an "I" which is still the form which expresses anonymity most faithfully, man and author little by little win the right to the third person, in proportion as existence becomes fate, and soliloquy becomes a Novel. Here the appearance of the "he" is not the starting point of History, it is the end of an effort which has been successful in extracting from a personal world made up of humours and tendencies, a form which is pure, significant, and which therefore vanishes as soon as it is born thanks to the totally conventional and ethereal decor of the third person. This certainly was the course displayed in the first novels of Jean Cayrol, whose case can be taken as an exemplar. But whereas in the classics — and we know that where writing is concerned classicism lasts until Flaubert — the withdrawal of the biological person testifies to the establishment of essential man, in novelists such as Cayrol, the invasion of the "he" is a progressive conquest over the profound darkness of the existential "I": so true it is that the Novel, identified as it is by its most formal signs, is a gesture of sociability; it establishes Literature as an institution.

Maurice Blanchot has shown, in the case of Kafka, that the elaboration of the impersonal narrative (let us notice, apropos of this term, that the "third person" is always presented as a negative degree of the person) was an act of fidelity to the essence of language, since the latter naturally tends towards its own destruction. We therefore understand how "he" is a victory over "I," inasmuch as it conjures up a state at once more literary and more absent. None the less this victory is ceaselessly threatened: the literary convention of the "he" is necessary to the belittling of the person, but runs at every moment the risk of encumbering it with an unexpected density. For Literature is like phosphorus: it shines with its maximum brilliance at the moment when it attempts to die. But as, on the other hand, it is an act which necessarily implies a duration — especially in the Novel — there can never be any Novel independently of Belles-Lettres. So that the third person in the Novel is one of the most obsessive signs of this tragic aspect of writing which was born in the last century, when under the weight of History, Literature became dissociated from the society which consumes it. Between the third person as used by Balzac and that used by Flaubert, there is a world of difference (that of 1848): in the former we have a view of History which is harsh, but coherent and certain of its principles, the triumph of an order; in the latter, an art which in order to escape its pangs of conscience either exaggerates conventions or frantically attempts to destroy them. Modernism begins with the search for a Literature which is no longer possible.

Thus we find, in the Novel too, this machinery directed towards both destruction and resurrection, and typical of the whole of modern art. What must be destroyed is duration, that is, the ineffable binding force running through existence: for order, whether it be that of poetic flow or of narrative signs, that of Terror or plausibility, is always a murder in intention. But what reconquers the writer is again duration, for it is impossible to develop a negative within time, without elaborating a positive art, an order which must be destroyed anew. So that the greater modern works linger as long as possible, in a sort of miraculous stasis, on the threshold of Literature, in this anticipatory state in which the breadth of life is given, stretched but not yet destroyed by this crowning phase, an order of signs. For instance, we have the first person in Proust, whose whole work rests on a slow and protracted effort towards Literature. We have Jean Cayrol, whose acquiescence to the Novel comes only as the very last stage of soliloquy, as if the literary act, being supremely ambiguous, could be delivered of a creation consecrated by society, only at the moment when it has at last succeeded in destroying the existential density of a hitherto meaningless duration.

The Novel is a Death; it transforms life into destiny, a memory into a useful act, duration into an orientated and meaningful time. But this transformation can be accomplished only in full view of society. It is society which imposes the Novel, that is, a complex of signs, as a transcendence and as the History of a duration. It is therefore by the obviousness of its intention, grasped in that of the narrative signs, that one can recognize the path which, through all the solemnity of art, binds the writer to society. The preterite and the third person in the Novel are nothing but the fateful gesture with which the writer draws attention to the mask which he is wearing. The whole of Literature can declare *Larvatus prodeo*[2] "As I walk forward, I point out my mask." Whether we deal with the inhuman experience of the poet, who accepts the most momentous of all breaks, that from the language of society, or with the plausible untruth of the novelist, sincerity here feels a need of the signs of falsehood, and of conspicuous falsehood in order to last and to be consumed. Writing is the product, and ultimately the source, of this ambiguity. This specialized language, the use of which gives the writer a glorious but none the less superintended function, evinces a kind of servitude, invisible at first, which characterizes any responsibility. Writing, free in its beginnings, is finally the bond which links the writer to a History which is itself in chains: society stamps upon him the unmistakable signs of art so as to draw him along the more inescapably in its own process of alienation.

Notes

1. The sentence which for Valéry epitomized the conventions of the novel.
2. *Larvatus prodeo* was the motto of Descartes.

8 Norman Friedman : *What Makes a Short Story Short?*

Although much has been written about specific short stories, the question that Norman Friedman poses in his title remains one that vexes those critics who grapple with the short story as a separate literary genre. Friedman's essay, first published in 1958, has become a classic on the form of the short story, one that provides a starting point for nearly all other discussions that have followed it, as we shall see when we come to Suzanne Ferguson's essay, "Defining the Short Story." Friedman makes his first controversial point in claiming that the forms of the short story and the novel differ "in degree but not in kind." He then claims that "a short story may be short" because "the material itself may be of small compass; or the material, being of broader scope, may be cut for the sake of maximizing the artistic effect." In one the object treated, and in the other the manner of presentation, produces brevity. Friedman concludes that to determine the answer to the title question, a reader must consider several possibilities and, in essence, ask not what makes *the* short story or *all* short stories short, but what makes *this* short story short. Such an orientation depends necessarily upon the author's initial claim that short stories differ from novels in degree but not in kind.

Norman Friedman (b. 1925), Professor of English at Queens College, at the City University of New York, is the author of *E. E. Cummings: The Art of His Poetry* (1960), *E. E. Cummings: The Growth of a Writer* (1964), *Logic, Rhetoric, and Style* (1963), and *Form and Meaning in Fiction* (1975).

The truth is that, just as in the other imitative arts one imitation is always of one thing, so in poetry the story, as an imitation of action, must represent one action, a complete whole. . . . Now a whole is that which has a beginning, middle, and end. A beginning is that which is not itself necessarily after anything else, and which has naturally something else after it; an end is that which is naturally after something itself, either as its necessary or usual consequent, and with nothing else after it; and a middle, that which is by nature after one thing and has also another after it. — Aristotle, *Poetics,* chapters 7 and 8.

A lthough the short story as a literary type gets a fair share of attention in classroom texts and writer's handbooks, it is still — tainted by commercialism and damned by condescension — running a poor fourth to poetry, drama, and novel-length fiction in the books and journals devoted to serious theoretical criticism. It is in the hope of making a beginning toward the evaluation of the short story as a worthy and noble art that I should like to attempt a frontal attack upon its basic problem — that of its shortness.

But it is not a question merely of defining "shortness," of fixing the upper and lower limits in terms of the number of words a work of fiction should have in order to be called a short story. Common sense tells us that, although the exact dividing lines cannot — and need not — be determined, we can pretty well distinguish, apart from marginal cases, between long, short, and medium fiction. We will not argue, then, about length in strictly quantitative terms, for most of us know what a short story is and can pull down from our shelves at a moment's notice a dozen anthologies containing stories of varying lengths — all called "short." To haggle over the borderlines is almost always fruitless, and that is one very good reason for not trying. I will simply assume without proof that the examples discussed in this paper as specimens of the type are indeed commonly regarded as short stories.

Nor is it a question of defining a different form, if by form we mean, as we usually do, certain materials unified to achieve a given effect, for the materials and their organization in a short story differ from those in a novel in degree but not in kind. To say, as has frequently been done, that short is distinguished from long fiction by virtue of its greater unity is surely to beg several questions at once. A fossil survivor of Poe's aesthetic, this notion confuses wholeness with singleness, unity with intensity. If unity implies that all the parts are related by an overall governing principle, there is certainly no reason why a short story should have more unity than a novel, although it may naturally have fewer parts to unify — a matter we shall examine in due course.

Nor may we say that a short story cannot deal with the growth of character, as has also been frequently done, or that it focuses upon culminations rather than traces developments, because the simple fact is that many stories do portray a character in the process of changing — Hemingway's "The Short Happy Life of Francis Macomber," for example, or Faulkner's "Barn Burning." Similarly, there is no reason why a story cannot deal with a change in thought, as in Steele's "How Beautiful with Shoes," or with a change in fortune, as in Fitzgerald's "Babylon Revisited." (Of course, some stories *are* static, and we shall discuss them below.) Nor may we say that stories are more commonly organized around a theme than novels, for some are, as Shirley Jackson's "The Lottery," and some are not, as Edith Wharton's "The Other Two." A story may arouse suspense and expectation, pity repugnance, hope, and fear, just as a novel may, and may resolve those emotions in a complete and satisfying way, just as a novel may.[1]

There is, of course, much truth in the approaches we have just touched upon, but none of them manages to include enough of the actual possibilities to be finally useful. Surely short stories contain fewer words than novels, but that measure is a misleading one because it centers on symptoms rather than causes; surely short stories may make a more singular impact upon the reader, but that is an effect having to do with questions other than simply unity as such; and just as surely a novel may deal at greater length with dynamic actions than a story, but there are ways in which a story may handle changes within its own sphere. Most of these principles, in brief, are too prescriptive. In order to understand how and why a short story gets to be short, therefore, I would like to propose a way of answering these questions which will apply to all examples of the type without prescribing beforehand what the characteristics of that type should be.

A story may be short, to begin with a basic distinction, for either or both of two fundamental reasons: the material itself may be of small compass; or the material, being of broader scope, may be cut for the sake of maximizing the artistic effect. The first reason has to do with distinctions as to the *object* of representation, while the second with distinctions as to the *manner* in which it is represented. We will thus discuss the size of the action (which may be large or small, and is not to be confused with the size of the *story,* which may be short or long), and its static or dynamic structure; and then the number of its parts which may be included or omitted, the scale on which it may be shown, and the point of view from which it may be told. A story may be short in terms of any one of these factors or of any combination, but for the sake of clarity and convenience we shall discuss them separately and give cross-references where necessary.

Elder Olson has provided us with a useful set of terms for discussing the question of size with some degree of clarity and precision.[2] A *speech,* he says, contains the continuous verbal utterance of a single character in a closed situation; the speaker is either talking to himself without interruption (soliloquy), or, if there are others present they neither reply nor make entrances and exits while he speaks (monologue). This is the kind of action shown in most short poems commonly called "lyric," as in Marvell's "To His Coy Mistress," for example, or Keats's "On First Looking Into Chapman's Homer," and many many others. A *scene* includes the continuous chain of utterance engendered between two or more speakers as one replies to the other (dialogue) in a closed situation, while an *episode* contains two or more such scenes centering around one main incident. A *plot,* finally, is a system of two or more such episodes. And a short story may conceivably encompass an action of any such size.

Naturally, a large action, such as the plot of *Great Expectations,* although unified in terms of its overall size, will contain smaller subactions, such as speeches, scenes, and episodes, unified in terms of *their* particular sizes; and these smaller subactions may be and often are detachable for certain purposes, as when an episode, for example, is extracted from a larger work for inclusion in an anthology. Actions of different sizes, that is to say, dovetail the smaller into the larger. The point is, however, that a speech, scene, or episode which is designed in itself to serve as the unifying basis of a single complete work must be fully independent, whereas in a larger work it is only partially so, necessarily containing elements binding it to what has gone before and what is to come after.

Why an author makes a certain initial choice regarding size we can only guess, except that he probably senses that he has a whole and complete action in itself and that this will suffice as a basis for separate treatment. This is a matter, then, of the original conception, and all that we can say is that a writer chooses to treat actions of different sizes because he feels, either by habit or deliberate choice or intuition or some combination, that any given one embodies all that is relevant to his purpose. An action of any given size, then, may be whole and complete in itself, and the smaller the action, the shorter its presentation may be.

The relevant parts of an action which is whole and complete, therefore, include those incidents which are needed to bring about and then display whatever necessary or probable consequences the writer wants to show his protagonist enacting or undergoing, and such other incidents as may be useful in casting these in their proper light. The size of that action, then, will depend upon what he wants his protagonist to do or suffer and upon how far back, correspondingly, he must go in the protagonist's experience to find those causes which are both necessary and sufficient to motivate and make credible that action. Clearly, a dynamic action will call into play a larger number of causes than a static one, and a more inclusive change will require a longer chain of causes than a less inclusive one. An action of whatever size is thus whole and complete whenever the delicate inter-linkage of causes and effects encompasses whatever is enough to make that action both understandable and likely.

The speech is best suited, obviously, to render a single moment or a brief succession of moments in any given chain of cause and effect. An immediate response, whether static or dynamic, to an immediate stimulus is the special province of lyric poetry. In Housman's "With Rue My Heart Is Laden," for example, the speaker responds with an expression of sor-row to the fact that many of his friends are now dead, while in Frost's "Stopping by Woods" the speaker responds to the mysterious attraction of the dark and snowy woods by first yielding to their temptation and then by resisting it. In the first we have a single but complete moment of lamenta-tion, while in the second we have a longer but equally complete succession of moments during the course of which the speaker makes up his mind about something, in the sense of choosing between alternatives. Either way, these particular actions are inherently small, and whatever is needed to make them clear and likely may therefore be encompassed in a rather short space.

As a result, such actions are rarely treated in fiction, even short fiction. We all know that the devices of the poetic art are especially capable of handling this sort of thing in an intensified manner, and that narrative prose, being especially flexible, is much more suited to larger actions where more has to be shown. I do know of two such actions in fiction, but they are the exceptions which prove the rule. Dorothy Parker's "A Tele-phone Call" presents a young lady in the throes of anxious anticipation as she awaits her boyfriend's belated phone call. And that is all there is to it: as far as we are concerned here, the entire story comprises her interior soliloquy as she waits for the phone to ring. E. B. White's "The Door" similarly presents practically nothing but the continuous mental states of its one and only character — presented sometimes indirectly by way of narration and sometimes directly by way of interior soliloquy — who is shown in a state of uncertainty and frustration regarding the contradictory values of modern civilization.

To present a single scene is much more feasible in short fiction, al-though even here pure examples are not as common as one might think. The best and clearest specimen with which I am familiar is Hemingway's

"Hills Like White Elephants," which shows a young American couple waiting in an isolated train station in the valley of the Ebro for the express from Barcelona. Except for the waitress who brings them drinks, the story encompasses only the single and continuous interchange of dialogue which occurs between the man and woman as they wait. The point of this story, which deals with a static situation, is, I think, to reveal to us by degrees the causes of the girl's plight, and through that to arouse our pity. Apparently unmarried, these two are on their way to get the girl an abortion. This is not, however, the source of the story's pathos; it lies, rather, in the fact that as the conversation progresses it becomes evident that her lover has no real feeling for her and her incipient need to extend their relationship to its normal fruition. Since that is all we need to know to get this particular effect, and since it can all be done within the bounds of a single conversation, that is all Hemingway had to show to unify this particular story.

And it is done, of course, with consummate skill. We read toward the end, for example: "He did not say anything but looked at the bags against the wall of the station. There were labels on them from all the hotels where they had spent nights." From this small detail we are allowed to infer worlds about the situation of this couple — the shallowness of their relationship, its rootlessness, its transiency. This allusion to the immediate past, although not formally a part of the whole action being shown (since the causes of the pathos are shown as the scene itself progresses), helps to place the situation in its proper light in the reader's mind. And notice how artfully it has been incorporated into the fabric of the present scene itself without authorial intrusion.

The episode is an even more commonly found size in the short story — indeed, its frequency may warrant our calling it the typical sort of action dealt with by this art. Hemingway's "Ten Indians," for example, contains five scenes centered around Nick's discovery of his Indian sweetheart's infidelity, his subsequent depression, and his final forgetfulness of his sorrow. He is, after all, rather young to allow heartbreak to affect him for more than a few hours at a time. This is a dynamic action involving changes in thought and feeling, and therefore requires — other things being equal — a larger action than a single scene for the establishing of its chain of cause and effect. It does, however, all take place within the span of a few hours and each of its scenes leads up to or away from a single central incident: (1) Nick is driving home late one afternoon from a Fourth of July celebration in town with the Garners and they kid him about his Indian girlfriend; (2) they arrive at the Garners, unload the wagon and Nick strikes out for his own home; (3) Nick is walking home; (4) his father gives him supper and tells him how he saw Prudie "having quite a time" in the woods with another boy, causing Nick to feel bad; (5) Nick goes unhappily to bed, but awakens contentedly later in the night to the sound of the wind and the waves, having forgotten his sorrow.

Thus a scene or episode requires less space in the telling, other things being equal, than the plot.

Another question regarding size is whether the action involves a change, and if so, whether that change is major or minor, and simple or complex. I hope it is clear by now that a short story may be either static or dynamic, but, as we have seen, an action which is static normally requires fewer parts than one which is dynamic and will therefore normally be shorter in the telling. That is to say, a static story simply shows its protagonist in one state or another and includes only enough to reveal to the reader the cause or causes of which this state is a consequence, while a dynamic story brings its protagonist through a succession of two or more states and thus must include the several causal stages of which these states are the consequences. Thus a static story will normally be shorter than a dynamic one.

Therefore, although not all short stories are static, most static actions are likely to be found in short stories — static situations expanded and elaborated to novel-length are comparatively rare (*Mrs. Dalloway* is an example). And there is a similar general correlation between static and dynamic actions and their various sizes. To achieve in fiction a change in the protagonist in an independent speech or scene is possible but not likely, and to extend a static situation through an entire independent episode or complete plot is also possible but equally unlikely. I would say, as a rule, that most static actions comprise a scene or a small episode.

Another example of a static story, in addition to "White Elephants" already discussed, is Sean O'Faoláin's "Sinners," in which a Catholic clergyman's mental anguish over the lies of a servant girl at confession is revealed. He is first shown twitching irritably at her stories during the confession, and then crying out in positive vexation later when he happens to overhear her admitting her lies at confession to her mistress. His emotional state is announced, as it were, in the first phase of the story, and confirmed in the second phase (because of transitions there are slightly more than two scenes here). Thus the reader is made to see his frustration, and then to understand it as having ample justification. And, in order to achieve this effect, the writer showed as much as he needed, two scenes or so, and no more.

Of course, he could have continued on with this story to show us the canon going through a subsequent change in feeling for the better, in which case he would have had to introduce a whole new line of causes working in that direction, and thus could have lengthened it; but if he had merely gone on with the same sort of thing, he would have blundered in exceeding the needs of his effect. It is this effect and the amount of action required to achieve it which determine the shortness of this story, when considered in itself as an independent work.

"Francis Macomber," "Barn Burning," "How Beautiful with Shoes," "Babylon Revisited," and "The Death of Ivan Ilyich" are short stories which comprise, on the other hand, dynamic actions. In the first, a cowardly man becomes finally courageous in the face of danger; in the second, a young boy decides to oppose at last his father's vindictive destruction of their landlord's property; in the third, an ignorant mountain girl becomes aware that man can be more than an animal; in the fourth, a reformed drunkard is frustrated temporarily in his plans to regain his estranged daughter; and in the fifth, a dying man sees his empty life truthfully for the first time. But there is a difference regarding magnitude even among dynamic actions, for all but the last are minor changes, not in the sense that they are unimportant or that their consequences are not serious or far-reaching, but rather in the sense that they call into play and require for their representation only one phase of their protagonists' lives. Thus a minor change will normally require less space than a major one.

Here again there may be a general correlation between inclusiveness and the size of an action, for most minor changes will involve but an episode, while a major change will involve a complete plot. In this sense, "Ilyich" has more in common with *Great Expectations* than with the other stories just mentioned; indeed, it even covers more aspects of its protagonist's life than the Dickens novel. Some episodes, then, are static, and some are dynamic, but plots tend almost always to be dynamic. And one of the differences between a short story plot and a novel plot need not, as we shall see below, be a difference in the intrinsic size of their actions but rather in the manner in which their actions are shown. In this sense, "Ilyich" is of course much closer in length to a short story than to a novel.

On the other hand, there is no reason why an action covering several episodes may not involve merely a minor change. We have thus to distinguish, on the basis of inclusiveness, minor and major plots (and I suppose an episode may deal with a major change, but I do not think this is likely). Fitzgerald points to this distinction as he narrates the experiences of Dexter Green in "Winter Dreams": "It is with one of those denials [the mysterious prohibitions in which life indulges] and not with his career as a whole that this story deals." And again, toward the end of the story: "This story is not his biography, remember, although things creep into it which have nothing to do with those dreams he had when he was young. We are almost done with them and with him now." Fitzgerald is saying, in effect, that this particular story finds its unity in treating only as many episodes as are required to show the reader the causes of Dexter's infatuation with Judy Jones and his subsequent disillusionment in her and the youthful possibilities she stands for in his mind, and that Dexter's other experiences (probably his business ventures and the like) are not particularly relevant thereto. He has guided himself, in consequence, largely by this original choice in matters of where to begin and end, and how much to include and omit. It is this limitation as to what phases of the protagonist's life are relevant to a given change which accounts for the shortness of this story.

The action of *The Great Gatsby,* on the other hand, although it is strikingly similar in its general outlines, because it deals with Gatsby's entire life, is a major plot. The obsession of Gatsby with Daisy and what she represents to him, that is to say, consumes all aspects of his career, and indeed costs him his very life at the end. The disillusionment of Gatsby, therefore, cannot be understood except in terms of his life as a whole, and that is why his story takes longer to tell than Dexter's. To have added Dexter's other interests to "Winter Dreams" would have been just as bad an artistic mistake as to have omitted Gatsby's from *The Great Gatsby:* the former would have resulted in irrelevance, while the latter would have caused a lack of clarity. Indeed, some critics of the novel have argued that it is too short even as it is to produce the requisite sense of probability or necessity in the reader, but that is quite another matter. (A rather different complaint has been raised against *For Whom the Bell Tolls,* which seems to some critics too *long* in proportion to the size of its action.)

There is a second difference regarding magnitude among dynamic actions which cuts across the one just examined between major and minor changes. A simple change brings its protagonist gradually from one state to another without reversals and is thus, since it calls into play only a single line of causation, a smaller action than a complex change, which brings its protagonist from one state into another and then into a third state opposite from the second, and which thus calls into play several lines of causation. The former, having consequently fewer parts, may be shorter in the telling.

All of the dynamic actions discussed so far are examples of the complex type, while Conrad's "An Outpost of Progress" illustrates a simple change. The moral characters of Kayerts and Carlier, weak and shallow to begin with, deteriorate swiftly and surely when brought to the acid test of prolonged and intimate contact "with pure unmitigated savagery" in the heart of Africa. If a short story can deal with the development of character, it can also deal, apparently, with its degeneration. It is interesting to contrast this story with "Heart of Darkness," for there, in making Kurtz a paragon of moral character *before* his surrender to the abyss, Conrad set himself a much harder job. But he also achieved more vivid results, because if the fall of Kayerts and Carlier is more probable, it is also by the same token less interesting. The second story, however, is almost three times longer than the first (the great length of "Heart of Darkness," incidentally, may also be explained in terms of its ruminative narrator — a topic to which we shall return below).

Thus, because it requires more "doing," a dynamic action tends to be longer than a static one; a major change, because it includes perforce more aspects of the protagonist's life, tends to be longer than a minor change; and a complex change, because it has more parts, tends to be longer than a simple one. But our principles must be continually qualified at every point because, as we shall see, we are dealing with a set of independent variables. A story which should be long in one way may actually be short in another; a story involving a major change, for example, which should be longer than one involving a minor change, all other things being equal, may actually turn out to be shorter because those other things are not equal.

A short story may be short, then, because its action is inherently small. But, as has been indicated, a story may encompass a larger action and still be short. If a writer has decided to show a plot, that is to say, he has a further option as to the manner in which he shall do so. And here he will be guided by his desire to maximize the vividness of his effect on the one hand, and to achieve that effect with the greatest economy of means on the other. He may decide, to begin with, that although a given part of his plot is relevant, he may best omit it and leave it to inference.

Since this question of selection can be discussed only in terms of how much of the whole action is put before the reader, and since we have defined "whole action" only generally, it behooves us to pause long enough to fill in our conceptions here. A whole action is, as we have seen, an action of a certain size — whether a speech, scene, episode, or plot — containing whatever is relevant to bringing the protagonist by probable or necessary stages from the beginning, through the middle, and on to the end of a given situation.

The question now under examination concerns how many of these parts are actually shown to the reader and how many are merely alluded to or left to inference. In Steinbeck's "Flight," for example, a young and hitherto rather shiftless boy, as a result of his first visit alone to the city, is forced to prove himself a man — even to the point of facing death bravely. In the actual telling of the story, however, Steinbeck chose to omit the boy's trip to Monterey entirely, bringing it in only later when the boy returns and tells his mother what happened there before he sets out for the mountains.

We are dealing with a complex dynamic action: what are the parts required for such an action to achieve its proper effect?

A complex change involves bringing the protagonist from one state to another by means of a reversal. What is required for clarity and belief, therefore, is (1) a precipitating cause to bring him into his first state, (2) a counterplot action to represent the consequences of that state, (3) an inciting cause which will serve to bring him out of the counterplot and on toward the opposite state, (4) a progressive action to represent him in the process of change, and (5) a culmination where the process is completed.[3] A simple change, as we have seen, involves bringing the protagonist from one state to another without a reversal, and therefore requires only the last three parts outlined above. And similar principles regarding selection may be applied to static actions in terms of the single states and relevant causes which they reveal.

Let us see how this scheme works for "Flight": (1) the boy is sent to Monterey for medicine by his mother; (2) he dons his father's hat and rides his father's saddle, boasting of his newfound manhood, and in Monterey drinks too much wine and gets into a fight; (3) he kills a man and must now either face the consequences like a man or run and hide "like a chicken"; (4) he returns home, tells his mother what happened, prepares himself for his journey, and suffers untold hardships for four days among the mountains; and (5) he dies finally with honor by facing, in his last extremity, his pursuers and accepting their vengeance. Most of phase two and all of three are omitted. Why?

We may say in the first place that, because probability demands that the protagonist tell his mother what happened anyway, Steinbeck simply acted in the interests of economy by avoiding repetition. That, however, is a rather mechanical explanation, although pertinent enough in its own way. More importantly, we may infer that Steinbeck intended to leave us with feelings of mingled pity and admiration for this boy as his story unfolds — pity for his suffering and death, and admiration for the noble manner in which he suffers and dies. This being the case, we may infer further that he left out most of the counterplot and the inciting incident because, in his effort to arouse our sympathies, he wanted consciously to avoid showing us his protagonist acting senselessly, without thought, and fatefully. By omitting these portions he also impresses us more vividly with the startling contrast between immaturity and maturity in his protagonist's behavior from the time he leaves in the morning till the time he returns at night. He is thus free to concentrate the greater portion of the reader's attention upon the boy's suffering and nobility rather than upon his rashness and immaturity. We must still *know,* however, what happened in Monterey, why the boy is taking to the mountains, and in what light to regard these events. And this we get from the boy's narration to his mother: the very fact that he tells her without hesitation and evasion is a sign of his real manhood. He was insulted, and so he killed before he knew what he was doing. Thus his ultimate death is made acceptable on the one hand and admirable on the other.

An instructive contrast to Steinbeck's wisdom in this matter is provided by a television adaptation of this story which I happened to see some time ago. Faced with wholly different technical problems, the television writer sought to enlarge his script not only by including those parts of the action which were left out of the original but also by elaborating upon and expanding them. The young boy was shown in Monterey — it was fiesta time and he got mixed up with a girl — and we see him getting insulted and killing his man. The fiesta allowed the insertion (intrusion would be a better word) of some dance productions as well as of some flicker of romantic interest. The flight itself was handled as honestly as possible, but even there the limitations of the medium necessitated the awkward device of having the boy talk to himself as he suffered, since he was, of course, alone and the fictional narrator was denied his function. The overall effect was distracting, to say the least: the only really relevant parts are the insult and the murder, so that the dancing and the girl, even though they were trumped up as the causes of his being insulted, simply came to nothing in terms of the rest of the story, and even with the insult and the murder it was quite upsetting actually to see our young hero draw blood; and the subsequent effort to elicit our sympathies for his suffering in the mountains was correspondingly vitiated. Perhaps because of the brevity of the original and its corresponding dependence upon narrative flexibility, the dramatized version of "Flight" was doomed from the outset.

The point to be made here is that a story may be short not because its action is inherently small, but rather because the author has chosen — in working with an episode or plot — to omit certain of its parts. In other words, an action may be large in size and still be short in the telling because not all of it is there. These gaps may be at the beginning of the action, somewhere along the line of its development, at the end, or some combination. Correspondingly, an action may be longer in the telling because more than its relevant parts are included.

Once he has decided what parts, of those which are relevant, he will include, the writer has a second option as to the scale on which he will show them. A given action, that is, may be made longer in the telling by expanding its parts, or shorter by contracting. What this implies is that, of all the things which actually "occur" or are present in a given scene — such as spoken dialogue, interior soliloquy, gesture, physical movement, clothing, and background setting — he may unfold them step by step or he may sum them up and mention only the high points. The contracted scale abstracts retrospectively from the event what is needed to advance the story and presents it in a condensed manner, while the expanded scale tries to give the illusion that the whole thing is being shown directly and in detail even as it happens. The contracted scale tends to cover a long timespan of action in a relatively short space, while the expanded scale tends to cover a short timespan in a relatively long space. And all this is, of course, actually a question of degree.

Flexibility, however, is one of the prime virtues of the fictional medium, and most narratives, whether long or short, vary the scale of presentation to suit the effect. Economy and vividness guide the writer here as before, but now the principle of proportion also comes into play. Those parts of the action which are more important than the others — and this, of course, will be related in each case to the effect intended — should naturally be emphasized by means of an expanded representation, and those which are less important should be condensed.

Although the amount of fictional time covered in the action has, as we shall see, no necessary connection with the length of its treatment, we can say that there is a general correlation, and that a writer who deals with actions covering a small timespan will normally choose the lesser magnitudes within which to work. The rule of economy tells the writer that, if the substance of his story takes place within the space of an hour, then a single scene will do the job. Likewise, if it covers several hours, a day, or a week, then an episode will be called for; and if it covers months or years, then a plot is needed. Joyce's *Ulysses,* however, reverses this correlation by expanding a single day into a full-length novel comprising many episodes, which merely emphasizes once again that we are dealing with a set of independent variables.

Tolstoy's "Death of Ivan Ilyich," on the other hand, is as good an example of a whole and full-sized plot condensed down to the length of a short story — albeit a rather long one — as can be found. It contains twelve numbered sections of varying lengths and, with some backtracking, takes its protagonist all the way from his childhood to his death in late middle age, and includes his schooling, courtship, marriage, career, and children. The whole action culminates in Ivan's first and final awareness, as he dies, of the reality of death and consequently of the hollowness of his entire life up to that point. Clearly, in order for this change to strike the reader with the proper intelligibility and force, Ivan's entire life has to be shown. The impact, that is to say, of Ivan's discovery depends for its point upon a knowledge of how his life has been lived previously and in terms of what values and attitudes.

But "Ivan Ilyich" is short (relatively) because, although the whole plot and more is shown, it is shown largely on a condensed scale. Likewise *Ulysses,* although it covers so much smaller a time span, is so much longer because its action is expanded to the last detail (apparently).

Economy is still the general principle in these cases, however. Even though Ivan's whole life must be shown, it is of such a repetitive and shallow character (which is exactly the point, of course) that to have shown it on a full scale would have bored the reader to extinction — although Tolstoy naturally does represent the more important parts of his plot on an expanded scale. Joyce, too, did what he had to do to get his effect, although it is of an altogether different sort. Since the work turns on the ironic contrast between man as he is and man as he would be, it is exactly the meanness and triviality of daily life which Joyce must emphasize. It follows, therefore, that an almost infinite expansion serves Joyce's purpose but would have hampered Tolstoy in the achievement of his.

Another instructive contrast between the two extremes is found in comparing "Ivan Ilyich," which utilizes, as we have seen, a high degree of contraction, with "White Elephants," which is almost as expanded as a single scene between two people covering thirty minutes or so can get. And the reasons for this difference should be clear by now: Tolstoy has a large action to show, but most of it is important only as it throws light upon the final few scenes; while Hemingway has only one scene to show, and show it he does. Thus a story may be short, even if it encompasses a large action, because much of its action is best shown on a contracted scale.

We may consider, finally, how the choice of a point of view is related to the question of length.[4] If a writer decides, for example, to allow his narrator complete omniscience, then several things will naturally follow. His narrator may editorialize, as in *Tom Jones* or *War and Peace,* and this of course will add significantly to the bulk of the work. Or, given omniscience, his narrator may analyze his characters' motives and states of mind at some length, and such commentary and exposition will also increase the bulk of the work. This is the reason why Mann's "Disorder and Early Sorrow" seems to cover so much more ground at first sight than it actually turns out to encompass upon close study: although it takes almost two hours to read, it actually includes an action whose timespan runs only from afternoon to evening of one day. Because, however, the action is shown through a screen of exposition and commentary regarding the Professor's states of mind, and even though the external action itself is rarely, as a consequence, shown directly and on an expanded scale, the story — although short — is a lengthy one in proportion to the time covered in the action.

Omniscience involves, on the other hand, features favorable to brevity. That is, a narrator who exists over and above the action itself may exercise, as they say, wide discretionary powers in matters of scale and selection. Because he is bound by no "mortal" limitations, he can manipulate his material at will. Thus he may shift the scene of the action in time and place, and, more importantly for the question in hand, may omit and/or sum up parts of the action which do not merit more explicit and detailed treatment. In the long run, then, omniscience is characterized by its flexibility and is equally at home in novels and short stories alike.

A character narrator may also be given to commentary and speculation, as is Marlow in "Heart of Darkness," and this too may add to the bulk of the work. The dramatic point of view similarly, because it is committed by definition to an expanded scale, as on the stage, tends toward length. Thus, an author who chooses the dramatic method for a short story had best work with an action of small size to begin with or, dealing with a larger one, omit certain of its parts.

To sum up, a story may be short because its action is intrinsically small; or because its action, being large, is reduced in length by means of the devices of selection, scale, and/or point of view. No one can tell in advance that, if a story is short, it is short because it has a certain number of words, or because it has more unity, or because it focuses upon culmination rather than development. All we can do, upon recognizing its shortness, is to ask how and why, keeping balanced simultaneously in our minds the alternative ways of answering these questions and their possible combinations. And then we may win increased understanding and hence appreciation of the specific artistic qualities of this curious and splendid but vastly underrated art.

Notes

1. Cf. R. S. Crane, "The Concept of Plot and the Plot of *Tom Jones,*" *Critics and Criticism: Ancient and Modern,* ed. R. S. Crane (Chicago: University of Chicago Press, 1952) pp. 616–47; and Theodore A. Stroud, "A Critical Approach to the Short Story," *Journal of General Education* 9 (1956): 91–100. The present essay may be read as a companion to Stroud's.
2. See Olson, "An Outline of Poetic Theory," in Crane, ed., *Critics and Criticism,* pp. 546–66, esp. p. 560.
3. Similar terms and concepts are used by Paul Goodman in his *Structure of Literature* (Chicago: University of Chicago Press, 1954), but in a slightly different way. I had arrived at my own position independently, before I read this brilliant but puzzling book.
4. See my "Point of View in Fiction: The Development of a Critical Concept," *PMLA* 70 (1955): 1160–84, for a full-length analysis of the varieties of this device.

9 Wayne Booth : *Distance and Point of View*

An Essay in Classification

Wayne Booth opens his essay by arguing that, while there have been many studies of narrative point of view in fiction, these have tended to be too descriptively particular or overtly prescriptive to generate useful guidelines for critical analysis. The former approach provides us with no terms to discuss the techniques of narrative point of view because they describe only individual works or artists; the latter provides too few terms because prescriptive critics reduce the "right" kind of narration to the techniques of which they approve. Frequently then, Booth charges, a work of fiction such as *Moby-Dick,* is criticized for "deviating" from the critic's model or is inadequately discussed because no terms exist to describe the narrative techniques actually employed.

Booth begins his discussion of specific terms by criticizing the too general use of the word "person." Beyond the phrases of "first person" and "third person," he argues, we need to consider such distinctions as *"dramatized* narrators and *undramatized* narrators"; we must also distinguish the "implied author" from the narrator. While explaining what he means by these distinctions, Booth also makes additional distinctions within these terms, such as one between dramatized narrators who are "mere *observers"* or *"narrator-agents."* He then discusses how "distance" pertains to the relationships among narrators and implied authors, narrators and readers, and implied authors and readers. Another crucial issue explored by Booth is that of reliable and unreliable narrators, a distinction that has caused major critical reassessments of such works as *The Great Gatsby* and *Huckleberry Finn.* Booth's exercise in classification, *The Rhetoric of Fiction* (1961), upon which this essay is based, helped to initiate — along with structuralist approaches to literary analysis — a major revaluation of the function of narrative. This has in turn led to the development of an entire sphere of literary theory called narratology.

Wayne C. Booth (b. 1921) is Professor of English Emeritus at the University of Chicago. In addition to *The Rhetoric of Fiction,* a revised version of which was published in 1983, he has published numerous other works, including *A Rhetoric of Irony* (1974) and *Critical Understanding: The Powers and Limits of Pluralism* (1979).

"But he [the narrator] little knows what surprises lie in wait for him, if someone were to set about analysing the mass of truth and falsehoods which he has
collected here." — "Dr. S.," in *Confessions of Zeno*

L ike other notions used in talking about fiction, point of view has
proved less useful than was expected by the critics who first brought
it to our attention. When Percy Lubbock hailed the triumph of Henry
James's dramatic use of the "central intelligence," and told us that "the
whole intricate question of method, in the craft of fiction," is governed by
"the relation in which the narrator stands to the story," he might have
predicted that many critics would, like E. M. Forster, disagree with him.
But he could hardly have predicted that his converts would produce, in
forty years of elaborate investigations of point of view, so little help to the
author or critic who must decide whether this or that technique in a particular work is appropriate to this or that effect. On the one hand we have been
given classifications and descriptions which leave us wondering why we
have bothered to classify and describe; the author who counted the number
of times the word "I" appears in each of Jane Austen's novels may be
more obviously absurd than the innumerable scholars who have traced in
endless detail the "*Ich-Erzählung,*" or "*erlebte Rede,*" or "*monologue
intérieur*" from Dickens to Joyce or from James to Robbe-Grillet. But he
is no more irrelevant to literary judgment. To describe particulars may be
interesting but it is only the preliminary to the kind of knowledge that
might help us explain the success or failure of individual works.

On the other hand, our efforts at formulating useful principles have
been of little more use because they have been overtly prescriptive. If to
count the number of times "I" occurs tells us nothing about how many
times "I" should occur, to formulate abstract appeals for more "showing"
and less "telling," for less authorial commentary and more drama, for
more realistic consistency and fewer arbitrary shifts which remind the
reader that he is reading a book, gives us the illusion of having discovered
criteria when we really have not. While it is certainly true that some effects
are best achieved by avoiding some kinds of telling, too often our prescriptions have been for "the novel" entire, ignoring what James himself knew
well: there are "5,000,000 ways to tell a story," depending on one's overall purposes. Too many Jamesians have tried to establish in advance the
precise degree of realistic intensity or irony or objectivity or "aesthetic
distance" his work should display.

It is true that dissenting voices are now heard more and more frequently, perhaps the most important being Kathleen Tillotson's recent inaugural lecture at the University of London, *The Tale and the Teller.* But the clichés about the superiority of dramatic showing over mere telling are still to be found everywhere: in scholarly journals, in the literary quarterlies, in the weekly reviews, in the latest book on how to read a novel, and in dust-jacket blurbs. "The author does not tell you directly but you find out for yourself from their [the characters'] every word, gesture, and act," a Modern Library jacket tells us about Salinger's *Nine Stories.* That this is praise, that Salinger would be in error if he were found telling us anything directly, is taken for granted.

Since the novelist's choices are in fact practically unlimited, in judging their effectiveness we can only fall back on the kind of reasoning used by Aristotle in the *Poetics: if* such-and-such an effect is desired, *then* such-and-such points of view will be good or bad. We all agree that point of view is in some sense a technical matter, a means to larger ends; whether we say that technique is the artist's way of discovering his artistic meaning or that it is his way of working his will upon his audience, we still can judge it only in the light of the larger meanings or effects which it is designed to serve. Though we all at times violate our own convictions, most of us are convinced that we have no right to impose on the artist abstract criteria derived from other kinds of work.

But even when we have decided to put our judgments in the hypothetical "if-then" form, we are still faced with an overwhelming variety of choices. One of the most striking features of our criticism is the casual way in which we allow ourselves to reduce this variety, thoughtlessly, carelessly, to simple categories, the impoverishment of which is evident whenever we look at any existing novel. On the side of effect critics at one time had a fairly large number of terms to play with — terms like tragedy, comedy, tragicomedy, epic, farce, satire, elegy, and the like. Though the neoclassical kinds were often employed in inflexible form, they did provide a frame of discourse which allowed the critic and artist to communicate with each other: "if the effect you want is what we have traditionally expected under the concept 'tragedy,' then your technique here is inadequate." If what we are working for is a first-rate comedy, Dryden tells us in "An Essay of Dramatic Poesy," then here are some rules we can count on; they may be difficult to apply, they may require painstaking discussion, and they will certainly require genius if they are to be made to work, but they can still be of help to artist and critic because they are based on an agreement about a recognized literary effect.

In place of the earlier kinds, we have generally substituted a criticism based on qualities that are supposed to be sought in all works. All novels are said to be aiming for a common degree of realistic intensity; ambiguity and irony are discussed as if they were always beauties, never blemishes. Point of view should always be used "consistently," because otherwise the realistic illusion will be destroyed.

When technical means are related to such simplified ends, it is hardly surprising that they are themselves simplified. Yet we all know that our experience of particular works is more complex than the simple terminology suggests. The prescriptions against "telling" cannot satisfy any reader who has experienced *Tom Jones, The Egoist, Light in August,* or *Ulysses* (the claim that the author does not address us directly in the last of these is one of the most astonishingly persistent myths in modern criticism). They explicitly contradict our experience of dozens of good novels of the past fifteen years which, like Joyce Cary's posthumous *The Captive and the Free,* have rediscovered for us how lively "telling" can be. We all know, of course, that "too much" of the author's voice is, as Aristotle said, unpoetic. But how much is too much? Is there an abstract rule applicable to "the novel," quite aside from the needs of particular works or kinds?

Our experience with the great novels tells us that there is not. Most novels, like most plays, cannot be purely dramatic, entirely shown as taking place in the moment. There are always what Dryden called "relations," narrative summaries of action that takes place "off-stage." And try as we will to ignore the troublesome fact, "some parts of the action are more fit to be represented, some to be related." But related by whom? When? At what length? The dramatist must decide, and his decision will be based in large part on the particular needs of the work in hand. The novelist's case is different mainly in that he has more devices to choose from; he may speak with all of the voices available to the dramatist, and he may also choose — some would say he is also tempted by — some forms of telling not easily adapted to the stage.

Unfortunately our terminology for the author's many voices has been inadequate. If we name over three or four of the great narrators — say Cervantes's Cid, Hamete Benengeli, Tristram Shandy, the "author" of *Middlemarch,* and Strether in *The Ambassadors* (with his nearly effaced "author" using his mind as a reflector of events) — we find again that to describe any of them with conventional terms like "first person" and "omniscient" tells us little about how they differ from each other, and consequently it tells us little about why they succeed while others, described in the same terms, fail. Some critics do, indeed, talk about the problem of "authority," showing that first-person tales produce difficulties in stories which do not allow any one person to know all that goes on; having made this point, which seems so obvious, they are often then driven to find fault with stories like *Moby-Dick,* in which the author allows his narrator to know of events that happen outside his designated sphere of authority.

We can never be sure that enriching our terms will improve our criticism. But we can be quite sure that the terms with which we have long been forced to work cannot help us in discriminating among effects too subtle — as are all actual literary effects — to be caught in such loose-meshed nets. Even at the risk of pedantry, then, it should be worth our while to attempt a richer tabulation of the forms the author's voice can take.

(1) Perhaps the most overworked distinction is that of "person." To say that a story is told in the first or the third person, and to group novels into one or the other kind, will tell us nothing of importance unless we become more precise and describe how the particular qualities of the narrators relate to specific desired effects. It is true that choice of the first person is sometimes unduly limiting; if the "I" has inadequate access to necessary information, the author may be led into improbabilities. But we can hardly expect to find useful criteria in a distinction that would throw all fiction into two, or at most three, heaps. In *this* pile we see *Henry Esmond,* "The Cask of Amontillado," *Gulliver's Travels,* and *Tristram Shandy.* In *that* we have *Vanity Fair, Tom Jones, The Ambassadors,* and *Brave New World.* But the commentary in *Vanity Fair* and *Tom Jones* is in the first person, often resembling more the intimate effect of *Tristram Shandy* than that of many third person works. And again, the effect of *The Ambassadors* is much closer to that of the great first-person novels, since Strether in large part "narrates" his own story, even though he is always referred to in the third person.

Further evidence that this distinction is ordinarily overemphasized is seen in the fact that all of the following functional distinctions apply to both first- and third-person narration alike.

(2) There are *dramatized* narrators and *undramatized* narrators. The former are always and the latter are usually distinct from the implied author who is responsible for their creation.

(a) *The implied author (the author's "second self").* Even the novel in which no narrator is dramatized creates an implicit picture of an author who stands behind the scenes, whether as stage manager, as puppeteer, or as an indifferent God, silently paring his fingernails. This implied author is always distinct from the "real man" — whatever we may take him to be — who creates a superior version of himself as he creates his work; any successful novel makes us believe in an "author" who amounts to a kind of "second self." This second self is usually a highly refined and selected version, wiser, more sensitive, more perceptive than any real man could be.

Insofar as a novel does not refer directly to this author, there will be no distinction between him and the implied, undramatized narrator; for example, in Hemingway's *The Killers* there is no narrator other than the implicit second self that Hemingway creates as he writes.

(b) *Undramatized narrators.* Stories are usually not as rigorously scenic as *The Killers;* most tales are presented as passing through the consciousness of a teller, whether an "I" or a "he." Even in drama much of what we are given is narrated by someone, and we are often as much interested in the effect on the narrator's own mind and heart as we are in learning what *else* the author has to tell us. When Horatio tells of his first encounter with the ghost in *Hamlet,* his own character, though never mentioned explicitly as part of the narrative event, is important to us as we listen. In fiction, as soon as we encounter an "I" we are conscious of an experiencing mind whose views of the experience will come between us and the event. When there is no such "I," as in *The Killers,* the inexperienced reader may make the mistake of thinking that the story comes to him unmediated. But even the most naive reader must recognize that something mediating and transforming has come into a story from the moment that the author explicitly places a narrator into the tale, even if he is given no personal characteristics whatever.

One of the most frequent reading faults comes from a naive identification of such narrators with the authors who create them. But in fact there is always a distinction, even though the author himself may not have been aware of it as he wrote. The created author, the "second self," is built up in our minds from our experience with all of the elements of the presented story. When one of those elements is an explicit reference to an experiencing narrator, our view of the author is derived in part from our notion of how the presented "I" relates to what he claims to present. Even when the "I" or "he" thus created is ostensibly the author himself — Fielding, Jane Austen, Dickens, Meredith — we can always distinguish between the narrator and the created author who presents him. But though the distinction is always present, it is usually important to criticism only when the narrator is explicitly dramatized.

(c) *Dramatized narrators.* In a sense even the most reticent narrator has been "dramatized" as soon as he refers to himself as "I," or, like Flaubert, tells us that "we" were in the classroom when Charles Bovary entered. But many novels dramatize their narrators with great fullness. In some works the narrator becomes a major person of great physical, mental, and moral vividness (*Tristram Shandy, Remembrance of Things Past,* and *Dr. Faustus*); in such works the narrator is often radically different from the implied author who creates him, and whose own character is built up in our minds partly by the way in which the narrator is made to differ from him. The range of human types that have been dramatized as narrators is almost as great as the range of other fictional characters — one must say "almost" because there are some characters who are unqualified to narrate or reflect a story.

We should remind ourselves that many dramatized narrators are never explicitly labeled as narrators at all. In a sense, every speech, every gesture, narrates; most works contain disguised narrators who, like Molière's *raisonneurs,* are used to tell the audience what it needs to know, while seeming merely to act out their roles. The most important unacknowledged narrators are, however, the third-person "centers of consciousness" through whom authors filter their narrative. Whether such "reflectors," as James sometimes called them, are highly polished, lucid mirrors reflecting complex mental experience, or the rather turbid, sense-bound "camera eyes" of much fiction since James, they fill precisely the function of avowed narrators.

> Gabriel had not gone with the others. He was in a dark part of the hall gazing up the staircase. A woman was standing near the top of the first flight, in the shadow also. He could not see her face but he could see the terra-cotta and salmon-pink panels of her skirt which the shadow made appear black and white. It was his wife. She was leaning on the banisters, listening to something. Gabriel was surprised at her stillness and strained his ear to listen also. But he could hear little save the noise of laughter and dispute on the front steps, a few chords struck on the piano and a few notes of a man's voice singing. . . . He asked himself what is a woman standing on the stairs in the shadow, listening to distant music, a symbol of.

The very real advantages of this method, for some purposes, have been a dominant note in modern criticism. Indeed, so long as our attention is on such qualities as naturalness and vividness, the advantages seem over-whelming. It is only as we break out of the fashionable assumption that all good fiction seeks these qualities in the same degree that we are forced to recognize disadvantages. The third-person reflector is only one mode among many, suitable for some effects but cumbersome and even harmful when other effects are desired.

(3) Among dramatized narrators, whether first-person or third-person reflectors, there are mere *observers* (the "I" of *Tom Jones, The Egoist, Troilus and Criseyde*), and there are *narrator-agents* who produce some measurable effect on the course of events (ranging from the minor in-volvement of Nick in *The Great Gatsby* to the central role of Tristram Shandy, Moll Flanders, Huckleberry Finn, and — in the third person — Paul Morel in *Sons and Lovers*). Clearly any rules we might discover about observers may or may not apply to narrator-agents, yet the distinc-tion is seldom made in talk about point of view.

(4) All narrators and observers, whether first or third person, can relay their tales to us primarily as *scene* (*The Killers, The Awkward Age*), pri-marily as *summary* or what Lubbock called "picture" (Addison's almost completely nonscenic tales in *The Spectator*), or, most commonly, as a combination of the two.

Like Aristotle's distinction between dramatic and narrative manners, the somewhat different modern distinction between telling and showing does cover the ground. But the trouble is that it pays for broad coverage with gross imprecision. Narrators of all shapes and shades must either report dialogue alone or support it with "stage directions" and description of setting. But when we think of the radically different effect of a scene reported by Huck Finn and a scene reported by Poe's Montresor, we see that the quality of being "scenic" suggests very little about literary effect. And compare the delightful summary of twelve years given in two pages of *Tom Jones* (III, i), with the tedious showing of even ten minutes of uncurtailed conversation in the hands of a Sartre when he allows his passion for "durational realism" to dictate a scene when summary is called for. We can only conclude that the contrast between scene and summary, between showing and telling — indeed, between any two dialec-tical terms that try to cover so much ground — is not prescriptive or norma-tive but loosely descriptive only. And as description, it is likely to tell us very little until we specify the kind of narrator who is providing the scene or the summary.

(5) Narrators who allow themselves to tell as well as show vary greatly depending on the amount and kind of *commentary* allowed in addition to a direct relating of events in scene and summary. Such commentary can, of course, range over any aspect of human experience, and it can be related to the main business in innumerable ways and degrees. To treat of it as if it were somehow a single device is to ignore important differences between commentary that is merely ornamental, commentary that serves a rhetorical purpose but is not part of the dramatic structure, and commentary that is integral to the dramatic structure, as in *Tristram Shandy*.

(6) Cutting across the distinction between observers and narrator-agents of all these kinds is the distinction between *self-conscious narrators,* aware of themselves as writers (*Tom Jones, Tristram Shandy, Barchester Towers, The Catcher in the Rye, Remembrance of Things Past, Dr. Faustus*), and narrators or observers who rarely if ever discuss their writing chores (*Huckleberry Finn*) or who seem unaware that they are writing, thinking, speaking, or "reflecting" a literary work (Camus's *The Stranger,* Lardner's *Haircut,* Bellow's *The Victim*).

(7) Whether or not they are involved in the action as agents, narrators and third-person reflectors differ markedly according to the degree and kind of *distance* that separates them from the author, the reader, and the other characters of the story they relate or reflect. Such distance is often discussed under terms like "irony," or "tone," but our experience is in fact much more diverse than such terms are likely to suggest. "Aesthetic distance" has been especially popular in recent years as a catchall term for any lack of identification between the reader and the various norms in the work. But surely this useful term should be reserved to describe the degree to which the reader or spectator is asked to forget the artificiality of the work and "lose himself" in it; whatever makes him aware that he is dealing with an aesthetic object and not real life increases "aesthetic distance," in this sense. What I am dealing with is more complex and more difficult to describe, and it includes "aesthetic distance" as one of its elements.

In any reading experience there is an implied dialogue among author, narrator, the other characters, and the reader. Each of the four can range, in relation to each of the others, from identification to complete opposition, on any axis or value or judgment: moral, intellectual, aesthetic, and even physical (does the reader who stammers react to the stammering of H. C. Earwicker as I do? Surely not). The elements usually discussed under "aesthetic distance" enter in of course; distance in time and space, differences of social class or conventions of speech or dress — these and many others serve to control our sense that we are dealing with an aesthetic object, just as the paper moons and other unrealistic stage effects of some modern drama have had an "alienation" effect. But we must not confuse these effects with the equally important effects of personal beliefs and qualities, in author, narrator, reader, and all others in the cast of characters. Though we cannot hope to deal with all of the varieties of control over distance that narrative technique can achieve, we can at least remind ourselves that we deal here with something more than the question of whether the author attempts to maintain or destroy the illusion of reality.

(a) The *narrator* may be more or less distant from the *implied author.* The distance may be moral (Jason versus Faulkner; the barber versus Lardner, the narrator versus Fielding in *Jonathan Wild*). It may be intellectual (Twain and Huck Finn, Sterne and Tristram Shandy in the matter of bigotry about the influence of noses, Richardson and Clarissa). It may be physical or temporal: most authors are distant from even the most knowing narrator in that they presumably know how "everything turns out in the end"; and so on.

(b) The *narrator* also may be more or less distant from the *characters* in the story he tells. He may differ, for example, morally, intellectually, and temporally (the mature narrator and his younger self in *Great Expectations* or *Redburn*), morally and intellectually (Fowler the narrator and Pyle the American in Greene's *The Quiet American,* both departing radically from the author's norms but in different directions), or morally and emotionally (Maupassant's "The Necklace," and Huxley's "Nuns at Luncheon," in which the narrators affect less emotional involvement than Maupassant and Huxley clearly expect from the reader).

(c) The *narrator* may be more or less distant from the *reader's* own norms, e.g., physically and emotionally (Kafka's *The Metamorphosis*); morally and emotionally (Pinkie in *Brighton Rock,* the miser in Mauriac's *Knot of Vipers;* the many moral degenerates that modern fiction has managed to make into convincing human beings).

One of the standard sources of plot in modern fiction — often advanced in the name of repudiating plot — is the portrayal of narrators whose characteristics change in the course of the works they narrate. Ever since Shakespeare taught the modern world what the Greeks had overlooked in neglecting character change (compare *Macbeth* and *Lear* with *Oedipus*), stories of character development or degeneration have become more and more popular. But it was not until we had discovered the full uses of the third-person reflector that we found how to show a narrator changing *as he narrates*. The mature Pip, in *Great Expectations,* is presented as a generous man whose heart is where the reader's is supposed to be; he watches his young self move away from the reader, as it were, and then back again. But the third-person reflector can be shown, technically in the past tense but in effect present before our eyes, moving toward or away from values that the reader holds dear. The twentieth century has proceeded almost as if determined to work out all of the permutations and combinations on this effect: start far and end near; start near and end far; start far, move close, but lose the prize and end far; start near, like Pip, move away, but see the light and return close; start far and move farther (many modern "tragedies" are so little tragic because the hero is too distant from us at the beginning for us to care that he is, like Macbeth, even further at the end); start near and end nearer. . . . I can think of no theoretical possibilities that haven't been tried; anyone who has read widely in modern fiction can fill in examples.

(d) The *implied author* may be more or less distant from the *reader.* The distance may be intellectual (the implied author of *Tristram Shandy,* not of course to be identified with Tristram, is more interested in and knows more about recondite classical lore than any of his readers), moral (the works of Sade), and so on. From the author's viewpoint, a successful reading of his book will reduce to zero the distance between the essential norms of his implied author and the norms of the postulated reader. Often enough there is very little distance to begin with; Jane Austen does not have to convince us that pride and prejudice are undesirable. A bad book, on the other hand, is often a book whose implied author clearly asks that we judge according to norms we cannot accept.

(e) The *implied author* (and reader) may be more or less distant from *other characters,* ranging from Jane Austen's complete approval of Jane Fairfax in *Emma* to her contempt for Wickham in *Pride and Prejudice.* The complexity that marks our pleasure in all significant literature can be seen by contrasting the kinds of distance in these two situations. In *Emma,* the *narrator* is noncommittal toward Jane Fairfax, though there is no sign of disapproval. The *author* can be inferred as approving of her almost completely. But the chief *reflector, Emma,* who has the largest share of the job of narration, is definitely disapproving of Jane Fairfax for most of the

way. In *Pride and Prejudice,* on the other hand, the narrator is noncommittal toward Wickham for as long as possible, hoping to mystify us; the author is secretly disapproving; and the chief reflector, Elizabeth, is definitely approving for the first half of the book.

It is obvious that on each of these scales my examples do not begin to cover the possibilities. What we call "involvement" or "sympathy" or "identification," is usually made up of many reactions to author, narrators, observers, and other characters. And narrators may differ from their authors or readers in various kinds of involvement or detachment, ranging from deep personal concern (Nick in *The Great Gatsby,* MacKellar in *The Master of Ballantrae,* Zeitblom in *Dr. Faustus*) to a bland or mildly amused or merely curious detachment (Waugh's *Decline and Fall*).

In talk about point of view in fiction, the most seriously neglected of these kinds of distance is that between the fallible or unreliable narrator and the implied author who carries the reader with him as against the narrator. If the reason for discussing point of view is to find how it relates to literary effects, then surely the moral and intellectual qualities of the narrator are more important to our judgment than whether he is referred to as "I" or "he," or whether he is privileged or limited, and so on. If he is discovered to be untrustworthy, then the total effect of the work he relays to us is transformed.

Our terminology for this kind of distance in narrators is almost hopelessly inadequate. For lack of better terms, I shall call a narrator *reliable* when he speaks for or acts in accordance with the norms of the work (which is to say, the implied author's norms), *unreliable* when he does not. It is true that most of the great reliable narrators indulge in large amounts of incidental irony, and they are thus "unreliable" in the sense of being potentially deceptive. But difficult irony is not sufficient to make a narrator unreliable. We should reserve the term unreliable for those narrators who are presented as if they spoke *throughout* for the norms of the book and who do not in fact do so. Unreliability is not ordinarily a matter of lying, although deliberately deceptive narrators have been a major resource of some modern novelists (Camus's *The Fall,* Calder Willingham's *Natural Child,* etc.). It is most often a matter of what James calls *inconscience;* the narrator is mistaken, or he pretends to qualities which the author denies him. Or, as in *Huckleberry Finn,* the narrator claims to be naturally wicked while the author silently praises his virtues, as it were, behind his back.

Unreliable narrators thus differ markedly depending on how far and in what direction they depart from their author's norms; the older term "tone," like the currently fashionable "distance," covers many effects that we should distinguish. Some narrators, like Barry Lyndon, are placed as far "away" from author and reader as possible, in respect to every virtue except a kind of interesting vitality. Some, like Fleda Vetch, the reflector in James's *The Spoils of Poynton,* come close to representing the author's ideal of taste, judgment, and moral sense. All of them make stronger demands on the reader's powers of inference than does reliable narration.

(8) Both reliable and unreliable narrators can be *isolated,* unsupported or uncorrected by other narrators (Gully Jimson in *The Horse's Mouth,* Henderson in Bellow's *Henderson the Rain King*) or supported or corrected (*The Sound and the Fury*). Sometimes it is almost impossible to infer whether or to what degree a narrator is fallible; sometimes explicit corroborating or conflicting testimony makes the inference easy. Support or correction differs radically, it should be noted, depending on whether it is provided from within the action, so that the narrator-agent might benefit (Faulkner's *Intruder in the Dust*) or is simply provided externally, to help the reader correct or reinforce his own view *as against the narrator's* (Graham Greene's *The Power and the Glory*). Obviously the effects of isolation will be radically different in the two cases.

(9) Observers and narrator-agents, whether self-conscious or not, reliable or not, commenting or silent, isolated or supported, can be either *privileged* to know what could not be learned by strictly natural means or *limited* to realistic vision and inference. Complete privilege is what we usually call omniscience. But there are many kinds of privilege, and very few "omniscient" narrators are allowed to know or show as much as their authors know.

We need a good study of the varieties of limitation and their function. Some limitations are only temporary, or even playful, like the ignorance Fielding sometimes imposes on his "I" (as when he doubts his own powers of narration and invokes the Muses for aid, e.g., *Tom Jones* XIII, i). Some are more nearly permanent but subject to momentary relaxation, like the generally limited, humanly realistic Ishmael in *Moby-Dick,* who can yet break through his human limitations when the story requires (" 'He waxes brave, but nevertheless obeys; most careful bravery that!' murmured Ahab" — with no one present to report to the narrator). And some are confined to what their literal condition would allow them to know (first person, Huck Finn; third person, Miranda and Laura in Katherine Anne Porter's stories).

The most important single privilege is that of obtaining an inside view, because of the rhetorical power that such a privilege conveys upon a narrator. A curious ambiguity in our notions of "omniscience" is ordinarily hidden by our terminology. Many modern works that we usually classify as narrated dramatically, with everything relayed to us through the limited views of the characters, postulate fully as much omniscience in the silent author as Fielding claims for himself. Our roving visitation into the minds of sixteen characters in Faulkner's *As I Lay Dying,* seeing nothing but what those minds contain, may seem in one sense not to depend on an omniscient narrator. But this method is omniscience with teeth in it: the implied author demands our absolute faith in his powers of divination. We must never for a moment doubt that he knows everything about each of these sixteen minds, or that he has chosen correctly how much to show of each. In short the choice of the most rigorously limited point of view is really no escape from omniscience — the true narrator is as "unnaturally" all-knowing as he ever was. If evident artificiality were a fault — which it is not — modern narration would be as faulty as Trollope's.

Another way of suggesting the same ambiguity is to look closely at the concept of "dramatic" story-telling. The author can present his characters in a dramatic situation without in the least presenting them in what we normally think of as a dramatic manner. When Joseph Andrews, who has been stripped and beaten by thieves, is overtaken by a stagecoach, Fielding presents the scene in what by some modern standards must seem an inconsistent and undramatic mode. "The poor wretch, who lay motionless a long time, just began to recover his senses as a stage-coach came by. The postilion hearing a man's groans, stopped his horses, and told the coachman, he was certain there was a dead man lying in the ditch. . . . A lady, who heard what the postilion said, and likewise heard the groan, called eagerly to the coachman to stop and see what was the matter. Upon which he bid the postilion alight, and look into the ditch. He did so, and returned, 'That there was a man sitting upright, as naked as ever he was born.' " There follows a splendid description, hardly meriting the name of *scene,* in which the selfish reactions of each passenger are recorded. A young lawyer points out that they might be legally liable if they refuse to take Joseph up. "These words had a sensible effect on the coachman, who was well acquainted with the person who spoke them; and the old gentleman above mentioned, thinking the naked man would afford him frequent opportunities of showing his wit to the lady, offered to join with the company in giving a mug of beer for his fare; till partly alarmed by the threats of the one, and partly by the promises of the other, and being perhaps a little moved with compassion at the poor creature's condition, who stood bleeding and shivering with the cold, he at length agreed." Once Joseph is in the coach, the same kind of indirect reporting of the "scene" continues, with frequent excursions, however superficial, into the minds and hearts of the assembly of fools and knaves, and occasional guesses when complete knowledge seems inadvisable. If to be dramatic is to show characters dramatically engaged with each other, motive clashing with motive, the outcome depending upon the resolution of motives, then this scene is dramatic. But if it is to give the impression that the story is taking place by itself, with the characters existing in a dramatic relationship vis-à-vis the spectator, unmediated by a narrator and decipherable only through inferential matching of word to word and word to deed, then this is a relatively undramatic scene.

On the other hand, an author can present a character in this latter kind of dramatic relationship with the reader without involving that character in any internal drama at all. Many lyric poems are dramatic in this sense and totally undramatic in any other. "That is no country for old men — " Who says? Yeats, or his "mask," says. To whom? To us. How do we know that it is Yeats and not some character as remote from him as Caliban is remote from Browning in "Caliban upon Setebos"? We infer it as the dramatized statement unfolds; the need for the inference is what makes the lyric *dramatic* in this sense. Caliban, in short, is dramatic in two senses; he is in a dramatic situation with other characters and he is in a dramatic situation over-against us. Yeats, or if we prefer "Yeats's mask," is dramatic in only one sense.

The ambiguities of the word dramatic are even more complicated in fiction that attempts to dramatize states of consciousness directly. Is *A Portrait of the Artist as a Young Man* dramatic? In some respects, yes. We are not told about Stephen. He is placed on the stage before us, acting out his destiny with only disguised help or comments from his author. But it is not his actions that are dramatized directly, not his speech that we hear unmediated. What is dramatized is his mental record of everything that happens. We see his consciousness at work on the world. Sometimes what it records is itself dramatic, as when Stephen observes himself in a scene with other characters. But the report itself, the internal record, is dramatic in the second sense only. The report we are given of what goes on in Stephen's mind is a monologue uninvolved in any modifying dramatic context. And it is an *infallible* report, even less subject to critical doubts than the typical Elizabethan soliloquy. We accept, by convention, the claim that what is reported as going on in Stephen's mind really goes on there, or in other words, that Joyce knows how Stephen's mind works. "The equation of the page of his scribbler began to spread out a widening tail, eyed and starred like a peacock's; and, when the eyes and stars of its indices had been eliminated, began slowly to fold itself together again. The indices appearing and disappearing were eyes opening and closing; the eyes opening and closing were stars . . . " Who says so? Not Stephen, but the omniscient, infallible author. The report is direct, and it is clearly unmodified by any "dramatic" context — that is, unlike a speech in a dramatic scene, we do not suspect that the report has here been in any way aimed at an effect on anyone but the reader. We are thus in a dramatic relation with Stephen only in a limited sense — the sense in which a lyrical poem is dramatic.

Indeed, if we compare the act of reporting in *Tom Jones* with the act of reporting in *Portrait,* the former is in one sense considerably more dramatic; Fielding dramatizes himself and his telling, and even though he is essentially reliable we must be constantly on our toes in comparing word to word and word to deed. "It is an observation sometimes made, that to indicate our idea of a simple fellow, we say, he is easily to be seen through: nor do I believe it a more improper denotation of a simple book. Instead of applying this to any particular performance, we choose rather to remark the contrary in this history, where the scene opens itself by small degrees; and he is a sagacious reader who can see two chapters before him." Our running battle to keep up with these incidental ironies in Fielding's narration is matched, in *Portrait,* with an act of absolute, unquestioning credulity.

We should note finally that the author who eschews both forms of artificiality, both the traditional omniscience and the modern manipulation of inside views, confining himself to "objective" surfaces only, is not necessarily identical with the "undramatized author" under (2) above. In *The Awkward Age,* for example, James allows himself to comment frequently, but only to conjecture about the meaning of surfaces; the author is dramatized, but dramatized as partially ignorant of what is happening.

(10) Finally, narrators who provide inside views differ in the depth and

the axis of their plunge. Boccaccio can give inside views, but they are extremely shallow. Jane Austen goes relatively deep morally, but scarcely skims the surface psychologically. All authors of stream-of-consciousness narration attempt to go deep psychologically, but some of them deliberately remain shallow in the moral dimension. We should remind ourselves that any sustained inside view, of whatever depth, temporarily turns the character whose mind is shown into a narrator; inside views are thus subject to variations in all of the qualities we have described above, and most importantly in the degree of unreliability. Generally speaking, the deeper our plunge, the more unreliability we will accept without loss of sympathy. The whole question of how inside views and moral sympathy interrelate has been seriously neglected.

Narration is an art, not a science, but this does not mean that we are necessarily doomed to fail when we attempt to formulate principles about it. There are systematic elements in every art, and criticism of fiction can never avoid the responsibility of trying to explain technical successes and failures by reference to general principles. But the question is that of where the general principles are to be found. Fiction, the novel, point of view — these terms are not in fact subject to the kind of definition that alone makes critical generalizations and rules meaningful. A given technique cannot be judged according to its service to "the novel," or "fiction," but only according to its success in particular works or kinds of work.

It is not surprising to hear practicing novelists report that they have never had help from critics about point of view. In dealing with point of view the novelist must always deal with the individual work: which particular character shall tell this particular story, or part of a story, with what precise degree of reliability, privilege, freedom to comment, and so on. Shall he be given dramatic vividness? Even if the novelist has decided on a narrator who will fit one of the critic's classifications — "omniscient," "first person," "limited omniscient," "objective," "roving," "effaced," and so on — his troubles have just begun. He simply cannot find answers to his immediate, precise, practical problems by referring to statements that the "omniscient is the most flexible method," or "the objective the most rapid or vivid," or whatever. Even the soundest of generalizations at this level will be of little use to him in his page-by-page progress through his novel. As Henry James's detailed records show, the novelist discovers his narrative technique as he tries to achieve for his readers the potentialities of his developing idea. The majority of his choices are consequently choices of degree, not kind. To decide that your narrator shall not be omniscient decides practically nothing. The hard question is, just how *inconscient* shall he be? To decide that you will use first-person narration decides again almost nothing. What kind of first person? How fully characterized? How much aware of himself as a narrator? How reliable? How much confined to realistic inference, how far privileged to go beyond realism? At what points shall he speak truth and at what points utter no judgment or even utter falsehood?

There are no doubt *kinds* of effect to which the author can refer — e.g., if he wants to make a scene more amusing, poignant, vivid, or ambiguous, or if he wants to make a character more sympathetic or more convincing, such-and-such practices may be indicated. But it is not surprising that in his search for help in his decisions, he should find the practice of his peers more helpful than the abstract rules of the textbooks: the sensitive author who reads the great novels finds in them a storehouse of precise examples, examples of how *this* effect, as distinct from all other possible effects, was heightened by the proper narrative choice. In dealing with the types of narration, the critic must always limp behind, referring constantly to the varied practice which alone can correct his temptations to overgeneralize.

10 Georg Lukács : *Marxist Aesthetics and Literary Realism*

In this excerpt from the preface to *Studies in European Realism* (1948; trans. 1950), Georg Lukács presents a Marxist analysis of European fiction, declaring Marxists to be "jealous guardians of our classical heritage in their aesthetics." They are able to evaluate the historical role of this heritage in the dialectical development of human culture, unlike "modern thinkers" who reject "the idea that there is any such thing as an unchanged general line of development." Lukács's purpose in studying the nineteenth-century realists, however, is less to emphasize their place in the world's cultural heritage than to defend "realism" as the highest form of fictional creation. Lukács claims a unique value for "realism" in literary production, one similar to Lionel Trilling's "moral realism." "Realism," he says, "is the recognition of the fact that a work of literature can rest neither on a lifeless average, as the naturalists suppose, nor on an individual principle which dissolves its own self into nothing."

Lukács argues that great literature must "depict the most important turning-points" of "the social and historical task humanity has to solve" (i.e., revolution). It can do this only by means of "realism," which enables it to create "types" that represent "the organic, indissoluble connection between man as a private individual and man as a social being, as a member of a community." Lukács does not claim, however, that a "great realist" must necessarily believe in Marxism and revolution. Conservative realists (Balzac) can be considered greater writers than left-wing naturalists (Zola) because the great realists "all have in common that they penetrate deeply into the great universal problems of their time and inexorably depict the true essence of reality as they see it." Lukács concludes his essay with a spirited defense of Russian realism, arguing that "never in all its history did mankind so urgently require a realist literature as it does today." While we may agree with Lukács's belief in literature's positive role in cultural development, we should ask whether only one form of literature can play such a role; and, in fact, whether "realist" fiction has actually played that role in any historical period.

Georg Lukács (1885–1971), a leading Marxist literary theorist, was born in Budapest. He returned there from Moscow after World War II to become professor of aesthetics at the University of Budapest. Although *Studies in European Realism* was the first of his Marxist books to be translated into English, his pre-Marxist work, *The Theory of the Novel* (1920; trans. 1971), is perhaps the best known of his translated criticism.

The Marxist philosophy of history is a comprehensive doctrine dealing with the necessary progress made by humanity from primitive communism to our own time and the perspectives of our further advance along the same road. As such, it also gives us indications for the historical future. But such indications — born of the recognition of certain laws governing historical development — are not a cookery book providing recipes for each phenomenon or period; Marxism is not a Baedeker of history, but a signpost pointing the direction in which history moves forward. The final certainty it affords consists in the assurance that the development of mankind does not and cannot finally lead to nothing and nowhere.

Of course, such generalizations do not do full justice to the guidance given by Marxism, a guidance extending to every topical problem of life. Marxism combines a consistent following of an unchanging direction with incessant theoretical and practical allowances for the deviousness of the path of evolution. Its well-defined philosophy of history is based on a flexible and adaptable acceptance and analysis of historical development. This apparent duality — which is in reality the dialectic unity of the materialist worldview — is also the guiding principle of Marxist aesthetics and literary theory.

Those who do not know Marxism at all or know it only superficially or at second hand, may be surprised by the respect for the classical heritage of mankind which one finds in the really great representatives of this doctrine and by their incessant references to that classical heritage. Without wishing to enter into too much detail, we mention as an instance, in philosophy, the heritage of Hegelian dialectics, as opposed to the various trends in the latest philosophies. "But all this is long out of date," the modernists cry. "All this is the undesirable, outworn legacy of the nineteenth century," say those who — intentionally or unintentionally, consciously or unconsciously — support the Fascist ideology and its pseudo-revolutionary rejection of the past, which is in reality a rejection of culture and humanism. Let us look without prejudice at the bankruptcy of the very latest philosophies; let us consider how most philosophers of our day are compelled to pick up the broken and scattered fragments of dialectic (falsified and distorted in this decomposition) whenever they want to say something even remotely touching its essence about present-day life; let us look at the modern attempts at a philosophical synthesis and we shall find them miserable, pitiful caricatures of the old genuine dialectic, now consigned to oblivion.

It is not by chance that the great Marxists were jealous guardians of our classical heritage in their aesthetics as well as in other spheres. But they do not regard this classical heritage as a reversion to the past; it is a necessary outcome of their philosophy of history that they should regard the past as irretrievably gone and not susceptible of renewal. Respect for the classical heritage of humanity in aesthetics means that the great Marxists look for the true highroad of history, the true direction of its development, the true course of the historical curve, the formula of which they know; and because they know the formula they do not fly off at a tangent at every hump in the graph, as modern thinkers often do because of their theoretical rejection of the idea that there is any such thing as an unchanged general line of development.

For the sphere of aesthetics this classical heritage consists in the great arts which depict man as a whole in the whole of society. Again it is the general philosophy (here: proletarian humanism) which determines the central problems posed in aesthetics. The Marxist philosophy of history analyses man as a whole, and contemplates the history of human evolution as a whole, together with the partial achievement, or non-achievement of completeness in its various periods of development. It strives to unearth the hidden laws governing all human relationships. Thus the object of proletarian humanism is to reconstruct the complete human personality and free it from the distortion and dismemberment to which it has been subjected in class society. These theoretical and practical perspectives determine the criteria by means of which Marxist aesthetics establish a bridge back to the classics and at the same time discover new classics in the thick of the literary struggles of our own time. The ancient Greeks, Dante, Shakespeare, Goethe, Balzac, Tolstoy all give adequate pictures of great periods of human development and at the same time serve as signposts in the ideological battle fought for the restoration of the unbroken human personality.

Such viewpoints enable us to see the cultural and literary evolution of the nineteenth century in its proper light. They show us that the true heirs of the French novel, so gloriously begun early in the last century, were not Flaubert and especially not Zola, but the Russian and Scandinavian writers of the second half of the century. The present volume contains my studies of French and Russian realist writers seen in this perspective.

If we translate into the language of pure aesthetics the conflict (conceived in the sense of the philosophy of history) between Balzac and the later French novel, we arrive at the conflict between realism and naturalism. Talking of a conflict here may sound a paradox to the ears of most writers and readers of our day. For most present-day writers and readers are used to literary fashions swinging to and fro between the pseudo-objectivism of the naturalist school and the mirage-subjectivism of the psychologist or abstract-formalist school. And inasmuch as they see any worth in realism at all, they regard their own false extreme as a new kind of near-realism or realism. Realism, however, is not some sort of middle way between false objectivity and false subjectivity, but on the contrary the true, solution-bringing third way, opposed to all the pseudo-dilemmas engendered by the wrongly posed questions of those who wander without a chart in the labyrinth of our time. Realism is the recognition of the fact that a work of literature can rest neither on a lifeless average, as the naturalists suppose, nor on an individual principle which dissolves its own self into nothingness. The central category and criterion of realist literature is the type, a peculiar synthesis which organically binds together the general and the particular both in characters and situations. What makes a type a type is not its average quality, not its mere individual being, however profoundly conceived; what makes it a type is that in it all the humanly and socially essential determinants are present on their highest level of development, in the ultimate unfolding of the possibilities latent in them, in extreme presentation of their extremes, rendering concrete the peaks and limits of men and epochs.

True great realism thus depicts man and society as complete entities, instead of showing merely one or the other of their aspects. Measured by this criterion, artistic trends determined by either exclusive introspection or exclusive extraversion equally impoverish and distort reality. Thus realism means a three-dimensionality, an all-roundness, that endows with independent life characters and human relationships. It by no means involves a rejection of the emotional and intellectual dynamism which necessarily develops together with the modern world. All it opposes is the destruction of the completeness of the human personality and of the objective typicality of men and situations through an excessive cult of the momentary mood. The struggle against such tendencies acquired a decisive importance in the realist literature of the nineteenth century. Long before such tendencies appeared in the practice of literature, Balzac had already prophetically foreseen and outlined the entire problem in his tragicomic story *Le chef d'oeuvre inconnu*. Here, experiment on the part of a painter to create a new classic three-dimensionality by means of an ecstasy of emotion and colour quite in the spirit of modern impressionism, leads to complete chaos. Fraunhofer, the tragic hero, paints a picture which is a tangled chaos of colours out of which a perfectly modeled female leg and foot protrude as an almost fortuitous fragment. Today a considerable section of modern artists has given up the Fraunhofer-like struggle and is content with finding, by means of new aesthetic theories, a justification for the emotional chaos of their works.

The central aesthetic problem of realism is the adequate presentation of the complete human personality. But as in every profound philosophy of art, here, too, the consistent following-up to the end of the aesthetic viewpoint leads us beyond pure aesthetics: for art, precisely if taken in its most perfect purity, is saturated with social and moral humanistic problems. The demand for a realistic creation of types is in opposition both to the trends in which the biological being of man, the physiological aspects of self-preservation and procreation are dominant (Zola and his disciples), and to the trends which sublimate man into purely mental, psychological processes. But such an attitude, if it remained within the sphere of formal aesthetic judgments, would doubtless be quite arbitrary, for there is no reason why, regarded merely from the point of view of good writing, erotic conflict with its attendant moral and social conflicts should be rated higher than the elemental spontaneity of pure sex. Only if we accept the concept of the complete human personality as the social and historical task humanity has to solve; only if we regard it as the vocation of art to depict the most important turning points of this process with all the wealth of the factors affecting it; only if aesthetics assign to art the role of explorer and guide, can the content of life be systematically divided up into spheres of greater and lesser importance; into spheres that throw light on types and paths and spheres that remain in darkness. Only then does it become evident that any description of mere biological processes — be these the sexual act or pain and sufferings, however detailed and, from the literary point of view, perfect it may be — results in a leveling-down of the social, historical, and moral being of men and is not a means but an obstacle to such essential artistic expression as illuminating human conflicts in all their complexity and completeness. It is for this reason that the new contents and new media of expression contributed by naturalism have led not to an enrichment but to an impoverishment and narrowing-down of literature.

Apparently similar trains of thought were already put forward in early polemics directed against Zola and his school. But the psychologists, although they were more than once right in their concrete condemnation of Zola and the Zola school, opposed another no less false extreme to the false extreme of naturalism. For the inner life of man, its essential traits and essential conflicts, can be truly portrayed only in organic connection with social and historical factors. Separated from the latter and developing merely its own immanent dialectic, the psychologist trend is no less abstract, and distorts and impoverishes the portrayal of the complete human personality no less than does the naturalist biologism which it opposes.

It is true that, especially regarded from the viewpoint of modern literary fashions, the position in respect of the psychologist school is at the first glance less obvious than in the case of naturalism. Everyone will immediately see that a description in the Zola manner of, say, an act of copulation between Dido and Aeneas or Romeo and Juliet would resemble each other much more closely than the erotic conflicts depicted by Virgil and Shakespeare, which acquaint us with an inexhaustible wealth of cultural and human facts and types. Pure introspection is apparently the diametrical opposite of naturalist leveling-down, for what it describes are quite individual, non-recurring traits. But such extremely individual traits are also extremely abstract, for this very reason of non-recurrence. Here, too, Chesterton's witty paradox holds good, that the inner light is the worst kind of lighting. It is obvious to everyone that the coarse biologism of the naturalists and the rough outlines drawn by propagandist writers deform the true picture of the complete human personality. Much fewer are those who realize that the psychologists' punctilious probing into the human soul and their transformation of human beings into a chaotic flow of ideas destroy no less surely every possibility of a literary presentation of the complete human personality. A Joyce-like shoreless torrent of associations can create living human beings just as little as Upton Sinclair's coldly calculated all-good and all-bad stereotypes.

Owing to lack of space this problem cannot be developed here in all its breadth. Only one important and at present often neglected point is to be stressed here because it demonstrates that the live portrayal of the complete human personality is possible only if the writer attempts to create types. The point in question is the organic, indissoluble connection between man as a private individual and man as a social being, as a member of a community. We know that this is the most difficult question of modern literature today and has been so ever since modern *bourgeois* society came into being. On the surface the two seem to be sharply divided, and the appearance of the autonomous, independent existence of the individual is all the more pronounced, the more completely modern *bourgeois* society is developed. It seems as if the inner life, genuine "private" life, were proceeding according to its own autonomous laws and as if its fulfillments and tragedies were growing ever more independent of the surrounding social environment. And correspondingly, on the other side, it seems as if the connection with the community could manifest itself only in high-sounding abstractions, the adequate expression for which would be either rhetoric or satire.

An unbiased investigation of life and the setting aside of these false traditions of modern literature lead easily enough to the uncovering of the true circumstances, to the discovery which had long been made by the great realists of the beginning and middle of the nineteenth century and which Gottfried Keller expressed thus: "Everything is politics." The great Swiss writer did not intend this to mean that everything was immediately tied up with politics: on the contrary, in his view — as in Balzac's and Tolstoy's — every action, thought, and emotion of human beings is insep-arably bound up with the life and struggles of the community, i.e., with politics; whether the humans themselves are conscious of this, uncon-scious of it, or even trying to escape from it, objectively their actions, thoughts, and emotions nevertheless spring from and run into politics.

The true great realists not only realized and depicted this situation — they did more than that, they set it up as a demand to be made on men. They knew that this distortion of objective reality (although, of course, due to social causes), this division of the complete human personality into a public and a private sector was a mutilation of the essence of man. Hence they protested not only as painters of reality, but also as humanists, against this fiction of capitalist society, however unavoidable this spontaneously formed superficial appearance. If as writers, they delved deeper in order to uncover the true types of man, they had inevitably to unearth and expose to the eyes of modern society the great tragedy of the complete human personality.

In the works of such great realists as Balzac we can again find a third solution opposed to both false extremes of modern literature, exposing as an abstraction, as a vitiation of the true poesy of life, both the feeble com-monplaces of the well-intentioned and honest propagandist novels and the spurious richness of a preoccupation with the details of private life.

This brings us face to face with the question of the topicality today of the great realist writers. Every great historical period is a period of transition, a contradictory unity of crisis and renewal, of destruction and rebirth; a new social order and a new type of man always come into being in the course of a unified though contradictory process. In such critical, transitional periods the tasks and responsibility of literature are exceptionally great. But only truly great realism can cope with such responsibilities; the accustomed, the fashionable media of expression, tend more and more to hamper literature in fulfilling the tasks imposed by history. It should surprise no one if from this point of view we turn against the individualistic, psychologist trends in literature. It might more legitimately surprise many that these studies express a sharp opposition to Zola and Zolaism.

Such surprise may be due in the main to the fact that Zola was a writer of the left and his literary methods were dominant chiefly, though by no means exclusively, in left-wing literature. It might appear, therefore, that we are involving ourselves in a serious contradiction, demanding on the one hand the politicization of literature and on the other hand attacking insidiously the most vigorous and militant section of left-wing literature. But this contradiction is merely apparent. It is, however, well suited to throw light on the true connection between literature and *Weltanschauung*.

The problem was first raised (apart from the Russian democratic literary critics) by Engels, when he drew a comparison between Balzac and Zola. Engels showed that Balzac, although his political creed was legitimist royalism, nevertheless inexorably exposed the vices and weakness of royalist feudal France and described its death agony with magnificent poetic vigour. This phenomenon, references to which the reader will find more than once in these pages, may at the first glance again — and mistakenly — appear contradictory. It might appear that the *Weltanschauung* and political attitude of serious great realists are a matter of no consequence. To a certain extent this is true. For from the point of view of the self-recognition of the present and from the point of view of history and posterity, what matters is the picture conveyed by the work; the question to what extent this picture conforms to the views of the authors is a secondary consideration.

This, of course, brings us to a serious problem of aesthetics. Engels, in writing about Balzac, called it "the triumph of realism"; it is a problem that goes down to the very roots of realist artistic creation. It touches the essence of true realism: the great writer's thirst for truth, his fanatic striving for reality — or expressed in terms of ethics: the writer's sincerity and probity. A great realist such as Balzac, if the intrinsic artistic development of situations and characters he has created comes into conflict with his most cherished prejudices or even his most sacred convictions, will, without an instant's hesitation, set aside these his own prejudices and convictions and describe what he really sees, not what he would prefer to see. This ruthlessness towards their own subjective world-picture is the hallmark of all great realists, in sharp contrast to the second-raters, who nearly always succeed in bringing their own *Weltanschauung* into "harmony" with reality, that is, forcing a falsified or distorted picture of reality into the shape of their own worldview. This difference in the ethical attitude of the greater and lesser writers is closely linked with the difference between genuine and spurious creation. The characters created by the great realists, once conceived in the vision of their creator, live an independent life of their own: their comings and goings, their development, their destiny is dictated by the inner dialectic of their social and individual existence. No writer is a true realist — or even a truly good writer, if he can direct the evolution of his own characters at will.

All this is however merely a description of the phenomenon. It answers the question as to the ethics of the writer: what will he do if he sees reality in such and such a light? But this does not enlighten us at all regarding the other question: what does the writer see and how does he see it? And yet it is here that the most important problems of the social determinants of artistic creation arise. In the course of these studies we shall point out in detail the basic differences which arise in the creative methods of writers according to the degree to which they are bound up with the life of the community, take part in the struggles going on around them, or are merely passive observers of events. Such differences determine creative processes which may be diametrical opposites; even the experience which gives rise to the work will be structurally different, and in accordance with this the process of shaping the work will be different. The question of whether a writer lives within the community or is a mere observer of it, is determined not by psychological, not even by typological factors; it is the evolution of society that determines (not automatically, not fatalistically, of course), the line the evolution of an author will take. Many a writer of a basically contemplative type has been driven to an intense participation in the life of the community by the social conditions of his time; Zola, on the contrary, was by nature a man of action, but his epoch turned him into a mere observer and when at last he answered the call of life, it came too late to influence his development as a writer.

But even this is as yet only the formal aspect of this problem, although no longer the abstractly formal. The question grows essential and decisive only when we examine concretely the position taken up by a writer. What does he love and what does he hate? It is thus that we arrive at a deeper interpretation of the writer's true *Weltanschauung,* at the problem of the artistic value and fertility of the writer's worldview. The conflict which previously stood before us as the conflict between the writer's worldview and the faithful portrayal of the world he sees, is now clarified as a problem within the *Weltanschauung* itself, as a conflict between a deeper and a more superficial level of the writer's own *Weltanschauung.*

Realists such as Balzac or Tolstoy in their final posing of questions always take the most important, burning problems of the community for their starting-point; their pathos as writers is always stimulated by those sufferings of the people which are the most acute at the time; it is these sufferings that determine the objects and direction of their love and hate and through these emotions determine also what they see in their poetic visions and how they see it. If, therefore, in the process of creation their conscious worldview comes into conflict with the world seen in their vision, what really emerges is that their true conception of the world is only superficially formulated in the consciously held worldview, and the real depth of their *Weltanschauung,* their deep ties with the great issues of their time, their sympathy with the sufferings of the people can find adequate expression only in the being and fate of their characters.

No one experienced more deeply than Balzac the torments which the transition to the capitalist system of production inflicted on every section of the people, the profound moral and spiritual degradation which necessarily accompanied this transformation on every level of society. At the same time Balzac was also deeply aware of the fact that this transformation was not only socially inevitable, but at the same time progressive. This contradiction in his experience Balzac attempted to force into a system based on a Catholic legitimism and tricked out with Utopian conceptions of English Toryism. But this system was contradicted all the time by the social realities of his day and the Balzacian vision which mirrored them. This contradiction itself clearly expressed, however, the real truth: Balzac's profound comprehension of the contradictorily progressive character of capitalist development.

It is thus that great realism and popular humanism are merged into an organic unity. For if we regard the classics of the social development that determined the essence of our age, from Goethe and Walter Scott to Gorki and Thomas Mann, we find *mutatis mutandis* the same structure of the basic problem. Of course every great realist found a different solution for the basic problem in accordance with his time and his own artistic personality. But they all have in common that they penetrate deeply into the great universal problems of their time and inexorably depict the true essence of reality as they see it. From the French Revolution onwards the development of society moved in a direction which rendered inevitable a conflict between such aspirations of men of letters and the literature and public of their time. In this whole age a writer could achieve greatness only in the struggle against the current of everyday life. And since Balzac the resistance of daily life to the deeper tendencies of literature, culture, and art has grown ceaselessly stronger. Nevertheless, there were always writers who in their life work, despite all the resistance of the day, fulfilled the demand formulated by Hamlet: "to hold the mirror up to nature," and by means of such a reflected image aided the development of mankind and the triumph of humanist principles in a society so contradictory in its nature that it on the one hand gave birth to the ideal of the complete human personality and on the other hand destroyed it in practice.

The great realists of France found worthy heirs only in Russia. All the problems mentioned here in connection with Balzac apply in an even greater measure to Russian literary development and notably to its central figure Leo Tolstoy. It is not by chance that Lenin (without having read Engels's remarks about Balzac) formulated the Marxist view of the principles of true realism in connection with Tolstoy. Hence there is no need for us to refer to these problems again here. There is all the more need, however, to call attention to the erroneous conceptions current in respect of the historical and social foundations of Russian realism, errors which in many cases are due to deliberate distortion or concealment of facts. In Britain, as everywhere else in Europe, the newer Russian literature is well known and popular among the intelligent reading public. But as everywhere else, the reactionaries have done all they could to prevent this literature from becoming popular; they felt instinctively that Russian realism, even if each single work may not have a definite social tendency, is an antidote to all reactionary infection.

Only if we have a correct aesthetic conception of the essence of Russian classical realism can we see clearly the social and even political importance of its past and future fructifying influence on literature. With the collapse and eradication of Fascism a new life has begun for every liberated people. Literature has a great part to play in solving the new tasks imposed by the new life in every country. If literature is really to fulfill this role, a role dictated by history, there must be as a natural prerequisite, a philosophical and political rebirth of the writers who produce it. But although this is an indispensable prerequisite, it is not enough. It is not only the opinions that must change, but the whole emotional world of men; and the most effective propagandists of the new, liberating, democratic feeling are the men of letters. The great lesson to be learnt from the Russian development is precisely the extent to which a great realist literature can fructifyingly educate the people and transform public opinion. But such results can be achieved only by a truly great, profound, and all-embracing realism. Hence, if literature is to be a potent factor of national rebirth, it must itself be reborn in its purely literary, formal, aesthetic aspects as well. It must break with reactionary, conservative traditions which hamper it and resist the seeping-in of decadent influences which lead into a blind alley.

In these respects the Russian writers' attitude to life and literature is exemplary, and for this, if for no other reason, it is most important to destroy the generally accepted reactionary evaluation of Tolstoy, and, together with the elimination of such false ideas, to understand the human roots of his literary greatness. And what is most important of all: to show how such greatness comes from the human and artistic identification of the writer with some broad popular movement. It matters little in this connection what popular movement it is in which the writer finds this link between himself and the masses; that Tolstoy sinks his roots into the mass of the Russian peasantry, and Gorki of the industrial workers and landless peasants. For both of them were to the bottom of their souls bound up with the movements seeking the liberation of the people and struggling for it. The result of such a close link in the cultural and literary sphere was then and is today that the writer can overcome his isolation, his relegation to the role of a mere observer, to which he would otherwise be driven by the present state of capitalist society. He thus becomes able to take up a free, unbiased, critical attitude towards those tendencies of present-day culture which are unfavourable to art and literature. To fight against such tendencies by purely artistic methods, by the mere formal use of new forms, is a hopeless undertaking, as the tragic fate of the great writers of the West in the course of the last century clearly shows. A close link with a mass movement struggling for the emancipation of the common people does, on the other hand, provide the writer with the broader viewpoint, with the fructifying subject matter from which a true artist can develop the effective artistic forms which are commensurate with the requirements of the age, even if they go against the superficial artistic fashions of the day.

These very sketchy remarks were required before we could express our final conclusion. Never in all its history did mankind so urgently require a realist literature as it does today. And perhaps never before have the traditions of great realism been so deeply buried under a rubble of social and artistic prejudice. It is for this reason that we consider a revaluation of Tolstoy and Balzac so important. Not as if we wished to set them up as models to be imitated by the writers of our day. To set an example means only: to help in correctly formulating the task and studying the conditions of a successful solution. It was thus that Goethe aided Walter Scott, and Walter Scott aided Balzac. But Walter Scott was no more an imitator of Goethe than Balzac was of Scott. The practical road to a solution for the writer lies in an ardent love of the people, a deep hatred of the people's enemies and the people's own errors, the inexorable uncovering of truth and reality, together with an unshakable faith in the march of mankind and their own people towards a better future.

There is today in the world a general desire for a literature which could penetrate with its beam deep into the tangled jungle of our time. A great realist literature could play the leading part, hitherto always denied to it, in the democratic rebirth of nations. If in this connection we evoke Balzac in opposition to Zola and his school, we believe that we are helping to combat the sociological and aesthetical prejudices which have prevented many gifted authors from giving their best to mankind. We know the potent social forces which have held back the development of both writers and literature: a quarter century of reactionary obscurantism which finally twisted itself into the diabolical grimace of the Fascist abomination.

Political and social liberation from these forces is already an accomplished fact, but the thinking of the great masses is still bedevilled by the fog of reactionary ideas which prevents them from seeing clearly. This difficult and dangerous situation puts a heavy responsibility on the men of letters. But it is not enough for a writer to see clearly in matters political and social. To see clearly in matters of literature is no less indispensable and it is to the solution of these problems that this book hopes to bring its contribution.

Beginning with a discussion of R. S. Crane's definition of plot, J. Arthur Honeywell develops an analysis of plot in the modern novel by contrasting it with the standard structure of eighteenth- and nineteenth-century British fiction. In particular, Honeywell stresses the changing treatment of temporal progression. In order to have a coherent structure, a novel must contain a "temporal progression" that meets three criteria: one, "it must have a definite beginning and a definite ending"; two, it "must somehow be sequential, that is, each event must arise out of preceding events and give rise to succeeding events"; three, "the events which make up the progression must all be somehow related in the more general sense of all belonging to the same 'world' or the same 'vision of reality.' " Although each condition must be present to ensure coherence, novelists usually emphasize one of the three, with the result that we can "distinguish three distinct kinds of plot."

Honeywell argues that eighteenth-century authors tended to organize their plots around "definite beginnings and endings," while in the nineteenth century, "novelists began to subordinate the problem of beginnings and endings to the problem of constructing a logical sequence of events, a sequence in which no event occurred without a reason or cause." In such novels attention shifts from the resolution of events to the forces and laws that govern situations and the "necessary" or logical outcome of such situations; but with the rise of modernism the focus shifts again. Twentieth-century plots are organized around a progression not so much through time as from "appearance" to "reality." Honeywell explains the initial difficulty we have in reading many modern novels by arguing that for authors "to construct plots which achieve a temporal synthesis by means of a movement from appearance to reality they must start by plunging the reader into the appearances . . . and let him discover for himself as he reads the structures of reality which gradually emerge."

J. Arthur Honeywell (b. 1928) is Professor of Philosophy at Skidmore College. In addition to "Plot in the Modern Novel" (1968), he has published essays on literature, poetics, ethics, and philosophy in such journals as *Ethics, New Scholasticism,* and the *Journal of Aesthetics and Art Criticism.*

Perhaps the clearest way to give a general indication of the nature of plot in the modern novel is to start by discussing briefly the concept of plot itself. In "The Concept of Plot and the Plot of *Tom Jones,*" one of the few recent attempts to develop the idea of plot as a central critical concept, R. S. Crane gives a short history of the term and then defines plot as "the particular temporal synthesis effected by the writer of the elements of action, character, and thought that constitute the matter of his invention."[1] This definition can serve as a starting point, since a brief analysis of the notion of plot as the temporal synthesis of the materials of the novel will reveal some of the possibilities of plot development and, by contrast with the other possibilities, how plot operates in many modern novels.

If plot is thought of as a temporal synthesis, then obviously it has two central characteristics. First, it operates as an organizing and unifying principle. It provides the synthesis which insures that the materials of a novel are experienced as all cohering into one unified object — the novel itself in its wholeness. Secondly, it operates in time. Since the experience of reading a novel is a temporal process and since the plot is the organization of this temporal process, the plot of a novel inevitably has the quality of developing in time. This raises the question of how temporal syntheses can be achieved.

For any temporal progression to be experienced as a significant and organized whole, three requirements must in some way be met. First, it must have a definite beginning and a definite ending. Otherwise, the progression cannot be distinguished from what went before and what comes after and so cannot be either conceived or experienced as a single thing. Secondly, the progression must somehow be sequential, that is, each event must arise out of preceding events and give rise to succeeding events. If this is not accomplished, then the result is a mixture of progressions rather than a single temporal progression. Thirdly, the events which make up the progression must all be somehow related in the more general sense of all belonging to the same "world" or the same "vision of reality." That is, there must be a general context which encompasses both the beginning and ending and the sequence of events and gives to them their significance. Otherwise there is no possibility of conceiving of or experiencing the events as parts of a coherent whole; they would be merely fortuitous results of random causal interactions having no meaningful interrelations. Although each of these requirements must somehow be met in any novel (or, in special cases where unusual effects are desired, must be deliberately neglected), it is usually the case that novelists place their emphasis on one of the three and subordinate the other two. As a result, it is possible to distinguish three distinct kinds of plot.

Novelists of the eighteenth century tended to construct their plots around definite beginnings and endings. The temporal progression of their novels was a movement from a natural starting point to a definitive ending — an ending of the "happy ever after" variety if the novel had a comic structure. The synthesis was that provided by a single action which moved, usually by way of reversals and discoveries, from a natural beginning point to a natural ending. This is the kind of plot which Aristotle analyzes in the *Poetics* and with which Professor Crane is concerned in his analysis of the plot of *Tom Jones.* One of the problems of constructing a plot of this kind is that of achieving the sense of finality which the ending requires, and eighteenth-century novelists tended to solve this problem with some variation of "poetic justice." The action is brought to a stage in which the good characters, after a period of difficulties, achieve on a permanent basis the conditions which insure their happiness and the bad characters are placed in conditions which insure their suffering. The major distinction which results is that between tragic and comic plots, although many variations of these two modes are possible. When the final and permanent happiness of the central characters is of a worldly sort, as in *Tom Jones* and *Humphry Clinker,* the action forms a comic plot. When the final and permanent happiness of the central character is of an other-worldly variety and is the result of worldly misfortune and death, as in *Clarissa,* the action forms a tragic plot. It follows also that plots of this kind require a certain kind of characterization. Most important, the central agents must be clearly characterized as virtuous, and thus deserving of happiness, or evil, and thus deserving of suffering. Only when this is done can the ending be constructed to provide that sense of justness which makes it definitive and final. Thus Fielding, Richardson, and Smollett all take pains to construct characters who are either virtuous or evil and to make the distinctions clear to their readers.

Early in the nineteenth century, most clearly with the novels of Sir Walter Scott, the fashion began to change. Novelists began to subordinate the problem of beginnings and endings to the problem of constructing a logical sequence of events, a sequence in which no event occurred without a reason or cause. The temporal progression of their novels tended to become a clearly articulated causal sequence from one state of affairs to another — in its more extreme form a "slice of life" in which both beginning and ending were arbitrary. The synthesis was achieved by establishing a single causal sequence in which each event is shown to be an effect of previous causes and the cause of subsequent effects. No longer are endings distinguished by their finality: rather they tend to become open-ended or at least ambiguous in terms of justice. Characteristic endings of this sort are those of *The Red and the Black, Crime and Punishment, Madame Bovary, The Return of the Native,* and *The Ambassadors.* The central problem of constructing plots of this sort is that of achieving the sense of causal or rational sequence which provides the organization of the events, and novelists tended to solve this problem by placing a specific type of character in a specific set of conditions and then letting the logic of the situation work itself out to its rational conclusion. What is important is not the ending but the insight into the operation of the causal laws and influences which condition human affairs. The major distinction which results is that between the realistic novel and the romance. When the set of conditions established is patterned on the details of ordinary life and the characters are presented as being for the most part passively influenced by these conditions, the novel tends toward the realistic or naturalistic mode. When, on the other hand, the set of conditions established includes the supernatural or at least the abnormal and the characters are presented as being active in manipulating or responding to these conditions, then the novel tends toward the mode of romance. The requirements of characterization also change. Central characters no longer have to be clearly virtuous or the reverse, but they do have to have clearly defined motives based on clearly defined passions and modes of behavior. Only with such characters can the causal sequence be made explicit. Characters such as Julian Sorel, Raskolnikov, Emma Bovary, Becky Sharp, Eustacia Vye, and Strether, although none are unambiguously virtuous or evil, are all constructed around passions and rules of action which bring them into conflict with the conditions surrounding them. The causal sequence is such that an ending of the final, "happy ever after" variety is inconceivable for any of the characters mentioned. Even death does not achieve the sense of finality and justness which Richardson manages in *Clarissa,* mainly because the conditions which make the death a logical conclusion are presented as still operating, whereas in *Clarissa* Richardson both eliminates the conditions which cause Clarissa's death and makes it clear that Clarissa achieves the supreme happiness of eternal bliss.

During the first two decades of the present century the fashion in plot development began changing again. Novelists lost interest in constructing logical or rational sequences and turned to the third possibility, that of structuring the events of the novel so as to present a coherent "world" or vision of reality. When the reader starts a novel like *Ulysses,* he is immediately confronted with a great variety of what appear to be incongruous, contradictory, and inconsequential facts. As he reads structural relations begin to emerge which tie the various facts together and give them significance. By the time he has finished, if not the first then the second or third reading, these structural relations are so firmly established that most of the facts have acquired significance and even the incongruities and contradictions can be seen to have meaning, to be a part of the reality of the world of the novel. The temporal progression of plots of this kind can then be described as a movement from appearance — the maze of apparently unrelated facts — to reality — the structural relations which, when apprehended, give significance and meaning to the facts. The synthesis is that established by the structural relations which emerge as the novel progresses and which are firmly established as the "reality" of the world of the novel by the time the novel ends.

An early example of this kind of plot is that of *The Good Soldier* by Ford Madox Ford. The novel begins with Dowell, the narrator, looking back at events of his past life which in his naiveté he has totally misunderstood. He has seen only the appearance of these events and has been blind to their real significance. The progression of the novel is that of Dowell's attempt to make sense of these past events. He fits together apparently unrelated facts, resolves apparent contradictions, gains insight into the motivation of the people involved, changes his evaluations of people and events, so that by the end of the novel he has a better insight into the realities of these past events than any of the other characters involved and has himself changed from being naive to being realistic. The reader, following Dowell's train of thought throughout the novel, moves in a similar way from the superficial appearances of the facts to an understanding of the realities of the situation and so of the real significance of the facts.

It should be stated at once that the fact that modern novelists tend to share basic assumptions about the construction of plots does not preclude a great diversity in the application of those assumptions. Like the novelists of the eighteenth and nineteenth centuries, they have achieved a wide variety of plot development within the limits of their shared assumptions. The central problem of constructing modern plots is that of establishing the structural relations which give coherence and significance to the at first apparently unrelated facts and which thus express a specific view of reality. But the patterns which emerge as structures of reality can take many forms. They can be universal patterns or archetypes which are presented as structuring the affairs of men at all times and places. Such archetypes are present in *Ulysses* (as the title itself suggests), *Finnegans Wake,* many of the novels of Thomas Mann, and other novels based upon mythical patterns. They can be social and institutional patterns which make sense of otherwise incongruous and inexplicable events. In *Absalom, Absalom!,* for example, the facts of the Sutpen story become significant and intelligible only as the social patterns of the South emerge during the course of the novel. In *The Good Soldier,* it is the sense of the social realities of Edwardian England which emerges as the facts of Dowell's story become intelligible. Or the structure of reality can be found in the subtle nuances and feelings, often incongruous and without rationale, which pervade even an ordinary mind on an ordinary day. The novels of Virginia Woolf and Nathalie Sarraute explore patterns of this kind. When the mind becomes less ordinary, such nuances become the feeling of nausea in the presence of existence explored by Sartre or the ironies and paradoxes of the life of the imagination explored by Nabokov in *Pale Fire.* The structure of reality, finally, can be found in underlying psychological patterns basic to the nature of men. The novels of D. H. Lawrence explore the degradations and victories of the psyche as it struggles to realize its true nature, while Lawrence Durrell's *Alexandria Quartet* makes use of the psychological complexities and patterns taken by love in modern society. Even this short list gives some indication of the diversity of structures which can be found to give coherence and significance to the "facts" of the human condition.

Since the time of Aristotle, the concept of plot has been associated with the concepts of discovery and reversal. There are discoveries and reversals in the better modern plots, but their nature is different from those used in the plots of earlier centuries. In eighteenth-century plots, formed as they were around a unified action, the appropriate kind of reversal was a reversal in the line of action from a movement toward one state of fortune to a movement toward another. In *Tom Jones,* for example, near the end of the novel the action seems to be moving unalterably toward Tom's disgrace and death when, as a result of certain discoveries, the line of action reverses itself completely and moves quickly to the highest state of fortune for Tom that he, or the reader, can imagine. The discoveries appropriate to such reversals of fortune consist of such things as the discovery of identity, of character, or of past events. In *Tom Jones* the discovery that Blifil had, in the past, concealed the evidence of Tom's parentage leads to the discovery of Tom's identity. This, in turn, leads to the recognition of Tom's virtuous character. This sequence of discoveries initiates the reversal of the action leading to Tom's final good fortune. Richardson, in *Clarissa,* handles reversals differently, but they are still reversals of the line of action. He constructs his plot around frequent changes of direction as Clarissa, and along with her the reader, given the changing information at her disposal, alternatively sees the action as moving toward good fortune or bad. The resulting constant fluctuation between hope and fear is central to the interest of the reader. The discoveries appropriate to these reversals are those made by Clarissa as she observes the actions and estimates the character of Lovelace and the other agents in a position to help or harm her.

Nineteenth-century plots, formed as they were around a causal sequence resulting from an opposition between the central characters and their surroundings, turned on reversals of intention and moral maxims. Typically the central character starts with one intention and one set of moral maxims, discovers that actions based on them lead to untenable conflicts with his surroundings, and ends by changing his intentions and his maxims. In *Crime and Punishment,* for example, Raskolnikov starts with the intention of improving the condition of men by murdering the old woman and with the utilitarian maxims he associates with such an intention. The act of murder, based on these convictions, leads to conflicts which were unforeseen and which soon become untenable. The reversal is completed in the last chapter where, sent to Siberia after his confession and trial, he is seen in the process of adopting convictions of a religiously humanitarian nature, convictions quite the reverse of those he held at the beginning. The discovery appropriate to such a reversal is generally the discovery of aspects of the surroundings left out of account by the original intention and maxims. In Raskolnikov's case it is the discovery of the religious side of life, in particular the sense of a more than merely utilitarian aspect to justice and mercy, which initiates his confession and subsequent reversal of convictions. In *The Ambassadors* the reversal and discovery take the same general form. Strether has come to Europe with the maxims of capitalistic New England and the intention of bringing Chad home. He gradually discovers aspects of Parisian life, in particular the aesthetic side of human life, which the New England maxims failed to take into account. Finding his original convictions untenable, he reverses his intention—he urges Chad to stay in Paris—and adopts a new maxim—that of gaining nothing for himself at the expense of other people—one he now sees as the reverse of the New England maxims.

Twentieth-century plots are formed around a movement from appearance to reality constituted by the emergence of structural patterns which give coherence and intelligibility to facts previously seen as unrelated and incongruous. These plots turn on reversals of perspective and reversals of valuation. What generally happens is that events and characters seen at one point in the novel in one perspective are seen at a later point in a different and often opposed perspective. The result of the reversal of perspective is often a reversal of valuation. In *The Good Soldier,* for example, Dowell (and the reader) at the beginning see Florence, Leonora, and Edward in the perspective of the superficial social conventions of Edwardian England. Since Edward is seen to have broken the conventions in such a way as to injure the others, he is evaluated as of relatively bad character while the two women are judged to be relatively innocent. By the end of the novel, as a result of the fuller understanding of the facts by Dowell (and the reader), these three characters are seen in another and more adequate perspective, a perspective centering on private virtues and motives rather than public conventions, with the result that Edward is now evaluated as relatively innocent and even virtuous in some ways and the two women are judged to be primarily guilty of the misfortunes which have affected them all. The discovery appropriate to this kind of reversal is the discovery of the realities of the situation. In *The Good Soldier* it is the discovery of the private lives and characters of the agents behind the public façade.

The same general type of reversal and discovery operates in a different manner in a novel like *Ulysses.* In *Ulysses* the title suggests at the beginning the perspective in which to evaluate Bloom; he is to be judged against Ulysses, a traditional hero. Seen in this perspective, Bloom is at first evaluated as a timid, inept, ignorant, vulgar, and overly docile character, lacking all the virtues of a traditional hero like Ulysses. As the reader follows Bloom through his day in Dublin, however, seeing him respond to the various episodes of the day and learning more about his private attitudes and convictions, the perspective and the evaluation tend to change. Judged not against the traditional hero but against the other Dubliners whom he meets during the day as he responds to the challenges of modern urban life, Bloom begins to be seen as something of a hero himself and to share with Ulysses some qualities — qualities such as curiosity, tolerance, a sense of adventure, a regard for wife and children — which many of his compatriots do not possess. He becomes a typical modern antihero.

One of the problems presented by a difficult novel like *Ulysses* is that most readers have been unable to perceive the reversal of perspective and evaluation during the first reading, which means they have been unable to follow the plot. Indeed the early critical judgments tended to see only the negative side of Bloom's character, his appearance of lacking all the qualities prominent in the traditional hero. It is only in recent years that critical opinion has recognized in Bloom the modern versions of some of the traditional heroic virtues found in Ulysses.

The concept of the antihero suggests some of the problems of characterization in modern novels resulting from the requirements of the new kind of plot. If the movement from appearance to reality is to involve a reversal of perspective and evaluation, then characters must be so constructed as to have two main aspects: a public side, that which is most apparent from the few facts in the reader's possession during the early parts of the novel, and a private side, that which emerges as the reader acquires more insight into the realities of the character and his situation. If the reversal of evaluation is to be pronounced, then the private side must be different from and even opposed to the public side. In terms of the publicly accepted and traditional conventions, Bloom is a nobody; in terms of his private aspirations and convictions, he is something of a modern hero. This doubling of character is itself a source of many of the apparent contradictions and incongruities which occur in modern novels and which have given it a reputation for obscurity.

The character of the antihero fits perfectly the requirements of modern plots. The antihero is a character who, judged by the publicly recognized conventions and standards of morality and importance and the traditional appearances of heroism, is evaluated as a person of no social importance, as often engaging in morally reprehensible actions, and as lacking all the qualities associated with the heroic. But the antihero also has a private side. When, as a result of the reader's insight into the realities of the world of the novel, he is judged in the perspective of more realistically grounded standards of morality and importance and the realities rather than the appearances of heroism, a reversed evaluation is made in which he becomes, in his own way, moral, important, and heroic. This is not to say that all modern novels contain antiheroes, but this mode of characterization fits the plot requirements so well that it is often used. This is why many modern novels are filled with characters existing on the outskirts of their society, characters who reject positions of social importance, who ignore the precepts of conventional morality, and who scoff at the traditional heroic postures. This also suggests the reason why in many modern novels the characters who hold the conventionally important public positions — the generals, priests, ministers, doctors, psychiatrists, government officials, and in general the leaders of society — often turn out in the end to be despicable characters lacking any true sense of morality and justice, any real importance on the personal or familial level, and any real heroism. In these cases the reversal of evaluation is working in the opposite direction, moving from high to low rather than from low to high.

One of the reasons why many modern novels have been called experimental is because the new type of plot has required innovations in technique. In nineteenth-century novels the reader is introduced immediately to the causal influences operating in the novel, since only then can he follow with understanding the causal sequence as it progresses. This requires narrative methods which follow the causal sequence of the story in its temporal progression. In modern novels, on the other hand, the reader must not be introduced immediately to the causal influences operating in the story, for it is his gradual insight into these influences as they emerge from the welter of facts that constitutes the plot of the novel. The new methods of narration were devised to achieve this gradual emergence of significance.

One procedure often used is the separation of the sequence of the presentation of the story from the story itself and its causal sequences. In *The Good Soldier,* for example, the story told is that of the complex affair involving Dowell, Edward, Florence, Leonora, and Nancy. The presentation of the story, on the other hand, consists of Dowell's attempt to make sense of the affair after the events have occurred. The result is that the causal sequence of the story itself is broken up as Dowell jumps backward and forward in time in his attempt to understand the significance of the facts he has to work with. The temporal movement of the presentation of the story follows a line of increasing significance and meaning, not the line of causal influences in the story itself. Such a method of narration is perfectly adapted to plots which move on a line of increasing significance and understanding from appearance to reality. *Absalom, Absalom!* uses similar methods. The Sutpen story is what is presented, but the presentation is done by Quentin and Shreve long after Sutpen has been dead and follows a line of increasing understanding rather than the line of causal influences.

Another procedure is the use of the stream of consciousness technique to record the events in the mind of one or more characters during short periods of time. In *Mrs. Dalloway,* for example, the reader is presented with events in Clarissa Dalloway's consciousness during a single day. The story being presented, however, includes many past events which Mrs. Dalloway remembers during that day. Similar techniques are used in a more complex way in *Ulysses* and *The Sound and the Fury.* The effect of all these techniques is to break up the causal sequence of the story and to allow the facts to emerge in such a way that the reader is involved in a movement of increasing understanding of the realities of the story.

One consequence of modern plots and their techniques is that the reader is involved in the plot to an unusual degree. The reader is presented with what seem to be contradictory and inconsequential facts; there is no narrator who understands the story and who can tell the reader what standards of morality are operating in the novel, what constitutes good or bad fortune for the characters, or what the cause and effect relations are. It is the job of the reader to actively contribute to the plot by seeking for the significant relations between the facts and by grasping the resulting patterns of reality as they emerge from the facts. In particular, he must, on the basis of the evidence he has, work out for himself the moral standards, the sources of happiness and suffering, and the operative causes in the world of each novel.

This analysis of modern plots and their consequences for characterization and methods of narration should explain why many modern novels are difficult to read and present the appearance of obscurity. It is not that modern novelists are interested in difficulty or obscurity for their own sake. It is rather that in order to construct plots which achieve a temporal synthesis by means of a movement from appearance to reality they must start by plunging the reader into the appearances, into the midst of seemingly unrelated, contradictory, incongruous, inconsequential, and even fantastic facts, and let him discover for himself as he reads the structures of reality which gradually emerge, if the reading is successful, to give meaning to the facts and coherence to the novel.

Note

1. R. S. Crane, "The Concept of Plot and the Plot of *Tom Jones,*" in *Critics and Criticism; Ancient and Modern,* ed. R. S. Crane (Chicago: University of Chicago Press, 1952), p. 620.

Point of View

In his essay on narrative point of view, Mitchell A. Leaska states that three major possibilities are open to the novelist. The first is omniscient narration, in which the author "may borrow, at will, the point of view of any of one or another character and observe things from that person's angle of perspective." The narrator may either *tell* the story or *dramatize* it, but in either case, the author establishes "a mediatory distance between the reader and the story."

Leaska sees modern fiction as tending toward the dramatic and less than omniscient perspectives, his second possibility. One form of limited narration is that of a "first-person observer," which emphasizes the narrator's personality and reliability. A variation is the "first-person narrator-participant," who is an actor in the development of the plot. This further narrows the perspective on events, because the narrator's own behavior affects his interpretation of actions. Another variation is that of "the third-person voice." Like first-person narration, "it does not permit of any direct account of the inner states of the characters under observation except in terms of surmise." Third-person narration, however, does not mean that the story is presented from a point of view outside the fiction. Leaska suggests that "perhaps the surest index to discovering the author's choice of vantage point is to consider the character on whom he focuses the reader's attention and on that character's relationship to the action of the story."

The third possibility abolishes the narrator altogether and confronts "the reader directly with the mental experience of a character" (Seymour Chatman discusses such stories later in this volume). "Non-narrated" stories may present a single perception of experience or "multiple inner points of view," but both preclude narrative summary. Leaska succinctly explains the difference between this method and that of omniscient narration: "While in the omniscient-author-point-of-view novel, the author looks into the minds of his characters and relates to the reader what is going on there, the information is presented as *he* sees and interprets it, rather than as his people see it. . . . In the multiple-point-of-view novel, however, the mental contents — the thoughts, feelings and perceptions of the *persona* — are rendered as they seem and feel to him." The character's inner mental processes are not filtered by any interpreting voice; instead, the responsibility for filtering, interpreting, and, in some cases, organizing the perceptions into a coherent plot devolves upon the reader.

Mitchell A. Leaska (b. 1934) is Professor of English at New York University. In addition to writing *Virginia Woolf's Lighthouse* (1970), from which this essay is excerpted, he is also the author of *The Voice of Tragedy* (1963) and *The Novels of Virginia Woolf: From Beginning to End* (1977).

T he question of who shall narrate the story or through whose eyes the reader shall see is one which every writer of the novel has had to face. The question does not seem to have been an especially vexing one to novelists of the past. But since the beginning of the modern novel — more specifically, since Henry James — with a more vigorous determination to achieve a greater reality of both the inner and the outer life to reveal the whole of experience, the choice of the angle or angles of narration, through which the story is to be transmitted, has created a great deal of difficulty and concern among literary craftsmen, artists, and critics alike.

In his critical prefaces, now collected as *The Art of the Novel* (1934), James was deeply concerned with problems of literary method, particularly the method of narrative presentation through a single consciousness — the "central intelligence" or the "sentient centre" or the "reflector," as he variously called it. Drawing principally from James's prefaces, Percy Lubbock, in *The Craft of Fiction* (1921), coherently formulated James's concepts about point of view — concepts which, since Lubbock, have become fairly rigid and consequently transmuted, by later critics of fiction, to a somewhat dogmatic statement of theory.

Wayne C. Booth, however, in his study *The Rhetoric of Fiction* (1961), in re-examining these earlier critical interpretations of method and procedure, has, by carefully pointing out weaknesses and fallacies in the doctrine, made perhaps the most significant single attempt at revising and modifying so important a concept as point of view. This critical evolution notwithstanding, however, it is important to recognize that as pioneer in and practitioner of the theory of point of view, Henry James was an advance guard of the new psychological fiction.

As every storyteller knows, a tale conceived in a particular way has certain affective potentialities over a reader's feelings and attitudes. But just how that tale is presented to the reader will determine whether those affective potentialities either become vivid or remain lifeless on the page. A useful way of considering point of view as a technical problem is to think of a novelist presenting his story as if he were a motion-picture director filming a script. The question to arise first is what angle or what combinations and variations of angles of vision will most effectively project the story for the viewer. After settling this question, the director must decide when to move the camera up close and when to increase the distance between the viewer and the viewed; when to reveal a scene slowly and when to quicken the pace; how to effect transitions smoothly from one angle to another so as to create a sense of continuity; whether to unfold the story chronologically or scramble the sequence while simultaneously building up a sense of relatedness and integration. All of these, and many more, are problems which must be dealt with if the story is to be transmitted intelligibly, vividly, and — most important — persuasively. The choices made will be determined, ultimately, by the choice of the angle or angles of vision.

Generally, for the novelist there are three broad possibilities open. The first of these is the point of view of the *omniscient narrator*. According to Beckson and Ganz, the omniscient view

> enables the writer to present the inner thoughts and feelings of his characters. God-like, he may survey from his Olympian position past and present so that the reader may come to know more of his imaginative world than any single character in it. In *Ulysses,* for example, a work that employs shifting points of view, Joyce reveals the inner thoughts of his three major characters through the stream of consciousness . . . and presents actions, unknown to the individual characters, going on in various parts of Dublin. Moreover, the omniscient author may sometimes openly comment on the behavior of his characters, as in Thackeray's *Vanity Fair. . . .*[1]

In omniscient narration, the author tells the story *after* it has happened. Moreover, the omniscient narrator may borrow, at will, the point of view of any of one or another character and observe things from that person's angle of perspective; and he may, with authorial responsibility, at other times, choose to abridge some part of the story, or comment on it, or take a panoramic view of it.

The opening lines from three different novels will illustrate the general tenor of omniscient narration:

from Hardy's *The Mayor of Casterbridge:*

> One evening of late summer, before the present century had reached its thirteenth year, a young man and woman, the latter carrying a child, were approaching the large village of Weydon-Priors, in Upper Wessex, on foot. They were plainly but

not ill clad, though the thick hoar of dust which had accumulated on their shoes and garments from an obviously long journey lent a disadvantageous shabbiness to their appearance just now.

from Jane Austen's *Pride and Prejudice:*

> It is a truth universally acknowledged that a single man in possession of a good fortune must be in want of a wife.
>
> However little known the feelings or views of such a man may be on his first entering a neighborhood, this truth is so well fixed in the minds of the surrounding families, that he is considered as the rightful property of some one or other of their daughters.

from Tolstoy's *Anna Karenina:*

> Happy families are all alike; every unhappy family is unhappy in its own way.[2]

One of the distinguishing features of an omniscient narrator is his power not only to inform the reader of the ideas and emotions of his characters, but also to reveal, in varying degrees, his own biases, whether by overt authorial intrusions or by the way in which he generalizes about life, morals, manners, and so on. This method of narration may very often be editorial in attitude; that is, the author not only reports ideas and events, but he criticizes and passes judgments on them as well.

I have been describing the omniscient narrator as primarily *telling* the story rather than dramatizing it. And in so far as *telling* is concerned, I have tried to emphasize the fact that summary narrative (as this mode of telling is often called) is characterized, in part, by the general manner in which events are reported; by the indefinite period of time such events cover; by the variety and freedom of locations where such events occur; by the tendency of the author-narrator to editorialize, to criticize, and, openly, even to judge.

The omniscient narrator, however, with all the latitude of storytelling he assumes, may choose to *dramatize,* to *show* the reader rather than to tell him. The method is theatrical, "objectified," as it were. When the omniscient narrator chooses to have his characters — with no one of their consciousness, now, open to view — act and speak equally before the reader, the authorial voice becomes neutral, the point of view impersonal, detached — "detached," that is, *only as it is possible in any work of fiction.*

When the author subdues his own vociferous presence, he, in a sense, forces the reader to deduce, from all the details he has seen and heard, his own generalizations as to what is going on and what his own attitude should be towards the spectacle placed before him. Because the reader, if he is to respond appropriately, requires from the scene the transmission of considerable data, one natural consequence of the stratagem is the presentation of a *specific* temporal and spatial framework capable of containing the concrete details and enclosing the dialogue — all of which are the *sine qua non* of the dramatic mode.

Because Flaubert favoured this impersonal stance of omniscient narrator, two scenes from *Madame Bovary* will serve to illustrate — the first, primarily dialogue; the second, primarily detail:

> He took her hand, and this time she did not withdraw it.
>
> "First prize for all-round farming!" cried the chairman.
>
> "Just this morning, for example, when I came to your house . . . "
>
> "To Monsieur Bizet, of Quincampoix."
>
> "Did I have any idea that I'd be coming with you to the show?"
>
> "Seventy francs!"
>
> "A hundred times I was on the point of leaving, and yet I followed you and stayed with you . . . "
>
> "For the best manures."
>
> " . . . as I'd stay with you tonight, tomorrow, every day, all my life!"
>
> "To Monsieur Caron, of Argueil, a gold medal!"
>
> "Never have I been so utterly charmed by anyone . . . "
>
> "To Monsieur Bain, of Givry-Saint-Martin!"
>
> " . . . so that I'll carry the memory of you with me . . . "
>
> "For a merino ram . . . "
>
> "Whereas you'll forget me; I'll vanish like a shadow."
>
> "To Monsieur Belot, of Notre-Dame . . . "
>
> "No, though! Tell me it isn't so! Tell me I'll have a place in your thoughts, in your life!"
>
> "Hogs: a tie! To Messieurs Leherisse and Cullembourg, sixty francs!"
>
> Rodolphe squeezed her hand, and he felt it all warm and trembling in his, like a captive dove that longs to fly away; but then, whether in an effort to free it, or in response to his pressure, she moved her fingers.
>
> "Oh! Thank God! You don't repulse me! How sweet, how kind! I'm yours; you know that now! Let me see you! Let me look at you!"

A gust of wind coming in the windows ruffled the cloth on the table; and down in the square all the tall headdresses of the peasant women rose up like fluttering white butterfly wings. (part 2, chapter 8)

But it was above all at mealtime that she could bear it no longer — in that small ground-floor room with its smoking stove, its squeaking door, its sweating walls and its damp floor tiles. All the bitterness of life seemed to be served up to her on her plate; and the steam rising from the boiled meat brought gusts of revulsion from the depths of her soul. Charles was a slow eater; she would nibble a few hazel-nuts, or lean on her elbow and draw lines on the oilcloth with the point of her table knife. (part 1, chapter 9)[3]

One important rhetorical function effected by the dramatic mode is to persuade the reader that he sees and ultimately judges for himself. This, in itself, has a great deal of appeal for the reader because a sense of immediacy has been achieved. It follows that if *showing*, unattended by authorial commentary and overt direction, effects a sense of immediacy, then one further difference between the narrative method and the dramatic is that in the narrative the distance between the story and the reader is considerably greater than it is in the dramatic, in which the very effect of impersonal presentation creates a more personal involvement of the reader with the story.

Suffice it to say, that in omniscient narration, the author has many advantages of dealing with both the story and the character in various descriptive and developmental ways. But one salient characteristic prevails with omniscient narration: namely, the author's readiness to place himself between the reader and the story to clarify a point, to make a confident interpretation of what otherwise might remain ambiguous and bothersome, and so on. And while no twentieth-century reader should be disturbed when something is made clear for him, if he is sufficiently conscious of some of the subtleties which obtain in all omniscience, he may become more alert as a reader when he begins to realize that even when the author is presenting something dramatically, he renders the scene through his own eyes rather than through the eyes of his characters — thus creating, however tenuous, a mediatory distance between the reader and the story.

The evolution toward direct presentation in the novel marks the chain of events in the course of which the novelist relinquishes some of his possible points of view; and by so doing, he also surrenders many sources of information which were available to him as an omniscient author. As he deprives himself of the privilege of commentary when he resorts to presenting his story dramatically, so the author denies himself any direct pronouncements in his fictional proceedings when he bequeaths his tale to a narrator who is either an observer or a participant in the story.

If the novelist chooses as his narrator a *first-person observer,* he restricts himself to some extent in that the narrator, as the observer, no longer has access to the inner states of the characters involved and, therefore, can report only what he witnessed or has genuinely discovered or, in extreme cases, has drawn inferences from. He may even guess. But he is not allowed entry into the minds of the principal characters of his story. The narrator-observer, moreover, although he views the story from what Friedman calls the "wandering periphery,"[4] like the omniscient narrator, is given the prerogative of presenting his material at any given point either as summary narrative or as scene. Thus the distances or variations in distance established between the reader and the story will, for the most part, be determined by the narrator's choice and manipulation of his modes of presentation — that is, whether by the narrative mode or the dramatic.

Because the narrator-observer, in reporting his story, is simultaneously interpreting that story, the reader's response to it and to his interpretation of it will inevitably be influenced by the impression he gets of the narrator, himself. It is necessary, therefore, to notice how, either before introducing the narrator or by endowing him with special self-evident characteristics such as honesty, perceptiveness, et cetera, the author persuades the reader that the narrator is worthy of his attention and trust.

Joseph Conrad in *Heart of Darkness,* for example, prepares us for Marlow's tale:

The yarns of seamen have a direct simplicity, the whole meaning of which lies within the shell of a cracked nut. But Marlow was not typical (if his propensity to spin yarns be excepted), and to him the meaning of an episode was not inside like a kernel but outside, enveloping the tale which brought it out only as a glow brings out a haze, in the likeness of one of these misty halos that sometimes are made visible by the spectral illumination of moonshine.

When there is no preparation, when the reader has no way of knowing about the narrator except from the process of his "acting himself out," there is apt to be trouble. One of Henry James's least popular novels,

The Sacred Fount, is a good example. The story is an account of a week-end party at a place called Newmarch; and it is told by an unnamed narrator who spends his entire time there trying to fathom the relationships between some of the guests. Very early in the novel, we learn that he sees close human relationships as a depletion of one individual for the enrichment of the other—metaphorically, as a "sacred fount" being drained.

From the very beginning, the reader is trapped in the consciousness of the narrator: there is no prelude or introductory information about him given from some other source. As a result, the reader is to the very end helplessly confined to only the evidence which the narrator chooses to furnish. And since he makes no bid for our sympathy in his rather unengaging search for depleted characters, we are at a loss as to how credible a witness he is. It takes no profound analysis to discover that the narrator is given to flights of fantasy; that he keeps a good deal of emotional distance between himself and others; that his drive for intellectual superiority is compulsive; and that he is obsessed with the notion that he is capable of "reading into mere human things an interest so much deeper than mere human things were in general prepared to supply." In fact, he reports what other characters in the story say of him: "You're abused by a fine fancy"; "You over-estimate the penetration of others"; " . . . people have such a notion of what you embroider on things that they're rather afraid to commit themselves or to lead you on"; and so on.

The reader, if he has managed to maintain enough interest to finish the novel, discovers at the end that nothing has been solved; in fact, nothing has actually happened that needs to be solved except for evaluating the narrator's ornate and highly suspect ruminations. Perhaps one of the surest pleasures to be derived from the work, either by the student of James or by the psychological critic, is in deducing the character and personality of an extremely complex and ambiguous narrator, because in this short novel James has pushed the impersonal aspect of the point-of-view method almost to the limits of absurdity. It is, therefore, small wonder that *The Sacred Fount* has never found either a wide or an enthusiastic reading public.

The long shelf of fiction is filled with stories told by *first-person narrator-participants;* that is, by narrators who have been actively involved in the events and reported, in their own voice, the story from a point in time *after* the experience itself. Moll Flanders, Huckleberry Finn,

Jane Eyre, Claudius, Holden Caulfield, David Copperfield mention only a few of these narrators who are also principal participants in the stories they tell. Quite often these narrators speak in the first-person voice, because that voice gives an impression of being livelier and more direct; and confidence can be more quickly established than with the use of the third-person voice.

When the "I" is used, however, the author denies himself more channels of information. More than that, he must surrender some of the vantage points the narrator-observer enjoyed from his "wandering periphery." Now the narrator-participant is centrally involved in the action, with his angle of perspective fixed at the centre of the experience he relates. In so far as concerns the source of his information, he is limited to his own thoughts, feelings, and perceptions. As Moll Flanders, for example, says very early in her "History and Misfortunes":

> This is too near the first hours of my life for me to relate anything of myself but by hearsay; 'tis enough to mention that, as I was born in such an unhappy place, I had no parish to have recourse to for my nourishment in my infancy; nor can I give the least account how I was kept alive, other than that, as I have been told, some relation of my mother took me away, but at whose expense, or by whose direction, I know nothing at all of it.

In subtler pieces of fiction however, the limitations set on available information are convincingly overcome by a narrator's capacity to speculate and to draw inferences. For example, Conrad works around the problem in the opening pages of *The Secret Sharer:*

> On my right hand there were lines of fishing stakes *resembling a mysterious* system of half-submerged bamboo fences, *incomprehensible* in its division of the domain of tropical fishes, and *crazy* of aspect *as if* abandoned forever. . . . To the left a group of barren islets, *suggesting* ruins of stone walls, . . . *There must have been* some glare in the air. . . .[5]

But the narrator-participant angle of view can offer problems to the reader. For one of the liveliest debates in contemporary criticism, we need only look at the conflicting interpretations given to the governess's story in James's *The Turn of the Screw.* The problem arises, among other things, from the fact not only that James has kept her impersonal, to the extent of leaving her unnamed — very much the same as the narrator in *The Sacred Fount* — but also that the reader's introduction to her by Douglas, the outer and indeed very favourable frame of reference, tends to cast her in a most auspicious light — a setting in which we are prepared even before meeting her to accept as absolute truth her testimony of the ghastly happenings at Bly.

But when readers' opinions of the governess range from that of a sexually repressed psychotic to that of an "honourable and fearless lady," as Rebecca West thinks of her, it is no longer a question of a reader's alertness or stupidity: it is rather more an issue of James's having willfully obscured his narrator-participant ("lucid reflector" seems inappropriate in this instance). The result is that few of us, as Booth remarks, "feel happy with a situation in which we cannot decide whether the subject is two evil children as seen by a naive but well-meaning governess or two innocent children as seen by a hysterical, destructive governess."[6]

It is ironic that of all novelists, it was Henry James who, in a letter to H. G. Wells, concerning the dangers of first-person narration, called it that "accursed autobiographic form which puts a premium on the loose, the impoverished, the cheap and the easy. Save in the fantastic and the romantic . . . it has no authority, no persuasive or convincing force. . . . "

Although thus far I have dealt exclusively with first-person narrator-observers and participants, a narrator — whether an observer or a participant — is employed very often, and as effectively, with the *third-person* voice. The method of narrator-observer, with no "I" to alert the reader that an experiencing mind is mediating between him and the event, is a subtle device which frequently causes the inexperienced reader to think that the fictional material is coming to him directly. Even though the author may give his narrator no personal characteristics, there are certainly effects which are produced by the undramatized narrator's tonal characteristics and the attitude he projects towards what he is reporting.

In this method of narration, everything depends directly on the presentation of background, external action, gesture, and speech. Since the method tends to transmit the story as a dramatic presentation of objective scenes, a sense of detachment and impersonality may be created. It shares, moreover, one basic limitation with the first-person narrator-observer: namely, that it does not permit of any direct account of the inner states of the characters under observation except in terms of surmise.

Because Hemingway creates perhaps the most rigorously impersonal stories by means of the undramatized narrator, the following passage from his short story, "Soldier's Home," will serve to illustrate:

He had tried so to keep his life from being complicated. Still, none of it had touched him. He had felt sorry for his mother and she had made him lie. He would go to Kansas City and get a job and she would feel all right about it. There would be one more scene maybe before he got away. He would not go down to his father's office. He would miss that one. He wanted his life to go smoothly. It had just gotten going that way. Well, that was all over now, anyway. He would go over to the schoolyard and watch Helen play indoor baseball.

When the *narrator-participant* is rendered in the *third person,* the unsuspecting reader, again, may confuse it with omniscient narration. D. H. Lawrence's *Sons and Lovers,* for example, is frequently thought of as narrated by the author; but if one stopped to consider where the fictional ballast lay, he would soon realize that the story, with the exception of the first three chapters, comes filtered almost entirely through Paul Morel, and it is his story — told in the third-person voice. Perhaps the surest index to discovering the author's choice of vantage point is to consider the character on whom he focuses the reader's attention and on that character's relationship to the action of the story. In the case of the third-person narrator-participant, if the selected character has no relation to a particular event, or if some occurrence is of no interest to him or is beyond his understanding, then no report of it is made.

Henry James's *The Ambassadors* is a worthy example of third-person-participant narration. In his discussion of that novel, Percy Lubbock says that James does not "tell the story of Strether's mind; he makes it tell itself, he dramatizes it."[7] He says further that everything in that work is rendered objectively: "whether it is a page of dialogue or a page of description nobody is addressing us, nobody is reporting his impression to the reader. The impression is enacting itself in the endless series of images that play over the outspread expanse of the man's mind and memory."[8] Perhaps the most important assertion Lubbock makes in his discussion of this Jamesian novel is that the presentation in time is integral to the objective method, because it requires the reader to "live" through the experience with the character — and at *his* pace.

Equally significant in the objective method is that it forces the reader to organize the story for himself, to make of it what he will. The French critic, Ramon Fernandez, suggests this aspect when he describes the novel as a "representation of events which take place in time, a representation submitted to the conditions of apparition and development of these events."[9]

The third-person narrator-participant method is particularly effective in *The Ambassadors* not only because the reader's sympathies are likely to be given up to Strether very early in the work, but also because the full awareness of his desires pitted against the restrictions of his conscience — the internal struggle dramatically depicted in the novel — is a conflict known to everyone at one time or another. *The Ambassadors* is, moreover, a perfect example of James's success in the fusion of form and content, because as a work of art it is an eloquent testimony of the dictum which occupies the very centre of James's aesthetic of the novel: and that is, to show something intensely, it must be shown from the appropriate angle of vision.

Finally, narrator-observers and participants, whether first person or third, have the privilege, at any given point, of summarizing the narrative or of presenting it dramatically, thereby modulating at will the distance between the reader and the story, by technical means. What is important here (as with omniscient narration) is the fact that distance — which in aesthetic terms is inversely proportional to involvement or sympathy or identification (critical terminology is inadequate on this point) — is ultimately the result of the author's or the narrator's or the character's effect on the reader. It makes no difference whether the voice is "I" or "he" or "she" or "we." The intellectual and moral and emotional qualities of the narrator, in the last analysis, will be more important in molding a reader's experience and judgment than the person of the voice. Our delight with Moll Flanders, our disapproval of Wickham in *Pride and Prejudice,* our pity for Anna Karenina, our disgust with Kafka's country doctor, our aversion to Faulkner's Jason Compson should indicate that the achievement of a literary effect has no fast or fixed rubric.

So long as there is a narrator, someone is mediating between the reader and the story. The next step in the direction of objectification is effected by doing away with the narrator altogether and dramatizing the inner state of a *persona* by *direct mental transmission;* that is, by confronting the reader directly with the mental experience of a character. One vivid example which illustrates direct transmission is found in James Joyce's *A Portrait of the Artist as a Young Man:*

When would he be like the fellows in Poetry and Rhetoric? They had big voices and big boots and they studied trigonometry. That was very far away. First came the vacation and then the next term and then again the vacation. It was like a train going in and out of tunnels and that was like the boys eating in the refectory when you opened and closed the flaps of the ears. Term, vacation; tunnel, out; noise, stop. How far away it was! It was better to go to bed to sleep. Only prayers in the chapel and then bed. (chapter I)

So thoroughly has Joyce given us the novel in terms of Stephen Dedalus, and so purged is the text of his own authorial presence, that readers coming to the work for the first time accept the fictional material to the extent that they frequently find themselves making only those value judgments which are shared by the narrator himself: for example, they share the profound seriousness with which he views himself; they accept the somewhat debauched version of aesthetic theory he offers; and they marvel, as much as Stephen himself, at his own artistry.[10]

When the mental atmospheres of two or more *personae* are presented, we have what might be called *multiple inner points of view.* The method of presentation — similar to that of a single consciousness — is almost entirely in the direction of scene, both of an inner view of the mind and of an outer view by means of speech and action. Erich Auerbach calls the method the "multipersonal representation of consciousness"[11] and points out that one of the possibilities of the multiple-consciousness method is its "obscuring and even obliterating the impression of an objective reality completely known to the author."[12] Discussing a passage from Virginia Woolf's *To the Lighthouse,* Professor Auerbach observes that Mrs. Woolf presents herself "to be someone who doubts, wonders, hesitates, as though the truth about her characters were not better known to her than it is to them or to the reader."[13] The statement is extremely significant in that it has to do not only with the author's attitude towards reality, but also, and more important, with the relationship between the form of the novel and how that form defines and communicates its meaning. This aspect will be discussed later in considerable detail.

In the multiple-point-of-view method, when a descriptive detail is necessary, it is supplied by way of "stage direction," as Norman Friedman calls it, or it is given through the thoughts and utterances of the *personae* themselves.

When the novelist maintains the third-person angle throughout, as does Virginia Woolf, in both *Mrs. Dalloway* and *To the Lighthouse,* one might legitimately ask how precisely this differs from an omniscient-author-point-of-view novel. The difference, though often not susceptible to detection, is chiefly this: While in the omniscient-author-point-of-view novel, the author looks into the minds of his characters and relates to the reader what is going on there, the information is presented as *he* sees and interprets it, rather than as his people see it. Moreover, in the traditional omniscient novel, the information is narrated as though it had already occurred. In the multiple-point-of-view novel (as I shall refer to it hereafter), however, the mental contents — the thoughts, feelings, and perceptions of the *persona* — are rendered as they seem and feel to him. In addition, the mental states are presented scenically as if the settings or situations which evoked those states were happening *now* before the reader, at the time of the reading. In brief, life is presented as it seems to the fictional people who are living it. As a consequence, the physical appearance of a character, what he does, what he thinks and feels — in short, all the fictional data — are communicated through the consciousness of someone present.

Notes

1. Karl Beckson and Arthur Ganz, *A Reader's Guide to Literary Terms* (New York: Noonday Press, 1960), p. 162.
2. Translated by Constance Garnett.
3. Translated by Francis Steegmuller.
4. Norman Friedman, "Point of View in Fiction: The Development of a Critical Concept," *PMLA* 70 (December 1955): 1160–84; reprinted in Robert Scholes, ed., *Approaches to the Novel* (San Francisco: Chandler Publishing, 1961), p. 130.
5. Italics are mine.
6. Wayne C. Booth, *The Rhetoric of Fiction* (Chicago: University of Chicago Press, 1961), p. 346.
7. Percy Lubbock, *The Craft of Fiction* (London: Jonathan Cape, 1921), p. 147.
8. Ibid., p. 170.
9. *Messages;* cited in Edwin Muir, *The Structure of the Novel* (London: Hogarth Press, 1928), pp. 119–20.
10. Booth, *The Rhetoric of Fiction,* pp. 323–36. For a detailed account of Joyce's method, see the unpublished dissertation by Erwin R. Steinberg, "The Stream-of-Consciousness Technique in James Joyce's *Ulysses*" (New York University, 1956).
11. Erich Auerbach, *Mimesis: The Representation of Reality in Western Literature,* trans. Willard Trask (New York: Doubleday, 1953), p. 474.
12. Ibid., p. 472.
13. Ibid.

13 William H. Gass : *The Concept of*
Character in Fiction

William Gass begins his discussion by claiming that "great character is the most obvious single mark of great literature. . . . A great character has an endless interest; its fascination never wanes." Character must be a constant source of new discovery, not only for the reader who picks up a novel for the first time, but also for the one who returns to the same novel for pleasure. Citing Aristotle as a case in point, Gass observes that character has not always been a major concern of critics or authors. Now, however, that character has become a focus of attention, does that mean that critics and authors have come to understand what constitutes a character and its relationship to reality? Gass thinks not. While many critics still follow Aristotle in upholding mimesis, Gass assures us that character is not "a mirror or a window onto life."

Having defined what character is *not* in the first part of his essay, Gass defines what it *is* in the third part (we have omitted the second part — eds.): "Characters are those primary substances to which everything else is attached." Here Gass breaks through the stereotype that "character" means *person,* by suggesting that it can also refer to natural objects, symbols, and even ideas. Gass observes paradoxically that, while we invariably think of characters as people, the proper names given to characters are initially the emptiest words used in a novel — "Mr. Smith" means nothing without description. Often, however, authors help us by providing proper names that are really descriptive words, such as Mr. Cashmore, and then reinforce their descriptions through the sounds they employ as well as the connotations of the common words used in proper names. It is this investiture of a fictional creation with verbal detail that makes characters not "a mirror or a window onto life," but a creation of language, which "freed from existence, can shine like essence, and purely Be." If we accept this nonmimetic concept of character, we might want to ask ourselves how it affects our view of Virginia Woolf's concern for "Mrs. Brown" or Lionel Trilling's concern for a "moral realism." Before answering that question, however, we might first want to decide whether or not we believe that art is mimetic. Georg Lukács, for instance, would no doubt condemn Gass's rejection of mimesis as another form of bourgeois decay.

William H. Gass (b. 1924) has taught philosophy at Washington University, St. Louis, for many years. He is well known as a novelist and literary critic, having produced such works as *Omensetter's Luck* (1966), *In the Heart of the Heart of the Country* (1968), and *Fiction and the Figures of Life* (1970), from which this essay is taken.

I have never found a handbook on the art of fiction or the stage, nor can I imagine finding one, that did not contain a chapter on the creation of character, a skill whose mastery, the author of each manual insists, secures for one the inner secrets of these arts: not, mind you, an easy thing: rather as difficult as the whole art itself, since, in a way, it is the whole art: to fasten in the memory of the reader, like a living presence, some bright human image. All well and good to paint a landscape, evoke a feeling, set a tempest loose, but not quite good enough to nail an author to his immortality if scheming Clarence, fat, foul-trousered Harry, or sweetly terraced Priss do not emerge from the land they huff and rage and eat in fully furnished out by Being; enough alive, indeed, to eat and huff in ours — dear God, more alive than that! — sufficiently enlarged by genius that they threaten to eat up and huff down everything in sight.

Talk about literature, when it is truly talk about something going on in the pages, if it is not about ideas, is generally about the people in it, and ranges from those cries of wonder, horror, pleasure, or surprise, so readily drawn from the innocently minded, to the annotated stammers of the most erudite and nervous critics. But it is all the same. Great character is the most obvious single mark of great literature. The rude, the vulgar, may see in Alyosha nothing more than the image of a modest, God-loving youth; the scholar may perceive through this demeanor a symbolic form; but the Alyosha of the untutored is somehow more real and present to him than the youth on his street whom he's known since childhood, loving of his God and modest too, equally tried, fully as patient; for in some way Alyosha's visionary figure will take lodging in him, make a model for him, so to reach, without the scholar's inflationary gifts, general form and universal height; whereas the neighbor may merely move away, take cold, and forget to write. Even the most careful student will admit that fiction's fruit survives its handling and continues growing off the tree. A great character has an endless interest; its fascination never wanes. Indeed it is a commonplace to say so. Hamlet. Ahab. Julien Sorel. Madame Bovary. There is no end to their tragedy. Great literature is great because its characters are great, and characters are great when they are memorable. A simple formula. The Danish ghost cries to remember him, and obediently — for we are gullible and superstitious clots — we do.

It hasn't always been a commonplace. Aristotle regarded character as a servant of dramatic action, and there have been an endless succession of opinions about the value and function of characters since — all dreary — but the important thing to be noted about nearly every one of them is that whatever else profound and wonderful these theories have to say about the world and its personalities, characters are clearly conceived as living outside language. Just as the movie star deserts herself to put on some press agent's more alluring fictional persona, the hero of a story sets out from his own landscape for the same land of romance the star reached by stepping there from life. These people — Huckleberry Finn, the Snopeses, Prince Myshkin, Pickwick, Molly Bloom — seem to have come to the words of their novels like a visitor to town . . . and later they leave on the arm of the reader, bound, I suspect, for a shabbier hotel, and dubious entertainments.

However, Aristotle's remark was a recommendation. Characters ought to exist for the sake of the action, he thought, though he knew they often did not, and those who nowadays say that given a sufficiently powerful and significant plot the characters will be dominated by it are simply answered by asking them to imagine the plot of *Moby-Dick* in the hands of Henry James, or that of *Sanctuary* done into Austen. And if you can persuade them to try (you will have no success), you may then ask how the heroes and the heroines come out. The same disastrous exercise can be given those who believe that traits make character like definitions do a dictionary. Take any set of traits you like and let Balzac or Joyce, Stendhal or Beckett, loose in a single paragraph to use them. Give your fictional creatures qualities, psychologies, actions, manners, moods; present them from without or from within; let economics matter, breeding, custom, history; let spirit wet them like a hose: all methods work, and none do. The nature of the novel will not be understood at all until this is: *from any given body of fictional text, nothing necessarily follows, and anything plausibly may*. Authors are gods — a little tinny sometimes but omnipotent no matter what, and plausible on top of that, if they can manage it.[1]

Though the handbooks try to tell us how to create characters, they carefully never tell us we are making images, illusions, imitations. Gatsby is not an imitation, for there is nothing he imitates. Actually, if he were a copy, an illusion, sort of shade or shadow, he would not be called a character at all. He must be unique, entirely himself, as if he had a self to be. He is required, in fact, to act *in character,* like a cat in a sack. No, theories of character are not absurd in the way representational theories are; they are absurd in a grander way, for the belief in Hamlet (which audiences often seem to have) is like the belief in God — incomprehensible to reason — and one is inclined to seek a motive: some deep fear or emotional need.

There are too many motives. We pay heed so easily. We are so pathetically eager for this other life, for the sounds of distant cities and the sea; we long, apparently, to pit ourselves against some trying wind, to follow the fortunes of a ship hard beset, to face up to murder and fornication, and the somber results of anger and love; oh, yes, to face up — *in books* — when on our own we scarcely breathe. The tragic view of life, for instance, in Shakespeare or in Schopenhauer, Unamuno, Sartre, or Sophocles, is not one jot as pure and penetratingly tragic as a pillow stuffed with Jewish hair, and if we want to touch life where it burns, though life is what we are even now awash with — futilely, stupidly drawing in — we ought not to back off from these other artifacts (wars, pogroms, poverty: men make them, too). But of course we do, and queue up patiently instead to see Prince Hamlet moon, watch him thrust his sword through a curtain, fold it once again into Polonius, that foolish old garrulous proper noun. The so-called life one finds in novels, the worst and best of them, is nothing like actual life at all, and cannot be; it is not more real, or thrilling, or authentic; it is not truer, more complex, or pure, and its people have less spontaneity, are less intricate, less free, less full.[2]

It is not a single cowardice that drives us into fiction's fantasies. We often fear that literature is a game we can't afford to play — the product of idleness and immoral ease. In the grip of that feeling it isn't life we pursue, but the point and purpose of life — its facility, its use. So Sorel is either a man it is amusing to gossip about, to see in our friends, to puppet around in our dreams, to serve as our more able and more interesting surrogate in further fanciful adventures; or Sorel is a theoretical type, scientifically profound, representing a deep human strain, and the writing of *The Red and the Black* constitutes an advance in the science of — what would you like? sociology?

Before reciting a few helpless arguments, let me suggest, in concluding this polemical section, just how absurd these views are which think of fiction as a mirror or a window onto life — as actually creative of living creatures — for really one's only weapon against Tertullians is ridicule.

There is a painting by Picasso which depicts a pitcher, candle, blue enamel pot. They are sitting, unadorned, upon the barest table. Would we wonder what was cooking in that pot? Is it beans, perhaps, or carrots, a marmite? The orange of the carrot is a perfect complement to the blue of the pot, and the genius of Picasso, neglecting nothing, has surely placed, behind that blue, invisible disks of dusky orange, which, in addition, subtly enrich the table's velvet brown. Doesn't that seem reasonable? Now I see that it must be beans, for above the pot — you can barely see them — are quaking lines of steam, just the lines we associate with boiling beans . . . or is it blanching pods? Scholarly research, supported by a great foundation, will discover that exactly such a pot was used to cook cassoulet in the kitchens of Charles the Fat . . . or was it Charles the Bald? There's a dissertation in that. And this explains the dripping candle standing by the pot. (Is it dripping? no? a pity. Let's go on.) For isn't Charles the Fat himself that candle? Oh no, some say, he's not! Blows are struck. Reputations made and ruined. Someone will see eventually that the pot is standing on a table, not a stove. But the pot has just come from the stove, it will be pointed out. Has not Picasso caught that vital moment of transition? The pot is too hot. The brown is burning. Oh, not *this* table, which has been coated with resistant plastic. Singular genius — blessed man — he thinks of everything.

Here you have half the history of our criticism in the novel. Entire books have been written about the characters in Dickens, Trollope, Tolstoy, Faulkner. But why not? Entire books have been written about God, his cohorts, and the fallen angels.

A character, first of all, is the noise of his name, and all the sounds and rhythms that proceed from him. We pass most things in novels as we pass things on a train. The words flow by like the scenery. All is change.[3] But there are some points in a narrative which remain relatively fixed; we may depart from them, but soon we return, as music returns to its theme. Characters are those primary substances to which everything else is attached. Hotels, dresses, conversations, sausage, feelings, gestures, snowy evenings, faces — each may fade as fast as we read of them. Yet the language of the novel will eddy about a certain incident or name, as Melville's always circles back to Ahab and his wedding with the white whale. Mountains are characters in Malcolm Lowry's *Under the Volcano,* so is a ravine, a movie, mescal, or a boxing poster. A symbol like the cross can be a character. An idea or a situation (the anarchist in *The Secret Agent,* bomb ready in his pocket), or a particular event, an obsessive thought, a decision (Zeno's, for instance, to quit smoking), a passion, a memory, the weather,

Gogol's overcoat — anything, indeed, which serves as a fixed point, like a stone in a stream or that soap in Bloom's pocket, functions as a character. Character, in this sense, is a matter of degree, for the language of the novel may loop back seldom, often, or incessantly. But the idea that characters are like primary substances has to be taken in a double way, because if any thing becomes a character simply to the degree the words of the novel qualify it, it also loses some of its substance, some of its primacy, to the extent that it, in turn, qualifies something else. In a perfectly organized novel, every word would ultimately qualify one thing, like the God of the metaphysician, at once the subject and the body of the whole.[4] Normally, characters are fictional human beings, and thus are given proper names. In such cases, to create a character is to give meaning to an unknown X; it is *absolutely* to *define;* and since nothing in life corresponds to these X's, their reality is borne by their name. They *are,* where it *is.*

Most of the words the novelist uses have their meanings already formed. Proper names do not, except in a tangential way. It's true that Mr. Mulholland could not be Mr. Mull, and Mr. Cashmore must bear, as best he can, the curse of his wealth forever, along with his desire for gain. Character has a special excitement for a writer (apart from its organizing value) because it offers him a chance to give fresh meaning to new words. A proper name begins as a blank, like a wall or a canvas, upon which one might paint a meaning, perhaps as turbulent and mysterious, as treacherous and vast, as Moby-Dick's, perhaps as delicate, scrupulous, and sensitive as that of Fleda Vetch.

I cannot pause here over the subject of rhythm and sound, though they are the heartbeat of writing, of prose no less than poetry.

> Their friend, Mr. Grant-Jackson, a highly preponderant pushing person, great in discussion and arrangement, abrupt in overture, unexpected, if not perverse, in attitude, and almost equally acclaimed and objected to in the wide midland region to which he had taught, as the phrase was, the size of his foot — their friend had launched his bolt quite out of the blue and had thereby so shaken them as to make them fear almost more than hope.[5]

Mr. Grant-Jackson is a preponderant pushing person because he's been made by *p*'s, and the rhythm and phrasing of James's writing here prepares and perfectly presents him to us. Certainly we cannot think of Molly Bloom apart from her music, or the gay and rapid Anna Livia apart from hers.

If one examines the texture of a fiction carefully, one will soon see that some words appear to gravitate toward their subject like flies settle on sugar, while others seem to emerge from it. In many works this logical movement is easily discernible and very strong. When a character speaks, the words seem to issue from him and to be acts of his. Description first forms a *nature,* then allows that nature to *perform.* We must be careful, however, not to judge by externals. Barkis says that Barkis is willing, but the expression *functions* descriptively to qualify Barkis, and it is Dickens's habit to treat speech as if it were an attribute of character, like tallness or honesty, and not an act. On the other hand, qualities, in the right context, can be transformed into verbs. Later in the book don't we perceive the whiteness of the whale as a design, an intention of Moby-Dick's, like a twist of his flukes or the smashing of a small boat?

Whether Mr. Cashmore was once real and sat by James at someone's dinner table, or was instead the fabrication of James's imagination,[6] as long as he came into being from the world's direction he once existed outside language. The task of getting him in I shall call the problem of rendering. But it must be stressed (it cannot be stressed too severely) that Mr. Cashmore may never have had a model, and may never have been imagined either, but may have come to be in order to serve some high conception (a Mr. Moneybags) and represent a type, not just himself, in which case he is not a reality *rendered,* but a universal *embodied.*[7] Again, Mr. Cashmore might have had still other parents. Meanings in the stream of words before his appearance might have suggested him, dramatic requirements may have called him forth, or he may have been the spawn of music, taking his substance from rhythm and alliteration. Perhaps it was all of these. In well-regulated fictions, most things are *over-determined.*

So far I have been talking about the function of a character in the direct stream of language, but there are these two other dimensions, the rendered and the embodied, and I should like to discuss each briefly.

If we observe one of J. F. Powers's worldly priests sharpening his eye for the pin by putting through his clerical collar, the humor, with all *its* sharpness, lives in the situation, and quite incidentally in the words.[8] One can indeed imagine Powers thinking it up independently of any verbal formula. Once Powers had decided that it would be funny to show a priest playing honeymoon bridge with his housekeeper, then his problem becomes the technical one of how best to accomplish it. What the writer must do, of course, is not only render the scene, but render the scene inseparable from its language, so that if the idea (the chaste priest caught in the clichés of marriage) is taken from the situation, like a heart from its body, both die. Far easier to render a real cornfield in front of you, because once that rendering has reached its page, the cornfield will no longer exist for literary purposes, no one will be able to see it by peering through your language, and consequently there will be nothing to abstract from your description. But with a "thought up" scene or situation, this is not the case. It comes under the curse of story. The notion, however amusing, is not literary, for it might be painted, filmed, or played. If we inquire further and ask why Powers wanted such a scene in the first place, we should find, I think, that he wanted it in order to embody a controlling "idea" — at one level of abstraction, the worldliness of the church, for instance. If he had nuns around a kitchen table counting the Sunday take and listening to the Cubs, *that* would do it. Father Burner beautifully embodies just such a controlling idea in Powers's celebrated story "The Prince of Darkness." Both rendering and embodying involve great risks because they require working into a scientific order of words what was not originally there. Any painter knows that a contour may only more or less enclose his model, while a free line simply and completely is. Many of the model's contours may be esthetically irrelevant, so it would be unwise to follow them. The free line is subject to no such temptations. Its relevance can be total. As Valéry wrote: There are no details in execution.

Often novelists mimic our ordinary use of language. We report upon ourselves; we gossip. Normally we are not lying; and our language, built to refer, actually does. When these selfsame words appear in fiction, and when they follow the forms of daily use, they create, quite readily, that dangerous feeling that a real Tietjens, a real Nickleby, lives just beyond the page; that through that thin partition we can hear a world at love.[9] But the writer must not let the reader out; the sculptor must not let the eye fall from the end of his statue's finger; the musician must not let the listener dream. Of course, he will; but let the blame be on himself. High tricks are possible: to run the eye rapidly along that outstretched arm to the fingertip, only to draw it up before it falls away in space; to carry the reader to the very edge of every word so that it seems he must be compelled to react as though to truth as told in life, and then to return him, like a philosopher liberated from the cave, to the clear and brilliant world of concept, to the realm of order, proportion, and dazzling construction . . . to fiction, where characters, unlike ourselves, freed from existence, can shine like essence, and purely Be.

Notes

1. This has already been discussed in "Philosophy and the Form of Fiction." In "Mirror, Mirror," I complain that Nabokov's omnipotence is too intrusive. [The essays to which Gass refers in all of these notes appear in W. H. Gass, *Fiction and The Figures of Life.*]

2. I treat the relation of fiction to life in more detail in "In Terms of the Toenail: Fiction and the Figures of Life." The problem is handled in other ways in "The Artist and Society," "Even if, by All the Oxen in the World," and "The Imagination of an Insurrection."

3. Of course nothing prevents a person from feeling that life is like this. See "A Spirit in Search of Itself."

4. There is no reason why every novel should be organized in this way. This method constructs a world according to the principles of Absolute Idealism. See "Philosophy and the Form of Fiction."

5. Henry James, "The Birthplace."

6. Some aspects of this imagination are dealt with in "The High Brutality of Good Intentions," and "In The Cage."

7. See "Philosophy and the Form of Fiction."

8. I enlarge on this aspect of Powers's work in "The Bingo Game at the Foot of the Cross."

9. See "The Medium of Fiction."

14 Gérard Genette : *Time and Narrative in* "A la recherche du temps perdu"

Gérard Genette outlines here the critical method he employs in *Narrative Discourse: An Essay in Method* (1972; trans. 1980). Genette is concerned in *Narrative Discourse* with what he considers the three main problems of narrative discourse: time, mode, and voice. This essay focuses exclusively on the problem of time, which the author subdivides into three parts: "the temporal *order* of the events that are being told and the pseudo-temporal order of the narrative," "the *duration* of the events and the duration of the narrative," and "the *frequency* of repetition between the events and the narrative, between history and story."

As Genette observes, literary narratives have in fact tended *not* to relay a plot in the chronological order in which the story's events occur. Epics tend to begin in the middle of things and then relate earlier events through flashbacks, while novels also use flashforwards. Genette identifies various elements of the narrative reshuffling of chronology and suggests some of the functions they serve. Flashbacks, for example, may either fill previous blank spaces in the narrative or serve as retrospections, emphasizing the importance of an event through repetition. Genette suggests, however, that such identifications can mislead the reader unless we also take duration into account. For example, Genette discovers that, as Marcel Proust's novel proceeds, more and more narrative ellipses occur, and an increasing number of pages are given over to episodes of decreasing chronological duration, resulting in an "increasing discontinuity of the narrative."

The third problem that concerns Genette is frequency. While the "singular narrative" — one that tells about each event once — is used most frequently, "repetitive narratives," which repeat key episodes or information at various points in the text, also exist. A third type is the "iterative narrative," in which "a single narrative assertion covers several recurrences of the same event or, to be more precise, of several analogical events considered only with respect to what they have in common." Genette focuses his attention on Proust and temporal structure precisely because, as Joseph Frank argues, modern literature, by breaking with traditional conceptions of chronology and narration, has learned to exploit alternative temporal ordering to create new ways for the reader to experience literature and, hence, perceive reality.

Gérard Genette (b. 1930) is a French critic and rhetorician, whose *Narrative Discourse* has been recognized as a major document of French structuralism. In addition to *Narrative Discourse,* his criticism has been translated into *Figures of Literary Discourse* (1982), *Narrative Discourse Revisited* (1988), *The Architext: An Introduction* (1992), and *Fiction and Diction* (1993).

I suggest a study of *narrative discourse* or, in a slightly different formulation, of *narrative* [*récit*] as *discourse* [*discours*]. As a point of departure, let us accept the hypothesis that all narratives, regardless of their complexity or degree of elaboration — and Proust's *A la recherche du temps perdu,* the text I shall be using as an example, reaches of course a very high degree of elaboration — can always be considered to be the development of a verbal statement such as "I am walking," or "He will come," or "Marcel becomes a writer." On the strength of this rudimentary analogy, the problems of narrative discourse can be classified under three main headings: the categories of *time* (temporal relationships between the narrative [story] and the "actual" events that are being told [history]); of *mode* (relationships determined by the distance and perspective of the narrative with respect to the history); and of *voice* (relationships between the narrative and the narrating agency itself: narrative situation, level of narration, status of the narrator and of the recipient, etc.). I shall deal only, and very sketchily, with the first category.

The time-category can itself be divided into three sections: the first concerned with the relationships between the temporal *order* of the events that are being told and the pseudotemporal order of the narrative; the second concerned with the relationships between the *duration* of the events and the duration of the narrative; the third dealing with relationships of *frequency* of repetition between the events and the narrative, between history and story.

Order

It is well known that the folk tale generally keeps a one-to-one correspondence between the "real" order of events that are being told and the order of the narrative, whereas literary narrative, from its earliest beginnings in Western literature, that is, in the Homeric epic, prefers to use the beginning *in medias res,* generally followed by an explanatory flashback. This chronological reversal has become one of the formal *topoi* of the epic genre. The style of the novel has remained remarkably close to its distant origin in this respect: certain beginnings in Balzac, as in the *Duchesse de Langeais* or *César Birotteau,* immediately come to mind as typical examples.

From this point of view, the *Recherche* — especially the earlier sections of the book — indicates that Proust made a much more extensive use than any of his predecessors of his freedom to reorder the temporality of events. The first "time," dealt with in the six opening pages of the book, refers to a moment that cannot be dated with precision but that must take place quite late in the life of the protagonist: the time at which Marcel, during a period when, as he says, "he often used to go to bed early," suffered from spells of insomnia during which he relived his own past. The first moment in the organization of the narrative is thus far from being the first in the order of the reported history, which deals with the life of the hero.

The second moment refers to the memory relived by the protagonist during his sleepless night. It deals with his childhood at Combray, or, more accurately, with a specific but particularly important moment of this child-hood: the famous scene that Marcel calls "the drama of his going to bed," when his mother, at first prevented by Swann's visit from giving him his ritualistic goodnight kiss, finally gives in and consents to spend the night in his room.

The third moment again moves far ahead, probably to well within the period of insomnia referred to at the start, or a little after the end of this period: it is the episode of the *madeleine,* during which Marcel recovers an entire fragment of his childhood that had up till then remained hidden in oblivion.

This very brief third episode is followed at once by a fourth: a second return to Combray, this time much more extensive than the first in temporal terms since it covers the entire span of the Combray childhood. Time segment (4) is thus contemporary with time segment (2) but has a much more extensive duration.

The fifth moment is a very brief return to the initial state of sleepless-ness and leads to a new retrospective section that takes us even further back into the past, since it deals with a love experience of Swann that took place well before the narrator was born.

There follows a seventh episode that occurs some time after the last events told in the fourth section (childhood at Combray): the story of Marcel's adolescence in Paris and of his love for Gilberte. From then on, the story will proceed in more closely chronological order, at least in its main articulations.

A la recherche du temps perdu thus begins with a zigzagging movement that could easily be represented by a graph and in which the relationship between the time of events and the time of the narrative could be summarized as follows: N(arrative) 1 = H(istory) 4; N_2 = H_2; N_3 = H_4; N_4 = H_2; N_5 = H_4; N_6 = H_1 (Swann's love); N_7 = H_3. We are clearly dealing with a highly complex and deliberate transgression of chronological order. I have said that the rest of the book follows a more continuous chronology in its main patterns, but this large-scale linearity does not exclude the presence of a great number of anachronisms in the details: *retrospections,* as when the story of Marcel's stay in Paris during the year 1914 is told in the middle of his later visit to Paris during 1916; or *anticipations,* as when, in the last pages of *Du côté de chez Swann,* Marcel describes what has become of the Bois de Boulogne at a much later date, the very year he is actually engaged in writing his book. The transition from the *Côté de Guermantes* to *Sodome et Gomorrhe* is based on an interplay of anachronisms: the last scene of *Guermantes* (announcing the death of Swann) in fact takes place later than the subsequent first scene of *Sodome* (the meeting between Charlus and Jupien).

I do not intend to analyze the narrative anachronisms in detail but will point out in passing that one should distinguish between *external* and *internal* anachronisms, according to whether they are located without or within the limits of the temporal field defined by the main narrative. The external anachronisms raise no difficulty, since there is no danger that they will interfere with the main narrative. The internal anachronisms, on the contrary, create a problem of interference. So we must subdivide them into two groups, according to the nature of this relation. Some function to fill in a previous or later blank (ellipsis) in the narrative and can be called *completive* anachronisms, such as the retrospective story of Swann's death. Others return to a moment that has already been covered in the narrative: they are *repetitive* or apparently redundant anachronisms but fulfill in fact a very important function in the organization of the novel. They function as *announcements* (in the case of prospective anticipations) or as *recalls* (when they are retrospective). Announcements can, for example, alert the reader to the meaning of a certain event that will only later be fully revealed (as with the lesbian scene at Montjouvain that will later determine Marcel's jealous passion for Albertine). Recalls serve to give a subsequent meaning to an event first reported as without particular significance (as when we find that Albertine's belated response to a knock on the door was caused by the fact that she had locked herself in with Andrée), or serve even more often to alter the original meaning—as when Marcel discovers after more than thirty years' time that Gilberte was in love with him at Combray and that what he took to be a gesture of insolent disdain was actually meant to be an advance.

Next to these relatively simple and unambiguous retrospections and anticipations, one finds more complex and ambivalent forms of anachronisms: anticipations within retrospections, as when Marcel remembers what used to be his projects with regard to the moment that he is now experiencing; retrospections within anticipations, as when the narrator indicates how he will later find out about the episode he is now in the process of telling; "announcements" of events that have already been told anticipatively or "recalls" of events that took place earlier in the story but that have not yet been told; retrospections that merge seamlessly with the main narrative and make it impossible to identify the exact status of a given section, etc. Finally, I should mention what is perhaps the rarest but most specific of all instances: structures that could properly be called *achronisms,* that is to say, episodes entirely cut loose from any chronological situation whatsoever. These occurrences were pointed out by J. P. Houston in a very interesting study published in *French Studies* (January 1962) entitled "Temporal Patterns in *À la recherche du temps perdu.*" Near the end of *Sodome et Gomorrhe,* as Marcel's second stay at Balbec draws to a close, Proust tells a sequence of episodes not in the order in which they took place but by following the succession of roadside-stops made by the little train on its journey from Balbec to La Raspelière. Events here follow a geographical rather than a chronological pattern. It is true that the sequence of places still depends on a temporal event (the journey of the train), but this temporality is not that of the "real" succession of events. A similar effect is achieved in the composition of the end of *Combray,* when the narrator successively describes a number of events that took place on the Méséglise way, at different moments, by following the order of their increasing distance from Combray. He follows the temporal succession of a walk from Combray to Méséglise and then, after returning to his spatial and temporal point of departure, tells a sequence of events that took place on the Guermantes way using exactly the same principle. The temporal order of the narrative is not that of the actual succession of events, unless it happens to coincide by chance with the sequence of places encountered in the course of the walk.

I have given some instances of the freedom that Proust's narrative takes with the chronological order of events, but such a description is necessarily sketchy and even misleading if other elements of narrative temporality such as duration and frequency are not also taken into account.

Duration

Generally speaking, the idea of an isochrony between narrative and "history" is highly ambiguous, for the narrative unit which, in literature, is almost always a narrative text cannot really be said to possess a definite duration. One could equate the duration of a narrative with the time it takes to read it, but reading times vary considerably from reader to reader, and an ideal average speed can only be determined by fictional means. It may be better to start out from a definition in the form of a relative quantity, and define isochrony as a uniform projection of historical time on narrative extension, that is, number of pages per duration of event. In this way, one can record variations in the speed of the narrative in relation to itself and measure effects of acceleration, deceleration, stasis, and ellipsis (blank spaces within the narrative while the flow of events keeps unfolding).

I have made some rather primitive calculations of the relative speed of the main narrative articulations, measuring on the one hand the narrative of the *Recherche* by number of pages and on the other hand the events by quantity of time. Here are the results.

The first large section, *Combray* or Marcel's childhood, numbers approximately 180 pages of the Pléiade edition and covers about ten years (let me say once and for all that I am defining the duration of events by general consensus, knowing that it is open to question on several points). The next episode, Swann's love affair with Odette, uses approximately 200 pages to cover about two years. The Gilberte episode (end of *Swann*, beginning of *Jeunes filles en fleurs*) devotes 160 pages to a duration that can be evaluated at two or three years. Here we encounter an ellipsis involving two years of the protagonist's life and mentioned in passing in a few words at the beginning of a sentence. The Balbec episode numbers 300 pages for a three-month-long time-span; then the lengthy section dealing with life in Paris society (*Côté de Guermantes* and beginning of *Sodome et Gomorrhe*) takes up 750 pages for two and a half years. It should be added that considerable variations occur within this section: 110 pages are devoted to the afternoon party at Mme. de Villeparisis's that lasts for about two hours, 150 pages to the dinner of nearly equal length at the Duchesse de Guermantes's, and 100 pages to the evening at the Princesse de Guermantes's. In this vast episode of 750 pages for two and a half years, 360 pages — nearly one-half — are taken up by less than ten hours of social life.

The second stay at Balbec (end of *Sodome*) covers approximately six months in 380 pages. Then the Albertine sequence, reporting the hero's involvement with Albertine in Paris (*La Prisonnière* and beginning of *La Fugitive*), requires 630 pages for an eighteen-month period, of which 300 deal with only two days. The stay in Venice uses 35 pages for a few weeks, followed by a section of 40 pages (astride *La Fugitive* and *Le Temps retrouvé*) for the stay in Tansonville, the return to the country of Marcel's childhood. The first extended ellipsis of the *Recherche* occurs here; the time-span cannot be determined with precision, but it encompasses approximately ten years of the hero's life spent in a rest home. The subsequent episode, situated during the war, devotes 130 pages to a few weeks, followed by another ellipsis of ten years again spent in a rest home. Finally, the concluding scene, the party at the Princesse de Guermantes's, devotes 190 pages to a two- or three-hour-long reception.

What conclusions can be derived from this barren and apparently useless enumeration? First of all, we should note the extensive shifts in relative duration, ranging from one line of text for ten years to 190 pages for two or three hours, or from approximately one page per century to one page per minute. The second observation refers to the internal evolution of the *Recherche* as a whole. It could be roughly summarized by stressing, on the one hand, the gradual slowing down of the narrative achieved by the insertion of longer and longer scenes for events of shorter and shorter duration. This is compensated for, on the other hand, by the presence of more and more extensive ellipses. The two trends can be easily united in one formula: increasing discontinuity of the narrative. As the Proustian narrative moves toward its conclusion, it becomes increasingly discontinuous, consisting of gigantic scenes separated from each other by enormous gaps. It deviates more and more from the ideal "norm" of an isochronic narrative.

We should also stress how Proust selects among the traditional literary forms of narrative duration. Among the nearly infinite range of possible combinations of historical and narrative duration, the literary tradition has made a rather limited choice that can be reduced to the following fundamental forms: (1) the *summary,* when the narrative duration is greatly reduced with respect to the historical duration; it is well known that the summary constitutes the main connective tissue in the classical *récit;* (2) the dramatic scene, especially the dialogue, when narrative and historical time are supposed to be nearly equal; (3) the narrative *stasis,* when the narrative discourse continues while historical time is at a standstill, usually in order to take care of a description; and (4) *ellipsis,* consisting of a certain amount of historical time covered in a zero amount of narrative. If we consider the *Recherche* from this point of view, we are struck by the total absence of summarizing narrative, which tends to be absorbed in the ellipses, and by the near-total absence of descriptive stasis: the Proustian descriptions always correspond to an actual observation-time on the part of the character; the time lapse is sometimes mentioned in the text and is obviously longer than the time it takes to read the description (three-quarters of an hour for the contemplation of the Elstir paintings owned by the Duc de Guermantes, when the description takes only four or five pages of the text). The narrative duration is not interrupted — as is so often the case with Balzac — for, rather than *describing,* Proust *narrates* how his hero perceives, contemplates, and experiences a given sight; the description is incorporated within the narrative and constitutes no autonomous narrative form. Except for another effect with which I shall deal at some length in a moment, Proust makes use of only two of the traditional forms of narrative duration: scene and ellipsis. And since ellipsis is a zero point of the text, we have in fact only one single form: the scene. I should add, however, without taking time to develop a rather obvious observation, that the narrative function of this traditional form is rather strongly subverted in Proust. The main number of his major scenes do not have the purely dramatic function usually associated with the classical "scene." The traditional economy of the novel, consisting of summarizing and nondramatic narrative alternating with dramatic scenes, is entirely discarded. Instead, we find another form of alternating movement toward which we must now direct our attention.

Frequency

The third kind of narrative temporality, which has in general received much less critical and theoretical attention than the two previous ones, deals with the relative frequency of the narrated events and of the narrative sections that report them. Speaking once more very schematically, the most obvious form of narration will tell once what happens once, as in a narrative statement such as: "Yesterday, I went to bed early." This type of narrative is so current and presumably normal that it bears no special name. In order to emphasize that it is merely one possibility among many, I propose to give it a name and call it the *singulative* narrative [*récit singulatif*]. It is equally possible to tell several times what happened several times, as when I say: "Monday I went to bed early, Tuesday I went to bed early, Wednesday I went to bed early," etc. This type of anaphoric narrative remains singulative and can be equated with the first, since the repetitions of the story correspond one-to-one to the repetitions of the events. A narrative can also tell several times, with or without variations, an event that happened only once, as in a statement of this kind: "Yesterday I went to bed early, yesterday I went to bed early, yesterday I tried to go to sleep well before dark," etc. This last hypothesis may seem a priori to be a gratuitous one, or even to exhibit a slight trace of senility. One should remember, however, that most texts by Alain Robbe-Grillet, among others, are founded on the repetitive potential of the narrative: the recurrent episode of the killing of the centipede, in *La jalousie*, would be ample proof of this. I shall call *repetitive* narrative this type of narration, in which the story repetitions exceed in number the repetitions of events. There remains a last possibility. Let us return to our second example: "Monday, Tuesday, Wednesday," etc. When such a pattern of events occurs, the narrative is obviously not reduced to the necessity of reproducing it as if its discourse were incapable of abstraction or synthesis. Unless a deliberate stylistic effect is aimed for, even the simplest narration will choose a formulation such as "every day" or "every day of the week" or "all week long." We all know which of these devices Proust chose for the opening sentence of the *Recherche*. The type of narrative in which a single narrative assertion covers several recurrences of the same event or, to be more precise, of several analogical events considered only with respect to what they have in common, I propose to call by the obvious name of *iterative* narrative [*récit itératif*].

My heavy-handed insistence on this notion may well seem out of place, since it designates a purely grammatical concept without literary relevance. Yet the quantitative amount and the qualitative function of the iterative mode are particularly important in Proust and have seldom, to my knowledge, received the critical attention they deserve. It can be said without exaggeration that the entire Combray episode is essentially an iterative narrative, interspersed here and there with some "singulative" scenes of salient importance such as the motherly goodnight kiss, the meeting with the Lady in the pink dress (a retrospective scene), or the profanation of Vinteuil's portrait at Montjouvain. Except for five or six such scenes referring to a single action and told in the historical past [*passé défini*], all the rest, told in the imperfect, deals with what used to happen at Combray regularly, ritualistically, every night or every Sunday, or every Saturday, or whenever the weather was good or the weather was bad, etc. The narrative of Swann's love for Odette will still be conducted, for the most part, in the mode of habit and repetition; the same is true of the story of Marcel's love for Swann's daughter Gilberte. Only when we reach the stay at Balbec in the *Jeunes filles en fleurs* do the singulative episodes begin to predominate, although they remain interspersed with numerous iterative passages: the Balbec outings with Mme. de Villeparisis and later with Albertine, the hero's stratagems at the beginning of *Guermantes* when he tries to meet the Duchess every morning, the journeys in the little train of the Raspelière (*Sodome, 2*), life with Albertine in Paris (the first eighty pages of *La Prisonnière*), the walks in Venice (*La Fugitive*), not to mention the iterative treatment of certain moments within the singulative scenes, such as the conversations about genealogy during the dinner at the Duchess's, or the description of the aging guests at the last Guermantes party. The narrative synthesizes these moments by reducing several distinct occurrences to their common elements: "the *women* were like this . . . the *men* acted like that; *some* did this, *others* that," etc. I shall call these sections *internal iterations,* in contrast with other, more common passages, in which a descriptive-iterative parenthesis begins in the middle of a singulative scene to convey additional information needed for the reader's understanding and which I shall call *external iterations.* An example would be the long passage devoted, in the middle of the first Guermantes dinner, to the more general and therefore necessarily iterative description of the Guermantes wit.

The use of iterative narrative is by no means Proust's invention; it is one of the most classical devices of fictional narrative. But the frequency of the mode is distinctively Proustian, a fact still underscored by the relatively massive presence of what could be called *pseudo-iterations,* scenes presented (mostly by the use of the imperfect tense) as if they were iterative, but with such a wealth of precise detail that no reader can seriously believe that they could have taken place repeatedly in this way, without variations. One thinks for example of some of the conversations between Aunt Léonie and her maid Françoise that go on for page after page, or of conversations in Mme. Verdurin's or Mme. Swann's salon in Paris. In each of these cases, a singular scene has arbitrarily, and without any but grammatical change, been converted into an iterative scene, thus clearly revealing the trend of the Proustian narrative toward a kind of inflation of the iterative.

It would be tempting to interpret this tendency as symptomatic of a dominant psychological trait: Proust's highly developed sense of habit and repetition, his feeling for the *analogy* between different moments in life. This is all the more striking since the iterative mode of the narrative is not always, as in the Combray part, based on the repetitive, ritualistic pattern of a bourgeois existence in the provinces. Contrary to general belief, Proust is less aware of the specificity of moments than he is aware of the specificity of places; the latter is one of the governing laws of his sensibility. His moments have a strong tendency to blend into each other, a possibility which is at the root of the experience of spontaneous recollection. The opposition between the "singularity" of his spatial imagination and, if I dare say so, the "iterativity" of his temporal imagination is nicely illustrated in the following sentence from *Swann*. Speaking of the Guermantes landscape, Proust writes: "[Its] specificity would *at times,* in my dreams, seize upon me with almost fantastical power" ("le paysage dont *parfois,* la nuit dans mes rêves, l'individualité m'étreint avec une puissance presque fantastique"). Hence the highly developed sense of *ritual* (see, for example, the scene of the Saturday luncheon at Combray) and, on the other hand, the panic felt in the presence of irregularities of behavior, as when Marcel, at Balbec, wonders about the complex and secret law that may govern the unpredictable absences of the young girls on certain days.

But we must now abandon these psychological extrapolations and turn our attention to the technical questions raised by the iterative narration.

Every iterative sequence can be characterized by what may be called its *delimitation* and its *specification.* The delimitation determines the confines within the flow of external duration between which the iterative sequence, which generally has a beginning and an end, takes place. The delimitation can be vague, as when we are told that "from a certain year on, Mlle. Vinteuil could never be seen alone" (1:147), or precise, defined — a very rare occurrence in Proust — by a specific date, or by reference to a particular event, as when the break between Swann and the Verdurins puts an end to an iterative sequence telling of Swann's encounters with Odette and starts off a new sequence. The specification, on the other hand, points out the recurring periodicity of the iterative unit. It can be indefinite (as is frequently the case in Proust who introduces an iterative statement by such adverbs of time as "sometimes," "often," "on certain days," etc.) or definite, when it follows an absolute and regular pattern such as: "every day," "every Sunday," etc. The pattern can also be more irregular and relative, as when the walks toward Méséglise are said to take place in bad or uncertain weather, or the walks toward Guermantes whenever the weather is good. Two or more specifications can of course be juxtaposed. "Every summer" and "every Sunday" combine to give "every Sunday in the summer," which is the iterative specification of much of the Combray section.

The interplay between these two dimensions of the iterative narrative varies and enriches a temporal mode threatened, by its very nature, by a degree of abstraction. Provided it has a certain length, an iterative section can very closely resemble an ordinary narrative, except for some grammatical traits. Yet it goes without saying that a narrative such as "Sunday at Combray" that would retain only events that *all* Sundays have in common would run the risk of becoming as dryly schematic as a stereotyped time-schedule. The monotony can be avoided by playing on the internal delimitations and specifications.

Internal delimitations: for instance, the diachronic caesura brought about by the story of the encounter with the "Lady in the pink dress" in the narration of Marcel's Sunday afternoon readings: this encounter will bring about a change of locale, after the quarrel between Marcel's parents and Uncle Adolphe has put the latter's room out of bounds. Another instance would be the change of direction in the hero's dreams of literary glory after his first encounter with the Duchess in the church of Combray. The single scene, in those instances, divides the iterative sequence into a *before* and an *after,* and so diversifies it into two subsequences which function as two *variants.*

Internal specifications: I mentioned the good weather/bad weather pattern which introduces a definite specification in the iterative series of the Sunday walks and determines the choice between Guermantes and Méséglise. Most of the time, however, the iterative narrative is diversified in indefinite specifications introduced by "sometimes . . . " or "one time . . . some other time . . . ," etc. These devices allow for a very flexible system of variations and for a high degree of particularization, without leaving the iterative mode. A characteristic example of this technique occurs toward the end of the *Jeunes filles en fleurs* in a description of Albertine's face (1:946–47). The iterative mode, indeed, applies just as well to the descriptive as to the narrative passages; half of Proust's descriptions make use of this mode:

Certains jours, mince, le teint gris, l'air maussade, une transparence violette descendant obliquement au fond de ses yeux comme il arrive quelquefois pour la mer, elle semblait éprouver une tristesse d'exilée. *D'autres jours,* sa figure plus lisse engluait les désirs à sa surface vernie et les empêchait d'aller au delà; *à moins que* je ne la visse tout à coup de côté, car ses joues mates comme une blanche cire à la surface étaient roses par transparence, ce qui donnait tellement envie de les embrasser, d'atteindre ce teint différent qui se dérobait. *D'autres fois,* le bonheur baignait ces joues d'une clarté si mobile que la peau, devenue fluide et vague, laissait passer comme des regards sous-jacents qui la faisaient paraître d'une autre couleur, mais non d'une autre matière, que les yeux; *quelquefois,* sans y penser, quand on regardait sa figure ponctuée de petits points bruns et où flottaient seulement deux taches plus bleues; C'était comme on eût fait d'un oeuf de chardonneret, *souvent* comme d'une agate opaline travaillée et polie à deux places seulement où, au milieu de la pierre brune, luisaient, comme les ailes transparentes d'un papillon d'azur, les yeux où la chair devient miroir et nous donne l'illusion de nous laisser, plus qu'en les autres parties du corps, approcher de l'âme. Mais *le plus souvent* aussi elle était plus colorée, et alors plus animée: *quelquefois* seul était rose, dans sa figure blanche, le bout de son nez, fin comme celui d'une petite chatte sournoise avec qui l'on aurait eu envie de jouer; *quelquefois* ses joues étaient si lisses que le regard glissait comme sur celui d'une miniature sur leur émail rose, que faisait encore paraître plus delicat, plus intérieur, le couvercle entr'ouvert et superposé de ses cheveux noirs; *il arrivait que* le teint de ses joues atteignît le rose violacé du cyclamen, et *parfois* même, quand elle était congestionnée ou fiévreuse, et donnant alors l'idée d'une complexion maladive qui rabaissait mon désir à quelque chose de plus sensuel et faisait exprimer à son regard quelque chose de plus pervers et de plus malsain, la sombre pourpre de certaines roses d'un rouge presque noir; et chacune de ces Albertin était différente, comme est différente chacune des apparitions de la danseuse dont sont transmutées les couleurs, la forme, le caractère, selon les jeux innombrablement variés d'un projecteur lumineux. (italics added)[1]

On *certain days,* slim, with grey cheeks, a sullen air, a violet transparency falling obliquely from her such as we notice sometimes on the sea, she seemed to be feeling the sorrows of exile. On *other days* her face, more sleek, caught and glued my desires to its varnished surface and prevented them from going any farther; *unless* I caught a sudden glimpse of her from the side, for her dull cheeks, like white wax on the surface, were visibly pink beneath, which made me anxious to kiss them, to reach that different tint, which thus avoided my touch. *At other times* happiness bathed her cheeks with a clarity so mobile that the skin, grown fluid and vague, gave passage to a sort of stealthy and sub-cutaneous gaze, which made it appear to be of another colour but not of another substance than her eyes; *sometimes,* instinctively, when one looked at her face punctuated with tiny brown marks among which floated what were simply two larger, bluer stains, it was like looking at the egg of a goldfinch — or *often* like an opalescent agate cut and polished in two places only, where, from the heart of the brown stone, shone like the transparent wings of a sky-blue butterfly her eyes, those features in which the flesh becomes a mirror and gives us the illusion that it allows us, more than through the other parts of the body, to approach the soul. But *most often of all* she shewed more colour, and was then more animated; *sometimes* the only pink thing in her white face was the tip of her nose, as finely pointed as that of a mischievous kitten with which one would have liked to stop and play; *sometimes* her cheeks were so glossy that one's glance slipped, as over the surface of a miniature, over their pink enamel, which was made to appear still more delicate, more private, by the enclosing though half-opened case of her black hair; *or it might happen that* the tint of her cheeks had deepened to the violet shade of the red cyclamen, and, *at times, even,* when she was flushed or feverish, with a suggestion of unhealthiness which lowered my desire to something more sensual and made her glance expressive of something more perverse and unwholesome, to the deep purple of certain roses, a red that was almost black; and each of these Albertines was different, as in every fresh appearance of the dancer whose colours, form, character, are transmitted according to the innumerably varied play of projected limelight. (1:708; italics added)

The two devices (internal delimitation and internal specification) can be used together in the same passage, as in this scene from *Combray* that deals in a general way with returns from walks. The general statement is then diversified by a delimitation (itself iterative, since it recurs every year) that distinguishes between the beginning and the end of the season. This second sequence is then again diversified by a single indefinite specification: "certains soirs. . . . " The following passage is built on such a system; very simple but very productive:

Nous rentrions *toujours* de bonne heure de nos promenades, pour pouvoir faire une
visite à ma tante Léonie avant le dîner. *Au commencement de la saison,* où le jour
finit tôt, quand nous arrivions rue du Saint-Esprit, il y avait encore un reflet du
couchant sur les vitres de la maison et un bandeau de pourpre au fond des bois du
Calvaire, qui se reflétait plus loin dans l'étang, rougeur qui, accompagnée souvent
d'un froid assez vif, s'associait, dans mon esprit, à la rougeur du feu au-dessus
duquel rôtissait le poulet qui ferait succéder pour moi au plaisir poétique donné par
la promenade, le plaisir de la gourmandise, de la chaleur et du repos. *Dans l'été, au
contraire,* quand nous rentrions le soleil ne se couchait pas encore; et pendant la
visite que nous faisions chez ma tante Léonie, la lumière qui s'abaissait et touchait
la fenêtre, était arrêtée entre les grands rideaux et les embrasses, divisée, ramifiée,
filtrée, et, incrustant de petits morceaux d'or le bois de citronnier de la commode,
illuminait obliquement la chambre avec la délicatesse qu'elle prend dans les sous-
bois. Mais, *certains jours forts rares,* quand nous rentrions, il y avait bien long-
temps que la commode avait perdu ses incrustations momentanées, il n'y avait plus,
quand nous arrivions rue du Saint-Esprit, nul reflet de couchant étendu sur les
vitres, et l'étang au pied du calvaire avait perdu sa rougeur, quelquefois il était déjà
couleur d'opale, et un long rayon de lune, qui allait en s'élargissant et se fendillait
de toutes les rides de l'eau, le traversait tout entier. (1:133; italics added)

We used *always* to return from our walks in good time to pay aunt Léonie a visit
before dinner. *In the first weeks of our Combray holidays,* when the days ended
early, we would still be able to see, as we turned into the Rue du Saint-Esprit, a
reflection of the western sky from the windows of the house and a band of purple at
the foot of the Calvary, which was mirrored further on in the pond; a fiery glow
which, accompanied often by a cold that burned and stung, would associate itself in
my mind with the glow of the fire over which, at that very moment, was roasting the
chicken that was to furnish me, in place of the poetic pleasure I had found in my
walk, with the sensual pleasures of good feeding, warmth and rest. *But in summer,*
when we came back to the house, the sun would not have set; and while we were
upstairs paying our visit to aunt Léonie its rays, sinking until they touched and lay
along her window-sill, would there be caught and held by the large inner curtains
and the bands which tied them back to the wall, and split and scattered and filtered;
and then, at last, would fall upon and inlay with tiny flakes of gold the lemonwood
of her chest-of-drawers, illuminating the room in their passage with the same
delicate, slanting, shadowed beams that fall among the boles of forest trees. *But on
some days, though very rarely,* the chest-of-drawers would long since have shed its
momentary adornments, there would no longer, as we turned into the Rue du Saint-
Esprit, be any reflection from the western sky burning along the line of window-

panes; the pond beneath the Calvary would have lost its fiery glow, sometimes indeed had changed already to an opalescent pallor, while a long ribbon of moonlight, bent and broken and broadened by every ripple upon the water's surface, would be lying across it, from end to end. (1:102; italics added)

Finally, when all the resources of iterative particularization have been exhausted, two devices remain. I have already mentioned pseudo-iteration (as in the conversations between Françoise and Aunt Léonie); this is admittedly a way of cheating or, at the very least, of stretching the reader's benevolence to the limit. The second device is more honest — if such ethical terminology can have any sense in the world of art — but it represents an extreme case leading out of the actually iterative mode: in the midst of an iterative section the narrator mentions a particular, singular occurrence, either as illustration, or example, or, on the contrary, as an exception to the law of repetition that has just been established. Such moments can be introduced by an expression such as "thus it happened that . . . " ("c'est ainsi que . . . ") or, in the case of an exception, "this time however . . . " ("une fois pourtant . . . "). The following passage from the *Jeunes filles* is an example of the first possibility: "*At times,* a kind gesture of one [of the girls] would awaken within me an expansive sympathy that replaced, for a while, my desire for the others. *Thus it happened that* Albertine, one day . . . " etc. (1:911).[2] The famous passage of the Martinville clock towers is an example of the second possibility. It is explicitly introduced as an exception to the habitual pattern: generally, when Marcel returns from walks, he forgets his impressions and does not try to interpret their meaning. "This time, however" (the expression is in the text), he goes further and composes the descriptive piece that constitutes his first literary work. The exceptional nature of an event is perhaps even more explicitly stressed in a passage from *La Prisonnière* that begins as follows: "*I will put aside,* among the days during which I lingered at Mme. de Guermantes's, one day that was marked by a small incident . . . ," after which the iterative narrative resumes: "*Except for this single incident,* everything went *as usual* when I returned from the Duchess's . . . " (3:54, 55).[3]

By means of such devices, the singulative mode merges, so to speak, with the iterative section and is made to serve it by positive or negative illustrations, either by adhering to the code or by transgressing it — which is another way of recognizing its existence.

The final problem associated with iterative temporality concerns the relationship between the duration or, rather, the internal diachrony of the iterative unit under consideration, and the external diachrony, that is, the flow of "real" and necessarily singulative time between the beginning and the end of the iterative sequence. A unit such as "sleepless night," made up of a sequence that stretches over several years, may very well be told in terms of its own duration from night to morning, without reference to the external passage of years. The typical night remains constant, except for internal specifications, from the beginning to the end of the sequence, without being influenced by the passage of time outside the particular iterative unit. This is, in fact, what happens in the first pages of the *Recherche*. However, by means of internal delimitations, the narrative of an iterative unit may just as readily encompass the external diachrony and narrate, for example, "a Sunday at Combray" by drawing attention to changes in the dominical ritual brought about by the passage of years: greater maturity of the protagonist, new acquaintances, new interests, etc. In the Combray episodes, Proust very skillfully plays upon these possibilities. J. P. Houston claimed that the narrative progresses simultaneously on three levels: with the duration of the day, of the season, and of the years. Things are perhaps not quite as clear and systematic as Houston makes them out to be, but it is true that, in the Sunday scenes, events taking place in the afternoon are of a later date than those taking place in the morning and that, in the narration of the walks, the most recent episodes are assigned to the longest itineraries. For the reader, this creates the illusion of a double temporal progression, as if the hero were a naïve little boy in the morning and a sophisticated adolescent at night, aging several years in the course of a single day or a single walk. We are touching here upon the outer limits of the iterative narrative mode.

Thus Proust appears to substitute for the *summary,* which typifies the classical novel, another form of synthesis, the iterative narrative. The synthesis is no longer achieved by acceleration, but by analogy and abstraction. The rhythm of Proust's narrative is no longer founded, as in the classical *récit,* on the alternating movement of dramatic and summarizing sections, but on the alternating movement of iterative and singular scenes. Most of the time, these alternating sections overlay a system of hierarchical subordinations that can be revealed by analysis. We already encountered two types of such systems: an iterative-explanatory section that is functionally dependent on an autonomous singular episode: the Guermantes wit (iterative) in the midst of a dinner at the duchess's (singular): and a singular-illustrative section dependent on an autonomous iterative sequence (in the scenes used as illustrations or exceptions). The hierarchical systems of interdependence can be more complex, as when a singular scene illustrates an iterative section that is itself inserted within another singulative scene: this happens, for example, when a particular anecdote (such as Oriane's wordplay on Taquin le Superbe) is used to illustrate the famous Guermantes wit: here we have a singulative element (Taquin le Superbe) within an iterative sequence (Guermantes wit) itself included in a singulative scene (dinner at Oriane de Guermantes's). The description of these structural relationships is one of the tasks of narrative analysis.

It often happens that the relationships are less clear and that the Proustian narrative fluctuates between the two modes without visible concern for their respective functions, without even seeming to be aware of the differences. Some time ago, Marcel Vigneron pointed out confusions of this sort in the section dealing with Marcel's love for Gilberte at the Champs-Elysées: an episode would start off in the historical past [*passé défini*], continue in the imperfect, and return to the historical past, without any possibility for the reader to determine whether he was reading a singular or an iterative scene. Vigneron attributed these anomalies to last-minute changes in the manuscript made necessary by publication. The explanation may be correct, but it is not exhaustive, for similar discrepancies occur at other moments in the *Recherche* when no such considerations of expediency can be invoked. Proust probably at times forgets what type of narrative he is using; hence, for example, the very revealing sudden appearance of a historical past within a pseudo-iterative scene (1:104, 722). He was certainly also guided by a secret wish to set the narrative forms free from their hierarchical function, letting them play and "make music" for themselves, as Proust himself said of Flaubert's ellipses. Hence the most subtle and admirable passages of all, of which J. P. Houston has mentioned a few, in which Proust passes from an iterative to a singular passage or uses an almost imperceptible modulation — such as an ambiguous imperfect of which it is impossible to know whether it functions iteratively or singularly, or the interposition of directly reported dialogue without declarative verb and, consequently, without determined mode, or a page of commentary by the narrator, in the present tense — to achieve the opposite effect; such a modulation, lengthily developed and to all appearances carefully controlled, serves as a transition between the first eighty pages of *La Prisonnière* that are in an iterative mode, and the singulative scenes that follow. I have particularly stressed the question of narrative frequency because it has often been neglected by critics and by theoreticians of narrative technique, and because it occupies a particularly prominent place in the work of Marcel Proust. A paper that deals so sketchily and provisionally with a single category of narrative discourse cannot hope to reach a conclusion. Let me therefore end by pointing out that, together with the daring manipulations of chronology I have mentioned in the first part of my paper and the large-sized distortions of duration described in the second, Proust's predilection for an iterative narrative mode and the complex and subtle manner in which he exploits the contrasts and relations of this mode with a singulative discourse combine to free his narrative forever from the constraints and limitations of traditional narration. For it goes without saying that, in an iterative temporality, the order of succession and the relationships of duration that make up classical temporality are from the very beginning subverted or, more subtly and effectively, *perverted*. Proust's novel is not only what it claims to be, a novel of time lost and recaptured, but also, perhaps more implicitly, a novel of controlled, imprisoned, and bewitched time, a part of what Proust called, with reference to dreams, "the formidable game it plays with Time" ("le jeu formidable qu'il fait avec le Temps").

Notes

1. All citations are from the Pléiade edition of *A la recherche du temps perdu*. The English version of this passage and of the passage on pp. 195–96 is from the translation by C. K. Scott Moncrieff, published by Random House. Translations in the text are by Paul De Man.

2. "*Parfois* une gentille attention de telle ou telle éveillait en moi d'amples vibrations qui éloignaient pour un temps le désir des autres. *Ainsi un jour* Albertine . . . "

3. "*Je mettrai à part,* parmi ces jours ou je m'attardai chez Mme. de Guermantes, un qui fût marqué par un petit incident . . . "; "*Sauf cet incident unique,* tout se passait *normalement* quand je remontais de chez la duchesse . . . "

William Freedman : *The Literary Motif*

A Definition and Evaluation

William Freedman takes a common but often vaguely defined critical term, "literary motif," and attempts to develop a comprehensive definition. He begins with a standard definition: "a theme, character, or verbal pattern which recurs in literature or folklore" and which may recur in a number of works or a single work; he then emphasizes that a motif may appear as a "verbal pattern" and may "act symbolically." In regard to being a verbal pattern, a motif, "although it may appear as something described, perhaps even more often forms part of the description." Thus, unlike a symbol, it may recur in a work without using the same object, image, or word each time. Freedman cites the repetition of varying references to money, finance, and economics in some of Henry James's and F. Scott Fitzgerald's novels. According to Freedman, a motif will fall into "one or more of three principal categories: cognitive, affective (or emotive), and structural." In addition, a motif must recur with sufficient frequency to make it recognizable, and its appearance must be avoidable or unlikely, so that it stands out from the general descriptive background.

Having established the appearance of a "motif," Freedman provides five criteria for evaluating its effectiveness: frequency, avoidability and unlikelihood, significance of context, the degree of the relevance and coherence of the motif as a whole, and — for those motifs that function symbolically — its appropriateness to what it symbolizes. After producing a working definition, Freedman discusses the literary value of the motif and its key contribution to artistic complexity: "the motif is a complex of separate parts subtly reiterating on one level what is taking place on another. It thus multiplies levels of meaning and interest." This evaluation is based on the premise "that subtlety, richness, and complexity are desirable qualities in a work of art," a premise that echoes James's belief that a work of fiction is only required to be "interesting." In this context, we may want to ask whether — just as it is possible for a work of fiction to be enhanced by complexity — it is possible for a work of fiction to be weakened by attempting too much subtlety and complexity, thereby sacrificing thematic content for artistic form.

William Freedman taught for many years at Brooklyn College. In 1969 he emigrated to Israel to become Senior Lecturer in English at the University of Haifa. In addition to "The Literary Motif" (1971), he has published essays on fiction, particularly American Jewish fiction, in such journals as *Modern Fiction Studies* and the *Mississippi Quarterly.*

Since the rise of the New Criticism in the Thirties, a criticism preoccupied with the work-in-itself and consequently with literary technique, there has been a steadily increasing flow of critical essays primarily
concerned with language. One important phase of this study of language
has been the attempt to discover clusters or families of related words or
phrases that, by virtue of their frequency and particular use, tell us something about the author's intentions, conscious or otherwise. Mark Schorer,
concerning himself only with families of metaphors, terms them "metaphoric substructures."[1] Reuben Brower, also mainly concerned with recurrent images or metaphors, terms them "continuities."[2] But although
most critics have concentrated primarily on the metaphoric members of
these language families, it seems obvious that the literal components, in
conjunction with the figurative, form a larger unit that may prove more
revealing still. And when we combine the literal and the figurative into a
single family unit, we emerge with what is perhaps most accurately called
the literary "motif."

Although there has been much discussion of the function of motifs in
specific works, so far as I know there has been nothing approaching a
detailed analysis of the device. I should like, therefore, to attempt such an
analysis, a description of what the literary motif is and how it functions.
And when I have done that I should like then to examine the question of its
literary value. It is a fairly automatic critical assumption that to demonstrate the existence of an elaborate motif in a given work is to demonstrate
something that enhances the value of that work. I agree. But at the same
time I think it advisable to inquire into the reasons behind this widespread
assent. It is not enough to show that an author has employed a motif or that
one has found its way into his work without at least inquiring why or if its
presence is an asset.

Perhaps as useful a starting point as any is the entry under "motif" in
one of the standard literary dictionaries:

A theme, character, or verbal pattern which recurs in literature or folklore. . . . A
motif may be theme which runs through a number of different works. The motif of
the imperishability of art, for example, appears in Shakespeare, Keats, Yeats, and
many other writers. A recurring element within a single work is also called a motif.

Among the many motifs that appear and reappear in Joyce's *Ulysses,* for example, are Plumtree's Potted Meat, the man in the brown mackintosh, and the one-legged sailor.[3]

My concern is with the latter part of this description, with the motif as it is employed within a single work. The statement in the *Reader's Guide* supplies a reasonable start toward a more complete definition of this kind of motif by accounting fairly well for the literal use of motifs, the repetition for emphasis of a self-contained, self-explanatory theme or the like. But it leaves much to be said. For one thing, it fails to make clear that the motif in a single work, like that which runs through many different works, may take the form of a verbal pattern. And it may be a family or, to borrow a term from Kenneth Burke, an "associational cluster," rather than merely a single, unchanging element. Second, it does not take into account what is perhaps the primary function of the motif as it is most often used and discussed, namely, to act symbolically. This description, in other words, does not encompass the money or finance motifs in James's *The Wings of the Dove* and *The Golden Bowl,* or Fitzgerald's *The Great Gatsby* and *Tender Is the Night.* The language of money, finance, and economics is indeed recurrent in these novels. But it recurs for a reason. Viewed collectively, this language refers to something outside itself, namely, the economic preoccupation of the society or some of its members. The motif, then, tells the reader something — to establish a convenient separation — about the action of the story (either its total structure or the events), the minds of the characters, the emotional import or the moral or cognitive content of the works. It tells him subtly what the incidents perhaps tell him bluntly. It is, in short, symbolic.

But this is not the same as saying that each instance of this language is a symbol, for two major lines of differentiation distinguish the symbolic motif from the symbol. First, the symbol may occur singly. The motif is necessarily recurrent and its effect cumulative. For this reason Steinbeck's symbolic turtle, which appears on the opening pages of *The Grapes of Wrath* and synecdochically foreshadows the movements and spirit of the Okies, is a symbol and not a motif. But if we were to find scattered throughout the book frequent references to, say, a turtleneck sweater which Tom Joad is never without or frequent reiterations of remarks to the effect that Ma Joad is hard-shelled or slow as a tortoise but equally persistent, then in this "associational cluster" we would have the makings of a motif. Here each reference to turtles, tortoises, or to things turtle-like or tortoise-like, would not necessarily be a symbol, for each reference would not always be a thing or event, but often only a symbolic way of talking about a thing or event.

This takes us to the second distinction. A symbol is something described; it is an event or it is a thing. It may be Melville's white whale or the mode of Ahab's death; it may be the New Testament's cross or the crucifixion of Christ upon it; or it may be the scarlet letter or little Pearl's peculiar reactions to it. But it is always a thing or event described. A motif, on the other hand, although it may appear as something described, perhaps even more often forms part of the description. It slips, as it were, into the author's vocabulary, into the dialogue, and into his imagery, often even at times when the symbolized referent is not immediately involved. For example, in our hypothetical case, Tom Joad's turtleneck sweater or Ma Joad's figurative hard shell might be referred to even when their perseverance is not at issue. Or, to cite a real example, Dreiser makes constant reference in *Sister Carrie* to Carrie's "dull little round" and Hurstwood's "exclusive circle" well before the question of circularity and futile, repetitive striving arises. The motif prepares us for the time when it will.

The motif, then, may become a part of the total perspective, pervading the book's atmosphere and becoming an important thread in the fabric of the work. Such permeation is achieved, for example, by the motif of circularity in *Sister Carrie*,[4] by the machine and animal motifs in *The Grapes of Wrath*,[5] by the isolation motif (doors, gates, fences, and so forth) in *The Sound and the Fury*,[6] and by the music motif in Sterne's *A Sentimental Journey*, to name but a very few of many.

The motif is not a symbol, but it may be symbolic. When it is, it acquires this character cumulatively and either by its relationship to the action (whether it be the total shape of the action or simply one or more of the events), to one or more of the characters, to the affective or cognitive content of the work, or to any combination of these possibilities. Whether the motif is symbolic or literal, however, it is through its service to one or more of these same aspects of the work that it achieves its purpose, and the motif therefore generally falls into one or more of three principal categories: cognitive, affective (or emotive), and structural. A motif may contribute to only one of these three aspects of the work. The motif of commerce and property in Austen's *Persuasion,* as an instance, is primarily cognitive. It serves to reveal to the reader the "social fact" that most characters in the novel measure value entirely in arithmetical and economic terms. Most motifs, however, relate to more than one of these aspects, although one may be of paramount importance. The motif of circularity in *Sister Carrie* is perhaps chiefly cognitive. It underscores Dreiser's presentation of the circular futility of human striving. But since this point is made largely by means of a repetitive circular patterning of the events of the novel, the motif relates to and underscores the novel's structure as well as its cognitive content. Although the chief function of the music motif in *A Sentimental Journey* is its enrichment of the emotive quality of the work, it is importantly related to both the cognitive content and structure as well. In *Tristram Shandy* it underscores the emotive quality, the structure and the cognitive content of the work, but principally its structure.

Two factors are indispensable to the establishment of a motif. The first is the frequency with which it recurs. The recurrence of references to finance in only two or three, or even five or ten, instances in a novel the size of, say, *The Golden Bowl,* would hardly constitute a motif. It might well be nothing more than coincidence or necessity. Obviously no specific numbers of references can possibly be fixed as requisite to the motif. That will vary with each work. But members of the family of references should occur often enough to indicate that purposiveness rather than merely coincidence or necessity is at least occasionally responsible for their presence. They should pervade the atmosphere sufficiently to assure that they will be at least subliminally felt.

Second is the avoidability and unlikelihood of the particular uses of a motif, or of its appearance in certain contexts, or of its appearance at all. References to hats in a novel about a milliner, for example, are all but unavoidable. Consequently, more than mere frequency of occurrence is required if hats are to function as a motif. This is not to say that their appearance or use must be unlikely to the point of inappropriateness. Quite the contrary, appropriateness is a basic test of efficacy. What I do mean is that the contexts in which the references appear or the uses to which they are put (extraliteral uses, for example) do not *demand* references from the field of the motif. In a novel about a milliner, a man's home, automobile, or other articles of clothing might serve equally well as indices of character, social status, or the like. The repeated use of hats to these symbolic purposes may, however, make these and other references to hats unexplainable as anything other than instances of a motif.

Assuming we have discovered a motif in a given work, our next concern is to measure its effectiveness. Five basic factors determine the efficacy of a motif. The first is again frequency. All other factors being equal and within limits to be adumbrated below, the greater the frequency with which instances of a motif recur the deeper the impression it is likely to make on the reader. The effect, of course, will also be increased the more extensive the individual references are. One need hardly be told that an extended metaphor or episode involving the motif subject is more likely to catch the reader's attention than a passing reference.

The second factor is again avoidability and unlikelihood. Clearly the more uncommon a reference is in a given context, the more likely it is to strike the reader, consciously or subconsciously, and the greater will be its effect. A reader might pass unnoticingly over a reference to a drummer, for example. But he is not so likely to remain unaffected by a metaphor that compares the impulse to pity to a musical instrument, a very common sort of metaphor in *A Sentimental Journey* and *Tristram Shandy*. For both of these criteria a qualification is needed. There would seem to be a law of diminishing returns here, the efficacy of the motif beginning to decline at the point where unlikelihood begins to shade into unsuitability or frequency into tedious repetition. Maximum power will therefore probably be achieved at the degree of frequency and improbability just short of this negative tendency, a point that varies from work to work.

A third factor determining the potency of a motif is the significance of the contexts in which it occurs. A motif that appears at most or all of the climactic points of a work, particularly if the symbolized referent of the motif is in the fore at these points, has greater effect than one that occurs only in less central passages, particularly if these passages do not overtly concern the tenor of the motif. The fact that the crucial event in the Benjy section of *The Sound and the Fury* — his misunderstood abuse of the passing schoolgirl — results from Benjy's opening the accidentally unlocked gate and that the crucial event in the Jason section concerns the stealing of the money he has locked in a strongbox, which he keeps in a dresser drawer inside a closet of his locked room, combines with the general pervasiveness of the motif of isolation and confinement to make that motif an important factor in the book and to ensure the fulfillment of its purpose.

A fourth factor is the degree to which all instances of the motif are relevant to the principal end of the motif as a whole and to which they fit together into a recognizable and coherent unit. If a unified effect is to be produced it will hardly be achieved by a motif in which all the parts are related only remotely and ramify into a variety of unrelated purposes: the closer the association between the components of the cluster the more unified their effect. The finance motif in *Tender Is the Night* is rendered more effective by the fact that its components point almost exclusively to the corrosive powers of money (as with Dick Diver's "emotional bankruptcy") rather than to several other possible qualities not related to the intended effect of either the motif or the work as a whole.

The fifth and final factor, which concerns only those motifs whose function is symbolic, is the appropriateness of the motif to what it symbolizes. Obviously a motif of circularity is more appropriate to a book about the circular repetitiveness of human fortune and behavior and the circular, futile strivings of the ill-equipped dreamer, as in *Sister Carrie,* than to one about, say, a love triangle. And again *The Sound and the Fury* is a good example. Constant references to doors, fences, gates, and the like are patently appropriate as symbolic representations of the Compsons' physical and spiritual isolation.

A possible criticism of the reader or critic who seems to find a motif in every cupboard is the observation that in certain instances the references seem virtually unavoidable. One may claim, for instance — and quite rightly — that James could hardly have written a novel like *The Golden Bowl* without alluding frequently to matters of finance. In the light of what has been said so far, however, this seems to me no very damaging accusation. If the reader can show satisfactorily that the presence of the motif is at least sometimes quite easily avoidable, that its overall frequency is greater than sheer coincidence or necessity might produce, that the separate members of the family or cluster operate together to a common end, and that they are singularly appropriate to a given aspect of the work in hand, he has, I think, shown both the existence and efficacy of a motif in that work. It is then virtually inevitable that the cumulative force of the motif, acting by association, must at least to some extent suffuse every occurrence of it, however unavoidable or insignificant any one may appear independently.

Perhaps now I may hazard a definition. A motif, then, is a recurrent theme, character, or verbal pattern, but it may also be a family or associational cluster of literal or figurative references to a given class of concepts or objects, whether it be animals, machines, circles, music, or whatever. It is generally symbolic — that is, it can be seen to carry a meaning beyond the literal one immediately apparent; it represents on the verbal level something characteristic of the structure of the work, the events, the characters, the emotional effects or the moral or cognitive content. It is presented both as an object of description and, more often, as part of the narrator's imagery and descriptive vocabulary. And it indispensably requires a certain minimal frequency of recurrence and improbability of appearance in order both to make itself at least subconsciously felt and to indicate its purposiveness. Finally, the motif achieves its power by an appropriate regulation of that frequency and improbability, by its appearance in significant contexts, by the degree to which the individual instances work together toward a common end or ends and, when it is symbolic, by its appropriateness to the symbolic purpose or purposes it serves.

But what of the literary value of a motif? What, if anything, does it contribute to the work it graces and to the reader's appreciation of that work? Everyone who writes about literature of course hopes that the nature and value of his efforts are self-evident. In most critical studies (book reviews and biographical and bibliographical notes usually excepted) this hope takes the form of an implicit syllogism that goes something like this: All works, or at least the one or ones here under consideration, are better if they possess a certain attribute or attributes or can be understood in certain terms. This book has these attributes or can be understood in these terms. Therefore, this is a better book than was previously supposed. As I've said, this syllogism is almost always implicit and only the minor premise is expressed in writing. In many cases the hidden assumptions might not be completely acceptable were they brought into the open, and although it is in such cases that exposure is most useful I think something may be gained by exposing even quite widely held evaluative assumptions in order that the reader may be a bit clearer about just what he is agreeing to.

Purely descriptive studies need not take a rear seat in the critical bus. The writer performs a worthwhile function when he attempts no more than to elucidate what he sees in the work, when he seeks to increase the reader's understanding of a work of art. The discovery of the motif should be as valuable — or at least nearly so — to the reader who sees no additional artistic merit accruing to the book as a result of the addition of this new information as it is to the reader who thinks it a better book therefore. If that hypothetical reader can be led to better understand what is going on in a given literary work, even to better understand why he does not like it, I think it will have been worth the effort. Nevertheless, let it be admitted that I do attach value to the motif. How widespread the approval of a well-handled motif in literature really is would seem to be a question for the pollsters. But while I can speak only for myself, I think it would be generally agreed that the discovery in a given work of a motif adequately fulfilling the criteria suggested above tends to enhance appreciation and alter judgment as well as increase understanding. The question then is "Why?" In what sense may we justifiably consider "motif" as a value term?

I think it is plain that unlike such terms as, say, "unity," or "order," "motif" is not an aesthetic primitive. That is to say our approval of the motif seems to derive by implication from several more fundamental premises or axioms. One such premise and one possible explanation of what I believe to be its acceptability as a term of implicit approbation may be found in Kenneth Burke's exaltation of the synecdoche. The synecdoche, as he defines it, is "the figure of speech wherein the part is used for the whole, the whole for the part, the container for the thing contained, the cause for the effect, the effect for the cause, etc."[7] Since the symbolic motif is basically microcosmic, since it is a part of a literary work that may often stand for the whole, it performs, I think, a synecdochic function. Consequently it may justly derive some of its appeal from that which Burke discovers in the synecdoche. "The more I examine both the structure of poetry and the structure of human relations outside of poetry," says Burke, "the more I become convinced that this is the 'basic' figure of speech, and that it occurs in many modes besides that of the formal trope" (pp. 23–24). As Burke points out, "we use the same word for sensory, artistic and political representation": our sensory abstractions "represent" the tree; the colors and forms in a painting "represent" the society as a whole. The fetish, the scapegoat, and perhaps above all the name are further instances of symbolic representatives of the whole. Clearly, then, the symbolic representation of a whole or of other parts by a single part forms an indispensable part of both the way we see things and the way we communicate them. This helps at least partially to explain why the literary motif, a subtle and elaborate variation of this figure in a work of art, would be likely to attract our interest and approval.

As I have defined it, the motif is a complex of separate parts subtly reiterating on one level what is taking place on another. It thus multiplies levels of meaning and interest. A second premise from which our approval of the motif may be derived, then, is that subtlety, richness, and complexity are desirable qualities in a work of art. This generalization does not always hold, for doubtless there are times when the barest simplicity is preferable. Nevertheless, we do take pleasure in at least a certain degree of subtlety, richness, and complexity. We say that *King Lear* is a greater achievement than any of Shakespeare's sonnets, and that Beethoven's Ninth Symphony is a greater achievement than his Second Piano Sonata, and one of the reasons is complexity. The reasons for complexity's hold upon us are not far to seek. Complication involves us more continually, more deeply, and more completely. It brings, as Coleridge said poetry must, "the whole soul of man into activity." But this is familiar stuff. Less often remarked (which is to say, I have never seen it mentioned) is the possible role of anthropomorphism. Spinoza once observed that if triangles had the power of intellectual conception they would conceive a triangular god. It seems equally likely that our attraction to complexity and its correlatives stems at least partially from the fact that the human organism is itself a highly subtle complex of parts functioning, to our own endless wonder, toward a single end: life. Clearly, human behavior and human relationships are no less complex. If, therefore, art is to function as an "imitation of life" (in whichever of the almost endless ways one might choose to interpret that phrase) and if it is to satisfy man's anthropomorphic inclinations and desires, complexity must be a part of it. So pervasive are these inclinations that the whole of organismic physics, the physics that was dominant from Aristotle through Newton and that to a certain extent persists to this day, has an anthropomorphic base; that is, it is based on the analogy between the human organism and the universe.[8] And just as anthropomorphism has served as a foundation for man's attempt to interpret the universe, so has it exerted an important influence on matters of desire and preference, although the anthropomorphic view of God and the universe is also, as more recent physics has shown, very likely a matter of preference as well as an attempt at understanding. Anthropomorphism has been suggested, for example, as a possible explanation for man's demonstrable affinity for symmetry in art and architecture. It seems to me at least as applicable to his preference for the qualities of richness and complexity.

Since all of the works cited here are novels and since the motif is chiefly a novelist's tool, it seems worthy of note that in two of the most useful definitions of the novel, or of a particular kind of novel, complexity occupies a central place. For Henry Fielding in his famous Preface to *Joseph*

Andrews, a comic romance — his term for the kind of novel he claimed to be writing and whose status he hoped to insure — "is a comic epic poem in prose: differing from comedy, as the serious epic from tragedy: its action being more extended and comprehensive; containing a much larger circle of incidents, and introducing a greater variety of characters." Two centuries later Ian Watt, defining in retrospect the genre as a whole, has this to say:

> Formal realism . . . is the narrative embodiment of a premise that Defoe and Richardson accepted very literally, but which is implicit in the novel form in general: the premise, or primary convention, that the novel is a full and authentic report of human experience, and is therefore under an obligation to satisfy its reader with such details of the story as the individuality of the actors concerned, the particulars of the times and places of their actions, details which are presented through a more largely referential use of language than is common in other literary forms.[9]

Watt's definition of the novel and Fielding's definition of his own kind of novel and of the form as he hoped it would evolve have very little in common. For as Watt makes clear it was the tradition of formal realism, not that of Fielding's classicism and polished artificiality, that finally won out. Nevertheless, although they agree in little else, they both insist on complexity. The principle of plenitude seems to apply to products of human no less than divine creation.

Perhaps one may sum up the value of the motif in the combination of its intellectual and affective appeals. Intellectually, since the motif usually points to a skillful author capable of subtlety and complexity, it first of all enhances the reader's respect for that author. This increased respect, I think, becomes inextricable from his impression of the work. We may not like to admit it — and admittedly all may not feel it — but for many of us the wonder we feel in the presence of, say, the genius of Shakespeare translates into increased appreciation of every evidence of that genius. I am prepared to suggest that the discovery that the tragedies are, after all, the issue of that infinite conglomeration of monkeys would in some degree diminish our response and appreciation. We are, at bottom, quite in love with ourselves as a species and are awed by what some of us, at least, can do. "Did one of us do that?" we wonder. And the fact that one of us did makes us love it all the more. We love the sign for what it points to as well as for what it is.

Second, and perhaps more basically, subtlety and complexity are themselves abundant sources of literary enjoyment and appreciation for reasons already discussed. And third, the motif appeals to whatever analytic interests we may have, to our sheer delight in discovering a technique and in watching it work both on its own and as a spoke in a well-oiled wheel. Affectively, assuming that the emotional effect or effects sought by any work are worth eliciting at all, it follows that the reinforcement of those effects on various levels, particularly the enrichment of the overall effect by means of a part, can only add scope and depth to the reading experience.

A final word about the motif, not as a literary device but as part of a critical approach. The kind of approach to fiction I have tried to outline here, it seems to me, performs that uncommon but useful coalescing function of bringing together under one roof the all too often disassociated schools of criticism. In its concentration on language, technique, and the text itself, the method is perhaps primarily what is generally called "New Critical." But insofar as it also investigates the possibility of authorial intention and awareness and, more important, the meaning of the motif to the contemporary audience and its probable effect on the given work's first readers, it attempts to make use of the abundant fruits of biographical and historical analysis as well.

Notes

1. Mark Schorer, "Fiction and the 'Matrix of Analogy,' " *Kenyon Review* 11 (1949): 539–60.
2. Reuben Brower, *The Fields of Light: An Experiment in Critical Reading* (New York: Oxford University Press, 1962). See particularly pp. 13, 14, 52–56, 103–17, 124–26, 148–50, 157–59, 161–63.
3. Karl Beckson and Arthur Ganz, *A Reader's Guide to Literary Terms* (New York: Noonday Press, 1960), p. 129.
4. William Freedman, "A Look at Dreiser as Artist: The Motif of Circularity in *Sister Carrie*," *Modern Fiction Studies* 8 (1962): 384–92.
5. Robert J. Griffin and William Freedman, "Machines and Animals: Pervasive Motifs in *The Grapes of Wrath*," *Journal of English and Germanic Philology* 62 (1963): 569–80.
6. Freedman, "Techniques of Isolation in *The Sound and the Fury*," *Mississippi Quarterly* 15 (1961): 21–26.
7. Kenneth Burke, *The Philosophy of Literary Form: Studies in Symbolic Action* (rev. ed.; New York: Vintage Books, 1957), pp. 22–23.

8. In *Philosophy of Science* (Englewood Cliffs, N.J.: Prentice-Hall, 1957), p. 119, Philipp Frank points out that "Newton explained the planetary motions by an analogy with the behavior of human beings, just as Aristotelian physics did." Similarly, Auguste Comte, in *Positive Philosophy* (trans. Harriett Martineau [London: George Bell & Sons, 1896]), book 3, chap. 1, remarks that "The spirit of all theological and metaphysical philosophy consists in conceiving all phenomena as analogous to the only one which is known through immediate consciousness — Life."

9. Ian Watt, *The Rise of the Novel* (Berkeley and Los Angeles: University of California Press, 1959), p. 32.

16 Gerald Prince : *Introduction to the Study of the Narratee*

Gerald Prince defines the narratee as "someone whom the narrator addresses," and as a "someone" who has been critically neglected. He argues that critical treatments of topics pertinent to the narratee have generally been subsumed in discussions of the narrator. But perhaps this is also due to a tendency to view listeners, readers, or narratees as passive recipients of the story rather than as active participants, as Mikhail Bakhtin would define them.

Prince suggests that we can find a phenomenal diversity of narratees in fiction and demonstrates the important differences between a narratee and the "real reader," "virtual reader," and "ideal reader." In order to describe the diversity of narratees, Prince creates a minimal portrait, that of "the zero-degree narratee," and observes how various fictions alter this "zero-degree" through certain narrative signals, as when the narrator of *Le Père Goriot* defines the narratee as white. Prince points out that the narrator may discuss such qualities in passages addressed to or overheard by the reader, rather than the narratee. But, as Prince emphasizes, "nevertheless, the portrait of a narratee emerges above all from the narrative addressed to him."

Having said this, Prince classifies fictional narratees according to types: (1) no one in particular, (2) a named or identified party who is not a character in the story, and (3) a character in the story. In the latter case, the narratee-character might play no other role than that of listener or might more actively participate in the plot. In either case, narratee-characters can either be affected by the stories related to them or remain unaffected. Furthermore, they can be essential, in that only a certain type of narratee will allow the story to be told, or interchangeable. Finally, they can be either listeners or readers.

After discussing their various functions, Prince concludes by claiming that "the narratee is one of the fundamental elements of all narration." Whether or not we agree with this claim, we can see the critical benefits to be gained from analyzing narratees. These benefits arise in part from perceiving fiction as a dialogue that occurs between author and reader and among narrator, characters, and narratee, rather than as a message simply received. Such perceptions recognize the recipients of fictional utterances, both internal and external to the text, as more active constructors of meaning than has been generally acknowledged.

Gerald Prince (b. 1941), Professor of French at the University of Pennsylvania, is author of *A Grammar of Stories: An Introduction* (1973), *Narratology: The Form and Functioning of Narrative* (1982), and *Narrative as Theme: Studies in French Fiction* (1992).

All narration, whether it is oral or written, whether it recounts real or mythical events, whether it tells a story or relates a simple sequence of actions in time, presupposes not only (at least) one narrator but also (at least) one narratee, the narratee being someone whom the narrator addresses. In a fiction-narration — a tale, an epic, a novel — the narrator is a fictive creation as is his narratee. Jean-Baptiste Clamence, Holden Caulfield, and the narrator of *Madame Bovary* are novelistic constructs as are the individuals to whom they speak and for whom they write. From Henry James and Norman Friedman to Wayne C. Booth and Tzvetan Todorov, numerous critics have examined the diverse manifestations of the narrator in fictive prose and verse, his multiple roles and his importance.[1] By contrast, few critics have dealt with the narratee and none to date has undertaken an in-depth study;[2] this neglect persists despite the lively interest raised by Benveniste's fine articles on discourse [*le discours*], Jakobson's work on linguistic functions, and the evergrowing prestige of poetics and semiology.

Nowadays, any student minimally versed in the narrative genre differentiates the narrator of a novel from its author and from the novelistic *alter ego* of the author and knows the difference between Marcel and Proust, Rieux and Camus, Tristram Shandy, Sterne the novelist, and Sterne the man. Most critics, however, are scarcely concerned with the notion of the narratee and often confuse it with the more or less adjacent notions of receptor [*récepteur*], reader, and arch-reader [*archilecteur*]. The fact that the word *narratee* is rarely employed, moreover, is significant.

This lack of critical interest in narratees is not inexplicable. Indeed, their study has been neglected, more than likely, because of a characteristic of the narrative genre itself; if the protagonist or dominant personality of a narration often assumes the role of the narrator and affirms himself as such (Marcel in *A la recherche du temps perdu,* Roquentin in *La Nausée,* Jacques Revel in *L'Emploi du temps*), there is no hero who is above all a narratee — unless one includes narrators who constitute their own narratee,[3] or perhaps a work like *La Modification.* Besides, it should not be forgotten that the narrator, on a superficial if not a profound level, is more responsible than his narratee for the shape and tone of the story as well as for its other characteristics. Finally, many problems of poetic narrative that might have been approached from the angle of the narratee have already been studied from the point of view of the narrator; after all, the individual who relates a story and the person to whom the story is told are more or less interdependent in any narration.

Whatever the case may be, narratees deserve to be studied. Major storytellers and novelists, as well as the less important, bear out this point. The variety of narratees found in fictive narrations is phenomenal. Docile or rebellious, admirable or ridiculous, ignorant of the events related to them or having prior knowledge of them, slightly naive as in *Tom Jones,* vaguely callous as in *The Brothers Karamazov,* narratees rival narrators in their diversity. Moreover, many novelists have in their own way examined the distinctions that should be maintained between the narratee and the receptor or between the narratee and the reader. In a detective novel by Nicholas Blake, for example, and in another by Philip Loraine, the detective succeeds in solving the crime when he realizes that the narratee and the receptor are not the same. In addition, there is no want of narratives that underscore the importance of the narratee, *A Thousand and One Nights* providing an excellent illustration. Scheherazade must exercise her talent as a storyteller or die, for as long as she is able to retain the attention of the caliph with her stories, she will not be executed. It is evident that the heroine's fate and that of the narration depend not only upon her capabilities as a storyteller, but also upon the humor of the narratee. If the caliph should become tired and stop listening, Scheherazade will die and the narrative will end.[4] The same fundamental situation can be found in the encounter of Ulysses with the Sirens,[5] as well as in a more recent work. Like Scheherazade, the hero of *La Chute* has a desperate need for a certain type of narratee. In order to forget his own guilt, Jean-Baptiste Clamence must find someone who will listen to him and whom he will be able to convince of everyone's guilt. He finds this someone at the Mexico City Bar in Amsterdam and it is at that moment that his narrative account begins.

The Zero-Degree Narratee

In the very first pages of *La Père Goriot,* the narrator exclaims: "That's what you will do, you who hold this book with a white hand, you who settle back in a well-padded armchair saying to yourself: perhaps this is going to be amusing. After reading about old Goriot's secret misfortunes, you'll dine with a good appetite attributing your insensitivity to the author whom you'll accuse of exaggeration and poetic affectation." This "you" with white hands, accused by the narrator of being egotistical and callous, is the narratee. It's obvious that the latter does not resemble most readers of *Le Père Goriot* and that consequently the narratee of a novel cannot be automatically identified with the reader: the reader's hands might be black or red and not white; he might read the novel in bed instead of in an armchair; he might lose his appetite upon learning of the old merchant's unhappiness. The reader of a fiction, be it in prose or in verse, should not be mistaken for the narratee. The one is real, the other fictive. If it should occur that the reader bears an astonishing resemblance to the narratee, this is an exception and not the rule.

Neither should the narratee be confused with the virtual reader. Every author, provided he is writing for someone other than himself, develops his narrative as a function of a certain type of reader whom he bestows with certain qualities, faculties, and inclinations according to his opinion of men in general (or in particular) and according to the obligations he feels should be respected. This virtual reader is different from the real reader: writers frequently have a public they don't deserve. He is also distinct from the narratee. In *La chute,* Clamence's narratee is not identical to the reader envisioned by Camus: after all, he's a lawyer visiting Amsterdam. It goes without saying that a virtual reader and a narratee can be alike, but once again it would be an exception.

Finally, we should not confuse the narratee with the ideal reader, although a remarkable likeness can exist between the two. For a writer, an ideal reader would be one who would understand perfectly and would approve entirely the least of his words, the most subtle of his intentions. For a critic, an ideal reader would perhaps be one capable of interpreting the infinity of texts that, according to certain critics, can be found in one specific text. On the one hand, the narratees for whom the narrator multiplies his explanations and justifies the particularities of his narrative are numerous and cannot be thought of as constituting the ideal readers dreamed up by a novelist. We need only think of the narratees of *Le Père Goriot* and *Vanity Fair.* On the other hand, these narratees are too inept to be capable of interpreting even a rather restricted group of texts within the text.

If narratees are distinct from real, virtual, or ideal readers,[6] they very often differ from each other as well. Nonetheless, it should be possible to describe each one of them as a function of the same categories and according to the same models. It is necessary to identify at least some of these characteristics as well as some of the ways in which they vary and combine with each other. These characteristics must be situated with reference to a sort of "zero-degree" narratee, a concept which it is now time to define.

In the first place, the zero-degree narratee knows the tongue [*langue*] and the language(s) [*langage(s)*] of the narrator. In his case, to know a tongue is to know the meanings [dénotations] — the signifieds as such and, if applicable, the referents — of all the signs that constitute it; this does not include knowledge of the connotations (the subjective values that have been attached to them). It also involves a perfect mastery of grammar but not of the (infinite) paragrammatical possibilities. It is the ability to note semantic and/or syntactic ambiguities and to be able to resolve these difficulties from the context. It is the capacity to recognize the grammatical incorrectness or oddness of any sentence or syntagm — by reference to the linguistic system being used.[7]

Beyond this knowledge of language, the zero-degree narratee has certain faculties of reasoning that are often only the corollaries of this knowledge. Given a sentence or a series of sentences, he is able to grasp the presuppositions and the consequences.[8] The zero-degree narratee knows narrative grammar, the rules by which any story is elaborated.[9] He knows, for example, that a minimal complete narrative sequence consists in the passage from a given situation to the inverse situation. He knows that the narrative possesses a temporal dimension and that it necessitates relations of causality. Finally, the zero-degree narratee possesses a sure memory, at least in regard to the events of the narrative about which he has been informed and the consequences that can be drawn from them.

Thus, he does not lack positive characteristics. But he also does not want negative traits. He can thus only follow a narrative in a well-defined and concrete way and is obliged to acquaint himself with the events by reading from the first page to the last, from the initial word to the final word. In addition, he is without any personality or social characteristics. He is neither good nor bad, pessimistic nor optimistic, revolutionary nor bourgeois, and his character, his position in society, never colors his perception of the events described to him. Moreover, he knows absolutely nothing about the events or characters mentioned and he is not acquainted with the conventions prevailing in that world or in any other world. Just as he doesn't understand the connotations of a certain turn of phrase, he doesn't realize what can be evoked by this or that situation, this or that novelistic action. The consequences of this are very important. Without the assistance of the narrator, without his explanations and the information supplied by him, the narratee is able neither to interpret the value of an action nor to grasp its repercussions. He is incapable of determining the morality or immorality of a character, the realism or extravagance of a description, the merits of a rejoinder, the satirical intention of a tirade. And how would he be able to do so? By virtue of what experience, what knowledge, or what system of values?

More particularly, a notion as fundamental as verisimilitude only counts very slightly for him. Indeed, verisimilitude is always defined in relation to another text, whether this text be public opinion, the rules of a literary genre, or "reality." The zero-degree narratee, however, is acquainted with no texts and in the absence of commentary, the adventures of Don Quixote would seem as ordinary to him as those of Passemurailles (an individual capable of walking through walls) or of the protagonists of *Une Belle Journée*.[10] The same would hold true for relations of implicit causality. If I learn in *La Légende de Saint Julien l'Hospitalier* that "Julien believes he has killed his father and faints," I establish a causal relationship between these two propositions founded upon a certain commonsense logic, my experience of the world, and my knowledge of certain novelistic conventions. We are, moreover, aware that one of the mechanisms of the narrative process "is the confusion of consecutiveness and consequence, what comes *after* being read in the narrative as *caused by. . . .* "[11] But the narratee with no experience and no common sense does not perceive relations of implicit causality and does not fall victim to this confusion. Finally, the zero-degree narratee does not organize the narrative as a function of the major codes of reading studied by Roland Barthes in *S/Z*. He doesn't know how to unscramble the different voices that shape the narration. After all, as Barthes has said: "The code is a convergence of quotations, a structural mirage . . . the resulting units . . . made up of fragments of this something which always has *already* been read, seen, done, lived: the code is the groove of this *already*. Referring back to what has been written, that is, to the Book (of culture, of life, of life as culture), the code makes the text a prospectus of this Book."[12] For the zero-degree narratee, there is no *already*, there is no Book.

The Signals of the Narratee

Every narratee possesses the characteristics that we have enumerated except when an indication to the contrary is supplied in the narration intended for him: he knows, for example, the language employed by the narrator, he is gifted with an excellent memory, he is unfamiliar with everything concerning the characters who are presented to him. It is not rare that a narrative might deny or contradict these characteristics: a certain passage might underline the language-related difficulties of the narratee, another passage might disclose that he suffers from amnesia, yet another passage might emphasize his knowledge of the problems being discussed. It is on the basis of these deviations from the characteristics of the zero-degree narratee that the portrait of a specific narratee is gradually constituted.

Certain indications supplied by the text concerning a narratee are sometimes found in a section of the narrative that is not addressed to him. One has only to think of *L'Immoraliste,* the two *Justines,* or *Heart of Darkness* to verify that not only the physical appearance, the personality, and civil status of a narratee can be discussed in this fashion, but also his experience and his past. These indications may precede the portion of the narrative intended for the narratee, or may follow, interrupt, or frame it. Most often, they confirm what the rest of the narration has revealed to us. At the beginning of *L'Immoraliste,* for example, we learn that Michel has not seen his narratees for three years and the story he tells them quickly confirms this fact. Nonetheless, sometimes these indications contradict the narrative and emphasize certain differences between the narratee as conceived by the narrator and as revealed by another voice. The few words spoken by Doctor Spielvogel at the end of *Portnoy's Complaint* reveal that he is not what the narrative has led us to believe.[13]

Nevertheless, the portrait of a narratee emerges above all from the narrative addressed to him. If we consider that any narration is composed of a series of signals directed to the narratee, two major categories of signals can be distinguished. On the one hand there are those signals that contain no reference to the narratee or, more precisely, no reference differentiating him from the zero-degree narratee. On the other hand, there are those signals that, on the contrary, define him as a specific narratee and make him deviate from the established norms. In *Un Coeur simple* a sentence such as "She threw herself on the ground" would fall into the first category; this sentence reveals nothing in particular about the narratee while still permitting him to appreciate the sorrow of Félicité. On the contrary, a sentence such as "His entire person produced in her that confusion into which we are all thrown by the spectacle of extraordinary men" not only records the reactions of the heroine in the presence of M. Bourais, but also informs us that the narratee has experienced the same feelings in the presence of extraordinary individuals. By interpreting all signals of the narration as a function of the narratee, we can obtain a partial reading of the text, but a well-defined and reproducible reading. By regrouping and studying the signals of the second category, we can reconstruct the portrait of the narratee, a portrait more or less distinct, original, and complete depending upon the text considered.

The signals belonging to the second category are not always easy to recognize or to interpret. In fact, if many of them are quite explicit, others are much less so. The indications supplied on the narratee at the beginning of *Le Père Goriot* are very clear and present no problem: "That's what you will do, you who hold this book with a white hand, you who settle back in a well-padded armchair. . . . " But the first two sentences of *The Sun Also Rises* present more difficulty. Jake does not explicitly state that, according to his narratee, to say that a man has been a boxing champion is to express admiration for him. It is enough for him to imply this: "Robert Cohn was once middleweight boxing champion of Princeton. Do not think that I am very much impressed by that as a boxing title, but it meant a lot to Cohn." A greater number of indications concerning this or that narratee are even more indirect. Obviously, any indication, whether explicit or indirect, should be interpreted on the basis of the text itself, using as a guide the language employed, its presuppositions, the logical consequences that it entails, and the already established knowledge of the narratee.

The signals capable of portraying the narratee are quite varied and one can easily distinguish several types that are worth discussing. In the first place, we should mention all passages of a narrative in which the narrator refers directly to the narratee. We retain in this category statements in which the narrator designates the narratee by such words as "reader" or "listener" and by such expressions as "my dear" or "my friend." In the event that the narration may have identified a specific characteristic of the narratee, for example, his profession or nationality, passages mentioning this characteristic should also be considered in this first category. Thus, if the narratee is a lawyer, all information concerning lawyers in general is pertinent. Finally, we should retain all passages in which the addressee is designated by second-person pronouns and verb forms.

Besides those passages referring quite explicitly to the narratee, there are passages that, although not written in the second person, imply a narratee and describe him. When Marcel in *A la recherche du temps perdu* writes: "Besides, most often, we didn't stay at home, we went for a walk," the "we" excludes the narratee. On the contrary, when he declares: "Undoubtedly, in these coincidences which are so perfect, when reality withdraws and applies itself to what we have dreamt about for so long a time, it hides it from us entirely," the "we" includes the narratee.[14] Often an impersonal expression or an indefinite pronoun can only refer to the narratee: "But, the work completed, perhaps one will have shed a few tears *intra muros* and *extra*."

Then again, there are often numerous passages in a narrative that, though they contain apparently no reference — even an ambiguous one — to a narratee, describe him in greater or lesser detail. Accordingly, certain parts of a narrative may be presented in the form of questions or pseudo-questions. Sometimes these questions originate neither with a character nor with the narrator who merely repeats them. These questions must then be attributed to the narratee and we should note what excites his curiosity, the kinds of problems he would like to resolve. In *Le Père Goriot,* for example, it is the narratee who makes inquiries about the career of M. Poiret: "What had he been? But perhaps he had been employed at the Ministry of Justice. . . . " Sometimes, however, the narrator addresses questions to the narratee himself, some of whose knowledge and defenses are thus revealed in the process. Marcel will address a pseudo-question to his narratee asking him to explain the slightly vulgar, and for that reason surprising, behavior of Swann: "But who has not seen unaffected royal princesses . . . spontaneously adopt the language of old bores? . . . "

Other passages are presented in the form of negations. Certain of these passages are no more the extension of a given character's statement than they are the response to a given narrator's question. It is rather the beliefs of the narratee that these passages contradict, his preoccupations that are attacked, and his questions that are silenced. The narrator of *Les Faux-Monnayeurs* vigorously rejects the theory advanced by the narratee to explain Vincent Molinier's nocturnal departures: "No, it was not to his mistress that Vincent Molinier went each evening." Sometimes a partial negation can be revelatory. In *A la recherche du temps perdu,* the narrator, while believing that the narratee's conjectures about the extraordinary suffering of Swann are well founded, at the same time finds them insufficient: "This suffering which he felt resembled nothing he had ever thought possible. Not only because in his hours of deepest doubt he had rarely imagined anything so painful, but because even when he imagined this thing, it remained vague, uncertain. . . . ''

There are also passages that include a term with demonstrative significance that instead of referring to an anterior or ulterior element of the narrative, refers to another text, to extra-textual experience [*hors-texte*] known to the narrator and his narratee. "He looked at the tomb and there buried his final tear as a young man . . . one of those tears which though they fall to the earth flow upward to the heavens." From these few lines, the narratee of *Le Père Goriot* recognizes the kind of tears buried by Rastignac. He has certainly already heard about them, without a doubt he has seen them, perhaps he has shed some himself.

Comparisons or analogies found in a narration also furnish us with information more or less valuable. Indeed, the second term of a comparison is always assumed to be known better than the first. On this basis, we can assume that the narratee of *The Gold Pot,* for example, has already heard the bursting of thunder ("The voice faded like the faraway muffled rumbling of thunder"), and we can accordingly begin the partial reconstruction of the type of universe with which he is familiar.

But perhaps the most revelatory signals and at times the most difficult to grasp and describe in a satisfactory way are those we shall call — for lack of a more appropriate term — *over-justifications* [*sur-justifications*]. Any narrator more or less explains the world inhabited by his characters, motivates their acts, and justifies their thoughts. If it occurs that these explanations and motivations are situated at the level of meta-language, meta-commentary, or meta-narration, they are over-justifications. When the narrator of *La Chartreuse de Parme* advises the narratee that at La Scala "it's customary for visits to the boxes to last only twenty minutes or so," he is only thinking about supplying the narratee with information necessary for the understanding of the events. On the other hand, when he asks to be excused for a poorly phrased sentence, when he excuses himself for having to interrupt his narrative, when he confesses himself incapable of describing well a certain feeling, these are over-justifications that he employs. Over-justifications always provide us with interesting details about the narratee's personality, even though they often do so in an indirect way; in overcoming the narratee's defenses, in prevailing over his prejudices, in allaying his apprehensions, they reveal them.

The narratee's signals — those that describe him as well as those that only provide him with information — can pose many problems for the reader who would wish to classify them in order to arrive at a portrait of the narratee or a certain reading of the text. It's not simply a question of their being sometimes difficult to notice, to grasp, or to explain, but in certain narratives, one can find contradictory signals. Sometimes they originate with a narrator who wishes to amuse himself at the expense of the narratee or underscore the arbitrariness of the text; often the world presented is a world in which the principles of contradiction known to us don't exist or are not applicable; finally, the contradictions — the entirely obvious ones — often result from the different points of view that the narrator strives to reproduce faithfully. Nonetheless it occurs that not all contradictory data can be entirely explained in this fashion. In these cases, they should be attributed to the author's ineptness — or temperament. In many pornographic novels, in the worst as well as in the best, the narrator, like the heroes of *La Cantatrice chauve,* will first describe a character as having blond hair, large breasts, and a bulging stomach and then on the following page will speak with as much conviction of her black hair, her flat stomach, and her small breasts. Coherence is certainly not an imperative for the pornographic genre in which a wild variation is the rule rather than the exception. It nonetheless remains that in these cases, it is difficult — if not impossible — to interpret the semantic material presented to the narratee.

Sometimes it is the signals describing the narratee that form a strangely disparate collection. Indeed, every signal relating to a narratee need not continue or confirm a preceding signal or announce a signal to follow. There are narratees who change much as narrators do or who have a rich enough personality to embrace various tendencies and feelings. But the contradictory nature of certain narratees does not always result from a complex personality or a subtle evolution. The first pages of *Le Père Goriot* indicate that a Parisian narratee would be able to appreciate "the particularities of this scene full of local observations and color." But these opening pages contradict what they have just asserted in accusing the narratee of insensitivity and in judging him guilty of mistaking reality for fiction. This contradiction will never be resolved. On the contrary, other contradictions will be added and it will become more and more difficult to know whom the narrator addresses. A case of ineptitude? Perhaps Balzac does not worry about technical details and sometimes commits errors which in a Flaubert or a Henry James would be shocking. But this is a revelatory instance of ineptitude: Balzac, who is obsessed with problems of identity—these problems are certainly very important in *Le Père Goriot*—does not manage to decide who will be his narratee.

Despite the questions posed, the difficulties raised, the errors committed, it is evident that the kinds of signals used, their respective numbers, and their distribution determine to a certain extent the different types of narrative.[15] Narratives in which explanations and motivations abound (*Don Quixote* and *Tristram Shandy, Les Illusions perdues* and *Le Temps retrouvé*) are very different from those in which explanations and motivations play a limited role (*The Killers, The Maltese Falcon, La Jalousie*). The former are often by narrators who find the dimension of discourse [*discours*] more important than that of narrative [*récit*] or who are acutely aware of the gratuitousness—and even the falseness—of any narrative or of a certain type of narrative and consequently try to exorcise it. The latter are produced by narrators who feel perfectly at ease in the narrative [*récit*] or who, for different reasons, wish to be transported from their usual surroundings. Moreover, explanations and motivations can present themselves for what they are or, on the other hand, can dissimulate their nature by disguising themselves more or less completely. A narrator of Balzac or Stendhal does not hesitate to declare the necessity of explaining a thought, an act, or a situation. "We are obliged at this point to interrupt for a moment the story of this bold undertaking in order to supply an indispensable detail which will explain in part the duchess's courage in advising Fabrice upon this quite dangerous flight." But Flaubert's narrators—in particular after *Madame Bovary*—often play upon ambiguity and we no longer know exactly if one sentence explains another or if it merely follows or precedes it: "He assembled an army. It became bigger. He became famous. He was sought after." Explanations can also be presented in the form of universal rules or general laws as in Balzac and Zola or can avoid as much as possible all generality as in the novels of Sartre and Simone de Beauvoir. Explanations can contradict or confirm one another, be repeated or used a single time, appear only at strategic moments or occur anywhere in the narrative. Each time a different type of narration is constructed.

Classification of Narratees

Thanks to the signals describing the narratee, we are able to characterize any narration according to the type of narratee to whom it is addressed. It would be useless, because too long, too complicated, and too imprecise, to distinguish different categories of narratees according to their temperament, their civil status, or their beliefs. On the other hand, it would be comparatively easy to classify narratees according to their narrative situation, to their position in reference to the narrator, the characters, and the narration.

Many narrations appear to be addressed to no one in particular: no character is regarded as playing the role of narratee and no narratee is mentioned by the narrator either directly ("Without a doubt, dear reader, you have never been confined in a glass bottle") or indirectly ("We could hardly do otherwise than pluck one of its flowers and present it to the reader"). Just as a detailed study of a novel such as *L'Education sentimentale* or *Ulysses* reveals the presence of a narrator who tries to be invisible and to intervene as little as possible in the course of the events, so too a thorough examination of a narration that appears to have no narratee — the two works mentioned above as well as *Sanctuary, L'Etranger,* and *Un Coeur simple* — permits his discovery. The narrator of *Un Coeur simple,* for example, does not refer a single time to a narratee in an explicit manner. In his narrative, nonetheless, there are numerous passages indicating more or less clearly that he is addressing someone. It is thus that the narrator identifies the individuals whose proper names he mentions: "Robelin, the farmer from Geoffosses . . . Liébard, the farmer from Touques . . . M. Bourais, a former lawyer." It cannot be for himself that he identifies Robelin, Liébard, or M. Bourais; it must be for his narratee. Moreover, the narrator often resorts to comparisons in order to describe a character or situate an event, and each comparison defines more precisely the type of universe known to the narratee. Finally, the narrator sometimes refers to extra-textual experiences ("that confusion into which we are all thrown by the spectacle of extraordinary men"), which provide proof of the narratee's existence and information about his nature. Thus, even though the narratee may be invisible in a narration, he nonetheless exists and is never entirely forgotten.

In many other narrations, if the narratee is not represented by a character, he is at least mentioned explicitly by the narrator. The latter refers to him more or less frequently and his references can be quite direct (*Eugene Onegin, The Gold Pot, Tom Jones*) or quite indirect (*The Scarlet Letter, The Old Curiosity Shop, Les Faux-Monnayeurs*). Like the narratee of *Un Coeur simple,* these narratees are nameless and their role in the narrative is not always very important. Yet because of the passages that designate them in an explicit manner, it is easy to draw their portrait and to know what their narrator thinks of them. Sometimes, in *Tom Jones,* the narrator supplies so much information about his narratee, takes him aside so often, lavishes his advice upon him so frequently, that the latter becomes as clearly defined as any character.

Often instead of addressing — explicitly or implicitly — a narratee who is not a character, the narrator recounts his story to someone who is (*Heart of Darkness, Portnoy's Complaint, Les Infortunes de la vertu*). This character can be described in a more or less detailed manner. We know practically nothing about Doctor Spielvogel in *Portnoy's Complaint,* except that he is not lacking in perspicacity. On the other hand, in *Les Infortunes de la vertu,* we are informed about all of Juliette's life.

The narratee-character might play no other role in the narrative than that of narratee (*Heart of Darkness*). But he might also play other roles. It is not rare, for example, for him to be at the same time a narrator. In *L'Immoraliste,* one of the three individuals listening to Michel writes a long letter to his brother. In this letter, he repeats the story told to him by his friend, entreats his brother to shake Michel from his unhappiness, and records his own reactions to the narrative as well as the circumstances that led to his being present at its telling. Sometimes the narratee of a story can be at the same time its narrator. He doesn't intend the narration to be for anyone other than himself. In *La Nausée,* for example, as in most novels written in the form of a diary, Roquentin counts on being the only reader of his journal.

Then again, the narratee-character can be more or less affected, more or less influenced by the narrative addressed to him. In *Heart of Darkness,* the companions of Marlow are not transformed by the story that he recounts to them. In *L'Immoraliste,* the three narratees, if they are not really different from what they were before Michel's account, are nonetheless "overcome by a strange feeling of malaise." And in *La Nausée,* as in many other works in which the narrator constitutes his own narratee, the latter is gradually and profoundly changed by the events he recounts for himself.

Finally, the narratee-character can represent for the narration someone more or less essential, more or less irreplaceable as a narratee. In *Heart of Darkness,* it's not necessary for Marlow to have his comrades on the *Nellie* as narratees. He would be able to recount his story to any other group; perhaps he would be able to refrain from telling it at all. On the other hand, in *L'Immoraliste,* Michel wished to address his friends and for that reason gathered them around him. Their presence in Algeria holds out hope: they will certainly not condemn him, they will perhaps understand him, and they will certainly help him get over his current situation. And in *A Thousand and One Nights,* to have the caliph as narratee is the difference between life and death for Scheherazade. If he refuses to listen to her, she will be killed. He is thus the only narratee whom she can have.

Whether or not he assumes the role of character, whether or not he is irreplaceable, whether he plays several roles or just one, the narratee can be a listener (*L'Immoraliste, Les Infortunes de la vertu, A Thousand and One Nights*) or a reader (*Adam Bede, Le Père Goriot, Les Faux-Monnayeurs*). Obviously, a text may not necessarily say whether the narratee is a reader or a listener. In such cases, it could be said that the narratee is a reader when the narration is written (*Hérodias*) and a listener when the narration is oral (*La Chanson de Roland*).

. . . We could probably think of other distinctions or establish other categories, but in any case, we can see how much more precise and more refined the typology of narrative would be if it were based not only upon narrators but also upon narratees. The same type of narrator can address very different types of narratees. Thus, Louis (*Le Noeud de vipères*), Salavin (*Journal de Salavin*), and Roquentin (*La Nausée*) are three characters who all keep a journal and who are very conscious of writing. But Louis changes narratees several times before deciding to write for himself; Slavin does not regard himself as the sole reader of his journal; and Roquentin writes exclusively for himself. Then again, very different narrators can address narratees of the same type. The narrators of *Un Coeur simple* and *La Condition humaine* as well as Meursault in *L'Etranger* all address a narratee who is not a character, who doesn't know them and who is not familiar with the individuals presented in the text nor with the events recounted.

Nonetheless, it is not only for a typology of the narrative genre and for a history of novelistic techniques that the notion of the narratee is important. Indeed, this notion is more interesting, because it permits us to study better the way in which a narration functions. In all narrations, a dialogue is established between the narrator(s), the narratee(s), and the character(s).[16] This dialogue develops — and consequently the narration also — as a function of the distance separating them from each other. In distinguishing the different categories of narratees, we have already used this concept, but without dwelling upon it too much: it is clear that a narratee who has participated in the events recorded is, in one sense, much closer to the characters than a narratee who has never even heard of them. But the notion of distance should be generalized. Whatever the point of view adopted — moral, intellectual, emotional, physical — narrator(s), narratee(s), and character(s) can be more or less close to each other ranging from the most perfect identification to the most complete opposition.

. . . As there are often several narrators, several narratees, and several characters in a text, the complexity of the rapports and the variety of the distances that are established between them can be quite significant. In any case, these rapports and these distances determine to a great extent the way in which certain values are praised and others are rejected in the course of a narration and the way in which certain events are emphasized and others are nearly passed over in silence. They determine as well the tone and the very nature of the narration. In *Les Cloches de Bâle,* for example, the tone changes completely — and cannot but change — once the narrator decides to proclaim his friendship for the narratee and to speak to him more honestly and more directly than he had previously: abandoning romantic extravagance, he becomes quasi-documentary; leaving behind false detachment, he becomes brotherly. On the other hand, many ironic effects in narration depend upon the differences existing between two images of the narratee or between two (groups of) narratees (*Les Infortunes de la vertu, Werther*), upon the distance existing between narrator and narratee on the one hand and character on the other (*Un Amour de Swann*), or yet again upon the distance existing between narrator and narratee (*Tom Jones*). The complexity of a situation results sometimes from the instability of the distances existing between the narrator, the narratee, and the characters. If Michel's guilt — or innocence — is not clearly established, it is partly because several times he shows himself capable of overcoming the distance separating him from his friends, or, if one prefers, because his friends are unsure of how much distance to put between themselves and him. . . .

The Narratee's Functions

The type of narratee that we find in a given narrative, the relations that tie him to narrators, characters, and other narratees, the distances that separate him from ideal, virtual, or real readers partially determine the nature of this narrative. But the narratee exercises other functions that are more or less numerous and important and are more or less specific to him. It will be worth the effort to enumerate these functions and to study them in some detail.

The most obvious role of the narratee, a role that he always plays in a certain sense, is that of relay between the narrator and the reader(s), or rather between the author and the reader(s). Should certain values have to be defended or certain ambiguities clarified, this can easily be done by means of asides addressed to the narratee. Should the importance of a series of events be emphasized, should one reassure or make uneasy, justify certain actions or underscore their arbitrariness, this can always be done by addressing signals to the narratee. In *Tom Jones,* for example, the narrator explains to the narratee that prudence is necessary for the preservation of virtue, an explanation that allows us to judge better his hero, virtuous but imprudent: "Prudence and circumspection are necessary even to the best men. . . . It is not enough that your designs, nay, that your actions, are intrinsically good, you must take care they shall appear so." Likewise, we know that although Legrandin is a snob, he is not lying when he protests against snobbery because Marcel says quite clearly to his narratee: "And indeed, that doesn't mean that Legrandin was not sincere when he inveighed against snobs." Indeed, the mediation doesn't always operate that directly: thus, narrator-narratee relations are sometimes developed in the ironic mode and the reader cannot always interpret literally the statements of the former to the latter. There exist other conceivable relays than direct and explicit asides addressed to the narratee, other possibilities of mediation between authors and readers. Dialogues, metaphors, symbolic situations, allusions to a particular system of thought or to a certain work of art are some of the ways of manipulating the reader, guiding his judgments, and controlling his reactions. Moreover, those are the methods preferred by many modern novelists, if not the majority of them; perhaps because they accord or seem to accord more freedom to the reader, perhaps because they oblige him to participate more actively in the development of the narrative, or perhaps simply because they satisfy a certain concern for realism. The role of the narratee as mediator is rather reduced in these cases. Everything must still pass via the narratee since everything — metaphors, allusions, dialogues — is still addressed to him; but nothing is modified, nothing is clarified for the reader by this passage. Whatever the advantages may be of this type of mediator it should nonetheless be recognized that from a certain point of view, direct and explicit statements by the narrator to the narratee are the most economical and the most effective sort of mediation. A few sentences suffice to establish the true significance of an unexpected act or the true nature of a character; a few words suffice to facilitate the interpretation of a complex situation. Although we can question indefinitely Stephen's esthetic maturity in *Portrait of the Artist as a Young Man* or the significance of a particular act in *A Farewell to Arms,* we always know exactly — or almost always — according to the text, what to think of Fabrice and la Sanseverina or of the intrigues of Mlle. Michonneau.[17]

Besides the function of mediation, the narratee exercises in any narration a function of characterization. . . . In the case of narrator-characters, the function of characterization is important although it can be reduced to a minimum even here: because he is at a distance from everything and from himself, because his strangeness and solitude depend upon this distance, Meursault would not know how to engage in a true dialogue with his narratee and, thus, cannot be described by this dialogue. Nonetheless, the relations that a narrator-character establishes with his narratee reveal as much — if not more — about his character than any other element in the narrative. In *La Religeuse,* Sister Suzanne, because of her conception of the narratee and her asides addressed to him, emerges as much less naive and much more calculating and coquettish than she would like to appear.

. . . Moreover, the relations between the narrator and the narratee in a text may underscore one theme, illustrate another, or contradict yet another. Often the theme refers directly to the narrative situation and it is the narration as theme that these relations reveal. In *A Thousand and One Nights,* for instance, the theme of narration as life is emphasized by the attitude of Scheherazade toward the caliph and vice versa: the heroine will die if her narratee decides not to listen to her any more, just as other characters in the narrative die because he will not listen to them: ultimately, any narrative is impossible without a narratee. But often, themes that do not concern the narrative situation — or perhaps concern it only indirectly — reveal the positions of the narrator and the narratee in relation to each other. In *Le Père Goriot,* the narrator maintains relations of power with his narratee. From the very beginning, the narrator tries to anticipate his narratee's objections, to dominate him, and to convince him. All means are used: the narrator coaxes, entreats, threatens, derides, and in the final analysis we suspect that he succeeds in getting the better of his narratee. In the last part of the novel, when Vautrin has been put in prison and Goriot is advancing more and more quickly toward death, the narrator rarely addresses his narratee. This is because the narrator has won the battle. He is now sure of his effects, of his domination, and he need no longer do anything but recount the story. This sort of war, this desire for power, can be found at the level of the characters. On the level of the events as well as on the level of narration, the same struggle takes place.

If the narratee contributes to the thematic of a narrative, he is also always part of the narrative framework, often of a particularly concrete framework in which the narrator(s) and narratee(s) are all characters (*Heart of Darkness, L'Immoraliste, The Decameron*). The effect is to make the narrative seem more natural. The narratee like the narrator plays an undeniable *verisimilating* [*vraisemblabilisant*] role. Sometimes this concrete framework provides the model by which a work or narration develops. In *The Decameron* or in *L'Heptameron,* it is expected that each of the narratees will in turn become a narrator. More than a mere sign of realism or an index of verisimilitude, the narratee represents in these circumstances an indispensable element for the development of the narrative.

. . . Finally it sometimes happens that we must study the narratee in order to discover a narrative's fundamental thrust. In *La Chute,* for example, it is only by studying the reactions of Clamence's narratee that we can know whether the protagonist's arguments are so powerful that they cannot be resisted, or whether, on the contrary, they constitute a skillful but unconvincing appeal. To be sure, the narratee doesn't say a single word throughout the entire novel and we don't even know if Clamence addresses himself or someone else: we only understand, from the narrator's remarks, that his narratee, like himself, is a bourgeois, in his forties, a Parisian, familiar with Dante and the Bible, a lawyer. . . . Nevertheless, this ambiguity emphasizing the essential duplicity of the protagonist's world does not represent a problem for the reader who would wish to discover the way in which Clamence is judged in the novel: whatever the identity of the narratee may be, the only thing that counts is the extent of his agreement with the theses of the hero. The latter's discourse shows evidence of a more and more intense resistance on the part of his interlocutor. Clamence's tone becomes more insistent and his sentences more embarrassed as his narrative progresses and his narratee escapes him. Several times in the last part of the novel he even appears seriously shaken. If at the end of *La Chute* Clamence is not defeated, he certainly has not been triumphant. If his values and his vision of the world and men are not entirely false, neither are they incontestably true. There are perhaps other professions than that of judge-penitent and there are perhaps other acceptable ways to live than Clamence's.

The narratee can, thus, exercise an entire series of functions in a narrative: he constitutes a relay between the narrator and the reader, he helps establish the narrative framework, he serves to characterize the narrator, he emphasizes certain themes, he contributes to the development of the plot, he becomes the spokesman for the moral of the work. Obviously, depending upon whether the narrator is skillful or inept, depending upon whether or not problems of narrative technique interest him, and depending upon whether or not his narrative requires it, the narratee will be more or less important, will play a greater or lesser number of roles, will be used in a way more or less subtle and original. Just as we study the narrator to evaluate the economy, the intentions, and the success of a narrative, so too we should examine the narratee in order to understand further and/or differently its mechanisms and significance.

The narratee is one of the fundamental elements of all narration. The thorough examination of what he represents, the study of a narrative work as constituted by a series of signals addressed to him, can lead to a more sharply delineated reading and a deeper characterization of the work. The study can lead also to a more precise typology of the narrative genre and a greater understanding of its evolution. It can provide a better appreciation of the way a narrative functions and a more accurate assessment of its success from a technical point of view. In the final analysis, the study of the narratee can lead us to a better understanding not only of the narrative genre but of all acts of communication.

Notes

1. See, for example, Henry James, *The Art of Fiction and Other Essays,* ed. Morris Roberts (New York: Oxford University Press, 1948); Norman Friedman, "Point of View in Fiction: The Development of a Critical Concept," *PMLA* 70 (Dec. 1955): 1160–84; Wayne C. Booth, *The Rhetoric of Fiction* (Chicago: University of Chicago Press, 1961); Tzvetan Todorov, "Poetique," in Oswald Ducrot et al., *Qu'est-ce que le structuralisme?* (Paris: Seuil, 1968), pp. 97–166; and Gérard Genette, *Figures,* vol. 3 (Paris: Seuil, 1972).

2. See, among others, Walker Gibson, "Authors, Speakers, Readers, and Mock Read-

ers," *College English* 9 (Feb. 1950): 265–69; Roland Barthes, "Introduction à l'analyse structurale des récits," *Communications* 8 (1966): 18–19; Tzvetan Todorov, "Les Categories du récit litteraire," *Communications* 8 (1966): 146–47; Gerald Prince, "Notes Towards a Categorization of Fictional 'Narratees,'" *Genre* 4 (March 1971): 100–105; and Genette, *Figures,* vol. 3, pp. 265–67.

3. In a certain sense, every narrator is his own narratee. But most narrators have other narratees as well.

4. See Tzvetan Todorov, "Les Hommes-récits," in *Poétique de la prose* (Paris: Seuil, 1971), pp. 78–91.

5. See Tzvetan Todorov, "Le Récit primitif," in ibid., pp. 66–77.

6. For convenience' sake, we speak (and will speak often) of readers. It is obvious that a narratee should not be mistaken for a listener — real, virtual, or ideal.

7. This description of the linguistic capabilities of the zero-degree narratee nonetheless raises many problems. Thus, it is not always easy to determine the meaning(s) [*dénotation(s)*] of a given term and it becomes necessary to fix in time the language [*langue*] known to the narratee, a task that is sometimes difficult when working from the text itself. In addition, the narrator can manipulate a language in a personal way. Confronted by certain idiosyncrasies that are not easy to situate in relation to the text, do we say that the narratee experiences them as exaggerations, as errors, or on the contrary do they seem perfectly normal to him? Because of these difficulties and many others as well, the description of the narratee and his language cannot always be exact. It is, nevertheless, to a large extent reproducible.

8. We use these terms as they are used in modern logic.

9. See in this regard, Gerald Prince, *A Grammar of Stories: An Introduction* (The Hague: Mouton, 1973). A formal description of the rules followed by all narratives can be found in this work.

10. On verisimilitude, see the excellent *Communications* 11 (1968).

11. Barthes, "Introduction à l'analyse structurale des récits," p. 10. It should be noted that while this confusion has been very much exploited, it is not at all necessary for the development of a narrative.

12. Roland Barthes, *S/Z* (Paris: Seuil, 1970), pp. 27–28.

13. We should undoubtedly distinguish the "virtual" narratee from the "real" narratee in a more systematic manner. But this distinction would perhaps not be very helpful.

14. Note that even an "I" can designate a "you."

15. See, in this regard, Gérard Genette, "Vraisemblance et motivation," in his *Figures,* vol. 2 (Paris: Seuil, 1969).

16. We follow here in modifying the perspective, Booth, *The Rhetoric of Fiction,* pp. 155ff.

17. See Booth, ibid.

Observing that " 'realism' seems to be a term from which there is no escaping in discussions of fiction, even now," George Levine sets out to redefine fictional realism. He notes that the term did not arise until the mid-nineteenth century, and that its short life has produced the strong counterreactions of modernism and the "self-consciously anti-realistic literature" of postmodernism, both of which are reactions against the idealist Victorian portrayal of reality. Levine argues, however, that despite its anti-realistic surface, "the idea that literature should be describing reality or truth is implicitly present still" in modern fiction.

To understand this apparent discrepancy between a commitment to reality and a rejection of realism, we must first distinguish between realism as a historical literary method and realism as an ideal. Understood in the first sense, realism "reflects both inherited conventions and a way of looking at the world, a metaphysic, as it were. It implies certain assumptions about the nature of the real world, assumptions which need not be made explicit in any realistic text but which certainly constitute a ground of meaning." By "a ground of meaning," Levine means that a fiction may be viewed as realistic in terms related to the author's effort to render observable details accurately, or in terms of the audience's comparison of the fiction's content with its own perception of social reality. When speaking of realism, Levine argues, we are therefore talking about how a work's content relates to a "dominant and shared notion of reality in operation," developed in contrast to "older and currently unsatisfying" conventions, and a consensus that "moral value" inheres in "the representation of that reality."

In order to move beyond this consensual conception of reality, Levine proposes ten assumptions to guide his discussion of realism, the paramount one, repeated first and last, being that "all fiction is fiction." This dictum can be understood as asserting that the beauty of art arises from imaginative lying: "The emphasis on lying should remind us of how much our admiration of great fictions depends not on their recording of life but on their creation of it through language and of how deeply all fiction is indebted to literature and its tradition." Levine carefully qualifies this remark by adding that "the pressures on literary form come not only from literary tradition but from the form of each writer's belief in the nature of reality." The issue, then, lies not in whether literature creates reality or reality creates literature, but in understanding how the two influence and alter each other, as in the case of the modernists, who both encouraged and reflected a rejection of Victorian values.

George Levine (b. 1931) is Professor of English at Rutgers University. In addition to editing several books, he has authored *The Boundaries of Fiction: Carlyle, Macaulay, Newman* (1968) and *The Realistic Imagination: English Fiction from Frankenstein to Lady Chatterley* (1981).

Realism would seem now to be a tired subject, and to revive it is to risk repetition and boredom. Unfortunately, however, the word "realism" is only tired, not dead, and whatever it refers to seems also more or less alive; certainly the problems raised by its meaning in literary contexts persist. In England there has been a continuous tradition of realistic writing, most recently in self-conscious repudiation of various modes of modernism, and in a very recent book David Lodge comes close to insisting on the almost precise overlap between realism and the novel as a form. Since, moreover, his point is to prove that the novel is not dead, he is also obliged to prove that realism, too, lives.[1] In any case, "realism" seems to be a term from which there is no escaping in discussions of fiction, even now.

It is, of course, a commonplace of criticism that "realism" is an elusive word, that it has been recklessly and carelessly used; but despite some very serious efforts, it has been impossible, finally, either to provide it with a consistently precise definition or to banish it. Even to argue that it describes a kind of phantom, something that is not and never has been, is to affirm a fairly comfortable position which has long since lost its shock value.[2] But it is important to note that the word has a relatively short history in English, appearing for the first time somewhere in the middle of the nineteenth century; and it developed, for the purposes of English fiction, on an analogy with French fiction.[3] And the very fiction it was used to describe — that, for instance, of Thackeray, or Mrs. Gaskell, or George Eliot — is regarded by modern artists as profoundly unrealistic in the sense that it surrendered to the happy ending and to coincidence, that it consistently omitted certain aspects of reality, that it tended to assume an intelligible universe.[4]

Part of the modern growth of self-consciously anti-realistic literature and criticism has surely been the result of a rejection of Victorian conceptions of reality, but the idea that literature should be describing reality or truth is implicitly present still. The most interesting fiction of our day frequently seems to be game-playing, to be enjoying — as in Borges, Barth, and Nabokov — the possibilities of language and pleasures of literary parody. But the games themselves, while suggesting powerfully the writers' consciousness of the way verbal structures intervene between us and reality, provide for us new possibilities of reality. Reality has become problematic in ways the Victorians could only barely imagine, yet much of the energy of modern fiction comes from sources similar to those which directed earlier realism: from a conscious rejection of the notions of reality implicit in earlier fictions and from a sense of the limits of the power of language to render reality at all. The method of Robbe-Grillet, as he himself has made clear, is an attempt to get more precise about reality as it is experienced by human consciousness.[5] With this notion of changing realities in mind, we can, moreover, make some sense of Erich Auerbach's treatment of Virginia Woolf as a great culmination of the tradition of literary realism.

Most of the confusions about the word "realism," I would argue, come from an initial confusion between an historically definable literary method and a more general (perhaps inescapable) attempt to be faithful to the real. Since reality is both inexhaustible and perpetually changing to human consciousness, the word "realism" had no chance of a stable meaning. Despite all its dangers, the word has the one virtue of forcing us to wrestle with some of the central problems of criticism and of art.

The question it poses initially is, not so simply, whether literature in any sense describes the real, extra-literary world. And that question, of course, leads to others: is it the function of literature to record reality or to illuminate, even create, new possibilities? What value can there be in a mere record of reality? Is it possible to render reality when perception can never be pure and the medium of language seems inevitably to influence its subject?[6] How can one judge literature on the basis of its fidelity to the real when the real itself is so elusive and variable? Questions like these are the province of philosophy and aesthetics, but they must enter into criticism, and they certainly underlie most of our assumptions of value. Every literary generation has to struggle with them, though I do not propose here to do so directly. Although much of what I say will remain at a high and dangerous level of abstraction, what I want to do here is help toward the development of a critical approach to fiction which will at once deal with our immediate or naive sense that fiction is somehow like life, that appropriate terms of judgment can be found in the comparison of fiction to what really happens in life, that the novel is the most mixed of literary forms and there-fore the one most responsive to extra-literary pressures, and with our more literary awareness of fiction as a structure of language working out from earlier structures and profoundly limited by the medium of language itself.

My bias, then, is historical, and I am convinced that criticism of fiction would profit from a fuller and more precise sense both of the traditions of the novel and of the changes in sensibility and perception which have affected those traditions. In its only even relatively precise sense, realism is an historical phenomenon, a literary method (or methods) rather than a literary or metaphysical ideal. Obviously, the second notion influenced the first, and historically speaking it is fair to say that writers thought that in adopting realism as a technique they were in fact moving closer to the truth. What is interesting here is that at one point in European history writers should have become so self-conscious about truth-telling in art (which I take to imply the growth of doubt about art in society) that they were led to raise truth-telling to the level of doctrine and to imply that previous literatures had not been telling it. Surely this is an important development in intellectual and cultural history, but surely, too, criticism is misled which works on the assumption that realistic novels — those of George Eliot, say — represent real life more accurately than do the narra-tives of Milton, or Melville, or even Fielding.

So extraordinary a book as Auerbach's *Mimesis* can itself be taken as fostering the confusion by implying that Western literature has been mov-ing constantly toward a finer and finer approximation to reality. If we read the book in that way, we can fall into the trap of assuming that there is some sort of absolute reality toward which artistic consciousness, in a kind of Hegelian dialectical movement, is progressively moving. Auerbach's great value lies not in his treatment of Virginia Woolf as the greatest "realist" because her techniques most precisely record the nature of psy-chological reality and the flux of experience, but in his wonderful treat-ment of the various styles of writers as they attempt to deal with new versions of reality, and in his implied assumption that the language of each writer creates the new reality. Perhaps the most fruitful approach to the problem is suggested by E. H. Gombrich's *Art and Illusion,*[7] a book which deals with the way in which artistic creation and audience perception are controlled by the conventions for the representation of reality within art and society. Artists have taught us to *see* differently; the way we see is culturally conditioned, so that lines suggesting depth to us may seem mere lines to those living in a different culture.[8]

Realism, like any literary method, reflects both inherited conventions and a way of looking at the world, a metaphysic, as it were. It implies certain assumptions about the nature of the real world, assumptions which need not be made explicit in any realistic text but which certainly constitute a ground of meaning. Among other things, it has, surely, implied that ordinariness is more real — at least more representative and therefore truthful — than heroism, that people are morally mixed rather than either good or bad, that the firmest realities are objects rather than ideas or imaginings. English realism, the type with which I will be most directly concerned, tended, moreover, to assume that the real is both meaningful and good, while French realism has consistently tended away from such moral assumptions to lead more directly to the notion of an indifferent universe and to that even more specialized kind of realism, naturalism.

Whatever the specific assumptions, one way to deal with the problem of realism is to locate those assumptions and to identify the conventions (including, in particular, assumptions about how literature ought to be affecting its audience). When a literary method comes to be called realistic it tends to imply several things: first, that there is a dominant and shared notion of reality in operation, upon which the writer and his audience can rely; second, that this notion is self-consciously replacing an older and currently unsatisfying one which is open to parody and rejection; third, that there is moral value (to be debated by those who continue to defend the older notion) in the representation of that reality. This obviously leads to confusions because the argument seems not to be about the nature of literary technique but about the nature of reality. Such confusion is redoubled by literary debates over whether, even if the artist's version of reality is accurate, the recording of that reality is rightfully the function of art. Much nineteenth-century criticism of realistic writers — of such different ones as George Eliot and Zola — was precisely of this kind. As Linda Nochlin suggests, such criticism assumed that writers "were doing no more than mirroring every-day reality. These statements derived from the belief that perception could be 'pure' and unconditioned by time or place."[9]

Just as realism implies certain metaphysical or quasi-metaphysical assumptions, so does criticism of it. In order to proceed with my argument, I need at this point to make clear as well as I can the assumptions upon which my analysis will — more or less ingenuously — be based. For economy's sake, I lay them out in propositional form, although they have not the rigor of philosophical argument. I do intend them as a coherent and gradually developing argument but believe it possible to accept some of the propositions without accepting all that precede or follow. I should, furthermore, preface them with two qualifying remarks: first, that the ideas apply most directly to the classical tradition of the nineteenth-century English novel (although I do believe them applicable, with some qualifications, to all fiction); and second, that like all truisms mine appear to me to be debatable or, at least, occasionally to disguise what is moot by leaving key words incompletely defined. At the risk then of either banality or obfuscation, let me begin.

1. All fiction is fiction.
2. All fiction emerges from the consciousness of the individual writer and is therefore shaped in the way that consciousness perceives.

   2a. The writer's consciousness will necessarily be deeply involved in the shared assumptions of his culture and in at least some of the traditions of fictional form.[10]

   2b. The writer's perceptions as well as his language will be largely controlled by these assumptions in combination with his private psychological needs.

3. The basic materials of fiction are words, and words are the means by which each consciousness constructs and orders its world and by which each private world is made shareable.

   3a. Words, as implied in 2a, are invested with the assumptions and history of the culture.

   3b. Words inevitably carry not only the burden of description (and perception) but the burden of value. A change in language implies a change both in perceptions and values — and, concomitantly, a change in the forms of fiction.

4. The fundamental form of fiction is, therefore, the working out in language of the possibilities imaginable by the writer in the direction of the most complete shareable fulfillment of his values.

   4a. Mimetic language, the language of "realistic" fiction, explores not only the possibilities of what is but the possibilities of what should be (as limited by the shareable assumptions implicit in the language, the culture, and the writer's mind).

   4b. Insofar as the descriptive and prescriptive tendencies of language and fiction are separable, the descriptive tends toward disorder, the prescriptive toward order, the one to integrity of detail, the other to coherence of design.[11]

5. The predominating energy in most fiction, however discursive, episodic, or apparently formless, is not the representation of reality but the shaping of the rendered experience. It is, in other words, formal, and manifests itself traditionally in plot, but also — as new critical analyses have suggested — in patterns of imagery, motifs, relationships.[12]

6. If romance can be stipulatively defined as a form in which pattern dominates over plausibility, in which the central figure achieves the fullest possible freedom from the limitations of a restricting context, in which ideal values are worked out and shown to be viable, romance is the underlying form of most fiction, whatever its ostensible mode.

6a. Romance is the translation of the writer's perceptions into narrative, that is, the imposition of form on experience.

6b. The imposition of form on experience is the mode by which literary conventions are transmitted. Curiously, the most intense and personal feelings and perceptions tend to take the most formally recognizable shapes. In Frye's convincing paradoxical formulation: "It has been a regular rule that the uninhibited imagination, in the structural sense, produces highly conventional art."[13]

6c. Romance is also the mode by which the particular psychic needs of the writer are most directly placed, as imaginative projections, in narrative.

7. Although novels may aspire to create the illusion of reality and to tell the truth, the most fruitful direct approach to fiction is through a focus on romance elements, the romance being the generator of form.

8. Form in any given novel is meaning since it determines the relations of the surface elements.

9. Patterning is the distinctive quality of fiction and of language, the material of fiction; and patterning is a reflection of the translation of experience into mind and feeling.

9a. There is no such thing as raw experience, since that implies some kind of experience undisturbed and unmodified — by mind or feeling.

9b. Fictional language differs from nonfictional rather in the degree to which engagement imposes meaning than in any formal way. Realism attempts to create the illusion of nonfiction as the writer struggles to come to terms with, as Frye puts it, "things as they are and not as the story-teller would like them to be for his convenience."[14]

10. All fiction is fiction.

Such abstract speculation on truth, reality, and perception is likely to miss out on the most obvious fact about fiction — its special power to amuse and engage us through narrative, to arouse expectations and provide satisfying resolutions.[15] And it is for this reason, among others, that I have insisted on the fictionality of fiction. Fiction is shaping, giving precedence to form over reality and even plausibility, when necessary.[16] It is the working out of imaginings and desires and needs, and its form is an expression of these. Traditionally, literature was taken as being both sweet and useful, *dulce et utile*. But the realist aesthetic tends to subsume both of these under the heading "form" as opposed to that of "truth." And a good part of the energy of English realist art was devoted to attempting to make it possible to combine the sweet and useful with the truthful.

By the end of the nineteenth century the difficulty of such an enterprise was clear. Oscar Wilde's wonderfully satiric and intelligent dialogue "The Decay of Lying" is a rich assertion of my rather more pallid propositions 4 through 4b, an attack on the conventions of realism dominating at the time and a recognition of an apparent incompatibility between form (coherence of design) and truth (integrity of detail). "What Art really reveals to us is Nature's lack of design," says Vivian.[17] The whole dialogue comes to equate imagination with lying, or, to put the better face on it, lying with imagination. It argues that what we value in art is the lying, not the mundane recording of a patternless and unattractive universe. "It is always the unreadable that occurs," Vivian says.[18] In this and the companion dialogue, "The Artist as Critic," Wilde suggests how the liar actually creates reality for us, although he would never allow himself so solemn a formulation. Wilde (or Vivian) goes on to suggest the virtues (heaven help us) of lying, and in so doing links together — beautifully for my purposes — the notion of entertainment, lying, imagination, and creativity:

For the aim of the liar is simply to charm, to delight, to give pleasure. He is the very basis of civilized society, and without him a dinner party, even at the mansions of the great, is as dull as a lecture at the Royal Society. . . . Nor will he be welcomed by society alone. Art, breaking from the prison-house of realism, will run to greet him, and will kiss his false, beautiful lips, knowing that he alone is in possession of the great secret of all her manifestations, the secret that Truth is entirely and absolutely a matter of style; while Life — poor, probable, uninteresting human life — tired of repeating herself for the benefit of Mr. Herbert Spencer, scientific historians, and the compilers of statistics in general, will follow meekly after him, and try to produce, in her own simple and untutored way, some of the marvels of which he talks.[19]

This is no joke.

The emphasis on lying should remind us of how much our admiration of great fictions depends not on their recording of life but on their creation of it through language and of how deeply all fiction is indebted to literature and its traditions: "Art," says Wilde, "finds her own perfection within, and not outside of, herself. She is not to be judged by any external standard of resemblance. She is a veil rather than a mirror."[20] This is a happier way of putting Frye's assertion that "literary shape cannot come from life; it comes only from literary tradition."

At the very least, these ideas seem valid in arguing that fiction is not to be judged "by any external standard of resemblance." Much of the weakness of criticism of the great novels in the central tradition of nineteenth-century realistic fiction is a result of the tendency to judge by such an external standard. We can see quite clearly now that disparagement of the "spontaneous combustion" episode in *Bleak House* because such things do not happen, or of the fairy-tale quality of *Jane Eyre* because it is mere wish fulfillment, is entirely beside the point of the special qualities of those books. To criticize in this way is to equate "realism" with "truth," and with "truth" as we happen to define it. Surely, the relation between art and truth is more complicated and interesting than that.

Of course, it will not do to dismiss entirely the mimetic element in the language of realism and simply to assimilate realism to romance. Frye is surely oversimplifying when he says that "literary shape cannot come from life," even though he means here overall structure rather than local detail. The pressures on literary form come not only from literary tradition but from the form of each writer's belief in the nature of reality. That this form is culturally influenced does not mean that it is exclusively shaped by literature — as witness, for example, the literary effects of *The Origin of Species*. The realistic method does develop out of conventions of empiricism. In her extremely interesting qualification of the views of Gombrich, Linda Nochlin, accepting our view that realism is an historically locatable technique rather than a direct expression of truth, points out that "if one takes the opposition between convention and empirical observation in art as a relative rather than an absolute criterion, one can see that in Realism the role played by observation is greater, that by convention smaller."[21] As an example, she shows how Constable, though he based his paintings of clouds partly on the work of Alexander Cozzens, an eighteenth-century engraver, nevertheless painted clouds as *he* saw them, and they are readily identifiable as to type, where Cozzens's clouds are not. I would argue, moreover, that the commitment to what was taken as observed reality significantly reshaped the larger structures and subject matters of fiction.

Yet patterning remains the distinctive quality of fiction, and it is with this patterning that novelists must, finally, come to terms, even if one of their initial motives is the telling of truth. For the truth must be the truth as they see it and in a mode whose traditions themselves entail a shape. The history of the novel in English from Defoe to the present reveals the dominance of "lying" in the convention of realism itself. Realism has been only one of the novel's modes, though a central mode, and its pressures have led the novelist to struggle — through all its transformations — to deal with "things as they are" rather than as he "would like them to be for his own convenience." But the struggle was never quite won because the obstacles realism itself created to the writers' imaginative needs led, inevitably, to its abandonment or at least radical revision. There developed a recognition, which we can see in Hardy, Conrad, Virginia Woolf, and others around the turn of the century, that things as they are are themselves a convention, and that the convention was a peculiarly painful one.

Notes

1. David Lodge, *The Novelist at the Crossroads* (London: Cornell University Press, 1971), p. 4.
2. For a discussion of the confusions surrounding the word realism see Erich Heller, "The Realistic Fallacy," *Listener* 53 (May 19, 1955): 188–89. Reprinted in George Becker, *Documents of Literary Realism* (Princeton: Princeton University Press, 1967). Heller suggests the emptiness of the word, as does my "Realism, or, In Praise of Lying: Some Nineteenth Century Novels," *College English* 31 (Jan. 1970): 355–65.
3. The word seems to have been borrowed from the French in the 1850s. See Richard Stang, *The Theory of the Novel in England, 1850–1870* (New York: Columbia University Press, 1959), p. 145; and two essays to which Stang alludes, R. G. Davis, "The Sense of the Real in English Fiction," *Comparative Literature* 3 (Summer 1951): 200–217; and "Balzac and His Writings," *Westminster Review* 60 (July 1853): 199–214. The latter essay still seems to assume a naive realism, but its brief discussion of the term is useful in suggesting — correctly — the close connection between realism and romanticism.
4. The most obvious and popular recent example of the attitude is in John Fowles's

The French Lieutenant's Woman; but, of course, while rejecting naive notions of realism and insisting instead on imaginative reality, Fowles exploits Victorian realistic techniques and writes a new best-seller.

5. Alain Robbe-Grillet, *Pour un nouveau roman* (Paris: Editions de Minuit, 1955). At one point he says, "Tous les écrivains pensent être realistes," and after a brief discussion he argues that "on doit conclure que tous ont raison" (p. 135).

6. See Linda Nochlin, *Realism* (Harmondsworth, Middlesex: Penguin, 1971): "The commonplace notion that Realism is a 'styleless' or transparent style, a mere simulacrum or mirror image of visual reality, is another barrier to its understanding as an historical and stylistic phenomenon. This is a gross simplification, for Realism was no more a mere mirror of reality than any other style, and its relation *qua* style to phenomenal data—the donnée—is as complex and difficult as that of Romanticism, the Baroque or Mannerism" (p. 14).

7. Ernst Gombrich, *Art and Illusion* (London: Phaidon Press, 1960). No summary can begin to cope with the argument of this brilliant book. Some of its orientation, however, is suggested by one key sentence: "Art is born of art, not of nature" (p. 21).

8. Linda Nochlin's book (see n. 6, above) is in part an attempt to qualify Gombrich's argument by showing that although realism is conventional, it differs from other conventions in its commitment to empirical truth: "It was not until the nineteenth century that contemporary ideology came to equate belief in the facts with the total content of belief itself; it is in this the crucial difference lies between nineteenth century Realism and all its predecessors" (p. 45).

9. Nochlin, *Realism,* p. 14.

10. See Lucien Goldmann, *The Human Sciences and Philosophy,* trans. Hayden White and Robert Anchor (London: Jonathan Cape, 1969): "Every manifestation is the work of its individual author and expresses his thought and way of feeling, but these ways of thinking and feeling are not independent entities with respect to the actions and behaviour of other men. They exist and may be understood only in terms of their inter-subjective relations which give them their whole tenor and richness" (p. 128). See also Henry James, "The Art of Fiction," p. 15 in this volume: "A novel is in its broadest definition a personal, a direct impression of life." Gombrich, however, writes, "If art were only, or merely, an expression of personal vision, there could be no history of art" (p. 4).

11. On points 4a and 4b Northrop Frye's essay "Myth, Fiction, and Displacement," in *Fables of Identity* (New York: Harcourt, Brace and World, 1963), is particularly helpful, and I should confess to a deep debt to its arguments, which have provoked (in both senses) much of my most recent thinking on the subject. Frye argues that "the realistic writer soon finds that the requirements of literary form and plausible content always fight against each other" (p. 36). The entire essay brilliantly explores the difference between imagination as a creative and structural power and imagination as a reproductive power, between "recognition of credibility, fidelity to experience," in fiction, and

"recognition of the identity of total design." In Frye's terms, art "deals, not with the world that man contemplates, but with the world that man creates" (p. 31). When art " 'imitates' nature it assimilates nature to human forms," a point not very different from the one that I am making. But Frye makes too sharp a distinction between literature and life by making too sharp a distinction between credibility and coherence.

12. Complicated qualifications would have to be made here because recent developments in fiction have self-consciously rejected or parodied the traditions of the great realistic novels of the nineteenth century. My major concern here is with the classical novel, from Richardson to Lawrence, but I would be prepared to argue that even for fictions like those of Nabokov, Barth, Butor, or Robbe-Grillet, this assertion is applicable.

13. Frye, "Myth, Fiction, and Displacement," p. 27.

14. Ibid.

15. See Sheldon Sacks, *Fiction and the Shape of Belief* (Chicago: University of Chicago Press, 1964). Sacks discusses the way in which genre imposes directions on narrative structure.

16. The traditional English realistic novel tended to work itself out so that the audience's aroused expectations would be satisfied by at least some rough poetic justice, usually distributed by virtue of appropriate coincidences. As an aspect of a changing vision of reality, the fiction of writers so different as Hardy and Zola tended, whether by coincidence or circumstantially realistic patterning, to make the absence of poetic justice precisely the aesthetic point of their fictions. The revised reality produced a revised aesthetic with its own kind of perversely satisfying resolutions and satisfactions. See Kenneth Graham's discussion of Zola as a romancer in *English Criticism of the Novel 1865–1900* (London: Oxford University Press, 1965), pp. 56–61.

17. "The Decay of Living," reprinted in Richard Ellmann, ed., *The Artist as Critic: Critical Writings of Oscar Wilde* (New York: Random House, 1968), p. 290.

18. Ellmann, ibid., p. 292.

19. Ibid., p. 305.

20. Ibid., p. 319.

21. Nochlin, *Realism*, p. 18.

Nonnarrated Stories

In his structuralist work *Story and Discourse: Narrative Structure in Fiction and Film* (1978), Seymour Chatman poses a crucial distinction between types of narrative statements: "Is the statement directly presented to the audience or is it mediated by someone — the someone we call the narrator?" Direct presentation assumes that the audience overhears the statement. Mediated narration, on the other hand, assumes a more or less express communication from narrator to audience. Because the latter kind of narrative statement predominates in works of fiction it has received a great deal of study, as some of the previous essays attest, but the nonnarrated story has received far less attention. Chatman's purpose is not to focus on what he calls "nonnarrated stories," but to introduce their existence as a possible means by which an author may present a story. In the course of a brief overview of the differences among "Real Author, Implied Author, Narrator, Real Reader, Implied Reader, and Narratee," Chatman concludes that "only the implied author and implied reader are immanent to a narrative, the narrator and narratee are optional."

Unlike Wayne Booth in his discussion of point of view, Chatman distinguishes between point of view and narrative voice: "Point of view is the physical place or ideological situation or practical life-orientation to which narrative events stand in relation. Voice, on the contrary, refers to the speech or other overt means through which events and existents are communicated to the audience." Thus, "the perspective and the expression need not be lodged in the same person." As a result of this distinction, we can understand the possibility of a nonnarrated story having a particular point of view, such as that of a single character, without having an identifiable narrative voice, since the story is directly presented to the audience. Chatman's distinction enables us to make sharper critical differentiations among the components comprising the expression, or "discourse," of the fiction's content, or "story."

Seymour Chatman (b. 1928) is Professor of Rhetoric at the University of California, Berkeley. He has also published, among other books, *Coming to Terms: The Rhetoric of Narrative in Fiction and Film* (1990) and *Reading Narrative Fiction* (1992).

Silence is become his mother tongue.
— Oliver Goldsmith, *The Good-Natured Man*

Every narrative — so this theory goes — is a structure with a content plane (called "story") and an expression plane (called "discourse"). . . . The expression plane is the set of narrative statements, where "statement" is the basic component of the form of the expression, independent of and more abstract than any particular manifestation — that is, the expression's substance, which varies from art to art. A certain posture in the ballet, a series of film shots, a whole paragraph in a novel, or only a single word — any of these might manifest a single narrative statement. I have proposed that narrative statements are of two kinds — process and stasis — corresponding to whether the deep narrative (not the surface linguistic) predicate is in the mode of existence (IS) or action (DOES).

Crosscutting this dichotomy is another: Is the statement directly presented to the audience or is it mediated by someone — the someone we call the narrator? Direct presentation presumes a kind of overhearing by the audience. Mediated narration, on the other hand, presumes a more or less express communication from narrator to audience. This is essentially Plato's distinction between *mimesis* and *diegesis,*[1] in modern terms between showing and telling. Insofar as there is telling, there must be a teller, a narrating voice.

The teller, the transmitting source, is best accounted for, I think, as a spectrum of possibilities, going from narrators who are least audible to those who are most so. The label affixed to the negative pole of narratorhood is less important than its reality in the spectrum. I say "nonnarrated"; the reader may prefer "minimally narrated," but the existence of this kind of transmission is well attested.

The narrator's presence derives from the audience's sense of some demonstrable communication. If it feels it is being told something, it presumes a teller. The alternative is a "direct witnessing" of the action. Of course, even in the scenic arts like drama and the ballet, pure mimesis is an illusion. But the degree of possible analogy varies. The main question is how the illusion is achieved. By what convention does a spectator or reader accept the idea that it is "as if" he were personally on the scene, though he comes to it by sitting in a chair in a theater or by turning pages and reading words. Authors may make special efforts to preserve the illusion that events "literally unfold before the reader's eyes," mostly by restricting the kinds of statements that can occur.

To understand the concept of narrator's voice (including its "absence") we need to consider three preliminary issues: the interrelation of the several parties to the narrative transaction, the meaning of "point of view" and its relation to voice, and the nature of acts of speech and thought as a subclass of the class of acts in general. These topics form a necessary prolegomena to the analysis of narrator's voice, upon which any discussion of narrative discourse rests.

Real Author, Implied Author, Narrator, Real Reader, Implied Reader, Narratee

That it is essential not to confuse author and narrator has become a commonplace of literary theory. As Monroe Beardsley argues, "the speaker of a literary work cannot be identified with the author — and therefore the character and condition of the speaker can be known by internal evidence alone — unless the author has provided a pragmatic context, or a claim of one, that connects the speaker with himself."[2] But even in such a context, the speaker is not the author, but the "author" (quotation marks of "as if"), or better the "author"-narrator, one of several possible kinds.

In addition, there is a demonstrable third party, conveniently dubbed, by Wayne Booth, the "implied author":

> As he writes, [the real author] creates not simply an ideal, impersonal "man in general" but an implied version of "himself" that is different from the implied authors we meet in other men's works. . . . Whether we call this implied author an "official scribe," or adopt the term recently revived by Kathleen Tillotson — the author's "second self" — it is clear that the picture the reader gets of this presence is one of the author's most important effects. However impersonal he may try to be, his reader will inevitably construct a picture of the official scribe.[3]

He is "implied," that is, reconstructed by the reader from the narrative. He is not the narrator, but rather the principle that invented the narrator, along with everything else in the narrative, that stacked the cards in this particular way, had these things happen to these characters, in these words or images. Unlike the narrator, the implied author can *tell* us nothing. He, or better, *it* has no voice, no direct means of communicating. It instructs us silently, through the design of the whole, with all the voices, by all the means it has chosen to let us learn. We can grasp the notion of implied author most clearly by comparing different narratives written by the same real author but presupposing different implied authors. Booth's example: the implied author of *Jonathan Wild* "is by implication very much concerned with public affairs and with the effects of unchecked ambition on the 'great men' who attain to power in the world," whereas the implied author "who greets us on page one of *Amelia*" conveys rather an "air of sententious solemnity."[4] The implied author of *Joseph Andrews,* on the contrary, sounds "facetious" and "generally insouciant." Not merely the narrator but the whole design of *Joseph Andrews* functions in a tone quite different from that of *Jonathan Wild* or *Amelia.* Henry Fielding created three clearly different implied authors.

The distinction is particularly evident in the case of the "unreliable narrator" (another of Booth's happy coinages). What makes a narrator unreliable is that his values diverge strikingly from that of the implied author's; that is, the rest of the narrative — "the norm of the work" — conflicts with the narrator's presentation, and we become suspicious of his sincerity or competence to tell the "true version." The unreliable narrator is at virtual odds with the implied author; otherwise his unreliability could not emerge.

The implied author establishes the norms of the narrative, but Booth's insistence that these are moral seems unnecessary. The norms are general cultural codes, whose relevance to story we have already considered. The real author can postulate whatever norms he likes through his implied author. It makes no more sense to accuse the real Céline or Montherlant of what the implied author causes to happen in *Journey to the End of the Night* or *Les Jeunes Filles* than to hold the real Conrad responsible for the reactionary attitudes of the implied author of *The Secret Agent* or *Under Western Eyes* (or, for that matter, Dante for the Catholic ideas of the implied author of the *Divine Comedy*). One's moral fibre cannot really be "seduced" by wily implied authors. Our acceptance of their universe is aesthetic, not ethical. To confound the "implied author," a structural principle, with a certain historical figure whom we may or may not admire morally, politically, or personally would seriously undermine our theoretical enterprise.[5]

There is always an implied author, though there might not be a single real author in the ordinary sense: the narrative may have been composed by committee (Hollywood films), by a disparate group of people over a long period of time (many folk ballads), by random-number generation by a computer, or whatever.[6]

The counterpart of the implied author is the *implied reader* — not the flesh-and-bones you or I sitting in our living rooms reading the book, but the audience presupposed by the narrative itself. Like the implied author, the implied reader is always present. And just as there may or may not be a narrator, there may or may not be a *narratee*.[7] He may materialize as a character in the world of the work: for example, the someone listening to Marlow as he unfolds the story of Jim or Kurtz. Or there may be no overt reference to him at all, though his presence is felt. In such cases the author makes explicit the desired audience stance, and we must give him the benefit of the doubt if we are to proceed at all. The narratee-character is only one device by which implied author informs the real reader how to perform as implied reader, which *Weltanschauung* to adopt. The narratee-character tends to appear in narratives like Conrad's whose moral texture is particularly complex, where good is not easily distinguished from evil. In narratives without explicit narratees, the stance of the implied reader can only be inferred, on ordinary cultural and moral terms. Thus, Hemingway's "The Killers" does not permit us to assume that we too are members of the Mob; the story just will not work if we do. Of course, the real reader may refuse his projected role at some ultimate level — nonbelievers do not become Christians just to read *The Inferno* or *Paradise Lost*. But such refusal does not contradict the imaginative or "as if" acceptance of implied readership necessary to the elementary comprehension of the narrative.

It is as necessary to distinguish among narratees, implied readers (parties immanent to the narrative), and real readers (parties extrinsic and accidental to the narrative) as it is among narrator, implied author, and real author. The "you" or "dear reader" who is addressed by the narrator of *Tom Jones* is no more Seymour Chatman than is the narrator Henry Fielding. When I enter the fictional contract I add another self: I become an implied reader. And just as the narrator may or may not ally himself with the implied author, the implied reader furnished by the real reader may or may not ally himself with a narratee. In *Tom Jones* or *Tristram Shandy* the alliance is reasonably close; in *Les Liaisons dangereuses* or *Heart of Darkness* the distance is great.

The situation of the narratee is parallel to that of the narrator: he ranges from a fully characterized individual to "no one." Again, "absence" or "unmarkedness" is put in quotation marks: in some sense every tale implies a listener or reader, just as it implies a teller. But the author may, for a variety of reasons, leave these components unmentioned, indeed, go out of his way to suggest that they do not exist.

We can now diagram the whole narrative-communication situation as follows:

Narrative text

Real — — → | Implied → (Narrator) → (Narratee) → Implied | — — → Real
author | author   reader | reader

The box indicates that only the implied author and implied reader are immanent to a narrative, the narrator and narratee are optional (parentheses). The real author and real reader are outside the narrative transaction as such, though, of course, indispensable to it in an ultimate practical sense. . . .

Point of View and Its Relation to Narrative Voice

It is the task of narrative theory, like any theory, to deal with the ambiguities and unclarities of terms passed down to it. To understand the concept of narrator's voice — including the case where one is "not" (or minimally) present — we must first distinguish it from "point of view," one of the most troublesome of critical terms. Its plurisignification must give pause to anyone who wishes to use it in precise discussion. At least three senses can be distinguished in ordinary use: (a) literal: through someone's eyes (perception); (b) figurative: through someone's worldview (ideology, conceptual system, *Weltanschauung,* etc.); (c) transferred: from someone's interest-vantage (characterizing his general interest, profit, welfare, well-being, etc.). The following sentences will illustrate these distinctions: (a) From John's point of view, at the top of Coit Tower, the panorama of the San Francisco Bay was breathtaking. (b) John said that from his point of view, Nixon's position, though praised by his supporters, was somewhat less than noble. (c) Though he didn't realize it at the time, the divorce was a disaster from John's point of view. In the first sentence, "The panorama of the Bay" is reported as acutally seen by John; he stands at the center of a half-circle of vision. Let us call that his *perceptual* point of view. In the second, there is no reference to his actual physical situation in the real world but to his attitudes or conceptual apparatus, his way of thinking, and how facts and impressions are strained through it. We can call that his *conceptual* point of view. In the third, there is no reference to John's mind at all, either to perceptual or conceptual powers. Since John is unaware of the mentioned consequences, he is not "seeing," in either the actual or the figurative sense; the term then is a simple synonym for "as far as John is concerned." Let us call this his *interest* point of view. What is confusing is that "point of view" may thus refer to an *action* of some kind — perceiving or conceiving — or to a *passive state* — as in the third sense.

Now texts, any kind of text, even ordinary conversation, may entail one or any combination of these senses. A simple description of an experiment or an explorer's account of a new island may convey only the literal perceptions of the author, but it may also entail his *Weltanschauung,* or his practical interests. A philosophical treatise on abstract issues does not usually entail perceptual point of view, but may express quite eloquently the author's personal interests in the matter, along with his ideology.

When we turn to narrative texts, we find an even more complicated situation, since as we have seen there is no longer a single presence, as in expository essays, sermons, political speeches, and so on, but two — character and narrator — not to speak of the implied author. Each of these may manifest one or more kinds of point of view. A character may literally perceive a certain object or event; and/or it may be presented in terms of his conceptualization; and/or his interest in it may be invoked (even if he is unconscious of that interest).[8]

Thus the crucial difference between "point of view" and narrative voice: point of view is the physical place or ideological situation or practical life-orientation to which narrative events stand in relation. Voice, on the contrary, refers to the speech or other overt means through which events and existents are communicated to the audience. Point of view does *not* mean expression; it only means the perspective in terms of which the expression is made. *The perspective and the expression need not be lodged in the same person.*[9] Many combinations are possible. Consider just literal, that is perceptual, point of view. Events and existents may be perceived by the narrator and recounted by him in his own first person: "I felt myself fall down the hill" or "I saw Jack fall down the hill" (in the first case, the narrator is protagonist, in the second, witness). Or the point of view may be assigned to a character who is not the narrator: then the separate narrating voice may or may not make itself heard — "Mary, *poor dear,* saw Jack fall down the hill" versus "Mary saw Jack fall down the hill." Or the event may be presented so that it is not clear who, if anyone, perceived it (or perception is not an issue): "Jack fell down the hill."

The "camera eye" names a convention (an "illusion of mimesis") which pretends that the events just "happened" in the presence of a neutral recorder. To call such narrative transmission "limited third person" is wrong because it specifies only the point of view, not the narrative voice. It is necessary to distinguish between "limited third person point of view voiced by a covert narrator," "limited third person point of view voiced by an overt narrator," and so on.

Perception, conception, and interest points of view are quite independent of the manner in which they are expressed. When we speak of "expression," we pass from point of view, which is only a perspective or stance, to the province of narrative voice, the medium through which perception, conception, and everything else are communicated. Thus point of view is *in* the story (when it is the character's), but voice is always outside, in the discourse. From *A Portrait of the Artist as a Young Man:* "A few moments [later] he found himself on the stage amid the garish gas and the dim scenery." The perceptual point of view is Stephen's, but the voice is the narrator's. Characters' perceptions need not be articulated — Stephen is not saying to himself the *words* "garish gas and dim scenery"; the words are the narrator's. This is a narrator's report. But in " 'He shivered a little, and I beheld him rise slowly as if a steady hand from above had been pulling him out of the chair by the hair' " (*Lord Jim*), not only the voice, but the perceptual point of view is the narrator's, Marlow's, not Jim's. And in "Coffin now. Got here before us, dead as he is. Horse looking round at it with his plume skewways. Dull eye: collar tight on his neck, pressing on a bloodvessel or something. Do they know what they cart out here every day?" ("Hades," *Ulysses*), the perceptual point of view is Leopold Bloom's, and so are the words, but he is no narrator. He is not telling a narratee anything. Indeed, he is not speaking even to himself: the convention argues that he is directly perceiving the coffin and the nag's dull eye, and nothing more. There *is* no narrator.

In all these cases the character perceives: his senses are directed outward upon the story-world. But when that perception is reported, as in the first two examples, there is necessarily presupposed another act of "seeing" with an independent point of view, namely that of the narrator, who has "peered into" the character's mind (metaphors are inevitable) and reports its contents from his *own* point of view. Can this kind of point of view be called "perceptual"? The word sounds strange, and for good reason. It makes sense to say that the character is literally perceiving something within the world of the work ("homodiegetically," as Genette would say). But what the narrator reports from his perspective is almost always outside the story (heterodiegetic), even if only retrospective, that is, temporally distant. Typically, he is looking back at his own earlier perception-as-a-character. But that looking-back is a conception, no longer a perception. The completely external narrator presents an even more purely conceptual view. He never *was* in the world of the work: discourse-time is not a later extension of story-time. He did not "perceive" in the same direct or diegetic sense that any character did. Literally speaking, he cannot have "seen" anything in that other world.

Thus the use of terms like "view" and "see" may be dangerously metaphorical. We "see" issues in terms of some cultural or psychological predisposition; the mechanism is entirely different from that which enables us to see cats or automobiles. Though it is true that preconceptions of various sorts affect our strictly physiological vision too (people may not see what is literally before their noses because they have compelling personal reasons not to), there remains an essential difference between perceptions and conceptions. Further, the narrator's is second-order or heterodiegetic conceptualizing *about* the story — as opposed to the first-order conceptualizing of a character within the story. These distinctions most clearly emerge where the two conflict, where the narrator is operating under a clearly different set of attitudes than those of the character. Then the narrator's conceptual point of view (except when he is unreliable) tends to override the character's, despite the fact that the latter maintains the center of interest and consciousness. An example is Conrad's *The Secret Agent:* the narrator is clearly unsympathetic to Verloc. Or, more precisely, the character has a conceptual point of view undermined by the narrator's manner of depicting it. Verloc's ideology (such as it is) reeks of indolence; the narrator carefully picks words to so characterize it. For example, Verloc does not simply stay in bed, he "wallows" in it. But the narrator (like all Conrad's narrators) is on the side of vigorous achievement. Similarly, he tells us that Verloc "remained undisturbed by any sort of aesthetic doubt about his appearance." From the narrator's conceptual point of view, implicitly communicated, Verloc's physical messiness is reprehensible and a clear analogue to moral sloth and political dishonesty. Or consider the difference between Verloc's and the narrator's attitudes toward female psychology. Verloc's unpleasant encounter with Mr. Vladimir brings him home in a towering rage. Forgetting that his wife is mourning the death of her brother, for which he is responsible, he is disappointed that she does not soothe him. Yet, immediately, he realizes that she is "a woman of few words." But his notion of his relationship with her, his conceptual point of view, is paraphrased in the narrator's superior diction: "[Winnie's] reserve, expressing in a way their profound confidence in each other, introduced at the same time a certain element of vagueness into their intimacy." Though the "profound confidence in each other" is the narrator's expression, not Verloc's, whose verbal style we know to be less elegant, it can only be Verloc's sentiment. His complacency, of course, turns out suicidal.

Disparity between the character's point of view and the narrator's expression of it need not entail ironic opposition. The narrator may verbalize neutrally or even sympathetically what (for reasons of youth, lack of education and intelligence, and so on) the character cannot articulate. This is the whole structural principle of James's *What Maisie Knew.* Maisie's uncertainly about when next she will visit her mother is expressed thusly: "Mama's roof, however, had its turn, this time, for the child, of appearing but remotely contingent. . . . " Clearly these are not phrases in Maisie's vocabulary. We accept them only because a sensitive little girl might have feelings that somehow matched the narrator's elegant terms. That is, we can "translate" into more childlike verbiage — for instance, "I don't expect to be at Mama's again very soon." The diction is sanctioned only by the convention of the "well-spoken narrator."

"Point of view" expressing someone's interests is even more radically distanced, since there is not even a figurative "seeing." The subject may be completely unconscious that events work for or against his interests (welfare, success, happiness). The identification of interest point of view may follow the clear specification of the character's perceptual and conceptual points of view. Once they are established, we continue identifying with his interests, by a process of inertia, even if he is unaware of something. In *The Ambassadors,* the narrator speaks of Maria Gostrey's powers of "pigeon-holing her fellow mortals": "She was as equipped in this particular as Strether was the reverse, and it made an opposition between them which he might well have shrunk from submitting to if he had fully suspected it." The narrator informs us of aspects of Maria's character that Strether does not know, yet it makes perfect sense to say that the sentence is "from his point of view." The focus of attention remains on him. Maria's traits are significant only in their implications for him — even though he is not aware of them.

Access to a character's consciousness is the standard entree to his point of view, the usual and quickest means by which we come to identify with him. Learning his thoughts insures an intimate connection. The thoughts are truthful, except in cases of willful self-deception. Unlike the narrator, the character can only be "unreliable" to himself.

At the same time, interest point of view can be established quite independently. The point of view may reside in a character who is "followed" in some sense, even if there is no reference at all to his thinking. If Jack and Peter are in the first scene, and Jack and Mary in the second, and Jack and Joseph in the third, we identify with Jack simply because he is the one continually on the scene. This has nothing to do with whether or not we care for him on human or other grounds.

The notion of interest point of view is not very meaningfully applied to an external narrator. His only interest is to get the narrative told. Other sorts of interest arise only if he is or was also a character. Then he may use the narrative itself as vindication, expiation, explanation, rationalization, condemnation, or whatever. There are hundreds of reasons for telling a story, but those reasons are the narrator's, not the implied author's, who is without personality or even presence, hence without motivation other than the purely theoretical one of constructing the narrative itself. The narrator's vested interests may be so marked that we come to think of him as unreliable.

The different points of view usually combine, but in important and interesting cases, they do not. Consider "autobiographical" or first-person narration, as in *Great Expectations.* The protagonist-as-narrator reports things from the perceptual point of view of his younger self. His ideology on the other hand tends to be that of his older self. The narrator is older and wiser for his experiences. In other narratives the ideology may not change; the narrator may exhibit substantially the same traits as characterized his earlier self. Where the narrator is a different person than the hero, he may present his own ideology, against which he judges his hero's actions, either overtly, as in *Tom Jones,* or covertly and inferentially, as in *The Ambassadors.* The narrator may utilize a perceptual point of view possible to no character, for example when he describes a bird's-eye view, or a scene with no one present, or what the character did *not* notice.

Notes

1. These terms are revived by Gérard Genette in "Frontières du récit," *Communications* 8 (1966).

2. In *Aesthetics* (New York, 1958), p. 240. Cf. Walker Gibson, "Authors, Speakers, Readers, Mock Readers," *College English* 11 (1950): 265–69; and Kathleen Tillotson, *The Tale and the Teller* (London: Rupert Hart-Davis, 1959).

3. *Rhetoric of Fiction,* pp. 70–71.

4. Ibid., p. 72.

5. There is an interesting discussion of the question in Susan Suleiman, "Ideological Dissent from Works of Fiction: Toward a Rhetoric of the *Roman a thèse,*" *Neophilologus* (April 1976): 162–77. Suleiman thinks that the implied author, as well as the narrator, can be unreliable, and thus we can accept imaginatively a narrative that we reject ideologically.

6. Christian Metz, *Film Language: A Semiotics of the Cinema,* trans. Michael Taylor (New York: Oxford University Press, 1974), p. 20.

7. The term was first coined, so far as I know, by Gerald Prince, "Notes Toward a Categorization of Fictional 'Narratees,' " *Genre* 4 (1971): 100–105. Booth's "postulated reader" is what I call the implied reader.

8. Another ambiguity of "point of view" was recognized by Sister Kristin Morrison in "James's and Lubbock's Differing Points of View," *Nineteenth-Century Fiction* 16 (1961): 245–56. Lubbock and his followers used the term in the sense of the narrative perspective of the speaker (the narrator), while James usually used it in the sense of the perspective of the knower or reader. Boris Uspensky in *Poetics of Composition,* trans. Valentina Zavarin and Susan Wittig (Berkeley: University of California Press, 1974), chap. 1, distinguishes various kinds of point of view along lines similar to mine. Some alternatives to "point of view" have been proposed: for instance, James's "central consciousness," Allen Tate's "post of observation," and Todorov's "*vision*" (derived from Jean Pouillon). The latter two continue the confusion between cognition and interest.

9. For example a recent article misreads "Eveline" by confusing character's point of view and narrator's voice (Clive Hart, "Eveline," in *James Joyce's Dubliners: Critical Essays* [London: Faber and Faber, 1969], p. 51). The author argues that Eveline is shallow and incapable of love — which may be true — but supports his argument with questionable evidence: "She over-dramatizes her association with Frank, calls it an 'affair' and him her 'lover'; she thinks of herself in pulp-literature terms as 'unspeakably' weary. But most obvious of all is the strong note of falsity in the language of the passage in which she reasserts her choice to leave: 'As she mused the pitiful vision of her mother's life laid its spell on the very quick of her being. . . . ' Dublin has so paralysed Eveline's emotions that she is unable to love, can think of herself and her situation only by means of a series of tawdry cliches." Surely the objectionable words are not Eveline's but the narrator's. It is he who is parodying pulp-literature sentimentality in tawdry cliches (as does the narrator of the "Nausicaa" section of *Ulysses*). Eveline may indeed feel maudlin sentiments, but "mused," "pitiful vision," "very quick of her being" are not in her vocabulary.

Tzvetan Todorov addresses a critical space he sees existing between the study of readers in "their social, historical, collective, or individual variability" and "the image of the reader . . . as character or as 'narratee.' " He defines this space as "the domain of the logic of reading," and he analyzes the reading of "so-called representative texts." According to Todorov, such reading "unfolds as a construction" because we tend to view the text as representing reality and we imaginatively create an appropriate world for that reality. Todorov is not concerned with arguing about the relationship of text and reality, but with answering the question: "How does a text get us to construct an imaginary world?" He employs a linguistic and structuralist method to answer this question, beginning by distinguishing between referential and nonreferential sentences, and arguing that readers use only the referential as construction material. Todorov then outlines how the narrative parameters of "time, point of view, and mode" serve different construction functions, their roles being reinforced by repetition, which enables the reader to "construct *one* event from *many* accounts."

Why is it so important to establish the concept of reading as construction? Todorov notes that no two readings of a novel are identical because each reader does not *receive* the novel's image of the universe, but *creates* his or her own image from partial and composite information. Part of the difference between two readers' readings results from the distinction between *signification* and *symbolization*. In the first, the reader is told of an event; in the second we are given clues, symbols, and implications that must be interpreted. We can see the validity of this distinction if we stop for a moment and consider how our reading of a work changes from the interpretations we make along the way to the interpretation we make at the end, when we reevaluate earlier symbolization in the context of the overall story. Todorov argues that just as readers construct different readings, so too the text may furnish us with readings through its characters or narrator. He calls this "construction as theme" and cites detective novels as an example: "a Watson figure constructs like the reader, but a Sherlock Holmes constructs better." As we can see from this example, not all constructions provided within a text need be helpful ones; some may purposely mislead the reader. Such a distinction helps us understand that while no single reading can be said to be "correct," not all readings construct their interpretations equally well or fully.

Tzvetan Todorov, born in 1939 in Sofia, Bulgaria, is Professor of Aesthetics at the Centre National de la Recherche Scientifique, Paris. He is the author of numerous books, among them *Symbolism and Interpretation* (trans. 1983), *Mikhail Bakhtin: The Dialogical Principle* (trans. 1984), *The Conquest of America: The Question of the Other* (trans. 1984), and *Genres of Discourse* (trans. 1990).

W hat is omnipresent is imperceptible. Nothing is more commonplace than the reading experience, and yet nothing is more unknown. Reading is such a matter of course that, at first glance, it seems there is nothing to say about it.

In literary studies, the problem of reading has been posed from two opposite perspectives. The first concerns itself with readers, their social, historical, collective, or individual variability. The second deals with the image of the reader as it is represented in certain texts: the reader as character or as "narratee." There is, however, an unexplored area situated between the two: the domain of the logic of reading. Although it is not represented in the text, it is nonetheless anterior to individual variation.

There are several types of reading. I shall pause here to discuss one of the more important ones: the one we usually practice when we read classical fiction or, rather, the so-called representative texts. This particular type of reading, and only this type, unfolds as a construction.

Although we no longer refer to literature in terms of imitation, we still have trouble getting rid of a certain way of looking at fiction; inscribed in our speech habits, it is a vision through which we perceive the novel in terms of representation, or the transposition of a reality that exists prior to it. This attitude would be problematic even if it did not attempt to describe the creative process. When it refers to the text itself, it is sheer distortion. What exists first and foremost is the text itself, and nothing but the text. Only by subjecting the text to a particular type of reading do we construct, from our reading, an imaginary universe. Novels do not imitate reality; they create it. The formula of the pre-Romantics is not a simple terminological innovation; only the perspective of construction allows us to understand thoroughly how the so-called representative text functions.

Given our framework, the question of reading can be restated as follows: How does a text get us to construct an imaginary world? Which aspects of the text determine the construction we produce as we read? And in what way? Let us begin with basics.

Referential Discourse

Only referential sentences allow construction to take place; not all sentences, however, are referential. This fact is well known to linguists and logicians, and we need not dwell on it.

Comprehension is a process different from construction. Take for example the following two sentences from *Adolphe:* "Je la sentais meilleure que moi; je me méprisais d'être indigne d'elle. C'est un affreux malheur que de n'être aimé quand on aime; mais c'en est un bien grand d'être aimé avec passion quand on n'aime plus."[1] The first sentence is referential: it evokes an event (Adolphe's feelings); the second sentence is not referential: it is a maxim. The difference between the two is marked by grammatical indices: the maxim requires a third-person present-tense verb, and contains no anaphores (words referring to preceding segments of the same discourse).

A sentence is either referential or nonreferential; there are no intermediary stages. However, the words that make up a sentence are not all alike in this respect; depending on the lexical choice, the results will be very different. Two independent oppositions seem pertinent here: the affective versus the nonaffective, and the particular versus the general. For example, Adolphe refers to his past as "au milieu d'une vie très dissipée." This remark evokes perceptible events but in an extremely general way. One could easily imagine hundreds of pages describing this very same fact. Whereas in the other sentence, "Je trouvais dans mon père, non pas un censeur, mais un observateur froid et caustique, qui souriait d'abord de pitié, et qui finissait bientôt la conversation avec impatience,"[2] we have a juxtaposition of affective versus nonaffective events: a smile, a moment of silence, are observable facts; pity and impatience are suppositions (justified, no doubt) about feelings to which we are denied direct access.

Normally, a given fictional text will contain examples of all these speech registers (although we know that their distribution varies according to period, schools of thought, or even as a function of the text's global organization). We do not retain nonreferential sentences in the kind of reading I call reading as construction (they belong to another kind of reading). Referential sentences lead to different types of construction depending on their degree of generality and on the affectivity of the events they evoke.

Narrative Filters

The characteristics of discourse mentioned thus far can be identified outside of any context: they are inherent in the sentences themselves. But in
reading, we read whole texts, not just sentences. If we compare sentences
from the point of view of the imaginary world which they help to construct, we find that they differ in several ways or, rather, according to
several parameters. In narrative analysis, it has been agreed to retain three
parameters: time, point of view, and mode. Here again, we are on relatively familiar ground (which I have already dealt with in my book *Poétique*); now it is simply a question of looking at the problems from the
point of view of reading.

Mode. Direct discourse is the only way to eliminate the differences
between narrative discourse and the world which it evokes: words are
identical to words, and construction is direct and immediate. This is not
the case with nonverbal events, nor with transposed discourse. At one
point, the "editor" in *Adolphe* states: "Notre hôte, qui avait causé avec un
domestique napolitain, qui servait cet étranger [i.e., Adolphe] sans savoir
son nom, me dit qu'il ne voyageait point par curiosité, car il ne visitait ni
les ruines, ni les sites, ni les monuments, ni les hommes."[3] We can imagine
the conversation between the editor-narrator and the host, even though it is
unlikely that the former used words (be it in Italian) identical to those
which follow the "he told me that" formula. The construction of the
conversation between the host and the servant, which is also evoked, is far
less determined; thus we have more freedom if we want to construct it
in detail. Finally, the conversations and the other activities common to
Adolphe and the servant are completely vague; only a general impression
is given.

The remarks of a fictional narrator can also be considered as direct
discourse, although on a different (higher) level. This is especially the case
if, as in *Adolphe,* the narrator is represented in the text. The maxim, which
we previously excluded from reading as construction, becomes pertinent
here — not for its value as an "énoncé" (i.e., a statement) but as "énoncia-
tion" (i.e., an utterance, implying a speaker and his circumstances). The
fact that Adolphe as narrator formulates a maxim on the misery of being
loved tells us something about his character, and therefore about the imaginary universe of which he is a part.

Time. The time of the fictional world ("story" time) is ordered chronologically. However, the sentences in the text do not, and as a rule cannot, absolutely respect this order; the reader undertakes therefore, unconsciously, the task of chronological reordering. Similarly, certain sentences evoke several events which are distinct yet similar ("iterative narrative"); in these instances we reestablish the plurality of the events as we construct.

Point of view. The "vision" we have of the events evoked by the text clearly determines our work of construction. For example, in the case of a positively slanted vision, we take into consideration (1) the event recounted, and (2) the attitude of the person who "sees" the event.

Furthermore, we know how to distinguish between information that a sentence gives concerning its object, and the information it gives concerning its subject; thus the "editor" of *Adolphe* can only think of the latter, as he comments on the story we have just read: "Je hais cette vanité qui s'occupe d'elle-même en racontant le mal qu'elle a fait, qui a la prétention de sa faire plaindre en se décrivant, et qui, planant indestructible au milieu des ruines, s'analyse au lieu de se repentir."[4] The editor constructs the subject of the narrative (Adolphe the narrator), and not its object (Adolphe the character, and Ellénore).

We usually do not realize just how repetitive, or rather how redundant, fiction is; we could, in fact, state almost categorically that each event is narrated at least twice. For the most part, these repetitions are modulated by the filters mentioned above: at one point a conversation may be reproduced in its entirety; at another, it may be alluded to briefly; action may be observed from several different points of view; it can be recounted in the future, in the present, and in the past. In addition, all these parameters can be combined.

Repetition plays an important role in the process of construction. We must construct *one* event from *many* accounts of it. The relationship between these different accounts varies, ranging from total agreement to downright contradiction. Even two identical accounts do not necessarily produce the same meaning (a good example of this is seen in Coppola's film *The Conversation*). The functions of these repetitions are equally varied: they help to establish the facts as in a police investigation, or to disprove the facts. Thus in *Adolphe,* the fact that the same character expresses contradictory views on the same subject at two different times which are quite close to each other, helps us to understand that states of mind do not exist in and of themselves, but rather in relationship to an interlocutor, to a partner. Constant himself expressed the law of this universe in the following manner: "L'objet qui nous échappe est nécessairement tout différent de celui qui nous poursuit."[5]

Therefore, if the reader is to construct an imaginary universe through his reading of the text, the text itself must be referential; in the course of reading, we let our imagination go to work, filtering the information we receive through the following types of questions: To what extent is the description of this universe accurate (mode)? When did the events take place (time)? To what extent is the story distorted by the various "centers of consciousness" through whom it is told (vision)? At this point, however, the job of reading has only begun.

Signification and Symbolization

How do we know what happens as we read? Through introspection; and if we want to confirm our own impressions, we can always have recourse to other readers' accounts of their own reading. Nevertheless, two accounts of the same text will never be identical. How do we explain this diversity? By the fact that these accounts describe, not the universe of the book itself, but this universe as it is transformed by the psyche of each individual reader. The stages of this transformation can be diagrammed as follows:

1. The author's account	4. The reader's account
↓	↑
2. The imaginary universe evoked by the author →	3. The imaginary universe constructed by the reader

We could question whether there really is a difference between stages 2 and 3, as is suggested by the diagram. Is there such a thing as nonindividual construction? It is easy to show that the answer must be positive. Everyone who reads *Adolphe* knows that Ellénore first lived with the Comte de p^{xxx}, that she left him, and went to live with Adolphe; they separated; she later joined him in Paris, etc. On the other hand, there is no way to establish with the same certainty whether Adolphe is weak or merely sincere.

The reason for this duality is that the text evokes facts according to two different modes, which I shall call signification and symbolization. Ellénore's trip to Paris is *signified* by the words in the text. Adolphe's (ultimate) weakness is *symbolized* by other factors in the imaginary universe, which are themselves signified by words. For example, Adolphe's inability to defend Ellénore in social situations is signified; this in turn symbolizes his inability to love. Signified facts are *understood:* all we need is knowledge of the language in which the text is written. Symbolized facts are *interpreted;* and interpretations vary from one subject to another.

Consequently, the relationship between stages 2 and 3, as indicated above, is one of symbolization (whereas the relationship between stages 1 and 2, or 3 and 4, is one of signification). In any case, we are not dealing with a single or unique relationship, but rather a heterogeneous ensemble. First, we always abbreviate as we read: stage 4 is (almost) always shorter than stage 1, whence stage 2 is richer than stage 3. Secondly, we often make mistakes. In both cases, studying the relationship between stages 2 and 3 leads to psychological projection: the transformations tell us about the reading subject. Why does he remember (or even add) certain facts and not others? But there are other transformations which provide information about the reading process itself, and these are the ones that will be our main concern here.

It is hard for me to say whether the situation I observe in the most varied kinds of fiction is universal or whether it is historically and culturally determined. Nevertheless, it is a fact that in every case, symbolization and interpretation (the movement from stage 2 to stage 3) imply the determinism of action. Would reading other texts, lyrical poems for example, require an effort of symbolization based on other presuppositions (e.g., universal analogy)? I do not know; the fact remains that in fiction, symbolization is based on the acknowledgment, either implicit or explicit, of the principle of causality. The questions we address, therefore, to the events that constitute the mental image of stage 2 are the following: What is their cause? What is their effect? We then add their answers to the mental image that constitutes stage 3.

Let us admit that this determinism is universal; what is certainly not universal is the form it takes in a given case. The simplest form, although one that we rarely find in our culture as a reading norm, consists in constructing another fact of the same type. A reader might say to himself, "If John killed Peter (a fact present in the story), it's because Peter slept with John's wife (a fact absent from the story)." This type of reasoning, characteristic of courtroom procedures, is not applied seriously to the novel; we assume that the author has not cheated and that he has provided (has signified) all the information we need to understand the story (*Armance* is an exception). The same is true as concerns effects or aftereffects: many books are sequels to others and tell the consequences of events in the imaginary universe represented in the first text; nevertheless, the content of the second book is generally not considered inherent in the first. Here again, reading practices differ from everyday habits.

When we read, we usually base our constructions upon another kind of causal logic; we look for the causes and consequences of a particular event elsewhere, in elements unlike the event itself. Two types of causal construction seem most frequent (as Aristotle already noted): the event is perceived as the consequence (and/or the cause) either of a character trait or of an impersonal or universal law. *Adolphe* contains numerous examples of both types of interpretation, and they are integrated into the text itself. Here is how Adolphe describes his father: "Je ne me souviens pas, pendant mes dix-huit premières années, d'avoir eu jamais un entretien d'une heure avec lui. . . . Je ne savais pas alors ce que c'etait que la timidité."[6] The first sentence signifies a fact (the absence of lengthy conversations). The second makes us consider this fact as symbolic of a character trait — timidity: if the father behaves in this way, it is because he is timid. The character trait is the cause of the action. Here is an example of the second case: "Je me dis qu'il ne fallait rien précipiter, qu'Ellénore était trop peu préparée à l'aveu que je méditais, et qu'il valait mieux attendre encore. Presque toujours, pour vivre en repos avec nous-mêmes, nous travestissons en calculs et en systèmes nos impuissances ou nos faiblesses: cela satisfait cette portion de nous qui est, pour ainsi dire, spectatrice de l'autre."[7] Here, the first sentence describes the event, and the second provides the reason — a universal law of human behavior, not an individual character trait. We might add that this second type of causality is dominant in *Adolphe:* the novel illustrates psychological laws, not individual psychologies.

After we have constructed the events that compose a story, we begin the task of reinterpretation. This enables us to construct not only the "personalities" of the characters but also the novel's underlying system of values and ideas. A reinterpretation of this type is not arbitrary; it is controlled by two series of constraints. The first is contained in the text itself: the author need but take a few moments to teach us how to interpret the events he evokes. This was the case in the passages from *Adolphe* cited earlier: once he has established a few deterministic interpretations, Constant can forgo naming the cause of the subsequent events; we have learned his lesson, and we shall continue to interpret in the way he has taught us. Such explicit interpretations have a double function: on the one hand, they tell us the reason behind a particular fact (exegetic function); on the other hand, they initiate us into the author's own system of interpretation, the one that will operate throughout the course of the text (meta-exegetic function).

The second series of constraints comes from the cultural context. If we read that so-and-so has cut his wife up into little pieces, we do not need textual indications to conclude that this is truly a cruel deed. These cultural constraints, which are nothing but the commonplaces of a society (its "set" of probabilities), change with time. These changes permit us to explain why interpretations differ from one period to another. For example, since extramarital love is no longer considered proof of moral corruption, we have trouble understanding the condemnations heaped upon so many fictional heroines of the past.

Human character and ideas: such entities are symbolized through action, but they can be signified as well. This was precisely the case in the passages from *Adolphe* quoted earlier: action symbolized shyness in Adolphe's father. Later, however, Adolphe signified the same thing, saying: My father was shy; that is also true of the general maxim. Human character and ideas can thus be evoked in two ways: directly and indirectly. During the course of his construction, the reader will compare the various bits of information obtained from each source and will find that they either tally or do not. The relative proportion of these two types of information has varied greatly during the course of literary history, as goes without saying: Hemingway did not write like Constant.

We must, however, differentiate between human character constructed in this way and the characters in a novel as such: not every character has a character, so to speak. The fictional character is a segment of the spatio-temporal universe represented in the text, nothing more; he/she comes into existence the moment referential linguistic forms (proper names, certain nominal syntagms, personal pronouns) appear in the text regarding an anthropomorphic being. In and of itself the fictional character has no content: someone is identified without being described. We can imagine — and there exist — texts where the fictional character is limited to just that: being the agent of a series of actions. But, as soon as psychological determinism appears in the text, the fictional character becomes endowed with character: he acts in a certain way, *because* he is shy, weak, courageous, etc. There is no such thing as character without determinism of this type.

The construction of character is a compromise between difference and repetition. On the one hand, we must have continuity: the reader must construct the *same* character. This continuity is already given in the identity of the proper name, which is its principal function. At this point, any and all combinations become possible: all actions might illustrate the same character trait, or the behavior of a particular character might be contradictory, or he might change the circumstances of his life, or he might undergo profound character modification. . . . So many examples come to mind that it is not necessary to mention them. Here again the choices are more a function of the history of styles than of the idiosyncrasies of individual authors.

Character, then, can be an effect of reading; there exists a kind of reading to which every text can be subjected. But in fact, the effect is not arbitrary; it is no accident that character exists in the eighteenth- and nineteenth-century novel and not in Greek tragedy or the folktale. A text always contains within itself directions for its own consumption.

Construction as Theme

One of the difficulties in studying reading is due to the fact that reading is so hard to observe: introspection is uncertain, psychosociological investigation is tedious. It is therefore with a kind of relief that we find the work of construction represented in fiction itself, a much more convenient place for study.

Construction appears as a theme in fiction simply because it is impossible to refer to human life without mentioning such an essential activity. Based on the information he receives, every character must construct the facts and the characters around him; thus, he parallels exactly the reader who is constructing the imaginary universe from his own information (the text, and his sense of what is probable); thus, reading becomes (inevitably) one of the themes of the book.

The thematics of reading can, however, be more or less emphasized, more or less exploited as a technique in a given text. In *Adolphe,* it is only partially the case: only the ethical undecidability of action is emphasized. If we want to use fiction to study construction, we must choose a text where construction appears as one of the principal themes. Stendhal's *Armance* is a perfect example.

The entire plot of the novel is, in fact, subjugated to the search for knowledge. Octave's erroneous construction functions as the novel's point of departure: based upon Armance's behavior (an interpretation deducing a character trait from an action), Octave believes that Armance is too concerned with money. This initial misunderstanding is barely settled when it is followed by a second one, symmetrical to but the reverse of the first: Armance now believes that Octave is too concerned with money. This initial mix-up establishes the pattern of the constructions that follow. Next, Armance correctly constructs her feelings for Octave, but it takes Octave ten chapters before he discovers that his feelings for Armance are called *love,* not *friendship.* For five chapters Armance believes that Octave doesn't love her; Octave believes that Armance doesn't love him during the book's fifteen main chapters; the same misunderstanding is repeated toward the end of the novel. The characters spend all their time searching for the truth, in other words, constructing the facts and the events around them. The tragic ending of the love relationship is not caused by impotence, as has often been said, but by ignorance. Octave commits suicide because of an erroneous construction: he believes that Armance doesn't love him anymore. As Stendhal says suggestively, "Il manquait de pénétration et non pas de caractère."[8]

We can see from this brief summary that several aspects of the construction process can vary. One can be agent or patient, a sender or receiver of information; one can even be both. Octave is an agent when he pretends or reveals, a patient when he learns or is mistaken. It is also possible to construct a fact ("first-level" construction), or someone else's construction of that same fact ("second-level" construction). Thus, Armance rejects the idea of marrying Octave when she contemplates what others might think of her. "Je passerais dans le monde pour une dame de compagnie qui a séduit le fils de la maison. J'entends d'ici ce que dirait Mme. la duchesse d'Ancre et même les femmes les plus respectables, par exemple la marquise de Seyssins qui voit dans Octave un époux pour l'une de ses filles."[9] Octave likewise rejects the idea of suicide when he envisions the possible constructions of others. "Si je me tue, Armance sera compromise; toute la société recherchera curieusement pendant huit jours les plus petites circonstances de cette soirée; et chacun de ces messieurs qui étaient présents sera autorisé à faire un récit différent."[10]

What we learn above all in *Armance* is the fact that a construction can be either right or wrong; if all right constructions are alike (they are the "truth"), wrong constructions vary, as do the reasons behind them: flaws in the transmitted information. The simplest type is the case of total ignorance: until a certain point in the plot, Octave hides the very existence of a secret concerning him (active role); Armance is also unaware of its existence (passive role). Afterwards, the existence of the secret may be learned, but without any additional information; the receiver may then react by inventing his own "truth" (Armance suspects Octave of having killcd somconc). Illusion constitutes yet a further degree of faulty information: the agent does not dissemble, but misrepresents; the patient is not ignorant or unknowing, but is in error. This is the most prevalent situation in the novel: Armance camouflages her love for Octave, claiming she will marry someone else; Octave thinks that Armance feels only friendship toward him. One may be both agent and victim of the travesty; thus Octave hides from himself the fact that he loves Armance. Finally, the agent can reveal the truth, and the patient can apprehend it.

Ignorance, imagination, illusion, and truth: here are at least three stages through which the search for knowledge passes before leading a character to a definitive construction. Obviously, the same stages are possible in the reading process. Normally, the construction represented in the text is isomorphic to the one that takes the text as its point of departure. What the characters don't know, the reader doesn't know either; of course, other combinations are possible as well. In the detective novel, a Watson figure constructs like the reader, but a Sherlock Holmes constructs better: the two roles are equally necessary.

Other Readings

The flaws in the reading construction do not in any way undermine its existence: we do not stop constructing because of insufficient or erroneous information. On the contrary, defects such as these only intensify the construction process. Nevertheless, it is possible that construction does not occur, and that other types of reading supersede it.

Discrepancies between readings are not necessarily found where we might expect. For example, there does not seem to be a big difference between construction based on a literary text and construction based on a referential but nonliterary text. This resemblance was implied in the propositions I advanced in the previous section; in other words, the construction of characters (from nonliterary material) is analogous to the reader's construction (from the text of a novel). "Fiction" is not constructed any differently from "reality." Both the historian and the judge, the former on the basis of written documents, the latter on that of oral testimony, reconstitute the facts; in principle, they do not proceed differently from the reader of *Armance;* this does not mean there are no differences as far as details are concerned.

A more difficult question, beyond the scope of this study, concerns the relationship between construction based on verbal information and construction based on other perceptions. From the smell of roast lamb, we construct the roast; similarly for a sound, a view, etc. Piaget calls this phenomenon "the construction of reality." In these instances the differences may be much greater.

We do not have to stray very far from the novel to find material requiring another type of reading. There are many literary texts, nonrepresentative texts, that do not lead to any construction at all. Several types can be distinguished here. The most obvious is a specific type of poetry, generally called lyric poetry, which does not describe events, which evokes nothing exterior to it. The modern novel, in turn, requires a different reading; the text is still referential, but construction does not occur because, in a certain sense, it is undecidable. This effect is obtained by a dismantling of any one of the mechanisms necessary for construction as we have described them. To take just one example: we have seen that a character's identity was a function of the identity and inambiguity of his name. Suppose now that, in a text, the same character is evoked successively by several different names, first "John," then "Peter," then "the man with the black hair," then "the man with the blue eyes," without any indication of co-reference between the two expressions; or, suppose again that "John" designates not one, but three or four characters; each time, the result is the same: construction is no longer possible because the text is representatively undecidable. We see the difference here between such impossibility of construction and the defective constructions mentioned earlier: we shift from the misunderstood to the unknowable. This modern literary practice has its counterpart outside of literature: schizophrenic discourse. Schizophrenic discourse preserves its representative intention, yet through a series of inappropriate procedures (which I have tried to classify elsewhere) it renders construction impossible.

This is not the place to study other types of reading; noting their place beside reading as construction will suffice. To perceive and describe reading as construction is all the more necessary, given that the individual reader, far from being aware of the theoretical nuances it exemplifies, reads the same text in several ways at the same time, or at different times. His activity is so natural to him that it remains imperceptible. Therefore, it is necessary to learn how to construct reading—whether it be as construction or as deconstruction.

Notes

1. "I felt that she was better than I; I scorned myself for being unworthy of her. It is a terrible misfortune not to be loved when one loves; but it is a far greater misfortune to be loved passionately when one no longer loves." All translations from *Adolphe* and *Armance* by Susan Suleiman.

2. "I found in my father not a censor, but a cold and caustic observer who would first smile in pity and soon finish the conversation with impatience."

3. "Our host, who had chatted with a Neapolitan servant who attended on that stranger [i.e., Adolphe] without knowing his name, told me that he was not at all traveling out of curiosity, for he visited neither the ruins, nor the natural sites, nor the monuments, nor his fellow-men."

4. "I hate that vanity which is preoccupied only with recounting the evil it has done, which has the pretension of inspiring pity by describing itself, and which, hovering indestructibly above the ruins, analyzes itself instead of repenting."

5. "The object that escapes us is of necessity altogether different from the one that pursues us."

6. "I cannot recall, during the first eighteen years of my life, ever having had an hour's conversation with him. . . . I did not know then what timidity was."

7. "I told myself that I mustn't be overhasty, that Ellénore was not sufficiently prepared for the confession I was planning and that it was better to wait some more. Almost always, to live in peace with ourselves, we hide our weaknesses and impotence beneath the guise of calculations and systems: this satisfies the part of ourselves which is, as it were, the spectator of the other."

8. "He lacked penetration, not character."

9. "The world would regard me as a lady's companion who seduced the son of the house. I can already hear what the duchesse d'Ancre would say, or even more respect-

able women like the marquise de Seyssins, who sees in Octave a husband for one of her daughters."

10.   "If I kill myself, Armance will be compromised. All of society will spend a week in tracking down the most minute circumstances of this evening; and every one of these gentlemen who were present will be authorized to give a different account of what happened."

20 John Barth : *The Literature of Replenishment*

John Barth states that "The Literature of Replenishment" (1980) is "meant as a companion and corrective" to "The Literature of Exhaustion" (1967). In the earlier essay Barth took a pessimistic view of late modernist literature. In "The Literature of Replenishment," he takes a more positive view of what he calls postmodernist literature. Barth begins by naming some of postmodernism's practitioners, such as himself, William Gass, John Hawkes, Donald Barthelme, Robert Coover, Thomas Pynchon, and Kurt Vonnegut, Jr. But even providing a list proves troublesome, much less attempting a definition. By its very nature, the term "postmodernism" requires some agreement about "modernism": a literary mode from which "postmodernism" proceeds and against which it reacts.

Barth attempts to define his term by beginning with Gerald Graff's delineation of modernism and discussing the ways in which postmodernism departs from it. The key to understanding modernism is "that one cardinal preoccupation of the modernists was the problematics, not simply of language, but of the medium of literature." For Barth, modernism was a repudiation of what Roland Barthes calls "bourgeois" fiction, and while postmodernism in part repudiates that repudiation, literature cannot simply consist of a movement of negations. Instead, Barth states: "My ideal postmodernist author neither merely repudiates nor merely imitates either his twentieth-century modernist parents or his nineteenth-century premodernist grandparents. . . . The ideal postmodernist novel will somehow rise above the quarrel between realism and irrealism, formalism and 'contentism,' pure and committed literature, coterie fiction and junk fiction." He ends his essay with the hope that postmodernist fiction may eventually be recognized as "a literature of replenishment."

John Barth (b. 1930), who teaches at Johns Hopkins University, has been hailed as one of the leading "postmodernists" in the United States, having published such novels as *Giles Goat-Boy* (1966), *The End of the Road* (1967), *The Sot-Weed Factor* (1967), and *Sabbatical: A Romance* (1982), as well as numerous short stories.

The word is not yet in our standard dictionaries and encyclopedias, but since the end of World War II, and especially in the United States in the latter 1960s and the 1970s, "postmodernism" has enjoyed a very considerable currency, particularly with regard to our contemporary fiction. There are university courses in the American postmodernist novel; at least one quarterly journal is devoted exclusively to the discussion of postmodernist literature; at the University of Tübingen last June (1979), the annual meeting of the Deutsche Gesellschaft für Amerikastudien took as its theme "America in the 1970s," with particular emphasis on American postmodernist writing. Three alleged practitioners of that mode — William Gass, John Hawkes, and myself — were even there as live exhibits. The December annual convention of the Modern Language Association, just held in San Francisco, likewise scheduled a symposium on "the self in postmodernist fiction," a subtopic that takes the larger topic for granted.

From all this, one might innocently suppose that such a creature as postmodernism, with defined characteristics, is truly at large in our land. So I myself imagined when, in preparation for the Tübingen conference, and in response to being frequently labeled a postmodernist writer, I set about to learn what postmodernism is. I had a sense of *déjà vu:* About my very first published fiction, a 1950 undergraduate effort published in my university's quarterly magazine, a graduate-student critic wrote: "Mr. Barth alters that modernist dictum, 'the plain reader be damned': He removes the adjective." Could that, I wondered now, be postmodernism?

What I quickly discovered is that while some of the writers labeled as postmodernists, myself included, may happen to take the label with some seriousness, a principal activity of postmodernist critics (also called "metacritics" and "paracritics"), writing in postmodernist journals or speaking at postmodernist symposia, consists in disagreeing about what postmodernism is or ought to be, and thus about who should be admitted to the club — or clubbed into admission, depending upon the critic's view of the phenomenon and of particular writers.

Who are the postmodernists? By my count, the American fictionists most commonly included in the canon, besides the three of us at Tübingen, are Donald Barthelme, Robert Coover, Stanley Elkin, Thomas Pynchon, and Kurt Vonnegut, Jr. Several of the critics I read widen the net to include Saul Bellow and Norman Mailer, different as those two writers would appear to be. Others look beyond the United States to Samuel Beckett, Jorge Luis Borges, and the late Vladimir Nabokov as engendering spirits of the "movement"; others yet insist upon including the late Raymond Queneau, the French "new novelists" Nathalie Sarraute, Michel Butor,

Alain Robbe-Grillet, Robert Pinget, Claude Simon, and Claude Mauriac, the even newer French writers of the Tel Quel group, the Englishman John Fowles, and the expatriate Argentine Julio Cortázar. Some assert that such filmmakers as Michelangelo Antonioni, Federico Fellini, Jean-Luc Godard, and Alain Resnais are postmodernists. I myself will not join any literary club that doesn't include the expatriate Colombian Gabriel García Márquez and the semi-expatriate Italian Italo Calvino, of both of whom more presently. Anticipations of the "postmodernist literary aesthetic" have duly been traced through the great modernists of the first half of the twentieth century—T. S. Eliot, William Faulkner, André Gide, James Joyce, Franz Kafka, Thomas Mann, Robert Musil, Ezra Pound, Marcel Proust, Gertrude Stein, Miguel de Unamuno, Virginia Woolf—through *their* nineteenth-century predecessors—Alfred Jarry, Gustave Flaubert, Charles Baudelaire, Stéphane Mallarmé, and E. T. A. Hoffmann—back to to Laurence Sterne's *Tristram Shandy* (1767) and Miguel de Cervantes's *Don Quixote* (1615).

On the other hand, among certain commentators the sifting gets exceedingly fine. Professor Jerome Klinkowitz of Northern Iowa, for example, hails Barthelme and Vonnegut as the exemplary "postcontemporaries" of the American 1970s and consigns Pynchon and myself to some 1960ish outer darkness. I regard the novels of John Hawkes as examples of fine late modernism rather than of postmodernism (and I admire them no less for that). Others might regard most of Bellow, and Mailer's *The Naked and the Dead,* as comparatively *pre*modernist, along with the works of such more consistently traditionalist American writers as John Cheever, Wallace Stegner, William Styron, or John Updike, for example (the last of whom, however, Ihab Hassan calls a modernist), or those of most of the leading British writers of this century (as contrasted with the Irish), or those of many of our contemporary American women writers of fiction, whose main literary concern, for better or worse, remains the eloquent issuance of what the critic Richard Locke has called "secular news reports." Even among the productions of a given writer, distinctions can be and often are invoked. Joyce Carol Oates writes all over the aesthetical map. John Gardner's first two published novels I would call distinctly modernist works; his short stories dabble in postmodernism; his polemical nonfiction is aggressively reactionary. Italo Calvino, on the other hand, began as an Italian new-realist (in *The Path to the Nest of Spiders* [1947]) and matured into an exemplary postmodernist (with, e.g., *Cosmicomics*

[1965] and *The Castle of Crossed Destinies* [1969] who on occasion rises, sinks, or merely shifts to modernism (e.g., *Invisible Cities* [1972]). My own novels and stories seem to me to have both modernist and postmodernist attributes, even occasional premodernist attributes.

One certainly does have a sense of having been through this before. Indeed, some of us who have been publishing fiction since the 1950s have had the interesting experience of being praised or damned in that decade as existentialists and in the early 1960s as black humorists. Had our professional careers antedated the Second World War, we would no doubt have been praised or damned as modernists, in the distinguished company listed above. Now we are praised or damned as postmodernists.

Well, but what *is* postmodernism? When one leaves off the mere recitation of proper names and makes due allowance for the differences among any given author's works, do the writers most often called postmodernist share any aesthetic principles or practices as significant as the differences between them? The term itself, like "postimpressionism," is awkward and faintly epigonic, suggestive less of a vigorous or even interesting new direction in the old art of storytelling than of something anticlimactic, feebly following a very hard act to follow. One is reminded of the early James Joyce's fascination with the word *gnomon* in its negative geometrical sense: the figure that remains when a parallelogram has been removed from a similar but larger parallelogram with which it shares a common corner.

My Johns Hopkins colleague Professor Hugh Kenner, though he does not use the term postmodernist, clearly feels that way in his study of American modernist writers (*A Homemade World* [1975]): After a chapter on William Faulkner entitled "The Last Novelist," he dismisses Nabokov, Pynchon, and Barth with a sort of sigh. The late John Gardner goes even farther in his tract *On Moral Fiction* (1978), an exercise in literary kneecapping that lumps modernists and postmodernists together without distinction and consigns us all to Hell with the indiscriminate fervor characteristic of late converts to the right. Irving Howe (*The Decline of the New* [1970]) and George P. Elliott (*The Modernist Deviation* [1971]) would applaud—Professor Howe perhaps less enthusiastically than Professor Elliott. Professor Gerald Graff of Northwestern University, writing in *Tri-Quarterly* in 1975, takes a position somewhat similar to Kenner's, as the titles of two of his admirable essays make clear: "The Myth of the Postmodernist Breakthrough" (*Tri-Quarterly* 26) and "Babbitt at the Abyss"

(*Tri-Quarterly* 33). Professor Robert Alter of Berkeley, in the same magazine, subtitles *his* essay on postmodernist fiction "reflections on the aftermath of modernism." Both critics proceed to a qualified sympathy for what they take to be the postmodernist program (as does Professor Ihab Hassan of the University of Wisconsin-Milwaukee in his 1971 study *The Dismemberment of Orpheus: Towards a Postmodern Literature*), and both rightly proceed *from* the premise that that program is in some respects an extension of the program of modernism, in other respects a reaction against it. The term *postmodernism* clearly suggests both; any discussion of it must therefore either presume that modernism in its turn, at this hour of the world, needs no definition — surely everybody knows what modernism is! — or else must attempt after all to define or redefine that predominant aesthetic of Western literature (and music, painting, sculpture, architecture, and the rest) in the first half of this century.

Professor Alter takes the former course: His aforementioned essay opens with the words: "Over the past two decades, as the high tide of modernism ebbed and its masters died off . . . " and proceeds without further definition to the author's reflections upon the ensuing low tide. Professor Graff, on the other hand, borrowing from Professor Howe, makes a useful quick review of the conventions of literary modernism before discussing the mode of fiction which, in his words, "departs not only from realistic conventions but from modernist ones as well."

It is good that he does, for it is not only *post*modernism that lacks definition in our standard reference books. My *Oxford English Dictionary* attests *modernism* to 1737 (Jonathan Swift, in a letter to Alexander Pope) and *Modernist* to 1588, but neither term in the sense we mean. My *American Heritage Dictionary* (1973) gives as its fourth and last definition of *modernism* "the theory and practice of modern art," a definition which does not take us very far into our American Heritage. My *Columbia Encyclopedia* (1975) discusses modernism only in the theological sense — the reinterpretation of Christian doctrine in the light of modern psychological and scientific discoveries — and follows this with an exemplary entry on *el modernismo*, a nineteenth-century Spanish literary movement which influenced the "Generation of '98" and inspired the *ultraísmo* of which Jorge Luis Borges was a youthful exponent. Neither my *Reader's Encyclopedia* (1950) nor my *Reader's Guide to Literary Terms* (1960) enters *modernism* by any definition whatever, much less *postmodernism*.

Now, as a working writer who cut his literary teeth on Eliot, Joyce,

Kafka, and the other great modernists, and who is currently branded as a postmodernist, and who in fact has certain notions, no doubt naive, about what that term might conceivably mean if it is to describe anything very good very well, I am grateful to the likes of Professor Graff for not regarding his categories as self-defining. It is quite one thing to compare a line of Verdi or Tennyson or Tolstoy with a line of Stravinsky or Eliot or Joyce and to recognize that you have put the nineteenth century behind you: "Happy families are all alike; every unhappy family is unhappy in its own way" (Leo Tolstoy, *Anna Karenina,* trans. Constance Garnett). " . . . riverrun, past Eve's and Adam's, from swerve of shore to bend of bay, brings us by a commodius vicus of recirculation back to Howth Castle and Environs" (James Joyce, *Finnegans Wake*). It is quite another thing to characterize the differences between those two famous opening sentences, to itemize the aesthetic principles — premodernist and modernist — from which each issues, and then to proceed to a great *post*modernist opening sentence and show where its aesthetics resemble and differ from those of its parents, so to speak, and those of its grandparents, respectively: "Many years later, as he faced the firing squad, Colonel Aureliano Buendia was to remember that distant afternoon when his father took him to discover ice" (Gabriel García Márquez, *One Hundred Years of Solitude,* trans. Gregory Rabassa).

Professor Graff does not do this, exactly, though no doubt he could if pressed. But I shall borrow his useful checklist of the characteristics of modernist fiction, add a few items to it, summarize as typical his and Professor Alter's differing characterizations of postmodernist fiction, disagree with them respectfully in some particulars, and then fall silent, except as a storyteller.

The ground motive of modernism, Graff asserts, was criticism of the nineteenth-century bourgeois social order and its worldview. Its artistic strategy was the self-conscious overturning of the conventions of bourgeois realism by such tactics and devices as the substitution of a "mythical" for a "realistic" method and the "manipulation of conscious parallels between contemporaneity and antiquity" (Graff is here quoting T. S. Eliot on James Joyce's *Ulysses*); also the radical disruption of the linear flow of narrative, the frustration of conventional expectations concerning unity and coherence of plot and character and the cause-and-effect "development" thereof, the deployment of ironic and ambiguous juxtapositions to call into question the moral and philosophical "meaning" of literary action, the adoption of a tone of epistemological self-mockery aimed at the naive pretensions of bourgeois rationality, the opposition of inward consciousness to rational, public, objective discourse, and an inclination to subjective distortion to point up the evanescence of the objective social world of the nineteenth-century bourgeoisie.

This checklist strikes me as reasonable, if somewhat depressing from our historical perspective. I would add to it the modernists' insistence, borrowed from their romantic forebears, on the special, usually alienated role of the artist in his society, or outside it: James Joyce's priestly, self-exiled artist-hero; Thomas Mann's artist as charlatan, or mountebank; Franz Kafka's artist as anorexic, or bug. I would add too, what is no doubt implicit in Graff's catalogue, the modernists' foregrounding of language and technique as opposed to straightforward traditional "content": We remember Thomas Mann's remark (in *Tonio Kröger,* 1903), "what an artist talks *about* is never the main point"; a remark which echoes Gustave Flaubert's to Louise Colet in 1852 — "what I could like to do . . . is write a book about nothing" — and which anticipates Alain Robbe-Grillet's *obiter dictum* of 1957: "the genuine writer has nothing to say . . . He has only a way of speaking." Roland Barthes sums up this fall from innocence and ordinary content on the part of modernist literature in *Writing Degree Zero* (1953): "the whole of literature, from Flaubert to the present day, became the problematics of language."

This is French hyperbole: It is enough to say that one cardinal preoccupation of the modernists was the problematics, not simply of language, but of the medium of literature.

Now, for Professor Alter, Professor Hassan, and others, *post*modernist fiction merely emphasizes the "performing" self-consciousness and self-reflexiveness of modernism, in a spirit of cultural subversiveness and anarchy. With varying results, they maintain, postmodernist writers write a fiction that is more and more about itself and its processes, less and less about objective reality and life in the world. For Graff, too, postmodern fiction simply carries to its logical and questionable extremes the antirationalist, antirealist, antibourgeois program of modernism, but with neither a solid adversary (the bourgeois having now everywhere co-opted the trappings of modernism and turned its defiant principles into mass-media kitsch) nor solid moorings in the quotidian realism it defines itself against. From this serious charge Graff exempts certain postmodernist satire, in particular the fiction of Donald Barthelme, Saul Bellow, and Stanley

Elkin, as managing to be vitalized by the same kitschy society that is its target.

I must say that all this sounds persuasive to me — until I examine more closely what I'm so inclined to nod my head yes to.

It goes without saying that critical categories are as more or less fishy as they are less or more useful. I happen to believe that just as an excellent teacher is likely to teach well no matter what pedagogical theory he suffers from, so a gifted writer is likely to rise above what he takes to be his aesthetic principles, not to mention what *others* take to be his aesthetic principles. Indeed, I believe that a truly splendid specimen in whatever aesthetic mode will pull critical ideology along behind it, like an ocean liner trailing seagulls. Actual artists, actual texts, are seldom more than more or less modernist, postmodernist, formalist, symbolist, realist, surrealist, politically committed, aesthetically "pure," "experimental," regionalist, internationalist, what have you. The particular work ought always to take primacy over contexts and categories. On the other hand, art lives in human time and history, and general changes in its modes and materials and concerns, even when not obviously related to changes in technology, are doubtless as significant as the changes in a culture's general attitudes, which its arts may both inspire and reflect. Some are more or less trendy and superficial, some may be indicative of more or less deep malaises, some perhaps healthy correctives of or reactions against such malaises. In any case, we can't readily discuss what artists aspire to do and what they end up doing except in terms of aesthetic categories, and so we should look further at this approximately shared impulse called postmodernism.

In my view, if it has no other and larger possibilities than those noted by, for example, Professors Alter, Graff, and Hassan, then postmodernist writing is indeed a kind of pallid, last-ditch decadence, of no more than minor symptomatic interest. There is no lack of actual texts illustrative of this view of the "postmodernist breakthrough"; but that is only to remind us that what Paul Valéry remarked of an earlier generation applies to ours as well: "Many ape the postures of modernity, without understanding their necessity." In my view, the proper program for postmodernism is neither a mere extension of the modernist program as described above, nor a mere intensification of certain aspects of modernism, nor on the contrary a wholesale subversion or repudiation of either modernism or what I'm calling premodernism: "traditional" bourgeois realism.

To go back a moment to our catalogue of the field-identification marks of modernist writing: Two other conspicuous ones are not yet there acknowledged, except by implication. On the one hand, James Joyce and the other great modernists set very high standards of artistry, no doubt implicit in their preoccupation with the special remove of the artist from his or her society. On the other hand, we have their famous relative difficulty of access, inherent in their antilinearity, their aversion to conventional characterization and cause-and-effect dramaturgy, their celebration of private, subjective experience over public experience, their general inclination to "metaphoric" as against "metonymic" means. (But this difficulty is *not* inherent, it is important to note, in their high standards of craftsmanship.)

From this relative difficulty of access, what Hassan calls their aristocratic cultural spirit, comes of course the relative unpopularity of modernist fiction, outside of intellectual circles and university curricula, by contrast with the fiction of, say, Dickens, Twain, Hugo, Dostoevsky, Tolstoy. From it comes also and notoriously the engenderment of a necessary priestly industry of explicators, annotators, allusion-chasers, to mediate between the text and the reader. If we need a guide, or a guidebook, to steer us through Homer or Aeschylus, it is because the world of the text is so distant from our own, as it presumably was not from Aeschylus's and Homer's original audiences. But with *Finnegans Wake* or Ezra Pound's *Cantos* we need a guide because of the inherent and immediate difficulty of the text. We are told that Bertolt Brecht, out of socialist conviction, kept on his writing desk a toy donkey bearing the sign *Even I must understand it;* the high modernists might aptly have put on their desks a professor-of-literature doll bearing, unless its specialty happened to be the literature of high modernism, the sign *Not even I can understand it.*

I do not say this in deprecation of these great writers and their sometimes brilliant explicators. If modernist works are often forbidding and require a fair amount of help and training to appreciate, it does not follow that they are not superbly rewarding, as climbing Mount Matterhorn must be, or sailing a small boat around the world. To return to our subject: Let us agree with the commonplace that the rigidities and other limitations of nineteenth-century bourgeois realism, in the light of turn-of-the-century theories and discoveries in physics, psychology, anthropology, technology, etc., prompted or fueled the great adversary reaction called modernist art — which came to terms with our new ways of thinking about the world at the frequent expense of democratic access, of immediate or at least ready delight, and often of political responsibility (the politics of Eliot, Joyce, Pound, Nabokov, and Borges, for example, are notoriously inclined either to nonexistence or to the far right). But in North America, in western and northern Europe, in the United Kingdom, in Japan, and in some of Central and South America, at least, these nineteenth-century rigidities are virtually no more. The modernist aesthetic is in my opinion unquestionably the characteristic aesthetic of the first half of our century — and in my opinion it *belongs* to the first half of our century. The present reaction against it is perfectly understandable and to be sympathized with, both because the modernist coinages are by now more or less debased common currency and because we really don't *need* more *Finnegans Wakes* and *Pisan Cantos,* each with its staff of tenured professors to explain it to us.

But I deplore the artistic and critical cast of mind that repudiates the whole modernist enterprise as an aberration and sets to work as if it hadn't happened; that rushes back into the arms of nineteenth-century middle-class realism as if the first half of the twentieth century hadn't happened. It *did* happen: Freud and Einstein and two world wars and the Russian and sexual revolutions and automobiles and airplanes and telephones and radios and movies and urbanization, and now nuclear weaponry and television and microchip technology and the new feminism and the rest, and except as readers there's no going back to Tolstoy and Dickens. As the Russian writer Evgeny Zamyatin was already saying in the 1920s (in his essay *On Literature, Revolution, and Entropy*): "Euclid's world is very simple, and Einstein's world is very difficult; nevertheless, it is now impossible to return to Euclid's."

On the other hand, it is no longer necessary, if it ever was, to repudiate *them,* either: the great premodernists. If the modernists, carrying the torch of romanticism, taught us that linearity, rationality, consciousness, cause and effect, naive illusionism, transparent language, innocent anecdote, and middle-class moral conventions are not the whole story, then from the perspective of these closing decades of our century we may appreciate that the contraries of those things are not the whole story either. Disjunction, simultaneity, irrationalism, anti-illusionism, self-reflexiveness, medium-as-message, political olympianism, and a moral pluralism approaching moral entropy — these are not the whole story either.

A worthy program for postmodernist fiction, I believe, is the synthesis or transcension of these antitheses, which may be summed up as premodernist and modernist modes of writing. My ideal postmodernist author neither merely repudiates nor merely imitates either his twentieth-century modernist parents or his nineteenth-century premodernist grandparents. He has the first half of our century under his belt, but not on his back. Without lapsing into moral or artistic simplism, shoddy craftsmanship, Madison Avenue venality, or either false or real naiveté, he nevertheless aspires to a fiction more democratic in its appeal than such late-modernist marvels (by my definition) as Beckett's *Texts for Nothing* or Nabokov's *Pale Fire*. He may not hope to reach and move the devotees of James Michener and Irving Wallace — not to mention the great mass of television-addicted nonreaders. But he *should* hope to reach and delight, at least part of the time, beyond the circle of what Mann used to call the Early Christians: professional devotees of high art.

I feel this in particular for practitioners of the novel, a genre whose historical roots are famously and honorably in middle-class popular culture. The ideal postmodernist novel will somehow rise above the quarrel between realism and irrealism, formalism and "contentism," pure and committed literature, coterie fiction and junk fiction. Alas for professors of literature, it may not need as much *teaching* as Joyce's or Nabokov's or Pynchon's books, or some of my own. On the other hand, it will not wear its heart on its sleeve, either; at least not its whole heart. (In a recent published exchange between William Gass and John Gardner, Gardner declares that he wants everybody to love his books; Gass replies that he would no more want his books to be loved by everybody than he'd want his daughter to be loved by everybody, and suggests that Gardner is confusing love with promiscuity.) My own analogy would be with good jazz or classical music: One finds much on successive listenings or close examination of the score that one didn't catch the first time through; but the first time through should be so ravishing — and not just to specialists — that one delights in the replay.

Lest this postmodern synthesis sound both sentimental and impossible of attainment, I offer two quite different examples of works which I believe approach it, as perhaps such giants as Dickens and Cervantes may be said to anticipate it. The first and more tentative example (it is not meant to be a blockbuster) is Italo Calvino's *Cosmicomics* (1965): beautifully written, enormously appealing space-age fables — "perfect dreams," John Updike has called them — whose materials are as modern as the new cosmology and as ancient as folktales, but whose themes are love and loss, change and permanence, illusion and reality, including a good deal of specifically Italian reality. Like all fine fantasists, Calvino grounds his flights in local, palpable detail: Along with the nebulae and the black holes and the lyricism, there is a nourishing supply of pasta, bambini, and good-looking women sharply glimpsed and gone forever. A true postmodernist, Calvino keeps one foot always in the narrative past — characteristically the Italian narrative past of Boccaccio, Marco Polo, or Italian fairy tales — and one foot in, one might say, the Parisian structuralist present; one foot in fantasy, one in objective reality, etc. It is appropriate that he has, I understand, been chastised from the left by the Italian communist critics and from the right by the Italian Catholic critics; it is symptomatic that he has been praised by fellow authors as divergent as John Updike, Gore Vidal, and myself. I urge everyone to read Calvino at once, beginning with *Cosmicomics* and going right on, not only because he exemplifies my postmodernist program, but because his fiction is both delicious and high in protein.

An even better example is Gabriel García Márquez's *One Hundred Years of Solitude* (1967): as impressive a novel as has been written so far in the second half of our century and one of the splendid specimens of that splendid genre from any century. Here the synthesis of straightforward-ness and artifice, realism and magic and myth, political passion and non-political artistry, characterization and caricature, humor and terror, are so remarkably sustained that one recognizes with exhilaration very early on, as with *Don Quixote* and *Great Expectations* and *Huckleberry Finn,* that one is in the presence of a masterpiece not only artistically admirable, but humanly wise, lovable, literally marvelous. One had almost forgotten that new fiction could be so *wonderful* as well as so merely important. And the question whether my program for postmodernism is achievable goes hap-pily out the window, like one of García Márquez's characters on flying carpets. Praise be to the Spanish language and imagination! As Cervantes stands as an exemplar of premodernism and a great precursor of much to come, and Jorge Luis Borges as an exemplar of *dernier cri* modernism and at the same time as a bridge between the end of the nineteenth century and the end of the twentieth, so Gabriel García Márquez is in that enviable succession: an exemplary postmodernist and a master of the storyteller's art.

A dozen years ago I published in these pages a much-misread essay called "The Literature of Exhaustion," occasioned by my admiration for the stories of Señor Borges and by my concern, in that somewhat apocalyptic place and time, for the ongoing health of narrative fiction. (The time was the latter 1960s; the place Buffalo, N.Y., on a university campus embattled by tear-gassing riot police and tear-gassed Vietnam War protesters, while from across the Peace Bridge in Canada came Professor Marshall McLuhan's siren song that we "print-oriented bastards" were obsolete.) The simple burden of my essay was that the forms and modes of art live in human history and are therefore subject to used-upness, at least in the minds of significant numbers of artists in particular times and places: in other words, that artistic conventions are liable to be retired, subverted, transcended, transformed, or even deployed against themselves to generate new and lively work. I would have thought that point unexceptionable. But a great many people—among them, I fear, Señor Borges himself—mistook me to mean that literature, at least fiction, is *kaput;* that it has all been done already; that there is nothing left for contemporary writers but to parody and travesty our great predecessors in our exhausted medium—exactly what some critics deplore as postmodernism.

That is not what I meant at all. Leaving aside the celebrated fact that, with *Don Quixote,* the novel may be said to *begin* in self-transcendent parody and has often returned to that mode for its refreshment, let me say at once and plainly that I agree with Borges that literature can never be exhausted, if only because no single literary text can ever be exhausted—its "meaning" residing as it does in its transactions with individual readers over time, space, and language. I like to remind misreaders of my earlier essay that written literature is in fact about 4,500 years old (give or take a few centuries depending on one's definition of literature), but that we have no way of knowing whether 4,500 years constitutes senility, maturity, youth, or mere infancy. The number of splendid sayable things—metaphors for the dawn or the sea, for example—is doubtless finite; it is also doubtless very large, perhaps virtually infinite. In some moods we writers may feel that Homer had it easier than we, getting there early with his rosy-fingered dawn and his wine-dark sea. We should console ourselves that one of the earliest extant literary texts (an Egyptian papyrus of ca. 2000 B.C., cited by Walter Jackson Bate in his 1970 study *The Burden of the Past and the English Poet*) is a complaint by the scribe Khakheperresenb that he has arrived on the scene too late: "Would I had phrases that are not known, utterances that are strange, in new language that has not been used, free from repetition, not an utterance that has grown stale, which men of old have spoken."

What my essay "The Literature of Exhaustion" was really about, so it seems to me now, was the effective "exhaustion" not of language or of literature, but of the aesthetic of high modernism: that admirable, not-to-be-repudiated, but essentially completed "program" of what Hugh Kenner has dubbed "the Pound era." In 1966–67 we scarcely had the term *postmodernism* in its current literary-critical usage — at least I hadn't heard it yet — but a number of us, in quite different ways and with varying combinations of intuitive response and conscious deliberation, were already well into the working out, not of the next best thing after modernism, but of the *best next* thing: what is gropingly now called postmodernist fiction; what I hope might also be thought of one day as a literature of replenishment.

Suzanne C. Ferguson begins by recognizing that critical theory in the 1980s remains at cross-purposes over how to define the short story as a discrete literary form. Is it one variant of prose fiction, like the novel, or is it a separate genre? Like Norman Friedman, Ferguson believes that "the main formal characteristics of the modern novel and the modern short story are the same," but the *modern* short story is even more heavily influenced by turn-of-the-century impressionism than the novel, and, hence, is more obviously distinct from earlier short fiction than is the modern novel from its prose precursors. But Ferguson, unlike Friedman, claims that in one specific element — plot — the modern short story is apparently unlike the modern novel. This claim depends in part upon the establishment of sufficient literary conventions known to the competent reader that enable the author to produce "elliptical plots" and "metaphorical plots" without rendering the short story incomprehensible. Ferguson builds her contention about short story plot in part upon Joseph Frank's distinction between spatially and temporally organized fictions, describing the modern short story as "a manifestation of impressionism rather than a discrete genre." But, like Friedman, Ferguson emphasizes this point in order to lead readers away from abstract generic debates and toward engagement with individual stories.

Suzanne C. Ferguson (b. 1939) is Professor of English at Wayne State University. She has authored *The Poetry of Randall Jarrell* (1971), edited *Critical Essays on Randall Jarrell* (1983), and coedited *Literature and the Visual Arts in Contemporary Society* (1986).

That there is no large and distinguished corpus of short story theory because the short story does not exist as a discrete and independent genre is a hypothesis — repugnant to many, of course — that ought to be taken seriously on occasion, if only to contemplate the perspective the hypothesis provides. "Intuition" or even "experience" may tell us that the "short story" exists, but defining it has proven surprisingly resistant to critical effort. A 1976 anthology, Charles May's *Short Story Theories,*[1] demonstrates the problematic situation. Short stories are defined in terms of unity (Poe, Brander Matthews, and others), techniques of plot compression (A. L. Bader, Norman Friedman, L. A. G. Strong), change or revelation of character (Theodore Stroud), subject (Frank O'Connor), tone (Gordimer), "lyricism" (Moravia), but there is no single characteristic or cluster of characteristics that the critics agree absolutely distinguishes the short story from other fictions. Thomas Gullason begins by lambasting Poe's formulas for "unity of effect" as "destructive," but ends up praising the short story for its "compact impact," which comes from "distillation" and "telescoping."[2] Norman Friedman's valiant effort to discover "What Makes a Short Story Short?" leaves the distinct impression that it is a short story because it is — well — *a short story.*[3]

A structuralist conception of fiction[4] tends to confirm the suspicion that there may be no rational way to distinguish "short story" from other narratives in the same mimetic mode: all stories, short and long, have certain required properties of narrativity — characters, place, events, a "beginning, middle, and an end," and coherence among the parts. All stories can be reduced to minimal statements of the required elements or expanded by the inclusion of optional developments in the narrative chain, as long as they maintain a discoverable coherence in their interrelationships. Like the sentence, the story has "slots" where various elements may be inserted; beyond a basic minimum of noun phrase plus verb phrase or existent plus event (character plus action), both the sentence and the story may be almost infinitely expanded. *Tristram Shandy* and *Ulysses* suggest an extreme range of options for the extrapolation of simple narrative sequences into long and complex ones. Similar expansion could be applied to any story, from "The Town Mouse and the Country Mouse" to "Indian Camp"; but of course the "best" short stories give us a sense of the inevitability of each sentence and persuade us that they are as complete as possible, that any addition or deletion would destroy their aesthetic wholeness. Whereas the omission of an entire sentence from Aesop's "The Town Mouse and the Country Mouse" would likely jeopardize its narrative coherence, we might add several without destroying its elegant symmetry or its moral. Indeed, its basic structure is the foundation of a number of nineteenth-century novels. We might remove one or more sentences from "The Fall of the House of Usher" or even (sacrilege!) "Araby" — providing we chose carefully — without altering its theme or quality for most readers.

What accounts, then, for the persistent notion that the "modern" short story is a new genre, something different from the tale and sketch that preceded it? In fact, the modern short story shows all the same shifts in sensibility and technique that affected the novel and the long story (or nouvelle) around the end of the nineteenth century, but these changes "look" different in the short story precisely because it is physically short. The main formal characteristics of the modern novel and the modern short story are the same: (1) limitation and foregrounding of point of view, (2) emphasis on presentation of sensation and inner experience, (3) the deletion or transformation of several elements of the traditional plot, (4) increasing reliance on metaphor and metonymy in the presentation of events and existents, (5) rejection of chronological time ordering, (6) formal and stylistic economy, and (7) the foregrounding of style. All these elements are associated with the literary movement called impressionism, or, more specifically in fiction, the tradition of Flaubert. I will argue that, just as impressionism dominates the mainstream of the novel in the late nineteenth and early twentieth centuries, so it does that of the short story. But the short story, because it has fewer "optional" narrative elements in its structural "slots," manifests its formal allegiances to impressionism even more obviously than does the novel and, consequently, seems more radically different from earlier short fiction than the impressionist novel seems different from the realistic novel that preceded it.

Let me take the characteristics in the order listed above, briefly illustrating each one. The limiting of point of view to that of a character or characters in the narrative and the emphasis on the presentation of sensation and inner experience are inextricably related. The same impulses that turned nineteenth-century philosophy away from positivism and toward phenomenology turned writers to the representation of experience *as* experienced by individuals. The importance of this philosophical shift in the interpretation of reality cannot be over-estimated in an attempt to understand what happened to writers' representations of reality. Imitation of how things "feel" or "seem" to the characters became the preferred subject of fiction rather than the imitation of "how things are" in the "real" world. Where the characters' attitudes and responses had always been a part of a more comprehensive view of the world, the subjectivity of "reality" now became the prevailing mode of understanding, and the exploration of subjectivity became the elusive "object" of fictional imitation.

In the impressionist short story, even more than in the impressionist novel, the author conceals himself, presenting the entire narrative from a point of view within the story, that of the characters' subjective experience of events, their "impressions," by using either first-person narration or the

Jamesian "method of the central intelligence." This emphasis on subjectivity inevitably affects the typical themes of modern fiction: alienation, isolation, solipsism, the quest for identity and integration. The characters, the experiencing subjects, are seen as isolated from other experiencing subjects, with only rare moments of communion or shared experience possible to them. Frank O'Connor's contention that the modern short story deals with outsiders, lonely individuals cut off from society, is true,[5] but that theme is equally typical of modern novels.

The preoccupation of impressionist authors with epistemological themes is another outgrowth of subjectivism, for when all we have in the world is our own experience of it, all received knowledge becomes suspect, and the very nature of knowledge becomes problematic. This uncertainty affects the concept of plot: the Aristotelian intertwining of knowledge with action is unraveled; protagonists become passive observers; the "absence" which impels the plot is absence of knowledge of some truth that could go beyond the merely personal to achieve a general validity. It is often the reader, rather than the character, who must directly confront the possibility that we cannot know anything for certain, that the processes we follow in search of truth may yield only fictions.[6]

Like the limiting of point of view and the theme of alienation, the quest for knowledge about reality is common to impressionist novels as well as short stories. In longer works of the earlier twentieth century, however, these features are usually less prominent than in shorter works because of the long works' elaboration of plot and character, their density of specification, and the like. Comparison of *Ulysses* with "The Dead" and of "The Dead" with "An Encounter" or "The Sisters" will clarify this contention. The theme of quest for reliable, transpersonal knowledge about the world is present in all three "genres" — novel, nouvelle, story — but there are complementary or ancillary themes in the longer works, along with multiplication of episodes in the plot, proliferation of detail in descriptions, and, in *Ulysses,* the diversification of styles in the texture of the work. Although all these factors actually do manifest the theme of the quest to define reality, the reader tends to be less aware of the theme as such and more engrossed in the richness of the longer works' texture. The compactness and focus of the short stories makes the theme more readily apparent.

It is in the realm of plot that the modern short story is most different from earlier short fiction and in which it appears to be most different from the novel. The deemphasis of physical action in impressionist fiction (or the disjunction of physical action from thought and feeling), which leaves adjustments of thought or feeling as the true "events" of the plot, makes the articulation of plot in many cases obscure. A related problem is the increasing expectation of the writers that their readers will have internalized the elements of traditional plots so thoroughly that the writers can presume readers will supply missing elements. The deletion of expected elements of the plot — from any "slot" in the story — is the hallmark of the late-nineteenth- and early-twentieth-century short story. There are two basic methods of deletion: that in which elements are simply omitted, which results in what I call "elliptical" plots, and that in which unexpected, dissonant existents or events are substituted for the omitted elements, which yields "metaphoric" plots.

Elliptical plots may omit the exposition and never get back to it (as in "Cat in the Rain" or "Hills Like White Elephants"); or pass over what would ordinarily be "dramatized" or extensively reported parts of the middle, episodes that develop the plot conflict (Kipling stories such as "Love O' Women" and "Mrs. Bathurst," or Faulkner's "A Rose for Emily"); or leave out closure (Chekhov's "On the Road" and many others). Impressionist novels more rarely begin *in medias res* without going back to fill in the beginning at some later point in the narrative, and they almost never omit important stages of the middle, because one of the basic principles of the novel is to develop and elaborate. Elements left out at their "normal" chronological point in the narrative sequence turn up elsewhere (as in *The Good Soldier*).

To understand the notion of "elliptical" plots, it is helpful to look at some actual stories and propose for them "hypothetical" plots that might form the "natural" or "deep structure" bases of the narratives. (By hypothetical plot I mean something more specifically formulable than the barebones structuralist "fabula": a counter-story, with a beginning, middle, and end, that tells "what happened" in chronological order.) In "Clay" a hypothetical plot is the story of Maria's life from the time when she had a "home" with Alphy and Joe's family, through the breakup of the family and her making a new "home" in the laundry, to the time of the actual story, at the end of which she (perhaps unconsciously) acknowledges her desolation, her "homelessness." The reader must to some extent construct this hypothetical plot in order for the actual story to seem meaningful. The act of constructing a hypothetical plot is what we ask students to perform when we ask them, "Who is Maria?"; "What is her relation to Alphy and

Joe?"; "Why does she live at the laundry?"; "How do we know she won't get married?"; and the like.[7]

The actual plot of "Clay" deletes expository material and neglects to provide episodes showing Maria's desire for a home and family to which she could belong. The past when she had a sort of home is referred to in only a few phrases, and the bleakness of her life in the laundry is seen only obliquely in Maria's deliberately optimistic view of herself in the role of "peacemaker" to the unruly laundresses. This actual plot consists of three episodes, two of them developing tension and the third climactic. Maria prepares for the All Hallows party, hoping to reconcile Joe and Alphy and thus restore the conditions of a past in which she was relatively happy; she travels to the party, buying a piece of cake as an "offering" and losing it en route because of the distraction of a man flirting with her; after causing some distress at the party because of her concern at losing the cake, she is rejected (tricked) by an unthinking neighbor girl and consoled by the appreciation of her wishful song. The parts of the hypothetical plot that are omitted are represented metonymically by the episodes Joyce has written. Maria's experience at the party is representative of her life, or so we interpret the story.

In "Eveline," the darling of structuralist analysts, a hypothetical plot might be said to begin with Eveline's loss of her mother's love (through death), to run through her opportunity to find a new love with Frank, and to end with her acknowledgment that she cannot throw off the bonds of habit that link her, without love, to her father and her home. Here the actual plot begins after Eveline has been offered the chance to escape but before she rejects it. Both "Clay" and "Eveline" begin almost at the crisis of the traditional, "hypothetical" plot. Eveline is on the brink of an action that would change her life; Maria has her plan to reconcile the brothers. Eveline cannot act; Maria is deflected. For Eveline there is a tumult, inevitable (though untold) recognition; for Maria there is a simple retreat. Only the reader recognizes that Maria means little to Joe's family, that her future is not to reconcile and reunite the family but to move on alone into death.

In both stories, the exposition and earlier stages of conflict are alluded to in the protagonists' memories, but only the climaxes are dramatized. Although aesthetic closure is achieved in "Eveline" in the concluding images of the inundating sea, and in "Clay" in Maria's rendition of "I Dreamt that I Dwelt in Marble Halls" and Joe's reaction to it, the themes keep on unraveling into the futureless future beyond the end of the stories.

The sense of a double plot in all such stories is strong; we recognize a story that has not been fully told lying behind the one that *is* told. Reading the stories, we become detectives, piecing together the main elements of the hypothetical plots in order to rationalize the actual plots.

In addition to stories in which parts of the plot are omitted, there are stories in which the elements of the hypothetical plot are represented at the surface level by sets of images or events — often trivial and unrelated to each other — that are analogous to and substitutes for events in the hypothetical plot; that is, they stand in relation to the theme of the story as the chain of events does in a normal plot, and the chain of events is left implicit. These I call "metaphoric" plots. "Ivy Day in the Committee Room" and "The Gambler, the Nun, and the Radio" are extreme examples. The surface events of these stories are disconnected and of little apparent significance, but they suggest a deep level at which themes of profound human import are developed.

The theme of "Ivy Day" is the debasement of Parnell's ideals in the behavior of his nominal followers. The conversation in the Committee Room exemplifies the dishonor while it implicitly evokes the image of Parnell and his struggle to give the Irish political freedom, an image the reader must remember independently of what is told in the actual story. Seen in retrospect, each separate, fragmentary episode is a small betrayal. As we read the story, however, we gather up seemingly random threads: the rejection of the old by the young, the chicaneries and temporizing of the political hacks, the disreputable activities of the clergy. A sort of climax is achieved in the plan to welcome Edward VII — opposite to Parnell, the "uncrowned king" — to Ireland on an official visit, although he represents not only English domination but womanizing, the pretext on which Parnell — the faithful lover of another man's wife — was brought down. The episodes of the plot are not only metaphoric in this case but ironic: the day that is meant to honor Parnell dishonors his memory. Joe Hynes's poem, banal but sincere, is the best a sorry lot can do to retrieve past heroism, and the popping corks of stout bottles complete the humans' feeble salute.

In Hemingway's story, the figures of the gambler and the nun are protagonists of auxiliary elliptical narratives within the actual plot, and they and the radio are vehicles of metaphors whose tenor is the theme of a general quest for the "opium of the people." Mr. Frazer, who plays the radio and contemplates the gambler and the nun, is in some obscure way the protagonist of another story of which we know too few details even to hypothesize a plot, as well as of the actual story, whose ironies bring him to a conclusion about the meaninglessness of experience and the nature of the opiums of the people.

Without our sense of how traditional plots work, these stories would simply be accounts of "what happened"; they seem to lack the obligatory coherence of existent and event of ordinary narrative. The disorder is of course intentional, and it imitates the surface disorder of the world in which we seek coherence. Combining our intuitive knowledge of "storiness" with a symbolic reading of the actual events and characters, we find the narrative element in the works and perceive them as short stories rather than random accounts of unrelated characters and happenings. A long impressionist fiction that would depend so heavily upon the reader's intensive interpretation of symbolic incidents and figures for the basis of its narrative sequence seems unworkable, and I am unable to name one. Metaphoric episodes or subplots are relatively common, however: the French architect episode in *Absalom, Absalom!*, the excursion to "M——" in *The Good Soldier,* and the owl-eyed man scenes of *The Great Gatsby* suggest themselves. The stylistic vagaries of *Ulysses* function similarly, although like other, later novels, *Ulysses* has already gone beyond the boundaries of impressionism in so many ways that one should probably not include it here. Instead of asking the reader to measure a subjective view against a traditional, "realistic" view, postimpressionist fiction denies the existence of the latter altogether.

Elliptical and metaphoric plots affirm Joseph Frank's conception of a spatially rather than a temporally organized form in modern fiction. In focusing on the crisis of a hypothetical narrative, or in representing that narrative only in figures or analogues, such plots devalue temporal sequence and the chain of cause and effect. The deemphasis of the orderly unfolding of an action through time is closely related to the emergence of "epiphany" as an ordering device. The notion of single "moments" of experience as determiners of the quality of a whole life appears to be mystical in origin, and in secular literature it goes back at least to Wordsworth, but it has become characteristic of modern fiction both as an item of belief and a structural principle. In the modern novel, we move from epiphany to epiphany, or in Woolf's image, along a series of small revelations, "matches struck unexpectedly in the dark."[8] In the short story, we frequently see only one such privileged moment, which takes the place of the traditional "turning point," the climax of the plot. Not much actual dramatized time passes, although in the memory and fantasy of the characters large reaches of "time" may be covered. The narrator of "A Rose for Emily" tells his story after Emily's funeral, and his "epiphany" takes place when someone picks an iron-grey hair from her pillow, but the "story" covers many years in the life of Miss Emily Grierson, not just or not even most importantly the moment of her death. The actual plot unfolds the story of the town's discovery; but the more interesting story is the hypothetical plot the reader must puzzle out and restore to its "natural" chronology in order to understand the actual story. Time is as malleable here as in *The Sound and the Fury* or *Absalom, Absalom!*, but we are not so much concerned with its operations. Nevertheless, we must make a conscious effort to restore chronology in order to understand Miss Emily's story. In the foregrounding of time and in the temporal displacements between the hypothetical and actual plots, "A Rose for Emily" is an extreme case of the deviousness of many modern stories, which overtly seem to disdain temporal order but covertly remind us how time-bound we are.

The use of setting in impressionist fiction is also different from that in earlier fiction. Insofar as impressionism is an extension of realism in its sensational, experiential aspect, settings are established through the use of detail to give verisimilitude. That these details are chosen as much or more to reflect the mood of the characters perceiving them as to convey a location for the action and the characters' social standing marks a significant difference between realism and impressionism. Drawing upon the romantic (even Gothic) tradition, impressionist settings are frequently used metaphorically to substitute for representation of action or analysis. The fragmentary description of the house, street, and alleys that forms the beginning of "Araby" has to convey more than just the location of the events; it must stand in place of hypothetical episodes in which the boy's character would be developed in the context of his family and his larger social environment; it must convey his class, his situation, his innocence, his predilection for romance: in short, his sensibility and his *need* to engage in some meaningful action. These initial paragraphs, though they record no specific events, substitute for the exposition of a traditional plot.

In the modern novel, setting is used for similar purposes, but in most novels it supplements rather than replaces other kinds of character and plot development. Although it is often difficult, even for purposes of analysis, to separate "setting" from some aspects of "characterization,"[9] it is probably true that setting is a more significant factor in the modern story than in the nouvelle and novel in terms of proportion of discourse space allotted to it.

Techniques of limiting point of view, constructing elliptical or metaphoric plots, using representative details for setting and character development go hand in hand with the impressionists' attention to stylistic economy and the foregrounding of style. In transforming the plot by deletion and substitution, writers also made their language more economical: dense with meaning as it is in poetry. From Flaubert forward, impressionist fiction foregrounds style in the emphasis on rhythmic prose, exact diction, and a high reliance on figures, particularly simile and metaphor. The author may disappear as commentator on the action, but he calls attention to himself through the special "signature" of his style.

Stylistic foregrounding has both negative and positive effects: although Hemingway's and Faulkner's highly mannered styles may grow tedious, even self-parodic, in their novels, in the stories they are a force for cohesiveness, imparting a special coloration or atmosphere that binds the often disparate events and characters together. Though Joyce said he wrote *Dubliners* in a style of "scrupulous meanness," few readers would agree; the beauty of Joyce's style, applied to the squalor of the subject, gives these stories their classic quality. By and large — except for Lawrence — the great short story writers have reputations as outstanding stylists, and much of the praise for their style, in terms of its "jewelling" or "polish," arises from a sense of the care lavished in the search for *le mot juste* by writers from Poe to Kipling, Joyce, Mansfield, Hemingway, Faulkner, Porter, Welty, both O'Connors, O'Faolain, Updike. The attribution of "lyricism" to the story also comes in large measure from the attention to style, the deliberation that is so apparent in manipulating diction, figuration, and syntactic and phonemic patterning to achieve precise tonal effects.

Even the association of the short story with certain national traditions — French, Russian, Irish, and American — can be seen to be linked with its impressionist elements rather than a particular national "gift." Turgenev and Chekhov, among the Russians, display in particular the foregrounding of setting, the reduction of physical action, and the elevation of mood changes to the status of plots; a recent book, in fact, treats Chekhov with James as an impressionist.[10] Among the French, Maupassant is preeminent in the short story; his techniques of compression and suggestion come directly from Flaubert, not from a tradition of the short story. Though Crane and James are the first Americans properly to be called impressionist writers, Poe and Hawthorne foreshadow impressionist techniques in the focus on inner states, the substitution of setting for action, and the use of fallible, ambivalent narrators in first-person (Poe) and third-person (Hawthorne) in both long and short fiction. George Moore follows Turgenev, Joyce follows Moore and Flaubert, in changing the mainstream of Irish short fiction from anecdote to impression.

What has made the modern short story seem distinct from the novel, in addition to the different distribution and proportion of narrative elements, is finally a matter of prestige. Given the emphasis on its status as a work of art and the insistence by many turn-of-the-century writers on stylistic elegance (a sure sign of "high" art!), the story began to be read more intensively. The deletion of traditional plot elements also demanded a more attentive reading, one in which the reader is conscious of narrative technique and style as keys to meaning. As the story became more obviously artful, its artistry was the more remarked in criticism. James and Wells thought in terms of a "golden age" or "millennium" of the short story, and writers began to establish reputations solely on the basis of their short fiction.

The idea that a "true" short story grew out of some older, amateurish form of the early nineteenth century is not borne out by the evidence. Although earlier there is a finer line between "popular" and highbrow stories, and though much nineteenth-century short fiction belongs to the specialized subgenres more characteristic of popular than serious fiction, the mainstream short story of the nineteenth century is as likely to deal with the same concerns as the novel of its time as the modern story and the modern novel are apt to deal with modern concerns. Brevity, however, is not well suited to the vision of Victorian fiction, in which men and women move through a complex society, posing goals and working toward them with greater or less success. One can imagine a short story about Dorothea Brooke or Willoughby, but not a very impressive one. Thus, though coherent and competently written, few Victorian short stories are of much interest to the modern reader.

In bringing to a close this sketch of the relations between impressionist conceptions and techniques and the forms of early modern fiction, I would like to focus on a point implicit in much of the rest of my argument. Comparison of nineteenth-century short and long fictions with their modern counterparts reveals one final way in which short stories seem different from longer ones in their formal identities. The less we are occupied with verisimilitude, with physical action, with extended characterization, the more obvious it is that the element which binds the whole *into* a whole is what readers perceive as a governing *theme* and often express as "the author's intention": in old-fashioned stories, the "moral." This "semantic" aspect of the story we abstract from its lexical aspect—the events, existents, and authorial commentary—as we see that organized in the syntactic aspect—plot, temporal ordering. Theme is what readers constitute as they study the significance and relationships of the various elements and locate the "storiness" emerging from the often obscure system the author provides. In realistic literature, the interplay of character and action in the plot is the primary vector of theme. In the modern, impressionist short story, in which plot is frequently suppressed, in which characterization is often achieved by having the characters perceive something or somebody "other" rather than acting or being themselves described by an implied author, in which setting may displace event, and in which the very sentence structures or figurative language may imply relationships not otherwise expressed, the readers' ability to recognize a theme is paramount to their acceptance of the work as belonging to the genre, "story." Oddly, this kind of narrative, whose most typical epistemology assumes the privacy of truth in individual experience, becomes the genre in which the readers' abstraction of theme—the statement of an interpretation—is a major factor in their differentiating it from other kinds of narrative. The moral is no longer an easily abstractable truism verified by an implied author, but a complex and hardly won proposition whose validity remains conditional and implicit, unconfirmed by the authorial voice, giving the story both "unity of effect" and a certain vagueness or mystery.

In attempting to show that the "modern short story" is a manifestation of impressionism rather than a discrete genre, I have cited many of the same characteristics that others have observed in arguing that the short story *is* a genre. That the short story *seems* very different from the novel in its plot, in the proportions of action to setting and character, or in the prominence of theme over vicarious experience, I concede, yet the context of impressionism seems to me a more comprehensive vantage point from which to interpret these differences than that of genre.

Any perspective, of genre or mode, is only a starting point in the interpretation and assimilation of a literary work. The complex adjustments in reading process we make in going from "The Town Mouse and the Country Mouse," Grimms' fairy tales, or "Wandering Willie's Tale" to "The Jolly Corner" or "The Gambler, the Nun, and the Radio" are considerable: greater, I would argue, than those we make in going from *The Good Soldier* or *To the Lighthouse* to "Soldier's Home" or "Ivy Day in the Committee Room." (Those who argue from a generic perspective would likely agree.) Nevertheless, our knowledge of Aesop or a fairy tale or Scott's tale — or any of the stories we heard as children or read in adolescence, no matter how crude or cheap — provide us with the basic knowledge of the fictional codes that we need to begin reading sophisticated modern short stories and their longer relatives. The question "What is a short story?" or even "What is an impressionist short story?" is probably not as important a question in the long run as other, specific questions we might ask about the relations of long and short stories, popular and highbrow stories, hypothetical and actual plots, or stories and reality. The object of such criticism is not, finally, to find generic or modal boxes to put stories into, but to open the boxes and let stories out for more illuminating scrutiny.

Notes

1. Charles E. May, ed., *Short Story Theories* (Athens: Ohio University Press, 1976).

2. Thomas Gullason, "The Short Story: An Underrated Art," in May, *Short Story Theories,* pp. 20–21, 30.

3. Norman Friedman, "What Makes a Short Story Short?" in May, *Short Story Theories*, pp. 131–46.

4. Beginning with V. K. Propp in *Morphology of the Folktale* (1928) and reaffirmed in later structuralist critics such as Claude Bremond and A. J. Greimas in *Communications* 8 (1966): 28–59 and 60–76; Roland Barthes, "An Introduction to the Structural Analysis of Narrative," trans. Lionel Duisit, *New Literary History* 6 (1975): 237–72; Seymour Chatman, *Story and Discourse* (Ithaca, N.Y.: Cornell University Press, 1978), pp. 43–48.

5. Frank O'Connor, from *The Lonely Voice* (1963), reprinted in May, *Short Story Theories*, pp. 86–89.

6. The fictionality of all (subjective) truth becomes an obsession in postmodern writing; it is a given in the work of Borges, Robbe-Grillet, Pynchon, and others, rather than an intuition against which the characters struggle, as in impressionist fiction.

7. These are types of questions it would be pointless to ask about the characters in

Borges or Barthelme, or even in such a relatively conservative postmodern story as Pynchon's "Entropy," for these characters *have* no "other" existence; the tie with a "real" world, in which we might imagine the characters as acting and suffering, is broken.

8. Virginia Woolf, *To the Lighthouse* (New York: Harcourt, Brace and World, 1955), p. 240.

9. Chatman, *Story and Discourse,* pp. 138–45.

10. Peter Stowell, *Literary Impressionism: James and Chekhov* (Athens: University of Georgia Press, 1980).

22 Henry Louis Gates, Jr. : *The Blackness of Blackness*

A Critique on the Sign and the Signifying Monkey

Henry Louis Gates, Jr.'s, "The Blackness of Blackness: A Critique on the Sign and the Signifying Monkey" begins by locating the concept of signification in the context of an African American "vernacular tradition that is approximately two centuries old." Gates then develops the figure of the "Signifying Monkey" as it evolved in African American mythic discourse, showing how it originated in the Yoruba mythology of West Africa. He carefully distinguishes African American signifying from French structural linguistics, which also is much concerned with signification. Within the African American literary tradition, Gates singles out Zora Neale Hurston's *Their Eyes Were Watching God*, not only because of its mythic tropes but also because of its intertextual relationships with other African American texts and writers. Gates also identifies Ralph Ellison as a key figure in this tradition, emphasizing the varieties of irony, parody, and Bakhtinian double-voicing that are found in his stories and especially in his novel *Invisible Man.*

Gates focuses most of his attention on Ishmael Reed's novel *Mumbo Jumbo*, explaining the importance of narrative voice in achieving the "carnivalization," especially parody, found there. He also shows that Reed is "signifying" on Ellison. What Gates finds most satisfying about Reed's work is that he has achieved his "canonical" status precisely through "his critique of the received, repeated tropes peculiar to that very canon." Perhaps Gates himself is signifying upon Reed to make a claim about, and simultaneously parody, his own canonical status as a major African American literary theorist. By placing African American literary production within a poststructuralist context, Gates reveals its unique, non-European, non-Western narrative features.

Henry Louis Gates, Jr., is W. E. B. Du Bois Professor of Humanities and Chair of the Afro-American Studies Department at Harvard University and a preeminent figure in African American literary and cultural studies. The essay excerpted here from *Figures in Black: Words, Signs, and the "Racial" Self* (1987) originally appeared in *Critical Inquiry*. He has also authored *The Signifying Monkey* (1988) and *Loose Cannons: Notes on the Culture Wars* (1992), and edited and co-edited numerous volumes, including *Black Literature and Literary Theory* (1984), *"Race," Writing and Difference* (1986), *Reading Black, Reading Feminist* (1990), and *Reading Rodney King/Reading Urban Uprising* (1993).

Signification is the Nigger's occupation. — Traditional[1]

Be careful what you do,
Or Mumbo-Jumbo, God of the Congo,
And all of the other
Gods of the Congo,
Mumbo-Jumbo will hoo-doo you,
Mumbo-Jumbo will hoo-doo you,
Mumbo-Jumbo will hoo-doo you. — Vachel Lindsay, *The Congo*

I need not trace in these pages the history of the concept of signification. Since Ferdinand de Saussure at least, signification has become a crucial aspect of much of contemporary theory. It is curious to me that this neologism in the Western tradition cuts across a term in the black vernacular tradition that is approximately two centuries old. Tales of the Signifying Monkey had their origins in slavery. Hundreds of these have been recorded since the nineteenth century. In black music, Jazz Gillum, Count Basie, Oscar Peterson, Oscar Browne, Jr., Little Willie Dixon, Nat "King" Cole, Otis Redding, Wilson Picket, and Johnny Otis — at least — have recorded songs called either "The Signifying Monkey" or simply "Signifyin(g)." My theory of interpretation, arrived at from within the black cultural matrix, is a theory of formal revisionism, it is tropological, it is often characterized by pastiche, and, most crucially, it turns on repetition of formal structures and their differences. Signification is a theory of reading that arises from Afro-American culture; learning how to signify is often part of our adolescent education. That it has not been drawn upon before as a theory of criticism attests to its sheer familiarity in the idiom. I had to step outside my culture, to defamiliarize the concept by translating it into a new mode of discourse, before I could see its potential in critical theory. My work with signification has now led me to undertake the analysis of the principles of interpretation implicit in the decoding of the signs used in the Ifá oracle, still very much alive among the Yoruba in Nigeria, in a manner only roughly related to Harold Bloom's use of the Kabbalah.

I Signifyin(g): Definitions

Perhaps only Tar Baby is as enigmatic and compelling a figure from Afro-American mythic discourse as is that oxymoron, the Signifying Monkey.[2]

The ironic reversal of a received racist image in the Western imagination of the black as simianlike, the Signifying Monkey — he who dwells at the margins of discourse, ever punning, ever troping, ever embodying the ambiguities of language — is our trope for repetition and revision, indeed our trope of chiasmus itself, repeating and reversing simultaneously as he does in one deft discursive act. If Vico and Burke, or Nietzsche, de Man, and Bloom, are correct in identifying four and six master tropes, then we might think of these as the master's tropes and of signifying as the slave's trope, the trope of tropes, as Bloom characterizes metalepsis, "a trope-reversing trope, a figure of a figure." Signifying is a trope in which are subsumed several other rhetorical tropes, including metaphor, metonymy, synecdoche, and irony (the master tropes), and also hyperbole and litotes, and metalepsis (Bloom's supplement to Burke). To this list we could easily add aporia, chiasmus, and catechesis, all of which are used in the ritual of signifying.

Signifying, it is clear, in black discourse means modes of figuration itself. When one signifies, as Kimberly W. Benston puns, one "tropes-a-dope." Indeed, the black tradition itself has its own subdivisions of signifying, which we could readily identify with the typology of figures received from classical and medieval rhetoric, as Bloom has done with his "map of misprision." The black rhetorical tropes, subsumed under signifying, would include marking, loud-talking, testifying, calling out (of one's name), sounding, rapping, playing the dozens, and so on.[3]

Let us consider received definitions of the act of signifying and of black mythology's archetypal signifier, the Signifying Monkey. The Signifying Monkey is a trickster figure, of the order of the trickster figure of Yoruba mythology (*Esu-Elegbara* in Nigeria and *Legba* among the Fon in Dahomey), whose New World figurations (*Exu* in Brazil, *Echu-Elegua* in Cuba, *Papa Legba* in the pantheon of the *loa* of *Vaudou* in Haiti, and *Papa La Bas* in the *loa* of *Hoodoo* in the United States) speak eloquently of the unbroken arc of metaphysical presupposition and patterns of figuration shared through space and time among black cultures in West Africa, South America, the Caribbean, and in the United States. These trickster figures, aspects of *Esu*, are primarily mediators: as tricksters they are mediators, and their mediations are tricks.[4]

The versions of *Esu* are all messengers of the gods: he who interprets the will of god to people, he who carries the desires of people to the gods. *Esu* is guardian of the crossroads, master of style and the stylus, phallic god of generation and fecundity, master of the mystical barrier that separates the divine from the profane worlds. He is known as the divine linguist, the keeper of *ase* (*logos*) with which Olodumare created the universe.

In Yoruba mythology, *Esu* always limps because his legs are of different lengths: one is anchored in the realm of the gods, and the other rests in this human world. The closest Western relative of *Esu*, of course, is Hermes; and, just as Hermes's role as interpreter lent his name readily to "hermeneutics," our metaphor for the study of the process of interpretation, so too can the figure of *Esu* stand as our metaphor for the act of interpretation itself for the critic of comparative black literature. In African and Latin American mythology, *Esu* is said to have taught *Ifa* how to read the signs formed by the sixteen sacred palmnuts which, when manipulated, configure into what is known as the signature of an *Odu*, two hundred and fifty-six of which comprise the corpus of *Ifa Divination*. The *Opon Ifa*, the carved wooden divination tray used in the art of interpretation, is said to contain at the center of its upper perimeter a carved image of *Esu*, meant to signify his relation to the act of interpretation, which we can translate either as *itumo* ("to unite or unknot knowledge") or as *yipada* ("to turn around or translate"). That which we now call close reading, the Yoruba call *Oda fa* ("reading the signs"). Above all else, *Esu* is the Black Interpreter, the Yoruba god of indeterminacy or *ariye-muye* (that which no sooner is held than it slips through one's fingers).[5] As Hermes is to hermeneutics, *Esu* is to *Esu tufunaalo* (bringing out the interstices of the riddle).

The *Esu* figures, among the Yoruba systems of thought in Dahomey and Nigeria, in Brazil and Cuba, in Haiti and at New Orleans, are divine; they are gods who function in sacred myths, as do characters in a narrative. *Esu*'s functional equivalent in Afro-American profane discourse is the Signifying Monkey, a figure who would seem to be distinctly Afro-American, probably derived from Cuban mythology, which generally depicts *Echu-Elegua* with a monkey at his side,[6] and who, unlike his Pan-African *Esu* cousins, exists in the discourse of mythology not primarily as a character in a narrative but rather as a vehicle for narration itself. It is from this corpus of narratives that signifying derives. The Afro-American rhetorical strategy of signifying is a rhetorical act that is not engaged in the game of information giving. Signifying turns on the play and chain of signifiers, and not on some supposedly transcendent signified. Alan Dundes suggests that the origins of signifying could "lie in African rhetoric." As anthropologists demonstrate, the Signifying Monkey is often called the Signifier, he who wreaks havoc upon the Signified. One is signified upon by the signifier. He is indeed the "signifier as such," in

Julia Kristeva's phrase, "a presence that precedes the signification of object or emotion."[7]

Scholars have for some time commented upon the peculiar use of the word "signifying" in black discourse. Though sharing some connotations with the standard English-language word, "signifying" has rather unique definitions in black discourse. Roger D. Abrahams defines it as follows:

> Signifying seems to be a Negro term, in use if not in origin. It can mean any of a number of things; in the case of the toast about the signifying monkey, it certainly refers to the trickster's ability to talk with great innuendo, to carp, cajole, needle, and lie. It can mean in other instances the propensity to talk around a subject, never quite coming to the point. It can mean making fun of a person or situation. Also it can denote speaking with the hands and eyes, and in this respect encompasses a whole complex of expressions and gestures. Thus it is signifying to stir up a fight between neighbors by telling stories; it is signifying to make fun of a policeman by parodying his motions behind his back; it is signifying to ask for a piece of cake by saying, "my brother needs a piece of cake."[8]

Essentially, Abrahams concludes, signifying is a "*technique* of indirect argument or persuasion," "a language of implication," "to imply, goad, beg, boast, by *indirect* verbal or gestural means." "The name 'signifying,' " he concludes, "shows the monkey to be a trickster, signifying being the language of trickery, that set of words or gestures achieving Hamlet's 'direction through indirection.' " The monkey, in short, is not only a master of technique, as Abrahams concludes; he *is* technique, or style, or the literariness of literary language; he is the great Signifier. In this sense, one does not signify something; rather, one signifies in some way.[9]

There are thousands of "toasts" of the Signifying Monkey, most of which commence with a variant of the following formulaic lines:

> Deep down in the jungle so they say
> There's a signifying monkey down the way
> There hadn't been no disturbin' in the jungle for quite a bit,
> For up jumped the monkey in the tree one day and laughed,
> "I guess I'll start some shit."[10]

Endings, too, tend toward the formulaic, as in the following:

> "Monkey," said the Lion,
> Beat to his unbooted knees,

"You and your signifying children
Better stay up in the trees."
Which is why today
Monkey does his signifying
A-way-up out of the way."[11]

In the narrative poems, the Signifying Monkey invariably repeats to his friend, the Lion, some insult purportedly generated by their mutual friend, the Elephant. The Lion, indignant and outraged, demands an apology of the Elephant, who refuses and then trounces the Lion. The Lion, realizing that his mistake was to take the monkey literally, returns to trounce the monkey. Although anthropologists and sociolinguists have succeeded in establishing a fair sample of texts of the Signifying Monkey, they have been less successful at establishing a consensus of definitions of black signifying.

In addition to Abraham's definitions, definitions of signifying by Zora Neale Hurston, Thomas Kochman, Claudia Mitchell-Kernan, Geneva Smitherman, and Ralph Ellison are of interest here for what they reveal about the nature of Afro-American narrative parody, which I shall attempt first to define and then to employ in a reading of Ishmael Reed's *Mumbo Jumbo* as a pastiche of the Afro-American narrative tradition itself. Kochman argues that signifying depends upon the signifier *repeating* what someone else has said about a third person, in order to *reverse* the status of a relationship heretofore harmonious; signifying can also be employed to *reverse* or *undermine* pretense or even one's opinion about one's own status.[12] This use of repetition and reversal (chiasmus) constitutes an implicit parody of a subject's own complicity in illusion. Claudia Mitchell-Kernan, in perhaps the most thorough study of the concept, compares the etymology of "signifying" in black usage with usages from standard English:

> What is unique in Black English usage is the way in which signifying is extended to cover a range of meanings and events which are not covered in its Standard English usage. In the Black community it is possible to say, "He is signifying" and "Stop signifying" — sentences which would be anomalous elsewhere.[13]

Mitchell-Kernan points to the ironic, or dialectic, relationship between identical terms in standard and black English, which have vastly different meanings:

The Black concept of *signifying* incorporates essentially a folk notion that dictionary entries for words are not always sufficient for interpreting meanings or messages, or that meaning goes beyond such interpretations. Complimentary remarks may be delivered in a left-handed fashion. A particular utterance may be an insult in one context and not another. What pretends to be informative may intend to be persuasive. The hearer is thus constrained to attend to all potential meaning-carrying symbolic systems in speech events — the total universe of discourse.[14]

This is an excellent instance of the nature of signifying itself. Mitchell-Kernan refines these definitions somewhat by suggesting that the Signifying Monkey is able to signify upon the Lion only because the Lion does not understand the nature of the monkey's discourse: "There seems something of symbolic relevance from the perspective of language in this poem. The monkey and the lion do not speak the same language; the lion is not able to interpret the monkey's use of language." The monkey speaks figuratively, in a symbolic code; the lion interprets or reads literally and suffers the consequences of his folly, which is a reversal of his status as King of the Jungle. The monkey rarely acts in these narrative poems; he simply speaks. As the Signifier, he determines the actions of the Signified, the hapless Lion and the puzzled Elephant.[15]

As Mitchell-Kernan and Zora Neale Hurston attest, signifying is a sexless rhetorical game, despite the frequent use in the "masculine" versions of expletives that connote intimate relations with one's mother. Hurston, in *Mules and Men,* and Mitchell-Kernan, in her perceptive "Signifying, Loud-talking and Marking," are the first scholars to record and explicate female signifying rituals.[16] Zora Neale Hurston is the first author of the tradition to represent signifying itself as a vehicle of liberation for an oppressed woman, and as a rhetorical strategy in the narration of fiction.

Hurston, whose definition of the term in *Mules and Men* (1935) is one of the earliest in the linguistic literature, has made *Their Eyes Were Watching God* into a paradigmatic signifying text, for this novel resolves that implicit tension between the literal and the figurative contained in standard English usages of the term "signifying." *Their Eyes* represents the black trope of signifying both as thematic matter and as a rhetorical strategy of the novel itself. Janie, the protagonist, gains her voice on the porch of her husband's store, not only by engaging with the assembled men in the ritual of signifying (which her husband had expressly forbidden her to do) but also by openly signifying upon her husband's impotency. His image wounded fatally, her husband soon dies of a displaced "kidney" failure. Janie "kills" her husband rhetorically. Moreover, Hurston's masterful use of the indirect discourse allows her to signify upon the tension between the two voices of Jean Toomer's *Cane* by adding to direct and indirect speech a strategy through which she can privilege the black oral tradition, which Toomer found to be problematical and dying. Hurston's is the "speakerly text."

The text of *Their Eyes,* moreover, is itself a signifying structure, a structure of intertextual revision, because it revises key tropes and rhetorical strategies received from precursory texts, such as W. E. B. Du Bois's *A Quest of the Silver Fleece* and Toomer's *Cane.* Afro-American literary history is characterized by tertiary formal revision: Hurston's text (1937) revises Du Bois's novel (1911), and Toni Morrison in several texts revises Ellison and Hurston; similarly, Ellison (1951) revises Wright (1940, 1945), and Ishmael Reed (1972), among others, revises both. It is clear that black writers read and critique other black texts as an act of rhetorical self-definition. Our literary tradition exists because of these precisely chartable formal literary relationships.

The key aspect of signifying for Mitchell-Kernan is "its indirect intent or metaphorical reference," a rhetorical indirection which she says is "almost purely stylistic." Its art characteristics remain foregrounded. By "indirection," Mitchell-Kernan means that "the correct semantic (referential interpretation) or signification of the utterance cannot be arrived at by a consideration of the dictionary meaning of the lexical items involved and the syntactic rules for their combination alone. The apparent significance of the message differs from its real significance. The apparent meaning of the sentence signifies its actual meaning."[17]

This rhetorical naming by indirection is, of course, central to our notions of figuration, troping, and of the parody of forms, or pastiche, in evidence when one writer repeats another's structure by one of several means, including a fairly exact repetition of a given narrative or rhetorical structure, filled incongruously with a ludicrous or incongruent content. T. Thomas Fortune's "The Black Man's Burden" is an excellent example of this form of pastiche, signifying as it does upon Kipling's "White Man's Burden":

What is the Black Man's Burden,
Ye hypocrites and vile,

Ye whited sepulchres
From th' Amazon to the Nile?
What is the Black Man's Burden,
Ye Gentile parasites,
Who crush and rob your brother
Of his manhood and his rights?

Dante Gabriel Rossetti's "Uncle Ned," a dialect verse parody of Stowe's *Uncle Tom's Cabin,* is a second example:

Him tale dribble on and on widout a break,
Till you hab no eyes for to see;
When I read Chapter 4 I had got a headache;
So I had to let Chapter 4 be.

Another example of formal parody is to suggest a given structure precisely by failing to coincide with it — that is, to suggest it by dissemblance. Repetition of a form and then inversion of the same through a process of variation is central to jazz. A stellar example is John Coltrane's rendition of "My Favorite Things" compared to Julie Andrews's vapid original. Resemblance, then, can be evoked cleverly by dissemblance. Aristophanes's *The Frogs,* which parodies the styles of both Aeschylus and Euripides; Cervantes's relationship to the fiction of knight-errantry; Henry Fielding's parody of the Richardsonian novel of sentiment in *Joseph Andrews,* and Lewis Carroll's double parody in *Hiawatha's Photographing* (which draws upon Longfellow's rhythms to parody the convention of the family photograph) all come readily to mind. Ralph Ellison defines the parody aspect of signifying in several ways relevant to our discussion below of the formal parody strategies at work in Ishmael Reed's *Mumbo Jumbo.*

In his complex short story "And Hickman Arrives" (1960), Ellison's narrator defines signifying in this way:

And the two men [Daddy Hickman and Deacon Wilhite] standing side by side, the one large and dark, the other slim and light brown, the other reverends rowed behind them, their faces staring grim with engrossed attention to the reading of the Word, like judges in their carved, high-backed chairs. And the two voices beginning their call and countercall as Daddy Hickman began spelling out the text which Deacon Wilhite read, playing variations on the verses just as he did with his trombone when he really felt like signifying on a tune the choir was singing.[18]

Following this introduction, the two ministers demonstrate the definition of signification, which in turn is a signification upon the antiphonal structure of the Afro-American sermon. This parody of form is of the same order as Richard Pryor's parody of both the same sermonic structure and Stevie Wonder's "Living for the City," which he effects by speaking the lyrics of Wonder's song in the form of and with the intonation peculiar to the Afro-American sermon in his "reading" of "The Book of Wonder." Pryor's parody is a signification of the second order, revealing simultaneously the received structure of the sermon (by its presence, demystified here by its incongruous content), the structure of Wonder's music (by the absence of his form and the presence of his lyrics), and the complex yet direct formal relationship between the black sermon and Wonder's music specifically, as well as that between black sacred and secular narrative forms generally.

Ellison defines signifying in other ways as well. In his essay on Charlie Parker, entitled "On Bird, Bird-Watching, and Jazz" (1962), Ellison defines the satirical aspect of signifying as one aspect of riffing in jazz:

> But what kind of bird was Parker? Back during the thirties members of the old Blue Devils Orchestra celebrated a certain robin by playing a lugubrious little tune called "They Picked Poor Robin." It was a jazz community joke, musically an extended signifying "riff" or melodic naming of a recurrent human situation, and was played to satirize some betrayal of faith or loss of love observed from the bandstand.[19]

Here again, the parody is twofold, involving a formal parody of the melody of "They Picked Poor Robin" as well as a ritual naming, and therefore a troping, of an action observed from the bandstand.

Ellison, of course, is our Great Signifier himself, naming things by indirection and troping throughout his works. In his well-known review of LeRoi Jones's *Blues People,* Ellison defines signifying in yet a third sense, then signifies upon Jones's reading of Afro-American cultural history, which he argues is misdirected and wrongheaded. "The tremendous burden of sociology which Jones would place upon this body of music," writes Ellison, "is enough to give even the blues the blues." Ellison writes that Lydia Maria Child's title, *An Appeal in Favor of That Class of Americans called Africans,*

> sounds like a fine bit of contemporary ironic signifying — "*signifying*" here meaning, in the unwritten dictionary of American Negro usage, "rhetorical understate-

ments." It tells us much of the thinking of her opposition, and it reminds us that as late as the 1890s, a time when Negro composers, singers, dancers and comedians dominated the American musical stage, popular Negro songs (including James Weldon Johnson's "Under the Bamboo Tree," now immortalized by T. S. Eliot) were commonly referred to as "Ethiopian Airs."[20]

Ellison's stress upon "the unwritten dictionary of American Negro usage" reminds us of the problem of definitions, of signification itself, when one is translating between two languages. The Signifying Monkey, perhaps appropriately, seems to dwell at this space between two linguistic domains. One wonders, incidentally, about this Afro-American figure and a possible French connection between *signe* ("sign") and *singe* ("monkey").

Ellison's definition of the relation his works bear to those of Richard Wright constitutes our definition of narrative signification, pastiche, or critical parody, although he employs none of these terms. His explanation of what we might call implicit formal criticism, however, comprises what we have sometimes called troping, after Geoffrey Hartman, and which we might take to be a profound definition of critical signification itself. Writes Ellison:

> I felt no need to attack what I considered the limitations of [Wright's] vision because I was quite impressed by what he had achieved. And in this, although I saw with the black vision of Ham, I was, I suppose, as pious as Shem and Japheth. Still I would write my own books and they would be in themselves, implicitly, criticisms of Wright's; just as all novels of a given historical moment form an argument over the nature of reality and are, to an extent, criticisms each of the other.[21]

Ellison in his fictions signifies upon Wright by parodying Wright's literary structures through repetition and difference. Although this is not the place for a close reading of this formal relationship, the complexities of the parodying can be readily suggested. The play of language, the signifying, starts with the titles. *Native Son* and *Black Boy* — both titles connoting race, self, and presence — Ellison tropes with *Invisible Man,* invisibility an ironic response of absence to the would-be presence of "blacks" and "natives," while "man" suggests a more mature, stronger status than either "sons" or "boy." Ellison signifies upon Wright's distinctive version of naturalism with a complex rendering of modernism; Wright's reacting protagonist, voiceless to the last, Ellison signifies upon with a nameless protagonist who is nothing but voice, since it is he who shapes, edits, and narrates his own tale, thereby combining action with the representation of action, thereby defining reality by its representation. This unity of presence and representation is perhaps Ellison's most subtle reversal of Wright's theory of the novel as exemplified in *Native Son,* since Bigger's voicelessness and powerlessness to act (as opposed to react) signify an absence, despite the metaphor of presence found in the novel's title; the reverse obtains in *Invisible Man,* where the absence implied by invisibility is undermined by the presence of the narrator as the narrator of his own text.

There are other aspects of critical parody at play here, too, one of the funniest being Jack's glass eye plopping into his water glass before him, which is functionally equivalent to the action of Wright's protagonist in "The Man Who Lived Underground," as he stumbles over the body of a dead baby, deep down in the sewer. It is precisely at this point in the narrative that we know Fred Daniels to be "dead, baby," in the heavy-handed way that Wright's naturalism was self-consciously symbolic. If Daniels's fate is signified by the objects over which he stumbles in the darkness of the sewer, Ellison signifies upon Wright's novella by repeating this underground scene of discovery but having his protagonist burn the bits of paper through which he has allowed himself to be defined by others. By explicitly repeating and reversing key figures of Wright's fictions, and by defining implicitly in the process of narration a sophisticated form more akin to Hurston's *Their Eyes Were Watching God,* Ellison exposes naturalism to be merely a hardened convention of representation of "the Negro problem" and perhaps part of the problem itself. I cannot emphasize enough the major import of this narrative gesture to the subsequent development of black narrative forms, since Ellison recorded a new way of seeing and defined both a new manner of representation and its relation to the concept of presence. The formal relation that Ellison bears to Wright, Ishmael Reed bears to both, but principally to Ellison. Once again, Ellison has formulated this complex and inherently polemical intertextual relationship of formal signifying, in a refutation of Irving Howe's critique of his work: "I agree with Howe that protest is an element of all art, though it does not necessarily take the form of speaking for a political or social program. It might appear in a novel as a *technical assault against the styles which have gone before* [emphasis added]."[22] This form of critical parody, of repetition and inversion, is what I define to be critical signification, or formal signifying, and is my metaphor for literary history.

This chapter is a reading of the tertiary relationship among Reed's "postmodern" *Mumbo Jumbo* as a signification upon Wright's "realism" and Ellison's "modernism." The set of intertextual relations that I chart through formal signification is related to what Mikhail Bakhtin labels double-voiced discourse, which he subdivides into parodic narration and the hidden, or internal, polemic. These two types of double-voiced discourse can merge together, as they do in *Mumbo Jumbo*. Although Bakhtin's discourse typology is familiar, let me cite his definition of hidden polemic. In hidden polemic,

the other speech act remains outside the boundaries of the author's speech, but it is implied or alluded to in that speech. The other speech act is not reproduced with a new intention, but shapes the author's speech while remaining outside its boundaries. Such is the nature of the hidden polemic. . . .

In hidden polemic the author's discourse is oriented toward its referential object, as in any other discourse, but at the same time each assertion about that object is constructed in such a way that, besides its referential meaning, the author's discourse brings a polemical attack to bear against another speech act, another assertion, on the same topic. Here one utterance focused on its referential object clashes with another utterance on the grounds of the referent itself. That other utterance is not reproduced; it is understood only in its import.[23]

Ellison's definition of the formal relationship his works bear to Wright's is a salient example of the hidden polemic: his texts clash with Wright's "on the ground of the referent itself." "As a result," Bakhtin continues, "the latter begins to influence the author's speech from within." This relationship Bakhtin calls double-voiced, whereby one speech act determines the internal structure of another, the second effecting the voice of the first, by absence, by difference.

Much of the Afro-American literary tradition can be read as successive attempts to create a new narrative space for representation of the recurring referent of Afro-American literature, the so-called black experience. Certainly, we read the relation of Sterling Brown's regionalism to Jean Toomer's lyricism in this way, Hurston's lyricism to Wright's naturalism in this way, and Ellison's modernism to Wright's naturalism in this way as well. We might represent this set of relationships in figure 1, which is intended in no sense other than to be suggestive.[24]

These relationships are reciprocal, because we are free to read in critical time machines, reading backwards, like Merlin moved through time. The

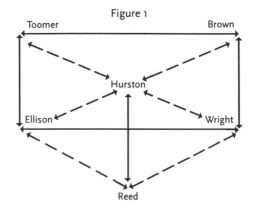

Figure 1

direct relation most important to my own theory of reading is the solid black line that connects Reed with Hurston. Reed and Hurston seem to relish the play of the tradition, while Reed's work seems to be a magnificently conceived play on the tradition. Both Hurston and Reed write myths of Moses, both draw upon black sacred and secular myths' discourse as metaphorical and metaphysical systems; both write self-reflexive texts which comment upon the nature of writing itself; both make use of the frame to bracket their narratives within narratives; and both are authors of fictions that I characterize as speakerly texts, texts that privilege the representation of the speaking black voice, of what the Formalists called skaz, and that Reed himself has defined as "an oral book, a talking book," a figure that occurs, remarkably enough, in four of the first five narratives in the black tradition in the eighteenth century.[25]

Reed's relation to these authors in the tradition is at all points double-voiced, since he seems to be especially concerned with employing satire to utilize literature in what Northrop Frye calls "a special function of analysis, of breaking up the lumber of stereotypes, fossilized beliefs, superstitious terrors, crank theories, pedantic dogmatisms, oppressive fashions, and all other things that impede the free movement . . . of society."[26] Reed, of course, seems to be most concerned with the free movement of writing itself. In Reed's work, parody and hidden polemic overlap in a process Bakhtin describes thusly: "When parody becomes aware of substantial resistance, a certain forcefulness and profundity in the speech act it parodies, it takes on a new dimension of complexity via the tones of the hidden polemic. . . . A process of inner dialogization takes place within the parodic speech act."[27]

This internal dialogization can have curious implications, the most interesting of which perhaps is what Bakhtin describes as "the splitting of double-voice discourse into two speech acts, into the two entirely separate and autonomous voices." The clearest evidence that Reed in *Mumbo Jumbo* is signifying through parody as hidden polemic is his use of the two autonomous narrative voices, which he employs in the manner of, and renders through, foregrounding, to parody the two simultaneous stories of detective narration, that of the present and that of the past, in a narrative flow that moves hurriedly from cause to effect. In *Mumbo Jumbo,* however, the second narrative, that of the past, bears an ironic relation to the first narrative, that of the present, because it comments upon both the other narrative and the nature of its writing itself, in what Frye describes in another context as "the constant tendency to self-parody in satiric rhetoric which prevents even the process of writing itself from becoming an oversimplified convention or ideal."[28] Reed's rhetorical strategy assumes the form of the relationship between the text and the criticism of that text, which serves as discourse upon that text.

II "Consult the Text"[29]

With these definitions of narrative parody and critical signification as a frame, let us read Ishmael Reed's third novel, *Mumbo Jumbo.* A close reading of Reed's corpus of works suggests strongly that he seems to be concerned with the received form of the novel, with the precise rhetorical shape of the Afro-American literary tradition, and with the relation that the Afro-American tradition bears to the Western tradition. Reed's concerns, as exemplified in his narrative forms, would seem to be twofold: on the one hand with that relation his own art bears to his black literary precursors, whom we can identify to include Zora Neale Hurston, Richard Wright, James Baldwin, and Ralph Ellison, and on the other hand the process of willing into being a rhetorical structure, a literary language, replete with its own figures and tropes, but one that allows the black writer to posit a structure of feeling that simultaneously critiques both the metaphysical presuppositions inherent in Western ideas and forms of writing and the metaphorical system in which the blackness of the writer and his experience have been valorized as a "natural" absence. In the short term, that is, through six demanding novels,[30] Reed has apparently decided to criticize, through signification, what he seems to perceive to be the received and conventional structures of feeling that he has inherited from the Afro-American tradition itself, almost as if the sheer process of the analysis can clear a narrative space for his generation of writers as decidedly as Ellison's narrative response to Wright and naturalism cleared a space for Leon Forrest, Toni Morrison, Alice Walker, James Alan McPherson, and especially Reed himself.

By undertaking the difficult and subtle art of pastiche, Reed criticizes the Afro-American idealism of a transcendent black subject, integral and whole, self-sufficient and plentiful, the "always already" black signified, available for literary representation in received Western forms as would be the water ladled from a deep and dark well. Water can be poured into glasses or cups or canisters, but it remains water just the same. Put simply, Reed's fictions concern themselves with arguing that the so-called black experience cannot be thought of as a fluid content to be poured into received and static containers. For Reed, it is the signifier that both shapes and defines any discrete signified. And it is the signifiers of the Afro-American tradition with whom Reed is concerned.

This is not the place to read all of Reed's works against this thesis. Nevertheless, Reed's first novel lends credence to this sort of reading and also serves to create what we may call a set of generic expectations through which we read the rest of his works. His first novel, *The Free-Lance Pallbearers,* is, above all else, a parody of the confessional mode which is the fundamental, undergirding convention of Afro-American narrative, received, elaborated upon, and transmitted in a chartable heritage from Briton Hammon's captivity narrative of 1760 through the antebellum slave narratives to black autobiography into black fiction, especially the fictions of Hurston, Wright, Baldwin, and Ellison.[31] This narrative of Bukka Doopeyduk is a pastiche of the classic black narrative of the questing protagonist's "journey into the heart of whiteness"; but it parodies this narrative form by turning it inside out, exposing the character of the originals, and thereby defining their formulaic closures and disclosures. Doopeyduk's tale ends with his own crucifixion. As the narrator of his own story, therefore, Doopeyduk articulates literally from among the dead an irony implicit in all confessional and autobiographical modes, in which any author is forced by definition to imagine himself or herself to be dead. More specifically, Reed signifies upon *Black Boy* and *Go Tell It on the Mountain* in a foregrounded critique which can be read as an epigraph to the novel: "*read growing up in Soulsville first of three install-*

ments/or what it means to be a backstage darkey." The "scat-singing voice" that introduces the novel Reed foregrounds against the "other" voice of Doopeyduk, whose "second" voice narrates the novel's plot. Here, Reed parodies both Hurston's use of free indirect discourse in *Their Eyes Were Watching God* and Ellison's use of the foregrounded voice in the prologue and epilogue of *Invisible Man,* which frame his nameless protagonist's picaresque account of his own narrative. In *Yellow Back Radio Broke Down,* Reed more fully and successfully critiques both realism and modernism, as exemplified in a kind of writing that one character calls "those suffering books I wrote about my old neighborhood and how hard it was."[32]

Reed's third novel, *Mumbo Jumbo,* is about writing itself; not only in the figurative sense of the post-modern, self-reflexive text but also in a literal sense: "So Jes Grew is seeking its words. Its text. For what good is a liturgy without a text?" (*Mumbo Jumbo,* p. 6.) *Mumbo Jumbo* is both a book about texts and a book of texts, a composite narrative composed of subtexts, pretexts, posttexts, and narratives within narratives. It is both a definition of Afro-American culture and its deflation. "The Big Lie concerning Afro-American culture," *Mumbo Jumbo*'s dust jacket informs us, "is that it lacks a tradition." The big truth of the novel, on the other hand, is that this very tradition is as rife with hardened convention and presupposition as is the rest of the Western tradition. Even this cryptic riddle of Jes Grew and its text parodies Ellison: *Invisible Man*'s plot is set in motion with a riddle, while the theme of the relationship between words and texts echoes a key passage from Ellison's short story "And Hickman Arrives": "Good. Don't talk like I talk, talk like I *say* talk. Words are your business boy. Not just *the* word. Words are everything. The key to the Rock, the answer to the question."[33]

Let us examine the book's dust jacket. The signifying begins with the book's title. "Mumbo jumbo" is the received and ethnocentric Western designation for both the rituals of black religions and all black languages themselves. A vulgarized Western translation of a Swahili phrase (*mambo, jambo*), "mumbo jumbo," as *Webster's Third International Dictionary* defines it, connotes "language that is unnecessarily involved and difficult to understand: *GIBBERISH.*" The *Oxford English Dictionary* cites its etymology as being "of unknown origin," implicitly serving here as the signified on which Reed's title signifies, recalling the myth of Topsy who "jes grew," with no antecedents, a phrase with which James Weldon

Johnson characterizes the creative process of black sacred music. *Mumbo Jumbo,* then, signifies upon Western etymology, abusive Western practices of deflation through misnaming, as well as Johnson's specious designation of the anonymity of creation, which indeed is a major component of the Afro-American cultural tradition.

But there is more parody in this title. Whereas Ellison tropes the myth of presence in Wright's titles of *Native Son* and *Black Boy* through his title of *Invisible Man,* inverting the received would-be correlation between blackness and presence with a narrative strategy that correlates invisibility (ultimate sign of absence) with the presence of self-narration and therefore self-creation, Reed parodies all three titles by employing as his title the English-language parody of black language itself. Whereas the etymology of "mumbo jumbo" has been problematical for Western lexicographers, any Swahili speaker knows that the phrase derives from the common greeting *jambo* and its plural, *mambo,* which loosely translated means "What's happening?" Reed is also echoing Vachel Lindsay's ironic poem *The Congo,* cited as an epigraph to this essay, which proved to be so fatally influencing to the Harlem Renaissance poets, as Charles Davis has shown.[34] From its title on, the novel serves as a critique of black and Western literary forms and conventions, and complex relationships between the two.

Let us proceed with our examination of the book's cover. A repeated and reversed image of a crouching, sensuous Josephine Baker sits back to back, superimposed upon a rose. Counterposed to this image is a medallion containing a horse with two riders. These signs adumbrate the two central oppositions of the novel's complicated plot: the rose and the double image of Josephine Baker together form a cryptic *vé vé.* A *vé vé* is a key sign in Vaudou, a sign drawn on the ground with sand, cornmeal, flour, and coffee to represent the *loa.* The *loa* are the deities who comprise the pantheon of Vaudou's gods. The rose is a sign of *Ezrulie,* goddess of love, home, and purity, as are the images of Josephine Baker, who became the French goddess of love in the late 1920s, in their version of the Jazz Age. The doubled image, as if mirrored, is meant to suggest the divine crossroads, where human beings meet their fate, but also at the center of which presides the *loa* Legba (Esu), guardian of the divine crossroads, messenger of the gods, the figure representing the interpreter and interpretation itself, the muse or *loa* of the critic. It is Legba who is master of that mystical barrier that separates the divine from the profane worlds. It is this complex yet cryptic *vé vé* that is meant both to placate Legba himself and to summon his attention and integrity in a double act of criticism and interpretation: that of Reed in the process of his representation of the tradition, to be found between the covers of the book, and that of the critic's interpretation of Reed's figured interpretation.*

. . .

But just as we can define orders of multiple substitution and signification for Reed's types and caricatures, as is true of allegory generally (e.g., Von Vampton, Van Vechten, "Hinken" Knackfuss), so too can we find all sorts of consistent levels of meaning with which we could attempt to find a closure to the text. I shall not do that here, however; the first decade of readers of *Mumbo Jumbo* have attempted to find one-to-one correlations with great energy, decoding its allegorical structure by finding analogues between the Harlem Renaissance and the Black Arts movement, for example. As interesting as such parallel universes are, I shall not attempt such a reading here, or even engage in one more rehearsal of its complex plots, since I can in these pages assume a large measure of reader familiarity with the text. I am concerned with its status as a rhetorical structure, as a mode of narration, and with relating this mode of narration to a critique of traditional notions of closure in interpretation. For Reed's most subtle achievement in *Mumbo Jumbo* is to parody, to signify upon, the notions of closure implicit in the key texts of the Afro-American canon itself. *Mumbo Jumbo,* in contrast, is a novel that figures and glorifies indeterminacy. The novel, in this sense, stands as a profound critique and elaboration upon this convention of closure in the black novel and its metaphysical implications. In its stead, Reed posits the notion of aesthetic play: the play of the tradition, the play on the tradition, the sheer play of indeterminacy itself.**

. . .

Both Ellison and Reed, then, critique the received idea of blackness as a negative essence, as a natural, transcendent signified; but implicit in such a critique is an equally thorough critique of blackness as a presence, which is merely another transcendent signified. Such a critique, therefore, is a critique of the structure of the sign itself and constitutes a profound cri-

---

*The following five-page discussion of *Mumbo Jumbo* has been omitted. — Editors

**Several pages of discussion of the narrative structure of *Mumbo Jumbo,* constituting the bulk of Section III, have been omitted. — Editors

tique. The Black Arts movement's grand gesture was to make of the trope of blackness a trope of presence. That movement willed it to be, however, a transcendent presence. Ellison's "text for today, the 'Blackness of Blackness,' " analyzes this gesture, just as surely as does Reed's text of blackness, the "Sacred Book of Thoth." In literature, blackness is produced in the text itself only through a complex process of signification. There can be no transcendent blackness, for it cannot and does not exist beyond manifestations in specific figures. Jes Grew, put simply, cannot conjure its texts; texts, in the broadest sense of this term (Charlie Parker's music, Ellison's fictions, Romare Bearden's collages, etc.), conjure Jes Grew.

Reed has in *Mumbo Jumbo* signified upon Ellison's critique of the central presupposition of the Afro-American literary tradition, by drawing upon Ellison's trope as a central theme of the plot of *Mumbo Jumbo* and making explicit Ellison's implicit critique of the nature of the sign itself, of a transcendent signified, an essence, which supposedly exists prior to its figuration. Their formal relationship can only be suggested by the relation of modernism to post-modernism, two overworked terms. Blackness exists, but only as a function of its signifiers. Reed's open-ended structure and his stress on the indeterminacy of the text demand that we, as critics, in the act of reading, produce a text's signifying structure. For Reed, as for his great precursor, Ellison, figuration is indeed "the Nigger's occupation."

IV

Reed's signifying relation to Ellison is exemplified in his poem "Dualism: in ralph ellison's invisible man":

i am outside of
history. i wish
i had some peanuts; it
looks hungry there in
its cage.

i am inside of
history. its
hungrier than i
thot.[35]

The figure of history here is the Signifying Monkey; the poem signifies upon that repeated trope of dualism figured initially in black discourse in W. E. B. Du Bois's essay "Of Our Spiritual Strivings," which forms the first chapter of *The Souls of Black Folk*. The dualism parodied by Reed's poem is that represented in the epilogue of *Invisible Man:* "now I know men are different and that all life is divided and that only in division is there true health" (p. 499). For Reed, this belief in the reality of dualism spells death. Ellison here has refigured Du Bois's trope, which bears full citation:

> After the Egyptian and Indian, the Greek and Roman, the Teuton and Mongolian, the Negro is a sort of seventh son, born with a veil, and gifted with second-sight in this American world, — a world which yields him no true self-consciousness, but only lets him see himself through the revelation of the other world. It is a peculiar sensation, this double-consciousness, this sense of always looking at one's self through the eyes of others, measuring one's soul by the tape of a world that looks on in amused contempt and pity. One ever feels his twoness, — an American, a Negro; two souls, two thoughts, two unreconciled strivings; two warring ideals in one dark body, whose dogged strength alone keeps it from being torn asunder.
>
> The history of the American Negro is the history of this strife, — this longing to attain self-conscious manhood, to merge his double self into a better and truer self. In this merging he wishes neither of the older selves to be lost.[36]

Reed's poem parodies profoundly both the figure of the black as outsider and the figure of the divided self. For, he tells us, even these are only tropes, figures of speech, rhetorical constructs like "double-consciousness," and not some preordained reality or thing. To read these figures literally, Reed tells us, is to be duped by figuration, just like the Signified Lion. Reed has secured his place in the canon precisely by his critique of the received, repeated tropes peculiar to that very canon. His works are the grand works of critical signification.

Notes

1. Quoted in Roger D. Abrahams, *Deep Down in the Jungle: Negro Narrative Folklore from the Streets of Philadelphia* (Chicago: Aldine, 1970), p. 53.
2. On "Tar Baby," see Ralph Ellison, *Shadow and Act* (New York: Vintage Books, 1964), p. 147; and Toni Morrison, *Tar Baby* (New York: Alfred A. Knopf, 1981). On

the black as quasi-simian, see Jean Bodin, *Method for the Easy Comprehension of History,* trans. Beatrice Reynolds (New York: Octagon Books, 1966), p. 105; Aristotle, *Historia Animalum,* trans. D'Arcy W. Thompson, in *The Works of Aristotle,* ed. J. A. Smith and W. D. Ross (Oxford: Oxford University Press, 1910), 4:606b; Thomas Herbert, *Some Years Travels* (London: R. Everingham, 1677), pp. 16–17; John Locke, *An Essay Concerning Human Understanding* (London: A. Churchill and A. Manship, 1721), book 3, chap. 6, sect. 23.

3. Geneva Smitherman defines these and other black tropes, then traces their use in several black texts. Smitherman's work, like that of Claudia Mitchell-Kernan and Roger Abrahams, is especially significant for literary theory. See Geneva Smitherman, *Talkin' and Testifyin': The Language of Black America* (Boston: Houghton Mifflin, 1977), pp. 101–67. See notes 12 and 13 below.

4. On versions of Esu, see Robert Farris Thompson, *Black Gods and Kings* (Bloomington: Indiana University Press, 1976), pp. 4/1–4/12, and *Flash of the Spirit* (New York: Random House, 1983); Pierre Verger, *Notes sur le culte des Orisa et Vodun* (Dakar: I.F.A.N., 1957); Joan Westcott, "The Sculpture and Myths of Eshu-Elegba," *Africa* 32.4: 336–53; Leo Frobenius, *The Voice of Africa* (London: Hutchinson, 1913); Melville J. and Frances Herskovits, *Dahomean Narrative* (Evanston: Northwestern University Press, 1958); Wande Abimbola, *Sixteen Great Poems of Ifa* (New York: UNESCO, 1975); William R. Bascom, *Ifa Divination* (Bloomington: Indiana University Press, 1969); Ayodele Ogundipe, "Esu Elegbara: The Yoruba God of Chance and Uncertainty" (Ph.D. diss., Indiana University, 1978); E. Bolaji Idowu, *Olódùmarè: God in Yoruba Belief* (London: Longman, 1962), pp. 80–85; and Robert Pelton, *The Trickster in West Africa* (Los Angeles: University of California Press, 1980).

5. On Esu and indeterminacy, see Robert Plant Armstrong, *The Powers of Presence: Consciousness, Myth, and Affecting Presence* (Philadelphia: University of Pennsylvania Press, 1981), p. 4. See p. 43 for a drawing of *Opon Ifa*; and Thompson, *Black Gods and Kings,* chap. 5.

6. On Esu and the monkey, see Lydia Cabrerra, *El Monte: Notes sobre las religiones, la magia, las supersticiones y el folklore de los negros criollos y el pueblo de Cuba* (Miami: Ediciones Universal, 1975), p. 84; and Alberto del Pozo, *Oricha* (Miami: Oricha, 1982), p. 1. On the Signifying Monkey, see Roger Abrahams, *Deep Down in the Jungle: Negro Narrative Folklore from the Streets of Philadelphia* (Chicago: Aldine, 1970), pp. 51–53, 66, 113–19, 142–47, 153–56, and especially 264; Bruce Jackson, *"Get Your Ass in the Water and Swim Like Me": Narrative Poetry from Black Oral Tradition* (Cambridge: Harvard University Press, 1974), pp. 161–80; Daryl Cumber Dance, *Shuckin' and Jivin': Folklore from Contemporary Black Americans* (Bloomington: Indiana University Press, 1978), pp. 197–99; Dennis Wepman, R. B. Newman, and M. B. Binderman, *The Life: The Lore and Folk Poetry of the Black Hustler* (Philadelphia: University of Pennsylvania Press, 1976), pp. 21–30; Lawrence W. Levine, *Black Culture and Black Consciousness: Afro-American Folk Thought from*

Slavery to Freedom (New York: Oxford University Press, 1977), pp. 364, 378–80, 438; and Richard M. Dorson, *American Negro Folktales* (New York: Fawcett, 1967), pp. 98–99.

7. Julia Kristeva, *Desire in Language: A Semiotic Approach to Literature and Art* (New York: Columbia University Press, 1980), p. 31.

8. See Abrahams, *Deep Down in the Jungle,* pp. 51–53, 66, 113–19, 142–47, 153–56, and especially 264; Roger D. Abrahams, "Playing the Dozens," *Journal of American Folklore* 75 (1962): 209–20; Roger D. Abrahams, "The Changing Concept of the Negro Hero," in *The Golden Log,* ed. Moady C. Boatright, Wilson M. Hudson, and Allen Maxwell (Dallas: Texas Folklore Society, 1962), pp. 125ff; and Roger D. Abrahams, *Talking Black* (Rowley, Mass.: Newbury House, 1976).

9. Abrahams, *Deep Down in the Jungle,* pp. 51–52, 66–67, 264. Abraham's awareness of the need to define uniquely black significations is exemplary; as early as 1964, when he published the first edition of *Deep Down in the Jungle,* he saw fit to add a glossary as an appendix of "Unusual Terms and Expressions," a title that unfortunately suggests the social scientist's apologia. (Emphasis added.)

10. Quoted in Abrahams, *Deep Down in the Jungle,* p. 113. In the second line of the stanza, "motherfucker" is often substituted for "monkey."

11. "The Signifying Monkey," in *Book of Negro Folklore,* ed. Langston Hughes and Arna Bontemps (New York: Dodd, Mead, 1958), pp. 365–66.

12. On signifying as a rhetorical trope, see Smitherman, *Talkin' and Testifyin',* pp. 101–67; Thomas Kochman, *Rappin' and Stylin' Out: Communication in Urban Black America* (Urbana: University of Illinois, 1972); and Thomas Kochman, " 'Rappin' in the Black Ghetto," *Trans-Action* 6.4 (Feb. 1969): 32; Alan Dundes, *Mother Wit from the Laughing Barrel* (Englewood Cliffs, N.J.: Prentice-Hall, 1973), p. 310; Ethel M. Albert, " 'Rhetoric,' 'Logic,' and 'Poetics' in Burund: Culture Patterning of Speech Behavior," in John J. Gumperz and Dell Hymes, eds., *The Ethnography of Communication," American Anthropologist* 66.6 (1964): 35–54. One example of signifying can be gleaned from the following anecdote. While writing this essay, I asked a colleague, Dwight Andrews, if he had heard of the Signifying Monkey as a child. "Why, no," he replied intently. "I never heard of the Signifying Monkey until I came to Yale and read about him in a book." I had been signified upon. If I had responded to Andrews, "I know what you mean; your Mama read to me from that same book the last time I was in Detroit," I would have signified upon him in return. See especially note 15 below.

13. Claudia Mitchell-Kernan, "Signifying," in Dundes, p. 313; and Claudia Mitchell-Kernan, "Signifying, Loud-Talking, and Marking," in Kochman, pp. 315–36. For Zora Neale Hurston's definition of the term, see *Mules and Men: Negro Folktales and Voodoo Practices in the South* (New York: Harper & Row, 1970), p. 161.

14. Mitchell-Kernan, "Signifying," p. 314.

15. Ibid., pp. 323–25.

16. Mitchell-Kernan, "Signifying, Loud-Talking, and Marking," pp. 315–36.

324   *Henry Louis Gates, Jr.*

17. Mitchell-Kernan, "Signifying," p. 325.
18. Ralph Ellison, "And Hickman Arrives," in *Black Writers of America*, ed. Richard Barksdale and Keneth Kinnamon (New York: Macmillan, 1972), p. 704.
19. Ralph Ellison, "On Bird, Bird-Watching, and Jazz," *Saturday Review*, July 20, 1962, reprinted in Ellison, *Shadow and Act*, p. 231.
20. Ralph Ellison, "Blues People," in Ellison, *Shadow and Act*, pp. 249, 250. The essay was first printed in the *New York Review of Books*, Feb. 6, 1964.
21. Ralph Ellison, "The World and the Jug," in Ellison, *Shadow and Act*, p. 117. The essay appeared first in the *New Leader*, Dec. 9, 1963.
22. Ellison, *Shadow and Act*, p. 137.
23. Mikhail Bakhtin, "Discourse Typology in Prose," in *Readings in Russian Poetics: Formalist and Structuralist Views*, ed. Ladislas Matejka and Krystyna Pomorska (Cambridge: MIT Press, 1971), pp. 176–99.
24. The use of interlocking triangles as a metaphor for the intertextual relationships of the tradition is not meant to suggest any form of concrete, inflexible reality. On the contrary, it is a systematic metaphor, as René Girard puts it, "systematically pursued." As Girard says: "The triangle is no *Gestalt*. The real structures are intersubjective. They cannot be localized anywhere; *the triangle has no reality whatever; it is a systematic metaphor, systematically pursued.* Because changes of size and shape do not destroy the identity of this figure, as we will see later, the diversity as well as the unity of the works can be simultaneously illustrated. The purpose and limitations of this structural geometry may become clearer through a reference to "structural models." The triangle is a model of a sort, or rather a whole family of models. But these models are not "mechanical" like those of Claude Lévi-Strauss. They always allude to the mystery, transparent yet opaque, of human relations. All types of structural thinking assume that human reality is intelligible; it is a *logos* and, as such, *it is an incipient logic, or it degrades itself into a logic.* It can thus be systematized, at least up to a point, however unsystematic, irrational, and chaotic it may appear even to those, or rather especially to those who operate the system" (emphasis added). René Girard, *Deceit, Desire, and the Novel: Self and Other in Literary Structure* (Baltimore: Johns Hopkins University Press, 1965), pp. 2–3.
25. For Ishmael Reed on "a talking book," see "Ishmael Reed: A Self Interview," *Black World*, June 1974, p. 25. For the slave narratives in which this figure appears, see James Albert Ukawsaw Gronniosaw, *A Narrative of the Most Remarkable Particulars of the Life of James Albert Ukawsaw Gronniosaw, An African Prince* (Bath, 1770); John Marrant, *Narrative of the Lord's Wonderful Dealings with John Marrant, a Black* (London: Gilbert and Plummer, 1785); Ottabah Cugoano, *Thoughts and Sentiments on the Evil and Wicked Traffic of the Slavery and Commerce of the Human Species* (London, 1787); and Olauduh Equino, *The Interesting Narrative of the Life of Olaudah Equino, or Gustavus Vassa, the African. Written by Himself.* (London: printed for the author, 1789).

26. Northrop Frye, *Anatomy of Criticism* (Princeton: Princeton University Press, 1971), p. 233.

27. Bakhtin, "Discourse Typology," p. 190.

28. Frye, p. 103.

29. Ellison, *Shadow and Act*, p. 140.

30. *The Free-Lance Pallbearers* (Garden City, N.Y.: Doubleday, 1967); *Yellow Back Radio Broke Down* (Garden City, N.Y.: Doubleday, 1969); *Mumbo Jumbo* (Garden City, N.Y.: Doubleday, 1972); *The Last Days of Louisiana Red* (New York: Random House, 1974); *Flight to Canada* (New York: Random House, 1976); and *The Terrible Twos* (New York: St. Martin's/Marek, 1982).

31. Neil Schmitz, "Neo-Hoodoo: The Experimental Fiction of Ishmael Reed," *20th Century Literature* 20.2 (Apr. 1974): 126–28. Schmitz's splendid reading is, I believe, the first to discuss this salient aspect of Reed's rhetorical strategy.

32. For an excellent close reading of *Yellow Back Radio Broke Down,* see Michel Fabre, "Postmodern Rhetoric in Ishmael Reed's *Yellow Back Radio Broke Down,*" in *The Afro-American Novel Since 1960,* ed. Peter Bruck and Wolfgang Karrer (Amsterdam: B. R. Gruner, 1982), pp. 167–88.

33. Ellison, "And Hickman Arrives," p. 701.

34. Charles T. Davis, *Black Is the Color of the Cosmos: Essays on Black Literature and Culture, 1942–1981,* edited by Henry Louis Gates, Jr. (New York: Garland, 1982), pp. 167–233.

35. Reed, *Conjure,* p. 50.

36. W. E. B. Du Bois, *The Souls of Black Folk* (New York: Fawcett, 1961), pp. 16–17.

23 Peter Brooks : *Reading for the Plot*

In "Reading for the Plot," Peter Brooks reacts against the structuralist emphasis on analyzing the specific features of literary texts by arguing for the singular importance of narrative in human culture. In his claim that narrative "need[s] to be considered as an operation important to our lives," Brooks asserts that there is a universal validity for foregrounding narrative in literary analysis. He defines narrative in terms of *plot,* which "is somehow prior to those elements most discussed by most critics." Invoking Aristotle, Forster, and others, Brooks claims that plot may well be the most fundamental formative element of narration.

If plot is "the organizing dynamic of a specific mode of human understanding," it therefore reflects the sensibility of a particular period in a given culture. For Brooks, then, how people plot the stories they tell reflects their most basic fears and beliefs. For Brooks, a plot encompasses not only the basic elements of the story, it also involves specific ways these elements are ordered in a text. Using ideas from the French structuralist Claude Lévi-Strauss and the Russian theorist Vladimir Propp—within a framework taken from Aristotle—Brooks criticizes those structuralists who emphasize linguistic models for narrative analysis and tend to separate the basic underlying story from the specific way its events are ordered. While Brooks finds some merit in the work of Roland Barthes and Gérard Genette, he still faults both of them for their failure to take sufficiently into account the fact that narrative is a temporal rather than a spatial medium.

Some important questions that arise from Brooks's argument, but are not resolved by it, pertain to the assertion that each age has its own particular anxieties about how plots get structured and resolved. How, for instance, do we evaluate the quality of a particular type of plot that was written in one age but read in another? In evaluating the quality of a literary work, should we be more concerned with how its plot represents the sensibility of its age, or how it satisfies a diverse range of readers' expectations?

Peter Brooks (b. 1938) is Professor of French and Comparative Literature at Yale University. In addition to *Reading for the Plot* (1984), from which this chapter is taken, he is also the author of *The Novel of Worldliness* (1969) and *The Melodramatic Imagination* (1976).

I

Our lives are ceaselessly intertwined with narrative, with the stories that we tell and hear told, those we dream or imagine or would like to tell, all of which are reworked in that story of our own lives that we narrate to ourselves in an episodic, sometimes semiconscious, but virtually uninterrupted monologue. We live immersed in narrative, recounting and reassessing the meaning of our past actions, anticipating the outcome of our future projects, situating ourselves at the intersection of several stories not yet completed. The narrative impulse is as old as our oldest literature: myth and folktale appear to be stories we recount in order to explain and understand where no other form of explanation will work. The desire and the competence to tell stories also reach back to an early stage in the individual's development, to about the age of three, when a child begins to show the ability to put together a narrative in coherent fashion and especially the capacity to recognize narratives, to judge their well-formedness. Children quickly become virtual Aristotelians, insisting upon any storyteller's observation of the "rules," upon proper beginnings, middles, and particularly ends. Narrative may be a special ability or competence that we learn, a certain subset of the general language code which, when mastered, allows us to summarize and retransmit narratives in other words and other languages, to transfer them into other media, while remaining recognizably faithful to the original narrative structure and message.

Narrative in fact seems to hold a special place among literary forms — as something more than a conventional "genre" — because of its potential for summary and retransmission: the fact that we can still recognize "the story" even when its medium has been considerably changed. This characteristic of narrative has led some theorists to suppose that it is itself a language, with its own code and its own rules for forming messages from the code, a hypothesis that probably does not hold up to inspection because narrative appears always to depend on some other language code in the creation of its meanings. But it does need to be considered as an operation important to all of our lives. When we "tell a story," there tends to be a shift in the register of our voices, enclosing and setting off the narrative almost in the manner of the traditional "once upon a time" and "they lived happily ever after": narrative demarcates, encloses, establishes limits, orders. And if it may be an impossibly speculative task to say what narrative itself is, it may be useful and valuable to think about the kinds of ordering it uses and creates, about the figures of design it makes. Here, I think, we can find our most useful object of attention in what has for centuries gone by the name of plot.

"Reading for the plot," we learned somewhere in the course of our schooling, is a low form of activity. Modern criticism, especially in its Anglo-American branches, has tended to take its valuations from study of the lyric, and when it has discussed narrative has emphasized questions of "point of view," "tone," "symbol," "spatial form," or "psychology." The texture of narrative has been considered most interesting insofar as it approached the density of poetry. Plot has been disdained as the element of narrative that least sets off and defines high art — indeed, plot is that which especially characterizes popular mass-consumption literature: plot is why we read *Jaws,* but not Henry James. And yet, one must in good logic argue that plot is somehow prior to those elements most discussed by most critics, since it is the very organizing line, the thread of design, that makes narrative possible because finite and comprehensible. Aristotle, of course, recognized the logical priority of plot, and a recent critical tradition, starting with the Russian formalists and coming up to the French and American "narratologists," has revived a quasi-Aristotelian sense of plot. When E. M. Forster, in the once influential *Aspects of the Novel,* asserts that Aristotle's emphasis on plot was mistaken, that our interest is not in the "imitation of an action" but rather in the "secret life which each of us lives privately," he surely begs the question, for if "secret lives" are to be narratable, they must in some sense be plotted, display a design and logic.[1]

There are evidently a number of different ways one might go about discussing the concept of plot and its function in the range of narrative forms. Plot is, first of all, a constant of all written and oral narrative, in that a narrative without at least a minimal plot would be incomprehensible. Plot is the principle of interconnectedness and intention which we cannot do without in moving through the discrete elements — incidents, episodes, actions — of a narrative: even such loosely articulated forms as the picaresque novel display devices of interconnectedness, structural repetitions that allow us to construct a whole; and we can make sense of such dense and seemingly chaotic texts as dreams because we use interpretive categories that enable us to reconstruct intentions and connections, to replot the dream as narrative. It would, then, be perfectly plausible to undertake a typology of plot and its elements from the *Iliad* and the *Odyssey* onward to the new novel and the "metafictions" of our time.[2] Yet it seems clear also that there have been some historical moments at which plot has assumed a greater importance than at others, moments in which cultures have seemed to develop an unquenchable thirst for plots and to seek the expression of central individual and collective meanings through narrative design. From sometime in the mid-eighteenth century through to the mid-twentieth century, Western societies appear to have felt an extraordinary need or desire for plots, whether in fiction, history, philosophy, or any of the social sciences, which in fact largely came into being with the Enlightenment and Romanticism. As Voltaire announced and then the Romantics confirmed, history replaces theology as the key discourse and central imagination in that historical explanation becomes nearly a necessary factor of any thought about human society: the question of what we are typically must pass through the question of where we are, which in turn is interpreted to mean, how did we get to be there? Not only history but historiography, the philosophy of history, philology, mythography, diachronic linguistics, anthropology, archaeology, and evolutionary biology all establish their claim as fields of inquiry, and all respond to the need for an explanatory narrative that seeks its authority in a return to origins and the tracing of a coherent story forward from origin to present.

The enormous narrative production of the nineteenth century may suggest an anxiety at the loss of providential plots: the plotting of the individual or social or institutional life story takes on new urgency when one no longer can look to a sacred masterplot that organizes and explains the world. The emergence of narrative plot as a dominant mode of ordering and explanation may belong to the large process of secularization, dating from the Renaissance and gathering force during the Enlightenment, which marks a falling-away from those revealed plots — the Chosen People, Redemption, the Second Coming — that appeared to subsume transitory human time to the timeless. In the last two books of *Paradise Lost,* Milton's angel Michael is able to present a full panorama of human history to Adam, concluding in redemption and a timeless future of bliss; and Adam responds:

How soon hath thy prediction, Seer Blest,
Measur'd this transient World, the Race of time,
Till time stand fixt: beyond is all abyss,
Eternity, whose end no eye can reach. (book 12, lines 553–56)

By the end of the Enlightenment, there is no longer any consensus on this prediction, and no cultural cohesion around a point of fixity which allows thought and vision so to transfix time. And this may explain the nineteenth century's obsession with questions of origin, evolution, progress, genealogy, its foregrounding of the historical narrative as par excellence the necessary mode of explanation and understanding.[3]

We still live today in the age of narrative plots, consuming avidly Harlequin romances and television serials and daily comic strips, creating and demanding narrative in the presentation of persons and news events and sports contests. For all the widely publicized nonnarrative or antinarrative forms of thought that are supposed to characterize our times, from complementarity and uncertainty in physics to the synchronic analyses of structuralism, we remain more determined by narrative than we might wish to believe. And yet, we know that with the advent of modernism came an era of suspicion toward plot, engendered perhaps by an over-elaboration of and overdependence on plots in the nineteenth century. If we cannot do without plots, we nonetheless feel uneasy about them, and feel obliged to show up their arbitrariness, to parody their mechanisms while admitting our dependence on them. Until such a time as we cease to exchange understandings in the form of stories, we will need to remain dependent on the logic we use to shape and to understand stories, which is to say, dependent on plot. A reflection on plot as the syntax of a certain way of speaking our understanding of the world may tell us something about how and why we have come to stake so many of the central concerns of our society, and of our lives, on narrative.

II

These sweeping generalizations will bear more careful consideration later on. It is important at this point to consider more closely just how we intend to speak of plot, how we intend to work with it, to make it an operative analytic and critical tool in the study of narrative. I want to urge a conception of plot as something in the nature of the logic of narrative discourse, the organizing dynamic of a specific mode of human understanding. This pursuit will in a moment take us into the discussion of narrative by a number of critics (of the type recently baptized narratologists), but perhaps the best way to begin is through a brief exercise in an old and thoroughly discredited form, the plot summary, in this case of a very old story. Here, then, is the summary of a story from the Grimm brothers, known in their version as "All-Kinds-of-Fur":[4]

A dying queen makes her husband promise that he will remarry only with a woman as beautiful as she, with the same golden hair. He promises, and she dies. Time passes, and he is urged by his councilors to remarry. He looks for the dead queen's equal, but finds no one; until, years later, his eyes light on his daughter, who looks just like her mother, with the same golden hair. He will marry her, though his councilors say he must not. Pressed to answer, the daughter makes her consent contingent on the performance of three apparently impossible tasks: he must give her three dresses, one as golden as the sun, one as silvery as the moon, the third as glittering as all the stars, plus a cloak made of a thousand different furs. The king, in fact, succeeds in providing these and insists on the marriage. The daughter then flees, blackens her face and hands, covers herself with the cloak of furs, and hides in the woods, where she is captured as a strange animal by the king of another country. She goes to work as a scullery maid in his kitchens, but on three successive occasions she appears at the king's parties clothed in one of her three splendid dresses and dances with him; and three times she cooks the king's pudding and leaves in the bottom of the dish one of the tokens she has brought from home (a golden ring, a golden spinning wheel, a golden reel). On the third repetition, the king slips the ring on her finger while they are dancing, and when she returns to the kitchen, in her haste she does not blacken one hand entirely. The king searches her out, notices the white finger and its ring, seizes her hand, strips off the fur cloak to reveal the dress underneath, and the golden hair, and claims her in marriage.

What have we witnessed and understood here? How have we moved from one desire that we, like the king's councilors, know to be prohibited, to a legitimate desire whose consummation marks the end of the tale? And what is the meaning of the process lying between beginning and end—a treble testing, with the supplemental requirement of the cloak; flight and disguise (using the cloak to become subhuman, almost a beast); then a sort of striptease revelation, also treble, using the three dresses provided by the father and the three golden objects brought from home (tokens, perhaps, of the mother), followed by recognition? How have we crossed from one kingdom to another through those woods which, we must infer, border on both of them? We cannot really answer such questions, yet we would probably all agree that the middle of the tale offers a kind of minimum satisfactory process that works through the problem of desire gone wrong and brings it to its cure. It is a process in which the overly eroticized object — the daughter become object of desire to the father — loses all erotic and feminine attributes, becomes unavailable to desire, then slowly, through repetition by three (which is perhaps the minimum repetition to suggest series and process), reveals her nature as erotic object again but now in a situation where the erotic is permitted and fitting. The tale is characterized by that laconic chasteness which Walter Benjamin found characteristic of the great oral stories, a refusal of psychological explanation and motivation.[5] It matter-of-factly takes on the central issues of culture — incest, the need for exogamy — without commentary. Like a number of the Grimms' tales, it seems to ask the question, Why do girls grow up, leave their homes and their fathers, and marry other men? It answers the question without explanation, through description of what needs to happen, the process set in motion, when normal forms are threatened, go awry: as in "Hawthorn Blossom" (the Grimms' version of "Sleeping Beauty"), we are given a kind of counter-example, the working-out of an antidote. The tale appears as the species of explanation that we give when explanation, in the logical and discursive sense, seems impossible or impertinent. It thus transmits a kind of wisdom that itself concerns transmission: how we pass on what we know about how life goes forward.

Folktale and myth may be seen to show narrative as a form of thinking, a way of reasoning about a situation. As Claude Lévi-Strauss has argued, the Oedipus myth may be "about" the unsolvable problem of man's origins — born from the earth or from parents? — a "chicken or egg" problem that finds its mythic "solution" in a story about generational confusion: Oedipus violates the demarcations of generations, becomes the "impossible" combination of son/husband, father/brother, and so on, subverting (and thus perhaps reinforcing) both cultural distinctions and categories of thought. It is the ordering of the inexplicable and impossible situation as narrative that somehow mediates and forcefully connects its discrete elements, so that we accept the necessity of what cannot logically be discoursed of. Yet I don't think we do justice to our experience of "All-Kinds-of-Fur" or the Oedipus myth in reducing their narratives — as Lévi-Strauss suggests all mythic narratives can be reduced — to their "atemporal matrix structure," a set of basic cultural antinomies that the narrative mediates.[6] Nor can we, to be sure, analyze these narratives simply as a pure succession of events or happenings. We need to recognize, for instance, that there is a dynamic logic at work in the transformations wrought between the start and the finish of "All-Kinds-of-Fur," a logic which makes sense of succession and time, and which insists that mediation of the problem posed at the outset takes time: that the meaning dealt with by narrative, and thus perhaps narrative's raison d'être, is of and in time. Plot as it interests me is not a matter of typology or of fixed structures, but rather a structuring operation peculiar to those messages that are developed through temporal succession, the instrumental logic of a specific mode of human understanding. Plot, let us say in preliminary definition, is the logic and dynamic of narrative, and narrative itself a form of understanding and explanation.

Such a conception of plot seems to be at least compatible with Aristotle's understanding of *mythos,* the term from the *Poetics* that is normally translated as "plot." It is Aristotle's claim that plot (*mythos*) and action (*praxis*) are logically prior to the other parts of dramatic fictions, including character (*ethos*). *Mythos* is defined as "the combination of the incidents, or things done in the story," and Aristotle argues that of all the parts of the story, this is the most important. It is worth quoting his claim once more:

> Tragedy is essentially an imitation not of persons but of action and life, of happiness and misery. All human happiness or misery takes the form of action; the end for which we live is a certain kind of activity, not a quality. Character gives us qualities, but it is in our actions — what we do — that we are happy or the reverse. In a play accordingly they do not act in order to portray the Characters: they include the Characters for the sake of the action. So that it is the action in it, i.e. its Fable or Plot, that is the end and purpose of the tragedy; and the end is everywhere the chief thing.[7]

Later in the same paragraph he reiterates, using an analogy that may prove helpful to thinking about plot: "We maintain, therefore, that the first essential, the life and soul, so to speak, of Tragedy is Plot; and that the Characters come second — compare the parallel in painting, where the most beautiful colours laid on without order will not give one the same pleasure as a simple black-and-white sketch of a portrait." Plot, then, is conceived to be the outline or armature of the story, that which supports and organizes the rest. From such a view, Aristotle proceeds to derive three consequences. First, the action imitated by the tragedy must be complete in itself. This in turn means that it must have a beginning, a middle, and an end — a point wholly obvious but one that will prove to have interesting effects in its applications. Finally, just as in the visual arts a whole must be of a size that can be taken in by the eye, so a plot must be "of a length to be taken in by the memory." This is important, since memory — as much in reading a novel as in seeing a play — is the key faculty in the capacity to perceive relations of beginnings, middles, and ends through time, the shaping power of narrative.

But our English term "plot" has its own semantic range, one that is interestingly broad and possibly instructive. The *Oxford English Dictionary* gives seven definitions, essentially, which the *American Heritage Dictionary* helpfully reduces to four categories:

1. (a) A small piece of ground, generally used for a specific purpose. (b) A measured area of land; lot.
2. A ground plan, as for a building; chart; diagram.
3. The series of events consisting of an outline of the action of a narrative or drama.
4. A secret plan to accomplish a hostile or illegal purpose; scheme.

There may be a subterranean logic connecting these heterogeneous meanings. Common to the original sense of the word is the idea of boundedness, demarcation, the drawing of lines to mark off and order. This easily extends to the chart or diagram of the demarcated area, which in turn modulates to the outline of the literary work. From the organized space, plot becomes the organizing line, demarcating and diagramming that which was previously undifferentiated. We might think here of the geometrical expression, plotting points, or curves, on a graph by means of coordinates, as a way of locating something, perhaps oneself. The fourth sense of the word, the scheme or conspiracy, seems to have come into English through the contaminating influence of the French *complot,* and became widely known at the time of the Gunpowder Plot. I would suggest that in modern literature this sense of plot nearly always attaches itself to the others: the organizing line of plot is more often than not some scheme or machination, a concerted plan for the accomplishment of some purpose which goes against the ostensible and dominant legalities of the fictional world, the realization of a blocked and resisted desire. Plots are not simply organizing structures, they are also intentional structures, goal-oriented and forward-moving.

Plot as we need and want the term is hence an embracing concept for the design and intention of narrative, a structure for those meanings that are developed through temporal succession, or perhaps better: a structuring operation elicited by, and made necessary by, those meanings that develop through succession and time. A further analysis of the question is suggested here by a distinction urged by the Russian formalists, that between *fabula* and *sjužet. Fabula* is defined as the order of events referred to by the narrative, whereas *sjužet* is the order of events presented in the narrative discourse. The distinction is one that takes on evident analytic force when one is talking about a Conrad or a Faulkner, whose dislocations of normal chronology are radical and significant, but it is no less important in thinking about apparently more straightforward narratives, since any narrative presents a selection and an ordering of material. We must, however, recognize that the apparent priority of fabula to sjužet is in the nature of a mimetic illusion, in that the fabula — "what really happened" — is in fact a mental construction that the reader derives from the sjužet, which is all that he ever directly knows. This differing status of the two terms by no means invalidates the distinction itself, which is central to our thinking about narrative and necessary to its analysis since it allows us to juxtapose two modes of order and in the juxtaposing to see how ordering takes place. In the wake of the Russian formalists, French structural analysts of narrative proposed their own pairs of terms, predominantly *histoire* (corresponding to fabula) and *récit,* or else *discours* (corresponding to sjužet). English usage has been more unsettled. "Story" and "plot" would seem to be generally acceptable renderings in most circumstances, though a structural and semiotic analysis will find advantages in the less semantically charged formulation "story" and "discourse."[8]

"Plot" in fact seems to me to cut across the fabula/sjužet distinction in that to speak of plot is to consider both story elements and their ordering. Plot could be thought of as the interpretive activity elicited by the distinction between sjužet and fabula, the way we *use* the one against the other. To keep our terms straight without sacrificing the advantages of the semantic range of "plot," let us say that we can generally understand plot to be an aspect of sjužet in that it belongs to the narrative discourse, as its active shaping force, but that it makes sense (as indeed sjužet itself principally makes sense) as it is used to reflect on fabula, as our understanding of story. Plot is thus the dynamic shaping force of the narrative discourse. I find confirmation for such a view in Paul Ricoeur's definition of plot as "the intelligible whole that governs a succession of events in any story."

Ricoeur continues, using the terms "events" and "story" rather than fabula and sjužet: "This provisory definition immediately shows the plot's connecting function between an event or events and the story. A story is *made out of* events to the extent that plot *makes* events *into* a story. The plot, therefore, places us at the crossing point of temporality and narrativity."[9] Ricoeur's emphasis on the constructive role of plot, its active, shaping function, offers a useful corrective to the structural narratologists' neglect of the dynamics of narrative and points us toward the reader's vital role in the understanding of plot.

The Russian Formalists presented what one might call a "constructivist" view of literature, calling attention to the material and the means of its making, showing how a given work is put together. "Device" is one of their favorite terms — a term for demonstrating the technical use of a given motif or incident or theme. Typical is Boris Tomachevsky's well-known illustration of the technical sense of "motivation": if a character in a play hammers a nail into the wall in act 1, then he or another character will have to hang himself from it in act 3. The work of Tomachevsky, Victor Shklovsky, and Boris Eichenbaum is invaluable to the student of narrative since it so often cuts through thematic material to show the constructed armature that supports it.[10] Perhaps the instance of the Russian formalists' work most compelling for our purposes is their effort to isolate and identify the minimal units of narrative, and then to formulate the principles of their combination and interconnection. In particular, Vladimir Propp's *The Morphology of the Folktale* merits attention as an early and impressive example of what can be done to formalize and codify the study of narrative.

Faced with the mass of material collected by folklorists and the inadequacy of attempts to order it through thematic groupings or patterns of derivation, Propp began with a gesture similar to that of Ferdinand de Saussure at the inception of modern linguistics, bracketing questions of origin and derivation and reference in order to find the principles of a morphology of a given body of material. Taking some one hundred tales classified by folklorists as fairy tales, he sought to provide a description of the fairy tale according to its component parts, the relation of these parts to one another and to the tale as a whole, and hence the basis for a comparison among tales. Propp claims that the essential morphological components are function and sequence. One identifies the functions by breaking down the tale into elements defined not by theme or character but rather according to the actions performed: function is "an act of character, defined from the point of view of its significance for the course of the action."[11] Functions will thus appear in the analysis as labels for kinds of action, such as "interdiction," "testing," "acquisition of the magical agent," and so on; whereas sequence will concern the order of the functions, the logic of their consecution. As a result of his study, Propp with a certain bravado puts forward four theses concerning the fairy tale:

1. The functions are stable, constant elements whoever carries them out.
2. The number of functions is limited (there are just thirty-one in the Russian fairy tale).
3. The sequence of functions is always identical (not all are present in every tale, but the sequence of those present is invariable).
4. All fairy tales are of one type in regard to their structure.

Whatever the validity of Propp's theses, the concept of function, and the "functionalist" view of narrative structure it implies, stresses in a useful way the role of verbs of action as the armature of narrative, their logic and articulation and sequence. Propp suggests an approach to the analysis of narrative actions by giving precedence to *mythos* over *ethos,* indeed by abstracting plot structure from the persons who carry it out. Characters for Propp are essentially agents of the action; he reduces them to seven "dramatis personae," defined by the "spheres of influence" of the actions they perform: the Villain, the Donor, the Helper, the Princess and her Father (who together function as a single agent), the Dispatcher, the Hero, and the False Hero. The names that an individual tale will assign to these agents — and the way it may combine or divide them — are relatively unimportant, as are their attributes and motivations. What counts is their role as vehicles of the action, their placement and appearance in order to make sure that the Hero is dispatched, for instance, or that he is presented with false claims that he must expose and overcome. Propp's analysis clearly is limited by the relatively simple and formulaic nature of the narratives he discusses. Yet something like the concept of "function" may be necessary in any discussion of plot, in that it gives us a way to think about what happens in narrative from the point of view of its significance to the course of the action as a whole, the articulation of narrative as a structure of actions.

Propp's insistence on sequence and function results in a "syntagmatic" analysis, that is, one concerned with the combination of units along a horizontal axis, as in a sentence. Within French structuralism, there has rather been a strong emphasis on the "paradigmatic," an attention to the vertical axis which represents the grammar and lexicon of narrative, the elements and sets of relations which an individual narrative must call upon and activate.[12] Lévi-Strauss's interest in the "atemporal matrix structure" of narrative, the basic set of relationships which underlies and generates any given mythic narrative, is an example. So is the work of the semiotician A. J. Greimas, who takes Propp's analysis and, in the spirit of Lévi-Strauss, tries to reformulate the seven "dramatis personae" in the form of a matrix structure, a set of symmetrical oppositions which defines a kind of field of force. Greimas offers a taxonomy whose inherent tensions generate the production of narrative. It looks like this:

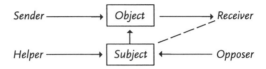

Without giving a full exposition of what Greimas calls his *modèle actantiel* — the dramatis personae have been rebaptized *actants,* emphasizing their quality of agency — one can see that the tale is conceived as a set of vectors, where the Hero's (the Subject's) search for the Object (the Princess, for instance) is helped or hindered, while the Object of the search itself (herself) is sent, or given, or put in the way of being obtained. The dotted line between Subject and Receiver indicates that very often these two coincide: the Hero is working for himself.[13]

The language used by Greimas — especially Subject and Object, but also Sender (*Destinateur*) and Receiver (*Destinataire*) — indicates that he is working also under the influence of a linguistic model, so central to structuralist thought in general. The work of Propp and other Russian formalists has proved susceptible of a reformulation by way of the linguistic model, by structuralists concerned to provide a general poetics of narrative (or "narratology"), that is, the conditions of meaning, the grammar and the syntax of narrative forms. Tzvetan Todorov (who more than anyone else introduced the ideas of the Russian formalists into French structuralism) works, for instance, from the postulate of a "universal grammar" of narrative.[14] Starting from a general analogy of narrative to a sentence writ large, Todorov postulates that the basic unit of narrative (like Propp's function) is a clause, while the agents are proper nouns, semantically void until predicated. The predicate terms are verbs (actions) and adjectives (states of being). His analysis proceeds largely with the study of verbs, the most important component of narrative, which have status (positive or negative), mood (imperative, optative, declarative, etc.), aspect (indicative, subjunctive), voice (passive or active). Clauses combine in different manners to form sequences, and complete narrative sequences are recognizable from their accomplishment of a transformation of the initial verb, now changed in status, mood, aspect, or by an added auxiliary verb.

Todorov best represents the linguistic model, applied to narrative analysis, in its most developed form. But such work is no doubt less valuable as a systematic model for analysis than as a suggestive metaphor, alerting us to the important analogies between parts of speech and parts of narrative, encouraging us to think about narrative as system, with something that approximates a grammar and rules of ordering that approximate a syntax. Perhaps the most challenging work to come out of narratology has used the linguistic model in somewhat playful ways, accepting it as a necessary basis for thought but opening up its implications in an engagement with the reading of texts. What I have most in mind here is Roland Barthes's *S/Z,* a book that combines some of the rigors of structuralist analysis, in its patient tracing of five codes through a tale broken down into 561 *lexias,* with interspersed speculative excurses on narrative and its reading.[15]

If we ask more specifically where in *S/Z* we find a notion approximating "plot," I think the answer must be: in some combination of Barthes's two irreversible codes — those that must be decoded successively, moving in one direction — the *proairetic* and the *hermeneutic,* that is: the code of actions ("Voice of the Empirical") and the code of enigmas and answers ("Voice of Truth"). The proairetic concerns the logic of actions, how their completion can be derived from their initiation, how they form sequences. The limit-case of a purely proairetic narrative would be approached by the picaresque tale, or the novel of pure adventure: narratives that give precedence to the happening. The hermeneutic code concerns rather the questions and answers that structure a story, their suspense, partial unveiling, temporary blockage, eventual resolution, with the resulting creation of a "dilatory space" — the space of suspense — which we work through toward what is felt to be, in classical narrative, the revelation of meaning that occurs when the narrative sentence reaches full predication. The clearest and purest example of the hermeneutic would no doubt be the detective story, in that everything in the story's structure, and its temporality, depends on the resolution of enigma. Plot, then, might best be thought of as an "overcoding" of the proairetic by the hermeneutic, the latter structuring the discrete elements of the former into larger interpretive wholes, working out their play of meaning and significance. If we interpret the hermeneutic to be a general gnomic code, concerned not narrowly with enigma and its resolution but broadly with our understanding of how actions come to be semiotically structured, through an interrogation of their point, their goal, their import, we find that Barthes contributes to our conception of plot as part of the dynamics of reading.

What may be most significant about *S/Z* is its break away from the somewhat rigid notion of structure to the more fluid and dynamic notion of structuration. The text is seen as a texture or weaving of codes (using the etymological sense of "text") which the reader organizes and sorts out only in provisional ways, since he never can master it completely, indeed is himself in part "undone" in his effort to unravel the text. The source of the codes is in what Barthes calls the *déjà-lu,* the already read (and the already written), in the writer's and the reader's experience of other literature, in a whole set of intertextual interlockings. In other words, structures, functions, sequences, plot, the possibility of following a narrative and making sense of it, belong to the reader's literary competence, his training as a reader of narrative.[16] The reader is in this view himself virtually a text, a composite of all that he has read, or heard read, or imagined as written. Plot, as the interplay of two of Barthes's codes, thus comes to appear one central way in which we as readers make sense, first of the text, and then, using the text as an interpretive model, of life. Plot — I continue to extrapolate from Barthes — is an interpretive structuring operation elicited, and necessitated, by those texts that we identify as narrative, where we know the meanings are developed over temporal succession in a suspense of final predication. As Barthes writes in an earlier essay ("Introduction to the Structural Analysis of Narrative"), what animates us as readers of narrative is *la passion du sens,* which I would want to translate as both the passion *for* meaning and the passion *of* meaning: the active quest of the reader for those shaping ends that, terminating the dynamic process of reading, promise to bestow meaning and significance on the beginning and the middle.[17]

But what Barthes discusses less well is the relation of the sensemaking operations of reading to codes outside the text, to the structuring of "reality" by textual systems. He tends to dismiss the referential or cultural code ("Voice of Science") as a "babble" conveying a society's received opinions and stereotypes. In particular, he does not pursue the questions of temporality raised by the irreversible nature of the proairetic and the hermeneutic codes. In the "Introduction to the Structural Analysis of Narrative," Barthes claims that time in narrative belongs only to the referent (to the fabula) and has nothing to do with the narrative discourse. And even in *S/Z*, which shows a diminished subservience to the paradigmatic model, Barthes's allegiances to the "writeable text" (*texte scriptible:* that which allows and requires the greatest constructive effort by the reader) and to the practice of "new new novelists" make him tend to disparage his irreversible codes as belonging to an outmoded ideology, and to reserve his greatest admiration for the symbolic ("Voice of the Text"), which allows one to enter the text anywhere and to play with its stagings of language itself.

Some correction of perspective is provided by Gérard Genette in *Narrative Discourse,* which along with the work of Todorov and Barthes constitutes the most significant contribution of the French structuralist tradition to thinking about narrative. In his careful and subtle study of the relationships among story, plot, and narrating, Genette pays close attention to the functioning of the infinitely variable gearbox that links the told to the ways of its telling, and how the narrative discourse — his principal example is Proust's *A la recherche du temps perdu* — works to subvert, replay, or even pervert the normal passages of time.[18] Noting the inescapable linearity of the linguistic signifier, Genette faces most directly the paradox of form and temporality when he points out that narrative as we commonly know it — as a book, for instance — is literally a spatial form, an object, but that its realization depends on its being gone through in sequence and succession, and that it thus metonymically "borrows" a temporality from the time of its reading: what he calls a "pseudo-time" of the text.[19]

Genette thus offers a kind of minimalist solution to the question of structure and temporality, and dissents in part from the structural narratologists' excessive emphasis on the paradigmatic, their failure to engage the movement and dynamic of narrative. Genette's solution may be too cautious. For not only does the reading of narrative take time; the time it takes, to get from beginning to end — particularly in those instances of narrative that most define our sense of the mode, nineteenth-century novels — is very much part of our sense of the narrative, what it has accomplished, what it means. Lyric poetry, we feel, strives toward an ideal simultaneity of meaning, encouraging us to read backward as well as forward (through rhyme and repetition, for instance), to grasp the whole in one visual and auditory image; and expository argument, while it can have a narrative, generally seeks to suppress its force in favor of an atemporal structure of understanding; whereas narrative stories depend on meanings delayed, partially filled in, stretched out. Unlike philosophical syllogisms, narratives ("All-Kinds-of-Fur," for example) are temporal syllogisms, concerning the connective processes of time. It is, I think, no accident that most of the great examples of narrative are long and can occupy our reading time over days or weeks or more: if we think of the effects of serialization (which, monthly, weekly, or even daily, was the medium of publication for many of the great nineteenth-century novels) we can per-haps grasp more nearly how time in the representing is felt to be a neces-sary analogue of time represented. As Rousseau contends in the preface to *La Nouvelle Héloïse,* a novel that in so many ways announces the nineteenth-century tradition, to understand his characters one must know them both young and old, and know them through the process of aging and change that lies in between, a process worked out over a stretch of pages.[20] And Proust's narrator says much the same thing at the end of *Le Temps retrouvé,* where — in the shadow of impending death — he resolves to ded-icate himself to the creation of a novel that will, of necessity, have "the shape of time."[21]

Plot as a logic of narrative would hence seem to be analogous to the syntax of meanings that are temporally unfolded and recovered, meanings that cannot otherwise be created or understood. Genette's study of narra-tive discourse in reference to Proust leads him to note that one can tell a story without any reference to the place of its telling, the location from which it is proffered, but that one cannot tell a story without indications of the time of telling in relation to the told: the use of verb tenses, and their relation one to another, necessarily gives us a certain temporal place in relation to the story. Genette calls this discrepancy in the situation of time and place a "dissymmetry" of the language code itself, "the deep causes of which escape us."[22] While Genette's point is valid and important in the context of linguistics and the philosophy of language, one might note that commonsensically the deep causes are evident to the point of banality, if also rather grim: that is, man is ambulatory, but he is mortal. Temporality is a problem, and an irreducible factor of any narrative statement, in a way that location is not: "All-Kinds-of-Fur" can be articulated from anywhere, but it needs to observe the sequence of tenses and the succession of events. It is my simple conviction, then, that narrative has something to do with time-boundedness, and that plot is the internal logic of the discourse of mortality.

Walter Benjamin has made this point in the simplest and most extreme way, in claiming that what we seek in narrative fictions is that knowledge of death which is denied to us in our own lives: the death that writes *finis* to the life and therefore confers on it its meaning. "Death," says Benjamin, "is the sanction of everything that the storyteller can tell."[23] Benjamin thus advances the ultimate argument for the necessary retrospectivity of narrative: that only the end can finally determine meaning, close the sentence as a signifying totality. Many of the most suggestive analysts of narrative have shared this conviction that the end writes the beginning and shapes the middle: Propp, for instance, and Frank Kermode, and Jean-Paul Sartre, in his distinction between living and telling, argued in *La Nausée,* where in telling everything is transformed by the structuring presence of the end to come, and narrative in fact proceeds "in the reverse"; or, as Sartre puts it in respect to autobiographical narration in *Les Mots,* in order to tell his story in terms of the meaning it would acquire only at the end, "I became my own obituary."[24] These are arguments to which we will need to return in more detail. We should here note that opposed to this view stand other analysts, such as Claude Bremond, or Jean Pouillon, who many years ago argued (as a Sartrean attempting to rescue narrative from the constraints Sartre found in it) that the preterite tense used classically in the novel is decoded by the reader as a kind of present, that of an action and a significance being forged before his eyes, in his hands, so to speak.[25] It is to my mind an interesting and not wholly resolvable question how much, and in what ways, we in reading image the pastness of the action presented, in most cases, in verbs in the past tense. If on the one hand we realize the action progressively, segment by segment, as a kind of present in terms of our experience of it — the present of an argument, as in my summary of "All-Kinds-of-Fur" — do we not do so precisely in anticipation of its larger hermeneutic structuring by conclusions? We are frustrated by narrative interminable, even if we know that any termination is artificial, and that the imposition of ending may lead to that resistance to the end which Freud found in his patients and which is an important novelistic dynamic in such writers as Stendhal and Gide.[26] If the past is to be read as present, it is a curious present that we know to be past in relation to a future we know to be already in place, already in wait for us to reach it. Perhaps we would do best to speak of the *anticipation of retrospection* as our chief tool in making sense of narrative, the master trope of its strange logic. We have no doubt forgone eternal narrative ends, and even traditional nineteenth-century ends are subject to self-conscious endgames, yet still we read in a spirit of confidence, and also a state of dependence, that what remains to be read will restructure the provisional meanings of the already read.

Notes

1. E. M. Forster, *Aspects of the Novel* (New York: Harcourt, Brace, 1927), p. 126.

2. One of the ambitions of Northrop Frye in *Anatomy of Criticism* (Princeton: Princeton University Press, 1957) is to provide such a typology in his *mythoi*. Yet there is in Frye a certain confusion between mythoi as plot structures and mythoi as myths or archetypes which to my mind makes his work less valuable than it might be.

3. On historical narrative as a form of understanding, see the fine essay by Louis O. Mink, "Narrative Form as Cognitive Instrument," in *The Writing of History: Literary Form and Historical Understanding,* ed. Robert H. Canary and Henry Kozicki (Madison: University of Wisconsin Press, 1978), pp. 129–49. Mink calls narrative "a primary and irreducible form of human comprehension" (p. 132). Of interest also is Dale H. Porter, *The Emergence of the Past* (Chicago: University of Chicago Press, 1981).

4. See "All-Kinds-of-Fur" (*Allerleirauh*), in *The Grimms' German Folk Tales,* trans. Francis P. Magoun and Alexander H. Krappe (Carbondale: Southern Illinois University Press, 1960), pp. 257–61.

5. See Walter Benjamin, "The Storyteller" (*Der Erzähler*), in *Illuminations,* trans. Harry Zohn (New York: Schocken Books, 1969), p. 91. On the place of incest and incest taboo in the Grimms' tales, see Marthe Robert, "The Grimm Brothers," in *The Child's Part,* ed. Peter Brooks (reprint, Boston: Beacon Press, 1972), pp. 44–56. One might offer the following diagram of the movement of the plot in "All-Kinds-of-Fur," from the initial overeroticization of the daughter (as the object of prohibited desires), through the underevaluation of the feminine (becoming the simulated beast), to the state of equilibrium achieved at the end: $+ + / - - / + -$. Without attaching too much importance to such a formula, one can see that it describes a process of working-out or working-through common to many tales.

6. On the Oedipus myth, see Claude Lévi-Strauss, "The Structural Study of Myth," in *Structural Anthropology* (Garden City, N.Y.: Anchor-Doubleday, 1967), pp. 202–25. On the "atemporal matrix structure," see Lévi-Strauss, "La Structure et la forme," *Cahiers de l'Institut de Science Economique Appliquée* 99, sér. M, no. 7 (1960): 29.

7. Aristotle, *Poetics,* trans. Ingram Bywater, in *Introduction to Aristotle,* 2d ed., ed. Richard McKeon (Chicago: University of Chicago Press, 1973), p. 678.

8. See Seymour Chatman, *Story and Discourse* (Ithaca: Cornell University Press, 1979). Chatman's book offers a useful summary, and attempt at synthesis, of narrative analysis in the structuralist tradition; he also gives extended bibliographical references. One can find an exposition of many of the issues that concern us here in Robert Scholes, *Structuralism in Literature* (New Haven: Yale University Press, 1974). *Fabula* and *sjužet* are rendered as "story" and "plot" by Lee T. Lemon and Marion Reis in their anthology *Russian Formalist Criticism* (Lincoln: University of Nebraska Press, 1965). Equating the fabula/sjužet distinction with story/plot is much criticized by Meir Sternberg in *Expositional Modes and Temporal Ordering in Fiction* (Baltimore: Johns Hopkins University Press, 1978), chap. 1. But Sternberg's understanding of the concept of plot is based exclusively on E. M. Forster's definition in *Aspects of the Novel,* where plot is distinguished from story by its emphasis on causality. To offer causality as the key characteristic of plot may be to fall into the error of the *post hoc ergo propter hoc,* as Roland Barthes suggests in "Introduction à l'analyse structurale des récits" (*Communications* 8 [1966], English trans. Stephen Heath, in *A Barthes Reader,* ed. Susan Sontag [New York: Hill and Wang, 1982]), and as Vladimir Propp implicitly demonstrates in *The Morphology of the Folktale,* 2d ed., trans. Laurence Scott (Austin: University of Texas Press, 1970); if plot appears to turn sequence into consequence, this may often be illusory; causality can be produced by new material, by changes in mood or atmosphere, by coincidence, by reinterpretation of the past, and so forth. Some of these issues will be taken up in chap. 10 [of *Reading for the Plot*]. Sternberg argues further that the sjužet is properly the whole of the text, whereas plot is an abstraction and reconstruction of it. But I think that sjužet as used by such Russian formalists as Boris Tomachevsky and Victor Shklovsky is similarly an abstraction and reconstruction of the logic of the narrative text and in this sense is quite close to Aristotle. For a useful discussion of the concept of plot, especially as related to the notion of mimesis, see Elizabeth Dipple, *Plot* (London: Methuen, 1970).

9. Paul Ricoeur, "Narrative Time" in *On Narrative,* ed. W. J. T. Mitchell (Chicago: University of Chicago Press, 1981), p. 167. Compare Louis O. Mink on historical narrative, when he argues that the past "is not an untold story but can be made intelligible only as the subject of stories we tell" ("Narrative Form as Cognitive Instrument," p. 148). Ricoeur offers a more extended presentation of his ideas in the recent *Temps et récit* (Paris: Editions du Seuil, 1983), which primarily concerns historical narrative and will be followed by a second volume devoted to fictional narrative.

10. The work I refer to here is available in English translation primarily in two anthologies: Lee T. Lemon and Marion Reis, eds., *Russian Formalist Criticism,* which contains Tomachevsky's essay in synthesis, "Thematics"; and Ladislav Matejka and Krystyna Pomorska, *Readings in Russian Poetics* (Cambridge: MIT Press, 1971). The major study of the Russian formalists remains Victor Erlich, *Russian Formalism* (The Hague: Mouton, 1955). See also the anthology in French translation edited by Tzvetan Todorov, *Théorie de la littérature* (Paris: Editions du Seuil, 1965).

11. Propp, *The Morphology of the Folktale,* p. 21.

12. The paradigmatic axis is the "axis of selection" in Roman Jakobson's terms, the set of rules and virtual terms that are activated along the syntagmatic axis, or "axis of combination." For a good discussion of the uses of the two axes, see Jakobson, "Closing Statement: Linguistics and Poetics," in *Style in Language,* ed. Thomas Sebeok (Cambridge: MIT Press, 1960), pp. 350–77.

13. See A. J. Greimas, *Sémantique structurale* (Paris: Larousse, 1966). One of Greimas's more amusing illustrations is Karl Marx's *Das Kapital,* which according to the model gives the following "actants": Subject: Man; Object: Classless Society; Sender: History; Receiver: Humanity; Helper: Proletariat; Opposer: Bourgeoisie.

14. See in particular Tzvetan Todorov, *Grammaire du Décameron* (The Hague: Mouton, 1969), and the essays of Poétique de la prose (Paris: Editions du Seuil, 1971), English trans. Richard Howard, *The Poetics of Prose* (Ithaca: Cornell University Press, 1977). On Todorov's contribution to the poetics of narrative, see Peter Brooks, "Introduction" to Todorov, *Poetics,* trans. Richard Howard (Minneapolis: University of Minnesota Press, 1981). See also Gerald Prince, *A Grammar of Stories* (The Hague: Mouton, 1973).

15. See Roland Barthes, *S/Z* (Paris: Editions du Seuil, 1970), English trans. Richard Miller (New York: Hill and Wang, 1974).

16. The notion of "literary competence," implicit in Barthes's view of reading, is very well discussed by Jonathan Culler in *Structuralist Poetics* (Ithaca: Cornell University Press, 1975), pp. 113–30. Culler's book as a whole offers a lucid and useful discussion of structuralist approaches to the study of literature.

17. Barthes, "Introduction à l'analyse structurale des récits," p. 27.

18. See Gérard Genette, "Discours du récit," in *Figures III* (Paris: Editions du Seuil, 1972), English trans. Jane Lewin, *Narrative Discourse* (Ithaca: Cornell University Press, 1980). To the histoire/récit (fabula/sjužet) distinction, Genette adds a third category, which he calls *narration* — "narrating" — that is, the level at which narratives sometimes dramatize the means and agency (real or fictive) of their telling. This category will prove of use to us later on. On the "perversion" of time in Proust, see "Discours du récit," p. 182.

19. Genette, "Discours du récit," pp. 77–78.

20. See Jean-Jacques Rousseau, "Seconde Préface," *La Nouvelle Héloïse* (Paris: Bibliothèque de la Pléiade, 1964), p. 18.

21. Marcel Proust, *A la recherche du temps perdu* (Paris: Bibliothèque de la Pléïade, 1954), 3:1045.

22. Genette, "Discours du récit," p. 228.

23. Benjamin, "The Storyteller," p. 94.

24. See Frank Kermode, *The Sense of an Ending* (New York: Oxford University Press, 1967); Jean-Paul Sartre, *La Nausée* (Paris: Gallimard, 1947), pp. 59–60; and Sartre, *Les Mots* (Paris: Gallimard, 1968), p. 171.

25. Jean Pouillon, *Temps et roman* (Paris: Gallimard, 1946). See also Claude Bremond, *Logique du récit* (Paris: Editions du Seuil, 1973).

26. On the resistance to the end, see D. A. Miller, *Narrative and Its Discontents* (Princeton: Princeton University Press, 1981). It is to Miller that I owe the term and concept "the narratable," which will be used frequently.

The relation of past and future to present is the subject of a famous meditation by Saint Augustine, in book 11 of the *Confessions,* where he finds a "solution" to the problem by the argument that there is a present of the past, in the form of memory, and a present of the future, in the form of anticipation or awaiting—a situation that he illustrates by the example of reciting a psalm. If Augustine does not solve the problem of temporality here, he surely offers a suggestive comment on the particular temporality of recitation or reading, its play of memory and anticipation. See the very rich analysis of Augustine's meditation in Ricoeur, *Temps et récit,* pp. 19–53.

24 David Lodge : *Mimesis and Diegesis in Modern Fiction*

David Lodge begins "Mimesis and Diegesis in Modern Fiction" by arguing that
we should avoid using ideological labels in discussing modern fiction. He proposes instead a pair of concepts as venerable and seemingly out of fashion as the
"plot" of which Peter Brooks speaks: mimesis (imitation) and diegesis (telling, or
explaining). Deriving from Aristotle and featured in some structuralist analyses,
they are terms that have recently fallen out of favor because of the postmodern
repudiation of referentiality. Barbara Foley claims that mimesis remains useful for
understanding realist fiction, but Lodge makes a claim that both mimesis and
diegesis are relevant to postmodernist fiction as well. He argues that they are
useful precisely because there has been a return to diegesis, or telling, in postmodernism, while in realist and modernist fiction mimesis was almost invariably the
dominant mode of representation. Henry James, among others, warned aspiring
authors to "show" rather than "tell."

In developing his argument, Lodge looks to Bakhtin, applying his theories of
narrative discourse to a range of novels from early realism to modernism (emphasizing James Joyce's *Ulysses*), before turning to postmodernist texts. Unlike
Hutcheon's emphasis on the epistemological questions raised by postmodernist
fiction — such as "how we know and come to terms with such a complex 'thing' "
as history — Lodge argues that postmodern literature's break with realism and
modernism can be found in its fundamental narrative strategies, specifically in a
return to diegesis: "not smoothly dovetailed with mimesis as in the classic realist
text, and not subordinated to mimesis as in the modernist text, but foregrounded
against mimesis." Can we now say, in reading Hutcheon alongside Lodge, that we
must distinguish not only between form and content in the literary work but
between modes of representing reality as well? And is this not, in essence, the
same question raised by Virginia Woolf some seventy years ago?

David Lodge (b. 1935) is noted as both a prominent British critic and a contemporary novelist. The first chapter of *After Bakhtin: Essays on Fiction and Criticism* (1990), reprinted here, originally appeared in *Contemporary Approaches to
Narrative* (1984), edited by Anthony Mortimer. Lodge is well known for such
novels as *The British Museum Is Falling Down* (1965), *How Far Can You Go*
(1983), and *Small World* (1985), and for such critical studies as *Graham Greene*
(1966) and *Working with Structuralism: Essays and Reviews on Nineteenth and
Twentieth Century Literature* (1981).

How does one begin to map a field as vast, as various as modern fiction? It seems a hopeless endeavor, and, in an absolute sense, it *is* hopeless. Even if one could hold all the relevant data in one's head at one time — which one cannot — and could formulate a typology into which they would all fit, some novelist would soon produce a work that eluded all one's categories, because art lives and develops by deviating unpredictably from aesthetic norms. Nevertheless the effort to generalize, to classify, has to be made; for without some conceptual apparatus for grouping and separating literary fictions criticism could hardly claim to be knowledge, but would be merely the accumulation of opinions about one damn novel after another. This is the justification for literary history, particularly that kind of literary history which has a generic or formal bias, looking for common conventions, strategies, techniques, beneath the infinite variety of subject matter. Such literary history breaks up the endless stream of literary production into manageable blocks or bundles, called "periods" or "schools" or "movements" or "trends" or "subgenres."

We are all familiar with a rough division of the fiction of the last 150 years into three phases, that of classic realism, that of modernism, and that of postmodernism (though, it hardly needs saying, these phases overlap both chronologically and formally). And we are familiar with various attempts to break down these large, loose groupings into more delicate and discriminating subcategories. In the case of postmodernist fiction, for instance: transfiction, surfiction, metafiction, new journalism, nonfiction novel, faction, fabulation, *nouveau roman, nouveau nouveau roman,* irrealism, magic realism, and so on. Some of those terms are synonyms, or nearly so. Most of them invoke or imply the idea of the new. British writing rarely figures on such maps of postmodern fiction. Our postmodernism, it is widely believed, has consisted in ignoring, rather than trying to go beyond, the experiments of modernism, reviving and perpetuating the mode of classic realism which Joyce, Woolf, and Co. thought they had dispatched for good.

This kind of map-making usually has an ideological and, in the Popperian sense of the word, historicist motivation. The mode of classic realism, with its concern for coherence and causality in narrative structure, for the autonomy of the individual self in the presentation of character, for a readable homogeneity and urbanity of style, is equated with liberal humanism, with empiricism, common sense, and the presentation of bourgeois culture as a kind of nature. The confusions, distortions, and disruptions of the postmodernist text, in contrast, reflect a view of the world as not merely subjectively constructed (as modernist fiction implied) but as absurd, meaningless, radically resistant to totalizing interpretation.

There is a certain truth in this picture, but it is a half-truth, and therefore a misleading one. The classic realist text was never as homogeneous, as consistent as the model requires; nor do postmodern novelists divide as neatly as it implies into complacent neorealist sheep and dynamic antirealist goats. (It hardly needs to be said that the ideology of the postmodernist avant-garde, reversing proverbial wisdom, prefers goats to sheep, John Barth's *Giles Goat-Boy* being one of its canonical texts.) Perhaps I have a personal interest in this issue, since I write as well as read contemporary fiction. I am dissatisfied with maps of contemporary fiction which take into account only the most deviant and marginal kinds of writing, leaving all the rest white space. But equally unsatisfactory is the bland, middlebrow, market-oriented reviewing of novels in newspapers and magazines which not only shies away from boldly experimental writing, but makes what one might call mainstream fiction seem technically less interesting and innovative than it often is.

Take, for example, the case of the contemporary British novelist Fay Weldon. She is a successful and highly respected writer, but her work rarely figures in any discussion of postmodernism in the literary quarterlies. Fay Weldon has been pigeonholed as a feminist novelist, and the criticism of her work is almost exclusively thematic. Now there is no doubt that she is a feminist writer, but her handling of narrative is technically very interesting and subtly innovative, and her feminism gets its force precisely from her ability to defamiliarize her material in this way. Typically, her novels follow the fortunes of a heroine, or a group of women, over a longish time span, from childhood in the 1930s and 1940s to the present. The narrator is usually revealed at some point to be the central character, but the narrative discourse mostly uses a third-person reference, typical of traditional authorial narration, often claiming the privileged insight into the interiority of several characters that belongs to that kind of narration, and not to the confessional autobiographical mode. The tense system is similarly unstable, switching erratically between the narrative preterite and the historical present. There is very artful use of condensed duration, that is, the summary narration of events which would have occupied a considerable length of time in reality, and which would be sufficiently important to the people involved to be worth lingering over in a more conventional kind of fiction. This creates a tone of comic despair about the follies and contradictions of human relations, and especially the fate of women. Here is a specimen from Fay Weldon's novel *Female Friends* (1975). Oliver is being promiscuously unfaithful to his wife Chloe and she complains.

> "For God's sake," he says, irritated, "go out and have a good time yourself. I don't mind."
>
> He lies in his teeth, but she doesn't know this. She only wants Oliver. It irks him (he says) and cramps his style. He who only wants her to be happy, but whose creativity (he says) demands its nightly dinner of fresh young female flesh.
>
> Gradually the pain abates, or at any rate runs underground. Chloe gets involved in Inigo's school: she helps in the library every Tuesday and escorts learners to the swimming pool on Fridays. She helps at the local birth control clinic and herself attends the fertility sessions, in the hope of increasing her own.
>
> Oh, Oliver! He brings home clap and gives it to Chloe. They are both soon and simply cured. His money buys the most discreet and mirthful doctors; Oliver himself is more shaken than Chloe, and her patience is rewarded: he becomes bored with his nocturnal wanderings and stays home and watches television instead.[1]

The first paragraph of this passage is a familiar kind of combination of direct speech and narrative, deviant only in the use of the present tense for the narrative. The second paragraph exerts the privilege of authorial omniscience somewhat paradoxically, since we know that Chloe is herself narrating the story. It also uses a deviant style of representing speech, apparently quoting Oliver in part, and reporting him in part. The effect of direct quotation arises from the congruence of tense between Oliver's speech and the narrator's speech ("it irks . . . he says"); the effect of reported speech arises from the use of the third-person pronoun ("it irks *him*"). This equivocation between quoted and reported speech allows the narrator to slide in a very loaded paraphrase of Oliver's stated need for young women—it is highly unlikely that he himself used that cannibalistic image, the "nightly dinner of fresh young female flesh." The penultimate paragraph uses a summary style of narration that seems quite natural because it is describing routine, habitual actions of little narrative interest. But summary is foregrounded in the last paragraph because applied to events which are full of emotional and psychological pain, embarrassment and recrimination—the sort of thing we are used to having presented scenically in fiction.

One way of describing this mode of writing would be to say that it is a mode of telling rather than showing, or, to use a more venerable terminology, of diegesis rather than mimesis. It seems to me a distinctively postmodern phenomenon in that it deviates from the norms of both classic realism and of modernism, as do, more spectacularly, the writers of the postmodernist avant-garde in America. Indeed, if we are looking for a formal, as distinct from an ideological, definition of postmodernism, we could, I believe, look profitably at its foregrounding of diegesis. The simple Platonic distinction between mimesis and diegesis, however, is inadequate to cope with all the varieties and nuances of novelistic discourse. In what follows I want to combine it — or refine it — with the more complex discourse typology of the Russian postformalists (who may have been one and the same person in some writings) Valentin Volosinov and Mikhail Bakhtin.

In Book III of *The Republic,* Plato distinguishes between diegesis, the representation of actions in the poet's own voice, and mimesis, the representation of action in the imitated voices of the character or characters. Pure diegesis is exemplified by dithyramb, a kind of hymn. (Later poeticians put lyric poetry into this category — a serious mistake according to Gérard Genette,[2] but one which need not concern us here.) Pure mimesis is exemplified by drama. Epic is a mixed form, combining both diegesis and mimesis, that is, combining authorial report, description, summary and commentary on the one hand, with the quoted direct speech of the characters on the other. It is important not to confuse "mimesis" in this sense with the wider application of the term by Plato (in, for instance, Book X of *The Republic*) and by Aristotle (in *The Poetics*), to mean imitation as opposed to reality. In that sense all art is imitation. In Book III Plato is concerned with two types of discourse by which verbal art imitates reality. To make the distinction clear, Plato (in the person of Socrates) cites the opening scene of *The Iliad,* where the Trojan priest Chryses asks the Greek leaders Menelaus and Agamemnon to release his daughter for a ransom.

> You know then, that as far as the lines
>> He prayed the Achaians all,
>> But chiefly the two rulers of the people,
>> Both sons of Atreus,
> the poet himself speaks, he never tries to turn our thoughts from himself or to
> suggest that anyone else is speaking; but after this he speaks as if he was himself

Chryses, and tries his best to make us think that the priest, an old man, is speaking and not Homer.[3]

In other words, the confrontation is introduced diegetically by the authorial narrator, and then presented mimetically in the speeches of the characters. To make the point even clearer, Plato rewrites the scene diegetically, transposing direct or quoted speech into indirect or reported speech, for example:

Agamemnon fell into a rage, telling him [Chryses] to go away now and not to come back, or his staff and the wreathings of the god might not help him; before he would give her up, he said, she should grow old with him in Argos; told him to be off and not to provoke him, if he wanted to get home safe.[4]

The original speech in Homer is translated by Rieu as follows:

"Old man" he said, "do not let me catch you loitering by the hollow ships today, nor coming back again, or you may find the god's staff and chaplet a very poor defence. Far from agreeing to set your daughter free, I intend her to grow old in Argos, in my house, a long way from her own country, working at the loom and sharing my bed. Off with you now, and do not provoke me if you want to save your skin."[5]

It is evident that, though there is a clear difference between the two passages, the individuality of Agamemnon's speech is not wholly obliterated by the narrator's speech in the Platonic rewriting, and could be obliterated only by some much more drastic summary, such as Gérard Genette suggests in his discussion of this passage: "Agamemnon angrily refused Chryses' request."[6] Plato conceived of the epic as a mixed form in the sense that it simply alternated two distinct kinds of discourse — the poet's speech and the characters' speech — and this is in fact true of Homer; but his own example shows the potential within narrative for a much more complex mixing, more like a fusing, of the two modes, in reported speech. This potential was to be elaborately exploited by the novel, which uses reported speech extensively — not only to represent speech, but to represent thoughts and feelings which are not actually uttered aloud. This is where Volosinov and Bakhtin are useful, because they focus on the way the novelistic treatment of reported speech tends towards an intermingling of authorial speech and characters' speech, of diegesis and mimesis.

In *Marxism and the Philosophy of Language* (1930) Volosinov distinguishes between what he calls (borrowing the terms from Wölfflin's art history) the linear style of reporting and the pictorial style. The linear style preserves a clear boundary between the reported speech and the reporting context (that is, the author's speech) in terms of information or reference, while suppressing the textual individuality of the reported speech by imposing its own linguistic register, or attributing to the characters exactly the same register as the author's. The linear style is characteristic of prenovelistic narrative and is associated by Volosinov especially with what he calls authoritarian and rationalistic dogmatism in the medieval and Enlightenment periods. I suggest that *Rasselas* (1759) affords a late example of what Volosinov calls the linear style:

> " . . . I sat feasting on intellectual luxury, regardless alike of the examples of the earth and the instructions of the planets. Twenty months are passed. Who shall restore them?"
>
> These sorrowful meditations fastened upon his mind; he passed four months in resolving to lose no more time in idle resolves, and was awakened to more vigorous exertion by hearing a maid, who had broken a porcelain cup, remark that what cannot be repaired is not to be regretted.
>
> This was obvious; and Rasselas reproached himself that he had not discovered it — having not known, or not considered, how many useful hints are obtained by chance, and how often the mind, hurried by her own ardor to distant views, neglects the truths that lie open before her. He for a few hours regretted his regret, and from that time bent his whole mind upon the means of escaping from the Valley of Happiness.[7]

In addition to the quoted direct speech of Rasselas at the beginning of the extract, there are two kinds of reported speech here: the reported utterance of the maid, and the reported inner speech, or thoughts, of Rasselas. All are linguistically assimilated to the dominant register of the authorial discourse. The author, Rasselas, and even the maid all seem to speak the same kind of language — balanced, abstract, polite; but the referential contours of the reported speech are very clearly demarcated and judged by the authorial speech. This is typical of Volosinov's linear style and Plato's diegesis: linguistic homogeneity — informational discrimination. It is one of the reasons why we hesitate to describe *Rasselas* as a novel, even though it postdates the development of the English novel. From a novel we expect a more realistic rendering of the individuality and variety of human speech than we get in *Rasselas* — both in direct or quoted speech and in reported speech or thought. (But note that there is a kind of tonal resemblance between the passage from *Rasselas* and the passage from Fay Weldon's *Female Friends* — the cool, confident, detached, ironic tone that is generated by the *summary* nature of the narrative discourse — summary being characteristic of diegesis, or what Volosinov calls the linear style.) For Volosinov, naturally influenced by Russian literary history, the rise of the novel virtually coincides with the development of the *pictorial* style of reported speech, in which author's speech and character's speech, diegesis and mimesis interpenetrate. The evolution of the English novel was more gradual.

The rise of the English novel in the eighteenth century began with the discovery of new possibilities of mimesis in prose narrative, through the use of characters as narrators — the pseudo-autobiographers of Defoe, the pseudo-correspondents of Richardson — thus making the narrative discourse a mimesis of an act of diegesis, diegesis at a second remove. These devices brought about a quantum leap in realistic illusion and immediacy, but they tended to confirm Plato's ethical disapproval of mimesis, his fears about the morally debilitating effects of skilful mimesis of imperfect personages. However highminded were the intentions of Defoe (which is doubtful) or of Richardson (which is not) there is no way in which the reader can be prevented from delighting in and even identifying with Moll Flanders or Lovelace in even their wickedest actions. Fielding, his mind trained in a classical school, restored the diegetic balance in his comic-epic-poem-in-prose: the individuality of characters is represented, and relished, in the reproduction of their distinctive speech — Fielding, unlike Johnson in *Rasselas,* does not make all the characters speak in the same register as himself — but the author's speech (and values) are quite clearly distinguished from the characters' speech and values; mimesis and diegesis are never confused. The same is true of Scott, in whose work there is, notoriously, a stark contrast between the polite literary English of the narrator's discourse, and the richly textured colloquial dialect speech of the Scottish characters — a disparity that becomes particularly striking in the shift from direct to reported speech or thought:

> "He's a gude creature," said she, "and a kind — it's a pity he has sae willyard a powny." And she immediately turned her thoughts to the important journey which she had commenced, reflecting with pleasure, that, according to her habits of life and of undergoing fatigue, she was now amply or even superfluously provided with the means of encountering the expenses of the road, up and down from London, and all other expenses whatever.[8]

The classic nineteenth-century novel followed the example of Fielding and Scott in maintaining a fairly even balance between mimesis and diegesis, showing and telling, scene and summary; but it also broke down the clear distinction between diegesis and mimesis in the representation of thought and feeling, through what Volosinov called the "pictorial style" of reported speech. In this, the individuality of the reported speech or thought is retained even as the author's speech "permeates the reported speech with its own intentions — humour, irony, love or hate, enthusiasm or scorn."[9] Let me illustrate this with a passage from *Middlemarch* (1871–72):

> She was open, ardent, and not in the least self-admiring; indeed, it was pretty to see how her imagination adorned her sister Celia with attractions altogether superior to her own, and if any gentleman appeared to come to the Grange from some other motive than that of seeing Mr. Brooke, she concluded that he must be in love with Celia: Sir James Chettam, for example, whom she constantly considered from Celia's point of view, inwardly debating whether it would be good for Celia to accept him. That he should be regarded as a suitor for herself would have seemed to her a ridiculous irrelevance. Dorothea, with all her eagerness to know the truths of life, retained very childlike ideas about marriage. She felt sure that she would have accepted the judicious Hooker, if she had been born in time to save him from that wretched mistake he made in matrimony: or John Milton when his blindness had come on; or any of the other great men whose odd habits it would have been glorious piety to endure; but an amiable handsome baronet, who said "Exactly" to her remarks even when she expressed uncertainty, — how could he affect her as a lover? The really delightful marriage must be that where your husband was a sort of father, and could teach you even Hebrew, if you wished it.[10]

Up to, and including, the sentence "Dorothea . . . retained very childlike ideas about marriage," this passage is diegetic: the narrator describes the character of Dorothea authoritatively, in words that Dorothea could not use about herself without contradiction (she cannot, for instance, acknowledge that her ideas are childlike without ceasing to hold them). Then the deixis becomes more problematical. The tag "she felt" is an ambiguous signal to the reader, since it can introduce either an objective report by the narrator or subjective reflection by the character. Colloquial phrases in the sequel, such as "that wretched mistake" and "when his blindness had come on" seem to be the words in which Dorothea herself would have articulated these ideas, though the equally colloquial "odd habits" does not. Why does it not? Because, in unexpected collocation with "great men" ("great men whose odd habits") it seems too rhetorical an irony for Dorothea — it is a kind of oxymoron — and so we attribute it to the narrator. But that is not to imply that Dorothea is incapable of irony. "Who said 'Exactly' to her remarks even when she expressed uncertainty" — do we not infer that Sir James's illogicality has been noted by Dorothea herself in just that crisp, dismissive way? Then what about the immediately succeeding phrase — "how could he affect her as a lover?" If the immediately preceding phrase is attributed to Dorothea, as I suggest, then it would be natural to ascribe this one to her also — but a contradiction then arises. For if Dorothea can formulate the question "How can Sir James affect me as a lover?" her alleged unconsciousness of her own attractions to visiting gentlemen is compromised. Is the question, then, put by the narrator, appealing directly to the reader, over the heroine's head, to acknowledge the plausibility of her behavior, meaning, "You do see, gentle reader, why it never crossed Dorothea's mind that Sir James Chettam was a possible match for her?" There *is* such an implication, but the reason given — that Sir James said "Exactly" when Dorothea expressed uncertainty — seems too trivial for the narrator to draw the conclusion, "How could he affect her as a lover?" The fact is that diegesis and mimesis are fused together inextricably here — and for a good reason: for there is a sense in which Dorothea knows what the narrator knows — namely, that Sir James is sexually attracted to her — but is repressing the thought, on account of her determination to marry an intellectual father figure. When Celia finally compels Dorothea to face the truth of the matter, the narrator tells us that "she was not less angry because certain details asleep in her memory were now awakened to confirm the unwelcome revelation." One of these details was surely that very habit of Sir James of saying "Exactly" when she expressed uncertainty — a sign of his admiration, deference, and anxiety to please rather than of his stupidity. Here, then, the character's voice and the author's voice are so tightly interwoven that it is impossible at times to disentangle them; and the author's irony, consequently, is affectionate, filled by a warm regard for Dorothea's individuality — very different from Johnson's judicial irony in the passage from *Rasselas*.

In the next stage of the novel's development, Volosinov observes, the reported speech is not merely allowed to retain a certain measure of autonomous life within the authorial context, but actually itself comes to dominate authorial speech in the discourse as a whole. "The authorial context loses the greater objectivity it normally commands in comparison with reported speech. It begins to be perceived and even recognizes itself as if it were subjective." Volosinov notes that this is often associated with the delegation of the authorial task to a narrator who cannot "bring to bear against [the] subjective position [of the other characters] a more authoritative and objective world."[11] In the Russian novel, it seems, Dostoevsky initiated this second phase in the development of the pictorial style. In the English novel I think we would point to the work of James and Conrad at the turn of the century: James's use of unreliable first-person narrators (*The Turn of the Screw*) or sustained focalization of the narrative through the perspective of characters whose perceptions are narrowly limited, with minimal authorial comment and interpretation ("In the Cage," *The Ambassadors*); Conrad's use of multiple framing via multiple narrators, none of whom is invested with ultimate interpretative authority (*Lord Jim, Nostromo*).

At this point it is useful to switch to Bakhtin's typology of literary discourse. There are three main categories:

1. *The direct speech of the author.* This corresponds to Plato's diegesis.
2. *Represented speech.* This includes Plato's mimesis — i.e., the quoted direct speech of the characters; but also reported speech in the pictorial style.
3. *Doubly oriented speech,* that is, speech which not only refers to something in the world but refers to another speech act by another addresser.

Bakhtin subdivides this third type of discourse into four categories, stylization, parody, *skaz* (the Russian term for oral narration) and what he calls "dialogue." Dialogue means here not the quoted direct speech of the characters, but discourse which alludes to an *absent* speech act. In stylization, parody, and *skaz,* the other speech act is "reproduced with a new intention"; in "dialogue" it "shapes the author's speech while remaining outside its boundaries." An important type of dialogic discourse in this sense is "hidden polemic," in which a speaker not only refers to an object in the world but simultaneously replies to, contests, or makes concessions to some other real or anticipated or hypothetical statement about the same object.

These categories all have their subcategories which can be combined and shifted around in the system in a somewhat bewildering way, but the basic distinctions are clear, and I think useful. Let me try and illustrate them with reference to *Ulysses,* a text as encyclopedic in this respect as in all others.

1. *The direct speech of the author.* This is the narrator who speaks in, for instance, the first lines of the book:

> Stately, plump Buck Mulligan came from the stairhead, bearing a bowl of lather on which a mirror and razor lay crossed.[12]

This is the purely diegetic plane of the text. The sentence describes Mulligan emerging onto the roof of the Martello tower not as Stephen Dedalus sees him (Stephen is below), nor as Mulligan sees himself, but as seen by an objective narrator. Since most narration in *Ulysses* is focalized, and stylistically colored, by a character's consciousness, or permeated by doubly oriented speech, such examples are comparatively rare. The author's speech as a distinct medium of communication is scarcely perceptible, in accordance with Joyce's aesthetic of impersonality: "The artist, like the God of the creation, remains within or behind or beyond or above his handiwork, invisible, refined out of existence, indifferent, paring his fingernails."[13]

2. *Represented speech.* This includes all the dialogue in the usual sense of that word — the quoted direct speech of the characters, which Joyce preferred to mark with an introductory dash, rather than the usual inverted commas. This category also includes all the passages of interior monologue — mimesis in Plato's terms, but representing thought instead of uttered speech. Molly Bloom's reverie in the last episode, "Penelope," is perhaps the purest example:

> Yes because he never did a thing like that before as ask to get his breakfast in bed with a couple of eggs since the City Arms hotel when he used to be pretending to be laid up with a sick voice doing his highness to make himself interesting for that old faggot Mrs Riordan that he thought he had a great leg of . . . (p. 608)

. . . and so on, for twenty thousand uninterrupted words.

The presentation of the thought of Stephen and Leopold Bloom is more varied and complex, combining interior monologue with free indirect speech[14] and focalized narration — in short, a mixture of mimesis and diegesis, in which mimesis dominates. Here, for example, is Bloom in the pork-butcher's shop in "Calypso":

> A kidney oozed bloodgouts on the willowpatterned dish: the last. He stood by the nextdoor girl at the counter. Would she buy it too, calling the items from a slip in her hand? Chapped: washingsoda. And a pound and a half of Denny's sausages. His eyes rested on her vigorous hips. Woods his name is. Wonder what he does. Wife is

oldish. New blood. No followers allowed. Strong pair of arms. Whacking a carpet
on the clothesline. She does whack it, by George. The way her crooked skirt swings
at each whack. (p. 48)

The various kinds of speech in this passage may be classified as follows:
A kidney oozed bloodgouts on the willowpatterned dish: Narrative (focal-
ized through Bloom).
the last. Interior monologue.
He stood by the nextdoor girl at the counter. Narrative (focalized through
Bloom).
Would she buy it too, calling the items from a slip in her hand? Free
indirect speech.
Chapped: washingsoda. Interior monologue.
And a pound and a half of Denny's sausages. Free direct speech (i.e., the
girl's words are quoted but not tagged or marked off typographically from
Bloom's).
His eyes rested on her vigorous hips. Narrative (focalized through Bloom).
Woods his name is, etc. (to end of paragraph). Interior monologue.

  3. *Doubly oriented speech.* In the later episodes of *Ulysses,* the authorial
narrator who, however self-effacing, was a stable, consistent and reliable
voice in the text, disappears; and his place is taken by various manifestations of Bakhtin's doubly oriented discourse. "Stylization" is well exemplified by "Nausicaa," in which Joyce borrows the discourse of cheap
women's magazines and makes it serve his own expressive purpose:

> Gerry was dressed simply but with the instinctive taste of a votary of Dame Fashion
> for she felt there was just a might that he might be out. A neat blouse of electric
> blue, self tinted by dolly dyes (because it was expected in the *Lady's Pictorial* that
> electric blue would be worn) with a smart vee opening down to the division and
> kerchief pocket (in which she always kept a piece of cottonwool scented with
> her favourite perfume because the handkerchief spoiled the sit) and a navy three
> quarter skirt cut to the stride showed off her slim graceful figure to perfection.
> (p. 287)

Who speaks here? Clearly it is not the author—he would not use such
debased, cliché-ridden language. But we cannot take it, either, to be the
author's report of Gerty's thought in free indirect speech. Free indirect
speech can always be transposed into plausible direct speech (first person,
present tense) and clearly that would be impossible in this case. It is a

written, not a spoken style, and a very debased one. It is neither diegesis nor mimesis, nor a blend of the two, but a kind of pseudodiegesis achieved by the mimesis not of a character's speech but of a discourse, the discourse of cheap women's magazines at the turn of the century. (In fact, the style of today's romantic fiction of the Mills & Boon type displays a remarkable consistency and continuity with Gerty's reading. Compare, for example: "Her dress was white, made from fine Indian cotton. Skimpy little shoulder-straps led to a bodice which was covered with layers of narrow, delicate lace finishing at the waist where it fitted Gina's slender figure to perfection." [15]) It is essential to the effect of "Nausicaa" that we should be aware of the style's double reference — to Gerty's experience, and to its own original discursive context. We are not to suppose that Gerty literally thinks in sentences lifted from the *Lady's Pictorial.* But the style of the *Lady's Pictorial* subtly manipulated, heightened, "objectified" (Bakhtin's word) vividly communicates a sensibility pathetically limited to the concepts and values disseminated by such a medium. The author, like a ventriloquist, is a silent presence in the text, but his very silence is the background against which we appreciate his creative skill.

This is stylization — not the same thing as parody. Parody, as Bakhtin points out, borrows a style and applies it to expressive purposes that are in some sense the reverse of the original purpose, or at least incongruous with it. For example, one of the headlines in "Aeolus" parodies the style of American tabloid journalism by applying it to an episode in classical antiquity recalled in more appropriate language by Professor MacHugh:

SOPHIST WALLOPS HAUGHTY HELEN

SQUARE ON PROBOSCIS. SPARTANS GNASH

MOLARS. ITHACANS VOW PEN IS CHAMP

— You remind me of Antisthenes, the professor said, a disciple of Georgias, the sophist. It is said of him that none could tell if he were bitterer against others or against himself. He was the son of a noble and a bondwoman. And he wrote a book in which he took away the palm of beauty from Argive Helen and handed it to poor Penelope. (p. 122)

The anonymous narrator of "Cyclops" provides an example of Irish *skaz* — the anecdotal chat of pubs and bars:

I was just passing the time of day with old Troy of the D. M. P. at the corner of Arbour Hill there and be damned but a bloody sweep came along and he near drove

his gear into my eye. I turned around to let him have the weight of my tongue when who should I see dodging along Stony Batter only Joe Hynes.
—Lo, Joe, says I. How are you blowing? Did you see that bloody chimney-sweep near shove my eye out with his brush? (p. 240)

We never discover who this narrator is, or to whom he is talking, or in what context. But clearly it is oral narration — *skaz*. There is no perceptible difference, either in syntax or type of vocabulary, between the discourse before and after the dash that in *Ulysses* introduces direct or quoted speech.

Of all the many styles in *Ulysses,* perhaps the most baffling to critical analysis and evaluation has been that of "*Eumaeus,*" a style which Stuart Gilbert classified as "Narrative: old." Rambling, elliptical, cliché-ridden, it is, we are told, meant to reflect the nervous and physical exhaustion of the two protagonists. As with "Nausicaa," we cannot read the discourse either as author's narration or as representation of Bloom's consciousness, though it does seem expressive of Bloom's character in some respects: his friendliness bordering on servility, his fear of rejection, his reliance on proverbial wisdom. Bakhtin's definition of "hidden polemic" seems to fit it very well: "Any speech that is servile or overblown, any speech that is determined beforehand not to be itself, any speech replete with reservations, concessions, loopholes and so on. Such speech seems to cringe in the presence, or at the presentiment of, some other person's statement, reply, objection." [16]

> *En route* to his taciturn, and, not to put too fine a point on it, not yet perfectly sober companion, Mr. Bloom who at all events, was in complete possession of his faculties, never more so, in fact, disgustingly sober, spoke a word of caution re the dangers of nighttown, women of ill fame and swell mobsmen, which, barely permissible once in a while though not as a habitual practice, was of the nature of a regular deathtrap for young fellows of his age particularly if they had acquired drinking habits under the influence of liquor unless you knew a little jiujitsu for every contingency as even a fellow on the broad of his back could administer a nasty kick if you didn't look out. (p. 502)

Let me return to the simple tripartite historical scheme with which I began — classic realism, modernism, postmodernism — and see what it looks like in the light of the discourse typology of Plato, Volosinov, and Bakhtin. The classic realist text, we may say, was characterized by a balanced and harmonized combination of mimesis and diegesis, reported speech and reporting context, authorial speech and represented speech. The modern novel evolved through an increasing dominance of mimesis over diegesis. Narrative was focalized through character with extensive use of "pictorial" reported speech or delegated to narrators with mimetically objectified styles. Diegesis, to be sure, does not completely disappear from the modernist novel, but it does become increasingly intractable. One can see the strain in those novelists who could least easily do without it: in Hardy, Forster, and Lawrence. Hardy hedges his bets, equivocates, qualifies or contradicts his own authorial dicta, uses tortuous formulae to avoid taking responsibility for authorial description and generalization. Forster tries to accommodate diegesis by making a joke of it:

> To Margaret—I hope that it will not set the reader against her—the station of King's Cross had always suggested Infinity [. . .] if you think this is ridiculous, remember that it is not Margaret who is telling you about it.[17]

At other times in *Howards End,* with less success, Forster tries to smuggle in his authorial comments as if they were his heroine's.

> Margaret greeted her lord with peculiar tenderness on the morrow. Mature as he was, she might yet be able to help him to the building of the rainbow bridge that should connect the prose in us with the passion. Without it we are meaningless fragments, half monks, half beasts, unconnected arches that have never joined into a man. With it love is born, and alights on the highest curve, glowing against the grey, sober against the fire.[18]

It is not just the rather purple diction, but the slide from narrative preterite to "gnomic present" in the tenses that gives away the author's voice.

Lawrence uses the same technique pervasively—for example in the famous passage where Lady Chatterley drives through Tevershall. She passes the school where a singing lesson is in progress:

> Anything more unlike song, spontaneous song, would be impossible to imagine; a strange bawling yell that followed the outlines of a tune. It was not like savages: savages have subtle rhythms. It was not like animals: animals mean something when they yell. It was like nothing on earth and it was called singing.[19]

The gnomic present tense—"savages *have,*" "animals *mean*"—indicates that this is not just a transcription of Connie Chatterley's thoughts—that the author is with her, speaking for her, lecturing us over her shoulder.

It has been often enough observed that Lawrence did not always live up to his own prescription that the novelist should keep his thumb out of the pan; but the prescription itself is very much in the spirit of modernism. Impersonality, "dramatization," "showing" rather than "telling" are the cardinal principles of the modernist fictional aesthetic, as variously formulated and practiced by James, Conrad, Ford, Woolf, and Joyce. This aesthetic required either the suppression or the displacement of diegesis: suppression by the focalization of the narrative through the characters; displacement by the use of surrogate narrators, whose own discourse is stylized or objectified—that is, deprived of the author's authority, made itself an object of interpretation. In James, Conrad, Ford, these narrators are naturalized as characters with some role to play in the story, but in *Ulysses* they do not have this validation: as I have tried to show they are conjured out of the air by the author's ventriloquism. This was the most radically experimental aspect of *Ulysses,* the aspect which even sympathetic friends like Pound and Sylvia Beach found hard to accept. They found it difficult to accept, I suggest, because these elaborate exercises in stylization and parody and dialogic discourse could not be justified, unlike the fragmentary, allusive passages of interior monologue, as a mimesis of character. It is still a common complaint among some readers of *Ulysses* that the introduction of a multiplicity of discourses which have no psychologically mimetic function in such episodes as "Sirens," "Cyclops," "Oxen of the Sun," and "Ithaca" is mere pedantry and self-indulgence, trivializing the human content of the book. But when we put the enterprise in the perspective of Bakhtin's poetics of fiction we immediately see that in opening up the novel to the play of multiple parodic and stylized discourses Joyce was aiming at a more comprehensive representation of reality than the stylistic decorum of the realist novel allowed; we see how this aim was organically linked to the project of writing a kind of modern epic, or mock epic, a comic inversion of and commentary upon the archetype of Homer. This is Bakhtin in "Epic and the Novel":

> any and every straightforward genre, any and every direct discourse—epic, tragic, lyric, philosophical—may and indeed must have itself become the object of representation, the object of a parodic, travestying "mimicry." It is as if such mimicry rips the word away from its object, disunifies the two, shows that a given straightforward generic word—epic or tragic—is one-sided, bounded, incapable of exhausting the object; the process of parodying forces us to experience those sides of

the object that are not otherwise included in a given genre or a given style. Parodic-travestying literature introduces the permanent corrective of laughter, of a critique on the one-sided seriousness of the lofty direct word, the corrective of reality that is always richer, more fundamental, and most importantly *too contradictory and heteroglot* to be fitted into a high and straightforward genre.[20]

Bakhtin might have been writing about *Ulysses* in that passage. In fact, he was writing about the fourth play of classical Greek drama, the satyr play, which traditionally followed the tragic trilogy and mocked its grandeur and seriousness. And he notes in passing that "the figure of the 'comic Odysseus,' a parodic travesty of his high epic and tragic image, was one of the most popular figures of satyr plays, of ancient Doric farce and pre-Aristophanic comedy, as well as of a whole series of minor comic epics."[21] Bloom has an ancient genealogy.

The resistance Joyce's readers often feel when they first encounter the later episodes of *Ulysses* is likely to be even greater in the case of *Finnegans Wake,* a book written entirely in doubly, or rather trebly, quadruply, multiply oriented discourse. Once again, Bakhtin's theory of the novel, and especially his emphasis on the crucial role of Rabelais in assimilating the folk tradition of carnival into literary narrative, seems very relevant. When Bakhtin writes about *Gargantua and Pantagruel,* he might be writing about *Finnegans Wake:*

we have the first attempt of any consequence to structure the entire picture of the world around the human conceived as a body . . . But it is not the individual human body, trapped in an irreversible life sequence that becomes a character — rather it is the impersonal body, the body of the human race as a whole, being born, living, dying the most varied deaths, being born again, an impersonal body that is manifested in its structure, and in all the processes of its life.[22]

The Rabelaisian body and surely, we must say, the body of HCE, is a body defined by the organs of self-transgression, the bowels and the phallus, mouth and anus, a body perpetually in the process of becoming, eating and defecating, copulating, giving birth, and dying at the same time through the displacements and condensations of carnival and dream (for what is dream but the carnival of the unconscious? what is carnival but a licensed communal waking dream?). According to Bakhtin, the two crucial ingredients in the Rabelaisian project, which made the novel possible, were *laughter* — the mockery of any and every type of discourse in the folk-carnival tradition — and what he called "polyglossia," the "interanimation of languages," such as obtained between Latin and the vernaculars at the Renaissance. Laughter and the interanimation of languages were also the vital ingredients of *Finnegans Wake.*

For most of his contemporaries, Joyce's greatest achievement was his mimetic rendering of the stream of consciousness within individual subjects, and this is what other novelists, like Woolf and Faulkner, tended to learn from him. "Let us present the atoms as they fall upon the mind in the order in which they fall, let us trace the pattern, however disconnected and incoherent in appearance, which each sight or incident scores upon the consciousness,"[23] exhorted Virginia Woolf in 1919, when the early episodes of *Ulysses* were first appearing in print. In principle, it was through interior monologue — the unvoiced, fragmentary, associative inner speech of the subject — that this program could be most completely fulfilled. Yet Virginia Woolf herself never used sustained interior monologue, except in *The Waves,* where it is so artificial as to have very little mimetic force. In her most characteristic work an impersonal but eloquent authorial narrator hovers over the characters and links together their streams of consciousness by a fluid blend of authorial report, free indirect speech, and fragments of free direct speech and interior monologue. Joyce himself, as I have already remarked, uses undiluted interior monologue only in "Penelope," and that to a large extent is what Dorrit Cohn calls a memory monologue[24] — that is, Molly is recalling past events rather than recording the atoms of experience in the order in which they fall upon her mind. *The Sound and the Fury* is also made up of memory monologues. The characters are narrating their stories to themselves, and we, as it were, overhear their narrations. The effect is not in essence very different from an old-fashioned epistolary or journal novel, though of course much more flexible and interiorized. In this way, mimesis turns back into a second-order diegesis — as it can hardly fail to do in narrative.

In pursuing mimetic methods to their limits, modernist fiction discovered that you cannot abolish the author, you can only suppress or displace him. Postmodernism says, in effect: so why not let him back into the text? The reintroduction of the author's speech, the revival of diegesis, has taken many forms. There is a conservative form — a return to something like the balanced combination of mimesis and diegesis of the nineteenth-century novel. The novels of Mauriac and Greene would be examples. "The exclusion of the author can go too far," said Greene in his 1945 essay on Mauriac. "Even the author, poor devil, has a right to exist, and M. Mauriac reaffirms that right."[25] The note is defensive, however, and Greene's own use of diegesis has been discreet. Very often in this kind of neorealist postmodern fiction the narrator is a character, but with little or no stylization of his discourse in Bakhtin's sense. The distance between the authorial norms and the character's norms is hardly perceptible. The narrator's perspective is limited, but as far as it goes, reliable. C. P. Snow's novels might be cited as an example.

More obviously continuous with modernism are those novels in which the discourse of the characterized narrator is doubly oriented in Bakhtin's sense: for example, stylized *skaz* in *The Catcher in the Rye,* parodic *skaz* in Mailer's *Why Are We in Vietnam?,* hidden polemic in Nabokov's *Pale Fire.* Some postmodernist novels combine a whole spectrum of stylized, parodic, and dialogic narrative discourses — e.g. John Barth's *Letters,* or Gilbert Sorrentino's *Mulligan Stew.*

How, then, does the postmodernist use of narrators differ from the modernist use of narrators? I would suggest that one difference is the emphasis on narration as such in postmodernist fiction. The narrators of modernist novels — e.g. the teacher of languages in Conrad's *Under Western Eyes,* or Dowell in Ford's *The Good Soldier,* must pretend to be *amateur* narrators, disclaiming any literary skill even while they display the most dazzling command of time shift, symbolism, scenic construction, etc. The narrators of postmodernist fiction are more likely to be explicit about the problems and processes involved in the act of narration, and very often the narrators are themselves writers with a close, sometimes incestuous relationship to the author. I find particularly interesting those postmodernist works in which diegesis is foregrounded by the explicit appearance in the text of the author as maker of his own fiction, the fiction we are reading. There is an instance of this toward the end of Margaret Drabble's recent novel *The Middle Ground* which brings out the distinction between modernist and postmodernist writing by reminding us of one of the great exponents of the former, Virginia Woolf:

> how good that it should end so well, and even as she was thinking this, look-
> ing round her family circle, feeling as she sat there a sense of immense calm,
> strength, centrality, as though she were indeed the centre of a circle, in the most old-
> fashioned of ways, a moving circle — oh, there is no language left to describe such
> things, we have called it all so much in question, but imagine a circle even so, a

circle and moving spheres, for this is her house and there she sits, she has everything and nothing, I give her everything and nothing.[26]

Here Margaret Drabble evokes a Woolfian epiphany (the allusion to Mrs. Ramsay's dinner party in *To the Lighthouse,* whether conscious or not, is inescapable) but at the same time wryly admits the arbitrariness of its construction. In this she shows herself to be not a neorealist (as she is usually categorized, and as her early work certainly encouraged one to think) but a postmodernist.

About three-quarters of the way through Joseph Heller's novel *Good as Gold,* one of its unnumbered chapters begins:

> Once again Gold found himself preparing to lunch with someone — Spotty Weinrock — and the thought arose that he was spending an awful lot of time in this book eating and talking. There was not much else to be done with him. I *was* putting him into bed a lot with Andrea and keeping his wife and children conveniently in the background. For Acapulco, I contemplated fabricating a hectic mixup which would include a sensual Mexican television actress and a daring attempt to escape in the nude through a stuck second-story bedroom window, while a jealous lover crazed on American drugs was beating down the door with his fists and Belle or packs of wild dogs were waiting below. Certainly he would soon meet a schoolteacher with four children with whom he would fall madly in love, and I would shortly hold out to him the tantalizing promise of becoming the country's first Jewish Secretary of State, a promise I did not intend to keep.[27]

Up to this point, Heller's novel, though its satirical comedy about Jewish family life and Washington politics is mannered and stylized, has consistently maintained an illusion of referring to the real world — it has, so to speak, challenged us to deny that the real world is as crazy as Heller represents it. But this passage violates the realistic code in two very obvious, and for the reader disconcerting, ways: firstly, by admitting that Gold is a character, in a book, and not a person, in the world; and secondly, by emphasizing that this character has no autonomy, but is completely at the disposition of his creator, who is not (or rather once was not) sure what to do with him. Two simple words have a powerful shock effect in this passage, because they have been hitherto suppressed in the narrative discourse in the interests of mimesis: *book* (referring to the novel itself) and *I* (referring to the novelist himself). The same words occur with similar, but even more startling, effect in Kurt Vonnegut's novel *Slaughterhouse Five.*

An American near Billy wailed that he had excreted everything but his brains. Moments later he said, "There they go, there they go." He meant his brains. That was I. That was me. That was the author of this book.[28]

Erving Goffman has designated such gestures "breaking frame." The Russian formalists called it "exposing the device." A more recent critical term is "metafiction." It is not, of course, a new phenomenon in the history of fiction. It is to be found in Cervantes, Fielding, Sterne, Thackeray, and Trollope, among others — but not, significantly, in the work of the great modernist writers. At least, I cannot think offhand of any instance in the work of James, Conrad, Woolf, and Joyce (up to and including *Ulysses*) where the fictitiousness of the narrative is exposed as blatantly as in my last few examples. The reason, I believe, is that such exposure foregrounds the existence of the author, the source of the novel's diegesis, in a way which ran counter to the modernist pursuit of impersonality and mimesis of consciousness. Metafictional devices are, however, all-pervasive in postmodernist fiction. I think for example of John Fowles's play with the authorial persona in *The French Lieutenant's Woman,* of Malcolm Bradbury's introduction of himself into *The History Man* as a figure cowed and dispirited by his own character, of B. S. Johnson's sabotage of his own fictionalizing in *Albert Angelo.* I think of the disconcerting authorial footnotes in Beckett's *Watt,* the flaunting of authorial omniscience in Muriel Spark, John Barth's obsessive recycling of his own earlier fictions in *Letters,* and the way the last page of Nabokov's *Ada* spills over on to the book jacket to become its own blurb. Perhaps, to conclude a list which could be much longer, I might mention my own novel *How Far Can You Go?,* in which the authorial narrator frequently draws attention to the fictitiousness of the characters and their actions, while at other times presenting them as a kind of history, and inviting the sort of moral and emotional response from the reader that belongs to traditional realistic fiction. For me, and I think for other British novelists, metafiction has been particularly useful as a way of continuing to exploit the resources of realism while acknowledging their conventionality. And need one say that the more nakedly the author appears to reveal himself in such texts, the more inescapable it becomes, paradoxically, that the author as a *voice* is only a function of his own fiction, a rhetorical construct, not a privileged authority but an object of interpretation?

To conclude: what we see happening in postmodernist fiction is a revival of diegesis: not smoothly dovetailed with mimesis as in the classic realist text, and not subordinated to mimesis as in the modernist text, but foregrounded against mimesis. The stream of consciousness has turned into a stream of narration — which would be one way of summarizing the difference between the greatest modernist novelist, Joyce, and the greatest postmodernist, Beckett. When the Unnameable says to himself, "You must go on. I can't go on. I'll go on," he means, on one level at least, that he must go on narrating.

Notes

1. Fay Weldon, *Female Friends* (New York: St. Martin's 1977), pp. 163–64.

2. Gérard Genette, *Introduction à l'architexte* (Paris: Seuil, 1979), pp. 14–15.

3. *Great Dialogues of Plato,* trans. W. H. D. Rouse (New York: New American Library, 1956), p. 190.

4. Ibid., p. 191.

5. Homer, *The Iliad,* trans. E. V. Rieu (Harmondsworth, Middlesex: Penguin, 1950), pp. 23–24.

6. Gérard Genette, *Narrative Discourse,* trans. Jane E. Lewin (Oxford: Oxford University Press, 1980), p. 170.

7. Samuel Johnson, *The History of Rasselas, Prince of Abissinia* (London: Carlton Classics, 1923), p. 23.

8. Sir Walter Scott, *The Heart of Midlothian* (New York: E. P. Dutton, Everyman, 1909), p. 265.

9. *Readings in Russian Poetics,* ed. Ladislav Matejka and Krystyna Pomorska (Cambridge, Mass.: Harvard University Press, 1979), p. 155. It is almost certain that the section of *Marxism and the Philosophy of Language* included in this anthology, which deals with the typology of narrative discourse, is directly or indirectly the work of Mikhail Bakhtin.

10. George Eliot, *Middlemarch* (Harmondsworth, Middlesex: Penguin, 1965), p. 32.

11. *Readings in Russian Poetics,* pp. 155–56.

12. James Joyce, *Ulysses,* ed. Walter Gabler (New York: Garland, 1986), p. 3. All page references are to this edition.

13. James Joyce, *A Portrait of the Artist as a Young Man* (New York: Viking, 1964), p. 215.

14. For an explanation of this term, see p. 360.

15. Claudia Jameson, *Lesson in Love* (London: Mills and Boon, 1982), p. 76.

16. *Readings in Russian Poetics,* p. 188. My account of Bakhtin's discourse typology is based mainly on this extract from Bakhtin's first book, *Problems of Dostoevsky's Art* (1929), later revised and expanded as *Problems of Dostoevsky's Poetics* (1963).

17. E. M. Forster, *Howards End* (Harmondsworth, Middlesex: Penguin, 1953), p. 13.

18. Ibid., p. 174.

19. D. H. Lawrence, *Lady Chatterley's Lover* (The Hague: Mouton, 1956), p. 139.

20. Mikhail Bakhtin, *The Dialogic Imagination,* ed. Michael Holquist, trans. Caryl Emerson and Michael Holquist (Austin: University of Texas Press, 1981), p. 55.

21. Ibid., p. 54.

22. Ibid., pp. 171–73.

23. Virginia Woolf, "Modern Fiction," reprinted in *Twentieth Century Literary Criticism: A Reader,* ed. David Lodge (New York: Longman, 1972), p. 89.

24. Dorrit Cohn, *Transparent Minds: Narrative Modes for Presenting Consciousness* (Princeton: Princeton University Press, 1978), pp. 247–55.

25. Graham Greene, *Collected Essays* (London: Faber and Faber, 1969), p. 116.

26. Margaret Drabble, *The Middle Ground* (London: Weidenfeld and Nicholson, 1980) pp. 246–47.

27. Joseph Heller, *Good as Gold* (New York: Knopf, 1980), p. 321.

28. Kurt Vonnegut, *Slaughterhouse Five* (New York: Delacorte, 1969), p. 109.

Breaking the Sequence

In her feminist analysis of women's writing Rachel Blau DuPlessis builds on the work of Virginia Woolf, from whom the title of this essay is taken: "Mary is tampering with the expected sequence. First she broke the sentence; now she has broken the sequence." For DuPlessis, this statement describes "a poetics of rupture and critique" that defines much of the literature written by women. For her, the breaking of the sentence indicates the rejection of "the structuring of the female voice by the male voice, female tone and manner by male expectations, female writing by male emphasis, female writing by existing conventions of gender. . . . Breaking the sentence is a way of rupturing language and tradition sufficiently to invite a female slant, emphasis, or approach." Women have been well represented as objects and characters in fiction, but DuPlessis, along with Woolf, argues that they have been underrepresented as subjects and authors.

DuPlessis argues further that, in addition to "breaking the sentence," the woman's voice in literature has also embarked on "breaking the sequence" in order to be heard. The "sequence" is the approved forms for fictional creation, the canonical genres recognized as "good" literature. In DuPlessis's words, "breaking the sequence is a rupture in habits of narrative order, that expected story told when 'love was the only possible interpreter' of women's textual lives." She suggests that this broken sequence can take the shape of "delegitimating the specific narrative and cultural orders of nineteenth-century fiction — the emphasis on successful or failed romance, the subordination of quest to love, the death of the questing female, the insertion into family life." In twentieth-century writing it can be seen as two major oscillations, one in "the gendering process" and the other in "the hegemonic process" — or, as we might say, in the domains of sexuality and power. DuPlessis analyzes the first oscillation through a radical critique of Freudianism. The second she analyzes through a discussion of feminist social theories, including a concept of women's development of a "double-consciousness," which arises from their marginal position as a muted group in patriarchal societies. In addition, then, to exploring the efforts of female writers to create an authentic "women's voice" through disrupting accepted norms, DuPlessis introduces us to feminist criticism, psychology, and social theory.

Rachel Blau DuPlessis (b. 1941) teaches English and women's studies at Temple University. She has published several books of poetry, experimental writing, and criticism, such as *American Women* (1972), *Writing Beyond the Ending: Narrative Strategies of Twentieth-Century Women Writers* (1985), from which this excerpt is taken; *H.D., The Career of That Struggle* (1986); *Tabula Rosa* (1987); and *The Pink Guitar: Writing As Feminist Practice* (1990).

I am almost sure, I said to myself, that Mary Carmichael is playing a trick on us. For I feel as one feels on a switchback railway when the car, instead of sinking, as one has been led to expect, swerves up again. Mary is tampering with the expected sequence. First she broke the sentence; now she has broken the sequence. . . . Perhaps she had done this unconsciously, merely giving things their natural order, as a woman would, if she wrote like a woman. But the effect was somehow baffling; one could not see a wave heaping itself, a crisis coming round the next corner. . . . For whenever I was about to feel the usual things in the usual places, about love, about death, the annoying creature twitched me away, as if the important point were just a little further on. — Virginia Woolf, *A Room of One's Own* (1929)

. . . Charlotte was gazing up into the dark eyes of Redmond. "My darling," he breathed hoarsely. Strong arms lifted her, his warm lips pressed her own. . . .
That was the way it was supposed to go, that was the way it had always gone before, but somehow it no longer felt right. I'd taken a wrong turn somewhere; there was something, some fact or clue, that I had overlooked. — Margaret Atwood, *Lady Oracle* (1976)

One approach to the feminist criticism of these modern writers is suggested in an analysis of "Mary Carmichael's first novel, *Life's Adventure*," a work and author invented by Virginia Woolf and explicated in *A Room of One's Own*.[1] This is a novel by the last of the series of ancestral mothers alluded to in the Elizabethan ballad of the Four Marys, which forms a frame for the essay. The first two are Mary Beton, with her legacy of money, and Mary Seton, who provides "room" — institutional and psychological space. Both are necessary for Mary Carmichael, the modern author, and all of them express the baffled and unmentioned Mary Hamilton, from the ages when women had no way to dissent, except through infanticide and anonymous song. Woolf scrutinizes this novel's style, plot, and purpose with a diffident casualness, finding "some fact or clue" of great importance: "Mary is tampering with the expected sequence. First she broke the sentence; now she has broken the sequence" (*AROO*, 85). In these matching statements are telescoped a poetics of rupture and critique.

The sentence broken is one that expresses "the ridicule, the censure, the assurance of inferiority" about women's cultural ineptitude and deficiencies.[2] To break the sentence rejects not grammar especially, but rhythm, pace, flow, expression: the structuring of the female voice by the male voice, female tone and manner by male expectations, female writing by male emphasis, female writing by existing conventions of gender — in short, any way in which dominant structures shape muted ones. For a woman to write, she must experiment with "altering and adapting the current sentence until she writes one that takes the natural shape of her thought without crushing or distorting it" (*G & R*, 81).[3]

At first it appeared as if Mary Carmichael would not be able to break this sentence and create her own. Her style was jerky, short, and terse, which "might mean that she was afraid of something; afraid of being called 'sentimental' perhaps; or she remembers that women's writing has been called flowery and so provides a superfluity of thorns . . . " (*AROO*, 85). Here she overcompensated for femaleness in deference to existing conventions.

But eventually, facing gender in an authentic way, the writer produces "a woman's sentence," the "the psychological sentence of the feminine gender," which "is used to describe a woman's mind by a writer [Dorothy Richardson] who is neither proud nor afraid of anything that she may discover in the psychology of her sex."[4] The sentence is "psychological" not only because it deepens external realism with a picture of consciousness at work but also because it involves a critique of her own consciousness, saturated as it is with discourses of dominance.

There is nothing exclusively or essentially female about "the psychological sentence of the feminine gender," because writers of both sexes have used that "elastic" and "enveloping" form. But it is a "woman's sentence" because of its cultural and situational function, a dissension stating that women's minds and concerns have been neither completely nor accurately produced in literature as we know it. Breaking the sentence is a way of rupturing language and tradition sufficiently to invite a female slant, emphasis, or approach. Similarly there is nothing innately gendered about the signifier "I," yet in *A Room of One's Own* the speaker's "I" is both female and plural — "a woman's voice in a patriarchal literary tradition" — and another "I," shadowing the page, is "polished, learned, well-fed," an explicitly male subject speaking of and from dominance.[5]

Woolf's "woman's sentence," then, has its basis not in biology, but rather in cultural fearlessness, in the attitude of critique — a dissent from, a self-conscious marking of, dominant statement. It can be a stress shifting, the kind of realignment of emphasis noted by Nancy Miller, following Luce Irigaray: "an italicized version of what passes for the neutral or standard face . . . a way of marking what has already been said."[6]

A "woman's sentence" is Woolf's shorthand term for a writing unafraid of gender as an issue, undeferential to male judgment while not unaware of the complex relations between male and female. A "woman's sentence" will thus be constructed in considered indifference to the fact that the writer's vision is seen as peculiar, incompetent, marginal. So Woolf summarizes "the first great lesson" mastered by Mary Carmichael: "she wrote as a woman, but as a woman who has forgotten that she is a woman" (*AROO*, 96). The doubled emphasis on woman, yet on forgetting woman, is a significant maneuver, claiming freedom from a "tyranny of sex" that is nonetheless palpable and dominant, both negated and affirmed.[7]

In both *A Room of One's Own* and the related "Women and Fiction," Woolf criticizes women for "resenting the treatment of [their] sex and pleading for its rights," because, in her view, this threatens the poise a writer achieves by the transcending of "indignation" on the one hand and "resignation" on the other, the "too masculine" here and the "too feminine" there.[8] This movement between complicity and critique expresses Woolf's version of a doubled dynamic that is, as we shall see momentarily, characteristic of other women writers.[9]

What binds these writers is their oppositional stance to the social and cultural construction of gender.[10] This opposition has a number of origins. Perhaps the most suggestive is that of marginality in two arenas.[11] When a female writer is black (Alice Walker, Zora Neale Hurston, Gwendolyn Brooks, Toni Morrison), colonial (Olive Schreiner, Doris Lessing, Jean Rhys), Canadian (Margaret Atwood), of working-class origin (Tillie Olsen, Marge Piercy), of lesbian or bisexual orientation (H.D., Virginia Woolf, Adrienne Rich, Joanna Russ), or displaced and déclassé (Dorothy Richardson), double marginalization can be produced. Either it compels the person to negate any possibility for a critical stance, seeking instead "conformity and inclusion" because the idea of an authoritative center is defensively affirmed, or it enlivens the potential for critique by the production of an (ambiguously) nonhegemonic person, one in marginalized dialogue with the orders she may also affirm.[12]

The woman writers studied here are further unified by their interested dissent from androcentric culture in nonfictional texts: essay, memoir, polemic, and social study. The texts will be seen, case by case, to contribute to their fictional elaborations and narrative stances.[13] Hence while hardly all of the writers would describe themselves as feminists, and some, indeed, resist that term, one may assert that any female cultural practice that makes the "meaning production process" itself "the site of struggle" may be considered feminist.[14] These authors are "feminist" because they construct a variety of oppositional strategies to the depiction of gender institutions in narrative. A writer expresses dissent from an ideological formation by attacking elements of narrative that repeat, sustain, or embody the values and attitudes in question. So after breaking the sentence, a rupture with the internalization of the authorities and voices of dominance, the woman writer will create that further rupture which is a center for this book: breaking "the sequence — the expected order" (*AROO,* 95).

Breaking the sequence is a rupture in habits of narrative order, that expected story told when "love was the only possible interpreter" of women's textual lives (*AROO,* 87). In her study of *Life's Adventure,* Woolf notes that the novelist Mary Carmichael alludes to "the relationship that there may be between Chloe and Roger," but this is set aside in favor of another bond, depicted "perhaps for the first time in literature" (*AROO,* 84, 86). "Chloe liked Olivia. They shared a laboratory together," begins Woolf (*AROO,* 87). The romance names with the allusions to Shakespearean transvestite characters are very suggestive, especially as opposed to the firmly heterosexual "Roger," with a whole history of slang behind him. One of these women is married, with children; the other is not. Their work — finding a cure for pernicious anemia — may suggestively beef up women's weakness of nerve with a good dose of female bonding.

The ties between Chloe and Olivia may be homosocial or, given the subsequent sexual-cultural metaphor of exploring the "serpentine cave" of women, they may be lesbian.[15] In either case, Woolf clearly presents a nonheterosexual relation nourished by the healthy vocation of women. She is also eloquent about the meaning of these changes. The women's friendship, based on their work life, will be "more varied and lasting because it will be less personal" (*AROO,* 88). "Personal" is Woolf's word (in essays throughout the twenties) for the privatization and exclusiveness that is part of the script of heterosexual romance. So the tie between Chloe and Olivia, a model for modern women writers, makes a critique of heterosexuality and the love plot, and offers (Woolf implies) a stronger and more positive sense of female quest. One is no longer allowed to "feel the usual things in the usual places, about love, about death" (*AROO*, 95). So breaking the sequence can mean delegitimating the specific narrative and cultural orders of nineteenth-century fiction — the emphasis on successful or failed romance, the subordination of quest to love, the death of the questing female, the insertion into family life. "The important point . . . just a little further on" that Mary Carmichael pushes her reader to see might be such narrative strategies as reparenting, female bonding, including lesbian ties, mother-child dyads, brother-sister pairs, familial transpositions, the multiple individual, and the transpersonal protagonist.

This study is also designed to suggest what elements of female identity would be drawn on to make plausible the analytic assumption that there is a women's writing with a certain stance toward narrative.[16] The narrative strategies of twentieth-century writing by women are the expression of two systemic elements of female identity — a psychosexual script and a sociocultural situation, both structured by major oscillations. The oscillations occur in the gendering process and in the hegemonic process. Oscillation is a swinging between two positions, a touching of two limits, or, alternately, a fluctuation between two purposes, states, centers, or principles. The narrative strategies I will present here all take basic elements of female identity, such as the gendering sequence, and realign their components.

The possibilities for heterosexual love and romance take shape in the object relations within the family, that is, in the ties of kinship forged between child and parent, and in the processes of gendering, all given very complete cultural and social support. As we know, there is a sequence that assists these arrangements — a psychosexual script that is one of our first dramas. The occasion of our "learning the rules of gendering and kinship" and the apparatus for the production of sexual personality is, of course, the oedipal crisis.[17]

Freudian theory, postulating the telos of "normal femininity" as the proper resolution of the oedipal crisis, bears an uncanny resemblance to the nineteenth-century endings of narrative, in which the female hero becomes a heroine and in which the conclusion of a valid love plot is the loss of any momentum of quest. The pitfalls to be avoided by a woman seeking normal femininity are very consistent with the traits of the female hero in narrative: defiance, activity, selfishness, heroic action, and identification with other women. For Freudian theory puts a high premium on female passivity and narcissism and on the "end" of husband, home, and male child. As for quest or individual aspiration, Freud poignantly realizes that the achievement of femininity has left "no paths open to [a woman] for further development; . . . [it is] as though, in fact, the difficult development which leads to femininity had exhausted all the possibilities of the individual."[18] By the repressions and sacrifices involved in becoming feminine, quest is at a dead end — a sentiment that we have seen replicated in narrative endings.

The "original bisexuality" or "bisexual disposition" of every individual is the major starting point for this account.[19] The oedipal crisis is a social process of gendering that takes "bisexual, androgynous," libidinally active, and ungendered infants and produces girls and boys, giving to the male future social and sexual domination, and to the female future domesticated status within the rules of the sex-gender system of its society.[20] Thus gender is a product. That there must be some kind of passage of an infant "into a social human being" is not at issue. It will involve the "[dialectical] process of struggle with and ultimate supersession (including integration) of symbolic figures of love, desire, and authority." As this citation from Ortner proposes, the theoretical possibility that the oedipal crisis is historically mutable must not be overlooked.[21] The drama might unfold with some alternate figures and some alternate products or emphases.

Another major element of the oedipal crisis for girls is the requisite shift of object choice from "phallic" or preoedipal mother — the mother of power — to a heterosexual object, the father. Little boys must shift generations, but not genders, in their object choice. The reason for the female shift has been contested. Freud postulated that a girl will turn from her mother, sometimes with hatred and hostility, when the mother is discovered to be bereft of the genital marker of male power. In feminist revisions of Freud, this revelation, called "penis envy" by Freud, has been viewed as the delivery of knowledge well beyond the perception of sheer genital difference, the shock of learning a whole array of psychosocial rules and orders valorizing maleness.

To Freud, the girl's tasks in the oedipal drama involve the repression of what he calls the "little man" inside her, that active, striving, clitoral self, and the repression of love for her mother, a person of her own sex. Yet even the Freudian account somewhat reluctantly presents a recurring tension between the oedipal and preoedipal phases for the female, whereas in most males (as far as the theory tells) the oedipus complex has a linear and cumulative movement. Freud has found that "Regressions to fixations at these pre-oedipal phases occur very often; in many women we actually find a repeated alternation of periods in which either masculinity or femininity has obtained the upper hand."[22] So the oedipal crisis can extend over years and follow an individual woman right into adulthood. Or, to say it another way, the "feminine" or "correct" resolution of women's gender identity comes easily unstuck and cannot be counted on.

A further elaboration of the oedipal crisis in women is available in Nancy Chodorow's analysis of mothering as a key institution in the social and psychic reproduction of gender. In her view, in the development of a girl, the preoedipal attachment to the mother is never entirely given up; it persists in coloring oedipalization, in shaping problems and issues of the female ego (boundlessness and boundary problems, "lack of separation or differentiation"), and in its influence on both the fact and the way that women mother. So while the gendering process is the "arena" where the goal of heterosexuality is "negotiated," it is also where the mother-daughter dyad and female bonding are affirmed.[23]

The narrative and cultural implications of this neo-Freudian picture of gendering are staggering. With no easy or one-directional passage to "normal femininity," women as social products are characterized by unresolved and continuous alterations between allegiance to males and to females, between heterosexuality and female-identified, lesbian, or bisexual ties. The "original bisexuality" of the individual female is not easily put to rest or resolved by one early tactical episode; rather the oscillation persists and is reconstituted in her adult identity. Further, the emotional rhythms of female identity involve repeated (and possibly even simultaneous) articulations of these two principles or states, which are taken (ideologically) as opposing poles.[24]

Twentieth-century women writers undertake a reassessment of the processes of gendering by inventing narrative strategies, especially involving sequence, character, and relationship, that neutralize, minimize, or transcend any oversimplified oedipal drama. This occurs by a recognition in various elements of narrative of the "bisexual oscillation" in the psychic makeup of characters, in the resolutions of texts, in the relationships portrayed. In twentieth-century narratives, effort is devoted to depicting masculine and feminine sides in one character — in Woolf's androgyny and in similar procedures in Richardson. Original bisexuality is extended the length of a character's life in H.D. and in Woolf. Women writers readjust the maternal and paternal in ways that unbalance the univocal sequence of object choices. This is why some female quest plots, like *To the Lighthouse* and *The Four-Gated City,* loop backward to mother-child attachments. Narratives of twentieth-century women, notably their *Künstlerromane,* may invent an interplay between the mother, the father, and the hero, in a "relational triangle."[25] These changes are often accompanied by pointed remarks about the plots, characters, and situations once expected in narrative: gender polarization, patrisexual romantic love, the arrest of female quest, the "happy ending" — remarks that, as we shall see, underline the self-consciousness of this critique of narrative scripts and the psychosexual drama that forms them.[26]

These representations of gendering could be achieved irrespective of whether any of the authors were aware of the exact terms of Freudian theory, although no doubt a number were, or whether they explicitly connected their narratives to any aspect of Freud's position (something that does occur in Woolf's *Orlando,* in H.D.'s *Helen in Egypt* and *Tribute to Freud,* and in Doris Lessing's *The Golden Notebook*).[27] For women artists, this sense of "remaining in the Oedipus situation for an indefinite period" would not have to be consciously understood.[28] One may simply postulate that the habit of living with an "unresolved" oedipus complex would lead the bearer to a greater identification of the unstable elements, greater intuitive knowledge of these components of one's interior life.

Indeed, Freud suggests a massive slippage of effectiveness, so that the learning of the rules of gender may need a good deal of extrafamilial reinforcement, especially where the girl is concerned. The formation of the superego — the acceptance of social rules, including those governing gender — is the result of "educative influences, of external intimidation threatening loss of love."[29] That is, education as an institution of gender, and culture as a whole, including literary products like narrative, channel the girl into dominant structures of the sex-gender system. The romance plot in narrative thus may be seen as a necessary extension of the processes of gendering, and the critique of romance that we find in twentieth-century female authors, as part of the oppositional protest lodged against both literary culture and a psychosexual norm.

The psychosexual oscillation of the gendering process, so distinctly theorized, interacts with another systemic aspect of female identity, which shows the same wavering, dialogic structure: a sociocultural oscillation of hegemonic processes. In the social and cultural arena, there is a constant repositioning between dominant and muted, hegemonic and oppositional, central and colonial, so that a woman may be described as (ambiguously) nonhegemonic or, with equal justice but less drama, as (ambiguously) hegemonic if her race, class, and sexuality are dominant. Virginia Woolf envisions this oscillating consciousness in *A Room of One's Own.* "It [the mind] can think back through its fathers or through its mothers, as I have said that a woman writing thinks back through her mothers. Again if one is a woman one is often surprised by a sudden splitting off of consciousness, say in walking down Whitehall, when from being the natural inheritor of that civilization, she becomes, on the contrary, outside of it, alien and critical" (*AROO,* 101). Note how Woolf passes from the oedipal-preoedipal division in object relations to the social oscillation, suggesting the relation of both processes to female identity. The debate between inheritor and critic is a movement between deep identification with dominant values and deep alienation from them. Whitehall, a street in London, is a synechdoche for British civil service and administrative agreements that endure beyond changes in specific governments, and thus is a metaphor for broad sociocultural agreement.

The shifting into alternative perspectives is taken by Woolf as a phenomenon peculiarly resonant for a woman. Her use of the word *natural* as opposed to the word *critical* sums the process up. *Natural* is what every ideology happily claims it is; the beliefs, social practices, sense of the self are second nature, assumed. The word *critical,* however, has the force of a severe and transgressive dissent from cherished mental structures and social practices. This contradictory quiver, this social vibrato creates a critical sensibility: dissent from the culture by which women are partially nourished, to which they are connected.

A major originating moment of Woolf's "outsider's feeling" came, significantly enough, in her confrontation at the turn of the century with the banal but forceful social and romantic expectations represented by George Duckworth, her half-brother and self-appointed substitute parent. At issue was her green dress, unconventionally made of upholstery fabric. From the moment of his anger at her appearance, from her as yet muted defiance, Woolf crystallizes that hegemonic set: proper dress, patterned feminine behavior, "tea table training," the absolute necessity for romance, the "patriarchal machinery" creating rigid, polarized male and female personalities. What astonished Woolf most was the female role of

passive, appreciative spectator and the acrobatic — almost Swiftean —
jumping through hoops demanded of males; the whole "circus" or "required act" was accomplished with no irony or critical questioning.[30]

Many commentators on women as a group and on female identity have
isolated as systemic some kind of dual relationship to the definitions offered by various dominant forces. Simone de Beauvoir sees the female
child "hesitating between the role of *object, Other,* which is offered to her,
and the assertion of her liberty" as subject.[31] John Berger argues that the
"social presence" of women and their ingenuity in living in "the keeping
of men" have created "two constituent yet always distinct elements of her
identity as a woman": the "surveyor and the surveyed."[32] The "duality of
women's position in society" is Gerda Lerner's explanation for the fact
that women as a group can be both victims and upholders of the status quo:
"Women live a duality — as members of the general culture and as partak-
ers of women's culture."[33] Nancy Cott similarly views "women's group
consciousness as a subculture uniquely divided against itself by ties to the
dominant culture."[34] Sheila Rowbotham describes the war of parts of the
self, given the attitudes of the dominant group on the Left. "One part of
ourselves mocked another, we joined in the ridicule of our own aspirations. . . . Part of us leapt over into their world, part of us stayed at
home. . . . We were never all together in one place, we were always in
transit, immigrants into alien territory."[35] And Alice Walker, in "In Search
of Our Mothers' Gardens," cites Woolf's *A Room of One's Own* to come
to terms with the "contrary instincts" in certain work by black women
from Phillis Wheatley to Zora Neale Hurston.[36] In sum, women writers as
women negotiate with divided loyalties and doubled consciousness, both
within and without a social and cultural agreement. This, in conjunction
with the psychosexual oscillation, has implications for "sentence" and
"sequence" — for language, ideology, and narrative.

Later in her career, Woolf continued her analysis of the source of wom-
en's sociocultural oscillation. In *Three Guineas,* Woolf finds that women's
structural position enables them to take an adversarial stance to institutions of dominance. Women, she argues, are basically outsiders, formed
by their nondominant ("unpaid for") education, as they observe the privileges of maleness and the sacrifices exacted from women themselves for
those privileges. The lived experience of women and men even from the
same social class differs so greatly that their world views and values are
irreconcilably distinct: "though we look at the same things, we see them
differently."[37]

Constituting a separate group within their social class, women should capitalize on this built-in zone of difference to think of themselves as an interested, coherent political bloc: an actual Society of Outsiders. They can and should refuse male society and its values (militarism, hierarchy, authoritarianism) even as they enter formerly all-male professions. And women have, Woolf is certain, less chance than men for being apologists for political, economic, and social oppression so intense that — her central point — the patriarchal politics of bourgeois liberalism is on a continuum with fascism and the authoritarian state. Being already outsiders, women should turn its negative markers ("poverty, chastity, derision, freedom from unreal loyalties") into positive markers of difference, and turn their marginal status to political advantage and analytic power (*TG*, 78).

The function of *Three Guineas* is to drive a politically motivated wedge of analysis and polemic between dominant and muted, inheritor and critic, class and gender allegiances, to try to convince educated women no longer to cooperate with the politics of their class. Indeed, in 1940 Woolf argued that women are in a position to make cross-class alliances with working-class men and women because their identification as "commoners, outsiders" will override apparent class distinctions.[38]

Yet the shift to the imperative mode and the call for a vow in *Three Guineas* betray the fact that women are not purely and simply Outsiders; otherwise one would not have to exhort them to remain so. They are, however, less integrated into the dominant orders than are men of their class. Women are a muted or subordinate part of a hegemonic process. Raymond Williams suggests that seeing hegemonic processes would be a way of visualizing culture to credit the internal debate between affirmation and critique. Hegemony includes a relationship in conflictual motion between the ideologies and practices of a dominant class or social group and the alternative practices, which may be either residual or emergent, of the muted classes or groups. Any set of hegemonic assumptions — notions orthodox in a given society and historical era — are "deeply saturating" and pervasive, "organized and lived," woven into the most private areas of our lives.[39] Still the hegemonic is always in motion, being "renewed, recreated, defended and modified."[40] These hegemonic processes are a site for both sociocultural reproduction and sociocultural dissent. The debate that women experience between the critic and the inheritor, the outsider and the privileged, the oppositional and the dominant is a major example of a hegemonic process, one whose results are evident in both social and narrative texts. Constantly reaffirmed as outsiders by others and sometimes by themselves, women's loyalties to dominance remain ambiguous, for they are not themselves in control of the processes by which they are defined.

Issues of control of voice and definition, then, allow Edwin Ardener's otherwise more static model to offer a complementary set of terms to define gender relations: the articulate or dominant men and then the non-dominant or muted women. The latter term recalls the muted sonority of a musical instrument — the sound different, tamped down, repressed, but still speaking, with the speech bearing the marks of partial silencing. Interestingly, giving voice to the voiceless and making visible the invisible are two prime maneuvers in feminist poetics. As Ardener would gloss this, "The muted structures are 'there' but cannot be 'realized' in the language of the dominant structure."[41] To depict these relationships, Ardener posits two almost overlapping circles, one standing for dominant vision, the other for muted. The larger uncontested space where the circles overlap is shared by men and women in a given society as parallel inhabitants of main culture. The tiny crescent-shaped band left over for women is their zone of difference. Visualizing the relationship between dominant and muted in this fashion suggests that women can oscillate between the two parts of the circle that represents them, between difference and dominance.

The concept of a "double-consciousness" that comes from one's oscillation between a main and a muted position is not, nor could it ever be, a way of describing women exclusively, but it offers a way of seeing the identity of any group that is at least partially excluded from or marginal to the historically current system of meaning, value, and power.[42] Feminist criticism, then, may be said to begin with W. E. B. Du Bois, postulating for blacks this double consciousness, born in negotiation with hegemonic processes.

Ellen Moers analyzed distinctive female stances based not on innate or essential femininity but on the shared cultural experiences of secondary status — constraints on travel, education, social mediations of childhood and motherhood — and reflected in particular uses of certain cultural tropes, such as the Gothic, the monster, the landscape.[43] This postulate was given forceful statement by Elaine Showalter: that women are parallel to other minority groups in their subcultural position "relative to a dominant society" and that this position leads to a unity of "values, conventions, experiences and behaviors" from which women draw and to which they respond with various fictional and biographical strategies.[44] Following Showalter's emphasis on formal and biographical strategies of response, Sandra Gilbert and Susan Gubar pose a repeated and reinvoked struggle as the master plot for women of the nineteenth century: in a dynamic generational confrontation in which dominant culture is the father and women are either sage daughters or mad wives in relation to patriarchal power. A nineteenth-century woman writer is the site of an internalized cultural debate: her own rage that she cannot speak and her culture's rage that she can. This contradiction is resolved in a powerful fictional motif: the madwoman, in whom expression struggles with repression.[45]

Where a reading of twentieth-century materials necessarily differs from the nineteenth-century texts most profoundly analyzed by Showalter and Gilbert and Gubar is that, by the twentieth century, middle-class women are technically — on paper — rather more part of the economic world, rather less legally and politically circumscribed than they were in the nineteenth. This changed position does not alter the negotiation process, but it does mean that women have an interior identification with dominant values (traditionally expressed as a rejection of female specialness) as well as an understanding of muted alternatives. Dominant and muted may be more equally balanced opponents in the twentieth century than in the nineteenth.

Mary Jacobus has also noted, and made central to her analysis of women's writing, the split between alien critic and inheritor that I have taken as a key text for this book. Jacobus further argues that, given this situation, "at once within culture and outside it," a woman writer must simultaneously "challenge the terms and work within them."[46] This precisely parallels my argument — that woman is neither wholly "subcultural" nor, certainly, wholly main-cultural, but negotiates differences and sameness, marginality and inclusion in a constant dialogue, which takes shape variously in the various authors, but with one end — a rewriting of gender in dominant fiction. The two processes in concert — the gendering and the hegemonic process — create mutual reinforcement for the double consciousness of women writers. This is the social and sexual basis of the poetics of critique.[47]

All forms of dominant narrative, but especially romance, are tropes for the sex-gender system as a whole.[48] Given the ideological and affirmative functions of narrative, it is no surprise that the critique of story is a major aspect of the stories told by twentieth-century women writers. . . . [49]

Notes

1. Virginia Woolf, *A Room of One's Own* (New York: Harcourt, Brace and World, 1957); abbreviated in the text as *AROO.* The epigraphs come from pp. 85 and 95.

2. Virginia Woolf, "Women and Fiction" (1929), in *Granite and Rainbow* (New York: Harcourt, Brace, 1958), p. 80; abbreviated as *G & R*.

3. The sentence is further qualified as being "too loose, too heavy, too pompous for a woman's use" (*G & R,* 81). A parallel, but slightly softened, statement about the sentence is found in *AROO*, p. 79, and an elaboration in the 1923 review of Dorothy Richardson, "Romance and the Heart," reprinted in *Contemporary Writers: Essays on Twentieth Century Books and Authors* (New York: Harcourt Brace Jovanovich, 1965), pp. 123–25. Working with these passages, Josephine Donovan also notes that the differences between "male" and "female" sentences exist in the tone of authority, the declaration of the insider in one, the under-the-surface life in the other, which rejects the authoritarian. Donovan also links Woolf's achievements in subjective realism to her critique of gender ideologies in narrative. "Feminist Style Criticism," in *Images of Women in Fiction: Feminist Perspectives,* ed. Susan Koppelman Cornillon (Bowling Green, Ohio: Bowling Green University Popular Press, 1972), pp. 339–52. A further note on the analysis of Woolf's "sentence." In this study as a whole, I am carefully (too?) agnostic on the subject of those actual disruptions of syntax, grammar, and words more characteristic of, say, Gertrude Stein; however, what Julia Kristeva calls the semiotic and symbolic registers may be another oscillation of dominant discourse in dialogue with marginality.

4. Richardson, "Romance and the Heart," pp. 124–25.

5. This is Nelly Furman's argument. "Textual Feminism," in *Women and Language in Literature and Society,* ed. Sally McConnell-Ginet, Ruth Borker, and Nelly Furman (New York: Praeger, 1980), pp. 50–51.

6. Nancy Miller, "Emphasis Added: Plots and Plausibilities in Women's Fiction," *PMLA* 96.1 (Jan. 1981): 38.

7. Woolf, "Women Novelists," reprinted in *Contemporary Writers,* p. 25.

8. Woolf, *Granite and Rainbow,* p. 80.

9. Here in the twenties, Woolf holds in conflictive tension her materialist and idealist views of writing. She argues that through art one may — indeed one must — transcend the cultural conditions of one's own formation. So in *A Room of One's Own,* Woolf combines a materialist analysis of the conditions that determine a woman's identity and capacity for work and an idealist vision of androgyny, a unity of the warring and unequal genders in luminous serenity. This point is made by Michele Barrett in her introduction to a collection of essays by Virginia Woolf, *Women and Writing* (New York: Harcourt Brace Jovanovich, 1979), pp. 20, 22.

10. For example, Woolf compared living with the institutions of gender as they are to living in "half-civilized barbarism," a slap at the meliorism of liberal ideology. Reply

to "Affable Hawk" from the *New Statesman* of 1920, in *The Diary of Virginia Woolf, Volume Two: 1920–1924,* ed. Anne Olivier Bell and Andrew McNeillie (New York: Harcourt Brace Jovanovich, 1978), p. 342.

11. Carolyn G. Heilbrun points toward the role of double determining when she suggests that "to be a feminist one had to have an experience of being an outsider more extreme than merely being a woman." *Reinventing Womanhood* (New York: W. W. Norton, 1979), pp. 20–24. Adrienne Rich describes the tension leading to a doubled vision: "Born a white woman, Jewish or of curious mind / —twice an outsider, still believing in inclusion—" *A Wild Patience Has Taken Me This Far* (New York: W. W. Norton, 1981), p. 39.

12. Myra Jehlen, "Archimedes and the Paradox of Feminist Criticism," *Signs* 6.4 (Summer 1981): 594. Jehlen makes this point about nineteenth-century American women, attempting to explain the literature of sentiment and limited challenge that they produced. "In this society, women stand outside any of the definitions of complete being; hence perhaps the appeal to them of a literature of conformity and inclusion." "(Ambiguously) nonhegemonic" from my essay "For the Etruscans: Sexual Difference and Artistic Production—the Debate over a Female Aesthetic," in *The Future of Difference,* ed. Hester Eisenstein and Alice Jardine (Boston: G. K. Hall, 1980). A further development of the phrase "(ambiguously) nonhegemonic" is found in Margaret Homans, " 'Her Very Own Howl': The Ambiguities of Representation in Recent Women's Fiction," *Signs* 9.2 (Winter 1983): 186–205. Homans suggests that "there is a specifically gender-based alienation from language" visible in thematic treatments of language in women's fiction, which derives from "the special ambiguity of women's simultaneous participation in and exclusion from a hegemonic group," p. 205.

13. For example, Olive Schreiner, *Women and Labour;* Charlotte Perkins Gilman, *The Man-Made World; or, Our Androcentric Culture and Women and Economics;* Virginia Woolf, *Three Guineas, A Room of One's Own,* and various essays; H.D., *Tribute to Freud, End to Torment,* and *The Gift;* Dorothy Richardson, essays on women; Adrienne Rich, *Of Woman Born* and *On Lies, Secrets and Silence;* Tillie Olsen, *Silences;* Doris Lessing, *A Small Personal Voice;* Alice Walker, *In Search of Our Mothers' Gardens.*

14. Annette Kuhn, *Women's Pictures: Feminism and Cinema* (London: Routledge and Kegan Paul, 1982), p. 17. The first chapter is a sterling exposition of feminist analysis of culture.

15. In the course of her research on the draft of *A Room of One's Own,* Alice Fox communicated to Jane Marcus that Woolf originally, wittily left a blank unfilled by the word *laboratory.* "Then she wrote that she was afraid to turn the page to see what they shared, and she thought of the obscenity trial for a novel." The allusion made and excised is to the contemporaneous trial of *The Well of Loneliness;* the implication that Woolf handled differently in her published text is that homophobic censorship and self-censorship alike conspire to mute discussion of relational ties between women.

Jane Marcus, "Liberty, Sorority, Misogyny," in *The Representation of Women in Fiction,* ed. Carolyn G. Heilbrun and Margaret R. Higonnet (Baltimore: Johns Hopkins University Press, 1983), p. 82.

16. Elaine Showalter proposed "that the specificity of women's writing [is] not . . . a transcient by-product of sexism but [is] a fundamentally and continually determining reality." "Feminist Criticism in the Wilderness," *Critical Inquiry* 8.2 (Winter 1981): 205.

17. Gayle Rubin, "The Traffic in Women: Notes on the 'Political Economy' of Sex," in *Toward an Anthropology of Women,* ed. Rayna [Rapp] Reiter (New York: Monthly Review Press, 1975), pp. 157–210.

18. Sigmund Freud, "The Psychology of Women" (1933), in *New Introductory Lectures on Psycho-Analysis,* trans. W. J. H. Sprott (New York: W. W. Norton, 1933), p. 184. The same essay is called "Femininity" in *The Standard Edition of the Complete Psychological Works of Sigmund Freud,* vol. 22, trans. James Strachey (London: Hogarth Press and The Institute of Psychoanalysis, 1964).

19. Freud, "The Psychology of Women," p. 158.

20. Rubin, "The Traffic in Women," p. 185.

21. Sherry B. Ortner, "Oedipal Father, Mother's Brother, and the Penis: A Review of Juliet Mitchell's *Psychoanalysis and Feminism,*" *Feminist Studies* 2, 2/3 (1975): 179. As Michele Barrett has remarked, "no substantial work has yet been produced that historicizes the [gendering] processes outlined in psychoanalytic theory." *Women's Oppression Today: Problems in Marxist Feminist Analysis* (London: Verso and New Left Books, 1980), p. 197.

22. Freud, "The Psychology of Women," p. 179. By female masculinity is meant the preoedipal object choice of a female; by femininity is meant the oedipal object choice of a male.

23. Nancy Chodorow, *The Reproduction of Mothering: Psychoanalysis and the Sociology of Gender* (Berkeley: University of California Press, 1978), p. 122.

24. Chodorow summarizes the female's "emotional, if not erotic bisexual oscillation between mother and father — between preoccupation with 'mother-child' issues and 'male-female' issues." *The Reproduction of Mothering,* p. 168. I am indebted to Chodorow for the concept of oscillation.

25. "The asymmetrical structure of parenting generates a female oedipus complex . . . characterized by the continuation of preoedipal attachments and preoccupations, sexual oscillation in an oedipal triangle, and the lack of either absolute change of love object or absolute oedipal resolution." Chodorow, *The Reproduction of Mothering,* pp. 133–34.

26. In an analysis related to my point here, Elizabeth Abel sees the theme and presence of same-sex friendship in literary works by women as an expression of female identity and the particularities of female oedipalization. As well, Abel offers striking remarks on the theory of literary influence that can be derived from Chodorow.

"(E)Merging Identities: The Dynamics of Female Friendship in Contemporary Fiction by Women," *Signs* 6.3 (Spring 1981): 413–35.

27. For example, H.D. was psychoanalyzed by Freud, and engaged, according to Susan Friedman, in a constant interior debate wtih Freud on several issues, including gender. *Psyche Reborn: The Emergence of H.D.* (Bloomington: Indiana University Press, 1981). Virginia Woolf noted her "very amateurish knowledge of Freud and the psychoanalysts" and admitted that "my knowledge is merely from superficial talk." In her circle, however, the talkers might have included James Strachey, the translator of Freud's *Complete Psychological Works*, cited in note 18. *The Letters of Virginia Woolf, Volume Five: 1932–1935*, ed. Nigel Nicolson and Joanne Trautmann (New York: Harcourt Brace Jovanovich, 1979), pp. 36 and 91.

28. Freud, "The Psychology of Women," p. 177.

29. Freud, "The Passing of the Oedipus-Complex," in *Collected Papers*, vol. 2 (London: Hogarth Press, 1957), p. 275. The paper dates from 1924.

30. Virginia Woolf, *Moments of Being*, ed. Jeanne Schulkind (New York: Harcourt Brace Jovanovich, 1978), pp. 132, 129, 132.

31. Simone de Beauvoir, *The Second Sex*, trans. H. M. Parshley (New York: Bantam Books, 1972), p. 47.

32. John Berger, *Ways of Seeing* (New York: Viking Press, 1972), p. 46.

33. Gerda Lerner, *The Majority Finds Its Past: Placing Women in History* (Oxford: Oxford University Press, 1979), pp. xxi, 52.

34. Nancy Cott, "Introduction," in *Root of Bitterness: Documents of the Social History of American Women* (New York: E. P. Dutton, 1972), p. 3.

35. Sheila Rowbotham, *Women's Consciousness, Man's World* (London: Penguin, 1973), pp. 30–31.

36. Alice Walker, "In Search of Our Mothers' Gardens," in *In Search of Our Mothers' Gardens* (San Diego: Harcourt Brace Jovanovich, 1983), p. 235.

37. Virginia Woolf, *Three Guineas* (New York: Harcourt, Brace and World, 1938), p. 5. Abbreviated in the text as *TG*.

38. Virginia Woolf, "The Leaning Tower," in *The Moment and Other Essays* (New York: Harcourt Brace Jovanovich, 1948), p. 154.

39. Raymond Williams, "Base and Superstructure in Marxist Cultural Theory," *New Left Review* 82 (Nov.–Dec. 1973): 7.

40. Raymond Williams, *Marxism and Literature* (Oxford: Oxford University Press, 1977), p. 112.

41. Edwin Ardener, "The 'Problem' Revisited," a coda to "Belief and the Problem of Women," in *Perceiving Women*, ed. Shirley Ardener (New York: John Wiley and Sons, 1975), p. 22. Elaine Showalter made Ardener's analysis available to feminist criticism in "Feminist Criticism in the Wilderness," *Critical Inquiry* 8.2 (Winter 1981), especially pp. 199–201.

42. "Double-consciousness" is, in fact, the influential formulation of black identity

made in 1903 by W. E. B. Du Bois in *The Souls of Black Folk* (in *Three Negro Classics,* ed. John Hope Franklin [New York: Avon Books, 1965], p. 215). "It is a peculiar sensation, the double-consciousness, this sense of always looking at one's self through the eyes of others, of measuring one's soul by the tape of a world that looks on in amused contempt and pity. One ever feels his twoness—an American, a Negro; two souls, two thoughts, two unreconciled strivings; two warring ideals in one dark body, whose dogged strength alone keeps it from being torn asunder." Richard Wright made a similar point in 1956: "First of all, my position is a split one, I'm black. I'm a man of the West. These hard facts condition, to some degree, my outlook." (*Presence Africaine* [Nov. 1956], cited in *The Black Writer in Africa and the Americas,* ed. Lloyd W. Brown [Los Angeles: Hennessey and Ingalls, 1973], p. 27).

43. Ellen Moers, *Literary Women: The Great Writers* (Garden City, N.Y.: Doubleday, 1976).

44. Elaine Showalter, *A Literature of Their Own: British Women Novelists from Brontë to Lessing* (Princeton: Princeton University Press, 1977), p. 11. The postulation of "unity" is also generally assumed in this study. However, other perspectives on women's writing might make other assumptions, now that "women's writing" is an accepted critical category.

45. Sandra M. Gilbert and Susan Gubar, *The Madwoman in the Attic: The Woman Writer and the Nineteenth-Century Literary Imagination* (New Haven: Yale University Press, 1979), p. 49.

46. Mary Jacobus, "The Difference of View," in *Women Writing and Writing about Women,* ed. Mary Jacobus (London: Croom Helm, 1979), pp. 19–20.

47. Myra Jehlen's summary of the relationship of women to culture is exemplary.

> Women (and perhaps some men not of the universal kind) must deal with their situation as a *pre*condition for writing about it. They have to confront the assumptions that render them a kind of fiction in themselves in that they are defined by others, as components of the language and thought of others. It hardly matters at this prior stage what a woman wants to write; its political nature is implicit in the fact that it is she (a "she") who will do it. All women's writing would thus be congenitally defiant and universally characterized by the blasphemous argument it makes in coming into being. And this would mean that the autonomous individuality of a woman's story or poem is framed by engagement, the engagement of its denial of dependence. We might think of the form this necessary denial takes (however it is individually interpreted, whether conciliatory or assertive) as analogous to genre, in being an issue, not of content, but of the structural formulation of the work's relationship to the inherently formally patriarchal language which is the only language we have. ("Archimedes," p. 582)

The proposal this book makes for the "structural formulation" analogous to genre is the act of critique, drawing on the oscillations of female identity.

48. The sex-gender system involves a linked chain of institutions such as the sexual

division of labor in production and in the socialization of children, valorized hetero-sexuality and the constraint on female sexuality, marriage and kinship, sexual choice and desire, gender asymmetry and polarization.

49. We have omitted a closing "survey of several contemporary works," which shows "how the critique of story is not only a thematic fact but an indication of the moral, ideological, and political desire to rescript the novel" (DuPlessis). — Editors

26 Barbara Foley : *The Documentary Novel and the Problem of Borders*

Barbara Foley concerns herself with a particular kind of literary fiction, in "The Documentary Novel and the Problem of Borders," that has been written for centuries, but has undergone transformations with the advent of modernism. Foley sees its taking two major forms: "the fictional autobiography" and "the metahistorical novel." Perhaps more important in her analysis than this distinction, however, is her argument that the documentary novel tradition has always overlapped with the mainstream tradition of the novel but has not been identical with it. Key to this nonidentity is that "the documentary novel is distinguished by its insistence that it contains some kind of specific and verifiable link to the historical world." This form of fiction, then, requires critics to address directly not only the issue of mimesis but also that of linguistic referentiality. Therefore, Foley claims that "to investigate the truth-telling claims of the documentary novel is thus to illuminate the assertive capacities of fiction in general."

While the issue of linguistic referentiality and the distinction between factual and fictional discourses has been a particularly prominent element of poststructuralist philosophy, Foley argues that their distinction has always been a concern in evaluating literary production and novelistic forms since the seventeenth century. Foley goes on to discuss various theories of mimesis and to posit a qualitative definition of the concept, turning to Gestalt psychology, as well as cognitive science, for assistance in explaining her conception. In her conclusion, Foley also introduces the issue of reader competence and assumptions that authors make about the reception capabilities of readers based on a mutual knowledge of generic conventions. Foley's argument can be defined as a type of genre analysis that takes both writing and reading strategies and competencies into account in relation to ongoing distinctions between fact and fiction. It also revives the concept of mimesis, in much the same way that Peter Brooks revives the concept of plot, as a counterargument to certain structuralist and poststructuralist claims about the indeterminacy and nonreferentiality of language.

Barbara Foley (b. 1948) is Professor of English at Rutgers University, Newark. In addition to *Telling the Truth* (1986), from which this excerpt is taken, she has also written *Radical Representations: Politics and Form in U.S. Proletarian Fiction, 1929–1991*.

Belief in fiction cannot be a matter of degree. We either accept the incidents of a story as if they were true, or we are aware of them as fiction. There can be no halfway house, no keeping an open mind, no suspending our judgment until further evidence is available. — Vivienne Mylne

The documentary novel constitutes a distinct fictional kind. It locates itself near the border between factual discourse and fictive discourse, but it does not propose an eradication of that border. Rather, it purports to represent reality by means of agreed-upon conventions of fictionality, while grafting onto its fictive pact some kind of additional claim to empirical validation. Historically, this claim has taken various forms. The pseudofactual novel of the seventeenth and eighteenth centuries simulates or imitates the authentic testimony of a "real life" person; its documentary effect derives from the assertion of veracity. The historical novel of the nineteenth century takes as its referent a phase of the historical process; its documentary effect derives from the assertion of extratextual verification. The documentary novel in the modernist era bifurcates into two distinct genres. The fictional autobiography represents an artist-hero who assumes the status of a real person inhabiting an invented situation; its documentary effect derives from the assertion of the artist's claim to privileged cognition. The metahistorical novel takes as its referent a historical process that evades rational formulation; its documentary effect derives from the assertion of the very indeterminacy of factual verification. Finally, the Afro-American documentary novel represents a reality submitting human subjects to racist objectification; its documentary effect derives from the presentation of facts that subvert commonplace constructions of reality. In all its phases, then, the documentary novel aspires to tell the truth, and it associates this truth with claims to empirical validation. If it increasingly calls into question the possibility of truth-telling, this skepticism is directed more toward the ideological assumptions undergirding empiricism than toward the capacity of fictive discourse to interpret and represent its referent.

Clearly the documentary novel, as I define it in this book, is not a minor subgenre that can be readily relegated to the margins of novelistic production in any given era. On the contrary: in the seventeenth and eighteenth centuries, the documentary novel is closely aligned with writing that Lennard J. Davis calls the "news/novel discourse";[1] in the nineteenth century, the documentary novel intersects with the major tradition of realism; in the early decades of the twentieth century, it participates in the principal concerns of modernism. Much writing in the entire domain of Afro-American prose fiction has a pronounced documentary quality. Thus central texts from each phase in the history of the novel (for example, *Moll Flanders, Pamela, Waverley, Henry Esmond, Orlando, A Portrait of the Artist as a Young Man, Native Son*) can be adjudged to be documentary novels. But while the documentary novel overlaps with the mainstream tradition of the novel, it is not identical with this tradition. Rather, the documentary novel is distinguished by its insistence that it contains some kind of specific and verifiable link to the historical world. (Whether or not this link succeeds in being "extratextual" in a larger sense remains to be seen.) It implicitly claims to replicate certain features of actuality in a relatively direct and unmediated fashion; it invokes familiar novelistic conventions, but it requires the reader to accept certain textual elements — characters, incidents, or actual documents — as possessing referents in the world of the reader. The documentary novel is not superior to other modes of fictional discourse in its capacity for assertion — all fictions assert their propositional content with equal force and sincerity, I believe — but it does raise the problem of reference for explicit consideration. To investigate the truth-telling claims of the documentary novel is thus to illuminate the assertive capacities of fiction in general.

. . . Factual and fictive discourses are not immutable essences but are historically varying types of writing, signaled by, and embodied in, changing literary conventions and generated by the changing structures of historically specific relations of production and intercourse. As M. M. Bakhtin has remarked, "The boundaries between fiction and nonfiction, between literature and nonliterature and so forth are not laid up in heaven. Every specific situation is historical. And the growth of literature is not merely development and change within the fixed boundaries of any definition; the boundaries themselves are constantly changing."[2] In examining the documentary novel's protean identity, I have had to abandon many prior conceptions about what constitutes fiction, the novel, history, and the elusive quality that I am terming the "documentary" effect. Modes of discourse do not remain within "fixed boundaries"; they change as much as do the modes of social and political representation in the worlds that they take as their referents.

I have discovered, nonetheless, that the distinction between fictional discourse and its various nonfictional counterparts — history, journalism, biography, autobiography — has remained a qualitative one. The need to distinguish between narratives held to be imaginary and those held to be directly representational would seem to be not a post-Cartesian phenomenon, testifying to the alienation of subject from object, but an abiding feature of discursive production. Even in the seventeenth and eighteenth centuries, when the documentary novel possessed its most ambiguous generic identity, the issue was not that prose fiction simply blended into purportedly veracious kinds of writing but that its primary locus, the romance, could not effectively assert the kind of truth that the early pseudofactual novelists wanted to tell. The pseudofactual novel's ambiguous generic status does not mean that writers and readers of the time inhabited an ontological haze but that they felt obliged to simulate veracious discourses if they hoped to appear credible to their readers. To say, as Bakhtin does, that the borderline between fiction and nonfiction is "constantly changing" does not mean that writers have not routinely respected such a borderline; it means, on the contrary, that writers have composed their fictions in contradistinction to one or more acknowledged forms of nonfictional writing. Fiction, I would propose, is intrinsically part of a binary opposition; it is what it is by virtue of what it is not.

. . . In this prolegomenon to my central theoretical and historical discussions, I shall confront the principal claims of my adversaries by arguing on logical grounds for the superiority of a qualitative view of mimesis. (By "qualitative" I mean different in kind rather than in degree.) In so doing, I run the risk of appearing to endorse an ahistorical or essentialist view of mimesis. Certainly it is true, as we shall see, that many defenses of the uniqueness of mimesis do in fact reify the realms of fictional and nonfictional discourse and deny their continually altering character. I believe, however, that a qualitative approach to the matter of defining fictionality is consonant with the premises of a materialist literary theory, so long as we remember that binary oppositions are dialectical oppositions as well.[3]

The view that fictional and nonfictional discourse cannot be qualitatively distinguished ordinarily rests on one of three arguments. The first of these, which I shall term the "spectrum" argument, centers on the claim that the significant qualities of factuality and fictionality inhere in separate facets of a literary work, rather than in any informing paradigm, and that the task of criticism is to assess the impact of these upon the work's rhetorical effect. Thus Paul Hernadi advocates a "microstructural theory of poetic discourse," which holds that any given literary work possesses aspects of various discourses and should be analyzed not as a text unified by a single generic frame but as a unity of multiple components reflecting the richness of literary discourse in general. Hernadi repudiates the investigation of "generic conventions as reflections of historically conditioned preferences of writers and readers." Instead, he asserts, "The finest generic classifications of our time make us look beyond their immediate concerns and focus on the order of literature, not on borders between literary genres."[4] Scholes and Kellogg, in *The Nature of Narrative,* reach a similar conclusion from the opposite direction, for they insist that it is such "historically conditioned preferences" that furnish the logical basis for a nonqualitative definition of mimesis. The novel has historically synthesized two narrative impulses, they argue, one directed toward the "empirical," or historical, and the other directed toward the "fictional," or imaginary. Empirical and fictional are blended tendencies, rather than distinctive kinds; history and fantasy stand as the poles of a narrative spectrum, with different narrative forms such as autobiography, realism, and romance occupying positions at various points along the scale. The "recording of specific fact, the representation of what resembles specific fact, and the representation of generalized types of actuality," declare Scholes and Kellogg, are all to be aligned along the empirical part of the narrative spectrum.[5]

A second type of nonqualitative argument, which I shall term the "family resemblance" argument, is based upon an invocation — albeit somewhat simplified — of Ludwig Wittgenstein's theory of linguistic reference. In his discussion of the definitive characteristics of concepts such as games, Wittgenstein points out the difficulties involved in the attempt to delineate a limited set of criteria that descriptively include all activities commonly held to be games and exclude all other activities: "Consider for example the proceedings we call 'games.' . . . What is common to them all? — Don't say, there *must* be something common, or they would not be called '*games*' — but *look* and *see* whether there is anything common to all. For if you look at them you will not see something that is common to *all,* but similarities, relationships, and a whole series at that." Drawing an analogy between games and the physical traits shared by the members of the same family, Wittgenstein concludes, "We see a complicated network of similarities overlapping and crisscrossing; sometimes overall similarities, sometimes similarities of detail."[6] For Wittgenstein, no fixed set of

properties defines the term "game," just as no fixed set of physical characteristics is shared by all members of the same family. For Wittgenstein,
language seduces us into believing that certain words denote actually
existing sets of relations, when all that these words really denote is concepts used to order the world of things.

Applied to the problem of defining mimesis, the "family resemblance"
argument proposes that qualitative distinctions between factual and fictional discourse are founded upon fallacious logic. Morris Weitz, for example, invokes Wittgenstein when he asserts that all aesthetic categories,
including the theory of literary kinds, are concepts with blurred edges and
that it is therefore impossible to formulate a clear description of mimetic
discourse. Asking himself whether an experimental fiction utilizing new
kinds of referential procedures can be classified as a "novel," he observes,
"What is at stake here is no factual analysis concerning necessary and
sufficient properties but a decision as to whether the work under examination is similar in certain respects to other works, already called 'novels,'
and consequently warrants the extension of the concept to cover the new
case." Every such classificatory decision is, however, necessarily an ad
hoc decision:

> "Art," itself, is an open concept. New conditions (cases) have constantly arisen and
> will undoubtedly constantly arise; new art forms, new movements will emerge,
> which will demand decisions on the part of those interested, usually professional
> critics, as to whether the concept should be extended or not. . . . Art, as the logic of
> the concept shows, has no set of necessary and sufficient properties, hence a theory
> of it is logically impossible and not merely factually difficult.[7]

Charles Stevenson, also invoking Wittgenstein, introduces a mathematical
model to solve the problem of fictional classification. Since fictionality is
signaled by a multiplicity of possibly relevant textual properties, he argues, and since no fictional work will possess all the traits associated with
mimesis, fictional representation consists of a "weighted average" of mimetic elements.[8] According to Stevenson, an arithmetical computation of
discernible features will yield the basis for a definitive decision about a
text's qualification for membership in the class of fictions. The "family
resemblance" argument claims for itself the virtues of both historicity and
empirical precision: to posit a fixed set of fictional features violates not
only the course of literary-historical development but also the diversity of
features present in any given fictional text.

Proponents of the spectrum and family resemblance approaches to generic definition quite correctly alert us to the danger of taking fictionality to reside in an immutable set of textual properties. But their arguments are only superficially empirical and historicist. The spectrum argument conflates the necessary recognition of historical shifts in the mimetic contract with the impossibility of logical classification, thereby precluding any inquiry into the historically varying epistemological bases of generic distinctions. Scholes and Kellogg quite rightly point out that the various modes of fictional, historical, and autobiographical discourse have adopted conventions signaled by widely varying textual features, and they convincingly demonstrate that certain markers of generic identity have even reversed their functions: the unwitnessed monologue, now a sure indicator of an author's fictional intentions, was once, they show, an accepted convention of heroic history. But a recognition of the relative — that is, historically variable — nature of the fact/fiction opposition does not mean that this opposition is denied absolute status at any given historical juncture. A spectrum of empirical possibilities is not the same thing as a spectrum of discursive kinds. As Barbara Herrnstein Smith puts it, "There is no principle of relative differentiation that could allow us to speak of any given composition as 'more' or 'less' fictive . . . and thereby assign it its proper place on the continuum. The distinction between natural and fictive is absolute."[9] The spectrum argument ends up treating generic categorization as a framework imposed a posteriori by literary critics, ruling out the possibility that it may constitute a necessary basis for the contracts formed between actual writers and readers.

The central problem with the family resemblance argument is that it treats all textual elements as having an equal claim upon the reader's attention, with no single trait being privileged by convention or authorial intention to exercise a dominant influence in the reader's apprehension of the text's generic identity. The text is, quite simply, the sum of its parts; if these parts cannot add up to a sufficient total, then the text is not recognizable as a member of the family of fictions. But to maintain that separate elements in factual or fictive works signal a certain family resemblance does not imply that qualitatively defined sets of relations among these elements cannot also be uncovered. Concepts with blurred edges are not necessarily concepts that lack a principle of unity; indeed, as Wittgenstein himself pointed out, concepts such as "games," while not readily definable in descriptive terms, are easily definable in practice, since clearly people know when they are playing games and when they are not. Wittgenstein's "insight into the looseness of our concepts, and its attendant jargon of 'family resemblance,' " remarks John Searle, "should not lead us into a rejection of the very enterprise of philosophical analysis."[10]

The third type of nonqualitative argument — the one developed recently with the most vehemence — has come from poststructuralist critics, who, invoking Nietzsche, propose that all our discourses about the material world, both factual and fictive, are circumscribed by the texts we construe in relation to that world. The very act of formulating an explanatory scheme is, for Barthes and Derrida, an enterprise inevitably shaped by language and ideology and is therefore fictive, in effect if not in intent. The project of criticism should not be to perpetuate the metaphysical dualisms of Western thought — among which the opposition of fiction and nonfiction figures centrally — but to reveal the inadequacy of reductive binary oppositions that privilege the products of the "creative" imagination, relegate (non)fiction to the margins of discourse, and ignore the textuality of all writing. Thus Roland Barthes has argued that "the only feature which distinguishes historical discourse from other kinds is a paradox: the 'fact' can exist linguistically only as a term in a discourse, yet we behave as if it were a simple reproduction of something on another plane of existence altogether, some extra-structural 'reality.' Historical discourse is presumably the only kind which aims at a referent "outside" itself that can in fact never be reached." Historical discourse is, therefore, a "fake performative, in which what claims to be the descriptive element is in fact only the expression of the authoritarian nature of that particular speech-act."[11] For Barthes, the insistence upon a referent beyond textuality is not simply a gesture of epistemological naïveté: it is an act of political repression.

Derrida develops the militantly antigeneric implications of Barthes's argument. The formulation of the binary opposition fiction/nonfiction produces, for Derrida, a "hierarchical axiology" that presupposes "an origin or . . . a 'priority' held to be simple, intact, normal, pure, standard, self-identical."[12] One aspect of the opposition (in this case, fiction) is implicitly valorized, and the other (nonfiction) is defined by subordination or exclusion — that is, by nonidentity. A deconstruction of such metaphysical categories reveals that what is excluded constitutes much more than nonidentity and that identity itself — as a pure essence beyond difference — is a specious category. When brought to bear upon the theory of discursive genres, the deconstructive project therefore reveals that

the law of the law of genre . . . is a principle of contamination. . . . The trait that
marks membership inevitably divides; the boundary of the set comes to form . . .
an internal pocket larger than the whole; and the outcome of this division and of this
overflowing remains as singular as it is limitless. . . . The principle of genre is
unclassifiable, it tolls the knell of the . . . classicum, of what permits one to call out
orders and to order, the manifold without a nomenclature. . . . [Genre designation]
gathers together the corpus and, at the same time . . . keeps it from closing, from
identifying itself with itself. This axiom of non-closure or non-fulfillment enfolds
within itself the condition for the possibility and the impossibility of taxonomy.[13]

For Derrida, the very attempt to formulate genre distinctions is undermined by the subversive nature of writing, which interpenetrates among
the epistemological categories that ideology sets up to delineate its terrain.

We may be grateful to Derridean deconstruction for calling our attention to the ideological agenda that is inevitably attached to the binary
opposition fiction/nonfiction. . . . The common valorization of "creative"
or "imaginative" writing does frequently imply a fetishization of mimetic
discourse and a positivist reduction of nonfictional discourse to the unmediated reportage of "what is." But, while I would certainly agree with
Barthes that historical discourse is in its way as saturated in ideology as is
mimetic discourse, I would not therefore conclude that historical and
mimetic discourse adopt equivalent representational procedures or constitute equivalent modes of cognition. And while I would grant Derrida's
point that Western philosophy is pervaded by abstract and ahistorical oppositions that, in the guise of reflecting transcendent essences, naturalize
dominant ideology, I would not therefore conclude that all inherited cognitive oppositions are equally ideological and equally fallacious. Some
oppositions — between fact and fiction, for instance — describe very real
(and, I believe, necessary) cognitive operations, in which actual historical
people engage and have engaged. Indeed, the Derridean project itself is
hardly exempt from the practice of binary opposition. Its universe is unre-
mittingly dualistic, with the forces of logocentrism, homogeneity, and
repression locked in combat with those of différance, heterogeneity, and
dispersal. If we recognize, as surely we must, that certain binary oppositions have been used to legitimate a hierarchical social order, the solution is not to jettison binary opposition altogether but to formulate a binary opposition to class dominance that will carry political force. In this
effort, it is not helpful to argue that all discourses are fictions or that the

goal of criticism is to formulate, in Derrida's words, "undecidables" that "can no longer be included within philosophical (binary) opposition, but which, however, inhabit philosophical opposition, resisting and disorganizing it, *without ever* constituting a third term."[14] The refusal to constitute a third term cannot go very far toward dislodging the "hierarchical axiology."

It should be apparent that, when one argues for a qualitative definition of fictionality, much more than the classification of discourse is involved: at stake, ultimately, is a whole debate about the relation between—and the context of—perception and cognition. I have no wish here to extend this debate. To support my assertion that fictional and nonfictional discourses are distinguishable not in degree but in kind, however, I would point out that most twentieth-century theories of cognition—in fields from psychology to the philosophy of science to linguistics—have found it necessary to postulate that the human mind characteristically uses polarity as an essential device in gaining understanding. Any given particular must be understood as part of a larger scheme, these theories tell us, if it is to be considered at all. The possible relevance of such theories to the problem of defining fictionality should be clear: the genres of fictional discourse engage informing paradigms qualitatively different from those of the various genres of nonfictional discourse, and even a presumably verifiable fact must be framed and contextualized before its signification can be determined.

From the field of Gestalt psychology, for example, we learn that perception ordinarily operates within qualitative and totalizing frames of reference. The rabbit-duck drawing, Gestalt psychologists would tell us, has two possible, and mutually exclusive, interpretations—it is either a rabbit or a duck. The viewer can readily enough grasp both perceptual possibilities but can process only one scheme at any particular instant. Any given detail in the drawing makes sense as part of either ordering scheme, but it demands wholly different interpretations when it is "read" from each perspective. Only a prior conventional context, external to the object of perception, can provide decisive criteria for adjudging the correctness of one or another interpretation. It is impossible, concludes E. H. Gombrich of this notorious example, to see "what is 'really there,' to see the shape apart from its interpretation."[15] There are no innocent perceptions: if perception is to produce cognition, it must invoke a framework of prior assumptions about what is being seen.

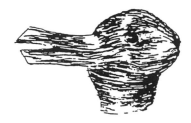

Gregory Bateson and Erving Goffman have argued that a great variety of human behaviors can be explained by means of the Gestalt model. Bateson proposes that, in activities such as play, fantasy, and psychotherapy, the participants agree upon "psychological frames" that perform a "metacommunicative function," giving the receiver "instructions or aids in his attempt to understand the messages included within the frame."[16] Psychological frames are, moreover, both exclusive and inclusive, excluding certain messages by including others and vice versa: according to Bateson, Gestalt paradigms are necessary for the unambiguous signaling of complex and overdetermined meanings. Goffman examines the operations of all sorts of social codes — from body language to advertising — in terms of what he calls "primary frameworks": "Each primary framework allows its user to locate, perceive, identify and label a seemingly infinite number of concrete occurrences defined in its terms. [The user] is likely to be unaware of such organized features as the framework has and unable to describe the framework with any completeness if asked, yet these handicaps are no bar to his easily and fully applying it."[17] Primary frameworks can also be transformed, or "keyed," in such a way that almost all the elements in the original activity signal an entirely new meaning when incorporated into a keyed context. Keying involves an agreement among the parties involved to bracket the keyed activity, pretending to follow the rules of the primary framework but actually following a set of very different rules. For Bateson and Goffman, then, the entire range of human behavior, serious and playful, is regulated by conventions that bear a "metacommunicative" relation to any given activity. An activity is understood as a *kind of thing,* and it is defined largely by contradistinction to what it is not.

Turning to the field of the philosophy of science, we may note that it has become axiomatic that scientists ordinarily hypothesize generalizations and then seek out the evidence that would validate, qualify, or refute those generalizations. Early bourgeois science proposed that human beings characteristically construct conceptual categories on the basis of inductively accumulated experience—a procedure that results, in Hume's words, in "that *perfect* habit, which makes us conclude in general, that instances, of which we have no experience, must necessarily resemble those of which we have."[18] T. S. Kuhn, by contrast, cautions that "no natural history can be interpreted in the absence of at least some implicit body of intertwined theoretical and methodological belief that permits selection, evaluation, and criticism."[19] Karl Popper, who sees the growth of scientific knowledge as a process of "conjecture and refutation," holds that the mind intrinsically possesses the "expectation of finding a regularity."[20] Michael Polanyi, rejecting those versions of Gestalt psychology that describe the perceiver as a passive receiver of preformed paradigms, declares, "I am looking at Gestalt . . . as the outcome of . . . an active shaping of experience performed in the pursuit of knowledge."[21] For these theorists, the scientific method consists in the constant evaluation of explanatory frames. Particulars do not yield up their meaning; they need to be located within a qualitatively defined larger scheme if they are to possess value as evidence.

Finally, it bears noting that such concepts as "tacit knowledge" and "primary frameworks" bear a distinct resemblance to Noam Chomsky's theory of linguistic competence, which posits that native speakers of a language are governed by an "abstract system underlying behavior, a system constituted by rules that interact to determine the form and intrinsic meaning of a potentially infinite number of sentences."[22] The process of acquiring language therefore means that "a child must devise a hypothesis compatible with presented data—he must select from the store of potential grammars a specific one that is appropriate to the data available to him."[23] Whenever a speaker utters a statement, then, he or she is invoking a "deep structure" that is the basis for the statement's being coherent and comprehensible (even if the statement is new to the listener). The goal of the study of the "universal grammar" of language, Chomsky concludes, is not simply to illuminate the procedures of language acquisition and communication; it is nothing less than the discovery of the general properties of human intelligence.[24]

These various descriptions of the relation of perception to cognition could, I suppose, be taken as evidence that human intelligence can never know reality, but that it merely imposes its fictions on what it encounters.

In my view, however, their implication is quite different. There is no reason to suppose that facts are created by interpretations if they are bound to them. We are free to see a duck or a rabbit, but not a giraffe; the Gestalt figure is not a Rorschach inkblot. The Copernican view of the solar system did not construct the data that rendered it a more powerful explanatory model than the Ptolemaic system. Nor is there any reason to conclude that any given "primary framework" or "tacit knowledge" or "deep structure" constitutes innate or transhistorical knowledge of a Kantian or Jungian kind. The human mind may have certain innate proclivities, but these are necessarily enacted through cognitive frames that are preeminently social constructs: the manifold variations in past and present human behavior testify to the embeddedness of any given conceptualization in a highly changeable social reality. These theories of cognition and language simply suggest that human intelligence characteristically operates in a configurational and — indeed — binary manner. Particulars must be grasped as functional components in qualitatively defined totalities — and excluded from other possible totalities — if they are to be grasped at all.

. . .

Both fictional discourse and nonfictional discourse make use of totalizing frames analogous to those explicitly formulated by psychology, linguistics, and the philosophy of science. Any given element in a narrative . . . must be scanned and interpreted as either factual or fictive in order to be read and understood. There is no specifically linguistic essence of fictionality that is immediately perceptible in the particulars of a text. As Victor Lange aptly puts it,

> Whether or not we are in the presence of a fictional field is . . . a matter of contextual analysis; it cannot be recognized unless we examine the specific aesthetic and logical uses to which the facts that sustain it have been put. The quality of the fact itself, whether it is related to any presumed actuality or is fanciful and nonrealistic, is of little concern for the determination of the fictional mode. The invented speeches in Tacitus are clearly part of a non-fictional intention; the actual letter which Rilke incorporated in *Malte Laurids Brigge* assumes, within the purposes of the novel, a distinctly fictional character.[25]

The writer assumes that the reader will possess the "competence" to know how to understand each particular, and that the "tacit knowledge" undergirding this competence is the knowledge of generic conventions shared by writer and reader alike. The nonfictional and fictional Gestalts employed by Tacitus and Rilke, respectively, are a function of the primary frameworks shared by readers of modern novels and ancient histories. I am arguing, in short, for a definition of mimesis as a contract, wherein writer and reader share an agreement about the conditions under which texts can be composed and comprehended. Even when writers take quantitative steps toward altering the terms of this agreement, they do so in the context of qualitatively defined discursive conventions. And the essence of mimesis — for it has an essence, *pace* Derrida and company — is that it is a social practice, whereby authors impart cognition of a particular kind to their readers.

The documentary novel, accordingly, is a species of fiction distinctly characterized by its adherence to referential strategies associated with nonfictional modes of discourse but also demanding to be read within a fictional Gestalt familiar to contemporaneous readers. Its dramatically altering strategies of representation do not mean that fictional discourse and nonfictional discourse are indistinguishable; they point instead to the changing terms of the fictional contract in different social formations. . . .

Notes

1. Lennard J. Davis, *Factual Fictions: The Origins of the English Novel* (New York: Columbia University Press, 1983).

2. M. M. Bakhtin, *The Dialogic Imagination: Four Essays,* ed. Michael Holquist, trans. Caryl Emerson and Michael Holquist (Austin: University of Texas Press, 1981), p. 33.

3. In chapters 1 to 4 of *Telling the Truth,* I frequently cite — and dispute — the views of critics who use the term "literature" or "poetry" where I use the term "fiction" or "mimesis." I am aware that this procedure may appear imprecise. The term "poetry," of course, often refers to verse; the term "literature" can be taken either as an honorific term denoting the quality of a text or as a highly general term denoting the whole province of "imaginative" writing — thus including a good deal of history, biography, autobiography, and journalism. In the discussions that follow, I have tried to adhere as closely as possible to the intentions of the critics cited: I have not adduced in support of my argument an opposition between "literature" and "nonliterature," for example, when its author means a distinction between "serious" and "popular" writing. It would have been incorrect, however, to confine my debates to those critics who use the terms "fiction" and "nonfiction," since critics often do mean "fictionality" when they discuss the essential feature(s) of "literary" or "poetic" discourse. For more on the

definition of "literature," see the various essays in Paul Hernadi's collection *What Is Literature?* (Bloomington: Indiana University Press, 1978); Raymond Williams, *Marxism and Literature* (Oxford: Oxford University Press, 1977), pp. 45–54; and Tzvetan Todorov, "The Notion of Literature," *New Literary History* 5 (Autumn 1973): 5–16. Note, also, that I use the term "mimesis" interchangeably with "fiction." Some theorists would include under the rubric of mimesis any discourse purporting to represent reality (that is, history, biography, autobiography, and so forth) but would exclude fictions of the more romantic or fantastic variety.

4. Paul Hernadi, *Beyond Genre: New Directions in Literary Classification* (Ithaca: Cornell University Press, 1972), p. 184.

5. Robert Scholes and Robert Kellogg, *The Nature of Narrative* (New York: Oxford University Press, 1969), pp. 86–87.

6. Ludwig Wittgenstein, *Philosophical Investigations,* 3d ed., trans. G. E. M. Anscombe (New York: Macmillan, 1956), 1:secs. 66–69.

7. Morris Weitz, "The Role of Theory in Aesthetics," *Journal of Aesthetics and Art Criticism* 15 (Sept. 1956): 28, 32.

8. Charles Stevenson, "On 'What Is a Poem?' " *Philosophical Review* 66 (July 1957): 329–62. Also see N. W. Visser, "The Generic Identity of the Novel," *Novel* 2 (Winter 1978): 101–14. For a persuasive critique of the application of the "family resemblance" concept to logical problems in aesthetic theory, see Maurice Mandelbaum, "Family Resemblances and Generalization Concerning the Arts," in *Problems in Aesthetics: An Introductory Book of Readings,* ed. Morris Weitz, 2d ed. (London: Macmillan, 1970), pp. 181–98. Mandelbaum argues that "family resemblance" theorists err in their focus upon "manifest features" rather than upon "relational attributes," which would require the critic to "consider specific art objects as having been created by someone for some actual or possible audience" (p. 187). In mathematics, as Stevenson observes, the quantitative approach to generic definition entails a repudiation of set theory. See Abraham Kaplan and H. F. Schott, "A Calculus for Empirical Classes," *Methods* 3 (1951): 165–90.

9. Barbara Herrnstein Smith, "On the Margins of Discourse," *Critical Inquiry* 1 (June 1975): 774. For a penetrating discussion of the changing boundary between autobiography and the novel, a distinction that is "dependent on distinctions between fiction and nonfiction, between rhetorical and empirical first-person narrative," see Elizabeth Bruss, *Autobiographical Acts: The Changing Situation of a Literary Genre* (Baltimore: Johns Hopkins University Press, 1976), 5–18.

10. John R. Searle, *Speech Acts: An Essay in the Philosophy of Language* (Cambridge: Cambridge University Press, 1970), 55. According to John M. Ellis, Wittgenstein's theory of language, properly understood, leads to the conclusion that literature can be qualitatively described by means of a "functional" definition. "When we seek a definition," he argues, "what we are seeking is not a statement of the feature held in common by the members of the category, but the appropriate circumstances for the use

of the word and the features of those circumstances that determine the willingness or unwillingness of the speakers of the language to use the word" (*The Theory of Literary Criticism: A Logical Analysis* [Berkeley: University of California Press, 1974], p. 34). Weitz is a crude Wittgensteinian, Ellis implies, for Weitz takes the impossibility of definition as the alternative to referential definition. The value of Ellis's theory is diminished, however, by his adherence to a nonassertive view of mimesis: the functionality of literary works, it turns out, consists in their being "used by society in such a way that the text is not taken as specifically relevant to the immediate context of its origin" (p. 43).

11. Roland Barthes, "Historical Discourse," in *Introduction to Structuralism*, ed. Michael Lane (New York: Basic, 1970), pp. 153, 154–55. For an instance of the political rhetoric that critics sympathetic with poststructuralism frequently attach to their discussions of the fact/fiction distinction, compare Suzanne Gearhart: "[All theories of literature and all theories of history] have consistently sought to fix the boundary between them and to establish once and for all the specificity of the fields in one of two ways: democratically, in that each accepts a mutually agreed on boundary which grants to each its own identity and integrity; or, just as often, imperialistically, in that each tries to extend its own boundary and to invade, engulf, or encompass the other. . . . In the second [case, the other genre] is overcome, cannibalized, incorporated into the sameness of the imperializing field" (*The Open Boundary of History and Fiction: A Critical Approach to the French Enlightenment* [Princeton: Princeton University Press, 1984], p. 4).

12. Jacques Derrida, "Limited Inc abc," in *Glyph: Johns Hopkins Textual Studies* 2 (Baltimore: Johns Hopkins University Press, 1977), p. 236. See also *Positions*, trans. Alan Bass (Chicago: University of Chicago Press, 1981), pp. 39–47.

13. Derrida, "The Law of Genre," quoted in Michael Ryan, *Marxism and Deconstruction: A Critical Articulation* (Baltimore: Johns Hopkins University Press, 1982), p. 19.

14. Derrida, *Positions*, p. 43. See also my "The Politics of Deconstruction," in the special issue "Deconstruction at Yale," *Genre* 17 (Spring–Summer 1984): 113–34.

15. E. H. Gombrich, *Art and Illusion: A Study in the Psychology of Pictorial Representation* (Princeton: Princeton University Press, 1960), p. 5.

16. Gregory Bateson, "A Theory of Play and Fantasy," in his *Steps to an Ecology of Mind: Collected Essays in Anthropology, Psychiatry, Evolution, and Epistemology* (San Francisco: Chandler, 1972), pp. 187–88. For more on the relations among Gestalt frames, play and fantasy, and fictionality, see Kendall L. Walton, "Fearing Fictions," *Journal of Philosophy* 75 (Jan. 1978): 5–27.

17. Erving Goffman, *Frame Analysis: An Essay on the Organization of Experience* (Cambridge, Mass.: Harvard University Press, 1976), p. 21.

18. David Hume, *Treatise of Human Nature*, ed. L. A. Selby-Bigge (Oxford: Clarendon, 1907), p. 135. For more on Hume's inductive argument, see also 1:3, vi and 1:3, xii.

19. T. S. Kuhn, *The Structure of Scientific Revolutions,* 2d ed. (Chicago: University of Chicago Press, 1970), pp. 16–17.

20. Karl Popper, *Conjectures and Refutations: The Growth of Scientific Knowledge* (New York: Basic, 1962), p. 47.

21. Michael Polanyi, *The Tacit Dimension* (Garden City, N.Y.: Doubleday, 1966), p. 6. In citing Polanyi, Kuhn, and Popper, I do not mean to imply that I endorse the particular theories of scientific method and development that these philosophers have evolved. I am simply noting the fact that modern philosophers of science of widely varying ideological orientations, neopositivist to intuitionist, have all found it necessary to posit that thought cannot take place in the absence of informing paradigms into which data — even anomalous data — must be incorporated. For a critique of both Popper's rationalism and Kuhn's irrationalism, see Larry Laudan, *Progress and Its Problems: Toward a Theory of Scientific Growth* (Berkeley: University of California Press, 1977).

22. Noam Chomsky, *Language and Mind* (New York: Harcourt, Brace & World, 1968), p. 62.

23. Noam Chomsky, *Aspects of the Theory of Syntax* (Cambridge, Mass.: MIT Press, 1965), p. 36.

24. Chomsky, *Language and Mind,* p. 24. For an application of Chomsky's theory of "deep structure" to the problem of mobilizing and perceiving generic distinction in imaginative literature, see Sheldon Sacks, "The Psychological Implications of Generic Distinction," *Genre* 1 (1968): 106–15.

25. Victor Lange, "The Fact in Fiction," *Comparative Literature Studies* 6 (Sept. 1969): 260. For other theories of fictional discourse explicitly invoking the concept of Gestalt, see Smith, 775–76; Ralph W. Rader, "The Concept of Genre in Eighteenth-Century Studies," in *New Approaches to Eighteenth-Century Literature: Selected Papers from the English Institute* (New York: Columbia University Press, 1974), pp. 84–86; and Norman Friedman, *Form and Meaning in Fiction* (Athens: University of Georgia Press, 1975), pp. 196–97.

27 Patrocinio P. Schweickart : *Reading Ourselves*

Toward a Feminist Theory of Reading

Patrocinio P. Schweickart begins "Reading Ourselves: Toward a Feminist Theory of Reading" with a discussion of three stories about reading, in all of which the storyteller ignores crucial elements because of his preconceptions. She then turns to Virginia Woolf's claim in *A Room of One's Own* that women tend to be absent from the philosophy, essays, and histories written by men. Woolf's conclusion is that "[w]oman herself must undertake the study of woman," a task which calls for a feminist theory of reading that studies writing written *by* women as well as writing written *about* women, while all along addressing the question of *how* women read.

Schweickart wishes to use reader-response criticism in her own study, but she finds that it needs the addition of feminist theory, because the material available to her for the most part omits a consideration of the race, class, and gender of the implied readers. She then presents a brief overview of trends in reader-response criticism, answering Elaine Showalter's assertion that the woman writer should be the primary focus of attention by asking, "[W]hy should the activity of the woman writer be more conducive to theory that the activity of the woman is?" It is Schweickart's belief that importing feminist criticism into reader-response criticism will bring such issues as "gender and politics" into that field. In conclusion, Schweickart argues that feminist reading invariably challenges the androcentric (male-centered) mode of most interpretive communities, becoming a "rereading" that helps women readers who are seeking to take "control of the reading process." Some questions that we might raise in response to Schweickart's argument are: Does her model apply regardless of the type of feminism a reader adopts in the reading process? Will readers find that certain feminist theories facilitate their reading of a particular text more than other theories? Should a woman always read first as a feminist?

Patrocinio P. Schweickart is Associate Professor of English at the University of New Hampshire. "Reading Ourselves: Toward a Feminist Theory of Reading" won the 1984 Florence Howe Award for Outstanding Feminist Scholarship.

Three Stories of Reading

A. Wayne Booth begins his presidential address to the 1982 MLA convention by considering and rejecting several plausible myths that might enable us "to dramatize not just our inescapable plurality but the validity of our sense that [as teachers and scholars of literature and composition] we belong together, somehow working on common ground." At last he settles on one story that is "perhaps close enough to our shared experience to justify the telling."[1]

Once upon a time there was a boy who fell in love with books. When he was very young he heard over and over the legend of his great-grandfather, a hard-working weaver who so desired knowledge that he figured out a way of working the loom with one hand, his legs, and his feet, leaving the other hand free to hold a book, and worked so steadily in that crooked position that he became permanently crippled. The boy heard other stories about the importance of reading. Salvation, he came to believe, was to be found in books. When he was six years old, he read *The Wizard of Oz*—his first *real* book—and was rewarded by his Great-Aunt Manda with a dollar.

When the boy grew up, he decided to become a teacher of "litcomp." His initiation into the profession was rigorous, and there were moments when he nearly gave up. But gradually, "there emerged from the trudging a new and surprising love, a love that with all my previous reading I had not dreamed of: the love of skill, of craft, of getting clear in my mind and then in my writing what a great writer had got right in his work" (Booth, p. 315). Eventually, the boy, now grown, got his doctorate, and after teaching for thirteen years in small colleges, he returned to his graduate institution to become one of its eminent professors.

Booth caps his narration by quoting from *The Autobiography of Malcolm X*. It was in prison that Malcolm learned to read:

> For the first time I could pick up a book and now begin to understand what the book was saying. Anyone who has read a great deal can imagine the new world that opened. Let me tell you something: from then until I left that prison, in every free moment I had, if I was not reading in the library, I was reading on my bunk. . . . [M]onths passed without my even thinking about being imprisoned. In fact, up to then, I never had been so truly free in my life. (As quoted by Booth, p. 317)

"Perhaps," says Booth, "when you think back now on my family's story about great-grandfather Booth, you will understand why reading about Malcolm X's awakening speaks to the question of where I got my 'insane love' [for books]" (p. 317).

B. When I read the Malcolm X passage quoted in Booth's address, the ellipsis roused my curiosity. What, exactly, I wondered, had been deleted? What in the original exceeded the requirements of a presidential address to the MLA? Checking, I found the complete sentence to read: "Between Mr. Muhammad's teachings, my correspondence, my visitors — usually Ella and Reginald — and my reading, months passed without my even thinking about being imprisoned."[2] Clearly, the first phrase is the dissonant one. The reference to the leader of the notorious Black Muslims suggests a story of reading very different from Booth's. Here is how Malcolm X tells it. While serving time in the Norfolk Prison Colony, he hit on the idea of teaching himself to read by copying the dictionary.

> In my slow, painstaking, ragged handwriting, I copied into my tablet every thing on that first page, down to the punctuation marks. . . . Then, aloud, to myself, I read back everything I'd written on the tablet. . . . I woke up the next morning thinking about these words — immensely proud to realize that not only had I written so much at one time, but I'd written words that I never knew were in the world. . . . That was the way I started copying what eventually became the entire dictionary. (p. 172)

After copying the dictionary, Malcolm X began reading the books in the prison library. "No university would ask any student to devour literature as I did when this new world opened to me, of being able to read and *understand*" (p. 173). Reading had changed the course of his life. Years later, he would reflect on how "the ability to read awoke inside me some long dormant craving to be mentally alive" (p. 179).

What did he read? What did he understand? He read Gregor Mendel's *Findings in Genetics* and it helped him to understand "that if you started with a black man, a white man could be produced; but starting with a white man, you never could produce a black man — because the white chromosome is recessive. And since no one disputes that there was but one Original Man, the conclusion is clear" (p. 175). He read histories, books by Will Durant and Arnold Toynbee, by W. E. B. Du Bois and Carter G. Woodson, and he saw how "the glorious history of the black man" had been "bleached" out of the history books written by white men.

> [His] eyes opened gradually, then wider and wider, to how the world's white men had indeed acted like devils, pillaging and raping and bleeding and draining the

whole world's non-white people. . . . I will never forget how shocked I was when I began reading about slavery's total horror. . . . The world's most monstrous crime, the sin and the blood on the white man's hands, are almost impossible to believe. (p. 175)

He read philosophy — the works of Schopenhauer, Kant, Nietzsche, and Spinoza — and he concluded that the "whole stream of Western Philosophy was now wound up in a cul-de-sac" as a result of the white man's "elaborate, neurotic necessity to hide the black man's true role in history" (p. 180). Malcolm X read voraciously, and book after book confirmed the truth of Elijah Muhammad's teachings. "It's a crime, the lie that has been told to generations of black men and white both. . . . Innocent black children growing up, living out their lives, dying of old age — and all of their lives ashamed of being black. But the truth is pouring out of the bag now" (p. 181).

Wayne Booth's story leads to the Crystal Ballroom of the Biltmore Hotel in Los Angeles, where we attend the protagonist as he delivers his Presidential Address to the members of the Modern Language Association. Malcolm X's love of books took him in a different direction, to the stage of the Audubon Ballroom in Harlem, where, as he was about to address a mass meeting of the Organization of Afro-American Unity, he was murdered.

C. As we have seen, an ellipsis links Wayne Booth's story of reading to Malcolm X's. Another ellipsis, this time not graphically marked, signals the existence of a third story. Malcolm X's startling reading of Mendel's genetics overlooks the most rudimentary fact of human reproduction: whether you start with a black man or a white man, without a woman, you get *nothing*. An excerpt from Virginia Woolf's *A Room of One's Own* restores this deleted perspective.[3]

The heroine, call her Mary, says Woolf, goes to the British Museum in search of information about women. There she discovers to her chagrin that woman is, "perhaps, the most discussed animal in the universe?"

Why does Samuel Butler say, "Wise men never say what they think of women"? Wise men never say anything else apparently. . . . Are they capable of education? Napoleon thought them incapable. Dr. Johnson thought the opposite. Have they souls or have they not souls? Some savages say they have none. Others, on the contrary, say women are half divine and worship them on that account. Some sages hold that they are shallower in the brain; others that they are deeper in consciousness. Goethe honoured them; Mussolini despises them. Wherever one looked men thought about women and thought differently. (pp. 29–30)

Distressed and confused, Mary notices that she has unconsciously drawn a picture in her notebook, the face and figure of Professor von X, engaged in writing his monumental work, *The Mental, Moral, and Physical Inferiority of the Female Sex.* "His expression suggested that he was labouring under some emotion that made him jab his pen on the paper as if he were killing some noxious insect as he wrote, but even when he had killed it that did not satisfy him; he must go on killing it. . . . A very elementary exercise in psychology . . . showed me . . . that the sketch had been made in anger" (pp. 31–32).

Nothing remarkable in that, she reflects, given the provocation. But "How explain the anger of the professor? . . . For when it came to analysing the impression left by these books, . . . there was [an] element which was often present and could not be immediately identified. Anger, I called it. . . . To judge from its effects, it was anger disguised and complex, not anger simple and open" (p. 32).

Disappointed with essayists and professors, Mary turns to historians. But apparently women played no significant role in history. What little information Mary finds is disturbing: "Wife-beating, I read, was a recognized right of a man, and was practiced without shame by high as well as low" (p. 44). Oddly enough, literature presents a contradictory picture.

If women had not existence save in fiction written by men, we would imagine her to be a person of utmost importance; very various; heroic and mean; splendid and sordid: infinitely beautiful and hideous in the extreme; as great as a man, some think even greater. But this is women in fiction. In fact, as Professor Trevelyan points out, she was locked up, beaten and flung about the room. (p. 45)

At last, Mary can draw but one conclusion from her reading. Male professors, male historians, and male poets can not be relied on for the truth about women. Woman herself must undertake the study of woman. Of course, to do so, she must secure enough money to live on and a room of her own.

Booth's story, we recall, is told within the framework of a professional ritual. It is intended to remind us of "the loves and fears that inform our daily work" and of "what we do when we are at our best," to show, if not a unity, then enough of a "center" "to shame us whenever we violate it." The principal motif of the myth is the hero's insane love for books, and the way this develops with education and maturity into "critical understanding," which Booth defines as that synthesis of thought and passion which should replace, "on the one hand, sentimental and uncritical identifications that leave minds undisturbed, and on the other, hypercritical negations that freeze or alienate" (pp. 317–18). Booth is confident that the experience celebrated by the myth is archetypal. "Whatever our terms for it, whatever our theories about how it happens or why it fails to happen more often, can we reasonably doubt the importance of the moment, at any level of study, when any of us — you, me, Malcolm X, my great-grandfather — succeeds in entering other minds, or 'taking them in,' as nourishment for our own?" (p. 318).

Now, while it is certainly true that something one might call "critical understanding" informs the stories told by Malcolm X and Virginia Woolf, these authors fill this term with thoughts and passions that one would never suspect from Booth's definition. From the standpoint of the second and third stories of reading, Booth's story is utopian. The powers and resources of his hero are equal to the challenges he encounters. At each stage he finds suitable mentors. He is assured by the people around him, by the books he reads, by the entire culture, that he is right for the part. His talents and accomplishments are acknowledged and justly rewarded. In short, from the perspective of Malcolm X's and Woolf's stories, Booth's hero is fantastically privileged.

Utopian has a second meaning, one that is by no means pejorative, and Booth's story is utopian in this sense as well. In overlooking the realities highlighted by the stories of Malcolm X and Virginia Woolf, Booth's story anticipates what might be possible, what "critical understanding" might mean for *everyone,* if only we could overcome the pervasive systemic injustices of our time.

Reader-Response Theory and Feminist Criticism

Reader-response criticism, as currently constituted, is utopian in the same two senses. The different accounts of the reading experience that have been put forth overlook the issues of race, class, and sex, and give no hint of the conflicts, sufferings, and passions that attend these realities. The relative tranquility of the tone of these theories testifies to the privileged position of the theorists. Perhaps, someday, when privileges have withered away or at least become more equitably distributed, some of these theories will ring true. Surely we ought to be able to talk about reading without worrying about injustice. But for now, reader-response criticism must confront the disturbing implications of our historical reality. Paradoxically, utopian theories that elide these realities betray the utopian impulses that inform them.

To put the matter plainly, reader-response criticism needs feminist criticism. The two have yet to engage each other in a sustained and serious way, but if the promise of the former is to be fulfilled, such an encounter must soon occur. Interestingly, the obvious question of the significance of gender has already been explicitly raised, and — this testifies to the increasing impact of feminist criticism as well as to the direct ideological bearing of the issue of gender on reader-response criticism — not by a feminist critic, but by Jonathan Culler, a leading theorist of reading: "If the experience of literature depends upon the qualities of a reading self, one can ask what difference it would make to the experience of literature and thus to the meaning of literature if this self were, for example, female rather than male. If the meaning of a work is the experience of a reader, what difference does it make if the reader is a woman?"[4]

Until very recently this question has not occurred to reader-response critics. They have been preoccupied with other issues. Culler's survey of the field is instructive here, for it enables us to anticipate the direction reader-response theory might take when it is shaken from its slumber by feminist criticism. According to Culler, the different models (or "stories") of reading that have been proposed are all organized around three problems. The first is the issue of control: Does the text control the reader, or vice versa? For David Bleich, Norman Holland, and Stanley Fish, the reader holds controlling interest. Readers read the poems they have made. Bleich asserts this point most strongly: the constraints imposed by the words on the page are "trivial," since their meaning can always be altered by "subjective action." To claim that the text supports this or that reading is only to "moralistically claim . . . that one's own objectification is more authoritative than someone else's."[5]

At the other pole are Michael Riffaterre, Georges Poulet, and Wolfgang Iser, who acknowledge the creative role of the reader, but ultimately take the text to be the dominant force. To read, from this point of view, is to create the text according to *its* own promptings. As Poulet puts it, a text, when invested with a reader's subjectivity, becomes a "subjectified object," a "second self" that depends on the reader, but is not, strictly speaking, identical with him. Thus, reading "is a way of giving way not only to a host of alien words, images and ideas, but also to the very alien principle which utters and shelters them. . . . I am on loan to another, and this other thinks, feels, suffers and acts within me."[6] Culler argues persuasively that, regardless of their ostensible theoretical commitments, the prevailing stories of reading generally vacillate between these reader-dominant and text-dominant poles. In fact, those who stress the subjectivity of the reader as against the objectivity of the text ultimately portray the text as determining the responses of the reader. "The more active, projective, or creative the reader is, the more she is manipulated by the sentence or by the author" (p. 71).

The second question prominent in theories of reading is closely related to the first. Reading always involves a subject and an object, a reader and a text. But what constitutes the objectivity of the text? What is "in" the text? What is supplied by the reader? Again, the answers have been equivocal. On the face of it, the situation seems to call for a dualistic theory that credits the contributions of both text and reader. However, Culler argues, a dualistic theory eventually gives way to a monistic theory, in which one or the other pole supplies everything. One might say, for instance, that Iser's theory ultimately implies the determinacy of the text and the authority of the author: "The author guarantees the unity of the work, requires the reader's creative participation, and through his text, prestructures the shape of the aesthetic object to be produced by the reader."[7] At the same time, one can also argue that the "gaps" that structure the reader's response are not built into the text, but appear (or not) as a result of the particular interpretive strategy employed by the reader. Thus, "there is no distinction between what the text gives and what the reader supplies; he supplies *everything*."[8] Depending on which aspects of the theory one takes seriously, Iser's theory collapses either into a monism of the text or a monism of the reader.

The third problem identified by Culler concerns the ending of the story. Most of the time stories of reading end happily. "Readers may be manipulated and misled, but when they finish the book their experience turns into knowledge . . . as though finishing the book took them outside the experience of reading and gave them mastery of it" (p. 79). However, some critics — Harold Bloom, Paul de Man, and Culler himself — find these optimistic endings questionable, and prefer instead stories that stress the impossibility of reading. If, as de Man says, rhetoric puts "an insurmountable obstacle in the way of any reading or understanding," then the reader "may be placed in impossible situations where there is no happy issue, but only the possibility of playing out the roles dramatized in the text" (Culler, p. 81).

Such have been the predominant preoccupations of reader-response criticism during the past decade and a half. Before indicating how feminist critics could affect the conversation, let me consider an objection. A recent and influential essay by Elaine Showalter suggests that we should not enter the conversation at all. She observes that during its early phases, the principal mode of feminist criticism was "feminist critique," which was counter-ideological in intent and concerned with the feminist as *reader*. Happily, we have outgrown this necessary but theoretically unpromising approach. Today, the dominant mode of feminist criticism is "gynocritics," the study of woman as *writer*, of the "history, styles, themes, genres, and structures of writing by women; the psychodynamics of female creativity; the trajectory of the individual or collective female career; and the evolution and laws of a female literary tradition." The shift from "feminist critique" to "gynocritics" — from emphasis on woman as reader to emphasis on woman as writer — has put us in the position of developing a feminist criticism that is "genuinely woman-centered, independent, and intellectually coherent."

> To see women's writing as our primary subject forces us to make the leap to a new conceptual vantage point and to redefine the nature of the theoretical problem before us. It is no longer the ideological dilemma of reconciling revisionary pluralisms but the essential question of difference. How can we constitute women as a distinct literary group? What is the *difference* of women's writing?[9]

But why should the activity of the woman writer be more conducive to theory than the activity of the woman reader is? If it is possible to formulate a basic conceptual framework for disclosing the "difference" of women's writing, surely it is no less possible to do so for women's reading. The same difference, be it linguistic, biological, psychological, or cultural, should apply in either case. In addition, what Showalter calls "gynocritics" is in fact constituted by feminist *criticism* — that is, *readings* — of female texts. Thus, the relevant distinction is not between woman as reader and woman as writer, but between feminist readings of male texts and feminist readings of female texts, and there is no reason why the former could not be as theoretically coherent (or irreducibly pluralistic) as the latter.

On the other hand, there are good reasons for feminist criticism to engage reader-response criticism. Both dispute the fetishized art object, the "Verbal Icon," of New Criticism, and both seek to dispel the objectivist illusion that buttresses the authority of the dominant critical tradition. Feminist criticism can have considerable impact on reader-response criticism, since, as Culler has noticed, it is but a small step from the thesis that the reader is an active producer of meaning to the recognition that there are many different kinds of readers, and that women — because of their numbers if because of nothing else — constitute an essential class. Reader-response critics cannot take refuge in the objectivity of the text, or even in the idea that a gender-neutral criticism is possible. Today they can continue to ignore the implications of feminist criticism only at the cost of incoherence or intellectual dishonesty.

It is equally true that feminist critics need to question their allegiance to text- and author-centered paradigms of criticism. Feminist criticism, we should remember, is a mode of *praxis*. The point is not merely to interpret literature in various ways; the point is to *change the world*. We cannot afford to ignore the activity of reading, for it is here that literature is realized as *praxis*. Literature acts on the world by acting on its readers.

To return to our earlier question: What will happen to reader-response criticism if feminists enter the conversation? It is useful to recall the contrast between Booth's story and those of Malcolm X and Virginia Woolf. Like Booth's story, the "stories of reading" that currently make up reader-response theory are mythically abstract, and appear, from a different vantage point, to be by and about readers who are fantastically privileged. Booth's story had a happy ending; Malcolm's and Mary's did not. For Mary, reading meant encountering a tissue of lies and silences; for Malcolm it meant the verification of Elijah Muhammad's shocking doctrines.

Two factors — gender and politics — which are suppressed in the dominant models of reading gain prominence with the advent of a feminist perspective. The feminist story will have *at least* two chapters: one concerned with feminist readings of male texts, and another with feminist readings of female texts. In addition, in this story, gender will have a prominent role as the locus of political struggle. The story will speak of the difference between men and women, of the way the experience and perspective of women have been systematically and fallaciously assimilated into the generic masculine, and of the need to correct this error. Finally, it will identify literature — the activities of reading and writing — as an important arena of political struggle, a crucial component of the project of interpreting the world in order to change it.

Feminist criticism does not approach reader-response criticism without preconceptions. Actually, feminist criticism has always included substantial reader-centered interests. In the next two sections of this paper, I will review these interests, first with respect to male texts, then with respect to female texts. In the process, I will uncover some of the issues that might be addressed and clarified by a feminist theory of reading.

The Female Reader and the Literary Canon

Although reader-response critics propose different and often conflicting models, by and large the emphasis is on features of the process of reading that do not vary with the nature of the reading material. The feminist entry into the conversation brings the nature of the text back into the foreground. For feminists, the question of *how* we read is inextricably linked with the question of *what* we read. More specifically, the feminist inquiry into the activity of reading begins with the realization that the literary canon is androcentric, and that this has a profoundly damaging effect on women readers. The documentation of this realization was one of the earliest tasks undertaken by feminist critics. Elaine Showalter's 1971 critique of the literary curriculum is exemplary of this work.

[In her freshman year a female student] . . . might be assigned an anthology of essays, perhaps such as *The Responsible Man,* . . . or *Conditions of Man,* or *Man in Crisis,* or again, *Representative Man: Cult Heroes of Our Time,* in which thirty-three men represent such categories of heroism as the writer, the poet, the dramatist, the artist, and the guru, and the only two women included are the actress Elizabeth Taylor, and the existential Heroine Jacqueline Onassis.

Perhaps the student would read a collection of stories like *The Young Man in American Literature: The Initiation Theme,* or sociological literature like *The Black*

Man and the Promise of America. In a more orthodox literary program she might study eternally relevant classics, such as *Oedipus;* as a professor remarked in a recent issue of *College English,* all of us want to kill our fathers and marry our mothers. And whatever else she might read, she would inevitably arrive at the favorite book of all Freshman English courses, the classic of adolescent rebellion, *A Portrait of the Artist as a Young Man.*

By the end of her freshman year, a woman student would have learned something about intellectual neutrality; she would be learning, in fact, how to think like a man. And so she would go on, increasingly with male professors to guide her.[10]

The more personal accounts of other critics reinforce Showalter's critique.

The first result of my reading was a feeling that male characters were at the very least more interesting than women to the authors who invented them. Thus if, reading their books as it seemed their authors intended them, I naively identified with a character, I repeatedly chose men; I would rather have been Hamlet than Ophelia, Tom Jones instead of Sophia Western, and, perhaps, despite Dostoevsky's intention, Raskolnikov not Sonia.

More peculiar perhaps, but sadly unsurprising, were the assessments I accepted about fictional women. For example, I quickly learned that power was unfeminine and powerful women were, quite literally, monstrous. . . . Bitches all, they must be eliminated, reformed, or at the very least, condemned. . . . Those rare women who are shown in fiction as both powerful and, in some sense, admirable are such because their power is based, if not on beauty, then at least on sexuality.[11]

For a woman, then, books do not necessarily spell salvation. In fact, a literary education may very well cause her grave psychic damage: schizophrenia "is the bizarre but logical conclusion of our education. Imagining myself male, I attempted to create myself male. Although I knew the case was otherwise, it seemed I could do nothing to make this other critically real."[12]

To put the matter theoretically, androcentric literature structures the reading experience differently depending on the gender of the reader. For the male reader, the text serves as the meeting ground of the personal and the universal. Whether or not the text approximates the particularities of his own experience, he is invited to validate the equation of maleness with humanity. The male reader feels his affinity with the universal, with the paradigmatic human being, precisely because he is male. Consider the famous scene of Stephen's epiphany in *A Portrait of the Artist as a Young Man.*

> A girl stood before him in midstream, alone and still, gazing out to sea. She seemed like one whom magic had changed into the likeness of a strange and beautiful seabird. Her long slender bare legs were delicate as a crane's and pure save where an emerald trail of seaweed had fashioned itself as a sign upon the flesh. Her thighs, fuller and softhued as ivory, were bared almost to the hips, where the white fringes of her drawers were like feathering of soft white down. Her slateblue skirts were kilted boldly about her waist and dovetailed behind her. Her bosom was a bird's, soft and slight, slight and soft, as the breast of some dark plummaged dove. But her long fair hair was girlish: and touched with the wonder of mortal beauty, her face.[13]

A man reading this passage is invited to identify with Stephen, to feel "the riot in his blood," and, thus, to ratify the alleged universality of the experience. Whether or not the sight of a girl on the beach has ever provoked similar emotions in him, the male reader is invited to feel his *difference* (concretely, *from the girl*) and to equate that with the universal. Relevant here is Lévi-Strauss's theory that woman functions as currency exchanged between men. The woman in the text converts the text into a woman, and the circulation of this text/woman becomes the central ritual that establishes the bond between the author and his male readers.[14]

The same text affects a woman reader differently. Judith Fetterley gives the most explicit theory to date about the dynamics of the woman reader's encounter with androcentric literature. According to Fetterley, notwithstanding the prevalence of the castrating bitch stereotype, "the cultural reality is not the emasculation of men by women, but the *immasculation* of women by men. As readers and teachers and scholars, women are taught to think as men, to identify with a male point of view, and to accept as normal and legitimate a male system of values, one of whose central principles is misogyny."[15]

The process of immasculation does not impart virile power to the woman reader. On the contrary, it doubles her oppression. She suffers "not simply the powerlessness which derives from not seeing one's experience articulated, clarified, and legitimized in art, but more significantly, the powerlessness which results from the endless division of self against self, the consequence of the invocation to identify as male while being reminded that to be male — to be universal — . . . is to be *not female*."[16]

A woman reading Joyce's novel of artistic awakening, and in particular the passage quoted above, will, like her male counterpart, be invited to identify with Stephen and therefore to ratify the equation of maleness with the universal. Androcentric literature is all the more efficient as an instrument of sexual politics because it does not allow the woman reader to seek refuge in her difference. Instead, it draws her into a process that uses her against herself. It solicits her complicity in the elevation of male difference into universality and, accordingly, the denigration of female difference into otherness without reciprocity. To be sure, misogyny is abundant in the literary canon.[17] It is important, however, that Fetterley's argument can stand on a weaker premise. Androcentricity is a sufficient condition for the process of immasculation.

Feminist critics of male texts, from Kate Millett to Judith Fetterley, have worked under the sign of the "Resisting Reader." Their goal is to disrupt the process of immasculation by exposing it to consciousness, by disclosing the androcentricity of what has customarily passed for the universal. However, feminist criticism written under the aegis of the resisting reader leaves certain questions unanswered, questions that are becoming ripe for feminist analysis: Where does the text get its power to draw us into its designs? Why do some (not all) demonstrably sexist texts remain appealing even after they have been subjected to thorough feminist critique? The usual answer—that the power of male texts is the power of the false consciousness into which women as well as men have been socialized—oversimplifies the problem and prevents us from comprehending both the force of literature and the complexity of our responses to it.

Fredric Jameson advances a thesis that seems to me to be a good starting point for the feminist reconsideration of male texts: "The effectively ideological is also at the same time necessarily utopian."[18] This thesis implies that the male text draws its power over the female reader from authentic desires, which it rouses and then harnesses to the process of immasculation.

A concrete example is in order. Consider Lawrence's *Women in Love,* and for the sake of simplicity, concentrate on Birkin and Ursula. Simone de Beauvoir and Kate Millet have convinced me that this novel is sexist. Why does it remain appealing to me? Jameson's thesis prompts me to answer this question by examining how the text plays not only on my false consciousness but also on my authentic liberatory aspirations—that is to say, on the very impulses that drew me to the feminist movement.

The trick of role reversal comes in handy here. If we reverse the roles of Birkin and Ursula, the ideological components (or at least the most egregious of these, e.g., the analogy between women and horses) stand out as absurdities. Now, if we delete these absurd components while keeping the roles reversed, we have left the story of a woman struggling to combine her passionate desire for autonomous conscious being with an equally passionate desire for love and for other human bonds. This residual story is not far from one we would welcome as expressive of a feminist sensibility. Interestingly enough, it also intimates a novel Lawrence might have written, namely, the proper sequel to *The Rainbow.*

My affective response to the novel Lawrence did write is bifurcated. On the one hand, because I am a woman, I am implicated in the representation of Ursula and in the destiny Lawrence has prepared for her: man is the son of god, but woman is the daughter of man. Her vocation is to witness his transcendence in rapt silence. On the other hand, Fetterley is correct that I am also induced to identify with Birkin, and in so doing, I am drawn into complicity with the reduction of Ursula, and therefore of myself, to the role of the other.

However, the process of immasculation is more complicated than Fetterley allows. When I identify with Birkin, I unconsciously perform the two-stage rereading described above. I reverse the roles of Birkin and Ursula and I suppress the obviously ideological components that in the process show up as absurdities. The identification with Birkin is emotionally effective because, stripped of its patriarchal trappings, Birkin's struggle and his utopian vision conform to my own. To the extent that I perform this feminist rereading *unconsciously,* I am captivated by the text. The stronger my desire for autonomous selfhood and for love, the stronger my identification with Birkin, and the more intense the experience of bifurcation characteristic of the process of immasculation.

The full argument is beyond the scope of this essay. My point is that *certain* (not all) male texts merit a dual hermeneutic: a negative hermeneutic that discloses their complicity with patriarchal ideology, and a positive hermeneutic that recuperates the utopian moment — the authentic kernel — from which they draw a significant portion of their emotional power.[19]

Reading Women's Writing

Showalter is correct that feminist criticism has shifted emphasis in recent years from "critique" (primarily) of male texts to "gynocritics," or the study of women's writing. Of course, it is worth remembering that the latter has always been on the feminist agenda. *Sexual Politics,* for example, contains not only the critique of Lawrence, Miller, and Mailer that won Millett such notoriety, but also her memorable rereading of *Villette*.[20] It is equally true that interest in women's writing has not entirely supplanted the critical study of patriarchal texts. In a sense "critique" has provided the bridge from the study of male texts to the study of female texts. As feminist criticism shifted from the first to the second, "feminist critique" turned its attention from androcentric texts per se to the androcentric critical strategies that pushed women's writing to the margins of the literary canon. The earliest examples of this genre (for instance, Showalter's "The Double Critical Standard" and Carol Ohmann's "Emily Brontë in the Hands of Male Critics") were concerned primarily with describing and documenting the prejudice against women writers that clouded the judgment of well-placed readers, that is, reviewers and critics.[21] Today we have more sophisticated and more comprehensive analyses of the androcentric critical tradition.

One of the most cogent of these is Nina Baym's analysis of American literature.[22] Baym observes that, as late as 1977, the American canon of major writers did not include a single woman novelist. And yet, in terms of numbers and commercial success, women novelists have probably dominated American literature since the middle of the nineteenth century. How to explain this anomaly?

One explanation is simple bias of the sort documented by Showalter, Ohmann, and others. A second is that women writers lived and worked under social conditions that were not particularly conducive to the production of "excellent" literature: "There tended to be a sort of immediacy in the ambitions of literary women leading them to professionalism rather than artistry, by choice as well as by social pressure and opportunity."[23] Baym adduces a third, more subtle, and perhaps more important reason. There are, she argues, "gender-related restrictions that do not arise out of the cultural realities contemporary with the writing woman, but out of later critical theories . . . which impose their concerns anachronistically, after the fact, on an earlier period."[24] If one reads the critics most instrumental in forming the current theories about American literature (Matthiessen, Chase, Feidelson, Trilling, etc.), one finds that the theoretical model for the canonical American novel is the "melodrama of beset manhood." To accept this model is also to accept as a consequence the exclusion from the canon of "melodramas of beset womanhood," as well as virtually all fiction centering on the experience of women.[25]

The deep symbiotic relationship between the androcentric canon and androcentric modes of reading is well summarized by Kolodny.

Insofar as we are taught to read, what we engage are not texts, but paradigms. . . . Insofar as literature is itself a social institution, so, too, reading is a highly socialized — or learned — activity. . . . We read well, and with pleasure, what we already know how to read; and what we know how to read is to a large extent dependent on what we have already read [works from which we have developed our expectations and learned our interpretive strategies]. What we then choose to read — and, by extension, teach and thereby "canonize" — usually follows upon our previous reading.[26]

We are caught, in other words, in a rather vicious circle. An androcentric canon generates androcentric interpretive strategies, which in turn favor the canonization of androcentric texts and the marginalization of gynocentric ones. To break this circle, feminist critics must fight on two fronts: for the revision of the canon to include a significant body of works by women, and for the development of the reading strategies consonant with the concerns, experiences, and formal devices that constitute these texts. Of course, to succeed, we also need a community of women readers who are qualified by experience, commitment, and training, and who will enlist the personal and institutional resources at their disposal in the struggle.[27]

. . .

Feminist Models of Reading: A Summary*

As I noted in the second section, mainstream reader-response theory is preoccupied with two closely related questions: (1) Does the text manipulate the reader, or does the reader manipulate the text to produce the meaning that suits her own interests? and (2) What is "in" the text? How can we distinguish what it supplies from what the reader supplies? Both of these questions refer to the subject-object relation that is established between reader and text during the process of reading. A feminist theory of reading also elaborates this relationship, but for feminists, gender — the gender inscribed in the text as well as the gender of the reader — is crucial.

*The preceding section, focusing on an essay by Adrienne Rich entitled "Vesuvius at Home: The Power of Emily Dickinson," has been omitted. — Editors

Hence, the feminist story has two chapters, one concerned with male texts and the other with female texts.

The focus of the first chapter is the experience of the woman reader. What do male texts *do* to her? The feminist story takes the subject-object relation of reading through three moments. The phrasing of the basic question signals the first moment. Control is conferred on the text: the woman reader is immasculated by the text. The feminist story fits well at this point in Iser's framework. Feminists insist that the androcentricity of the text and its damaging effects on women readers are not figments of their imagination. These are implicit in the "schematized aspects" of the text. The second movement, which is similarly consonant with the plot of Iser's story, involves the recognition of the crucial role played by the subjectivity of the woman reader. Without her, the text is *no-thing*. The process of immasculation is latent in the text, but it finds its actualization only through the reader's activity. In effect, the woman reader is the agent of her own immasculation.[28]

Here we seem to have a corroboration of Culler's contention that dualistic models of reading inevitably disintegrate into one of two monisms. Either the text (and, by implication, the author) or the woman reader is responsible for the process of immasculation. The third moment of the subject-object relation — ushered in by the transfiguration of the heroine into a feminist — breaks through this dilemma. The woman reader, now a feminist, embarks on a critical analysis of the reading process, and she realizes that the text has power to structure her experience. Without androcentric texts she will not suffer immasculation. However, her recognition of the power of the text is matched by her awareness of her essential role in the process of reading. Without her, the text is nothing — it is inert and harmless. The advent of feminist consciousness and the accompanying commitment to emancipatory praxis reconstitutes the subject-object relationship within a dialectical rather than a dualistic framework, thus averting the impasse described by Culler between the "dualism of narrative" and the "monism of theory." In the feminist story, the breakdown of Iser's dualism does not indicate a mistake or an irreducible impasse, but the necessity of *choosing* between two modes of reading. The reader can submit to the power of the text, or she can take control of the reading experience. The recognition of the existence of a choice suddenly makes visible the normative dimension of the feminist story: She *should* choose the second alternative.

But what does it mean for a reader to take control of the reading experience? First of all, she must do so without forgetting the androcentricity of the text or its power to structure her experience. In addition, the reader taking control of the text is not, as in Iser's model, simply a matter of selecting among the concretizations allowed by the text. Recall that a crucial feature of the process of immasculation is the woman reader's bifurcated response. She reads the text both as a man and as a woman. But in either case, the result is the same: she confirms her position as other. Taking control of the reading experience means reading the text as it was *not* meant to be read, in fact, reading it against itself. Specifically, one must identify the nature of the choices proffered by the text and, equally important, what the text precludes — namely, the possibility of reading as a woman *without* putting one's self in the position of the other, of reading so as to affirm womanhood as another, equally valid, paradigm of human existence.

All this is easier said than done. It is important to realize that reading a male text, no matter how virulently misogynous, could do little damage if it were an isolated event. The problem is that within patriarchal culture, the experience of immasculation is paradigmatic of women's encounters with the dominant literary and critical traditions. A feminist cannot simply refuse to read patriarchal texts, for they are everywhere, and they condition her participation in the literary and critical enterprise. In fact, by the time she becomes a feminist critic, a woman has already read numerous male texts — in particular, the most authoritative texts of the literary and critical canons. She has introjected not only androcentric texts, but also androcentric reading strategies and values. By the time she becomes a feminist, the bifurcated response characteristic of immasculation has become second nature to her. The feminist story stresses that patriarchal constructs have objective as well as subjective reality; they are inside and outside the text, inside and outside the reader.

The pervasiveness of androcentricity drives feminist theory beyond the individualistic models of Iser and of most reader-response critics. The feminist reader agrees with Stanley Fish that the production of the meaning of a text is mediated by the interpretive community in which the activity of reading is situated: the meaning of the text depends on the interpretive strategy one applies to it, and the choice of strategy is regulated (explicitly or implicitly) by the canons of acceptability that govern the interpretive community.[29] However, unlike Fish, the feminist reader is also aware that the ruling interpretive communities are androcentric, and that this androcentricity is deeply etched in the strategies and modes of thought that have been introjected by all readers, women as well as men.

Because patriarchal constructs have psychological correlates, taking control of the reading process means taking control of one's reactions and inclinations. Thus, a feminist reading — actually a rereading — is a kind of therapeutic analysis. The reader recalls and examines how she would "naturally" read a male text in order to understand and therefore undermine the subjective predispositions that had rendered her vulnerable to its designs. Beyond this, the pervasiveness of immasculation necessitates a collective remedy. The feminist reader hopes that other women will recognize themselves in her story and join her in her struggle to transform the culture.[30]

Notes

I would like to acknowledge my debt to David Schweickart for the substantial editorial work he did on this chapter.

1. Wayne Booth, presidential address, "Arts and Scandals 1982," *PMLA* 98 (1983): 313. Subsequent references to this essay are cited parenthetically in the text.

2. *The Autobiography of Malcolm X,* written with Alex Haley (New York: Grove Press, 1964), p. 173. Subsequent references are cited parenthetically in the text.

3. Virginia Woolf, *A Room of One's Own* (New York: Harcourt Brace Jovanovich, 1981). Subsequent references are cited parenthetically in the text.

4. Jonathan D. Culler, *On Deconstruction: Theory and Criticism after Structuralism* (Ithaca: Cornell University Press, 1982), p. 42. (Subsequent references are cited parenthetically in the text.) Wayne Booth's essay "Freedom of Interpretation: Bakhtin and the Challenge of Feminist Criticism," *Critical Inquiry* 9 (1982): 45–76, is another good omen of the impact of feminist thought on literary criticism.

5. David Bleich, *Subjective Criticism* (Baltimore: Johns Hopkins University Press, 1978), p. 112.

6. Georges Poulet, "Criticism and the Experience of Interiority," trans. Catherine and Richard Macksey, in *Reader-Response Criticism: From Formalism to Structuralism,* ed. Jane Tompkins (Baltimore: Johns Hopkins University Press, 1980), p. 43. Poulet's theory is not among those discussed by Culler. However, since he will be useful to us later, I mention him here.

7. This argument was advanced by Samuel Weber in "The Struggle for Control: Wolfgang Iser's Third Dimension," cited by Culler in *On Deconstruction,* p. 75.

8. Stanley E. Fish, "Why No One's Afraid of Wolfgang Iser," *Diacritics* 11 (1981): 7. Quoted by Culler in *On Deconstruction*, p. 75.

9. Elaine Showalter, "Feminist Criticism in the Wilderness," *Critical Inquiry* 8 (1981): 182–85. Showalter argues that if we see feminist critique (focused on the reader) as our primary critical project, we must be content with the "playful pluralism" proposed by Annette Kolodny: first because no single conceptual model can comprehend so eclectic and wide-ranging an enterprise, and second because "in the free play of the interpretive field, feminist critique can only compete with alternative readings, all of which have the built-in obsolescence of Buicks, cast away as newer readings take their place" (p. 182). Although Showalter does not support Wimsatt and Beardsley's proscription of the "affective fallacy," she nevertheless subscribes to the logic of their argument. Kolodny's "playful pluralism" is more benign than Wimsatt and Beardsley's dreaded "relativism," but no less fatal, in Showalter's view, to theoretical coherence.

10. Elaine Showalter, "Women and the Literary Curriculum," *College English* 32 (1971): 855. For an excellent example of recent work following in the spirit of Showalter's critique, see Paul Lauter, *Reconstructing American Literature* (Old Westbury, N.Y.: Feminist Press, 1983).

11. Lee Edwards, "Women, Energy, and *Middlemarch,*" *Massachusetts Review* 13 (1972): 226.

12. Ibid.

13. James Joyce, *A Portrait of the Artist as a Young Man* (London: Jonathan Cape, 1916), p. 195.

14. See also Florence Howe's analysis of the same passage, "Feminism and Literature," in *Images of Women in Fiction: Feminist Perspectives,* ed. Susan Koppelman Cornillon (Bowling Green, Ohio: Bowling Green State University Press, 1972), pp. 262–63.

15. Judith Fetterley, *The Resisting Reader: A Feminist Approach to American Fiction* (Bloomington: Indiana University Press, 1978), p. xx. Although Fetterley's remarks refer specifically to American literature, they apply generally to the entire traditional canon.

16. Fetterley, *Resisting Reader,* p. xiii.

17. See Katherine M. Rogers, *The Troublesome Helpmate: A History of Misogyny in Literature* (Seattle: University of Washington Press, 1966).

18. Fredric Jameson, *The Political Unconscious: Narrative as a Socially Symbolic Act* (Ithaca: Cornell University Press, 1981), p. 286.

19. In *Woman and the Demon: The Life of a Victorian Myth* (Cambridge: Harvard University Press, 1982), Nina Auerbach employs a similar — though not identical — positive hermeneutic. She reviews the myths and images of women (as angels, demons, victims, whores, etc.) that feminist critics have "gleefully" unmasked as reflections and instruments of sexist ideology, and discovers in them an "unexpectedly

empowering" mythos. Auerbach argues that the "most powerful, if least acknowledged creation [of the Victorian cultural imagination] is an explosively mobile, magic
woman, who breaks the bounds of family within which her society restricts her. The
triumph of this overweening creature is a celebration of the corporate imagination that
believed in her" (p. 1). See also Auerbach, "Magi and Maidens: The Romance of the
Victorian Freud," *Critical Inquiry* 8 (1981): 281–300. The tension between the positive and negative feminist hermeneutics is perhaps most apparent when one is dealing with the "classics." See, for example, Carol Thomas Neely, "Feminist Modes
of Shakespeare Criticism: Compensatory, Justificatory, Transformational," *Women's
Studies* 9 (1981): 3–15.

20. Kate Millet, *Sexual Politics* (New York: Avon Books, 1970).

21. Elaine Showalter, "The Double Critical Standard and the Feminine Novel," chap.
3 in *A Literature of Their Own: British Women Novelists from Brontë to Lessing*
(Princeton: Princeton University Press, 1977), pp. 73–79; Carol Ohmann, "Emily
Brontë in the Hands of Male Critics," *College English* 32 (1971): 906–13.

22. Nina Baym, "Melodramas of Beset Manhood: How Theories of American Fiction
Exclude Women Authors," *American Quarterly* 33 (1981): 123–39.

23. Ibid., p. 125.

24. Ibid., p. 130. One of the founding works of American literature is "The Legend of
Sleepy Hollow," about which Leslie Fiedler writes: "It is fitting that our first successful homegrown legend would memorialize, however playfully, the flight of the
dreamer from the shrew" (*Love and Death in the American Novel* [New York: Criterion, 1960] p. xx).

25. Nina Baym's *Women's Fiction: A Guide to Novels by and about Women in America, 1820–1870* (Ithaca: Cornell University Press, 1978) provides a good survey of
what has been excluded from the canon.

26. Annette Kolodny, "Dancing through the Minefield: Some Observations on the
Theory, Practice, and Politics of a Feminist Literary Criticism," *Feminist Studies* 6
(1980): 10–12. Kolodny elaborates the same theme in "A Map for Rereading: Or,
Gender and the Interpretation of Literary Texts," *New Literary History* 11 (1980):
451–67.

27. For an excellent account of the way in which the feminist "interpretive community" has changed literary and critical conventions, see Jean E. Kennard, "Convention
Coverage, or How to Read Your Own Life," *New Literary History* 8 (1981): 69–88.
The programs of the MLA Convention during the last twenty-five years offer more
concrete evidence of the changes in the literary and critical canons, and of the ideological and political struggles effecting these changes.

28. Iser writes:

> Text and reader no longer confront each other as object and subject, but instead the
> "division" takes place within the reader [herself]. . . . As we read, there occurs an

artificial division of our personality, because we take as a theme for ourselves something we are not. Thus, in reading there are two levels — the alien "me" and the real, virtual "me" — which are never completely cut off from each other. Indeed, we can only make someone else's thoughts into an absorbing theme for ourselves provided the virtual background of our personality can adapt to it. ("The Reading Process: A Phenomenological Approach," in Tompkins, *Reader Response Criticism*, p. 67)

Add the stipulation that the alien "me" is a male who has appropriated the universal into his maleness, and we have the process of immasculation described in the third section.

29. Stanley E. Fish, *Is There a Text in This Class? The Authority of Interpretive Communities* (Cambridge: Harvard University Press, 1980), especially part 2.

30. Although the woman reader is the "star" of the feminist story of reading, this does not mean that men are excluded from the audience. On the contrary, it is hoped that on hearing the feminist story they will be encouraged to revise their own stories to reflect the fact that they, too, are gendered beings, and that, ultimately, they will take control of their inclination to appropriate the universal at the expense of women.

28 Joanne S. Frye : *Politics, Literary Form, and a Feminist Poetics of the Novel*

In "Politics, Literary Form, and a Feminist Poetics of the Novel," Joanne S. Frye analyzes the relationship between the popularity and mimetic characteristics of the novel as well as the appropriateness of "gender-based interpretation." Her claim that narrative is central to life echoes Peter Brooks, while her concern for how the novel's representational character affects it as a popular literary genre parallels Barbara Foley's discussion of mimesis and referentiality. Frye's focus on gender aligns her with Patrocinio Schweickart and Susan Lanser. Unlike Barbara Foley, however, Frye's attention to representation has more to do with "the novel's capacity to interpret and participate in cultural change" than with its ability to be documentary. Frye draws much of her analysis of the novel's flexibility and its role in cultural change from the theories of Mikhail Bakhtin. Bakhtin's name recurs throughout the later essays in this volume, suggesting the degree to which critics have integrated his ideas into contemporary theory and criticism. Defining how certain features of the novelistic tradition create possibilities for feminist criticism, Frye explains that it is through a close concern with the structural features of the novel that we can learn "to speak of women's lives and of the possibilities for changing women's lives." In a sense, then, Frye is concerned with novelistic "poetics" less to focus internally on the novel as text than to focus on how the novel works as a social force in altering consciousness and behavior. The ways in which specific novelistic structures have evolved through time may well contribute to how they function as a social force.

But Frye recognizes that the novel cannot exert pressure on society without readers. She therefore concludes that "a key agent in this contemporary reopening of conventions . . . is the presence of a feminist interpretive community." A feminist poetics of the novel, then, would have to pay attention not only to the conditions of literary production but also to the contemporary critical responses specific texts have received. Frye's essay, like Foley's, indicates how some feminist critics and theorists are now reviewing literary concepts that many structuralists and poststructuralists sought to jettison, reclaiming them for the feminist enterprise by rethinking and redefining them in terms of their ability to effect social transformation.

Joanne S. Frye (b. 1944) is Professor of English at the College of Wooster. In addition to *Living Stories, Telling Lives* (1986), from which this excerpt is taken, she has also published essays in such journals as *Studies in Short Fiction* and *Contemporary Literature.*

I

As a genre, the novel is of initial interest to feminist critics because it has some rather direct links to the kinds of discourse used in people's daily lives and, therefore, to both interpretations and reinterpretations of women's lives. Four prominent qualities of the novel suggest its direct connection to life experiences: its narrative form, its flexibility, its popularity, and its concern with the individual. As a narrative form, the novel is closely tied to the multiple narrative processes by which human beings daily shape their experience. As a flexible form, it is rather immediately responsive to patterns of cultural change. As a popular form, it is capable of speaking to and for people in their ordinary daily living. And as a form based in individual experience, it is especially able to seek out new interpretations of experience that defy the "normal." Each of these qualities participates in an initial view of the novel as related to lived experience and peculiarly open to gender-based interpretation.

Consider, first, the centrality of narrative to both the novel and the daily storytelling by which people often make sense of their experience. As anthropologists have made us acutely aware, the need to narrate is an apparently pervasive human need: the need to tell stories, hear stories, read stories; the need to make sense of lived experience through setting events in narrative relationship to each other. We use narrative to assess cause and effect in a pattern of significance, to relate ourselves to a sense of purpose, to claim a shared reality with other people, and to identify a specificity and a continuity of self through memory. In short we use the process of creating narrative shape to identify our place in the world.[1]

The need children often feel at the end of the day not just to hear a bedtime story but also to tell the events of their own day is precisely this narrative need to give meaning and pattern to those events. Doris Lessing represents this life narrative situation vividly in her characterization of a conversation between Anna Wulf and her daughter Janet in *The Golden*

An introductory section on theoretical issues in American feminist criticism has been omitted. — Editors

Notebook. The familiar childhood plea, "Tell me a story," prompts Anna to respond, "There once was a little girl called Janet" and to proceed with the tale of "how this little girl went to school on a rainy day, did lessons, played with the other children, quarrelled with her friend." The sequence continues as, in Anna's words, "Janet eats dreamily, . . . listening while I create her day, give it form."[2] The entire process, giving form to an ordinary day, is crucial to Janet's evolving self-awareness: her attempt to place herself in the world and assess her experiences as part of a meaningful pattern.

Lessing thus draws on the common awareness of children's need for narrative pattern, their primary human relationship to storytelling. The significance of this form giving in the novel — Anna's knowledge that she creates Janet's day by giving it form — is doubly powerful because Anna herself, in recording this experience in her journal, is shaping her own experience as she tells of having shaped Janet's. Her journal serves for her the same function that the story serves for Janet. Through narrative construction, both Janet and Anna are assessing their personal experiences; through narrative construction they engage in the human process of meaning making. In doing so, they have "created" their experience as a part of an interpretive construct.

Such construction is accomplished in large measure through the identification of perceived beginnings and endings, for we assess our current situation in terms of its previous causes and its projected effects. People interpret and even choose their courses of action according to their anticipated ends: projected "conclusions" such as graduation, marriage, separations, departures, births, and deaths. All such demarcating events, in anticipation, shape the human choices prior to them and, in retrospect, shape the understanding of subsequent human experiences. Narrative construction, built as it is on the interpretation of cause and effect, beginnings and endings, becomes a primary means by which we decide what constitutes a cause or effect, a beginning or an ending. Ulric Neisser's assessment of the general process of cognition implicitly identifies how narrative becomes a cognitive instrument in our daily lives: "When we choose one *action* rather than another the embedding schema usually includes some anticipation of our own future situation; like a cognitive map it contains the ego."[3] We act, that is, according to our narrative construction of experience, future as well as past. As Barbara Hardy puts it, "In order really to live, we make up stories about ourselves and others, about the personal as well as the social past and future."[4] We create experiential narratives as a way of understanding or *making* a relationship among the events in our lives.

Narrative can thus be claimed as a crucial human means for understanding lived experience, what Louis Mink explicitly calls the "cognitive" function of narrative.[5] Although cultures vary widely in their perceptions of reality and in the symbolic systems by which they make experiences perceptible, there are no known cultures which lack storytelling as a participant in those systems. As Mink puts it, "story-telling is the most ubiquitous of human activities, and in any culture it is the form of complex discourse that is earliest accessible to children and by which they are largely acculturated";[6] like Janet, children learn how to interpret their experiences through the culturally available narrative patterns. Robert Alter makes a similar point: the human being "as the language-using animal is quintessentially a teller of tales, and narration is his [or her] way of *making* experience, or . . . of making nonverbal experience distinctly human."[7] Human beings, in other words, claim and define our experiences as our own — *make* them — through the stories by which we assign them meaning. It is in this process that narrative becomes, in Frederic Jameson's phrase, "the central function or *instance* of the human mind."[8]

Because "natural narratives and literary narratives are similar in both structure and style," as Susan Lanser reminds us,[9] the novel participates in this central human activity as both model and enactment of our daily stories. We see in the novel the kinds of interpretive patterning by which we narrate our daily experiences to each other; we learn from the novel the culturally available patterning by which to structure and understand the data of our lives. As the longest and most modern narrative form, the novel serves as a crucial exemplar for the process of interpreting and giving form to lived experience. In addition, as novelistic narrative is an agent of interpretation, it becomes as well a possible agent of *re*interpretation, not only giving form but also altering accepted forms — the process central to all feminist scholarship.

The interpretive process inherent in narrative is augmented by a second characteristic of the novel: its extraordinary flexibility as a form. Introduced as "the novel," it remains in many ways "the new." Although, as literature, the novel shares the conventional nature of all literary forms, it is incomplete to say, as Northrop Frye does, "Poetry can only be made out of other poems; novels out of other novels."[10] I would dispute such an absolute claim even with regard to poetry, but it is a still less accurate claim for novels. Quite simply, the language we use in our daily lives and in the stories we tell in our daily lives is the language predominant in most novels. As "a hybrid of narrative and discursive forms,"[11] the novel is continually bending its conventions to include issues at stake in the culture in which it was written. Walter Reed goes so far as to make this feature of the novel definitionally central: the novel, he says, is "a long prose fiction which opposes the forms of everyday life, social and psychological, to the conventional forms of literature, classical or popular, inherited from the past. The novel is a type of literature suspicious of its own literariness; it is inherently anti-traditional in its literary code."[12] He goes on to assert that the "novel explores the difference between the fictions which are enshrined in the institution of literature and the fictions, more truthful historically or merely more familiar, by which we lead our daily lives."[13] The literariness that encodes and encapsulates the novel is thus especially permeable to other cultural codes of its own time; its words carry a weight similar to the weight of words used in ordinary human efforts to communicate. It is true that the reader and writer share a sort of contractual agreement shaped by the conventions of literary genre,[14] but it is also true that they share a language coded as well to the experience of daily social life: a language with the referential impact of communication.

This is not to say that language in the novel *refers* in any direct or unitary way but rather to find in its flexibility a portion of the novel's capacity to interpret and participate in cultural change. Mikhail Bakhtin's highly suggestive analysis of the novel's development traces the historical evolution of this capacity to a developing consciousness of multiple languages — "heteroglossia" — and the resulting awareness that a given language must be seen as no more than "a working hypothesis for comprehending and expressing reality."[15] In Bakhtin's view, this human recognition that *all* language acts as hypothesis evolves into the novel's special dialogic capacity to interact with its contemporary surroundings: "an indeterminacy, a certain semantic openendedness, a living contact with unfinished still-evolving contemporary reality (the openended present)" (p. 7). Thus does the novel reveal an "orientation that is contested, contestable and contesting" (p. 332). Thus, too, does its flexibility yield new interaction with social reality, new comprehension of cultural change. From a feminist perspective Bakhtin's analysis rings true: the novel has evolved in interaction with the social realities of women's and men's lives. But more crucially, the analysis points toward the significance of that flexibility now: the novel's dialogic capacity enables it to engage in "eternal re-thinking and re-evaluating" (p. 31) as it interacts with its social environment.

The incorporation of multiple languages in a dialogical form and the resulting openness to the languages and codes of lived experience have no doubt also contributed to the third characteristic I have claimed as vital to a feminist poetics of the novel: its evolution as a popular form in many ways prompted by and correlated to the rise in general literacy. In the eighteenth century, the century of its official birth in many literary histories, the novel was already a form available to a broad "social and educational spectrum."[16] Its growth and evolution over the subsequent two centuries, especially in its English-language versions, has depended on a broad readership and at least a partial incorporation of multi-class experience. Though its expressions have often privileged white middle-class experience and been shaped by male-dominant assumptions, its very multiplicity has opened its characterizations to a broader popular base, as its readership, at least into the mid-twentieth century, has incorporated a broad popular audience.

Many claims for the novel's feminist possibilities derive directly from the recognition of its popularity: its rise correlates with a rise in female literacy and middle-class leisure; its historical form is closely associated with varieties of personal relationships and the particularities of women's domestic and emotional lives; in comparison with other genres, a disproportionate number of prominent English novelists have been women, as have been a significant number of its most financially successful practitioners. Many historians of the novel have noted the primacy of women readers in eighteenth- and nineteenth-century authors' thinking about audience. Many feminist critics have noted the long and prominent association of the novel with women: as characters, as readers, as authors.[17] Decidedly, these correlations provide rich material for feminist analysis.

The correlations, however, are not without their attendant hazards for a feminist poetics. For if the novel has grown up in association with women, it has also grown up in association with the given cultural assumptions about women's lives. A tinge of irony colors feminist claims that the domestic novel freed women to enter literature as it broke down the limits of epic form: no longer defined by the feats of the [male] hero in a mythical world of fixed values, the novel now opened extended narrative to enquire into the complex and immediate experience of women's daily lives. The claims are crucial but not yet sufficient. For the realist strand of the novel, grounded in domestic detail and personal relationships, risks assault from both sides of the straits of feminist understanding of language: appropriation into the language and sexual ideology of the status quo and separatism into the world of female "difference." One assault comes from the recognition that the realist novel will not "seem credible" if it diverges radically from "people's beliefs about reality" and is redoubled in the formulaic expressions of many overtly "popular" novels.[18] The other assault comes from the claims, built upon assumptions of "difference," that women are especially good at writing novels because of their unique gifts for observation and relationship, qualities then trivialized by a male-dominant value system.[19] Obviously, the challenges can be inverted in the hands of women choosing to value difference and seek alternative ways of expressing it, but the risk still attends the novelistic perceptions of women's lives.

The potential for irony increases when we acknowledge that, as a popular form closely associated with women and often claimed by feminist criticism, the novel seems nonetheless to resist the most urgent feminist concern: the need for cultural change and the opening of possibilities in the lives of women. Thus, in contrast to a celebratory tone in some feminist analysis, a tone of resignation or despair pervades the work of a number of other significant analysts. Nancy K. Miller, for example, concludes *The Heroine's Text* with the statement that until the culture at large changes, we must either continue to read the old plots or perhaps "stop reading novels."[20] And Myra Jehlen argues that because the novel has its ideological base in the social structures of patriarchal society, it can be of little use to feminist needs for change and of little interest to feminist writers.[21]

These crucial warnings about the confinements of the traditional realist novel are joined by a warning implicit in the general academic study of the Anglophone novel: criticism of the twentieth-century novel has canonized far more male than female novelists and has simultaneously developed a more elitist view of the novel as form. On the one hand, the realist novel, with its assumptions of a popular audience, seems doomed to reinforce the status quo; on the other hand, developments away from the realist novel seem to resist women's full participation and to deny any vital connection with immediate lives of ordinary people.

How, then, can the popularity of the novel form be a resource, rather than a liability, to a feminist poetics of the novel? One answer derives from the kind of claim that Ann Barr Snitow makes for the realist novel in implementing cultural redefinitions: "The realist novel has always been the novel of such first phases. Since the inception of the form, novels have been 'how-to' manuals for groups gathering their identity through self-description."[22] Once a group has begun to redefine its beliefs about reality — once women have begun to reach new and shared understandings of their experience — the novel has the capacity to make those understandings available to a broad popular audience. But more than this: precisely because its flexibility interacts with its popularity, the novel is by definition disposed to incorporate developing perceptions and evolving kinds of discourse; its dialogic capacity, its openness to contemporary reality, its inclination toward a "decentering of the ideological world"[23] interact with its ties to popular and broad-based experience. It bears within its evolution as a popular form the protean capacity to resist cultural fixity and to reinterpret the lives of women. As a popular form, the novel has often tended to center in female characters and personal relationships; as a popular and flexible form, it has the capacity to criticize its historical limits and reassess the very lives it is sometimes accused of "fixing." Precisely as a popular form, the novel retains the capacity to evade the hazards of its popularity and help shape new understandings of women's lives.

A fourth characteristic, the novel's defining concern with individual experience, has similarly problematic but ultimately fruitful implications for feminist criticism, as it contributes to the novel's relationship to lived experience. The historical association of the novel with the notion of individualism has been noted by multiple analysts of the novel, with divergent measures of approval and disapproval: Walter Benjamin, Lucien Goldmann, Terence Hawkes, Edward Said, and Ian Watt, to name a few. Benjamin, for example, notes the birth of the novel in the isolated individual, as contrasted with the communal basis for storytelling.[24] More positively, Watt speaks of the subject matter of the novel as "individual self-definition,"[25] and Said calls the self the "primordial discovery of the novel."[26] This focus is, in part, because the novel, as an extended printed document, centers in the individual reader, alone with the book,[27] and in part because the idea of the novel has centered in the individuation of its characters.

An emphasis on the individual is decidedly troubling from a point of view, such as that of feminism, that views social forces as major determinants of human activity and that also rests on the need to claim a communal identity. Marxists, both feminist and nonfeminist, are central in the critique of individualism, for clear ideological and methodological reasons. Mary Poovey's Marxist feminist assessment of "the promises of love" in Jane Austen aptly identifies the problem with individualism as the view "that the personal can be kept separate from the social, that one's 'self' can be fulfilled in spite of — and in isolation from — the demands of the marketplace."[28] Such awarenesses seem to argue against any possibility of seeing the novel as participant in feminist change. Indeed, that too is one of Jehlen's conclusions in her analysis of the novel: the novel's "organically individualistic" form, she argues, is posited on "the special form that sexual hierarchy has taken in modern times"; the form itself precludes female characters from "becoming autonomous."[29]

But while such an argument is provocative, I think it is not, finally, compelling. For it requires a relatively static view of the novel, which ignores its flexibility as "the new," its capacity for self-criticism,[30] its historically persistent incorporation of multiple perceptions. Indeed, I am convinced that the novel's very basis in individualism has rich possibilities from a feminist perspective, initially because feminism, like the novel, is intimately tied to issues of individual self-definition.[31] By social definition — in which the novel has itself been historically implicated — women have been denied individual selfhood, have been refused the right to autonomous action and self-definition. As outsiders in a patriarchal culture, women have also been held in relative isolation from each other and from a sense of social consensus. Thus the need for a sense of individual strength and agency and for the inclusion of female experience in the cultural definition of the individual becomes crucial to overcoming the cultural falsification of female experience. It is in this process that the novel's centering in the individual can be especially fruitful for feminist analysis. I share Jehlen's view that the achievement of female autonomy has radical implications,[32] as does any redefinition of individualism to include female autonomy. Through its individualism, the novel opens onto a capacity to offer new narrative interpretations of the female individual, not as isolated and self-serving but as a strong and complex human being in social interaction with other human beings.

Again this capacity is not simply claimed, for the notion of the individual often brings with it associations of unity, sameness, identity as stasis — associations that can be used to limit women to an essentialist concept of femininity. In feminist as in other literary analysis, the self-evident accuracy of Bakhtin's assertion that "an individual cannot be completely incarnated into the flesh of sociohistorical categories" (p. 37) is often overlooked in the urge to systematize the functional interaction between plot and character. But because the novel's distinctive narrative form is multiple and flexible, it can yield an alternative notion of the human individual as multiple and flexible, rather than unitary and fixed. If the novelistic individual extends beyond the boundaries of our sociohistorical and linguistic categories, it follows that what Bakhtin calls "an unrealizable surplus of humanness" (p. 37) becomes a leading edge onto new possibilities in the ever-reopening future. In a feminist poetics, this notion of the individual as a defining center of the novel's narrative form frees the idea of an individual woman from established sociohistorical categories of femininity and allows the possibility for a redefined individualism. Once more Bakhtin's terms, if not his male bias, point the way.

> The epic wholeness of an individual disintegrates in a novel. . . . A crucial tension develops between the external and internal man [or woman], and as a result the subjectivity of the individual becomes an object of experimentation and representation. . . . This disintegration of the integrity that an individual had possessed in epic (and in tragedy) combines in the novel with the necessary preparatory steps toward a new, complex wholeness. (pp. 37–38)

The point to be taken here is the recognition that individualism in the novel, like the literary form itself, is a function of ceaseless and open-ended interaction. As the tension in an individual between external and internal — between established "categories" and a "surplus of humanness" — is inherent to the novel's dialogic form, so the notion of the complex and protean individual is an effect of that form.

In this sort of novelistic individualism, a feminist poetics can find a further expansion of the novel's capacity to speak to social concerns. Because the novel form is concerned with the lives of individuals, it opens immediately onto the social reality of both its author and its readers. Because it speaks from individual to individual — as Lessing says, "in a small personal voice" and "directly, in clear words"[33] — it affirms the possibility of social communication and of shared understanding. But because it is structured as process and shows us the "surplus of humanness," its individualism neither binds us to the known social reality nor limits its shared understanding to the absolutism that shadows the notion of "clear words." The novel's individualism itself can answer the feminist need to speak of women's lives and of the possibilities for changing women's lives.*

III

What we often take to be the formal conventions of the novel are more precisely those conventions that evolved as a part of the nineteenth-century novel's concern to represent social reality in a world subject to rapid shifts in shared cultural assumptions. As "truth" was under seige by the rise in scientific, industrial, economic, and eventually psychological sophistication, so the novel evolved conventions by which to assess human experience in the midst of such complexity. But, as critics such as George Levine and Robert Alter have pointed out, nineteenth-century novelists were themselves self-consciously aware that their novels were not re-presentations of reality but rather representational fictions shaped by conventions.[34] We could even say that the entire history of the novel is defined by this same tension: the urge to speak meaningfully of human experience in a social context coupled with the recognition that meaning is partial and equivocal. At any rate, the origin of the novel can be traced to this central recognition of uncertainty: a historical break with the univocal narratives of myth or epic, in which the old idea of narrative had been merged with an absolutist world view.[35]

From a feminist perspective, the break with mythic and epic visions is manifestly important to an understanding of novelistic conventions, for this break provides the initial departure from a vision of a social world in which women are mere objects of exchange in the battles among men or one in which women's only power is mysterious or magical. To depart from such narrative traditions and to enter instead a narrative of social complexity is to open the narrative possibilities evident in ordinary human interaction. By definition, the conventions of novelistic narrative initiate feminist understanding as they reject the fixity of meaning.

The positions of the two sexes in the stories of epic heroes underline the importance of relinquishing epic certainty: men fighting battles in which

---

*Section II has been omitted. In it, Frye discusses the movement toward developing a feminist poetics of the novel, with special attention to Sandra Gilbert and Susan Gubar's *The Madwoman in the Attic*. —Editors women serve only as booty or provocation. Helen of Troy, though most renowned, is scarcely alone either in serving this narrative function or in the mythic weight borne by the power of her beauty. Nor is Odysseus singular in encountering various and violent adventures that give shape and substance to his wanderings: as a hero of epic proportions he gains narrative presence through the completed actions of his series of conquests. Although I oversimplify to make my point, the pattern is decisive enough to need little illustration: men and women have clear sex-marked roles in the narrative forms of the epic, and for women, these roles are bound by the available images of female sexuality.

In myth and fairy tale, women are more likely to be significant agents of the tale, but here too the available roles are marked out by definitions of female sexuality and by the assumptions of univocality. It is by now nearly a cliché, evolving out of early feminist work on images of women, that these patterns of myth, legend, and fairy tale have characterized women in one of two dominant polar patterns: saint or witch, virgin or whore, angel or monster. On either side of the polarity, the vision of woman, even when she does act, is basically an objectification through her sexuality, a denial of her own complex subjective reality, a fixed perspective on her as an outsider rather than an agent of her own reality.[36] She is either the good and passive Snow White or the wicked queen her stepmother; she is Eve the temptress or she is the Virgin Mary.[37]

When the novel arises as a major narrative form, it breaks with these limitations in significant ways. As it develops what Bakhtin calls "the zone of maximal contact with the present" (p. 11), it breaks down the notions of absolute sameness in character and of absolute conclusiveness in plot.[38] In doing so it not only opens itself to notions of change and uncertainty; it also requires a reinterpretation of notions of gender. As men are no longer presented as identical with themselves, so women can no longer be easily presented as incarnations of sexually bound traits: their humanness exceeds the boundaries of sociohistorical categories.

This is why the novel's popularity, flexibility, and focus on the individual are all such powerful resources for new understandings of women's lives in the eighteenth and nineteenth centuries. This is also why the evolution of novelistic understanding turned naturally to personal relationships and hence to a more complex awareness of the dailiness of women's as well as men's lives. And this is at least one reason why women in the nineteenth century found in the novel a genre that was responsive to their own perspectives on human experience: Jane Austen, the Brontë sisters, George Eliot, and many lesser-known women novelists claimed the resources of this narrative genre to convey their own human visions.

But the sociohistorical context for these novelists remained male-dominant. They could, to some extent, write of their own experiences and perceptions but the social realities continued to set boundaries to their novelistic world. The primary arena for women's actions, in the novel as in life, was by definition domestic; and the most favored plot — also by definition — was the cultural plot for a woman's favored destiny: the "love story."

This brief historical excursus provides some explanation of why the nineteenth-century realist novel is simultaneously in favor and under attack in contemporary feminist criticism. The realist novel gave women writers access to literary voice and hence shows us the experiences of women's lives, but it also constrained their notions — and ours — of women's lives within the assumptions and values of a decidedly patriarchal society. Its conventions were both those by which women gained access to literary expression and those by which we have come to see women's lives defined as primarily domestic and relational.

But, of course, the evolution of the novel did not stop in the nineteenth century, and a feminist understanding of its resources must also take into account the issues raised by novelists of the twentieth century in interaction with their own social context. Not surprisingly, we can find in Virginia Woolf's "Modern Fiction" a crucial moment in the evolution of novelistic conventions as she rejected what she saw as the limiting conventions of novelistic form: "The writer seems constrained, not by his [or her] own free will, but by some powerful and unscrupulous tyrant who has him [or her] in thrall to provide a plot, . . . But sometimes . . . we suspect a momentary doubt, . . . Is life like this? Must novels be like this?"[39] Rejecting the realist novel, Woolf, like many another modernist, was reacting to a sense of dramatic cultural change: the breaking up of many shared cultural values, the fragmentation of modern life, the inability to trust that one's own perceptions might hold true for anyone else. She felt, too, the inadequacy of literary conventions of the realist novel to the reality of subjective experience. With the cultural change, she felt the urgency for a new literary form to characterize the altered sense of life.

Current feminist interest in Woolf has emphasized the importance of reclaiming her identity as a socialist, a political feminist, a lesbian. This is work that is extremely important and restorative after half a century of denying or obscuring these parts of her life and work. But her concern with literary conventions — her efforts at formal experimentation by which she has achieved a place as a major modernist writer — are also of crucial significance to a feminist point of view.[40] For though her observations on form are cast in a generalizing "human" context — and share, as I have said, the concerns of male modernists as well — they are of particular use in a redefinition of the novel as a way of redefining female experience. Woolf's concern was with the reshaping of novelistic conventions in order that they might better "represent" the complexities of lived experience; the modernist recognition that "life isn't like this" joins the feminist recognition that though the historical premises of "representation" are inadequate, the novel's concern to "represent" lived experience remains fundamental.[41]

To represent by redefining the premises of representation: this, then, was the problem Woolf saw in her own relationship to her social context and to novelistic conventions, as it is the problem I have made central to a feminist understanding of the novel. As Woolf was well aware, the shifting of novelistic conventions can only be an ongoing process, not something that can be accomplished by feminist fiat. But novelists have always used literary conventions and been aware that readers bring conventional expectations to their novel reading; and the self-conscious play with these expectations has participated in our sense of the novel's malleability and its potential for portraying experience in new ways. With this knowledge, contemporary feminist critics, novelists, and novel readers can follow Woolf and find in the historical shifting of these conventions a peculiarly useful access to ways of redefining our cognitive strategies: not a feminist fiat but a feminist claiming of the culturally available strategies for change.

The premises of novelistic representation are not bound by strongly defined formal conventions, but our understanding of the realist novel is nonetheless structured by novelistic conventions in four broadly defined areas: plot, character, reality, and thematic unity.[42] The modernist breaking up of the codes and expectations in these areas was a clear refusal of the world view offered in the great novels of nineteenth-century realism and a denial that that view of "reality" had a special claim on the "real." Alain Robbe-Grillet's characterization of the "old novel" is indicative of what his predecessors in the twentieth century were rejecting before him: a "Balzacian character," "chronological plot," and "transcendent humanism."[43] Furthermore, like his predecessors, he also rejects the notion that reality is "already entirely constituted" and asserts that "not only does each of us see in the world his [or her] own reality, but . . . the novel is precisely what creates it."[44] Thus the conventions of representation in the nineteenth-century novel are seen as unviable for interpreting complex lived experience, especially in the modern world.

These "old" novelistic conventions are also the conventions that have been demonstrably problematic for any view of autonomous women characters and for characterizing female experience outside the assumptions of male dominance. Women have been bound by the anticipated resolution of plot difficulties in marriage, death, or painful isolation, by the definition of character in terms of the traits of "femininity," by the presentation of reality as the relational and domestic social context that the dominant sexual ideology presumes for women, and by the coherence of the love story. Thus a feminist poetics of the novel can usefully join modernists and postmodernists in rejecting such conventions. But since the necessity of a shared community, the desire for a meaningful place in the world, and the importance of assessing actual lived experience are also central to a feminist view, much of the postmodernist movement toward self-contained structures of verbal play or Robbe-Grillet's object-centered texts will not in itself meet the feminist need for a redefined capacity to represent. A feminist poetics of the novel needs, then, to understand, to subvert, and finally to reinterpret the formal resources of novelistic representation. If we understand these conventions as having only the pretense of stability or self-assurance, we can avoid reifying them and find instead their available resources as cognitive strategies, self-consciously invoked in the attempt to interpret and represent a social experience that defies a full representation.

. . .

In a feminist redefinition of the conventions, then, social reality derives from the recognition that the structuring activity is a shared human need and is the effect of the culturally available paradigms by which people interpret the world around them. For women writers and readers the claiming of subjective experience and the development of narrative explanations for what is specifically female in that experience becomes a crucial way of identifying an altered social reality. Through a paradigm centered in female experience (thus raising to visibility, among other things, the previously invisible qualities of women's strength and agency) the novelistic claim to portray a view of social reality becomes a means of access to newly shared experience and provides the possibility, through the writer-character-reader triad, for a sense of community in the new shared reality.

In this view, it is not that there is no reality, as in extreme versions of postmodernist thought, but that the novelistic constitution of reality is a part of the endless interaction between information and interpretation by which we all live. Adding the previously obscured information of explicitly female experience requires a new interpretive paradigm for social reality; the development of new paradigms makes accessible new information. In voicing their own multiple subjective versions of the world, women thus come to identify their reality not in the "femininity" of the dominant paradigm, but in a shared basis of female experience at the heart of the sense-making process. This is a commitment not to an unchanging reality but to a reality of shared interpretation in process.

Implicit in the dialogical form of the novel, the refusals of determinate reality, character, and plot are thus all a part of the process by which women can "extend the real rather than dissolve it"[45] through renewing novelistic conventions for feminist understanding. In this context, the conventions of thematic unity operate pervasively in our reading of all the other narrative conventions and in their transfer to our reading of lives. The principle of thematic unity is the governing principle for selection of events by which the plot — or even the "story" — is constituted, of characteristics by which characters are concretized, of objects and information by which the external world is made present. In each case, the selection process for the reader reading and for the writer writing is based on the anticipation of thematic unity. Clearly the reading at which we will arrive — either of the life experience or of the novelistic world — is crucially dependent on the governing principle by which these selections are made. In the traditional portrayal of women, it is almost inevitably the defining unity of the love interest; the narrative coherence depends on our assumptions that the novelistic lives of women will be centered in their relationship to men. But through altered novelistic conventions, the shift in thematic unity, and particularly the insistence on multiple thematic unities emphasized by the modernist refusal of determinate form, enables the perception that women's lives can have multiple centers. It thus becomes possible to construct alternative thematic unities based on female autonomy and informed by female experience. The emphasis once again is on process rather than product, a further evolution of the fundamental novelistic understanding: explanatory structures have referential power and value but must always be subject to alteration.

A key agent in this contemporary reopening of conventions to process is the presence of a feminist interpretive community. In her analysis of the functioning of interpretive conventions, Jean Kennard hypothesizes that "literary conventions change when their implications conflict with the vision of experience of a new 'interpretive community.' " She argues convincingly that we must recognize the "nonliterary as well as literary influences" by which literary conventions are changed, and she suggests that contemporary feminist perspectives have enabled us to read differently the possibilities in earlier works such as *The Awakening,* even though readers of its own time could not see it as an expression of "women's search for self-fulfillment."[46] She sees this convention as operating in more recent novels first as a development of the concept of self-fulfillment and then as a convention that itself needed to be broken.

Implicit in Kennard's argument, though not actually worked out, is the recognition that such conventions create new cultural paradigms by which women readers read both novels and their lives and by which women writers read their perspectives on life into their novels. The feminist literary community thus provides a necessary link in the dialogic process involved in literary and cultural change: in perpetually evolving interchange, the culture and the individual interact through the formation and use of interpretive paradigms and with the intervention of newly evolved shared perceptions. The dominant culture text, the grid of expectations, is changed by the interpretive participation of individuals in the act of developing new shared conventions: women gain cultural support from other women and thus gain the perceptual capacities for forming new literary conventions and for reading lives in new ways.

In an early manifesto of feminist literary criticism, Adrienne Rich gave powerful definition to its experiential basis: "A radical critique of literature, feminist in its impulse, would take the work first of all as a clue to how we live, how we have been living, how we have been led to imagine ourselves, how our language has trapped as well as liberated us, how the very act of naming has been till now a male prerogative and how we can begin to see and name — and therefore live — afresh."[47] In spite of the differences among feminist critics, Rich's rationale for feminist criticism continues to define our unifying concerns: the affirmation of literature's interpretive power, the recognition of language as both constraint and liberation, the need to claim the agency of vision and voice in resistance to male dominance. Current work in feminist literary criticism seems most concerned with the difficulty of meeting these goals and with the recognition that language and literature continue to act powerfully as constraint.

But even these recognitions do not require the rejection of those early values or of the experiential basis for feminist criticism; they only require that our analyses are cognizant of the complexities of literary form as it both shapes and is shaped by experience. Mary Poovey has pointed out that ideology is enabling as well as restricting;[48] so, too, is literary form as long as we recognize not only its potential imposition of stasis, but also its enabling power in yielding new understandings of women's lives.

Through claiming the novel's capacity both to "represent" and to re-define the premises of representation, a feminist poetics of the novel, then, reclaims the historical potential of the novel and addresses precisely those political concerns that gave original impetus to feminist literary criticism: the fuller understanding of women's lives and the commitment to cultural change. Eagleton's claim for the distinctiveness of feminist criticism, from which I took my point of departure in this chapter, thus becomes a claim for the "life" of literary theory rather than the "death" he proclaimed in his "obituary." What is our interest in and commitment to the study of literature? Why should we want to engage with it? Enriched by the recognitions implicit in feminist literary criticism's new sophistication, the old answer reasserts itself: because it tells us something about how we live and how we might live. It helps give us that capacity "to see and name — and therefore live — afresh."

Notes

1. My view of the human importance of narrative is pervasively indebted to Frank Kermode, *The Sense of an Ending: Studies in the Theory of Fiction* (New York: Oxford University Press, 1967). In the face of more recent work in narratology, this work retains its interest as it affirms the human and dynamic rather than the structural and static elements of narrative. For an important recent effort to restore considerations of narrative to a more dynamic awareness of human needs, see Peter Brooks, *Reading for the Plot: Design and Intention in Narrative* (Oxford: Oxford University Press, 1984).

2. Doris Lessing, *The Golden Notebook* (1962; reprint, New York: Bantam, 1973), p. 363.

3. Ulric Neisser, *Cognition and Reality: Principles and Implications of Cognitive Psychology* (San Francisco: W. H. Freeman, 1976), p. 182.

4. Barbara Hardy, "An Approach Through Narrative," in *Towards a Poetics of Fiction*, ed. Mark Spilka (Bloomington: Indiana University Press, 1977), p. 31.

5. Louis Mink, "Narrative Form as Cognitive Instrument," in *The Writings of His-*

tory: Literary Form and Historical Understanding, ed. Robert H. Canary and Henry Kozicki (Madison: University of Wisconsin Press, 1978), pp. 129–49.

6. Ibid., p. 133.

7. Robert Alter, *Partial Magic: The Novel as a Self-Conscious Genre* (1975; reprint, Berkeley: University of California Press, 1978), p. 64.

8. Fredric Jameson, *The Political Unconscious: Narrative as a Socially Symbolic Act* (Ithaca: Cornell University Press, 1981), p. 13. Cf. also Christa Wolf's impassioned conviction that "[s]torytelling is humane and achieves humane effects" and "[s]tory-telling is the assignment of meaning." *Cassandra: A Novel and Four Essays,* trans. Jan Van Heurck (London: Virago, 1984), pp. 173–74.

9. Susan Sniader Lanser, *The Narrative Act: Point of View in Prose Fiction* (Princeton: Princeton University Press, 1981), p. 65.

10. Northrop Frye, *The Anatomy of Criticism* (1957; reprint, Princeton: Princeton University Press, 1971), p. 97.

11. J. Paul Hunter, "The Loneliness of the Long-Distance Reader," *Genre* 10 (Winter 1977): 481.

12. Walter Reed, "The Problem with a Poetics of the Novel," in *Towards a Poetics of Fiction,* p. 64.

13. Ibid., p. 65.

14. Cf., for example, Frye, *Anatomy of Criticism,* pp. 95–98.

15. Mikhail M. Bakhtin, *The Dialogic Imagination: Four Essays,* ed. Michael Holquist, trans. Caryl Emerson and Michael Holquist (Austin: University of Texas Press, 1981), p. 61. Subsequent references will be indicated in the text.

16. Hunter, "Loneliness," p. 459.

17. See, for example, Ellen Moers, *Literary Women: The Great Writers* (Garden City, N.Y.: Anchor Books, 1977), p. 182. See, too, Ian Watt's suggestion that the "rise of the novel . . . would seem to be connected with the much greater freedom of women in modern society." *The Rise of the Novel: Studies in Defoe, Richardson, and Fielding* (1957; reprint, Berkeley: University of California Press, 1965), p. 138.

18. Carol Pearson and Katherine Pope, *The Female Hero in American and British Literature* (New York: R. R. Bowker, 1981), p. 11; see also pp. 6–7 on the conservatism of popular literary forms.

19. See Showalter, "Women Writers and the Double Standard," in *Woman in Sexist Society: Studies in Power and Powerlessness,* ed. Vivian Gornick and B. K. Moran (1971; reprint, New York: New American Library, 1972), pp. 452–79.

20. Nancy K. Miller, *The Heroine's Text: Readings in the French and English Novel, 1722–1782* (New York: Columbia University Press, 1980), p. 158.

21. Myra Jehlen, "Archimedes and the Paradox of Feminist Criticism," *Signs* 6.4 (Summer 1981): 600. Although I disagree with a number of her major conclusions, I find Jehlen's analysis provocative and much more complex than my use of it here implies.

22. Ann Barr Snitow, "The Front Line: Notes on Sex in Novels by Women, 1969–1979," *Signs* 5.4 (Summer 1980): 705. Snitow also concludes that women novelists will continue to find "social realism" a fruitful form (p. 718).

23. See Bakhtin, *The Dialogic Imagination*, especially p. 367.

24. Walter Benjamin, "The Storyteller," in *Illuminations*, trans. Harry Zohn (New York: Schocken, 1969), p. 87.

25. Watt, "Serious Reflections on *The Rise of the Novel*," in *Towards a Poetics of Fiction*, p. 102.

26. Edward Said, *Beginnings: Intention and Method* (Baltimore: Johns Hopkins University Press, 1975), p. 141.

27. See Hunter, "Loneliness," esp. p. 471.

28. Mary Poovey, "*Persuasion* and the Promises of Love," in *The Representation of Women in Fiction*, ed. Carolyn G. Heilbrun and Margaret R. Higonnet (Baltimore: Johns Hopkins University Press, 1983), p. 172.

29. Jehlen, "Archimedes," p. 595.

30. Bakhtin speaks repeatedly of the novel's distinctive capacity to criticize itself (e.g., *The Dialogic Imagination*, pp. 6, 49, and 412).

31. I share Eagleton's view that a concern for "the experience of the human subject" is participant in the political basis of feminist criticism because "sexism and gender roles are questions which engage the deepest personal dimensions of life" (p. 149).

32. Jehlen, "Archimedes," p. 600.

33. Lessing, *A Small Personal Voice*, ed. Paul Schlueter (New York: Alfred A. Knopf, 1974), p. 21.

34. George Levine, *The Realistic Imagination: English Fiction from Frankenstein to Lady Chatterley* (Chicago: University of Chicago Press, 1981); Alter.

35. For an extended treatment of this historical break, see the essay titled "Epic and Novel: Toward a Methodology for the Study of the Novel," Bakhtin, *The Dialogic Imagination*, pp. 3–40.

36. See Sherry Ortner's anthropological analysis of women's cultural position as "both under and over (but really simply outside of) the sphere of culture's hegemony." "Is Female to Male as Nature Is to Culture?" in *Woman, Culture, and Society*, ed. Michelle Zimbalist Rosaldo and Louise Lamphere (Stanford: Stanford University Press, 1974), pp. 66–87, esp. p. 86.

37. For a powerful reading of this pattern, see Gilbert and Gubar, *The Madwoman in the Attic: The Woman Writer and the Nineteenth-Century Literary Imagination* (New Haven: Yale University Press, 1979), pp. 3–44.

38. Following Bakhtin, I recognize that "novelization" evolved gradually and was evident well before the development of what we generally recognize as the genre of the novel. See especially "From the Prehistory of Novelistic Discourse," pp. 41–83.

39. Virginia Woolf, "Modern Fiction," in *Collected Essays* (New York: Harcourt, Brace and World, 1967), 2:106.

452 Joanne S. Frye

452 Joanne S. Frye

40. Cf. Gillian Beer, "Beyond Determinism: George Eliot and Virginia Woolf," in *Women Writing and Writing about Women:* "The eschewing of plot as an aspect of her feminism" (p. 95).

41. Cf. Carolyn A. Durham's argument that women's experimental uses of narrative form, as evident in Marie Cardinal, are different from the New Novel because they are concerned with lived experience. "Feminism and Formalism: Dialectical Structures in Marie Cardinal's *Une Vie pour deux*," *Tulsa Studies in Women's Literature* 4.1 (Spring 1985): 94. I am indebted to Durham for insights in conversation on the novel and its experimental forms, as well as on feminism.

42. For analysis of more specific "codes" that can be grouped into these areas, see Barthes, "An Introduction to the Structural Analysis of Narrative," and his analysis of Balzac in *S/Z*, trans. Richard Miller (New York: Hill and Wang, 1974); see, too, Jonathan Culler's summary of structuralist codes in *Structuralist Poetics: Structuralism, Linguistics, and the Study of Literature* (Oxford: Oxford University Press, 1977), pp. 173–79; his assessment of the interaction between narrative conventions of causation is particularly suggestive (pp. 176–77).

43. Alain Robbe-Grillet, *For a New Novel: Essays on Fiction,* trans. Richard Howard (New York: Grove, 1965), p. 168.

44. Ibid., pp. 160, 161.

45. This is Robert Anchor's suggestion for what will happen if contemporary realism makes effective use of the possibilities evident in postmodernist literature. "Realism and Ideology: The Question of Order," *History and Theory* 22.2 (May 1983): 119.

46. Jean E. Kennard, "Convention Coverage or How to Read Your Own Life," *New Literary History* 13.1 (Autumn 1981): 84, 71, and 71–72, respectively.

47. Adrienne Rich, "When We Dead Awaken: Writing as Re-Vision," in *On Lies, Secrets, and Silence* (New York: Norton, 1979), p. 33.

48. Poovey, "*Persuasion* and the Promises of Love," p. 178.

Susan S. Lanser : *Toward a Feminist*
Narratology

While it can be said that critics like Peter Brooks and Barbara Foley have developed their theories by reacting against prominent trends within structuralism and poststructuralism, others have developed theirs as extensions and syntheses of existing theories. Such is the case, for instance, with Schweickart's responsive feminist reader, Frye's poetics of social transformation, and the essay by Susan Lanser, "Toward a Feminist Narratology." Lanser builds on work she herself initiated in *The Narrative Act,* a book in which she elaborated a poetics that could address the subtle ways a woman writer's subversive voice operates within standard novelistic conventions. Narratology, particularly in Gérard Genette's theories, developed through the conceptions of voicing and double-voicing developed by Bakhtin. Lanser extends these conceptions in order to focus on "the notions of public and private levels as an additional category" of narrative analysis that is especially pertinent "to the study of women's texts."

Lanser claims that "for women writers, as feminist criticism has long noted, the distinction between private and public contexts is a crucial and complicated one." She believes that developing a feminist theory of narratology will enable us to differentiate "between purely formal and contextual approaches to meaning in narrative." Many contemporary theorists of fiction share Lanser's concern that differences in geography and time are constantly working against any belief in universal and unchanging critical categories. What Lanser does not address, since it is not her purpose, is the question of whether contextualizing of narrative and genre needs to be conducted from such additional perspectives as race, class, and sexual orientation. Henry Louis Gates, Jr.'s "The Blackness of Blackness" suggests one answer to this question.

Susan S. Lanser is Professor of Comparative Literature and English and Affiliate Professor of Women's Studies at the University of Maryland. She is the author of *The Narrative Act: Point of View in Prose Fiction* (1981), and *Fictions of Authority: Women Writers and Narrative Voice* (1992). She has also coedited with the Folger Collective *Women Critics, 1660–1820* (1996).

What you choose and reject theoretically, then, depends upon what you are practically trying to do. This has always been the case with literary criticism: it is simply that it is often very reluctant to realize the fact. In any academic study we select the objects and methods of procedure which we believe the most important, and our assessment of their importance is governed by frames of interest deeply rooted in our practical forms of social life. Radical critics are no different in this respect: it is just that they have a set of social priorities with which most people at present tend to disagree. This is why they are commonly dismissed as "ideological," because "ideology" is always a way of describing other people's interests rather than one's own.

— Terry Eagleton, *Literary Theory*

. . .

I would like to begin the movement toward a feminist narratology by identifying some of the questions a feminist reading might raise for narratology. I will emphasize here not so much the fruitful applications which narratology could currently offer but the questions that it does not yet seem to have addressed. I have chosen, instead of a typical piece of fiction, a far more anomalous work because it presents many complexities in a short space of text and allows me to examine several aspects of women's writing and writing in general. The text is a letter, allegedly written by a young bride whose husband censored her correspondence. It appeared in *Atkinson's Casket* in April 1832, sandwiched between a discussion of angels and directions for "calisthenic exercises."[1] No indication is given of the letter's source, authenticity, or authorship. I am assuming, but cannot be certain, that it is apocryphal; I make no assumptions about the author's sex. Here is the text as it appears in the *Casket:*

FEMALE INGENUITY

Secret Correspondence. — A young Lady, newly married, being obliged to show her husband all the letters she wrote, sent the following to an intimate friend.

I cannot be satisfied, my Dearest Friend!
blest as I am in the matrimonial state.
unless I pour into your friendly bosom,
which has ever been in unison with mine,
the various deep sensations which swell
with the liveliest emotions of pleasure
my almost bursting heart. I tell you my dear

The ellipses indicate omission of the introductory section on the history of the relationship of feminism and narratology. — Editors

husband is one of the most amiable of men,
I have been married seven weeks, and
have never found the least reason to
repent the day that joined us, my husband is
in person and manners far from resembling
ugly, crass, old, disagreeable, and jealous
monsters, who think by confining to secure;
a wife, it is his maxim to treat as a
bosom-friend and confidant, and not as a
plaything or menial slave, the woman
chosen to be his companion. Neither party
he says ought to obey implicitly; —
but each yield to the other by turns —
An ancient maiden aunt, near seventy,
a cheerful, venerable, and pleasant old lady,
lives in the house with us — she is the delight of both young and old — she is civil to all the neighborhood round,
generous and charitable to the poor —
I know my husband loves nothing more
than he does me; he flatters me more
than the glass, and his intoxication
(for so I must call the excess of his love)
often makes me blush for the unworthiness
of its object, and I wish I could be more deserving
of the man whose name I bear. To
say all in one word, my dear, and to
crown the whole, my former gallant lover
is now my indulgent husband, my fondness
is returned, and I might have had
a Prince, without the felicity I find with
him. Adieu! May you be as blest as I am unable to wish that I could be more
happy.

N.B. — The key to the above letter is to read the first and then every alternate line.

For purposes of easy reference, I reproduce below the decoded subtext that this reading of alternate lines will yield:

I cannot be satisfied, my Dearest Friend!
unless I pour into your friendly bosom,
the various deep sensations which swell
my almost bursting heart. I tell you my dear
I have been married seven weeks, and
repent the day that joined us, my husband is
ugly, crass, old, disagreeable, and jealous[;]
a wife, it is his maxim to treat as a
plaything or menial slave, the woman
he says ought to obey implicitly; —
An ancient maiden aunt, near seventy,
lives in the house with us — she is the devil to all the neighborhood round.
I know my husband loves nothing more
than the glass, and his intoxication
often makes me blush for the unworthiness
of the man whose name I bear. To
crown the whole, my former gallant lover
is returned, and I might have had
him. Adieu! May you be as blest as I am unhappy.

Written for two readers (the prying husband and the intimate friend) this letter is in an unusually obvious sense a double construction, a blatant specimen of writing over and under censorship. The surface text and subtext are strikingly different both in story and narration, and a narrative theory adequate for describing the whole will have to account for both and for the narrative frame that binds them. In particular, such a text raises for discussion questions about narrative voice, narrative situation, and plot.

Perhaps the most obvious difference between the letters, apart from their contrasting stories, is the difference between the two voices. Some linguists have argued that there is a "woman's language" or a discourse of the powerless:[2] speech that is "polite, emotional, enthusiastic, gossipy, talkative, uncertain, dull, and chatty" in contrast to men's speech or powerful speech, which is "capable, direct, rational, illustrating a sense of humor, unfeeling, strong (in tone and word choice) and blunt" (Kramarae, p. 58). The two letters illustrate many of the differences between these two modes of speech. The surface text is virtually a sampler of "women's language": its self-effacing narrator praises the "more deserving" husband and blushes for her own "unworthiness"; her "liveliest emotions" generate a discourse of repetition, hyperbole, convolution, and grammatical anomaly. It is the voice of one who clearly can*not* "say all in one word," who can assert herself only in empty phrases and a syntax of negativity. The voice of the subtext is, by contrast, strikingly simple and direct, in the kind of language that commands (an all-too-ready) authority.[3] This second narrator shows herself angry, strong, decisive, sure of her judgments, acutely aware of her husband's deficiencies and of her own lost opportunities. Her speech acts — "I repent," "I know," "she is the devil," "I am unhappy" — are acts of conviction; such a voice requires enormous confidence and would probably be accorded an immediate credibility. Beneath the "feminine" voice of self-effacement and emotionality, then, lies the "masculine" voice of authority that the writer cannot inscribe openly. The subtext also exposes the surface text, and hence the surface voice, as a subterfuge, revealing the "feminine style" to be a caricature donned to mask a surer voice in the process of communicating to a woman under the watchful eyes of a man. But this also means that the powerless form called "women's language" is revealed as a potentially subversive — hence powerful — tool.

In *The Narrative Act* I called for a poetics that would go beyond formal classifications in order to describe the subtle but crucial differences between voices like these. For in structural terms the two voices are similar: both are first-person/protagonist (autodiegetic) narrators (though they are addressing different narratees). Most of the qualities that distinguish the two voices have yet to be codified by narratology. One might ask, for example, what kinds of illocutionary acts the narrator undertakes and whether she undertakes them in a discourse of "presence" or "absence," if we take "absence" to encompass such practices as "irony, ellipsis, euphemism, litotes, periphrasis, reticence, pretermission, digression, and so forth" (Hamon, p. 99). This question, in turn, might lead to a (much-needed) theory that would define and describe *tone* in narrative. Tone might be conceived at least in part as a function of the relationship between the deep and superficial structures of an illocutionary act (e.g., the relationship between an act of judgment and the language in which the judgment is expressed).

This double text recalls an even sharper lesson about narrative voice, the lesson formulated by Bakhtin: that in narrative there is no single voice, that in far subtler situations than this one, voice impinges upon voice, yielding a structure in which discourses of and for the other constitute the discourses of self; that, to go as far as Wayne Booth does, "We are constituted in polyphony" (p. 51). The blatant heteroglossia of this letter — and I shall suggest below that it is even more layered than it at first appears — is but a sharper version of the polyphony of all voice and, certainly in visible ways, of the female voices in many women's narratives. For the condition of being woman in a male-dominant society may well necessitate the double voice, whether as conscious subterfuge or as tragic dispossession of the self. Thus in a text like Charlotte Perkins Gilman's "The Yellow Wallpaper," the narrator speaks her desires underneath a discourse constructed for her by her husband John; in Susan Glaspell's "A Jury of Her Peers" two women protect a third from a conviction for murder by communicating in "women's language" under the watchful but unseeing eyes of the Law; in novel after novel Jane Austen constitutes a narrative voice that cannot be pinned down, that can be read according to one's own desires; a novel like Marge Piercy's *Small Changes* builds a double structure through which both its author and its protagonist work out the necessity of living in a world of double discourse (Hansen). A narratology adequate to women's texts (and hence to all texts, though polyphony is more pronounced and more consequential in women's narratives and in the narratives of other dominated peoples) would have to acknowledge and account for this polyphony of voice, identifying and disentangling its strands, as recent studies by Graciela Reyes and Michael O'Neal begin to do.

If we return with this understanding of voice to the double-text letter, it is easy to identify those verbal features that distinguish one from the other by examining the forms of "excess" that were pared away in the decoding process. The first and less significant is a combination of repetition and hyperbole that serves as "filler," yielding phrases like "which has ever been in unison with mine" and "with the liveliest emotions of pleasure." The second is more important, for it creates the syntactic hinge that binds and finally transforms the whole: a series of negations that the subtext will reverse.

I . . . have *never* found the least reason to repent
my husband is . . . *far from* resembling . . . monsters
a wife, it is his maxim to treat . . . *not* as a plaything
Neither party, he says ought to obey implicitly
I am *unable* to wish that I could be more happy —

This negativity is more than the link between two texts; it is the means by which the two letters finally yield a third: a story, a third voice, a third audience. For the negativity makes of the surface text not one narrator's simple proclamation of happiness but the indictment of an entire social system. What indeed, does the surface paint but the very portrait of marriage that it claims to erase? Each negative statement suggests departure from a social norm, a norm in which brides repent their marriages, husbands are monstrous, women are treated as playthings or slaves, and women's desires are unthinkable. In other words, the surface text, by saying what one particular marriage is not, shows the terrible contours of what its narrator expected marriage to be. While the subtext condemns one man and laments one woman's fate, the surface letter condemns an entire society, presenting as typical the conditions which the subtext implies to be individual. The subtext, then, becomes an instance of the surface text rather than its antithesis; the two versions reveal not opposing but related truths. It is fitting, then, that they meet at their point of dissatisfaction, at the single line — the first — that does not change: "I cannot be satisfied, my dearest Friend!"

In the light of this reading, women's language becomes not simply a vehicle for constructing a more legitimate (masculine, powerful) voice but the voice through which the more global judgment of patriarchal practices is exercised. This text differs from the "palimpsestic" discourse feminist criticism frequently describes in which "surface designs" act simply as a cover to "conceal or obscure deeper, less accessible (and less socially acceptable) levels of meaning" (Gilbert and Gubar, p. 73). Here the "surface design" turns out to be a more damning discourse than the text it purports to protect. The text designed for the husband conceals an undertext (the text designed for the confidante), but the undertext, in turn, creates a new reading of the surface text and hence a third text designed, I would argue, for yet another addressee. This third text is the one constituted by the *public* "display-text"[4] that is the letter *as it appeared* in *Atkinson's Casket.* Its addressee is the *literary* reader; she is neither the duped male nor the sister-confidante but the unidentified public narratee of either sex who can see beyond the immediate context of the writer's epistolary circumstance to read the negative discourse as covert cultural analysis. Thus the literary context of this text provides a third and entirely different reading from the readings yielded to the private audiences of husband and friend. At the same time, it is *the knowledge of* the other two texts, the access to the private texts, that opens the third reading, in a version, perhaps, of what Genette calls *hypertextualité* (*Palimpsestes,* p. 11).

The fact that this letter has several narratees suggests the importance of recognizing the narrative levels a text may contain. Gérard Genette has made an extremely important contribution to narratology in distinguishing the multiple diegetic levels possible in a single text because one narrative may enclose or generate another (Genette, *Narrative Discourse,* pp. 227–37; *Nouveau discours,* pp. 55–64). Genette speaks of the outermost level as the *extradiegetic,* of a narrative incorporated within this one as *intradiegetic,* and of a third narrative level as *metadiegetic.* Extradiegetic narrators, says Genette, are usually "author-narrators" — Jane Eyre, George Eliot's "third person" voice — and "as such they occupy the same narrative level as their public — that is, as you and me" (*Narrative Discourse,* p. 229). But as Genette also makes clear, there is no *necessary* connection between extradiegetic narration and a public audience; letter-writers and diarists (Pamela, Werther) may also be extradiegetic narrators. Intradiegetic (and metadiegetic) narrators — Rochester when he is telling Jane Eyre the story of Bertha Mason, the characters in *Middlemarch* — are conventionally able to address only narratees inscribed *within* the text. In *Frankenstein* Walton's letters to his sister constitute an extradiegetic narrative; Frankenstein's story, told to Walton, is intradiegetic, and the monster's history, narrated to Frankenstein and enclosed within the tale he tells Walton, is metadiegetic. Genette's notion of levels provides a precise way of speaking about such embedded narratives and identifying their narratees — and for describing transgressions across narrative levels (called metalepses) like those Diderot's narrator commits in *Jacques le fataliste.*

But Genette himself recognizes that narrative level has been made too much of, and that indeed it does not take us very far. In the *Nouveau discours* he makes clear just how relative the distinction of levels is by generating an imaginary scene in which three men sit down, one offers to tell the others a story which he warns will be long, and the storyteller begins, " 'For a long time I used to go to bed early' " (p. 64). With a frame of only a sentence, says Genette, the entirety of Proust's *A la recherche* suddenly becomes an intradiegetic narration. If we look at the letter in terms of Genette's levels, we could identify as either an extradiegetic narrator or simply as an editor the voice that presents the letter as a specimen of "Female Ingenuity" and explains both its context and its secret code to the readers of *Atkinson's Casket.*[5] The diegetic level of the letter is then contingent on this initial decision. And both the surface letter and the subtext, being interlinear, exist on the same level, in an unusual case of double diegesis. Genette's notion of levels does not allow us to say much about the narrative situation of this letter because it applies only to internal relations among parts of a text. It does not describe any individual narrative act per se, and it closes off the text from considerations external and contextual.

To provide a more complete analysis of narrative level, I would propose as a complement to Genette's system a distinction between public and private narration. By public narration I mean simply narration (implicitly or explicitly) addressed to a narratee who is external (that is, heterodiegetic)[6] to the textual world and who can be equated with a public readership; private narration, in contrast, is addressed to an explicitly designated narratee who exists only within the textual world. Public narration evokes a direct relationship between the reader and the narratee and clearly approximates most closely the nonfictional author-reader relationship, while in private narration the reader's access is indirect, as it were "through" the figure of a textual persona. Such a distinction, combined with Genette's notions of both level and person, would yield the typology shown in Table 1.

I propose this notion of public and private narrative levels as an additional category particularly relevant to the study of women's texts. For women writers, as feminist criticism has long noted, the distinction between private and public contexts is a crucial and a complicated one. Traditionally speaking, the sanctions against women's writing have taken the form not of prohibitions to write at all but of prohibitions to write for a public audience. As Virginia Woolf comments, "Letters did not count": letters were private and did not disturb a male discursive hegemony. Dale Spender takes the distinctions even further, arguing that the notions of public and private concern not only the general context of textual production but its gender context as well: that is, writing publicly becomes synonymous with writing for and to men. Spender comments:

> The dichotomy of male/female, public/private is maintained by permitting women to write . . . for themselves (for example, diaries) and for each other in the form of letters, 'accomplished' pieces, moral treatises, articles of interest for other women—particularly in the domestic area—and even novels for women. . . . There is no contradiction in patriarchal order while women write for women and therefore remain within the limits of the private sphere; the contradiction arises only when women write for men. (p. 192)

The bride's letter both illustrates Spender's formulation and expands it in important ways. The only public level of narration here is the narration that presents the letter in the *Casket* as the "display" of a correspondence.

Table 1

LEVEL	PERSON	PUBLIC	PRIVATE
extradiegetic	heterodiegetic (third-person)	narration of *Emma* or *Middlemarch*	moments of "metalepse" in *Jacques le fataliste* when narrator consorts with his characters
	homodiegetic (first-person)	Jane Eyre's narration	letters of Walton or Werther
intradiegetic or metadiegetic	heterodiegetic (third-person)	?	tales of the *Heptameron* or *Scheherezade*
	homodiegetic (first-person)	the "found" memoir of Lionel Verney in Mary Shelley's *The Last Man* or Pirandello's *Six Characters*	narratives of Frankenstein and the Monster

In relation to this level, the letter itself is a private text, designed for a private readership. Yet the surface letter is intended by its narrator to be an eminently *public* text in relation to the subtext, which is the private text she urgently hopes will *not* be available to the "public" who is her husband. In terms of the I-narrator's intentions, the "public" text is indeed designed for the man, the private (indeed secret) text for the female friend. One must already, then, redefine the simple distinction of public and private to create a category in which a narration is private but is designed to be read as well by someone other than its officially designated narratee;[7] I will call this a semi-private narrative act. To the extent that the surface letter is in some sense public, it dramatizes the way in which women's public discourse may be contaminated by internal or external censorship. This, in turn, helps to explain why historically women writers have chosen, more frequently than men, private forms of narration — the letter, the diary, the memoir addressed to a single individual — rather than forms that require them to address a public readership, and why public and private narratives by women employ different narrative strategies.[8] The concept could also be applied fruitfully to texts in which the narrative level is unclear, as in Gilman's "The Yellow Wallpaper" and Craik's *A Life for a Life,* which seem to implicate a public narratee while purporting to write a private diary.

The application of the distinction public/private to literary texts requires us to think in more complex ways about the dichotomy of gender that Spender attaches to private and public discourse. Here again the letter is illustrative. For if my analysis is persuasive in suggesting the existence of a third text available only to one who has read both the second and the first, and read in the light of a particular understanding both of women and of textuality, then the public text — that is, the one which is directed by the extradiegetic narrator or editor to "anyone" — is also the most hidden text, the hardest to see, for nothing really points to its existence except itself, and it requires a reader who brings to it particular kinds of knowledge. Since it is at the public level of narration that the ideal reading becomes possible, the letter *presented as a display text* also *escapes* the gender associations of the original structure of the intradiegetic narrative (in which it seems that public = male and private = female), suggesting a kind of paradigm for reading "as a woman" that encompasses but is not determined by the question of sex. Equally, when women write novels that use private narrative forms, they are nonetheless writing for a public, and a public that cannot entirely be dichotomized in gender terms. How individual writers negotiate this complex context of gender and public-ity constitutes another important area to investigate.

The difference between Genette's formulation of narrative levels and my own illustrates, I hope, the difference between purely formal and contextual approaches to meaning in narrative. Just as speech act theory understood that the minimal unit of discourse was not the sentence but the *production* of the sentence in a specific context, so the kind of narratology I am proposing would understand that the minimal narrative is the narrative as produced. In the case of the letter that appears in the *Casket,* questions of context are closely related to interpretive possibilities. For depending on whether one sees the letter as a historical document or as a text written deliberately for display — and whether, if "display text," an imitation or a parody — different readings of the letter emerge. If the text is an authentic document, a letter actually written by an unhappy wife that somehow came into the hands of the *Casket,* then the text might become important historical evidence of the ways in which women's writing is conditioned by censorship. If the text were constructed as imitation, it stands as evidence of the *perception,* if not the historical fact, of censorship. But the letter may well have been intended as a parody of the "female style." Indeed, the history of this style, and its connection to the epistolary, provides the context for an interesting possibility. Historically, the letter has such overdetermined associations with women that what became thought of as the "female style," a style acclaimed for its artlessness, its sense of immediacy and lack of forethought, was a style tied to the epistolary mode (Donovan, "The Silence is Broken," pp. 212–14). If the letter is in fact a "display text," it may well be a display of "female ingenuity" not only in the obvious sense of a clever composition that finds a "woman's way" around censorship, but in the service of a broader and literary design: to make mockery of the assumptions about women's "artless" epistolary style, to reveal woman as man's equal in intellectual capacity. For "ingenuity," the *OED* tells us, means not only the (oxymoronic) union of straightforward openness with the genius for skillful, inventive design but also the quality or condition of being a free-born man. And if the letter was written by its own editor, it also provided a convenient and safe vehicle for criticizing male dominance, since an editor need take no responsibility for a private "found" text.

The rhetorical complexity of the letter reminds us that narrative meaning is also a function of narrative circumstance. Narratology has not yet provided satisfying language through which to make distinctions of rhetorical context;[9] feminist criticism, in its concern with questions of authenticity and authorship, might find it difficult even to talk about a text this uncertain in origin. A feminist narratology might acknowledge the existence of multiple texts, each constructed by a (potential) rhetorical circumstance. To the extent that such questions determine the very *meaning* of narrative, they are questions for narratology.

The final element of my discussion of difference between the bride's two letters — the question of story or plot — I will treat only sketchily here, for it lies outside my area of expertise. In traditional terms, the surface text — the one written for the husband — can barely be said to have a plot, and one might of course argue that it is not a narrative at all. There is not a singular verb tense in the text; every independent predication is cast in the stative or iterative mode. All the action that the text implies, hence all there is of story, precedes the narrative moment; by the time of the writing all conflict — the gap between expectations and reality — has already been resolved (and not by the protagonist's actions at all). Notions of both plot and character are strained by such a structure in which the *actant* is really a recipient, in which nothing whatever is predicted of which the fulfillment would constitute plot as it is narratologically defined. And although one could also see this stasis as the basis for a plot left to the reader's imagination, to the extent that plot is a function of modalized predication and hence of desire (Costello, Brooks), the surface text refuses even the possibility of plot: "I am *unable to wish* that I could be more happy."

Thus the first text creates stasis of both event and character, an idyll of harmony in which the "indulgent husband," as "bosom friend," is a synthesis of the confidante with her "friendly bosom" and the "gallant lover": all characters but the protagonist coalesce into one idealized whole. But the subtext does offer the elements of a possible plot. Here we have a full-blown triangle — husband, lover, wife — in which the necessity for a confidante becomes logical. The plot of this subtext is actually highly conventional: drunken husband, sinister maiden aunt,[10] gallant suitor in the wings. But here too the expectations for story, though more fully roused, are shunted aside. While there is one singular event — "my former gallant lover is returned" — the narrator says, "I *might have* had him," suggesting that there is no real possibility of change.

Can one speak narratologically of plot or even story in these two letters, or is one condemned simply to negative definitions — plotlessness, or story without plot? Narratology is rich in its efforts to pin down the nature of plot. The formulations of Propp, Bremond, Todorov, Costello, Pavel, Prince, all offer useful ways to talk about large numbers of texts, perhaps of most (premodernist) texts. But in the case of the letter, each schema fails. Although the subtext is a catalogue of acts of villainy, for example, one cannot say of it as Propp says of his folktales that "each new act of villainy, each new lack creates a new move" (92). In his canon movement is possible; here it is not.[11] The units of anticipation and fulfillment or problem and solution that structure plot according to narrative theorists of plot assume that textual actions are based on the (intentional) deeds of protagonists; they assume a power, a possibility, that may be inconsistent with what women have experienced both historically and textually, and perhaps inconsistent even with women's desires. A radical critique like Mária Brewer's suggests that plot has been understood as a "discourse of male desire recounting itself through the narrative of adventure, project, enterprise, and conquest," the "discourse of desire as separation and mastery" (pp. 1151, 1153).

If standard narratological notions of plot do not adequately describe (some) women's texts, then what is needed is a radical revision in theories of plot. For one thing, as Katherine Rabuzzi notes (in Donovan, "Jewett's Critical Theory," p. 218), " 'by and large, most women have known a nonstoried existence.' " Women's experience, says Donovan, often seems, when held against the masculine plot, "static, and in a mode of waiting. It is not progressive, or oriented toward events happening sequentially or climactically, as in the traditional masculine story plot" (pp. 218–19). This letter, or a novel like Sarah Orne Jewett's *The Country of the Pointed Firs,* can thus only be defined as a "plotless text." (Donovan, "Women's Poetics," 106). Similarly, some of Grace Paley's finest stories (for example, "Friends" and "Ruthy and Edie" in the most recent collection, *Later the Same Day*), which a traditional narratology would describe as "plotless," are constituted by plots of women's attempts to "make sense" of their world.[12] A contemporary popular novel like Meg Wolitzer's *Hidden Pictures,* which sets up negative possibilities that neither occur nor are noted *not* to occur, when measured against plot theories becomes a "flawed" story making worrisome predictions that it does not fulfill. Yet one could also see this plot as a structure of anxiety and (gradual) relief that corresponds to real-world experiences of women in the difficult circumstances of this novel's protagonists, a lesbian couple raising a son in suburbia. If again and again scholars of women's writing must speak in terms of the "plot*less*" (usually in quotation marks, suggesting their dissatisfaction with the term), then perhaps something is wrong with the notions of plot that have followed from Propp's morphology. Perhaps narratology has been mistaken in trying to arrive at a single definition and description of plot. We will learn more about women's narratives — and about scores of twentieth-century texts — if we make ourselves find language for describing their plots in positive rather than negative terms.

There is another level of plot, too, that the bride's letter urges us to think about. There is, in fact, one sequence of anticipation and fulfillment that this text does fully constitute, and it occurs in the act of writing. In the case of both letters, whether the narrator's life is happy or miserable, what she "cannot be satisfied" without is, simply, *the telling* — narrative itself. The act of writing becomes the fulfillment of desire, telling becomes the single predicated act, as if to tell were in itself to resolve, to provide closure. *Récit* and *histoire,* rather than being separate elements, converge, so that telling becomes integral to the working out of story. Communication, understanding, being understood, becomes not only the objective of the narration but the act that can transform (some aspect of) the narrated world. In a universe where waiting, inaction, reception, predominate, and action is only minimally possible, the narrative act itself becomes the source of possibility.

What happens in the letter, then, is that the wish for the other's happiness substitutes for the possibility of change in one's own life; the writer's experience serves as a (positive or negative) stimulus to the reader's own story. The confidante thus becomes an active participant not simply in narration, but in plot itself; the wish for the narratee's happiness transfers the imperatives of plot, so that the possibilities of change and fulfillment are given over to the narratee. The letter thus suggests a plot behind women's "plotless" narrative, the subversive plot of sharing an experience so that the listener's life may complete the speaker's tale. I would be eager for narratology to talk about such a crossing of the plot of narration with the story plot.

My analysis of this coded letter suggests in sketchy ways aspects of narrative that a revised poetics might scrutinize and codify. A comprehensive theory of voice would develop a framework for describing the elements that constitute polyphony and would formulate a linguistically based theory of narrative tone. Attention to the rhetorical context of narrative — its generic status and the public or private level of the narration — would be understood as important determinants of narrative meaning. And theories of plot and story would be reexamined to find alternatives to the notion of plot as active acquisition or solution and to incorporate the plot that may be generated by the relationship between narrator and narratee. Once it is clear that some (women's) texts cannot be adequately described by traditional, formalist narratology, we begin to see that other texts — postmodernist texts, texts by writers of Asia and Africa, perhaps — may be similarly unaccounted for. It is only, I believe, such an expansive narratology that can begin to fulfill the wish Gerald Prince expresses at the end (p. 164) of his *Narratology:* that "ultimately, narratology can help us understand what human beings are."

Notes

1. I discovered this letter quite accidently. While browsing through the stacks of the University of Wisconsin-Madison library several years ago, I came across an odd compendium titled *The Genteel Female,* edited by Clifton Furness. Its endpapers consist of the page from *Atkinson's Casket* that contains the letter.

2. There are three controversies embedded in this topic: whether there is in fact a "women's language," whether it is exclusive to women, and whether it is a negative characteristic. In 1975 Robin Lakoff suggested that women use language forms that differ from men's and that this language reinforces the social and political powerlessness of women. Other critics have argued that "women's language" is a fiction constructed upon sex stereotypes and that women do not actually speak differently from men. Still others agree that there is difference, but rather than seeing the difference as negative, they consider "women's language" better oriented to concern for others and to the careful contextualizing of one's beliefs (rather than the "masculine" assertion of universals). For a sense of this controversy, see Spender, pp. 32–51. A related question is whether it is more accurate to speak of "women's language" or of "powerless language." On the basis of empirical study in a courtroom context, O'Barr and Atkins found far more credibility accorded to female witnesses speaking in the "powerful style" than to those speaking in the "powerless style."

3. Richard Sennett believes that simple, direct discourse in the active voice bespeaks a confidence that frequently inspires a too-easy and hence dangerous obeisance. See *Authority,* chap. 5.

4. Mary Louise Pratt uses the term to designate a text or speech act whose relevance lies in its tellability, and which is thus detachable from its immediate circumstances of production. Literary texts and jokes are examples. See Pratt, pp. 136–48.

5. I thank Harold Mosher for the suggestion that this figure is not actually a narrator at all but merely an editor. I had been considering this voice to be similar to the one that introduces, say, the governess's narrative in *The Turn of the Screw.* The problem, I believe, lies at least in part with Genette's own system, which does not distinguish an editor from an extradiegetic narrator. Such a narrator, after all, may appear only briefly to introduce a major intradiegetic narrative and may do so in the guise of an editor.

6. I am suggesting that not only narrators but also narratees can be heterodiegetic or homodiegetic — that is, within or outside the fictional world — and that a homodiegetic narrator can address a heterodiegetic narratee (although it would constitute a narrative transgression for a heterodiegetic narrator to address a homodiegetic narratee). I have decided not to use these terms, however, in order to avoid confusion with heterodiegetic and homodiegetic narrators and because of my commitment to simplify narrative terminology.

7. This is somewhat different from the case of a letter that is intercepted by a character for whom it was not destined, as happens frequently, say, in *Clarissa.* The difference is

that in this case the narrator *knows* her text will be intercepted and has structured the surface narrative accordingly.

8. The difference between private and public narration in narratives by women are a major focus of the book I am now completing on women writers and narrative voice.

9. As Susan Léger has pointed out to me, a book like Ross Chambers's *Story and Situation* is a healthy exception to this norm.

10. I am aware that my analysis of the letters has omitted any discussion of the maiden aunt and that her "maidenness" makes her a particularly interesting figure in the context of the portraits of marriage in these letters.

11. One could argue that the presence of a lover in the subtext keeps eternally open the possibility of action, even if that action seems to be thwarted by the given text. Such a possibility testifies to the power of the desire for plot.

12. For the example of these Paley stories I am indebted to Alan Wilde, whose book *Middle Ground: Studies in Contemporary American Fiction* (Philadelphia: University of Pennsylvania Press, 1987) includes a chapter on her work.

Works Cited

Bakhtin, M. M. "Discourse in the Novel." In *The Dialogic Imagination: Four Essays,* edited by Michael Holquist, translated by Caryl Emerson and Michael Holquist, pp. 259–422. Austin: University of Texas Press, 1981.

Bal, Mieke. *Femmes imaginaires: l'ancien testament au risque d'une narratologie critique.* Paris: Nizet; Montreal: HMH, 1986.

———. "The Narrating and the Focalizing: A Theory of the Agents in Narrative." *Style* 17 (1983): 234–69.

———. "Sexuality, Semiosis and Binarism: A Narratological Comment on Bergen and Arthur." *Arethusa* 16.1–2 (1983): 117–35.

———. "Sexuality, Sin, and Sorrow: The Emergence of Female Character (A Reading of Genesis 1–3)." In *The Female Body in Western Culture,* edited by Susan Rubin Suleiman, pp. 317–38. Cambridge: Harvard University Press, 1986.

Booth, Wayne C. "Freedom of Interpretation: Bakhtin and the Challenge of Feminist Criticism." *Critical Inquiry* 9 (1982): 45–76.

Bremond, Claude. *Logique du récit.* Paris: Seuil, 1973.

Brewer, Mária Minich. "A Loosening of Tongues: From Narrative Economy to Women Writing." *MLN* 99 (1984): 1141–61.

Brooks, Peter. "Narrative Desire." *Style* 18 (1984): 312–27.

———. *Reading for the Plot.* New York: Knopf, 1984.

Chambers, Ross. *Story and Situation: Narrative Seduction and the Power of Fiction.* Minneapolis: University of Minnesota Press, 1984.

Costello, Edward. "Modality and Narration: A Linguistic Theory of Plotting." Ph.D. diss., University of Wisconsin, 1975.

Donovan, Josephine. "Sarah Orne Jewett's Critical Theory: Notes Toward a Feminine Literary Mode." In *Critical Essays on Sarah Orne Jewett.* Edited by Gwen L. Nagel. Boston: Hall, 1984.

———. "The Silence is Broken." In *Women and Language in Literature and Society,* edited by Sally McConnell-Ginet et al., pp. 205–18. New York: Praeger, 1980.

———. "Toward a Women's Poetics." *Tulsa Studies in Women's Literature* 3.1–2 (1984): 99–110.

DuPlessis, Rachel Blau. *Writing Beyond the Ending: Narrative Strategies of Twentieth-Century Women Writers.* Bloomington: Indiana University Press, 1985.

Eagleton, Terry. *Literary Theory: An Introduction.* Minneapolis: University of Minnesota Press, 1983.

"Female Ingenuity." *Atkinson's Casket or Gems of Literature, Wit, and Sentiment.* No. 4, Philadelphia, Apr. 1832: 186.

Fish, Stanley. *Is There a Text in This Class? The Authority of Interpretive Communities.* Boston: Harvard University Press, 1980.

Furman, Nelly. "The Politics of Language: Beyond the Gender Principle?" In *Making a Difference: Feminist Literary Criticism,* edited by Gayle Greene and Coppelia Kahn, pp. 59–79. London: Methuen, 1985.

———. "Textual Feminism." In *Women and Language in Literature and Society,* edited by Sally McConnell-Ginet et al., pp. 45–54. New York: Praeger, 1980.

Furness, Clifton, ed. *The Genteel Female.* New York: Knopf, 1931.

Genette, Gérard. *Narrative Discourse: An Essay in Method.* Translated by Jane E. Lewin. Ithaca: Cornell University Press, 1980. Translation of "Discours du récit," in *Figures III.* Paris: Seuil, 1972.

———. *Nouveau Discours du récit.* Paris: Seuil, 1982.

———. *Palimpsestes: la littérature au second degré.* Paris: Seuil, 1982.

Gilbert, Sandra, and Susan Gubar. *The Madwoman in the Attic: The Woman Writer and the Nineteenth-Century Literary Imagination.* New Haven: Yale University Press, 1979.

Hamon, Philip. "Text and Ideology: For a Poetics of the Norm." *Style* 17 (1983): 95–119.

Hansen, Elaine Tuttle. "The Double Narrative Structure of *Small Changes.*" In *Contemporary American Women Writers: Narrative Strategies.* Edited by Catherine Rainwater and William J. Scheick. Lexington: University Press of Kentucky, 1985.

Jefferson, Ann. "*Mise en abyme* and the Prophetic in Narrative." *Style* 17 (1983): 196–208.

Kotin, Armine Mortimer. "Narrative Closure and the Paradigm of Self-Knowledge in *La Princesse de Clèves.*" *Style* 17 (1983): 181–95.

Kramarae, Cheris. "Proprietors of Language." In *Women and Language in Literature and Society,* edited by Sally McConnell-Ginet et al., pp. 58–68. New York: Praeger, 1980.

Lakoff, Robin. *Language and Woman's Place.* New York: Harper and Row, 1975.

Lanser, Susan Sniader. *The Narrative Act: Point of View in Prose Fiction.* Princeton University Press, 1981.

——, and Evelyn Torton Beck. "(Why) Are There No Great Women Critics? — And What Difference Does it Make?" In *The Prism of Sex: Essays in the Sociology of Knowledge,* edited by Julia Sherman and Evelyn T. Beck, pp. 79–91. Madison: University of Wisconsin Press, 1979.

Lévi-Strauss, Claude. *Myth and Meaning.* New York: Schocken, 1978.

Lodge, David. *Small World.* New York: Macmillan, 1984.

McConnell-Ginet, Sally, Ruth Borker, and Nelly Furman, eds. *Women and Language in Literature and Society.* New York: Praeger, 1980.

Medvedev, P. N., and M. M. Bakhtin. *The Formal Method in Literary Scholarship: A Critical Introduction to Sociological Poetics,* translated by Albert J. Wehrle. Baltimore: Johns Hopkins University Press, 1978.

Meese, Elizabeth A. *Crossing the Double-Cross: The Practice of Feminist Criticism.* Chapel Hill: University of North Carolina Press, 1986.

Miller, Nancy K. "Emphasis Added: Plots and Plausibilities in Women's Fiction." *The New Feminist Criticism: Essays on Women, Literature, and Theory,* edited by Elaine Showalter, pp. 339–60. New York: Pantheon, 1985.

Newton, Judith. "Making — and Remaking — History: Another Look at 'Patriarchy'." *Tulsa Studies in Women's Literature* 3.1–2 (1984): 125–41.

O'Barr, William M., and Bowman K. Atkins. " 'Women's Language' or 'Powerless Language'?" *Women and Language in Literature and Society,* edited by Sally McConnell-Ginet et al., pp. 93–110. New York: Praeger, 1980.

O'Neal, Michael. "Point of View and Narrative Technique in the Fiction of Edith Wharton." *Style* 17 (1983): 270–89.

Pavel, Thomas G. *The Poetics of Plot: The Case of English Renaissance Drama.* Minneapolis: University of Minnesota Press, 1985.

Pratt, Mary Louise. *Toward a Speech Act Theory of Literary Discourse.* Bloomington: Indiana University Press, 1977.

Prince, Gerald. *Narratology: The Form and Function of Narrative.* Berlin: Mouton, 1982.

Propp, Vladimir. *Morphology of the Folktale,* edited by Louis A. Wagner. 2d ed. Austin: University of Texas Press, 1968.

Reyes, Graciela. *Polifonía textual: La citación en el relato literario.* Madrid: Greos, 1984.

Rimmon-Kennan, Shlomith. *Narrative Fiction: Contemporary Poetics.* London: Methuen, 1983.

Schor, Naomi. *Breaking the Chain: Women, Theory, and French Realist Fiction.* New York: Columbia University Press, 1985.

Sennett, Richard. *Authority.* New York: Knopf, 1980.

Showalter, Elaine, ed. *The New Feminist Criticism: Essays on Women, Literature, and Theory.* New York: Pantheon, 1985.

———. "Women's Time, Women's Space; Writing the History of Feminism Criticism." *Tulsa Studies in Women's Literature* 3.1–2 (1984): 29–43.

Spender, Dale. *Man Made Language.* London: Routledge and Kegan Paul, 1980.

Torgovnick, Marianna. *Closure in the Novel.* Princeton: Princeton University Press, 1981.

Warhol, Robyn R. "Toward a Theory of the Engaging Narrator: Earnest Interventions in Gaskell, Stowe, and Eliot." *PMLA* 101 (1986): 811–18.

Weinsheimer, Joel. "Theory of Character: *Emma.*" *Poetics Today* 1.1–2 (1979): 185–211.

30 Linda Hutcheon : *"The Pastime of Past Time"*

Fiction, History, Historiographical Metafiction

In " 'The Pastime of Past Time': Fiction, History, Historiographic Metafiction,"
Linda Hutcheon approaches the same issue that Barbara Foley addresses — the
distinction between historical and fictional events — but she does so from an
alternative direction. Hutcheon concerns herself with how postmodernist readings
of history and realist fiction demonstrate that they rely more on verisimilitude than
factuality. Whereas Foley looks at a particular type of realist fiction, the documentary novel, Hutcheon turns her attention to types of novels that she defines as
"historiographic metafiction": that is, "novels that are intensely self-reflexive."
She suggests that they are attentive to their own artifice as literary texts, "but that
[they] also both reintroduce historical context into metafiction and problematize
the entire question of historical knowledge." In other words, Hutcheon analyzes
novels that rely for their authority less on apparent historical accuracy than on
calling into question history's alleged ability to provide any authoritative commentary at all.

Hutcheon studies several examples of historiographic metafiction to display
their variety, and she determines that their skepticism plays a positive role by
opening up both fiction and history to interrogation by the present. Unlike the
traditional historical novel, postmodern works always question not only the *facts*
themselves but also the systems by which such facts are constructed, connected,
and rendered coherent. Toward the end of her essay Hutcheon makes the point that
the study of how narrative functions is key to unraveling not only the formal
complexities of postmodern fiction but the problem of representation as well. She
thus shares a concern prominent among theorists of fiction throughout the past
decade: that fiction, despite its permutations, remains fundamentally a story about
the world and our participation in it.

Linda Hutcheon (b. 1947) is Professor of English and Comparative Literature
at the University of Toronto, Canada. A major theorist and critic of the postmodern, she has authored *Narcissistic Narrative* (1980), *A Theory of Parody* (1985),
The Canadian Postmodern (1988), *A Poetics of Postmodernism* (1988), *The Politics of Postmodernism* (1989), and *Splitting Images: Contemporary Canadian
Ironies* (1991).

474   *Linda Hutcheon*

I

We theoreticians have to know the laws of the peripheral in art.
The peripheral is, in fact, the non-esthetic set.
It is connected with art, but the connection is not causal.
But to stay alive, art must have new raw materials. Infusions of the
peripheral. — Viktor Shklovsky

In the nineteenth century, at least before the rise of Ranke's "scientific
history," literature and history were considered branches of the same
tree of learning, a tree which sought to "interpret experience, for the
purpose of guiding and elevating man" (Nye, p. 123). Then came the
separation that resulted in the distinct disciplines of literary and historical
studies today, despite the fact that the realist novel and Rankean histor-
icism share many similar beliefs about the possibility of writing factually
about observable reality (Hayden White, "Fictions," p. 25). However, it is
this very separation of the literary and the historical that is now being
challenged in the theory and art of what we seem to want to label as
postmodernism. Recent postmodern readings of both history and realist
fiction have focused more on what the two modes of writing share than on
how they differ. They have both been seen to derive their force more from
verisimilitude than from any objective truth; they are both identified as linguistic constructs, highly conventionalized in their narrative forms, and
not at all transparent, either in terms of language or structure; and they appear to be equally intertextual, deploying the texts of the past within their
own complex textuality. But these are also the implied teachings of what I
would like to call postmodern "historiographic metafiction" — novels that
are intensely self-reflexive but that also both re-introduce historical context into metafiction and problematize the entire question of historical
knowledge. Like those recent theories of both history and fiction, this kind
of novel — *G., Midnight's Children, Ragtime, The French Lieutenant's
Woman, The Name of the Rose* — forces us to recall that history and fiction
are themselves historical terms and their definitions and interrelations are
historically determined and vary with time (see Seamon, pp. 212–16).

In the last century, as Barbara Foley has shown, historical writing and
historical novel writing influenced each other mutually: Macauley's debt
to Scott was an overt one, as was Dickens's to Carlyle in *A Tale of Two
Cities* (Foley, pp. 170–71). Today, the new skepticism and suspicion about
the writing of history that one finds in the work of Hayden White, Michel

de Certeau, Paul Veyne, Lionel Gossman, Dominick LaCapra, and others are mirrored in the challenges to historiography in novels like *Shame, The Public Burning,* or *A Maggot:* they share the same questioning stance toward their common use of conventions of narrative, of reference, of the inscribing of subjectivity, of their identity as textuality, and even of their implication in ideology.

In both fiction and history writing today, our confidence in empiricist and positivist epistemologies has been shaken — shaken, but perhaps not yet destroyed. And this is what accounts for the skepticism rather than any real denunciation; it also accounts for the defining paradoxes of postmodern discourses. Postmodernism is a contradictory cultural enterprise, one that is heavily implicated in that which it seeks to contest. It uses and abuses the very beliefs it takes to task; it installs and only then subverts the conventions of genre. Historiographic metafiction, for example, keeps distinct its formal autorepresentation from its historical context, and in so doing problematizes the very possibility of historical knowledge, because there is no reconciliation, no dialectic here — just unresolved contradiction.

The history of the discussion of the relation of art to historiography is therefore relevant to any poetics of postmodernism, for the separation is a traditional one, even if it is being reformulated in a different context today. To Aristotle (*Poetics,* 1451a–b), the historian could only speak of what has happened, of the particulars of the past; the poet, on the other hand, spoke of what could or might happen and so could deal more with universals. Freed of the linear succession of history writing, the poet's plot could have different unities. This was not to say that historical events and personages could not appear in tragedy: "nothing prevents some of the things that have actually happened from being of the sort that might probably or possibly happen" (1451b). History-writing was seen to have no such conventional restraints of probability or possibility. Nevertheless, many historians since have used the techniques of fictional representation to create imaginative versions of their historical, real worlds (see Holloway; Levine; Braudy; Henderson). The postmodern novel has done the same, and the reverse. It is part of the postmodernist stand to confront the paradoxes of fictive versus historical representation, the particular vs. the general, and the present versus the past. And its confrontation is itself contradictory, for it refuses to recuperate or dissolve either side of the dichotomy, yet it is willing to exploit both.

History and fiction have always been notoriously porous genres, of course. At various times both have included in their elastic boundaries such forms as the travel tale and various versions of what we now call sociology (Veyne, p. 30). It is not surprising that there would be overlappings of concern and even mutual influences between the two genres. In the eighteenth century, the focus of this commonality of concern tended to be the relation of ethics (not factuality) to truth in narrative. Both journalism and novels could be equally "false" in ethical terms. (Only with the passing of the Acts of Parliament that defined libel did the notion of historical "fact" enter this debate [Davis].) It is not accidental that, in one critic's words, "[f]rom the start the writers of novels seemed determined to pretend that their work is not *made,* but that it simply exists" (Josipovici, p. 148); in fact, it was safer, in legal and ethical terms. Defoe's works made claims to veracity and actually convinced some readers that they were factual, but most readers today (and many then) had the pleasure of a double awareness of both fictiveness and a basis in the "real" — as do readers of contemporary historiographic metafiction.

In fact, J. M. Coetzee's recent novel, *Foe,* addresses precisely this question of the relation of "story" and "history" writing to "truth" and exclusion in the practice of Defoe. There is a direct link here to a familiar assumption of historiography: "that every history is a history of some entity which existed for a reasonable period of time, that the historian wishes to state what is literally true of it in a sense which distinguishes the historian from a teller of fictitious or mendacious stories" (Morton White, p. 4). *Foe* reveals that storytellers can certainly silence, exclude, and absent certain past events — and people — but it also suggests that historians have done the same: where are the women in the traditional histories of the eighteenth century? Coetzee offers the teasing fiction that Defoe did not write *Robinson Crusoe* from information from the historical castaway, Alexander Selkirk, or from other travel accounts, but from information given him by a subsequently "silenced" woman, Susan Barton, who had also been a castaway on "Cruso" 's [sic] island. It had been Cruso who had suggested that she tell her story to a writer who would add "a dash of colour" to her tale. She resists because she wants the "truth" told, and Cruso admits that a writer's "trade is in books, not in truth" (p. 40). But Susan sees the problem: "If I cannot come foreward, as author, and swear to the truth of my tale, what will be the worth of it? I might as well have dreamed it in a snug bed in Chichester" (p. 40).

Susan tells Foe (he added the "de" only later, and so lost Coetzee's irony) her tale and his response is that of a novelist. Susan replies: "You remarked it would have been better had Cruso rescued not only musket and powder and ball, but a carpenter's chest as well, and built himself a boat. I do not wish to be captious, but we lived on an island so buffeted by wind that there was not a tree did not grow twisted and bent" (p. 55). In frustration, she begins her own tale, "The Female Castaway, Being a True Account of a Year Spent on a Desert Island. With Many Strange Circumstances Never Hitherto Related" (p. 67), but discovers that the problems of writing history are not unlike those of writing fiction: "Are these enough strange circumstances to make a story of? How long before I am driven to invent new and stranger circumstances: the salvage of tools and muskets from Cruso's ship; the building of a boat . . . a landing by cannibals . . . ?" (p. 67). Her final decision is, however, that "what we accept in life we cannot accept in history" (p. 67) — that is, lies and fabrications.

The linking of "fictitious" to "mendacious" stories (and histories) is one that other historiographic metafictions also seem to be obsessed with: *Famous Last Words, Legs, Waterland,* and *Shame.* In the latter, Salman Rushdie's narrator addresses openly the possible objections to his position as insider/outsider (i.e., an immigrant) writing about the events of Pakistan from England — and in English:

> *Outsider! Trespasser! You have no right to this subject!* . . . I know: nobody ever arrested me [as they did the friend of whom he has just written]. Nor are they ever likely to. *Poacher! Pirate! We reject your authority. We know you, with your foreign language wrapped around you like a flag: speaking about us in your forked tongue, what can you tell but lies?* I reply with more questions: is history to be considered the property of the participants solely? In what courts are such claims staked, what boundary commissions map out the territories? (p. 28)

The eighteenth-century concern for lies and falsity becomes a postmodern concern for the multiplicity and dispersion of truth(s), truth(s) relative to the specificity of place and culture. Yet the paradox is still there: when Pakistan was formed, the *Indian* history had to be written out of the Pakistani past. But who did this work? History was rewritten by immigrants — in Urdu and English, the imported tongues. As the narrator of *Shame* puts it, he is forced — by history — to write in "this Angrezi . . . and so for ever alter what is written" (p. 38).

There has also been another, long tradition, dating (as we have seen) from Aristotle, that makes fiction not only separate from, but also superior to, history, a mode of writing which can only narrate the contingent and particular. The romantic and modernist assertions of the autonomy and supremacy of art led, however, as Jane Tompkins has shown so convincingly, to a marginalization of literature, one that extremes of metafiction (like American surfiction) only exacerbate. Historiographic metafiction, in deliberate contrast to what I would call such late modernist radical metafiction, attempts to demarginalize the literary through confrontation with the historical, and it does so both thematically and formally.

For example, Christa Wolf's *No Place on Earth* is about the fictionalized meeting of two historical figures, dramatist Heinrich von Kleist and poet Karoline von Günderrode: "The claim that they met: a legend that suits us. The town of Winkel, on the Rhine, we saw it ourselves." The "we" of the narrating voice, in the present, underlines the metafictive historical reconstruction on the level of form. But on the thematic level too, life and art meet, for this is the theme of the novel, as Wolf's Kleist tries to break down the walls between "literary fantasies and the actualities of the world" (p. 12), contesting his colleagues' separation of poets from praxis: "Of all the people here, perhaps there is none more intimately bound to the real world than I am" (p. 82). It is he who is trying to write a romantic historical work about Robert Guiscard, Duke of Normandy. The metafictive and the historiographic also meet in the intertexts of the novel, for it is through them that Wolf fleshes out the cultural and historical context of the fictive meeting. The intertexts range from Günderrode's own letters to canonic romantic works like Hölderlin's *Hyperion,* Goethe's *Torquato Tasso,* and Brentano's *Gedichte* — but, in all, the theme is the relation, or rather the conflict, between art and history, between literature and life. This novel reminds us, as did Roland Barthes much earlier, that the nineteenth century gave birth to both the realist novel and history, two genres which share a desire to select, construct, and render self-sufficient and closed a narrative world that would be representational but still separate from changing experience and historical process. Today, history and fiction share a need, if not really a desire, to contest these very assumptions.

II

To the truth of art, external reality is irrelevant. Art creates its own reality, within which truth and the perfection of beauty is the infinite refinement of itself. History is very different. It is an empirical search for external truths, and for the best, most complete, and most profound external truths, in a maximal corresponding relationship with the absolute reality of the past events. — David Hackett Fischer

These words are not without their ironic tone, of course, as Fischer is describing what he sees as a standard historian's preconceptions about art and history. But it is not far from a description of the basic assumptions of many kinds of formalist criticism: "literature is not a discourse that can or must be false . . . it is a discourse that, precisely, cannot be subjected to the test of truth; it is neither true nor false, to raise this question has no meaning: this is what defines its very status as 'fiction' " (Todorov, p. 18). Historiographic metafiction suggests that truth and falsity may indeed not be the right terms in which to discuss fiction, but not for the reasons offered above. Postmodern novels like *Flaubert's Parrot, Famous Last Words,* and *A Maggot* imply that there are only truths in the plural, and never one truth; and there is rarely falseness per se, just other truths. Fiction and history are narratives distinguished by their frames (see Smith), frames which historiographic metafiction both asserts and then crosses. It posits both the generic contracts of fiction (as self-sufficient, autonomous metafiction) and of history. The postmodern paradoxes here are complex. The interaction of the historiographic and the metafictional foregrounds the rejection of the claims of both "authentic" representation and "inauthentic" copy alike, and the very meaning of artistic originality is as challenged as is the transparency of historic referentiality.

Postmodern fiction suggests that to re-write or to re-present the past in fiction and in history is, in both cases, to open it up to the present, to prevent it from being conclusive and teleological. Such is the teaching of novels like Susan Daitch's *L.C.*, with its double layer of historical reconstruction, both of which are presented with metafictional self-consciousness. Parts of the journal of (fictive) Lucienne Crozier, implicated yet marginalized witness of the (real) 1848 revolution in Paris, are edited and translated twice: once by Willa Rehnfield and once by her younger assistant after her death. The recent interest in archival women's history is given an interesting new twist here, for the two translations of the end of Lucienne's diary are so vastly different that the entire activity of translation, as well as research, is called into question. In the more traditional Willa's version, Lucienne dies of consumption in Algiers, abandoned by her revolutionary lover. In the version of her more radical assistant (a veteran of Berkeley in

1968, being sought by the police for a bombing), Lucienne stops writing, while also awaiting arrest for her own revolutionary activities. The only common denominator appears in the image that, in the Arab world of Algiers, Lucienne feels *like an invalid* — sequestered and marginalized.

The problematizing of the nature of historical knowledge, in novels like this or like Ian Watson's *Chekhov's Journey,* points both to the need to separate and the danger of separating fiction and history as narrative genres. This problematizing has also been in the foreground of much contemporary literary theory (on Lentricchia, de Man, and Derrida, see Parker) and philosophy of history, from Hayden White to Paul Veyne. When the latter calls history "un roman vrai" (p. 10), he is signaling the two genres' shared conventions: selection, organization, diegesis, anecdote, temporal pacing, and emplotment (p. 14, 15, 22, 29, 46–48). But this is not to say that history and fiction are part of the "same order of discourse" (Lindenberger, p. 18). They are different, though they share social, cultural, and ideological contexts, as well as formal techniques. Novels (with the exception of some extreme surfictions) incorporate social and political history to some extent, and that extent will vary (Hough, p. 113), just as historiography is often as structured, coherent, and teleological as any narrative fiction. It is not only the novel but history too that is "palpably betwixt and between" (Kermode, "Novel," p. 235). Both historians and novelists *constitute* their subjects as possible objects of narrative representation, as Hayden White ("Historical Text," p. 57) has argued (for history alone, however). And they do so by the very structures and language they use to present those subjects. In Jacques Ehrmann's extreme formulation: "[H]istory and literature have no existence in and of themselves. It is we who constitute them as the object of our understanding" (p. 153).

Postmodernism deliberately confuses the notion that history's problem is verification, while fiction's is veracity (Berthoff, p. 272). Both are signifying systems ·in our culture, what Doctorow once called modes of "mediating the world for the purpose of introducing meaning" ("False Documents," p. 24). And it is both the constructed, imposed nature of that meaning and the seemingly absolute necessity for us to make meaning that historiographic metafiction like Coover's *The Public Burning* reveals. This novel teaches that "history itself depends on conventions of narrative, language, and ideology in order to present an account of 'what really happened' " (Mazurek, p. 29). Both history and fiction are cultural sign systems, ideological constructions whose ideology includes their appearance of being autonomous and self-contained. It is the metafictionality of these novels that underlines Doctorow's notion that "history is a kind of fiction in which we live and hope to survive, and fiction is a kind of speculative history . . . by which the available data for the composition is seen to be greater and more various in its sources than the historian supposes" (p. 25).

Fredric Jameson has argued that historical representation is as surely in crisis as is the linear novel, and for much the same reasons:

> The most intelligent "solution" to such a crisis does not consist in abandoning historiography altogether, as an impossible aim and an ideological category all at once, but rather—as in the modernist aesthetic itself—in reorganizing its traditional procedures on a different level. Althusser's proposal seems the wisest in this situation: as old-fashioned narrative or "realistic" historiography becomes problematic, the historian should reformulate her vocation—not any longer to produce some vivid representation of history 'as it really happened,' but rather to produce the *concept* of history. ("Periodizing," p. 180)

There is only one word I would change in this: the word "modernist" seems to me to be less apt than "postmodernist," though Jameson would never agree (see "Postmodernism and Consumer Society" and "Postmodernism or The Cultural Logic"). Postmodern historiographic metafiction has done exactly what Jameson calls for here, though it is more the problematizing than just the production of a "*concept* of history" (and fiction) that results. The two genres may be textual constructs, narratives which are both nonoriginary in their reliance on past intertexts and also unavoidably ideologically laden, but they do not, in historiographic metafiction at least, "adopt equivalent representational procedures or constitute equivalent modes of cognition" (Foley, p. 35). However, there are (or have been) combinations of history and fiction which do attempt such equivalence.

III

> [T]he binary opposition between fiction and fact is no longer relevant: in any differential system, it is the assertion of the space *between* the entities that matters. — Paul de Man

Perhaps. But historiographic metafiction suggests the continuing relevance of such an opposition, even if it be a problematic one. It both installs and then blurs the line between fiction and history. This kind of generic blurring has been a feature of literature back to the classical epic and the Bible (see Weinstein, p. 263), but the simultaneous assertion and crossing of boundaries is more postmodern. Umberto Eco has claimed that there are three ways to narrate the past: the romance, the swashbuckling tale, and the historical novel. He has added that it was the latter that he intended to write in *The Name of the Rose* (pp. 74–75). Historical novels, he feels, "not only identify in the past the causes of what came later, but also trace the process through which those causes began slowly to produce their effects" (p. 76). This is why his medieval characters, like John Banville's in his *Doctor Copernicus,* are made to talk like Wittgenstein. I would say, however, that this device points to a fourth way of narrating the past: historiographic metafiction — and not historical fiction — because of the intensely self-conscious way in which all this is done.

What is the difference between postmodern fiction and what we usually think of as nineteenth-century historical fiction, though its forms persist today (see Fleishman)? It is difficult to generalize about this latter complex genre because, as theorists have pointed out, history plays a great number of distinctly different roles, at different levels of generality, in its various manifestations. There seems little agreement as to whether the historical past is always presented as individualized, particularized and past (i.e., different from the present) (see Shaw, pp. 26, 48, 148) or whether that past is offered as typical and therefore present, or at least as sharing values through time with the present (Lukács). While acknowledging the difficulties of definition (see Turner; Shaw) that the historical novel shares with most genres, we might define historical fiction as that which is modeled on historiography to the extent that it is motivated and made operative by a notion of history as a shaping force (in the narrative and in human destiny) (see Fleishman). However, it is Georg Lukács's influential and more particular definition that theorists most frequently have to confront in their defining, and I am no exception.

Lukács felt that the historical novel could enact historical process by presenting a microcosm which generalizes and concentrates (p. 39). The protagonist, therefore, should be a type, a synthesis of the general and particular, of "all the humanly and socially essential determinants." From this definition, it is clear that the protagonists of historiographic metafiction are anything but types: they are the ex-centrics, the marginalized, the peripheral figures of fictional history — the Coalhouse Walkers (in *Ragtime*), the Saleem Sinais (in *Midnight's Children*), the Fevvers (in *Nights at the Circus).* Even the historical personages take on different, particularized, and ultimately ex-centric status: Doctor Copernicus (in the novel of the same name), Houdini (in *Ragtime*), Richard Nixon (in *The Public Burning*). Historiographic metafiction espouses a postmodern ideology of pluralism and recognition of difference; "type" has little function here, except as something to be ironically undercut. The protagonist of a postmodern novel like Doctorow's *Book of Daniel* is overtly specific, individual, culturally and familially conditioned in his response to history, both public and private. The narrative form enacts the fact that Daniel is not a type of anything, no matter how much he may try to see himself as representing the New Left or his parents' cause.

Related to this notion of type is Lukács's belief that the historical novel was defined by the relative unimportance of its use of detail, which he saw as "only a means of achieving historical faithfulness, for making concretely clear the historical necessity of a concrete situation" (p. 59). Therefore, accuracy or even truth of detail was irrelevant. Many readers of historical fiction would disagree, I suspect, as have writers of it (John Williams, pp. 8–11). Postmodern fiction contests this defining characteristic in two different ways. First of all, historiographic metafiction, as we have seen, plays upon the truth and lies of the historical record. In novels like *Foe, Burning Water,* or *Famous Last Words,* certain known historical details are deliberately falsified in order to foreground the possible mnemonic failures of recorded history and the constant potential for both deliberate and inadvertent error. The second difference lies in the way in which postmodern fiction actually uses detail or historical data. Historical fiction (*pace* Lukács) usually incorporates and assimilates these data in order to lend a patina of verifiability or an air of dense specificity and particularity to the fictional world. Historiographic metafiction incorporates, but rarely assimilates the data. More often the process of *attempting* to assimilate is what is foregrounded. Historiographic metafiction acknowledges the paradox of the *reality* of the past but its (only) *textualized* accessibility to us today.

Lukács's third major defining characteristic of the historical novel is its relegation of historical personages to secondary roles. Clearly, in postmodern novels like *Doctor Copernicus, Kepler, Legs* (Jack Diamond), and *Antichthon* (Giordano Bruno), this is hardly the case. In many historical novels, the real figures of the past are deployed to validate or authenticate the fictional world by their presence, as if to hide the joins between fiction and history in a formal, ontological sleight of hand. The metafictional self-reflexivity of postmodern novels prevents any such subterfuge, and poses that ontological join as a problem: how do we know the past? what do (what can) we know of it now? Sometimes the manipulation of historical personages is so blatant and in conflict with known fact that the reader is forced to ask the reason behind, for instance, John Barth's rewriting of John Smith's rescue of Pocahontas in *The Sot-Weed Factor.* It is never too difficult to see that reason, thanks to the overt metafictionality: here, it is the demystification of the heroic — and falsifying — view of history that has passed into legend. Similarly Coover does considerable violence to the history of the Rosenbergs in *The Public Burning,* but he does so to satiric ends, in the name of social critique. I do not think that he intends to construct a wilful betrayal of politically tragic events; perhaps, however, he does want to make a connection to the real world of political action through the reader — through our awareness of the need to question received versions of history.

While the debates still rage about the definition of the historical novel, in the 1960s a new variant on the history/fiction confrontation came into being: the nonfictional novel. This differed from the treatment of recent factual events recounted as history, as in William Manchester's *The Death of a President.* It was a form of documentary narrative which deliberately used techniques of fiction in an overt manner and which usually made no pretense of objectivity of presentation. In the work of Hunter S. Thompson, Tom Wolfe, and Norman Mailer, the authorial structuring experience was often in the forefront as the new guarantee of "truth," as we watched the narrator's individual attempts to perceive and impose pattern on what he saw about him. This metafictionality and provisionality in the nonfictional novel obviously link it to historiographic metafiction, but there are, as we shall see, significant differences.

It is probably not accidental that this form of the New Journalism, as it was called, was an American phenomenon. The Vietnam War had brought with it a real distrust of official "facts" as presented by the military and the media, and the ideology of the sixties had licensed a revolt against homogenized forms of experience (Hellmann, p. 8). The result was a kind of overtly personal and provisional journalism, autobiographical in impulse and performative in impact. The famous exception was Truman Capote's *In Cold Blood,* which is a modern rewriting of the realist novel — universalist in assumptions and omniscient in narrative technique. But in works like *The Electric Kool-Aid Acid Test, Fear and Loathing: On the Campaign Trail '72*, and *Of a Fire on the Moon*, there was a very "sixties" kind of direct confrontation with social reality in the present (Hollowell, p. 10). The impact of the new mixing of fiction and fact is clear on popular, if not academic, history in the years following: in *John Brown's Journey*, Albert Fried broke the rules and showed the tentative groping movement of his becoming interested in his historical topic. The book is "marked by the feeling of a historian in the act of grappling with his subject" (Weber, p. 144), as the subtitle underlines: *Notes and Reflections on His America and Mine.*

The nonfictional novel of the sixties and seventies did not just record the contemporary hysteria of history, as Robert Scholes has claimed (p. 37). It did not just try to embrace "the fictional element inevitable in any reporting" and then try to imagine its "way toward the truth" (p. 37). What it did was seriously question who determined and created that truth, and it was this particular aspect of it that perhaps enabled historiographic metafiction's more paradoxical questioning. A number of critics have seen parallels in the nonfictional novel and contemporary metafiction, but they seem to disagree completely on the form that parallel takes. For one, both stress the overt, totalizing power of the imagination of the writers to create unities (Hellmann, p. 16); for another, both refuse to neutralize contingency by reducing it to unified meaning (Zavarzadeh, p. 41). I would agree with the former as a designation of the nonfictional novel, though not of all metafiction; and the latter certainly defines a lot of contemporary self-reflexive writing more accurately than it does the New Journalism. Historiographic metafiction, of course, fits both definitions: it installs totalizing order, only to contest it, by its radical provisionality, intertextuality, and, often, fragmentation. In many ways, the nonfiction novel is a late modernist creation (see Smart, p. 3) in the sense that both its self-consciousness about its writing process and its stress on subjectivity (or psychological realism) recall Woolf and Joyce's experiments with limited, depth vision in narrative, though, in the New Journalism, it is the author whose historical presence as participant authorizes subjective response. Postmodern novels like Rudy Wiebe's *The Scorched-Wood People* parody this stance, however. The participant in the historical action was real, but is still fictionalized: he is made to tell the tale of Louis Riel from a point in time *after* his own death, with the insights of retrospection and access to information he could not possibly have had as participant.

IV

History is three-dimensional. It partakes of the nature of science, art, and philosophy. — Louis Gottschalk

Historiographic metafictions raise a number of specific issues regarding the interaction of historiography and fiction that deserve more detailed study: issues surrounding the nature of identity and subjectivity; the question of reference and representation; the intertextual nature of the past; the ideological implications of writing about history; narrative emplotting; and the status of historical documents, not to mention "facts."

First of all, historiographic metafictions appear to privilege two modes of narration, both of which problematize the entire notion of subjectivity: multiple points of view (as in Thomas's *The White Hotel*) or an overtly controlling narrator (as in Swift's *Waterland*). In neither, however, do we find a subject confident of his/her ability to know the past with any certainty. This is not a transcending of history, but a problematized inscribing of subjectivity into history. In a novel like *Midnight's Children,* nothing, not even the self's physical body, survives the instability caused by the rethinking of the past in nondevelopmental, noncontinuous terms. To use the (appropriate) language of Michel Foucault, Saleem Sinai's body is exposed as "totally imprinted by history and the process of history's destruction of the body" (p. 148). Postmodernism establishes, differentiates, and then disperses stable narrative voices (and bodies) that use memory to try to make sense of the past. It both installs and then subverts traditional concepts of subjectivity; it both establishes and is capable of shattering "the unity of man's being through which it was thought that he could extend his sovereignty to the events of the past" (Foucault, p. 153). The protagonist's psychic disintegration in *Waterland* reflects this shattering; but his strong narrative voice asserts that same selfhood, in a typically postmodern and paradoxical way. The second epigraph of Swift's novel is from *Great Expectations* (a retrospectively ironic source for a book about no expectations and about the past). *Waterland* shares with Dickens's novel a locale (the marshy fenlands) and a preoccupation with the past, but Swift reveals none of Dickens's confidence that one could learn from that past. Indeed, his history teacher protagonist knows better — from both global and personal experience. This kind of intertextuality, often parodic in its ironies, is typical of postmodern fiction. It is a way of literally incorporating the textualized past into the text of the present.

Postmodern intertextuality is a formal manifestation of both a desire to close the gap between past and present for the reader and a desire to rewrite the past in a new context. It is not a modernist desire to order the present through the past or to make the present look spare in contrast to the richness of the past (see Antin, pp. 106–14). It is not an attempt to void or avoid history. Instead, it directly confronts the past of literature — and of historiography, for it too derives from other texts (documents). It uses and abuses those intertextual echoes, inscribing their powerful allusions and then subverting that power through irony. In all, there is little of the modernist sense of a unique, symbolic, visionary "work of art"; there are only texts, already written ones. Intertexts can be both historical and aesthetic in their nature and function.

To what, though, does the very language of historiographic metafiction refer? To a world of history or one of fiction? It is commonly accepted that there is a radical disjunction between the basic assumptions underlying these two notions of reference. History's referents are presumed to be real; fiction's are not. But what postmodern novels teach is that, in both cases, they actually refer at the first level to other texts: we only know the past (which really did exist) through its textualized remains. They problematize the activity of reference by refusing either to bracket the referent (as surfiction might) or to revel in it (as nonfictional novels might). This is not an emptying of the meaning of language, as Gerald Graff seems to think (p. 397). The text still communicates — in fact, it does so very didactically. There is not so much "a loss of belief in a significant external reality" (p. 403) as there is a loss of faith in our ability to (unproblematically) *know* that reality, and therefore to be able to represent it in language. Fiction and history are not different in this regard.

Historiographic metafiction also poses new questions about reference. The issue is no longer: "to what empirically real object in the past does the language of history refer?"; it is more: "to which discursive context could this language belong? to which prior textualizations must we refer?" Postmodern art is more complex and more problematic than extreme late modernist autorepresentation might suggest, with its view that there is no presence, no external truth which verifies or unifies, that there is only self-reference (Smith, pp. 8–9). Historiographic metafiction self-consciously states this, but then immediately points to the discursive nature of all reference — both literary and historiographical. The referent is always already inscribed in the discourses of our culture. This is no cause for despair; it is the text's major link with the "world," but one that acknowledges its identity as construct, rather than as simulacrum of some "real" outside. Once again, this does not deny that the past "real" existed; it only conditions our mode of knowledge of that past — we can only know it through its traces, its relics. The question of reference depends on what John Searle (p. 330) calls a shared "pretense" and what Stanley Fish calls being party to a set of "discourse agreements which are in effect decisions as to what can be stipulated as a fact" (p. 242). A "fact" is discourse-defined; an "event" is not.

Postmodern art is not so much ambiguous as it is doubled and contradictory, as can be seen in novels like Pynchon's *Gravity's Rainbow*, whose overassertion of reference "dissipates its own referentiality" (Bradbury, p. 178). There is clearly a rethinking of the modernist tendency to move away from representation (Harkness, p. 9) by both installing it materially and subverting it. In the visual arts, as in literature, there has been a rethinking of the sign/referent relation in the face of the realization of the limits of self-reflexivity's separation from social practice (Menna, p. 10). Historiographic metafiction shows fiction to be historically conditioned and history to be discursively structured, and in the process manages to broaden the debate about the ideological implications of the Foucaldian conjunction of power and knowledge — for readers and for history itself as a discipline. As the narrator of Rushdie's *Shame* puts it: "History is natural selection. Mutant versions of the past struggle for dominance; new species of fact arise, and old saurian truths go to the wall, blindfolded and smoking last cigarettes. Only the mutations of the strong survive. The weak, the anonymous, the defeated leave few marks. . . . History loves only those who dominate her: it is a relationship of mutual enslavement" (p. 124).

The question of whose history survives is one that obsesses postmodern novels like Timothy Findley's *Famous Last Words*. In problematizing almost everything the historical novel once took for granted, historiographic metafiction destabilizes concepts of both history and fiction. The premise of postmodern fiction is the same as that articulated by Hayden White regarding history: "every representation of the past has specifiable ideological implications" (*Tropics*, p. 69). But the ideology of postmodernism is paradoxical, for it depends upon and draws its power from that which it contests. It is not truly radical; nor is it truly oppositional (as Martin, pp. 44–46, claims for the novel as a genre). But this does not mean it has no critical clout. The Epiloguist of *A Maggot* may claim that what we have read is indeed "a maggot, not an attempt, either in fact or in language, to reproduce known history" (p. 449), but that does not stop him from extended ideological analyses of eighteenth-century social, sexual, and religious history. Similarly, contemporary philosophers of history like Michel de Certeau have reminded historiographers that no research of the past is free of socioeconomic, political, and cultural conditions (p. 65). Novels like *The Public Burning* or *Ragtime* do not trivialize the historical and the factual in their "game-playing" (Robertson) but rather politicize them through their metafictional rethinking of the epistemological and ontological relations between history and fiction. Both are acknowledged as part of larger social and cultural discourses which formalist literary criticism had formerly relegated to the extrinsic and irrelevant. This said, it is also true that it is part of the postmodern ideology not to ignore cultural bias and interpretive conventions and to question authority — even its own.

All of these issues — subjectivity, intertextuality, reference, ideology — underlie the problematized relations between history and fiction in post-modernism. But many theorists today have pointed to narrative as the one concern that envelops all of these, for the process of narrativization has come to be seen as a central form of human comprehension, of imposition of meaning and formal coherence on the chaos of events (Hayden White, "Narrativization," p. 795; Jameson, *Political*, p. 13; Mink, 132). Narrative is what translates knowing into telling (Hayden White, "Value," p. 5), and it is precisely this translation that obsesses postmodern fiction. The conventions of narrative in both historiography and novels, then, are not constraints, but enabling conditions of possibility of sense-making (Martin). Their disruption or challenging will be bound to upset such basic structuring notions as causality and logic — as happens with Oskar's drumming in *The Tin Drum:* narrative conventions are both installed and subverted. The refusal to integrate fragments (in novels like *Z.* or *The White Hotel*) is a refusal of the closure and telos which narrative usually demands (see Kermode, *Sense*). In postmodern poetry too, as Marjorie Perloff has argued, narrative is used in works like Ashbery's "They Dream Only of America" or Dorn's *Gunslinger,* but used in order to question "the very nature of the *order* that a systematic plot structure implies" (p. 158).

The issue of narrativity encompasses many others that point to the postmodern view that we can only know "reality" as it is produced and sustained by cultural representations of it (Owens, p. 21). In historiographic metafictions, these need not be directly verbal representations, for *ekphrases* (or verbal representations of visual representations) often have central representational functions. For example, in Carpentier's *Explosion in a Cathedral,* Goya's "Desastres de la guerra" series provides the works of visual art that are actually the sources of the novel's descriptions of revolutionary war. The seventh of that series, plus the "Dos de Mayo" and "Tres de Mayo," are particularly important, for their glorious associations are left aside by Carpentier, as an ironic signal of his own point of view. Of course, literary intertexts function in the narrative in a similar way. The details of Estaban and Sofía's house in Madrid come, in fact, from Torres Villaroel's *Vida,* a book which Estaban had read earlier in the novel (see Saad, pp. 120–22).

Historiographic metafictions, like both historical fiction and narrative history, cannot avoid dealing with the problem of the status of their "facts" and of the nature of their evidence, their documents. And, obviously, the related issue is that of how those documentary sources are deployed: can they be objectively, neutrally related? or does interpretation inevitably enter with narrativization? The epistemological question of how we know the past joins the ontological one of the status of the traces of that past. Needless to say, the postmodern raising of these questions offers few answers, but this provisionality does not result in some sort of historical relativism or presentism. It rejects projecting present beliefs and standards onto the past and asserts, in strong terms, the specificity and particularity of the individual past event. Nevertheless, it also realizes that we are epistemologically limited in our ability to know that past, since we are both spectators of and actors in the historical process. Historiographic metafiction suggests a distinction between "events" and "facts" that is one shared by many historians. Events are configured into facts by being related to "conceptual matrices within which they have to be imbedded if they are to count as facts" (Munz, p. 15). Historiography and fiction, as we saw earlier, *constitute* their objects of attention; in other words, they decide which events will become facts. The postmodern problematization points to our unavoidable difficulties with the concreteness of events (in the archive, we can find only their textual traces to make into facts) and their accessibility (do we have a full trace or a partial one? what has been absented, discarded as nonfact material?). Dominick LaCapra has argued that all documents or artifacts used by historians are not neutral evidence for reconstructing phenomena which are assumed to have some independent existence outside them. All documents process information and the very way in which they do so is itself a historical fact that limits the documentary conception of historical knowledge (p. 45).

I do not mean to suggest that this is a radical, new insight. In 1910, Carl Becker wrote that "the facts of history do not exist for any historian until he creates them" (p. 525), that representations of the past are selected to signify whatever the historian intends. It is this very difference between events (which have no meaning in themselves) and facts (which are given meaning) that postmodernism foregrounds. Even documents are selected as a function of a certain problem or point of view (Ricoeur, p. 108). Historiographic metafiction often points to this process by using the paratextual conventions of historiography (especially footnotes) to both inscribe and undermine the authority and objectivity of historical sources and explanations.

Unlike the documentary novel as defined by Barbara Foley, what I have been calling postmodern fiction does not "aspire to tell the truth" (Foley, p. 26) as much as to question *whose* truth gets told. It does not so much associate "this truth with claims to empirical validation" as contest the ground of any claim to such validation. How can a historian (or a novelist) check any historical account against past empirical reality in order to test its validity? Facts are not given but are constructed by the kinds of questions we ask of events (Hayden White, *Tropics*, p. 43). In the words of *Waterland*'s history teacher, the past is a "thing which cannot be eradicated, which accumulates and impinges" (p. 109). What postmodern discourses — fictive and historiographic — ask is how we know and come to terms with such a complex "thing."

Works Cited

Antin, David. "Modernism and Postmodernism: Approaching the Present in American Poetry." *Boundary 2* 1.1 (Fall 1972): 98–133.

Aristotle. *Poetics*, translated by James Hutton. London: Norton, 1982.

Barthes, Roland. *Writing Degree Zero*, translated by Annette Lavers and Colin Smith. London: Jonathan Cape, 1967.

Becker, Carl. "Detachment and the Writing of History." *Atlantic Monthly* 106 (1910): 534–36.

Berthoff, Warner. "Fiction, History, Myth: Notes toward the Discrimination of Narrative Forms." In *The Interpretation of Narrative: Theory and Practice*, edited by M. W. Bloomfield, pp. 263–87. Cambridge: Harvard University Press, 1970.

Bloomfield, M. W., ed. *The Interpretation of Narrative: Theory and Practice.* Cambridge: Harvard University Press, 1970.

Bradbury, Malcolm. *The Modern American Novel.* Oxford: Oxford University Press, 1983.

Braudy, Leo. *Narrative Form in History and Fiction: Hume, Fielding, and Gibbon.* Princeton: Princeton University Press, 1970.

Bremner, Robert H., ed. *Essays on History and Literature.* N.p.: Ohio State University Press, 1966.

Canary, Robert H., and Henry Kozicki, eds. *The Writing of History: Literary Form and Historical Understanding.* Madison: University of Wisconsin Press, 1978.

Certeau, Michel de. *L'Écriture de l'histoire.* Paris: Gallimard, 1975.

Coetzee, J. M. *Foe.* Toronto: Stoddardt, 1986.

Daitch, Susan. *L.C.* London: Virago, 1986.

Davis, Lennard. *Factual Fictions: The Origins of the English Novel.* New York: Columbia University Press, 1983.

Doctorow, E. L. "False Documents." In *E. L. Doctorow: Essays and Conversations,* edited by Richard Trenner, pp. 16–27. Princeton: Ontario Review Press, 1983.

Eco, Umberto. Postscript to *The Name of the Rose.* Trans. William Weaver. San Diego: Harcourt, Brace, Jovanovich, 1983, 1984.

Ehrmann, Jacques. "The Death of Literature." Trans. A. James Arnold. In Federman, pp. 229–53.

Federman, Raymond, ed. *Surfiction: Fiction Now . . . and Tomorrow.* 2d ed. Chicago: Swallow Press, 1981.

Fish, Stanley. *Is There a Text in This Class? The Authority of Interpretive Communities.* Cambridge: Harvard University Press, 1980.

Fleishman, Avrom. *The English Historical Novel: Walter Scott to Virginia Woolf.* Baltimore: Johns Hopkins University Press, 1971.

Fletcher, Angus, ed. *The Literature of Fact.* New York: Columbia University Press, 1976.

Foley, Barbara. *Telling the Truth: The Theory and Practice of Documentary Fiction.* Ithaca: Cornell University Press, 1986.

Foster, Hal, ed. *The Anti-Aesthetic: Essays on Postmodern Culture.* Port Townsend, Wash.: Bay Press, 1983.

Foucault, Michel. *Language, Counter-Memory, Practice.* Trans. D. F. Bouchard and S. Simon. Ithaca: Cornell University Press, 1977.

———. *This Is Not a Pipe.* Trans. and ed. James Harkness. Berkeley: University of California Press, 1982.

Fowles, John. *A Maggot.* Toronto: Collins, 1985.

Graff, Gerald. "The Myth of the Postmodernist Breakthrough." *TriQuarterly* 26 (Winter 1973): 383–417.

Harkness, James. "Translator's Introduction." In Foucault, *This Is Not a Pipe,* pp. 1–12.

Hellmann, John. *Fables of Fact: The New Journalism as New Fiction.* Urbana: University of Illinois Press, 1981.

Henderson, Harry B. *Versions of the Past: The Historical Imagination in American Fiction.* Oxford: Oxford University Press, 1974.

Holloway, John. *The Victorian Sage.* New York: Norton, 1953.

Hollowell, John. *Fact and Fiction: The New Journalism and the Nonfiction Novel.* Chapel Hill: University of North Carolina Press, 1977.

Hook, Sidney, ed. *Philosophy and History: A Symposium.* New York: New York University Press, 1963.

Hough, Graham. *An Essay on Criticism.* New York: Norton, 1966.

Jameson, Frederic. *The Political Unconscious: Narrative as a Socially Symbolic Act.* Ithaca: Cornell University Press, 1981.

————. "Postmodernism and Consumer Society." In *The Anti-Aesthetic: Essays on Postmodern Culture,* edited by Hal Foster, pp. 111–25. Port Townsend, Wash.: Bay Press, 1983.

————. "Postmodernism, or The Cultural Logic of Late Capitalism." *New Left Review* 146 (July–Aug. 1984): 53–92.

————. "Periodizing the 60s." In *The 60s Without Apology,* edited by Sohnya Sayres, et al., pp. 178–209. Minneapolis: University of Minnesota Press and *Social Text,* 1984.

Josipovici, Gabriel. *The World and the Book: A Study of Modern Fiction.* London: Macmillan, 1971.

Kermode, Frank. "Novel, History, and Type." *Novel* 1 (1968): 231–38.

————. *The Sense of an Ending.* New York: Oxford University Press, 1970.

LaCapra, Dominick. "On Grubbing in My Personal Archives: An Historiographical Exposé of Sorts (Or How I Learned to Stop Worrying and Love Transference)." *Boundary 2,* 2.3 (1985): 43–67.

Levine, George. *The Boundaries of Fiction: Carlyle, Macaulay, Newman.* Princeton: Princeton University Press, 1968.

Lindenberger, Herbert. "Toward a New History in Literary Study." *Profession* 84 (1984): 16–23.

Lukács, Georg. *The Historical Novel.* Translated by Hannah and Stanley Mitchell. London: Merlin, 1962.

Martin, Wallace. *Recent Theories of Narrative.* Ithaca: Cornell University Press, 1986.

Mazurek, Raymond A. "Metafiction, the Historical Novel, and Coover's *The Public Burning.*" *Critique* 23.3 (1982): 29–42.

Menna, Filiberto. "Gli anni Settanta," *Il Verri* 1–2, 7th ser. (marzo/giugno 1984): 9–14.

Mink, Louis O. "Narrative Form as a Cognitive Instrument." In *The Writing of History: Literary Form and Historical Understanding,* edited by Robert H. Canary and Henry Kozicki, pp. 129–49. Madison: University of Wisconsin Press, 1978.

Munz, Peter. *The Shapes of Time*. Middletown, Conn.: Wesleyan University Press, 1977.

Nye, Russel B. "History and Literature: Branches of the Same Tree." In *Essays on History and Literature,* edited by Robert H. Bremner, pp. 123–59. N.p.: Ohio University Press, 1966.

Owens, Craig. "Representation, Appropriation, and Power." *Art in America* 70.5 (May 1982): 9–21.

Parker, Andrew. " 'Taking Sides' (On History): Derrida Re-Marx." *Diacritics* 11 (1981): 57–73.

Perloff, Marjorie. *The Dance of the Intellect: Studies in the Poetry of the Pound Tradition*. Cambridge: Cambridge University Press, 1985.

Ricoeur, Paul. *Time and Narrative*. Vol. 1. Translated by Kathleen McLaughlin and David Pallauer. Chicago: University of Chicago Press, 1984.

Robertson, Mary F. "Hystery, Herstory, History: 'Imagining the Real' in Thomas's *The White Hotel.*" *Contemporary Literature* 25.4 (Winter 1984): 452–77.

Rushdie, Salman. *Shame*. London: Picador, 1984.

Saad, Gabriel. "L'Histoire et la révolution dans *Le Siècle des lumières.*" In *Quinze Études autour de El Siglo de las luces de Alejo Carpentier,* pp. 113–22. Paris: L'Harmattan, 1983.

Sayres, Sohnya, et al., eds. *The 60s Without Apology*. Minneapolis: University of Minnesota Press and *Social Text,* 1984.

Scholes, Robert. "Double Perspective on Hysteria." *Saturday Review* 24 (Aug. 1968): 37.

Seamon, Roger G. "Narrative Practice and the Theoretical Distinction between History and Fiction." *Genre* 16 (1983): 197–218.

Searle, John. "The Logical Status of Fictional Discourse." *New Literary History* 6 (1975): 319–32.

Shaw, Harry E. *The Forms of Historical Fiction: Sir Walter Scott and His Successors*. Ithaca: Cornell University Press, 1983.

Smart, Robert Augustin. *The Nonfiction Novel*. Lanham, N.Y.: University Press of America, 1985.

Smith, Barbara Herrnstein. *On the Margins of Discourse: The Relation of Literature to Language*. Chicago: University of Chicago Press, 1978.

Swift, Graham. *Waterland*. London: Heinemann, 1983.

Todorov, Tzvetan. *Introduction to Poetics*. Translated by Richard Howard. Minneapolis: University of Minnesota Press, 1981.

Tompkins, Jane. "The Reader in History: The Changing Shape of Literary Response." In *Reader-Response Criticism: From Formalism to Post-Structuralism,* edited by Jane Tompkins, pp. 201–33. Baltimore: Johns Hopkins University Press, 1980.

———, ed. *Reader-Response Criticism: From Formalism to Post-Structuralism*. Baltimore: Johns Hopkins University Press, 1980.

Trenner, Richard, ed. *E. L. Doctorow: Essays and Conversations*. Princeton: Ontario Review Press, 1983.

Turner, Joseph W. "The Kinds of Historical Fiction." *Genre* 12 (1979): 333–55.

Veyne, Paul. *Comment on écrit l'histoire*. Paris: Seuil, 1971.

Weber, Ronald. *The Literature of Fact: Literary Nonfiction in American Writing*. Athens, Ohio: Ohio University Press, 1980.

Weinstein, Mark A. "The Creative Imagination in Fiction and History." *Genre* 9.3 (1976): 263–77.

White, Hayden. "The Fictions of Factual Representation." In *The Literature of Fact*, edited by Angus Fletcher, pp. 21–44. New York: Columbia University Press, 1976.

———. "The Historical Text as Literary Artifact." In *The Writing of History: Literary Form and Historical Understanding*, edited by Robert A. Canary and Henry Kozicki, pp. 41–62. Madison: University of Wisconsin Press, 1978.

———. *Tropics of Discourse: Essays in Cultural Criticism*. Baltimore: Johns Hopkins University Press, 1978.

———. "The Value of Narrativity in the Representation of Reality." *Critical Inquiry* 7.1 (Autumn 1980): 5–27.

———. "The Narrativization of Real Events." *Critical Inquiry* 7.4 (Summer 1981): 793–98.

White, Morton. "The Logic of Historical Narration." In *Philosophy and History: A Symposium*, edited by Sidney Hook, pp. 3–31. New York: New York University Press, 1963.

Williams, John. "Fact in Fiction: Problems for the Historical Novelist." *Denver Quarterly* 7.4 (1973): 1–12.

Wolf, Christa. *No Place on Earth*. Translated by Jan Van Heurck. New York: Farrar, Straus and Giroux, 1982.

Zavarzadeh, Mas'ud. *The Mythopoeic Reality: The Postwar American Nonfiction Novel*. Urbana: University of Illinois Press, 1976.

Index

Permissions

1. "The Art of Fiction," by Henry James, is reprinted from *The Future of the Novel,* ed. Leon Edel, Vintage 1956, with permission of Leon Edel.

2. "Mr. Bennett and Mrs. Brown" is reprinted from Virginia Woolf, *The Captain's Death Bed and Other Essays,* by permission of Harcourt Brace Jovanovich, Inc., copyright 1950.

3. "Flat and Round Characters" is reprinted from E. M. Forster, *Aspects of the Novel,* by permission of Harcourt Brace Jovanovich, Inc., copyright 1927, 1954.

4. "Epic and Novel" is reprinted from *The Dialogic Imagination: Four Essays by M. M. Bakhtin,* ed. Michael Holquist, trans. Caryl Emerson and Michael Holquist. Reprinted with permission of the University of Texas Press, copyright 1981.

5. "Spatial Form in Modern Literature," by Joseph Frank, is reprinted from *Sewanee Review* 53.2–3 (1945). Copyright 1945, 1983, University of the South. Reprinted with permission of the editor of the *Sewanee Review.*

6. "Manners, Morals, and the Novel" is reprinted from Lionel Trilling, *The Liberal Imagination* (Viking, 1950; Harcourt Brace Jovanovich, 1978). Copyright 1950 Lionel Trilling. Reprinted with permission of Mrs. Diana Trilling.

7. "Writing and the Novel," originally published in French in 1953, is reprinted from Roland Barthes, *Writing Degree Zero,* English translation by Annette Lavers and Colin Smith. Translation copyright 1967 Jonathan Cape Ltd. Reprinted with permission of Hill and Wang, a division of Farrar, Straus & Giroux, Inc.

8. "What Makes a Short Story Short?" by Norman Friedman is reprinted with permission from *Modern Fiction Studies* 4 (1958). Copyright 1958 Purdue Research Foundation, West Lafayette, Ind. 47907.

9. "Distance and Point-of-View: An Essay in Classification," by Wayne C. Booth, is reprinted from *Essays in Criticism* 11 (1961) with permission of Wayne C. Booth.

10. "Marxist Aesthetics and Literary Realism" is reprinted from Georg Lukács, *Studies in European Realism* (1950), trans. Edith Bone, with permission of Grosset and Dunlap, copyright 1964.

11. "Plot in the Modern Novel," by J. Arthur Honeywell, originally appeared in *Critical Approaches to Fiction,* ed. Shiv Kumar and Keith McKean. Reprinted with permission of McGraw-Hill Book Co., copyright 1968.

12. "The Concept of Point of View" is reprinted from Mitchell A. Leaska, *Virginia Woolf's Lighthouse.* Copyright 1970 Columbia University Press. Reprinted with permission of Mitchell A. Leaska.

13. "The Concept of Character in Fiction" is reprinted from William H. Gass, *Fiction and The Figures of Life,* with permission of William H. Gass, copyright 1970, 1971.

14. "Time and Narrative in *A la recherche du temps perdu,*" by Gérard Genette, trans. Paul De Man, is reprinted with permission from *Aspects of Narrative,* ed. J. Hillis Miller. Copyright 1971 Columbia University Press.

15. "The Literary Motif: A Definition and Evaluation," by William Freedman, is reprinted with permission of the editors of *Novel* 5 (Winter 1971).

16. "Introduction to the Study of the Narratee," by Gerald J. Prince, originally appeared in *Poetique* 14 (1973) and was translated by Francis Mariner for *Reader-Response Criticism*, ed. Jane P. Tompkins (Baltimore: Johns Hopkins University Press, 1980). It is reprinted here with permission of Gerald Prince.

17. "Realism Reconsidered," by George Levine, is reprinted from *The Theory of the Novel: New Essays*, ed. John Halperin, by permission of Oxford University Press, copyright 1974.

18. "Discourse: Nonnarrated Stories" is reprinted from Seymour Chatman, *Story and Discourse: Narrative Structure in Fiction and Film*. Copyright 1978 Cornell University. Reprinted with permission of Cornell University Press.

19. "Reading as Construction," by Tzvetan Todorov, originally appeared in *The Reader in the Text: Essays on Audience and Interpretation*, ed. Susan R. Suleiman and Inge Crosman. Reprinted with permission of Princeton University Press, copyright 1980.

20. "The Literature of Replenishment," originally published in the *Atlantic*, January 1980, is reprinted from John Barth, *The Friday Book*, ©copyright 1984 by John Barth, reprinted by permission of Wylie, Aitken & Stone, Inc.

21. "Defining the Short Story: Impressionism and Form," by Suzanne C. Ferguson, is reprinted with permission from *Modern Fiction Studies* 28.1 (1982). Copyright 1982 by Purdue Research Foundation, West Lafayette, Ind. 47907.

22. "The Blackness of Blackness: A Critique on the Sign and the Signifying Monkey" is reprinted from Henry Louis Gates, Jr., *Figures in Black: Words, Signs, and the "Racial" Self,* copyright 1987 Oxford University Press. Reprinted by permission of Oxford University Press and the author.

23. "Reading for the Plot," parts I and II, is reprinted from Peter Brooks, *Reading for the Plot,* copyright 1984 by Peter Brooks. Reprinted by permission of Alfred A. Knopf, Inc.

24. "Mimesis and Diegesis in Modern Fiction" is reprinted from David Lodge, *After Bakhtin: Essays on Fiction and Criticism,* copyright 1990 by Routledge. Reprinted by permission of Routledge and the author.

25. "Breaking the Sentence; Breaking the Sequence" is reprinted from Rachel Blau DuPlessis, *Writing Beyond the Ending.* Copyright 1985 by Rachel Blau DuPlessis. Reprinted with permission of Rachel Blau DuPlessis and Indiana University Press.

26. "The Documentary Novel and the Problem of Borders" is reprinted from Barbara Foley, *Telling the Truth: The Theory and Practice of Documentary Fiction,* copyright 1986 by Cornell University Press. Used by permission of Cornell University Press.

27. "Reading Ourselves: Toward a Feminist Theory of Reading," by Patrocinio P. Schweickart, is reprinted from *Gender and Reading: Essays on Reading, Texts, and Con-*

Michael J. Hoffman is Professor of English at the University of California, Davis.

Patrick D. Murphy is Professor of English at the Indiana University of Pennsylvania.